The Palgrave Handbook of Disability Sport in Europe

Caroline van Lindert • Jeroen Scheerder •
Ian Brittain
Editors

The Palgrave Handbook of Disability Sport in Europe

Policies, Structures and Participation

Editors
Caroline van Lindert
Mulier Institute
Utrecht, The Netherlands

Jeroen Scheerder
Department of Movement Sciences
KU Leuven
Leuven, Belgium

Ian Brittain
Coventry University
Centre for Business in Society
Coventry, UK

ISBN 978-3-031-21758-6   ISBN 978-3-031-21759-3 (eBook)
https://doi.org/10.1007/978-3-031-21759-3

© The Editor(s) (if applicable) and The Author(s), under exclusive licence to Springer Nature Switzerland AG 2023

This work is subject to copyright. All rights are solely and exclusively licensed by the Publisher, whether the whole or part of the material is concerned, specifically the rights of translation, reprinting, reuse of illustrations, recitation, broadcasting, reproduction on microfilms or in any other physical way, and transmission or information storage and retrieval, electronic adaptation, computer software, or by similar or dissimilar methodology now known or hereafter developed.

The use of general descriptive names, registered names, trademarks, service marks, etc. in this publication does not imply, even in the absence of a specific statement, that such names are exempt from the relevant protective laws and regulations and therefore free for general use.

The publisher, the authors, and the editors are safe to assume that the advice and information in this book are believed to be true and accurate at the date of publication. Neither the publisher nor the authors or the editors give a warranty, expressed or implied, with respect to the material contained herein or for any errors or omissions that may have been made. The publisher remains neutral with regard to jurisdictional claims in published maps and institutional affiliations.

Cover illustration: © South_agency / Getty Images

This Palgrave Macmillan imprint is published by the registered company Springer Nature Switzerland AG.
The registered company address is: Gewerbestrasse 11, 6330 Cham, Switzerland

Foreword by the President of IFAPA

It is my sincere pleasure to write the foreword for this important and significant publication.

Adapted physical activity and disability sport have evolved significantly in the past 40 years and this book provides an opportunity from a cross-national perspective to share how disability sport at the grassroots level has addressed varying challenges and opportunities. The profiles of 19 nations herein include evidence related to policy and structure and general participation and more specifically how this relates to inclusion.

I am particularly pleased with the publication of this book in my role as the President of the International Federation of Adapted Physical Activity (IFAPA). IFAPA is an international scientific organisation of higher education scholars, practitioners and students dedicated to promoting adapted physical activity. The fundamental purposes of IFAPA are

- to encourage international cooperation in the field of physical activity to the benefit of individuals of all abilities;
- to promote, stimulate and support research in the field of adapted physical activity throughout the world;
- and to make scientific knowledge of and practical experiences in adapted physical activity available to all interested persons, organisations and institutions.

At our 2021 International Symposium of Adapted Physical Activity held online by the University of Jyväskylä in Finland, the lead authors, along with chapter authors from Spain, Lithuania and Norway, organised a workshop focusing on the preliminary results of the book.

IFAPA members are clearly interested in sport and recreation participation and policies and specifically those related to inclusion for persons experiencing disability and most certainly at the grassroots level of participation. This handbook will thus make an important contribution by enabling the development and exchange of knowledge in these areas among practitioners, policymakers and researchers.

This book also provides an important point of connection between academics in the world of adapted physical activity, sport sociology, sport policy and sport participation, of which there is tremendous crossover and potential for further collaboration.

My sincere congratulations to the editors and authors for producing a high-quality, informative and interesting compilation that will serve our movement and those experiencing disability with better programmes and opportunities in sport and recreation.

International Federation of Adapted Physical Activity   David Legg
Champaign, IL, USA

Foreword by the President of EUFAPA

The European Union (EU) is an international organisation that links 27 countries and operates with a broad influence to formulate, shape and implements European policy. The EU promotes the inclusion and active participation of people with disability in society, in line with the EU's human rights approach to disability issues. However, having a disability or illness is the third most frequently mentioned reason in Europe for not practising sports more regularly. The removal of social, physical and psychological barriers is an important policy priority for the European Commission, since participation in sport has proved to be a powerful tool for the health and well-being of people with disabilities. Also, it is the responsibility of each of us professionally involved in adapted physical activity as academics, researchers or practitioners to strive that these barriers are limited, and removed in future.

In my capacity as the President of the European Federation of Adapted Physical Activity (EUFAPA), I would like to extend my thanks to all authors, representing 19 European countries, for their contribution in writing this book. EUFAPA is a European organisation concerned with promotion and dissemination of experiences, results and findings in the fields of adapted physical activity and sport science, and their practical application to the benefit of individuals across the life span. Thanks to this book we can better understand the large diversity in disability sport systems, policies and adapted sport programmes across the different regions in Europe.

In some EU countries special study programmes have been developed at higher education settings delivering extensive research and scientific innovations in the area of sport for persons with disability, while in other countries local programmes are successfully implemented with limited professional or governmental assistance. The EUFAPA especially welcomes the information and analysis carried out in this book. This can help us to assess the main achievements and challenges in the field of sport for persons with disability in Europe. Such information should enable our colleagues across Europe to promote future initiatives in this field. Moreover, it is important to achieve an EU-level dialogue between various colleagues from different professional areas providing physical activity services for persons with disability.

My sincere gratitude to colleagues, editors and all who contributed to the preparation of this book. This publication could only be reached thanks to the support of the partnership of professionals from different countries and adapted sport sectors.

European Federation of Adapted Physical Activity   Aija Klavina
Olomouc, Czech Republic

Foreword by the President of EASS

Within the sports world, there is a political wish to promote the human rights policy and expand diversity in sport. But wishes must be fulfilled through knowledge and action, and this very important handbook, focusing on disability, provides a strong foundation for promoting the human right to sport for participants with any kind of physical, mental, intellectual or sensory disability.

It is a great honour for me, as the President of the European Association of Sociology of Sport (EASS), to write this foreword for the *Palgrave Handbook of Disability Sport in Europe*. The idea to start this project arose during an EASS conference in Bordeaux, France, in 2018. We promoted the idea during a POLIS (Policy and Politics In Sport) workshop in Arnhem, the Netherlands, and during an EASS conference in Bö, Norway, in 2019, where the editors held a presentation during a MEASURE (Meeting for European Sport Participation and Sport Culture Research) network session. Around half of the contributing authors are familiar with EASS and other contributing authors come from other networks, such as EUFAPA (adapted physical activity). With this handbook, two fields of expertise have been combined to create the unique field of disability sport policy and participation.

In the handbook, the authors examine various ways grassroots sports for persons with a disability (pwd) are delivered throughout Europe. The book is written from a cross-national perspective, with a collection of 19 country-specific chapters from different regions in Europe, with both up-to-date data and in-depth descriptions and analyses, based on a common theoretical and conceptual framework. Two main topics are covered:

- Policy and structure: Which agents (different levels and types) are involved in delivering sport for pwd and what are the relationships between these agents? What kind of policies and legislation apply to sport for pwd and to what extent do they promote inclusion in sport among pwd?
- Participation in sport: How, and to what extent do pwd participate in sport? What are the facilitators and barriers towards their participation in sport? What are the methods and methodological challenges in data collection on the sport participation of pwd?

The handbook contains brilliant chapters on 19 countries and their perspective on the two main topics. The book provides us with a comprehensive overview of these topics and allows us to compare the similarities and differences in sport policy and sport practice.

I would like to give my compliments to and thank the editors Caroline van Lindert (Mulier Institute), Jeroen Scheerder (KU Leuven) and Ian Brittain (Coventry University), for all their excellent work as editors of this *Palgrave Handbook of Disability Sport in Europe*. I also applaud the respective authors of the country chapters. Their work gives us not only a unique and new insight into disability sport in Europe, but also new theoretical and empirical insights. The handbook is one of a kind; it includes general chapters, country-specific chapters, cross-national and cross-temporal analyses, and so on. It is a must-read and must-have for sociologists interested in sport and disability from a participatory, governance and policy perspective!

This handbook is relevant to all EASS members, and I want to stress the value of the book to (sport) sociologists and social scientists, in general, as well as to scholars and practitioners in the field of disability sport.

European Association of Sociology of Sport   Laila Ottesen
Copenhagen, Denmark

Acknowledgements

The idea behind this handbook arose during discussions within different networks about research on sport participation of persons with a disability (pwd) and the underlying policies in regard to the inclusion of pwd in sport. It became apparent that books comparing both subjects across countries were scarce. The first ideas for a book like this were presented at a special session of the Policy and Politics In Sport (POLIS) network at Papendal, the Netherlands, in 2018. The ideas were further elaborated during conferences of the European Association of Sociology of Sport (EASS) and within the Meeting for European Sport Participation and Sport Culture Research network (MEASURE). The connection was soon made with the international network of researchers and practitioners in the field of disability sport that gather biannually at the Disability Sport Conference, held at Coventry University in the United Kingdom. Furthermore, ideas about the handbook were exchanged with colleagues from both the European and the International Federation of Adapted Physical Activity (EUFAPA and IFAPA). This enabled an encounter between the 'worlds' of sport participation and sport policy research and that of human rights, diversity and inclusion in disability sport and Paralympic studies. We would like to thank the colleagues within these networks for their support in elaborating the ideas for this handbook.

This publication would not have been possible without the support and cooperation of the following organisations and people. We thank the Dutch Ministry of Health, Welfare and Sports for its support in covering the initial editorial costs incurred by the Mulier Institute. This support helped us getting started and gave the project a solid base. We are furthermore grateful for the supportive roles of the Mulier Institute itself, and the University of Leuven and the University of Coventry for letting the editors do their work.

We thank Sharla Plant from Palgrave for her enthusiastic response to our first ideas for this handbook and support in pushing it forward. And many thanks to Sarah Hills and her colleagues from Springer Nature for transforming our manuscript to a handbook that hopefully will be a valuable source of knowledge for anyone working in the fields of disability sport, whether as a practitioner, policymaker or scholar.

The handbook would not have been possible without the contributions from the authors, who dedicated their time and energy to bring together valuable data and knowledge regarding the various ways disability sport is delivered in their respective countries. We are grateful for their trust, cooperation and patience. We hope this network will continue to exist and exchange knowledge moving forward.

Thank you also to Juno Prent, student assistant from the Mulier Institute, for helping finalize details during the final phase of the submission process.

And last but not least, we gratefully thank Maxine de Jonge, former researcher at the Mulier Institute, for her enthusiastic help, good ideas, proofreading and tireless support throughout the entire journey of our handbook project.

Utrecht, The Netherlands	Caroline van Lindert
Leuven, Belgium	Jeroen Scheerder
Coventry, UK	Ian Brittain

Contents

1 **Introduction: Sport Participation a Human Right for Persons with a Disability**... 1
Caroline van Lindert, Jeroen Scheerder, and Ian Brittain

2 **Understanding Disability, Disability Sport and Inclusion**.......... 25
Ian Brittain, Caroline van Lindert, and Jeroen Scheerder

3 **Participation in Sport and Physical Activity Amongst People with a Disability: A Pan-European Comparative Approach**........ 55
Jeroen Scheerder, Kobe Helsen, Caroline van Lindert, and Ian Brittain

4 **Denmark: Disability Sports Policy at Arm's Length**.............. 79
Christian Røj Voldby and Karsten Elmose-Østerlund

5 **Finland: Facts Behind the Long and Complicated Process of Disability Inclusion in Sports**............................. 101
Kati Lehtonen and Aija Saari

6 **Disability and Sport in Iceland** 125
Ingi Þór Einarsson and Vidar Halldorsson

7 **Norway**... 145
Marit Sørensen and Nina Kahrs

8 **Beyond Inclusion: Opportunity Structures in Sports for All in Sweden**... 169
Kim Wickman and Linda Torége

9 **Ireland** 193
Catherine Carty and Paul Kitchin

10 **Northern Ireland: Disability Sport in a Shared Space** 217
Paul Kitchin and Catherine Carty

11	**United Kingdom: An Inclusionary Approach to Sport** .... 237 Matej Christiaens, Ian Brittain, and Christopher Brown	
12	**Austria: Half Way to Inclusion?** .... 267 Torsten Wojciechowski and Claudia Stura	
13	**Disability Sport in Belgium/Flanders: From a Fragmented Mosaic Towards a More Inclusive Landscape** .... 295 Debbie Van Biesen and Jeroen Scheerder	
14	**Complexity and Coexistence: Disability Sport in Germany** .... 325 Jürgen Mittag	
15	**The Netherlands: Towards Inclusive Sport for People with a Disability** .... 349 Caroline van Lindert and Maxine de Jonge	
16	**Switzerland** .... 385 Julia Albrecht, Siegfried Nagel, and Christoffer Klenk	
17	**Hungary: Rise of Attention Given to Disability Sports** .... 411 Szilvia Perényi and Zsuzsanna Szilárd	
18	**Disability Sport in Lithuania** .... 437 Jurate Pozeriene and Diana Reklaitiene	
19	**Structure of the Analysis on the Development and Situation of Disability Sports Policy in Slovenia**. .... 461 Mojca Doupona and Simona Kustec	
20	**Portugal: Pathways of Sport for People with Disabilities** .... 485 Leonardo José Mataruna-Dos-Santos, Anabela Vitorino, and Nuno M. Pimenta	
21	**Disability Sport in Spain** .... 513 Javier Pérez Tejero and Cati Lecumberri Gómez	
22	**Turkey (Republic of Turkey): Disability Sports, Policies and Implementations** .... 537 Yeşim Albayrak Kuruoğlu	
23	**The Landscape of Sport for Persons with a Disability: A System Within a System** .... 561 Caroline van Lindert, Jeroen Scheerder, and Ian Brittain	

Index. 599

Notes on Contributors

Julia Albrecht is a project coordinator at the National Center for Tumor Diseases Heidelberg, Germany. She received her PhD in 2020 from the Institute of Sport Science, University of Bern, Switzerland, where she was a research assistant from 2015 to 2020. The title of her dissertation is 'Participation of People Experiencing Disabilities in Organized Sports'. Her main areas of research are the social integration of people with disabilities and migration background. She contributed to the implementation of the European project 'Social Integration and Volunteering in Sports Clubs in Europe' (led by Barne Ibsen and Karsten Elmose-Østerlund) in Switzerland. Her most recent publication, together with the Swiss co-authors Christoffer Klenk and Siegfried Nagel, with the title 'Just taking part or fully participate with others!? Social integration of members with disabilities in mainstream sports clubs', was published in *Sport und Gesellschaft*,18(3), 253–279. https://doi.org/10.1515/sug-2021-0021

Ian Brittain has formerly been an executive board member of the International Stoke Mandeville Wheelchair Sports Federation and was the sports coordinator for the International Wheelchair and Amputee Sports Federation World Games in Rio de Janeiro, 2005. He is the Heritage Advisor to the International Wheelchair and Amputee Sports Federation (IWAS) (now World Abilitysport) and has attended five Summer Paralympic Games, from Sydney 2000 to Rio 2016. He is an associate professor at the Centre for Business in Society, Coventry University, UK, where his research focuses upon sociological, historical and sports management aspects of Paralympic and disability sport. He has authored four books and edited three others on the subject of Paralympic and disability sport, and legacies and mega-events.

Christopher Brown is Senior Lecturer in Sports Development at the University of Hertfordshire, UK. Chris specializes in disability sport, with a particular interest in Paralympic Games legacies and the sport spectator experiences of disabled people. Chris is the founder of Disability Sport Info, an initiative that communicates insights on disability sport to a non-academic audience. His podcasts are available via the following link: https://disabilitysportinfo.buzzsprout.com/. Chris's three most recent publications are as follows:

Brown, C. (2022, August 26). London 2012 Paralympics was not a gamechanger for disabled people's sports participation – here's why. *The Conversation*. https://theconversation.com/london-2012-paralympics-was-not-a-gamechanger-for-disabled-peoples-sports-participation-heres-why-189027

Brown, C., & Pappous, A. S. (2022). Leveraging the London 2012 Paralympic Games to increase sports participation: The role of voluntary sports clubs. *Managing Sport and Leisure*, 1–17. https://doi.org/10.1080/23750472.2022.2105253

Brown, C. & Pappous, A. (2021). Are mega-events a solution to address physical inactivity? Interrogating the London 2012 Paralympic sport participation legacies among people with disabilities. *European Journal for Sport and Society*, *18*(1), 18–43. https://doi.org/10.1080/16138171.2020.1792112

Catherine Carty is the UNESCO Chair Manager on Inclusive Sport at Munster Technological University (MTU). She leads a global consortium to advance the inclusive policy actions of UNESCO's sport work. She focuses on advancing human rights, sustainable development and the principle of no one left behind. Catherine led a three-day session at Expo2020 Dubai on this topic, bringing together UN and multi-lateral agencies, governments, the sports sector, development banks and human rights institutions. Catherine is strategically involved in advancing UNESCO's Fit for Life flagship. She was on the guidelines development group of WHO's 2020 Physical Activity and Sedentary Behaviour Guidelines. Catherine sits on the steering group for Measuring Sports Contribution to the Sustainable Development Goals; the advisory group of the Centre of Sport and Human Rights; the UN Interagency Group for Sport for Development and Peace; the Global Action on Disability (GLAD) Network; #WeThe15 Steering Group; and the OECD's Towards an Integrated Policy Approach advisory group.

Dr. Matej Christiaens is a Senior Lecturer in Sport Business at Liverpool John Moores University in the UK. His research focuses on sports equality for marginalized groups and the social and political dimensions of sports. He recently published an article in European Sport Management Quarterly on the implementation of inclusion policies for disabled people in non-disabled voluntary community sports clubs, highlighting the complexities of achieving inclusivity in practice. In his upcoming publication co-authored with A. Konkel, he analyses the struggle for recognition of female ski jumpers, exploring the gendered dynamics of sports participation. Through his work, Dr. Christiaens contributes to broader conversations about equity and social justice in sports.

Maxine de Jonge currently works as a policy adviser for the municipality of Nieuwegein, the Netherlands. She worked as a researcher for the Mulier Institute from 2018 until 2023. She has an academic background in adapted physical activity and kinesiology. Her work focuses on the sport participation of children and adults with a disability, and specifically the factors that stimulate or hinder participation among this group.

Mojca Doupona is Full Professor of Sport Sociology at the University of Ljubljana. Her research focuses on gender differences in sport, national identity, violence in sport and dual careers of athletes. She has coordinated and participated in several national, European and international research projects. She is leading the Collaborative Partnerships Erasmus+ project 'Meter Matters' (2022–2024). The main purpose of the Meter Matters project is to develop a model with criteria for co-funding inclusion in sport. Acting as Director General for sport at the Slovenian Ministry of Education, Science and Sport (2020–2022), she coordinated activities and events for the enhancement of active lifestyles and sports participation of Slovenian citizens.

Ingi Þór Einarsson is a lector at the Sport Science department of Reykjavik University. His teaching includes, among other courses, adapted physical activity and exercise physiology. His main research interests are functional aquatic resistance training, physical activity and health among disabled children, and performance analyses among athletes. Ingi is also a successful swimming coach and has worked with many Paralympic medallists from Iceland. He is also a high-performance director for National Paralympic Committee (NPC) Iceland and is responsible for the high-performance strategy in Para sport in Iceland. Ingi was also for many years a classifier for World Para-swimming and took part in designing and evolving the classification systems used in Para-swimming.

Karsten Elmose-Østerlund is Associate Professor of Sports Sociology in the Department of Sports Science and Clinical Biomechanics, University of Southern Denmark. Karsten's primary research topics include sports participation and movement habits; the organization of sport, including sports clubs; and social integration in sport. From 2015 to 2017, he was the project leader for the European research project 'Social Inclusion and Volunteering in Sports Clubs in Europe', with the participation of ten European countries. Based on this project, Karsten has recently co-edited a book with Springer titled *Functions of Sports Clubs in European Societies. A Cross-national Comparative Study* and had had published a number of journal articles regarding the role of migration and disability status for participation in sports clubs and voluntary work. Karsten is working on the national project 'Moving Denmark', which examines the movement habits of the adult population.

Cati Lecumberri Gómez holds a degree in Pedagogy (1999) and a PhD in Physical Activity and Sports Sciences from the National Institute of Physical Education of Barcelona (2009). In 2013 she obtained the accreditation of assistant doctor by the National Agency of Evaluation of the Quality and Accreditation (ANECA). She has been, since the 2007–2008 academic year, Professor of Teaching and Physical Activity and Sports Sciences at the University of Vic—Central University of Catalonia. She has specialized in research areas related to sports as an educational tool in contexts of exclusion and social vulnerability, collaborating with the Futbol Club Barcelona Foundation, the Rafa Nadal Foundation and the Aldeas Infantiles project. She has coordinated the emerging Group of Research in Physical Education of the University of Vic—Central University of Catalonia between 2011 and 2018 (ID 2017SGR260). She holds the position of deputy director of Educational Quality and Innovation, National Institute of Physical Education of Catalonia (INEFC), Faculty of the University of Barcelona.

Vidar Halldorsson is Professor of Sociology at the University of Iceland. His research and teaching emphasize a wide range of sociological topics such as sports, team culture, adolescents, substance use, expertise, public discourse and popular culture, within the paradigms of cultural sociology, the sociology of knowledge and symbolic interaction. His research focus is on collective behaviour and the cultural production of achievement. Vidar is the author of books about the sport success of Iceland and visual analysis of modern society. Vidar is working on a book on the impact of social atmosphere on what we think, how we feel and what we do.

Kobe Helsen is a scientific researcher in the Policy in Sports & Physical Activity Research Group, Department of Movement Sciences, KU Leuven, Belgium. Since 2017, he has participated in research projects concerning the policy and management issues regarding local sports federations, and concerning the multitude of impacts of sports events. Kobe functioned as researcher in the Erasmus+ research project RUN for HEALTH (2018–2020) and investigated the local effects of the 2021 Union Cycliste Internationale (UCI) Road World Championships that were held in Flanders. He is co-editor of *The Rise and Size of the Fitness Industry in Europe: Fit for the Future?* (2020, Palgrave Macmillan). Kobe's research interests are in the field of the societal impacts of sports events.

Nina Kahrs is a former associate professor at the Norwegian School of Sport Sciences, Oslo, Norway. Her research interests have been adapted physical activity (APA) and special education, spanning from organization of disability sport, guiding of blind persons, classification in winter sledge sport and swimming through physical activity for children with congenital heart diseases. She has been active in organizing sport programmes for people with a disability in wheelchair basket, swimming and archery as well as in serving as a coach and a guide. She has wide experience from developing educational programmes in APA both in Norway and internationally, for example, a programme at the University of Western Cape, South Africa. She served in the Thematic Network of Adapted Physical Education and was involved in building the European Master in Adapted Physical Education/ERASMUS EMDAPA. She served as vice-president in the Norwegian Sport Organisation for Disabled (NHIF) and has worked to develop international disability sport organisations (International Blind Sports Association [IBSA] and the sport organisation for the blind in Uganda).

Recent publications: (1) Sørensen, M & Kahrs, N. (2011) En idrett for alle? (A sport for all?) In: V. Hanstad et al. (Eds.). Norsk idrett- indre spenning og ytre press. (Norwegian Sport, inner tension and outward pressure), Oslo, Akilles. (2) Trude Halvorsen, Nina Kahrs (2017. 2. Ed) Fra leik i vann til svømming. Om svømmeopplæring og Funksjonsnedsettelser (From play in water to swimming. About disabilities and teaching people with disabilities to swim) Bondi Forlag/Norges Svømmeforbund (The Norwegian Organisation of Swimming), Oslo.

Paul Kitchin is Senior Lecturer in Sport Management at Ulster University, Northern Ireland. His twin areas of research coalesce around the use of sport to either engage or exclude marginalized groups of people. Track one is positioned at the nexus of disability, accessibility and the built environment of sport. He has a long-standing research interest in the engagement of disabled people and ageing populations in and through sport and leisure. In particular, his research examines the supply-side barriers that reinforce inequality and inaccessibility for these marginalized groups. Track two is focused on social determinants of health and, in particular, the relationship between gambling harm and gambling industry marketing tactics. His research aims to provide co-produced and pragmatic solutions to address concerns around these relevant areas. A member of the European Sport Management Association since 2009, he is a senior fellow of the (UK) Higher Education Academy.

Christoffer Klenk is a senior lecturer at the Institute of Sport Science, University of Bern, Switzerland. His research interests are in voluntary sport organizations and community sport development. More recently, his research focus is on social inclusion and diversity management in sport clubs. Christoffer Klenk is a member of the Swiss and German Society for Sport Science (SGS, Deutscher Versehrtensportverband [DVS]) and reviewer for various sport sociology and management journals.

Yeşim Albayrak Kuruoğlu is an assistant professor at the School of Physical Education and Sports, Haliç University, Istanbul, Turkey. She obtained her MSc and PhD degrees in the field of Physical Activity and Health from the Institute of Health Sciences, Marmara University, Istanbul. She attended the '37th & 39th Sessions of Young Participants' and '6th Post-Graduate Session on Olympic Studies' at the International Olympic Academy in Greece. She worked as a Vice Dean, Senator of the Faculty of Sport Sciences and the Head of Health, Culture and Sports Department, besides teaching tasks in her career. Her academic interests are Olympism, physical activity and health in special populations, physically demanding industrial work and sport for sustainable development. She is a member of the general board of Fenerbahçe Sports Club, Sports Sciences Association of Turkey and the International Olympic Academy Participants Association (IOAPA).

Simona Kustec serves as a full professor at the Faculty of Management, University of Primorska. Prof. Kustec is a political sciences researcher, with a rich and diverse body of work in the fields of governance, elections, and set of specific public policy studies, among them especially of sport policies. She has been involved in several research project groups in Slovenia and abroad. Professor Kustec also served as a member of the National Assembly of the Republic of Slovenia and leader of the leading coalition deputy group (2014–2018), as the Minister of Education, Science and Sport (2020–2022), and in the second half of 2021 as the president of the EU Council for Education, Youth, Culture and Sport, and for Competitiveness (for the field of research).

Kati Lehtonen is a principal researcher at Jamk University of Applied Sciences in Finland and adjunct professor of sport governance and management in Tampere University. Her research interests are focusing on sport systems, organizations, sport policy, networks, management and governance as well as on civic activity of sport. Lehtonen is a member of the Finnish Society of Sport Sciences and the

National Sport Council's Research, Foresight and Evaluation Section. Her most recent publications are related to collaborative governance, gender and gender equality in Finnish sport policy.

Leonardo José Mataruna-Dos-Santos is an associate professor at the Canadian University Dubai, Faculty of Management in the United Arab Emirates and Full Professor at Salgado de Oliveira University in Brazil. He has a PhD in Sport Management – Physical Education (Gama Filho University, Brazil). He has a postdoc in Contemporary Culture (Federal University of Rio de Janeiro, Brazil), in Sport for Development (Coventry University, UK), and Sport Management (Technical University of Munich, Germany). He received a Marie Curie Fellow – European Union to study the social legacy of London Games. Mataruna has an MSc in Adapted Physical Activity (Unicamp, Brazil), PGCert in Conflict Resolution (Coventry University), PG Diploma in Olympic Studies (International Olympic Academy, Greece/Loughborough University, UK). He is a research member of Stradeos Group of University of Lille (France) and UNESCO advisor. He is a Member of the World Anti-Doping Agency (WADA) Education Committee, and in the Social Science Research Expert Advisory Group of WADA. He is a member of the Portugal Olympic Academy and postdoc research fellow at University of Trás-os-Montes and Alto Douro (UTAD). Mataruna is a member of Education Board of the UAE Judo Federation and Brazilian Committee of Pierre de Coubertin. He is an Associate Research Fellow at Coventry University (UK), Salgado de Oliveira University (Brazil) and Autonomy University of Occident, Mexico. He is also a journalist specialized in Sports acting in the United Arab Emirates (Abu Dhabi National Oil Company – ADNOC Pro-League), Roshn Saudi Arabia (Saudi Pro League) Football Leagues, Brazil, Germany and Portugal.

Jürgen Mittag (born 1970) studied Political Science, Medieval and Modern History, and German Literature at the Universities of Cologne, Bonn and Oxford (1992–1997). He obtained his PhD from the University of Cologne in 2000 and worked from 1997 to 2003 as a research assistant at the Jean Monnet-Chair for Political Science, University of Cologne. From 2003 to 2010 he was the Managing Director (wiss. Geschäftsführer) at the Institute for Social Movements, Ruhr University Bochum. Since 2011 he is the chair holder and head of the Institute of European Sport Development and Leisure Studies, German Sport University Cologne, and was appointed as Jean Monnet Professor in 2011. His major fields of research are: sports systems and (international) sport politics, European integration, parties and trade unions, and tourism studies. He has been a visiting professor at the European University Institute, Florence; at Boğaziçi Üniversitesi (Bosporus University), Istanbul (DAAD Lectureship); at Beijing Sport University, Peking; and at Shanghai University of Sport.

Siegfried Nagel is a full professor at the University of Bern and director of the Institute of Sport Science. His main fields of interest are sport organization research, particularly in sports clubs and federations, as well as sports participation research. He is the leader of several research projects in sport sociology and sport management that mainly focus on social integration in organized sport, sport club development, volunteering and professionalization. Prof. Nagel is the president of the Swiss Society of Sport Science and former president of the European Association for Sociology of Sport (EASS). He has recently authored—together with co-authors—the published book *Functions of Sports Clubs in European Societies. A Cross-national Comparative Study*.

Szilvia Perényi is an associate professor at the Hungarian University of Sports Sciences, Budapest; she completed her PhD from Semmelweis University and MSc in Sports Management as a Fulbright scholar from Florida State University, USA. Szilvia has experience from different levels of sports with governmental, non-governmental and private entities, and frequently serves on Local Organising Committees (LOCs) of international sporting events. Her research work is connected to sports participation and policy, volunteerism and non-profit organizations in sports, along with topics related to event management, and she participates in Erasmus + Sports partnerships. She is a member of the Hungarian Society for Sports Sciences and extended board member of the European Association for the Sociology of Sports.

Nuno M. Pimenta is a full adjunct professor and researcher at the Sport Sciences School of Rio Maior—Polytechnic Institute of Santarém (ESDRM), where he is the coordinator of the European Bachelor's in Physical Activity and Lifestyle. He works in the field of sports sciences, particularly in the assessment and promotion of health-related fitness and health-enhancing physical activity. Nuno is committed to working on relevant contributions to people's lives through research and development. Nuno is part of interdisciplinary research teams in several national and European R&D projects, namely VASelfCare (https://vaselfcare.rd.ciencias.ulisboa.pt); Train4Health (https://www.train4health.eu), focusing on promoting healthy lifestyles; and SEDY2 (https://www.inholland.nl/inhollandcom/about-inholland/sedy2), focusing on promoting physical activity and inclusion in sport for children with disabilities. Nuno is a member of the board of the Portuguese Society for the Study of Obesity and is part of the multidisciplinary Prediabetes Study Group within the Portuguese Society of Diabetology.

Jurate Pozeriene is an associate professor and vice rector of Lithuanian Sports University. She has Bachelor's and Master's degree in Physiotherapy from the Lithuanian Academy of Physical Education, and a PhD diploma in Social Sciences, Education. Most of her studies and scientific publications were done in the field of physical, psychological and social rehabilitation of the disabled and their empowerment through adapted physical activity. She has authored more than 40 published scientific papers and is co-author of 10 textbooks, participated in more than 25 conferences, and was involved in more than 15 national and international academic and research projects. During the last 25 years she has been practising, teaching and researching in the field of physical, psychological and social rehabilitation of the disabled and their empowerment through adapted physical activity. She was the General Secretary of Lithuanian Special Olympics for ten years and until now is the president of Lithuanian Association of Adapted Physical Activity.

Diana Reklaitiene is a professor at and rector of Lithuanian Sports University. During the last 20 years she has been practising, teaching and researching in the field of adapted physical activity: rehabilitation, quality of life of people with different impairments and inclusive education.

She has Bachelor's and Master's degrees in Physiotherapy from the Lithuanian Academy of Physical Education. Her working experience was in a foster home for children with intellectual disabilities as a physical therapist and special physical education teacher, and at Lithuanian Sports University as a lecturer and later as an associate professor in the Department of Adapted Physical Activity. She has a PhD diploma in Social Sciences, Education. She was also actively involved in more than 20 national and international academic and research projects, authored more than 50 published research papers and is co-author of 8 textbooks. She is a board member of Lithuanian Adapted Physical Activity Association and Lithuanian Neurodynamic Therapy Association.

Aija Saari started her career in Finnish disability sports in 1990. During her early years she became interested in disability inclusion, which led her to find answers from research. She completed her PhD in 2011 from Jyväskylä University. She has authored several practically oriented published guidebooks, with a focus on disability inclusion in sports and recreation, as well as national evaluation reports of disability inclusion in Finnish sports, participation of people with disabilities and accessibility. She works as a research manager at the Finnish Paralympic Committee and is an active member of both national and international adapted physical activity networks.

Jeroen Scheerder has an educational background in Sport Sociology (PhD), Social & Cultural Anthropology (MA), Movement & Sport Sciences (MSc), and Marketing (FC). He is Professor of Sport Policy and Sport Sociology in the Department of Movement Sciences at the KU Leuven, Belgium, and is the academic coordinator of the *KU Leuven Sport Policy & Sport Management Master Programme*. He was the head of the *Policy in Sports & Physical Activity Research Group* (2012–2023) and the promotor-coordinator of the *Interuniversity Policy Research Centre on Sports* financed by the Flemish government (2017–2023). From 2014 to 2016 he was president of the European Association for Sociology of Sport (EASS), and from 2005 to 2007 he was visiting Professor of Sport Sociology at the Faculty of Political & Social Sciences, Ghent University, Belgium. Jeroen Scheerder lectures in the fields of sport governance, sport policy/politics, sport sociology and leisure sciences. His research interests lie in management-related, political and sociological aspects of sport and leisure-time physical activity. Together with colleagues from the Dutch Mulier Institute and the German Sport University Cologne, he has founded the European MEASURE (Meeting for European Sport Participation and Sport Culture Research network) and POLIS (Policy and Politics In Sport) research networks, which focus on sport participation and sport policy/sport politics respectively. Jeroen Scheerder is (co-)editor of eight international academic books and three special issues of the *European Journal for Sport & Society*, (co-)author of +100 articles in peer-reviewed journals, and (co-)author of +40 chapters in international academic books (see https://lirias.kuleuven.be/cv?u=u0008762). So far, he has (co-)supervised 18 doctoral theses in the fields of sport governance, sport management, sport policy and/or sport sociology. He is the lead editor of the *KU Leuven Sport, Policy & Management Studies* (see https://faber.kuleuven.be/sportmanagement).

Marit Sørensen is a professor emerita at the Norwegian School of Sport Sciences, Oslo, Norway. Her research interests combine adapted physical activity and sport and exercise psychology, spanning from organization of disability sport, through motivational interventions to increase physical activity, to mental health and physical activity. She is a fellow of the International Society of Sport Psychology (ISSP) and the International Association of Applied Psychology (IAAP). She is a section editor of the *European Journal of Adapted Physical Activity* (EUJAPA) and serves on the editorial board of the journal *Mental Health and Physical Activity* (MENPA). Recent publications include: Sørensen, M., Bentzen, M. & Farholm, A. Motivational physical activity intervention for psychiatric inpatients: A two-phased single-cases experimental study. *European Journal of Adapted Physical Activity* 2021;Volum 14(2). Sørensen, M., Roberts, G. & Farholm, A. Motivational climate in the home: Implications for physical activity, psychosocial outcomes and family relations. *International Journal of Sport Psychology* 2021;Volum 52(1) s. 71–89.

Claudia Stura is a professor and vice-director of studies at the University of Applied Sciences in Kufstein, Austria, and holds a PhD in International Conflict Management from Kennesaw State University, USA. Her research focus is on migration and sports. For example, she has worked with migrating professional athletes and the respective confederations to facilitate their acculturation process. She leads an EU project on supporting professionals who work with unaccompanied and separated children as well as a project on organized sports and intercultural competence and social capital in Tyrol, Austria. Recent publications include "Waiting for Godot (no more?): Institutional Innovation under Test in Response to Humanitarian Crises" (Plank & Stura, 2023) and "Sports confederations & legitimacy development: integration efforts as expression of social responsibility" (Stura, 2021).

Zsuzsanna Sáringerné Szilárd is a habilitated college professor at the Semmelweis University Pető András Faculty in Hungary. She graduated from the Hungarian University of Physical Education with a degree in Physical Education and swimming coaching. In 2006, she obtained a PhD degree in Education from the Doctoral School of Education, Eötvös Loránd University. Her dissertation was written on the topic of motion studies in childhood and habilitated in 2017 at the University of Physical Education. Since 2003, at the Semmelweis University András Pető Faculty, her main educational topics are: physical education, integrated physical education, adapted physical education, Parasport, and sports and quality of life. She authored published articles and books on her research interests, conducted research studies on integration, info-communication accessibility, and health and sport and quality of life.

Javier Pérez Tejero is a university professor in the Department of Health and Human Performance, Faculty of Physical Activity and Sports Sciences—INEF, Universidad Politécnica de Madrid (UPM), Spain, teaching Adapted Physical Activities and Sports for People with Disabilities (and related subjects) at Bachelor's and Master's levels. He is the director of the 'Sanitas Foundation' Chair of Studies on Inclusive Sports (CEDI) since 2009 at UPM (www.deporteinclusivo.com). He is a founding member and director (since 2022) of the recognized research group Physical Activity in Specific Populations Actividad Físico-deportiva en Poblaciones Específicas (AFIPE, UPM), visiting professor in different Master's degrees (both international and national levels) and principal investigator in several research projects. He was a wheelchair basketball coach at national and international levels (1998–2014) and responsible for this sport in the Spanish Federation of Sports for People with Physical Disabilities (FEDDF, 2014–2020). Author of numerous publications (books, book chapters and scientific articles) on sport for people with disabilities. He was one of the five recipients (as work coordinators) of the National Sports Award in the category of Arts and Sciences applied to sport by the Spanish Ministry of Culture and Sports for the publication of the work "The White Book of sport for people with disabilities in Spain" in 2019. Javier is also president-elect of the European Federation of Adapted Physical Activity since June 2022.

Linda Torége is a development manager at Parasport Sweden, Sweden. With a Bachelor's in Sport and a Master's in Africa Studies, she has been to many parts in the world, where she has worked in sport and societal development. In Norway, as a member of staff at the Norwegian Olympic and Paralympic Committee and the Confederation of Sports, she followed the inclusion process of Parasport into traditional sport federations. When she started working in Sweden with the Parasport Federation and the Swedish Paralympic Committee, one of the learnings from Norway was to try to facilitate a partnership with academia at an early stage of the inclusion process. Her work is all about policy and to be attentive to how practice can be shaped by policy and the other way around. A critical part of policy and development of practice in Parasport is research.

Debbie Van Biesen is a postdoctoral researcher and lecturer in the research unit Adapted Physical Activity and Psychomotor Rehabilitation, Department of Rehabilitation Sciences, KU Leuven, Belgium. Since January 2021 she divides her time across KU Leuven and Virtus World Intellectual Impairment Sport. She was appointed as the Virtus Academy manager, leveraging on international and evidenced-based knowledge of elite athletes with intellectual disability and autism. She has an extensive record of peer-reviewed published scientific articles in top journals in her field. During her PhD, she contributed to the development of evidence-based classification systems for elite athletes with intellectual disabilities, which led to their re-inclusion in the Paralympic Games. She was involved in other research projects related to coaching Para athletes, psychosocial aspects of disabilities, health-enhancing physical activity, disability sport participation and performance optimization.

Caroline van Lindert is educated in Leisure Studies (BA) and in Cultural Anthropology (MSc). She worked as a senior researcher at the Mulier Institute in the Netherlands since 2007. Prior to 2007, Caroline was Lecturer in Sports Management at the Academy for Leisure and Events, Breda University for Applied Sciences. The Mulier Institute is a non-profit, scientific sport-research institute in the Netherlands. As such, the Mulier Institute is engaged in fundamental, practice-focused and policy-relevant social-scientific sport research. It monitors the developments within the Dutch sports sector. As a cultural anthropologist, Caroline is interested in the underlying preferences, motivations and obstacles that influence sport participation of disadvantaged groups, in particular people with disabilities, and how their inclusion in sport can be stimulated through policy measures and interventions. Caroline is seen as an expert in disability sport (research) in the Netherlands. Educated in qualitative research methods, Caroline is interested in the lived experiences of persons with a disability and their involvement as experts by experience. At the Mulier Institute, Caroline coordinates research projects on different aspects of disability sport in the Netherlands, for example, sport policy evaluation studies, sport participation surveys, studies on the inclusion in sport and the impact of community sport coaches. Caroline has been a critical friend for policymakers and practitioners on disability sport at the national and local level for more than ten years and is a valued expert in meetings on the subject. Caroline coordinated two nation wide surveys on disability sport in 2008 and 2013, subsidized by the Dutch ministry of Health, Welfare and Sport, and has been working on a follow-up of these studies as a result of the increased interest for inclusion in sport for people with disabilities in the Netherlands.

Anabela Vitorino is a full adjunct professor and researcher at the Sport Science School of Rio Maior (ESDRM), Polytechnic Institute of Santarém (IPSantarém), member of the Research Center in Sport, Health and Human Development (CIDESD), and holds a PhD in Sport Sciences from the University of Trás-os-Montes e Alto Douro (UTAD) and a EuroPsy-European Certificate in Psychology by European Federation of Psychologists' Associations and practical degree in Special Psychopedagogy (Specialist) from Polytechnic Institute of Santarém, Leiria and Coimbra. Anabela is part of an interdisciplinary research team in SEDY2 Project ERAMUS+ (https://www.inholland.nl/inhollandcom/about-inholland/sedy2), focusing on promoting physical activity and inclusion in sport for children with disabilities (2020–2022). Her research interests and her academic research field are linked to motivational determinants in sport and exercise and behavioural change, with special focus on sedentary behaviour, physical activity, healthy lifestyles, well-being, exercise adherence, drop-out and persistence in sport, and specifically in sport for people with disabilities.

Christian Røj Voldby is a PhD candidate in the Department of Sports Science and Clinical Biomechanics, University of Southern Denmark. In his PhD, Christian examines similarities and differences in municipal disability policies and their role in disability sport. Christian's primary research interests include disability sport; sports policies; organizational learning, including sports club development;

coaching development; and cooperation between voluntary and municipal institutions. Besides several research reports, he recently authored published journal articles on how to develop coaching education through action research, with a particular focus on young coaches and on how sports clubs build and sustain organizational capacity based on longitudinal data.

Kim Wickman is a senior lecturer and associate professor at the Department of Education, Umeå University. Her subject competence extends across several areas, including special education, gender, sport and disability studies. Her research and teaching interests are identity constructions and power relations within the field of sport and special education with particular reference to ability, disability, gender and equality. For example, she is interested in how inclusion/exclusion, normality/deviation and equality/inequality is performed, maintained and challenged. Currently, Kim is engaged in a research project with colleagues, called Equal conditions in Sweden's largest popular movement (FORTE Dnr 2018-01759). Through qualitative and quantitative data collection methods the project investigates, on individual, group and organizational levels, opportunities and barriers for a change process towards equal conditions in sports. She is also the coordinator of interdisciplinary research collaboration for Special Education at Umeå University in Sweden.

Torsten Wojciechowski is a professor at EHiP – European University of Applied Sciences for Innovation and Perspective in Backnang, Germany, and Dean of the Faculty of Health, Sport and Nutrition. He studied Sport and Political Science and holds a doctorate from the University of Stuttgart, Germany. His research focus is on sport development, sport organizations, sport management, sport sociology, sport policy and health research. He is a member of the German Association for Sport Science, the European Association for Sociology of Sport, the Sport Organisation Research Network (SORN), and the Policy and Politics in Sport Network (POLIS). His recent publications include an edited volume on sport associations which he has co-edited with Lutz Thieme.

Abbreviations

ADEPS	General sport administration/Administration Générale du Sport
ADHD	Attention deficit hyperactivity disorder
ADL	Activities of Daily Living/Algemene Dagelijkse Levensverrichtingen
AFAPA	Austrian Federation of Adapted Physical Activity
AFFSS	Association for the French-speaking Federations for School Sport
AHLMSD	Association of the Heads of Lithuanian Municipal Sports Departments
APA	Adapted Physical Activity
APPC	Portuguese Association of Cerebral Palsy/Associação Portuguesa de Paralisia Cerebral
ASD	Autism Spectrum disorder
ASKÖ	Working Group for Sports and Physical Culture in Austria/Arbeitsgemeinschaft für Sport und Körperkultur in Österreich
ASPr	Swiss Association for Paralytics and Rheumatics
ASVÖ	General Sports Association Austria/Allgemeiner Sportverband Österreich
AUVA	General Accident Insurance Institution/Allgemeine Unfallversicherungsanstalt
BAR	German Association for Rehabilitation/Bundesarbeitsgemeinschaft für Rehabilitation
BASPO	Federal Office of Sport/Bundesamt für Sport
BDC	Belgian Deaf Sport Committee
BehiG	Disability Equality Act/Behindertengleichstellungsgesetz, Bundesgesetz über die Beseitigung von Benachteiligungen von Menschen mit Behinderungen
BFS	Federal Statistical Office/Bundesamt für Statistik
BGB	German Civil Code/Bürgerliches Gesetzbuch

BGStG	Federal Law for the Equality of People with Disabilities/Bundes-Behindertengleichstellungsgesetz
BISp	Federal Institute for Sports Science/Bundesinstitut für Sportwissenschaft
BMAS	Federal Ministry of Labour and Social Affairs/Bundesministerium für Arbeit und Soziales
BMI	Federal Ministry of the Interior/Bundesministerium des Inneren
BNMO	Dutch Military War and Service Victims Association/Bond van Nederlandse Militaire Oorlog- en Dienstslachtoffers
BOA	British Olympic Association
BOE	Spanish Official Gazette/Boletín Oficial del Estado
BOIC	The Belgian Olympic and Interfederal Committee
BPA	British Paralympic Association
BPC	Belgian Paralympic Committee
BRSNW	North Rhine-Westphalia Association of Sport for the Disabled and Rehabilitation/Behinderten- und Rehabilitationssportverband Nordrhein-Westfahlen
BSFG	National Law on Sports Promotion/Bundes-Sportförderungsgesetz
BSO	Austrian Sports Organisation/Österreichische Bundes-Sportorganisation
BSV	Federal Office of Social Insurance/Bundesamt für Sozialversicherungen
BSVG	Belgian Sports Federation for the Disabled
Bufdir	The Norwegian Directory for Children, Youth and Families/Barne og Ungdoms og familie Direktoratet
CAS	Court of Arbitration for Sport
CBS	Statistics the Netherlands/Centraal Bureau voor de Statistiek
CERMI	Spanish Committee of Representatives of People with Disabilities/Comité Estatal de Representantes de Personas con Discapacidad
CGFNI	Commonwealth Games Federation NI
CHF	Swiss Francs/Schweizer Franken
CHS	Continuous Household Survey
CI	Coaching Ireland
CIA	Central Intelligence Agency
CISS	International Committee for the Silent Sports/Comité International des Sports des Sourds
CMO	Chief Medical Officer
COE	Spanish Olympic Committee/Comité Olímpico Español
CONDA	National Congress in Adapted Sport/Congreso Nacional de Deporte Adaptado
CPE	Spanish Paralympic Committee/Comité Paralímpico Español
CPISRA	Cerebral Palsy International Sports and Recreation Association

Abbreviations xxix

CPP	Portuguese Paralympic Committee/Comité Paralímpico de Portugal
CRPD	The Convention on the Rights of Persons With Disabilites
CSC	Community sport coaches/Buurtsportcoaches
CSD	Higher Sports Council/Consejo Superior de Deportes
CSR	Corporate social responsibility
DBS	German Disabled Sports Association/Deutscher Behindertensportverband
DBSB	German Chess Federation for the Blind and Visually Impaired/Deutscher Blinden-und Sehbehinderten-Schachbund
DBSJ	German Disabled Sports Youth/Deutsche Behindertensport Jugend
DBSV	German Association for the Blind and Disabled/Deutscher Blinden- und Sehbehindertenverband
DCMS	Department for Culture Media and Sport
DFIF	Danish Association of Company Sports/Dansk Firmaidrætsforbund
DGI	Danish Gymnastics and Sports Association/Danske Gymnastik- og Idrætsforeninger
DGRh	German Society for Rheumatology/Deutsche Gesellschaft für Rheumatologie
DGS	German Deaf Sport Association/Deutscher Gehörlosen-Sportverband
DGUV	German Social Accident Insurance/Deutsche Gesetzliche Unfallversicherung
DIF	Sports Confederation of Denmark/Danmarks Idrætsforbund
Disability Sport NI	Disability Sport Northern Ireland
DKThR	German Curatorship for Therapeutic Riding/Deutsches Kuratorium für Therapeutisches Reiten
DoC	Department of Communities
DOSB	German Olympic Sports Confederation/Deutscher Olympischer Sportbund
DP	Disabled Person/People
DRS	German Wheelchair Sports Association/Deutscher Rollstuhl-Sportverband
DSF	Disability Sport Federation
DSF(s)	Disability Sport Federation(s)
DSG	Disability Stakeholder Group
DSSS	German Schools Sports Foundation/Deutsche Schulsportstiftung
DSSV	German Sports Association for the Hard of Hearing/Deutscher Schwerhörigen Sportverband
DVE	German Association of Occupational Therapists/Deutscher Verband der Ergotherapeuten

DVGS	German Association for Health Sports and Sports Therapy/Deutscher Verband für Gesundheitssport und Sporttherapie
DVS	German Disabled Sports Association (old term)/Deutscher Versehrtensportverband
DZ-RS	National Assembly of the Republic of Slovenia/Državni zbor Republike Slovenije
EB	Eurobarometer
EBGB	Federal Office for the Equality of Persons with Disabilities/Eidgenössisches Büro für die Gleichstellung von Menschen mit Behinderungen
EBH	Equal Treatment Authority/Egyenlő Bánásmód Hatóság
EBSED	Association of Sports and Educational Sciences in Disabled Individuals/Engelli Bireylerde Spor ve Eğitim Derneği
EDAD	Survey on disabilities, personal autonomy and dependency situations/Encuesta de Discapacidad, Autonomía personal y situaciones de Dependencia
EDI	Federal Department of the Interior/Eidgenössisches Department des Inneren
EHIS	European Health Interview Survey
EqA 2010	Equality Act 2010
ESS	European Social Survey
EU	European Union
EU-SILC	European Statistics of Income and Living Conditions
EVS	European Values Study
FAI	Football Association of Ireland
FCP	OPorto Football Club/Futebol Clube do Porto
FEDC	Spanish Federation of Sports for the Blind/Federación Española de Deportes para Ciegos
FEDDF	Spanish Sports Federation for People with Physical Disabilities/Federación Española de Deportes para Personas con Discapacidad Física
FEDDI	Spanish Sports Federation for People with Intellectual Disabilities/Federación Española de Deportes para Personas con Discapacidad Intelectual
FEDPC	Spanish Federation of Sports for People with Cerebral Palsy/Federación Española de Deportes para Personas con Parálisis Cerebral
FEDS	Spanish Sports Federation Sports for the Deaf/Federación Española de Deportes para Sordos
Féma	Adapted Multisports Federation/Fédération Multisports Adaptés
FEMP	Spanish Federation of Municipalities and Provinces/Federación Española de Municipios y Provincias

Abbreviations xxxi

FIHO	Foundation for Funding Disability and Humanitarian Organisations/Fundacija za financiranje invalidskih in humanitarnih organizacij v Republiki Sloveniji
FIPFA	Federation Internationale De Powerchair Football Association
FMSZ	Hungarian Federation for Sportorganisations of People with Disabilities/Fogyatékkal élők Sportszervezeteinek Magyarországi Szövetsége
FODISZ	Disability Student and Leisure Sports Association/Fogyatékosok Diák-, és Szabadidősport Szövetség
FONESZ	National Sports Federation for the Disabled/Fogyatékosok Nemzeti Sportszövetsége
FOVESZ	Competition Sports Association of the Disabled/Fogyatékosok Versenysport Szövetség
FPDD	Portuguese Federation of Sport for People with Desabilities/Federação Portuguesa de Desporto para Pessoas com Deficiência
FPG	Federation Disabled Horse riding/Federatie Paardrijden Gehandicapten *(dissolved)*
FSG	Disability Sport Fund/Fonds Gehandicaptensport
FSN	Family Support Network
FŠO	Sports Foundation/Fundacija za šport
fte	Fulltime equivalent
GAA	Gaelic Athletic Association
GALI	Global Activity Limitation Indicator
GAPPA	Global Action Plan on Physical Activity
GDP	Gross Domestic Product
GDPR	General Data Protection Regulation
GE/LSMA	National health survey/biannual national lifestyle monitor/Gezondheidsenquête/Leefstijlmonitor
GFBS	Company for the Promotion of Disability Sport/Gesellschaft zur Förderung des Behindertensports
GoB	Governing Body
GOV	Governmental
GSN	Disability Sport Netherlands/Gehandicaptensport Nederland
G-sport	Disability sport
HBS	Household Budget Survey
HCL	Healthy Life Centres/Frisklivssentraler
HDI	Human Development Index
HDI	UN Human Development Index
HEAL	Healthy Eating Active Living
HETUS	Harmonised European Time Use Surveys
HI	Hearing impairment
HODR	Name of a sports club for individuals with visual impairments named after an ancient god
HSE	Health Service Executive

HUY	The High Perfomance Unit/Huippu-urheiluyksikkö
IBSA	International Blind Sports Association
ICF	International Classification of Functioning, Disability and Health (framework)
ICIDH	International Classification of Impairments, Disabilities and Handicaps
ICRPD	Convention on the Rights of Persons with Disabilities
ICSD	The International Committee of Sport for the Deaf
IDA	Industrial Development Authority
ÍF	National sports federation for disabled athletes/Íþróttasamband Fatlaðra
IFCPF	International Federation of CP-Football
IHREC	Irish Human Rights and Equality Commission
II	Intellectual impairment
IIS	Irish Institute of Sport
INAS	International (sports) Federation for Athletes/Persons with an Intellectual Impairment/Disability
INE	Spanish Statistical Office/Instituto Nacional de Estadística
INIDD	National Survey on Incapacities, Disabilities and Disadvantages/Inquérito Nacional de Incapacidades, Deficiências e Desvantagens
INR	National Institute for Rehabilitation/Instituto Nacional para a Reabilitação
INSOS	branch association of social institutions with services for people with disabilities in Switzerland/Soziale Institutionen für Menschen mit Behinderungen Schweiz
Int	Intermediary
IPC	International Paralympic Committee
IPDJ	Portuguese Institute of Sport and Youth/Instituto Português do Desporto e Juventude
IQ	Intelligence quotient/Intelligentiequotiënt
IRFU	Irish Rugby Football Union
ISC	Irish Sports Council
ÍSÍ	The National Olympic and Sport Association of Iceland/Íþróttasamand Íslands
ISM	Irish Sports Monitor
ISSP	International Social Survey Programme
IV	Disability Insurance/Invalidenversicherung
IWA	Irish Wheelchair Association
IWAS	International Wheelchair and Amputee Sports Association
IWBF	International Wheelchair Basketball Federation
IWRF	International Wheelchair Rugby Federation
J+S	Youth and Sports/Jugend und Sport
JTFO	Jugend trainiert für Olympia
JTFP	Jugend trainiert für Paralympics

Abbreviations

KADA	Career Afterwards/Karriere Danach
KAP	Kazan Action Plan
KCB	Knowledge Centre on Disability/Videnscenter for Handicap
KCSB	Knowledge Centre for Sport and Physical Activity/Kenniscentrum voor Sport en Bewegen
KIHU	KIHU Olympic Research Institute/Kilpa- ja huippu-urheilun tutkimuskeskus
KNDSB	(Royal) Deaf Sport Federation/(Koninklijke) Nederlandse Doven Sport Bond
KVL	Finnish Association on Intellectual and Developmental Disabilities/Kehitysvammaliitto
LAM	Local Activity Means/Lokale aktivitetsmidler
LBSF	Lithuanian Blind Sports Federation
LETR	Law Enforcement Torch Run
LFSIG	National Federation Sport Open days Disabled/Landelijke Federatie Sport Instuiven Gehandicapten *(dissolved)*
LGBTQ+	Lesbian, gay, bisexual, transgender, queer and others. The 'plus' represents other sexual identities.
LHF	French-speaking Handisport League/League Handisport Francophone
LIKES	LIKES Research Centre for Physical Activity and Health/Liikunnan ja kansanterveyden tutkimuskeskus
LNOP	Lithuanian National Olympic Committee
LOK	The local activity sport support system/Statligt lokalt aktivitetsstöd
LPC	Lithuanian Paralympic Committee
LSFD	Lithuanians Sports Federation for the Disabled
LSP	Local Sports Partnership
LSS	The Act concerning Support and Service to Persons with Certain Functional Disabilities/Lag (199, p. 387) om stöd och service till vissa funktionshindrade
LTAD	Long-Term Athletes Development model
LTS	Finnish Society of Sport Sciences/Liikuntatieteellinen Seura
MATP	Motor Activity Training Programme
MCD	Ministry of Culture and Sport/Ministerio de Cultura y Deporte
MDDSZ	Ministry of Labour, Family, Social Affairs and Equal Opportunities/Ministrstvo za delo, družino, socialne zadeve in enake možnosti
MDS	Model Disability Survey
MDSZ	National Student Sport Federation/Magyar Diáksport Szövetség
MEHM	Minimum European Health Module
MEOSZ	National Association of Disabled People's Associations/Magyar Országos Szövetsége

MÉS	Sportfederation for People with mental Disabilities/Magyar Értelmi Fogyatékosok Sportszövetsége
MHB	Hungarian Helsinki Committee/Magyar Helsinki Bizottság
MHD	Mental health disorder
MINEPS	International Conference of Ministers and Senior officials Responsible for PE and Sports
MinOCW	Ministry of Education, Culture and Sciences/Ministerie van Onderwijs, Cultuur en Wetenschappen
MinVWS	Ministry of Health, Welfare and Sport/Ministerie van Volksgezondheid, Welzijn en Sport
MIZŠ	Ministry of Education, Science and Sport/Ministrstvo za izobraževanje, znanost in šport
MLMS	Hungarian Sports Federation of Visually Impaired and Disabled Persons/Magyar Látássérültek és Mozgáskorlátozottak Sportszövetsége
MP	The Green Party/Miljöpartiet
MPB	Hungarian Paralympic Committee/Magyar Paralimpiai Bizottság
MPCE	Ministry of the Presidency, Relations with the Courts and Equality/Ministerio de Presidencia, Relaciones con las Cortes e Igualdad
MPSZ	Hungarian Parasport Federation/Magyar Parasport Szövetség
MRC Aardenburg	Military Rehabilitation Centre Aardenburg/Militair Revalidatie Centrum Aardenburg
MSA	Ministry of Social affairs
MSOB	National Special Olympics Federation/Magyar Speciális Olimpiai Bizottság
MSOSZ	Hungarian Special Olympic Association/Magyar Speciális Olimpiai Szövetség
MSSSZ	Hungarian Deaf Sports Federation/Magyar Siketek Sportszövetsége
MSZSZ	National Leisure sports Federation/Magyar Szabadidősport Szövetség
MSZSZ	Hungarian Transplant Association—for Sport, Culture and Advocacy/Magyar Szervátültetettek—Országos Sport, Kulturális és Érdekvédelmi—Szövetsége
MTU	Munster Technological University
MZ	Ministry of Health/Ministrstvo za zdravje
NASAK	National Sports Facility Concept/Nationales Sportanlagenkonzept
NAV	The Norwegian Labour and Welfare Administration/Norges arbeids- og velferds administrasjon
NDIS	National Disability Inclusion Strategy
NDPB	Non-Departmental Public Bodies
NDSF	National Disability Sport Federation

Abbreviations

NDSO	National Disability Sport Organisation
NEBAS	Dutch Association for Adapted Sport/Nederlandse Bond voor Aangepast Sporten *(dissolved)*
NFI	The Norwegian Sports Federation for the disabled/Norges Funksjonshemmedes Idrettsforbund
NFSG	National Disability Sport Fund/Stichting Nationaal Fonds Sport Gehandicapten *(dissolved)*
NFSOG	Federation for Disability Sport & Outdoor Recreation for People with Intellectual Disability
NGB	National Governing Body (of Sport)
NGO's	Non-governmental Organizations
NHIF	The Norwegian Federation for Disability Sports/Norges Handicapidrettsforbund
NHSSS	The Norwegian School of Sport Sciences
NI	Northern Ireland
NIF	The Norwegian Sports Confederation and Olympic-and Paralympic Committee/Norges idrettsforbund og olympiske og paralympiske komité
NIH	The Norwegian School of Sport Sciences/Norges idrettshøgskole
NIS	Dutch Disabled Sport Federation/Nederlandse Invaliden Sportbond *(dissolved)*
NISB	Dutch Institute for Sport and Physical activity/Nederlands Instituut voor Sport en Bewegen *(dissolved)*
NISF	Northern Ireland Sports Forum
NISRA	Northern Ireland Research and Statistics Agency
NIVEL	Dutch Institute for Health Services Research/Stichting Nederlands Instituut voor Onderzoek van de Gezondheidszorg
NKL	Federation for the Visually Impaired/Näkövammaisten liitto
NOC	National Olympic Committee
NOC*NSF	Netherlands Olympic Committee*Dutch Sports Federation/ Nederlands Olympisch Comité*Nederlandse Sport Federatie
Non-Gov	Non-Governmental
NPA	National Prevention Agreement/Nationaal Preventie Akkoord
NPAP	National Physical Activity Plan
NPC	National Paralympic Committee
NPŠŠ	National branch sports schools/nacionalne panožne športne šole
NPŠZ	National branch sports federations/nacionalne panožne športne zveze
NRK	The Norwegian Broadcasting Corporation/Norges Rikskringkasting
NRZ	National Swimming Council/Nationale Raad Zwembaden
NSA	National Sport Agreement/Nationaal Sport Akkoord
NSCF	National Sport Confederation

NSF	National Sport Federation/Nationale Sport Federatie (Bond)
NSF(s)	National Sport Federation(s)
NSG	National Sport Federation for the intellectually impaired/Nederlandse Sportbond voor Geestelijk gehandicapten (*dissolved*)
NSIOS	National Council of Disability Organisations of Slovenia/Nacionalni svet invalidskih organizacij Slovenije
NSR	Dutch Sport Council/Nederlandse Sport Raad
NSVG	Dutch-speaking Sports Federation for Visually Handicapped People
NYSE	Sports Association of Cripples/Nyomorékok Sport Egyesülete
ÖBR	Austrian Disability Council/Österreichischer Behindertenrat
ÖBSV	Austrian Disability Sports Organisation/Österreichischer Behindertensportverband
OCD	Obsessive-compulsive disorder
OCI	Olympic Council of Ireland
OECD	Organisation for Economic Co-operation and Development
ÖGSV	Austrian Deaf Sports Confederation/Österreichischer Gehörlosen Sportverband
OK	National Olympic Committee/Suomen Olympiakomitea
OKM	The Ministry of Education and Culture/Opetus- ja kulttuuriministeriö
OKS-ZŠZ	National Olympic Committee—Association of Sport Federations/Olimpijski komite Slovenije—Združenje športnih zvez
ONCE	Spanish Association for the Blind/Organización Nacional de Ciegos Españoles
OORI	National Institute of Medical Rehabilitation/Országos Orvori és Rehabilitációs Intézet
ÖPC	Austrian Paralympic Committee/Österreichisches Paralympisches Komitee
ÖSB	Austrian Association of Cities/Österreichischen Städtebund
ÖVP	Conservative Austrian Peoples Party/Österreichische Volkspartei
ÖVSV	Austrian Invalidity Sports Association/Österreichische Versehrtensportverband
PA	Physical activity
Para Group	Swiss Grouping for Paraplegics
Paralympics GB	Paralympics Great Britain and Northern Ireland
PCI	Paralympic Council of Ireland
PE	Physical education
PI	Physical impairment
PIP	Personal Independence Payment
Pwd	Person with a disability
PWD	Persons with disabilities

Abbreviations

Pwd	People with a disability/mensen met een beperking
PwD	Persons/people with disabilities
Pwds	Persons with a disability
RC Kriens	Wheelchair Club Kriens/Rollstuhlclub Kriens
RF	Swedish Sports Confederation/Riksidrottsförbundet
RFEC	Royal Spanish Cycling Federation/Real Federación Española de Ciclismo
RIM	Biennial general meeting/Riksidrottsmötet
RIVM	National Institute for Public Health and the Environment/Rijks Instituut voor Volksgezondheid en Milieu
ROI	Republic of Ireland
RSS	Wheelchair Sports Switzerland/Rollstuhlsport Schweiz
S	The Democratic Party/Socialdemokraterna
SAPAS	Sport and Physical Activity Survey
SBV	Saxon Association of Sport for the Disabled and Rehabilitation/Sächsischer Behinderten- und Rehabilitationssportverband
scUK	Sports Coach United Kingdom
SDG's	Sustainable Development Goals
SDI	The Swedish Deaf Sports Federation/Svenska Dövidrottsförbundet
SGB	Social Code/Sozialgesetzbuch
SH Geneva	Sport Handicap Geneva
SIDO	Sports Inclusion Disability Officer
SINOSZ	National Deaf and Mute Sports Federation/Siketek és Nagyothallók Országos Szövetsége
SIU	Finnish Association of Sports for the Disabled/Suomen Invalidien Urheiluliitto
SIVSCE	Social Inclusion and Volunteering in Sports Clubs in Europe
SKLU	Finnish Association of Sports for Intellectual Disabilities/Suomen Kehitysvammaisten Liikunta ja Urheilu
SKUL	Finnish Athletic Association of the Deaf/The Sports Federation for the Deaf/Kuurojen Urheiluliitto
SLOBO	Organisation for After-School Sport in Special Education
SMK	Conference of Sports Ministers of the Länder/Sportministerkonferenz
SNI	Special Educational Needs/Sajátos Nevelési Igény
SNR	National Rehabilitation Secretariat/Secretariado Nacional de Reabilitação
SOB	Special Olympics Belgium
SOD	Special Olympics Germany/Special Olympics Deutschland
SOL	Special Olympics Lithuanian
SON	Special Olympics Netherlands/Special Olympics Nederland
SOÖ	Special Olympics Austria
SOU	Special Olympics Ulster

SoveLi	Finnish Adapted Physical Activity Federation/Soveltava liikunta SoveLi
SPEAK	Sport Ireland Strategic Planning, Evaluation and Knowledge
SPÖ	Social Democratic Party of Austria/Sozialdemokratische Partei Österreichs
SpoFöG	Sports Promotion Act/über die Förderung von Sport und Bewegung
Sport NI	Sport Northern Ireland
SPV	Swiss Paraplegics Association/Schweizer Paraplegiker-Vereinigung
SRK	Sports Minister Conference/Sportministerkonferenz
SSB	Statistics Norway/Statistisk sentralbyrå
StMAS	Bavarian State Ministry of Labour and Social Affairs/Bayerisches Staatsministerium für Familie, Arbeit und Soziales
STUI	State department for Youth and Sport/Statens ungdoms- og idrettskontor
SVBS	Swiss Federation for Disability Sport/Schweizerischer Verband für Behindertensport
SVGN	Sport federation for the visually impaired/Sportfederatie Visueel Gehandicapten Nederland *(dissolved)*
SVIS	Swiss Sports Federation for Invalids/Schweizerischer Verband für Invalidensport
SWG	Foundation Water sport for Disabled/Stichting Watersport met Gehandicapten
TAO	Financial support scheme for tax deduction of companies supporting sport/Társasági adó és osztalékadó
TASZ	Society for Civil Liberties/Társaság a Szabadságjogokért
TDA	Turkish Disability Act
TESYEV	Turkey Disabled Sports, Education, Assistance and Education Foundation/Türkiye Engelliler Spor Yardım ve Eğitim Vakfı
TFEU	Treaty on the Functioning of the European Union
THL	The National Institute of Health and Welfare/Terveyden ja hyvinvoinnin laitos
TMOK	National Olympic Committee of Turkey/Türkiye Milli Olimpiyat Komitesi
UK	United Kingdom
UN	United Nations
UNCRPD	United Nations Convention on the Rights of Persons with Disabilities
UNESCO	United Nations Educational, Scientific and Cultural Organization
UNICEF	United Nations Children's Fund
URI-Soča	The University Rehabilitation Institute, Republic of Slovenia/Univerzitetni rehabilitacijski Inštitut Republike Slovenije—Soča

VAU	Finnish Sports Federation of Persons with Disabilities/Suomen Vammaisurheilu ja—liikunta VAU
VDSB	Flemish Deaf Sport League
VI	Visual impairment
VLG	Flemish Disability Sports League/Vlaamse Liga Gehandicaptensport
VLN	National Sports Council/Valtion liikuntaneuvosto
VNG	Association of Dutch Municipalities/Vereniging Nederlandse Gemeenten
VSF	Flemish Sports Federation/Vlaamse sport federatie
VSG	Association of Sport and Municipalities/Vereniging Sport en Gemeenten
VTS	Flemish trainer school/Vlaamse trainersschool
WG	Washington Group on Disability Statistics
WG-SS	Washington Group on Disability Statistics Short Set
WHO	World Health Organization
WMO	Social Support Act/Wet Maatschappelijke Ondersteuning
YST	Youth Sport Trust
ZŠRS Planica	The Institute of Sport of the Republic Slovenia Planica/Zavod za šport Republike Slovenije Planica
Zveza ŠIS-SPK	Sports Federation for the Disabled of Slovenia/Zveza za šport invalidov Slovenije—Slovenski paralimpijski komite
ZVK	German Association for Physiotherapy/Deutscher Verband für Physiotherapie
	National Paralympic Committee/Suomen Paralympiakomitea
	The Social Services Act/Socialtjänstlagen, 2020
	Swedish Parasport Federation/Svenska Parasportförbundet

List of Figures

Fig. 1.1	Comparative framework for each country chapter throughout the book. Source: editors' own elaboration based on the conceptual framework of Scheerder et al. (2017)	10
Fig. 1.2	Participating countries per region and corresponding chapter numbers. Source: Mulier Institute, this work	18
Fig. 2.1	Disability and the triangle of violence. Source: adapted from Galtung (1990)	27
Fig. 2.2	The ICF model for disability. Source: adapted from World Health Organization (2002)	35
Fig. 2.3	Classification of disabilities in the handbook. Source: adapted from Von Heijden-Brinkman et al. (2013)	37
Fig. 2.4	Self-reported long-term limitations in daily activities due to health problems, population 16 years and older, population EU-27 countries and participating countries in the handbook (% share of population, 2020). *United Kingdom and Iceland data from 2018. For practical reasons Northern Ireland is regarded as a separate unit in the handbook. In the EU-data, Northern Ireland will be regarded part of the UK and therefore is missing in the figure. Source: Eurostat (2022a) (HLTH_SILC_12)	41
Fig. 2.5	Distribution of persons aged 15 years and older with physical and sensory functional activity limitations, population EU-27 countries and participating countries in the handbook (% share of population, 2014). Data not available for the Netherlands, Belgium and Switzerland. For practical reasons Northern Ireland is regarded as a separate unit in the handbook. In the EU-data, Northern Ireland will be regarded part of the UK and therefore is missing in the figure. Source: Eurostat (2021) (HLTH_EHIS_PL1E)	42

Fig. 2.6	Preliminary model for disability sport in the handbook. Source: adapted from LTAD model for athletes with a disability (Higgs & Legg, n.d.; Higgs et al., 2019) and the Church model of sports (Scheerder et al., 2011)	48
Fig. 3.1	Sports participation in (former) EU28 member states amongst people with and without a disability or illness aged 15 and over according to country (2013–2017), percentages of total population. *Note*: Due to a low number of cases in at least one of the two EB data sets (less than 50 respondents with disability in the respective country), the numbers of Estonia, Latvia, Lithuania, Slovakia, Slovenia, Croatia, Cyprus, Malta, Luxembourg and Ireland need to be treated with caution. *Source*: Authors' own calculations, based on Eurobarometer data (European Commission, 2014, 2018)	65
Fig. 3.2	Sports participation in (former) EU28 member states amongst people with and without a disability or illness aged 15 and over according to region (2013–2017), percentages of total population. Source: Authors' own calculations, based on Eurobarometer data (European Commission, 2014, 2018)	66
Fig. 3.3	Participation in a sports club in (former) EU28 member states amongst people with and without a disability or illness aged 15 and over according to region (2013–2017), percentages of total population. Source: Authors' own calculations, based on Eurobarometer data (European Commission, 2014, 2018)	67
Fig. 3.4	Participation in a fitness centre in (former) EU28 member states amongst people with and without a disability or illness aged 15 and over according to region (2013–2017), percentages of total population. *Source*: Authors' own calculations, based on Eurobarometer data (European Commission, 2014, 2018)	68
Fig. 3.5	Representation of people with a disability in sports clubs from ten European countries (2015), percentages of total number of sports clubs. *Note:* Numbers between brackets below the bars in the figure concern the number of people with a disability for each specific country. *Source*: Authors' own calculations, based on Nagel et al. (2020)	69
Fig. 3.6	Non-representation of specific population groups in sports clubs from ten European countries (2015), percentages of total number of sports clubs. *Note1:* Numbers between brackets below the bars in the figure concern the number of people with a disability for each specific country. *Note2:* For readability reasons, only the percentages related to people with a disability are shown. *Source*: Authors' own calculations, based on Nagel et al. (2020)	69

List of Figures

Fig. 3.7	Number of sports clubs with special initiatives for specific population groups in ten European countries (2015), percentages of total number of sports clubs. *Note1:* Numbers between brackets below the bars in the figure concern the number of people with a disability for each specific country. *Note2:* For readability reasons, only the percentages related to people with a disability are shown. *Source*: Authors' own calculations, based on Nagel et al. (2020)	70
Fig. 3.8	Association between income inequality (2010–2017, quintile ratios) and rate of sports participation amongst people with a disability 15 years of age and over (2017) in EU27 (due to a lack of data, Malta cannot be included in this dispersion diagram) countries. *Note:* $r_{\text{Pearson}} = -0.62$ ($p<0.01$). *Source*: Authors' own calculations, based on European Commission (2018) and UNDP (2020)	73
Fig. 4.1	Disability sport framework for Denmark. Abbreviations used: KCD (Knowledge Centre on Disability); DGI (Danish Gymnastics and Sports Association); DIF (Sports Confederation of Denmark); NSFs (National Sports Federations)	85
Fig. 4.2	Number of days per week the respondents do sport or are physically active for at least 30 minutes, grouped by type and severity of the disability (%, n = 20,451). Source: Amilon et al. (2017)	93
Fig. 4.3	Whether the respondents are active in sport or exercise in general and in any of the three organisational forms: sports club, fitness centre or self-organised, grouped by type and severity of the disability (%, n = 18,957). Source: Østerlund et al. (2014)	94
Fig. 4.4	The distribution of sports club members according to whether they have a disability and which disability (%, n = 3163). Source: van der Roest et al. (2017)	95
Fig. 5.1	The birth and re-structure of various disability sports associations in Finland	106
Fig. 5.2	The structure of the Finnish disability sports landscape. Arrows are showing financial relationships	108
Fig. 6.1	The overall structure of disability sport in Iceland	132
Fig. 7.1	The organisation of The Norwegian Confederation of Sports and Olympic and Paralympic Committee (NIF, 2019a)	148
Fig. 7.2	Timeline of the development of disability sport in Norway	152
Fig. 7.3	Organisation of disability sport in Norway	154
Fig. 7.4	How finances from the National Lottery surplus were distributed for 2020 (NIF, 2020c)	155
Fig. 7.5	Participation and medals in summer and winter Paralympic games from 2004 to 2018	158
Fig. 7.6	Numbers of members active in para sport (NIF, 2020a)	158
Fig. 7.7	Clubs with active para sport members from 2002 to 2017 (Dale, 2019)	159

Fig. 7.8	Factors that need to be in place for integration (Sørensen et al., 1999)	161
Fig. 8.1	The Swedish Sport organisation (The Federation of Deaf Sport is one of 72 special sports federations)	173
Fig. 8.2	The emergence of parasport in Sweden	176
Fig. 8.3	The funding and co-dependency of the national, regional and local sports between the different geographical levels of the governmental, intermediate and non-governmental levels of sport in Sweden	177
Fig. 8.4	The governance model of the Swedish Parasport Federation	180
Fig. 10.1	Disability sport framework for NI	222
Fig. 11.1	Map of the UK	238
Fig. 11.2	The (disability) sport structure in the UK	245
Fig. 11.3	Inactivity by impairment type. Source: adapted from Active Lives Online, 2020	258
Fig. 12.1	The development of disability sports in Austria	274
Fig. 12.2	The structure of disability sports in Austria. Notes: *AUVA* General Accident Insurance Institution, *BSO* Austrian Sports Organisation; Bundes-Sport *GmbH* Federal Sports Ltd., *GFBS* Company for the Promotion of Disability Sport, *ÖBR* Austrian Disability Council, *ÖBSV* Austrian Disability Sports Association, *ÖGSV* Austrian Deaf Sports Confederation, *ÖPC* Austrian Paralympic Committee, *ÖSB* Austrian Association of Cities, *SOÖ* Special Olympics Austria, *SRK* Sports Minister Conference	275
Fig. 12.3	Membership in disability sports in Austria (data from the membership statistics of the BSO; memberships of ÖBSV and ÖGSV). Source: https://www.sportaustria.at/de/ueber-uns/mitglieder/mitgliederstatistik/	284
Fig. 13.1	Agents involved in the disability sports landscape in Belgium. Note: dotted arrows indicate financing; full arrows indicate relationship (membership/partnership). Sources: Claes et al. (2017); Scheerder et al. (2011); Scheerder et al. (2021); Scheerder and Vos (2013); Marin-Urquiza et al. (2020)	304
Fig. 13.2	The inclusion continuum. Note: definitions adapted from 'General Comment No. 4' of the UN Convention on the Rights for Persons with Disability (2016) in the context of education. Source: Burns and Johnston (2020)	312
Fig. 13.3	The social status pyramid of disability sport. Source: data derived from Scheerder et al. (2018b)	317
Fig. 14.1	The disability sport system in Germany*. *N.B.: the German sport system in disability sport is characterised by only limited forms of direct hierarchy and formal control	332

List of Figures

Fig. 15.1 Timeline history of disability sport in the Netherlands*. *BNMO=Dutch Military War and Service Victims Association; (K)NDSB=(Royal) Dutch Deaf Sports Federation; NIS=Dutch Disabled Sports Federation; NSG=Dutch Sports Federation for persons with intellectual disability; (N)FSG=(National) Disability Sport Fund; NEBAS=Dutch Association for Adapted Sports; NPC=National Paralympic Committee; NOC*NSF=Netherlands Olympic Committee*Dutch Sports Federation. Source: authors' own work 356

Fig. 15.2 Agents involved in the Dutch disability sport landscape. Source: Van Lindert & De Jonge, 2022: adapted by the authors 358

Fig. 15.3 Weekly participation in categories of sport, including walking and cycling for pleasure, by disability and chronic condition, population aged 18–79 (2017–2019, in percentages). ¹Physical disability (one or more) is a combination of mobility, visual and/or hearing disability. Sources: Gezondheidsenquête/Leefstijlmonitor CBS in cooperation with RIVM (2017–2019), in: Van den Dool et al., 2022: adapted by the authors 375

Fig. 16.1 The emergence of disability sport in Switzerland. Organisations in bold are among the founders of Swiss disability sport. Underlined organisations still exist... 390

Fig. 16.2 Disability sport framework for Switzerland 392

Fig. 17.1 Disability sports framework for Hungary. *As of June 2022 the State Secretariat of Sports from the Ministry of Human Resources was transferred under the Ministry of Defence. Source: Developed by author as an adaptation to disability sport using Perényi (2013)... 420

Fig. 17.2 State support for the Hungarian Paralympic Committee (MPB) between 2005 and 2020 in million HUF. Source: MPB (Hungarian Paralympic Committee) 428

Fig. 18.1 Disability sport structure Lithuania 445

Fig. 19.1 Pyramid structure of sport as defined in the NPŠRS 2014–2023 (Jurak, 2014), with adds for disability sport. Source: Jurak, 2014 (left side), authors' own work (right side) 468

Fig. 19.2 Sport framework of Slovenia. Source: Scheerder et al. (2007) 469

Fig. 20.1 Organogram of able-bodied sport governance in Portugal (GOV—Governmental, Int—intermediary, Non-Gov—Non-governmental agents; arrows represent hierarchical and/or financial relationships). Source: authors' own artwork; data publicly available online on institutional websites of the Portuguese Institute of Sport and Youth (https://ipdj.gov.pt) and the Portuguese Olympic Committee (https://comiteo limpicoportugal.pt) 489

Fig. 20.2	Percentage of the population without and with disabilities by disability type in Portugal. Source: data of Census 2001 (INE, 2001)	490
Fig. 20.3	Historical timeline of disability sport emergence and rise. Source: authors' own artwork, adapted from (Sousa et al., 2013)	492
Fig. 20.4	Organogram of disability sport governance in Portugal (GOV—Governmental, Int—intermediary, Non-Gov—Non-governmental agents; arrows represent a hierarchical and/or financial relationship). Source: authors' own artwork; data publicly available online on institutional websites of the Portuguese Institute of Sport and Youth (https://ipdj.gov.pt), the Portuguese Paralympic Committee (https://paralimpicos.pt), the National Institute of Rehabilitation (https://www.inr.pt/inicio) and the Portuguese Federation of Sport for Persons with Disabilities (https://fpdd.pt/novo/)	495
Fig. 21.1	The structure of disability sport in Spain	518
Fig. 21.2	Percentage of people with disabilities that would like to spend their leisure time in a given activity but cannot because of disability. Source: EDAD, INE, 2008	528
Fig. 22.1	Agents of disability sports in Turkey. Sources: Canpolat (2020a), Ministry of Foreign Affairs (www.mfa.gov.tr)	547
Fig. 23.1	Composite framework for disability sport in Europe. Source: Authors' own interpretation based on data from Chaps. 4–22	568
Fig. 23.2	Examples of secondary agents involved in disability sport in Europe. Source: Authors' own interpretation based on data from Chaps. 4–22	572
Fig. 23.3	Typologies of governing sport for pwds by non-governmental agents. Source: Authors' own interpretation based on data from Chaps. 4–22	573
Fig. 23.4	Relationships between agents with regard to disability sport. Source: Authors' own interpretation based on data from Chaps. 4–22	579
Fig. 23.5	Countries on a continuum of mainstreaming, from mainly 'disability-based' to mainly 'sport-based' (indicative). Source: Authors' own interpretation based on data from Chaps. 4–22	581
Fig. 23.6	Socio-ecological model applied to sport participation amongst persons with a disability. Source: Adapted by the authors from a.o. McLeroy et al. (1988), Mehtälä et al. (2014), Sallis et al. (2008)	591

List of Tables

Table 3.1	Classification of (former) EU member states (N = 28) according to their geographical location	61
Table 3.2	Participation in physical activity, (club-organised) sport and fitness in (former) EU27/EU28 member states amongst people with a disability or illness aged 15 and over (2009–2017), percentages of total population	63
Table 3.3	Participation in physical activity, (club-organised) sport and fitness in (former) EU27/EU28 member states amongst people without a disability or illness aged 15 and over (2009–2017), percentages of total population	63
Table 3.4	Physical activity (PA), overall sports participation and sports participation in different organisational settings in (former) EU27/EU28 member states amongst people with a disability or illness aged 15 and over according to background characteristics (2009–2017), percentages of total population	71
Table 3.5	Physical activity (PA), overall sports participation and sports participation in different organisational settings in (former) EU27/EU28 member states amongst people without a disability or illness aged 15 and over according to background characteristics (2009–2017), percentages of total population	72
Table 4.1	Facts and statistics for Denmark	80
Table 4.2	Sport profile for Denmark	81
Table 4.3	Facts and statistics on disability in Denmark regarding the adult population, aged 16–64 years (estimated % of population, n=20,386)	83
Table 5.1	Facts and statistics of Finland	102
Table 5.2	Sport profile of Finland	104
Table 5.3	Changes of disability sports terminology from 1980 until today, from Finnish to English	105

Table 5.4	Statistics on activity limitation (disability) in Finland, % of population, 20 years or older, based on FinSote 2017–2018 ($n = 26,405$)	105
Table 6.1	Facts and statistics about Iceland	126
Table 6.2	Sport profile of Iceland	128
Table 7.1	Facts and statistics of Norway	146
Table 7.2	Sport profile of Norway	149
Table 7.3	Disability in Norway: estimates by type of disability. NB! This is not a complete overview of all disabilities	150
Table 7.4	Distribution of grants from the Ministry of Culture (post 5) within NIF	156
Table 7.5	Number of para sport members within the 15 most popular sports 2019	159
Table 8.1	Facts and statistics of Sweden	171
Table 8.2	Sport profile of Sweden	172
Table 8.3	Changes of disability sports terminology from 1980 until today, from Swedish to English	174
Table 9.1	Fact and statistics of Ireland Republic	195
Table 9.2	Sport profile of Ireland up to 2020/21 Republic of Ireland	196
Table 9.3	Statistics on disability in Ireland (aged <1 to 85+) in 2016	198
Table 9.4	Population (number) by difficulty in tasks of daily living, Census Year 2016	198
Table 9.5	Early disability sport organisations in Ireland by year of establishment	199
Table 9.6	Recommendations for promoting the participation of people with disabilities in physical activity and sport in Ireland (2005)	200
Table 9.7	Disability sport framework for Ireland	201
Table 9.8	Disability NGBs and LSPs supported directly by Sport Ireland in 2020	206
Table 9.9	Key 2019 Sport Ireland funding of sport for people with disabilities	206
Table 9.10	Irish sports monitor participation %, 2013–2019	209
Table 9.11	Barriers to participation in physical activity and sport by people with disabilities in Ireland	211
Table 9.12	Facilitators of participation in physical activity by people with disabilities in Ireland	211
Table 10.1	Facts and statistics of Northern Ireland	219
Table 10.2	Sport profile of Northern Ireland 2019	219
Table 10.3	All population figures: general health	220
Table 10.4	Statistics on disability in Northern Ireland	221
Table 10.5	SAPAS 2010 key performance indicator (KPI) results	226
Table 11.1	Facts and characteristics of the UK	240
Table 11.2	Sport profile of the UK	241
Table 11.3	Sport priorities in the UK	242

List of Tables

Table 11.4	Disability prevalence in the UK	243
Table 11.5	Disability terminology	243
Table 11.6	National disability sport organisations (NDSOs) in the UK	246
Table 11.7	Additional laws and regulations in the UK	250
Table 11.8	The economic importance of sport in the UK	252
Table 12.1	Facts and descriptives of Austria	269
Table 12.2	Sports profile of Austria	271
Table 12.3	Disability in Austria	272
Table 12.4	National funding of Austrian disability sports organisations (2019)	281
Table 12.5	Sports and physical activity of people with disabilities in Austria (minimum 10 minutes/week)	286
Table 12.6	Cycling of people with disabilities in Austria (minimum 10 minutes/week)	286
Table 12.7	Muscle-strengthening activities of people with disabilities in Austria	287
Table 13.1	Facts and statistics for Belgium, Brussels-Capital Region, Flanders, Wallonia and East Belgium (most recently available data included)	297
Table 13.2	Sports profile for Belgium, Flanders, Wallonia and East Belgium (most recently available data included)	299
Table 13.3	Prevalence of people with disabilities in Flanders/Belgium according to the type of impairment	302
Table 13.4	Sports participation of people with disabilities in Flanders	315
Table 13.5	Self-reported barriers towards sports participation by people with disabilities in Flanders, according to the type of impairment	319
Table 14.1	Facts and descriptives of Germany	327
Table 14.2	Sport profile of Germany	328
Table 14.3	Severely disabled people in Germany by gender and age (*Schwerbehinderung*)	330
Table 15.1	Facts and statistics of the Netherlands	351
Table 15.2	Sport profile of the Netherlands	352
Table 15.3	Facts and statistics on disability and chronic conditions in the Netherlands	354
Table 15.4	Weekly sport participation population aged 18–79, by disability (OECD indicator, moderate and severe) and chronic condition (per year, in percentages)	370
Table 15.5	Weekly sport participation, by socio-demographic and health variables, persons with physical disabilities (OECD indicator, moderate and severe) and chronic condition, population aged 18–79 (2017–2019, in percentages)	372
Table 15.6	Details of sport participation by disability and chronic condition, population aged 18–79 (2019, in percentages)	374
Table 16.1	Figures of Switzerland	386

Table 16.2	Sport profile of Switzerland	387
Table 16.3	Facts and statistics on disability in Switzerland (2017; population aged 15 and over in private households)	388
Table 17.1	Statistical data of Hungary based on the 2021 census	412
Table 17.2	Sport country profile of Hungary	414
Table 17.3	Disability forms by age and proportion in relation to total population in 2011	416
Table 17.4	Available state funding for disability sports (in million Euro) between 2018 and 2020	427
Table 17.5	Total number of participants affiliated with disability sports umbrella organisations (year of 2018)	430
Table 17.6	Total number of registered participants with disabilities in national sports federations with capital and countryside breakdown (2018)	431
Table 18.1	Facts and statistics of Lithuania	438
Table 18.2	Sport profile of Lithuania	441
Table 18.3	Changes of disability sports terminology from 1991 until today, from Lithuanian to English	442
Table 18.4	School setting of children with special needs in Lithuania	443
Table 18.5	Budget for sports organizations in Lithuania	450
Table 19.1	Facts and statistics of Slovenia	462
Table 19.2	Sport profile of Slovenia	464
Table 19.3	Facts and statistics on disability in Slovenia, age 6 to 26	464
Table 19.4	Number of athletes included in the Zveza ŠIS-SPK 2020 by age	465
Table 19.5	FIHO tenders for disability organisations by year (2015–2020) and the number of participants in funded sports programmes	475
Table 19.6	Financing of the Zveza ŠIS-SPK according to the source of financing in the period 2017–2019	476
Table 19.7	Co-financed disability sports programmes at the local level in the period 2016–2018 in EUR	476
Table 20.1	Demographic data and country characteristics	487
Table 20.2	Quality of life index in Portugal—2021	488
Table 20.3	Disability sport participation in numbers only of people with disabilities in mainstream (regular) sport federations, in 2019	503
Table 21.1	Facts and statistics of Spain	514
Table 21.2	Sport profile of Spain	515
Table 21.3	Facts and statistics on disability in Spain	516
Table 21.4	Number of athletes with disability with a licence at a given Spanish disability sport federation by gender, year 2019	529
Table 21.5	Number of licences for athletes with disabilities in mainstream Spanish sports federations by gender	530
Table 22.1	Facts and statistics of Turkey	538
Table 22.2	Sport profile of Turkey	541

Table 22.3	Chronological establishment of schools for students with various disabilities between the late Ottoman and early Republic of Turkey	541
Table 22.4	Type of impairments, population and prevalence	542
Table 22.5	Changes of the terms disability and disability sports from Turkish to English	544
Table 22.6	Policies and stakeholders regarding sport for disadvantaged people emphasised in the National Youth and Sports Policy Document of Turkey	551
Table 22.7	Financial aid received by the disability sports federations according to the 2017 Activity Report of Directorate General for Sports Services	551
Table 22.8	Number of participants in four major disability sports federations of Turkey, in 2019	553
Table 22.9	Sport branches of the disabled sport federations in Turkey	554
Table 23.1	Available types of data sources for sport participation among persons with a disability in the countries involved in the handbook	585
Table 23.2	Individual factors that may influence sport participation by pwds	591
Table 23.3	Interpersonal factors that may influence sport participation by pwds	592
Table 23.4	Organisational factors that may influence sport participation by pwds	592
Table 23.5	Community factors that may influence sport participation by pwds	593
Table 23.6	Policy factors that may influence sport participation by pwds	593

Chapter 1
Introduction: Sport Participation a Human Right for Persons with a Disability

Caroline van Lindert, Jeroen Scheerder, and Ian Brittain

> Persons with disabilities have the right to have good conditions in the workplace, to live independently, to equal opportunities, to participate fully in the life of their community. All have a right to a life without barriers. And it is our obligation, as a community, to ensure their full participation in society, on an equal basis with others.
> Commission President Von der Leyen in the Union of Equality: Strategy for the Rights of Persons with Disabilities 2021–2030 (European Commission, 2021: 1).

In this handbook we examine the various ways grassroots sports for persons with a disability (hereafter pwds) is delivered throughout Europe. The focus is on countries in the European Region, not exclusively European Union (EU) member countries. This handbook is important for several reasons.

First of all, according to estimations of the World Health Organization (WHO) and the World Bank, over 1 billion people live with some form of disability (physical, mental, intellectual or sensory). This corresponds to 15% of the world's population, the majority of which live in low- and middle-income countries. Up to 3.8% of people 15 years and older experience significant difficulties in functioning, often requiring specific health care services (World Health Organization, 2022; World Health Organization & The World Bank, 2011; see also Martin Ginis et al., 2021). In the WHO European Region, an estimated 135 million people live with a

C. van Lindert (✉)
Mulier Institute, Utrecht, The Netherlands
e-mail: c.vanlindert@mulierinstituut.nl

J. Scheerder
Department of Movement Sciences, KU Leuven, Leuven, Belgium

Policy Research Centre on Sports on behalf of the Flemish Government, Leuven, Belgium
e-mail: jeroen.scheerder@kuleuven.be

I. Brittain
Centre for Business in Society, Coventry University, Coventry, UK
e-mail: aa8550@coventry.ac.uk

© The Author(s), under exclusive license to Springer Nature Switzerland AG 2023
C. van Lindert et al. (eds.), *The Palgrave Handbook of Disability Sport in Europe*, https://doi.org/10.1007/978-3-031-21759-3_1

disability (World Health Organization Regional Office for Europe, 2022). In the 27-EU member countries, a quarter of the population, approximately 87 million persons (aged 16 years and older) experience limitations in the execution of daily activities due to health problems (European Commission, 2021; Grammenos & Priestley, 2020). People with lower income, lower education or who are unemployed are at an increased risk of disability or long-term illness. Disability is also more prevalent among women and the elderly (Grammenos & Priestley, 2020; World Health Organization & The World Bank, 2011). With an aging population and a global increase in chronic health conditions, such as diabetes, cardiovascular diseases or mental disorders, the number of pwds globally and in the European Region is growing (European Commission, 2021; Grammenos & Priestley, 2020; World Health Organization & The World Bank, 2011). Almost everyone will experience some form of disability, either temporarily or permanently, at some point in life. It is argued that disability can therefore be seen as part of the human condition (World Health Organization & The World Bank, 2011). Following the International Classification of Functioning, Disability and Health (hereafter ICF) (World Health Organization, 2002), the experience of disability varies greatly, as a disability results from the dynamic interaction between someone's health condition or impairments, which are often invisible, and contextual factors, both personally and environmentally (European Commission, 2021; World Health Organization & The World Bank, 2011).

Persons with disabilities experience disadvantages in various areas of life. They have a higher probability of being discriminated against, have a higher risk of poverty, poorer quality of life, poorer health, higher health care costs and are at greater risk of injury. They are more likely to experience health consequences due to physical inactivity or sedentary lifestyles compared to persons without disability (Blauwet, 2019; European Commission, 2021; European Union, 2019; Kantar, 2019; Leung et al., 2021; Martin Ginis et al., 2021; United Nations, 2019; World Health Organization & The World Bank, 2011). The Covid-19 pandemic may have amplified the disadvantages (De Boer et al., 2021; European Commission, 2021). These inequalities are attributable to various factors. One of which is social exclusion, where possibilities and opportunities to participate in society are unevenly distributed over social groups based on income, education, age, gender and/or mental or physical abilities (Elling & Claringbould, 2005). Pwds are excluded from different domains of life as a result of a denial or lack of, or barriers in, access to resources, rights, goods and services, for example, healthcare, education, employment or recreation. And they are underrepresented in decision-making and political participation. This is specifically the case for women and girls with a disability (European Commission, 2021; United Nations, 2019). These barriers also negatively impact the possibilities for pwds to participate in sport and physical activity (hereafter PA) (Brittain et al., 2020; European Commission, 2021; European Union, 2010). It is observed that pwds have lower rates of participation in sport and PA compared with their peers without disabilities (Blauwet, 2019; Borland et al., 2020; De Hollander & Proper, 2018; Hoekstra et al., 2019; Leung et al., 2021; Martin Ginis et al., 2021). Consequently, they will be less able to experience the physical, mental and social benefits that are associated with sport and PA (Bull et al., 2020; Darcy & Dowse, 2013; De Boer et al., 2021; Ecorys, 2018; Leung et al., 2021; Martin Ginis et al., 2016; Smith et al., 2018; World Health Organization, 2020). These lower sport participation rates combined with associated poorer health are of high concern worldwide and call for more inclusive practices and sport programmes accessible to pwds (Bull et al., 2020; Darcy et al., 2017; Hoekstra et al., 2019; Leung et al., 2021).

With the adoption of the United Nations Convention on the Rights of Persons with Disabilities (hereafter UNCRPD) in 2006, minimum standards were set to promote, protect and ensure that all pwds have the right to participate in society on an equal basis, including in sport (United Nations, 2006). Article 30.5 of the UNCRPD states that State Parties are responsible for (a) encouraging and promoting participation of pwds in mainstream sporting activities at all levels; (b) ensuring that pwds have the opportunity to organise, develop and participate in disability-specific sporting and recreational activities and encourage the provision on an equal basis with others of appropriate instruction, training and resources; (c) ensuring that pwds have access to sporting venues; (d) ensuring that children with disabilities have equal access with other children to participation in play, recreation, leisure and sporting activities, including those activities in the school system; and (e) ensuring that pwds have access to services from those involved in the organisation of sporting activities.

The WHO and United Nations (UN) are committed to ensuring access to sport and physical education for all at the global level. For instance, through the Global Action Plan on Physical Activity (GAPPA, 2018–2030), the WHO encourages member states to support development of national sports policies that prioritise investments in sports programmes which also target pwds (World Health Organization, 2018). The UN has included pwds in its Sustainable Development Goals (SDGs), in which sport is seen as an important enabler of sustainable development (United Nations, 2015). Through the International Charter of Physical Education, Physical Activity and Sport, the United Nations Educational, Scientific and Cultural Organisation (UNESCO) promotes inclusive access to sport by all, including pwds (UNESCO, 2015). UNESCO installed a special chair in Inclusive Physical Education, Sport, Fitness and Recreation at the Institute of Technology, Tralee (Ireland), to further enable inclusion of pwds in physical education (hereafter PE), sport, fitness and physical recreation by means of education, advocacy and collaboration of various organisations (Sportanddev.org, 2015, see for more information Chap. 9. Ireland). To make a shift from merely policy intents to concrete actions, at the UNESCO 6th International Conference of Ministers and Senior officials Responsible for PE and Sports (MINEPS) in 2017, the Kazan Action Plan (KAP) was adopted. One of the main policy areas the KAP is structured around is developing a comprehensive vision of inclusive access for all. The plan marks the commitment to link sport policy development to the SDGs, as well as to support an overarching sport policy follow-up framework and international and national multi-stakeholder cooperation (UNESCO, 2021).

The EU and its member states are parties to the UNCRPD. The treaty entered into force for the EU in January 2011 and has guided the content of the European disability strategy 2010–2020 through which the EU worked on implementation of the UNCRPD. This strategy aimed to empower pwds so that they can enjoy their full rights and benefit from participation in society and the European economy (European Commission, 2010). One of the areas of action was participation, including the participation of pwds in sport. The strategy also identifies the support needed for funding, research, raising awareness, statistics and data collection. In March 2021, the European Commission adopted the Union of Equality: Strategy for the rights of persons with disabilities 2021–2030, which builds on previous strategies (European Commission, 2021).

The EU claims that the European Disability Strategy 2010–2020 has contributed to improving the situation in a number of areas, in particular accessibility for pwds and promoting their rights by putting disability high on the EU agenda (European Commission, 2020). However, pwds still face numerous barriers to their full inclusion and participation in various domains of life, including the fields of sport and PA (European Union, 2019; United Nations, 2019). In regard to sport and PA, some common barriers are pain and fatigue, low self-efficacy, lack of family support, lack of financial resources, inadequate or inaccessible facilities and transport, lack of appropriate programmes and negative attitudes towards pwds (Darcy et al., 2017; Ecorys, 2018; Jaarsma et al., 2014; Martin Ginis et al., 2021; Yu et al., 2022).

The objective of the renewed strategy is to improve the lives of pwds in the coming decade, in the EU and beyond, and aims to progress on all areas of the UNCRPD. In line with Article 1 of the UNCRPD, the strategy takes account of the diversity of disability comprising long-term physical, mental, intellectual or sensory impairments. The strategy also promotes an intersectional perspective in line with the UN 2030 Agenda for SDGs (United Nations, 2015) as pwds face the risk of multiple disadvantages due to a potential combination of identities (gender, racial, ethnic, sexual, religious and/or socioeconomic). The European Commission will support member states in shaping their national strategies and action plans to further implement the UNCRPD and EU legislation in various domains, such as ensuring equal opportunities and access to sport. The strategy leans on the European Pillar of Social Rights (European Union, 2017) and is part of the action plan adopted by the Commission (European Union, 2021). The basis for combatting discrimination and establishing equality within EU policies is anchored in EU legislation, for example, the Treaty on the Functioning of the European Union (TFEU) (European Union, 2016) and the Charter of Fundamental Rights of the European Union (European Union, 2012). In addition, since 1975, the human right to participate in 'sport for all' has been part of the European Sports (for all) Charter.[1] EU member states are

---

[1] 24 September 1975 the 'European Sport for All Charter' was adopted at the Conference of European Ministers responsible for Sport. This first charter was updated in 1992 and 2001 as the 'European Sports Charter' (the Charter) and was updated again in 2021. The successive versions of this charter have provided an essential basis for governmental policies in the field of sport and enabled individuals to exercise their right to participate in sport (see Council of Europe, 2021).

encouraged to ensure, for example, that all members of a local community have opportunities to take part in sport and that, where necessary, additional measures are taken aimed at enabling disadvantaged individuals or groups and pwds to make effective use of such opportunities (Council of Europe, 2021).

The role of sport for social inclusion is highlighted in the 2010 Conclusions of the Council of the European Union, in which the 'sport for all' principle is supported (European Union, 2010). The Council bears in mind that access to sport for all is important, including the accessibility and availability of sport facilities, infrastructures and venues to as many people as possible, in particular to pwds, as well as the importance of enabling pwds to participate on an equal basis with others in recreational, leisure and sporting activities and invites member states to promote actions related to that (European Union, 2010). The rights of pwds to participate in sporting activities on an equal basis with people without disabilities are also emphasised in the European Commission Communication to Develop the European Dimension of Sport (European Commission, 2011). The 2019 Council conclusions of the European Union on Access to sport for pwds further emphasise the importance and necessity of member states to take far-reaching measures to ensure the inclusion of pwds in sport (European Union, 2019).

Although numerous national governments, worldwide and in the European Region, have ratified the UNCRPD and are working on improving equal rights for pwds, sport participation levels among pwds, as mentioned before, still lag far behind that of the general population in European countries. This is shown by a small-scale mapping research commissioned by the EU to develop insight into (barriers to) participation in sport by pwds and knowledge of best practices across EU member states (Ecorys, 2018). Within the EU there is considerable variation in the scope of data availability in relation to sport participation by pwds, as shown by the small-scale mapping research. This makes it difficult to compare the rates of sport participation across the EU (Ecorys, 2018). However, in the cross-national surveys on sport and PA in the EU member states, disability and illness are often mentioned as reasons for not participating in sport and PA (European Commission, 2018). In Chap. 3 of this handbook the challenge of making cross-national comparisons based on available data will be discussed.

Another in-depth mapping of general sports statistics and data at both EU and national levels in the EU-27 also reveals shortcomings in the collection of data on levels of sport participation by pwds (Pletosu et al., 2021). Both mappings make clear that there is need for more consistent approaches to data collection across the EU that would enable cross-national comparisons (Ecorys, 2018). This also applies to data on sport policy and programmes focusing on pwds. Various sport programmes and interventions, targeted towards pwds in general, as well as towards different types of disability, are identified within the EU. It seems that general sport programmes are increasingly developing a strong disability component. However, there is a strong variation in levels of funding allocated to sport participation programmes across the EU (Ecorys, 2018).

(Academic) literature and research on disability sport policy and grassroots sport participation by pwds are scarce or fragmented compared to the literature on sport participation and sport policy in the general population (Nicholson et al., 2011; Scheerder et al., 2017). In addition, within the disability sport discourse, Paralympic Sport, para sports and the Paralympic movement seem to receive more attention than grassroots sport participation and policies that promote sport participation in general for pwds. With the exception of Paralympic studies, exchanging knowledge or data on disability sport among scholars across Europe seems to not yet be common practice (see Brittain & Beacom, 2018). However, disability sport has begun to get more attention in university bachelor and master programmes and from both academic scholars and scientific journals in recent years. This growing interest is obviously related to the global concerns about the underrepresentation of pwds in sport and increased calls to action for inclusive practices worldwide. The development of disability studies as an academic discipline, where scholars examine the meaning, nature and consequences of disability as a complex social phenomenon (DISN, n.d.), could have also contributed to this trend.

We note that studies with a primary focus on measuring rates of participation in (grassroots and competitive) sport in pwds and comparing these data with general populations are still scarce. This is in contrast to studies with a focus on levels of PA in pwds and the associated health benefits (De Boer et al., 2021; Martin Ginis et al., 2016). Sport participation studies, if they exist, differ greatly in size, scope or subject. For example, some focus on specific subgroups, for example, people with intellectual disability (Borland et al., 2020; Robertson et al., 2018); some focus on a specific sport intervention, for example, sitting volleyball (Leung et al., 2021), or some are intended for readers in the specific country for which data was collected (Scheerder et al., 2018; Von Heijden-Brinkman et al., 2013). Quite a number of empirical and academic studies are focussed on the experienced barriers and facilitators towards participation in sport by pwds (Carbone et al., 2021; Darcy et al., 2017; Scheerder et al., 2018; Von Heijden-Brinkman et al., 2013) and on the integration process of disability sport (Sørensen & Kahrs, 2006) or the inclusiveness of (policy) programmes and interventions (Christiaens & Brittain, 2021). A recent overview of national policies on disability sport and on sport participation data for pwds across the European Region however still is largely lacking. Studies that shed some light on these two subjects are for instance the aforementioned small-scale EU-mapping research (Ecorys, 2018) and a comparative study of the provision of disability sport based on questionnaire data among representatives from 19 European countries in 2010 (Thomas & Guett, 2014). The authors found that the organisation and structure of disability sport throughout Europa at the time were fragmented, complex and cumbersome. They observed a policy climate characterised by a largely uncoordinated and differential commitment to disability sport (Thomas & Guett, 2014). Therefore, despite the significance of previous studies, there is need to examine specific aspects of disability sport policy and participation in more detail.

Key Reasons for the Handbook

To summarise, the following reasons led to the composition of this handbook: first, the fact that disability is part of the human condition and that many of us will at some point in life experience some form of disability; second, pwds face numerous barriers that hinder their full inclusion in sport, resulting in lower rates of participation compared to their peers without disabilities; third, pwds consequently will be less able to experience the benefits associated with sport and PA; fourth, pwds have the right to participate in sport on an equal basis with others, as promoted amongst others by the UNCRPD; fifth, progress in minimising the gap in sport participation between persons with and without disabilities is slow, despite efforts made by governments and organisations globally and in the European Region; and sixth, the need to gather, analyse and compare national data to provide a better picture of the various ways disability sport is delivered throughout Europe.

1.1 Aim and Key Benefits

In order to bring the opportunities for pwds to participate in sport on equal footing with opportunities for persons without disabilities, it is important to draw attention to this group's underrepresentation in (organised) sport and the lack of consistent data in this area of research. A review and cross-national comparison of existing sport participation data and policy systems for disability sport can contribute to a recognition of the problem. Therefore, this handbook aims to *explore the various ways sport for pwds is governed and organised across Europe, as well as the extent to which and how pwds participate in sport.*

The book will also identify various methods of data collection in sport participation research, as well as challenges in data collection in this population. This handbook is written from a cross-national perspective based upon a collection of 19 country-specific chapters from different regions in Europe, with both up-to-date data and in-depth descriptions and analyses, based upon a rigorous theoretical and conceptual framework. This format allows for the identification of similarities and differences between the respective countries in their policies, infrastructure and participation levels with respect to sport for pwds. The handbook is mainly descriptive in nature, but it is the editors' hope that the findings from this cross-national comparison will ultimately contribute to a better understanding of how national, regional and local policies and organisational settings with regard to sport for pwds (can) contribute to the integration and inclusion of pwds in sport as promoted by the UNCRPD and EU policy on disability sport.

The following questions have led the editors and contributing authors in their work:

- At national, regional and local level, which governmental, intermediate and non-governmental agents are involved in delivering sport for pwds, what are their roles and what is the nature of the relationships between the relevant agents in the disability sport system?
- At national, regional and local level, what kind of policies and legislation apply to sport for pwds and to what extent do they promote inclusion in sport among pwds?

- How, and to what extent, do pwds participate in sport and what are the facilitators and barriers towards their participation in sport?
- What are the methods and challenges in collecting sport participation data with regard to pwds?

It is anticipated that the depth and breadth of this handbook, together with its theoretical and cross-national perspective approach, will ensure its location as a valuable resource for academic study across a range of sport and disability-related programmes, as well as a point of reference for researchers and policymakers working in this area. It will contribute to the understanding of the issues concerning sport policy, structure and organisation in disability sport, (data collection in) sport participation by pwds and developments in the integration and inclusion process of pwds in sport. With the present handbook, the editors seek to improve the understanding of the differences and similarities between European countries concerning these issues and provide an incentive to share examples concerning research topics and methods as well as policy-related issues. In addition, the intention is to demonstrate the importance of including 'disability' as a variable in (statistical) data collection on sport and sport participation, and to raise interest for further research about sport for pwds across Europe.

This handbook partly aligns with the design by Scheerder, Willem & Claes' edited volume *Sport Policy Systems and Sport Federations. A cross-National Perspective* (2017). The work of Scheerder et al. (2017) also includes country-specific chapters, however, the focus is on general sport policy systems. In our handbook, an overview of country-specific descriptions of sport policy systems with special attention to disability sport and sport participation among pwds is presented. To the best of our knowledge, no other book on either topic that covers examples from European countries is presently available. Our handbook provides added value to the Palgrave Handbook of Paralympic Studies (Brittain & Beacom, 2018), and other volumes on the global sports arena and Paralympic Games. In this handbook, the focus lies on the grassroots and participatory level of disability sport, and the key benefit is that it introduces concepts of disability, disability sport, social inclusion and sport policy to a wider audience and also covers a broad selection of examples from European countries in this regard.

1.2 Outline and Short Introduction of Terms

In the following sections of this chapter, the comparative framework that serves as a guideline for the description of the policy system on disability sport in each country will be presented, followed by an overview of the countries selected for this handbook.

In this handbook and throughout the country-specific chapters, the concepts of 'disability' and 'disability sport' will be frequently used. In Chap. 2, these concepts are introduced in more detail. Chap. 2 serves as an introduction for the following country-specific contributions. Moreover, parts of it have been used by the contributors as they represent different academic disciplines and/or professional backgrounds and were not necessarily familiar either with disability-specific concepts or sport policy-specific concepts. These explanatory texts were part of an instructions document with guidelines to write a country-specific chapter (Van Lindert et al., 2020).

Chapter 3 consists of a secondary analysis by comparing cross-national data on sport participation among pwds. More specifically, for this chapter, available data are used from the Eurobarometer Survey on sport (European Commission, 2018). Chapters 4–22 will cover the 19 country-specific cases with regard to disability sport policy and participation. In the following section of this chapter the structure for the country-specific cases is explained. Chapter 23 is the final chapter with conclusions and recommendations for future research on disability sport policy and participation that are largely drawn from the country-specific chapters.

Use of Terms

In this handbook pwds are referred to as persons with impairments or disorders in mental and/or physical functions. Disability is conceptualised using the ICF-model (World Health Organization, 2002). Other disability models and their meaning will be explained in Chap. 2. For readability, in this handbook we prefer to use the term disability and persons with a disability or with disabilities, instead of disorders or impairments. In the ICF-model, the term 'handicap' or 'disability' refers to the social aspects of human functioning (see Chap. 2). Having a disability is not so much a characteristic of the individual, as it is caused by circumstances in society. Society must then ensure the optimal participation of persons with disabilities in social life. Social changes, in particular in the fields of sport and PA, are necessary to make this possible. We prefer to use person first language as much as possible (person with a disability instead of disabled person), as we recognise, bearing the UNCRPD in mind, that every person is valued primarily for who he or she is and is not judged purely for having a disorder or impairment. But as the reader will notice, the terms 'disabled person' and 'person with a disability' will also be used interchangeably, as the term 'disabled person' is widely used, for example, in the United Kingdom (UK). We recognise the possibility that different meanings can be assigned to the terms in the respective countries. Thus, we leave room for contributing authors to align with local parlance in regard to this concept.

As for the term 'disability sport', this is defined broadly and was discussed beforehand with the contributing authors (Van Lindert et al., 2020). For the purpose of this handbook we define disability sport as (see also Chap. 2): the system that delivers, supports and promotes the participation of sport and PA in a sporting context by pwds at all levels, both mainstream and adapted, sport-based and disability-based, at a grassroots and recreational level, but also at a competitive and elite sport level, as well as the infrastructure that supports these practices. The main focus of the book, however, is on the systems that support or promote sport participation of pwds at a grassroots or sport for all level.

To improve readability, throughout the handbook we use the words 'disability sport', 'disability sport system' or 'disability sport policy'. However, this does not necessarily mean that, in the respective countries, there is a separate system for sport for pwds with its own unique elements. This can be the case, but there may also be settings in which there is little difference in the way sport is delivered for pwds and persons without disabilities. With regard to the terms used in the book, we seek common ground and are aware of the possible sensitivities in their use with the reader.

1.3 Comparative Approach of the Handbook

In this handbook, the analysis focuses on the policy and organisational landscape of disability sport, or in short the policy system of disability sport, and on the sport participation by pwds, as well as the facilitators and barriers they experience towards active participation and involvement in sport and PA. The country-specific chapters represent the current state and body of knowledge, and are structured following a standardised framework to enable cross-national comparison (see Fig. 1.1). In the handbook, country chapters are organised by region. The framework is partly based on earlier work published by Scheerder et al. (2017) in their cross-national comparison of sport policy systems and sport federations in Europe. The main focus for the

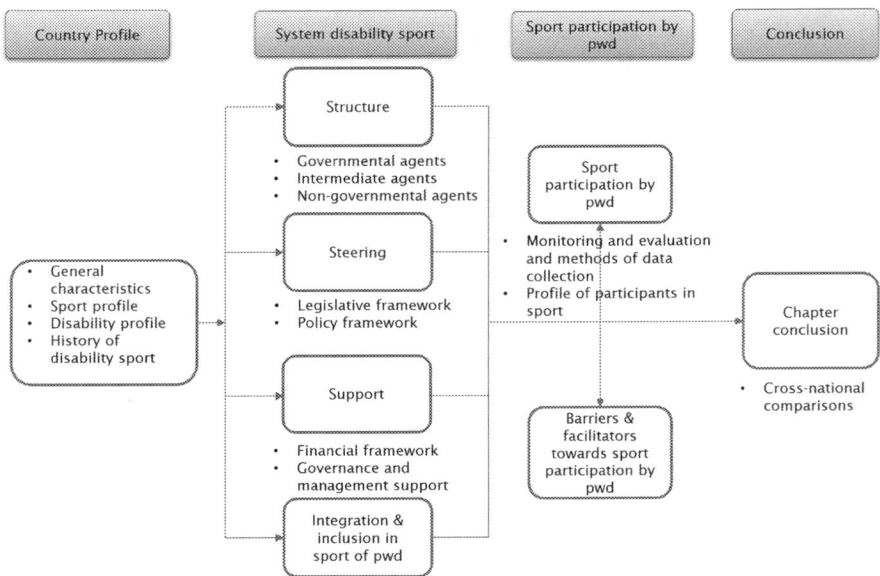

Fig. 1.1 Comparative framework for each country chapter throughout the book. Source: editors' own elaboration based on the conceptual framework of Scheerder et al. (2017)

analysis in Scheerder et al. (2017) was on the relationship between sport (con)federations and governmental bodies, more precisely on the position and the power of national sport(con)federations in 13 different countries. These relationships will be part of the analysis in the present handbook too, but will not be the primary focus. In this handbook the editors added elements to the original framework of Scheerder et al. (2017) which consisted of the country profile, the sport policy system (structure, steering and support) and chapter conclusions. Sport participation was added as a distinct topic, as well as elements related to disability in general and disability sport and inclusion in sport by pwds.

The chapter contributors were asked to address questions regarding the following eight main topics:

1. Country profile
2. Structure of disability sport
3. Steering of disability sport
4. Support for disability sport
5. Level of integration or inclusion in sport by pwds
6. Sport participation by pwds
7. Barriers and facilitators for sport participation by pwds
8. Country-specific conclusions

Country Profile

First of all, chapter contributors were asked to include a short country profile. This first section is significant as it provides a clear insight into the cultural, economic, political and social context in which the policy and organisational structure of disability sport and sport participation levels for pwds in the respective countries are generated. This enables the reader to understand differences and similarities between countries. In particular, this section consists of four topics following the framework provided by Scheerder et al. (2017) and the guidelines provided by the editors (Van Lindert et al., 2020):

(a) a brief description of the general characteristics of the country outlining the geographic, demographic, political, economic and social-cultural situation;
(b) a brief description of the general (mainstream) sport system with its main agents, including the levels of participation in sport by the general population;
(c) a brief overview of the definition and prevalence of disability and the social position of pwds in the respective countries (see also Chap. 2 for more details);
(d) the emergence or rise of disability sport in the specific country.

The latter two topics were added to the original framework of Scheerder et al. (2017) because in the present work the focus is on disability sport. The way society views (persons with a) disability and existing laws and legislation regarding pwds may influence the position and participation of this group in society and in sport, possibly resulting in differences in the (evolution of) disability sport systems in the respective countries (see Chap. 2).

Structure of Disability Sport

Secondly, as part of the disability sport system, contributors were invited to describe and analyse the organisational structure of disability sport in their country, including (a) governmental, (b) intermediate and (c) non-governmental structures at the national, regional and local levels. As in Scheerder et al. (2017), this section is based on the framework used by Hallmann and Petry (2013) which was based on earlier work from Tokarski et al. (2004).

The framework used is a simplified reproduction of reality, but it aims to help readers to understand who the main players are in the landscape of disability sport, whether this differs or corresponds to the general sport system in the respective countries and what the nature of the relationship is (hierarchical, membership/partnership or financial) between the various players. The focus is primarily on the agents that have a direct role in creating sport policies and/or sport programmes for pwds. Authors were asked to pay attention to sport-related as well as non-sport related agents. As further outlined in Chap. 2, sport for recreational purposes may also be delivered by non-sport-related agents, for example, schools, community or rehabilitation centres. Contributors, however, were asked to refrain from including non-sport-related organisations in the figure that do not directly contribute to the creation of policies and programmes specifically dedicated towards pwds. If these organisations play an indirect role in the disability sport system, for example, in the recruitment of participants or the referral of pwds to sport offers for pwds elsewhere, these agents are mentioned separately in the text, namely as secondary agents. By governmental agents, we mean various administrative bodies that have been established by the government and perform tasks for the government, such as ministries, (sub)departments, provinces, counties, cities or municipalities. These could be sport related, but can also have a link to other policy domains, for example, health and welfare, economics, tourism and so on. By intermediate agents we mean organisations that function as a link between the government and non-governmental agents, such as an independent administrative body that performs a governmental task, but has an independent statutory function. These intermediate agents can serve as agents with an advisory or executive role, supporting the creation of sport programmes by the non-governmental agents. The presence of these agents may vary by country. Examples of these agents include, among others, national sport councils, advisory boards, science-related institutes, umbrella organisations of municipalities and so on. Non-governmental agents are more focused on the implementation or delivery of sport programmes for pwds. They have an independent status, and include civic organisations as well as private and commercial organisations that are active in the domain of disability sport. In addition, organisations with a semi-public task, such as educational or healthcare institutions, could also be included, if they implement (out of school) sport programmes for their students or clients. Civic organisations concern a wide area of social profit organisations acting in public life, independently from government and business. They represent the interests and values of their members or other citizens. Examples here are sport (con)federations and sport clubs, as well as social profit foundations and social clubs. Private and commercial organisations are, for instance, fitness and wellness clubs.

Steering of Disability Sport

Thirdly, again following the framework of Scheerder et al. (2017), country contributors were asked to describe the mechanisms used by governing bodies to steer (non) sport agents with regard to disability sport in their country. This section is divided in three parts: (a) relationships, (b) the legislative framework and (c) the policy framework. Steering is about the relationships between the government and non-governmental (sport) agents and under what conditions these relationships are built. The country-specific contributions provide a description of the financial, membership/partnership and hierarchical relationships, and what legislation (laws and acts) are relevant to disability sport in the specific country. This can also include non-sport-related legislation, for example, with regard to human rights or inclusion of pwds in society. In regard to the policy framework, authors describe what kind of policies are relevant to (disability) sport, what the main government policy objectives and programmes are in regard to disability sport, and how other agents in the landscape relate to these policies. Also, answers are given to whether countries have their own policies and whether they are involved in implementing government policies.

Based on theoretical insights from Scheerder et al. (2017), in this handbook two main theories are used for analysing the relationships between various stakeholders in the disability sport landscape. The first theory concerns the so-called principal-agent approach. "A [principal-agent] relationship has arisen between two (or more) parties when one, designated as the agent, acts for, on behalf of, or as a representative for the other, designated the principal, in a particular domain of decision problems" (Ross, 1973: 134). The principal-agent model allows for an analysis of the relation between governmental actors as principals and civil society actors (e.g. sport federations or other non-governmental sport bodies) as agents. The principal-agent approach thus emphasises the arm's length and asymmetrical relationship between government and sport organisations (Goodwin & Grix, 2011). It is essentially based on the hierarchical position of governments.

The second theoretical approach implies the so-called co-governance perspective fitting with the network governance mode of policy-making and implementing (Skelcher, 2000). Here, the question relates to what extent and in which form sport (con)federations are involved in the country's processes of sport policy-making and service delivery (Groeneveld, 2009). Thus, co-governance implies direct interaction between the government and voluntary sport organisations in the development of public policy, both within policy-making and in the implementation processes. Contributors of the country chapters are invited to reflect theoretically on the disability sport system in their specific country in general, and, more specifically, on the relationship between governmental and non-governmental sporting bodies regarding sport for pwds in particular. Whether a principal-agent relationship or a co-involvement policy mechanism is in operation within a specific country depends on the particular sport system in that country. Both forms of policy relationship contain advantages and disadvantages. It is hypothesised that in countries with an interventionist sport legislation, meaning a policy system with a strong intervention by governmental actors, principal-agent relationships are dominant, whereas in countries with a non-interventionist sport legislation co-governance relationships are more likely to occur.

Support of Disability Sport

As part of the disability sport system, the chapter contributors were also asked to analyse the ways in which sport agents in the disability sport landscape are supported in their operations. Following again Scheerder and colleagues' framework (Scheerder et al., 2017), contributors were asked to provide, where possible, an overview of the financial framework in their country regarding disability sport. What are the subsidising mechanisms and financial resources for (sport) agents involved in disability sport? Agents involved in disability sport can also be supported in their governance and management by the government or respective sport governing bodies, including in training and education of staff and coaches, with practical tools and guidelines for implementing policy plans, in exchanging knowledge and so on.

Integration or Inclusion in Sport of Persons with a Disability

Considering the analysis given by the contributors in regard to the country profile and disability sport system (the previous four elements of the framework), authors were asked to briefly draw some conclusions regarding the provision of sport for pwds in their country and whether the developments in their country contributed to the integration or inclusion of pwds in sport. Contributors were asked to answer questions like: how can pwds participate in sport (activities), do they have equal access to sport and/or what kind of adapted sport opportunities are there? This element of the comparative framework was added to the original framework of Scheerder et al. (2017).

Sport Participation by Persons with a Disability

In this handbook, another element was added to the original framework of Scheerder et al. (2017). Because of the observed lack of data on the levels of sport participation by pwds in Europe, contributors were encouraged to give an overview of the existing data in their country. For this section we rely partly on previous comparative studies regarding sport participation in the general population (e.g. Hallmann & Petry, 2013; Helsen & Scheerder, 2021; Nicholson et al., 2011; Scheerder et al., 2011). In Hallmann and Petry's (2013) comparative study on systems, participation and public policy, the focus was on existing national participation surveys per country, including topics, for example, definitions of how sport participation is usually measured, participation rates in general and based on socio-demographic characteristics, trends in sport participation rates, top ten most practised sports, organisational forms and so on. Comparing sport participation research turns out to be difficult and this lies, according to Hallman and Petry, within the research itself and how sport participation is defined. Earlier work from Nicholson et al. (2011) mentions issues relating to inconsistent definitions between countries and over time and no coordination body or federation being responsible for sport participation. Scheerder et al. (2011) and Helsen and Scheerder (2021) also emphasised different research traditions in sport participation in the European Union. Comparative studies on disability sport participation are mostly lacking, except for the beforementioned small-scale mapping research commissioned by the European Commission in 2018 (Ecorys, 2018). In the Ecorys study the aim was to identify data collected at the EU member state level on participation in sport by pwds and for different types of disabilities. Data from 11 countries were involved in this study (Belgium, France, Germany, Ireland, Italy, Latvia, the Netherlands, Romania, Sweden and Spain). The country reviews revealed a strong variation in the range of data relating to sport participation for pwds. Country-level data on participation of pwds in sport ranged from detailed data available on different levels of activity (e.g. from inactive to fairly active and active) for different disability groups to broader measures of participation in sport (e.g. numbers of people doing a sport) for all disabilities. Other measures included numbers of clubs offering disability sport and numbers of club members. The authors observed that in some cases, data was not collected on a regular basis at the national level (Ecorys, 2018).

For our handbook, we asked contributors to review whether data on sport participation amongst pwds in the respective countries were already available. In cases where no data were available authors were asked to reflect on the reasons for this. In this section the focus was on two topics: (a) monitoring and evaluation and (b) sport participation. Contributors were asked to describe first whether the national government or any other central agent (has plans to) invest(s) in or stimulate(s) the monitoring of trends in sport participation by pwds in their country and whether there is a tradition in evaluating disability sport programmes and what kind of methods for data collection were used. To be able to compare data from the various countries, authors were asked to describe the following topics (depending on available data):

(a) definitions or indicators that were used to measure sport (e.g. what kind of activities are considered as sport in the survey or data?), sport participation (e.g. times per year, month or week?) and disability (when is a person considered as having a disability in the study?);
(b) participation rates for pwds in general and compared to the general population, per type of impairment and severity of disability, by sociodemographic variables (e.g. age, gender, income and education levels, etc.);
(c) type of activity (e.g. football, swimming, etc.; and to what extent the sport is adapted to the needs of pwds or not);
(d) social setting (whether pwds participate in disability-specific groups or in a non-disabled social setting);
(e) organisational setting (membership of a sport club or participation in other (non)organisational settings; and whether pwds are members of disability-specific clubs and/or mainstream clubs).

As we explain in Chap. 2, the extent to which and how pwds participate in sport may vary immensely, as the reader will also experience in the individual country chapters. Countries will also differ in the amount of data that are available regarding the previously mentioned topics. The aim of this handbook is to reveal this diversity and identify gaps and challenges in this regard.

To provide a more general picture of the sports participation amongst pwds in Europe, in Chap. 3 we present results from a secondary analysis of data from the Eurobarometer survey on sport.

Barriers and Facilitators Towards Sport Participation by Persons with a Disability

The last section, besides the conclusions, was focussed on giving an overview per country on the most important mediating or moderating factors for participation in sport by pwds. As mentioned earlier, pwds are less likely to participate in sport compared to persons without disabilities and experience various barriers towards participation. The UNCRPD and the European Disability Strategy are focussed on removing barriers towards participation in society (and in sport) for pwds. In order to be successful as a country in stimulating inclusion in sport, knowledge of these barriers is of utmost importance. Contributors were therefore asked to give (again depending on available data in the country) an overview of (a) the reasons (motivations) for pwds to participate in sport and (b) the barriers pwds are experiencing to be/become active participants in sport. Authors were asked if possible, according to the ICF-framework (see Chap. 2), to make a distinction between personal factors that influence sport participation (e.g. perceived health, self-image, attitudes towards

1 Introduction: Sport Participation a Human Right for Persons with a Disability

sport, etc.) and external or environmental factors (e.g. accessibility of transport, facilities, programmes, the availability or absence of trained volunteers and coaches, etc.). As the reader will experience, some contributors also described barriers and facilitators in regard to the disability sport system (e.g. experienced barriers by agents involved).

Chapter Conclusions

The last part of the country-specific chapters are the concluding remarks. Contributors were asked to draw conclusions in regard to the relationship between the disability sport system in the respective countries and sport participation levels of pwds. Authors raise questions for future research and indicate possible implications for future development of disability sport in their country and beyond. They were also asked to add a brief note on the possible influence of the Covid-19 pandemic on the participation in sport by pwds. Beyond the requested topics, authors were invited to add data on particular situations regarding disability sport in their country.

1.4 Selection of Countries

This handbook covers case studies from 19 countries in the European Region, EU member and non-member states. The objective is to explore the various ways sport for pwds is governed and organised across Europe, as well as the extent to which and how pwds participate in sport. The aim is to exchange knowledge and learn from each other. The comparative nature of this handbook required a selection of countries based on the following criteria: (a) focus on countries in the European region and (b) a geographical distribution over five regions in Europe (Northern Europe, Western Europe, Central Europe, Eastern Europe and Southern Europe, see Fig. 1.2). This classification into five regions can be helpful in identifying similarities and differences between groups of countries that more or less share similar social, welfare, economic, cultural or political characteristics (see also the concluding chapter of this handbook, Chap. 23). There is a certain correspondence of our proposed geographical classification with Esping-Andersen's (1990) typology of welfare states. Esping-Andersen (1990) distinguishes between universalist or social democratic welfare states (see Northern Europe), liberal or so-called Anglo-Saxon welfare states (see Western Europe), conservative-corporate welfare states (see Central Europe), Mediterranean welfare states (see Southern Europe) and so-called post-communist welfare states (see Eastern Europe). In Chap. 3 too, reference is made to Esping-Andersen's typology and a similar geographical classification is used in comparing EU-based data on sport participation amongst pwds.

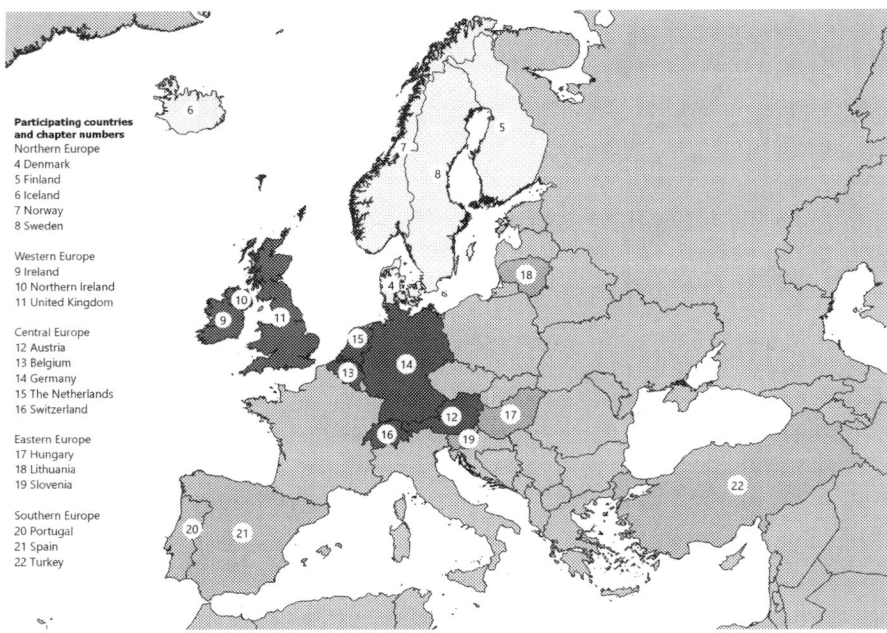

Fig. 1.2 Participating countries per region and corresponding chapter numbers. Source: Mulier Institute, this work

As for the European focus, the critical reader might suggest to expand the focus of the handbook to countries outside Europe (e.g. countries in the Middle East, Russia or China) as the cross-national differences in religion, governance and geopolitics might be larger. It would be interesting to compare many different countries around the world because of the varying backgrounds. However, for this handbook the editors deliberately chose to focus on countries in the European Region. As mentioned earlier in this chapter, the EU is a signatory of the UNCRPD which requires from EU member states to take appropriate and effective measures towards social inclusion of pwds in and through sports. The Convention requires from signatories to enable pwds to participate on an equal basis with others in recreational, leisure and sporting activities. The European strategy on disability furthermore aims to empower pwds so that they can enjoy their full rights and benefit fully from participation in society and the European economy, including in sport and recreation. Even in Europe there is a lack of research and data collection regarding disability sport and the question is whether a European dimension towards disability sport policy, structure and participation could be identified. In general, Scheerder et al. (2017) talk about the existence of a 'European sport model' which is characterised by strong government involvement in sport. However, there are striking differences concerning the organisation and structure of sport within Europe. If this is also true for disability sport, this makes it interesting to keep the analysis focussed on the European Region alone.

During the preparatory phase of this handbook potential contributors from various countries in all regions of Europe were contacted, resulting in the list of countries presented in Fig. 1.2. The participating countries are divided into the beforementioned five regions and their order in this handbook is according to this classification: Northern Europe (Chaps. 4–8), Western Europe (Chaps. 9–11), Central Europe (Chaps. 12–16), Eastern Europe (Chaps. 17–19) and Southern Europe (Chaps. 20–22). Certain regions are more comprehensively covered than others. Lack of time and/or lack of data have prevented some academics from participating in this handbook. This means we are missing the perspective of some countries, mainly representing Eastern and Southern Europe. Countries that have more 'history' in promoting disability sport at a grassroots level and have a greater 'track record' in policy-making in this field and monitoring of sport participation data were in a better position to write a chapter. To encourage countries that are less far along in this process to participate, the editors left open the possibility to participate even if not all requested data were available. These differences between the country chapters are taken into account in the comparison of the disability sport systems in Europe in the concluding chapter.

References

Blauwet, C. A. (2019). More than just a game. *American Journal of Physical Medicine & Rehabilitation, 98*(1), 1–6. https://doi.org/10.1097/PHM.0000000000001063

Borland, R. L., Hu, N., Tonge, B., Einfeld, S., & Gray, K. M. (2020). Participation in sport and physical activity in adults with intellectual disabilities. *Journal of Intellectual Disability Research, 64*(12), 908–922. https://doi.org/10.1111/jir.12782

Brittain, I., & Beacom, A. (Eds.). (2018). *The Palgrave handbook of paralympic studies*. Palgrave Macmillan. https://link.springer.com/book/10.1057/978-1-137-47901-3

Brittain, I., Biscaia, R., & Gérard, S. (2020). Ableism as a regulator of social practice and disabled peoples' self-determination to participate in sport and physical activity. *Leisure Studies, 39*(2), 209–224. https://doi.org/10.1080/02614367.2019.1694569

Bull, F. C., Al-Ansari, S. S., Biddle, S., Borodulin, K., Buman, M. P., Cardon, G., Carty, C., Chaput, J., Chastin, S., Chou, R., Dempsey, P. C., DiPietro, L., Ekelund, U., Firth, J., Friedenreich, C. M., Garcia, L., Gichu, M., Jago, R., Katzmarzyk, P. T., & Willumsen, J. F. (2020). World Health Organization 2020 guidelines on physical activity and sedentary behaviour. *British Journal of Sports Medicine, 54*(24), 1451–1462. https://doi.org/10.1136/bjsports-2020-102955

Carbone, P. S., Smith, P. J., Lewis, C., & LeBlanc, C. (2021). Promoting the participation of children and adolescents with disabilities in sports, recreation, and physical activity. *Pediatrics, 148*(6), e2021054664. https://doi.org/10.1542/peds.2021-054664

Christiaens, M., & Brittain, I. (2021). The complexities of implementing inclusion policies for disabled people in UK non-disabled voluntary community sports clubs. *European Sport Management Quarterly, 1–21*. https://doi.org/10.1080/16184742.2021.1955942

Council of Europe. (2021). *Recommendation CM/Rec(2021)5 of the Committee of Ministers to member States on the Revised European Sports Charter*. Council of Europe. https://www.coe.int/en/web/sport/european-sports-charter

Darcy, S., & Dowse, L. (2013). In search of a level playing field – The constraints and benefits of sport participation for people with intellectual disability. *Disability & Society, 28*(3), 393–407. https://doi.org/10.1080/09687599.2012.714258

Darcy, S., Lock, D., & Taylor, T. (2017). Enabling inclusive sport participation: Effects of disability and support needs on constraints to sport participation. *Leisure Sciences, 39*(1), 20–41. https://doi.org/10.1080/01490400.2016.1151842

De Boer, D. R., Hoekstra, F., Huetink, K. I. M., Hoekstra, T., Krops, L. A., & Hettinga, F. J. (2021). Physical activity, sedentary behavior and well-being of adults with physical disabilities and/or chronic diseases during the first wave of the COVID-19 pandemic: A rapid review. *International Journal of Environmental Research and Public Health, 18*, 6342. https://doi.org/10.3390/ijerph18126342

De Hollander, E. L., & Proper, K. I. (2018). Physical activity levels of adults with various physical disabilities. *Preventive Medicine Reports, 10*(August 2017), 370–376. https://doi.org/10.1016/j.pmedr.2018.04.017

DISN. (n.d.). *Disability Studies as an academic discipline*. Retrieved April 11, 2022, from https://disabilitystudies.nl/en/disability-studies-academic-discipline

Ecorys. (2018). *Mapping on access to sport for people with disabilities. A report to the European Commission*. Publications Office of the European Union. https://op.europa.eu/en/publication-detail/-/publication/09e457a0-04d7-11e9-adde-01aa75ed71a1

Elling, A., & Claringbould, I. (2005). Mechanisms of inclusion and exclusion in the Dutch sports landscape: Who can and wants to belong? *Sociology of Sport Journal, 22*(4), 498–515. https://doi.org/10.1123/ssj.22.4.498

Esping-Andersen, G. (1990). *The three worlds of welfare capitalism*. Princeton University Press.

European Commission. (2010). *European strategy on disability 2010–2020*. European Commission. https://eur-lex.europa.eu/LexUriServ/LexUriServ.do?uri=COM%3A2010%3A0636%3AFIN%3Aen%3APDF

European Commission. (2011). *Developing the European dimension in sport*. European Commission Communication. https://eur-lex.europa.eu/legal-content/EN/TXT/HTML/?uri=CELEX:52011DC0012&from=FR

European Commission. (2018). *Special Eurobarometer 472 Report – Sport and physical activity* (Vol. 8, Issue December 2017, p. 133). European Commission. https://doi.org/10.2766/483047.

European Commission. (2020). *Commission staff working document evaluation of the European Disability Strategy 2010–2020. SWD(2020) 289 final/2*. European Commission.

European Commission. (2021). *Union of equality: Strategy for the rights of persons with disabilities 2021–2030*. European Commission. https://eur-lex.europa.eu/legal-content/EN/TXT/?uri=COM%3A2021%3A101%3AFIN#:~:text=Union_of_Equality%3A_Strategy_for_the_Rights_of,have_a_right_to_a_life_without_barriers

European Union. (2010). *Council conclusions of 18 November 2010 on the role of sport as a source of and a driver for active social inclusion (2010/C 326/04)*. European Union. https://eur-lex.europa.eu/legal-content/EN/TXT/PDF/?uri=CELEX:52010XG1203(04)&from=EN

European Union. (2012). *The charter of fundamental rights of the European Union. 2012/C 326/02*. European Disability Expertise. https://eur-lex.europa.eu/legal-content/EN/TXT/?uri=CELEX:12012P/TXT

European Union. (2016). *Consolidated versions of the treaty on European Union and the treaty on the functioning of the European Union. 2016/C 202/02*. Publications Office of the European Union. https://eur-lex.europa.eu/legal-content/EN/TXT/?uri=celex%3A12016ME%2FTXT

European Union. (2017). *European pillar of social rights*. https://ec.europa.eu/info/sites/default/files/social-summit-european-pillar-social-rights-booklet_en.pdf

European Union. (2019). *Conclusions of the Council of the European Union and the representatives of the member states meeting within the council on access to sport for persons with disabilities (2019/C 192/06)*. European Union. https://eur-lex.europa.eu/legal-content/EN/TXT/PDF/?uri=CELEX:52019XG0607(03)

European Union. (2021). *The European pillar of social rights action plan*. European Commission. https://op.europa.eu/webpub/empl/european-pillar-of-social-rights/downloads/KE0921008ENN.pdf

Goodwin, M., & Grix, J. (2011). Bringing structures back in. The 'governance narrative', the 'decentred approach' and 'asymmetrical network governance' in the education and sport policy communities. *Public Administration, 89*(2), 537–556. https://doi.org/10.1111/j.1467-9299.2011.01921.x

Grammenos, S., & Priestley, M. (2020). *Master tables concerning EU 2020: Year 2018. Statistics on persons with disabilities (2018)*. European Disability Expertise. https://www.disability-europe.net/downloads/1046-ede-task-2-1-statistical-indicators-tables-eu-silc-2018

Groeneveld, M. (2009). European sport governance, citizens, and the state. *Public Management Review, 11*(4), 421–440. https://doi.org/10.1080/14719030902989516

Hallmann, K., & Petry, K. (Eds.). (2013). Comparative sport development. systems, participation and public policy. In *Sport economics, management and policy* (Vol. 8). Springer. https://link.springer.com/book/10.1007/978-1-4614-8905-4

Helsen, K., & Scheerder, J. (2021). Sports participation, physical (in)activity and overweight in the European Union. A comparative study based on pan-European data 2002–2017. In *Sport policy & management studies* (Vol. 67). KU Leuven/Policy in Sports & Physical Activity Research Group. https://gbiomed.kuleuven.be/english/research/50000737/groups/policy-in-sports-physical-activity-research-group/bms-studies/bms67.pdf

Hoekstra, F., Roberts, L., Van Lindert, C., Martin Ginis, K. A., Van der Woude, L. H. V., & McColl, M. A. (2019). National approaches to promote sports and physical activity in adults with disabilities: Examples from the Netherlands and Canada. *Disability and Rehabilitation, 41*(10), 1217. https://doi.org/10.1080/09638288.2017.1423402

Jaarsma, E. A., Dijkstra, P. U., Geertzen, J. H. B., & Dekker, R. (2014). Barriers to and facilitators of sports participation for people with physical disabilities: A systematic review. *Scandinavian Journal of Medicine & Science in Sports, 24*(6), 871–881. https://doi.org/10.1111/sms.12218

Kantar. (2019). *Special Eurobarometer 493. Discrimination in the European Union*. European Union. https://europa.eu/eurobarometer/surveys/detail/2251

Leung, K. M., Chung, P. K., Chu, W., & Ng, K. (2021). Physical and psychological health outcomes of a sitting light volleyball intervention program on adults with physical disabilities: A non-randomized controlled pre-post study. *BMC Sports Science, Medicine and Rehabilitation, 13*(1), 100. https://doi.org/10.1186/s13102-021-00328-7

Martin Ginis, K. A., Ma, J. K., Latimer-Cheung, A. E., & Rimmer, J. H. (2016). A systematic review of review articles addressing factors related to physical activity participation among children and adults with physical disabilities. *Health Psychology Review, 10*, 478–494. https://doi.org/10.1080/17437199.2016.1198240

Martin Ginis, K. A., Van der Ploeg, H. P., Foster, C., Lai, B., McBride, C. B., Ng, K., Pratt, M., Shirazipour, C. H., Smith, B., Vásquez, P. M., & Heath, G. W. (2021). Participation of people living with disabilities in physical activity: A global perspective. *The Lancet, 398*(10298), 443–455. https://doi.org/10.1016/S0140-6736(21)01164-8

Nicholson, M., Hoye, R., & Houlihan, B. (Eds.). (2011). *Participation in sport. International policy perspectives*. Routledge.

Pletosu, T., Airaghi, E., & Goffredo, S. (2021). *Mapping of sport statistics and data in the EU final report to the European Commission*. Publications Office of the European Union. https://op.europa.eu/en/publication-detail/-/publication/25c4dfc8-19bf-11ec-b4fe-01aa75ed71a1/language-en/format-PDF/source-249167352

Robertson, J., Emerson, E., Baines, S., & Hatton, C. (2018). Self-reported participation in sport/exercise among adolescents and young adults with and without mild to moderate intellectual disability. *Journal of Physical Activity and Health, 15*(4), 247–254. https://doi.org/10.1123/jpah.2017-0035

Ross, S. (1973). The economic theory of agency: The principal's problem. *American Economic Review, 63*(2), 134–139.

Scheerder, J., Vandermeerschen, H., Van Tuyckom, C., Hoekman, R., Breedveld, K., & Vos, S. (2011). *Understanding the game: Sport participation in Europe. Facts, reflections and recommendations*. Katholieke Universiteit Leuven.

Scheerder, J., Vanlandewyck, Y., Van Biesen, D., Cans, E., Lenaerts, L., Meganck, A. S., & Cornelissen, J. (2018). *Onderzoek naar de actieve sportdeelname van personen met een beperking in Vlaanderen en het Brussels Hoofdstedelijk Gewest. Een nulmeting [Research into active participation in sport among persons with a disability in Flanders and the Brussels Capital Reg].* KU Leuven/Policy in Sport & Physical Activity Research Group. https://limo.libis.be/primo-explore/fulldisplay?docid=LIRIAS1689711&context=L&vid=Lirias&search_scope=Lirias&tab=default_tab&fromSitemap=1

Scheerder, J., Willem, A., & Claes, E. (Eds.). (2017). *Sport policy systems and sport federations. A cross-national perspective.* Palgrave Macmillan.

Skelcher, C. (2000). Changing images of the state: Overloaded, hollowed-out, congested. *Public Policy and Administration, 15*(3), 3–19. https://doi.org/10.1177/095207670001500302

Smith, B., Kirby, N., Skinner, B., Wightman, L., Lucas, R., & Foster, C. (2018). *Physical activity for general health benefits in disabled adults: Summary of a rapid evidence review for the UK Chief Medical Officers' update of the physical activity guidelines about Public Health England.* Public Health England.

Sørensen, M., & Kahrs, N. (2006). Integration of disability sport in the Norwegian sport organizations: Lessons learned. *Adapted Physical Activity Quarterly, 23*(2), 184–202. https://doi.org/10.1123/apaq.23.2.184

Sportanddev.org. (2015). *The UNESCO chair in inclusive physical education, sport, fitness and recreation.* https://www.sportanddev.org/en/article/news/unesco-chair-inclusive-physical-education-sport-fitness-and-recreation

Thomas, N., & Guett, M. (2014). Fragmented, complex and cumbersome: A study of disability sport policy and provision in Europe. *International Journal of Sport Policy and Politics, 6*(3), 389–406. https://doi.org/10.1080/19406940.2013.832698

Tokarski, W., Steinbach, D., Petry, K., & Jesse, B. (Eds.). (2004). *Two players. One goal? Sport in the European Union.* Meyer & Meyer Sport.

UNESCO. (2015). *International charter of physical education and sport.* UNESCO. https://unesdoc.unesco.org/ark:/48223/pf0000235409

UNESCO. (2021). *MINEPS VI – Kazan 2017.* https://en.unesco.org/mineps6/kazan-action-plan

United Nations. (2006). *Convention on the rights of persons with disabilities (CRPD).* https://www.un.org/development/desa/disabilities/convention-on-the-rights-of-persons-with-disabilities.html

United Nations. (2015). *Transforming our world: The 2030 agenda for sustainable development. A/RES/70/1.* United Nations.

United Nations. (2019). *Disability and development report. Realizing the sustainable development goals by, for and with persons with disabilities. 2018.* United Nations.

Van Lindert, C., Scheerder, J., & Brittain, I. (2020). *Instructions to write a country-specific chapter (internal document).* Mulier Institute.

Von Heijden-Brinkman, A., Van den Dool, R., Van Lindert, C., & Breedveld, K. (2013). *(On) beperkt sportief 2013: Monitor sport-en beweegdeelname van mensen met een handicap.* https://www.mulierinstituut.nl/publicaties/12543/onbeperkt-sportief-2013/

World Health Organization. (2002). *Towards a common language for functioning, disability and health. International classification of functioning, disability and health (ICF).* https://www.who.int/publications/m/item/icf-beginner-s-guide-towards-a-common-language-for-functioning-disability-and-health

World Health Organization. (2018). *Global action plan on physical activity 2018–2030. More active people for a healthier world.* World Health Organization.

World Health Organization. (2020). *2020 WHO guidelines on physical activity and sedentary behavior.* World Health Organization. https://www.who.int/publications/i/item/9789240015128

World Health Organization. (2022). *Disability and health, factsheet.* https://www.who.int/news-room/fact-sheets/detail/disability-and-health#:~:text=Over_1_billion_people_are_estimated_to_live,difficulties_in_functioning%2C_often_requiring_healthcare_services

World Health Organization, & The World Bank. (2011). *World report on disability*. World Health Organization. https://www.who.int/teams/noncommunicable-diseases/sensory-functions-disability-and-rehabilitation/world-report-on-disability

World Health Organization Regional Office for Europe. (2022). *Facts on disability*. https://www.who.int/europe/news-room/fact-sheets/item/disability

Yu, S., Wang, T., Zhong, T., Qian, Y., & Qi, J. (2022). Barriers and facilitators of physical activity participation among children and adolescents with intellectual disabilities: A scoping review. *Healthcare, 10*(2), 233. https://doi.org/10.3390/healthcare10020233

Chapter 2
Understanding Disability, Disability Sport and Inclusion

Ian Brittain, Caroline van Lindert, and Jeroen Scheerder

2.1 Introduction

The country-specific chapters in this book give a comparative overview of the different ways various countries across Europe attempt to include persons with a disability (pwds) in sport, and the policies they adopt to try and promote this. Before going any further therefore, it would appear pertinent to try and explain some of the reasons why such policies are necessary and why pwds might feel excluded from such opportunities in the first place.

The Paralympic Movement and, we believe, modern-day grassroots sporting opportunities for pwds owe much of their existence to the Stoke Mandeville Games, started in the United Kingdom by Sir Ludwig Guttmann in 1948 as a form of rehabilitation for spinally injured service personnel from World War II (Brittain, 2014). Guttmann (1976, p. 12–13) cited three underpinning philosophies for his introduction of sport into the rehabilitation process.

Sport as a Curative Factor Guttmann believed that sport can be invaluable in restoring the overall fitness, including strength, speed, co-ordination and endurance,

---

I. Brittain (✉)
Centre for Business in Society, Coventry University, Coventry, UK
e-mail: aa8550@coventry.ac.uk

C. van Lindert
Mulier Institute, Utrecht, The Netherlands
e-mail: c.vanlindert@mulierinstituut.nl

J. Scheerder
Department of Movement Sciences, KU Leuven, Leuven, Belgium

Policy Research Centre on Sports on behalf of the Flemish Government, Leuven, Belgium
e-mail: jeroen.scheerder@kuleuven.be

of someone receiving a disabling injury, because it represents the most natural form of exercise that can greatly complement other forms of remedial exercise. It was for this reason that archery was the first sport to appear at the Stoke Mandeville Games, because Guttmann felt that it represented "immense value in strengthening, in a very natural way, just those muscles of the upper limbs, shoulders and trunk, on which the paraplegic's well-balanced, upright position depends" (Guttmann, 1952, p. 8).

The Recreational and Psychological Value of Sport Guttmann claimed that the big advantage of sport for pwds over other remedial exercises lies within its recreational and psycho-emotional value, pointing out that much of the restorative power of sport is lost if the pwd does not enjoy their participation in it. As long as enjoyment is derived from the activity, then Guttmann claims that sport can help develop an active mind, self-confidence, self-dignity, self-discipline, competitive spirit and camaraderie, all of which are essential in helping to overcome the physical and emotional consequences that can occur, particularly with the onset of sudden traumatic disability.

Sport as a Means of Social Re-Integration There are certain sports where pwds are capable of competing alongside their peers without a disability, for example, archery, bowls and table tennis, as Paula Fantato of Italy proved when she competed from a wheelchair in archery at the 1996 Olympic Games in Atlanta. Guttmann claimed that this helps create a better understanding between pwds and their peers without disability, and aids in their social re-integration through the medium of sport.

2.2 Why Are Persons with a Disability Excluded from Society?

In order to try and explain why pwds feel excluded from society it is important to highlight the way many pwds are treated and viewed by the wider society. To a large extent pwds are still viewed by many as a 'class or category' with little appreciation or understanding of the unique nature of each person, regardless of the disability. The adaptation of Galtung's Triangle of Violence, below, highlights some of the ways in which pwds have historically been 'victims' of various kinds of 'violence' or discrimination around the world (see Fig. 2.1). For the purpose of this chapter violence is defined by the World Health Organization (WHO) as "the intentional use of physical force or power, threatened or actual, against oneself, another person, or against a group or community, that either results in or has a high likelihood of resulting in injury, death, psychological harm, maldevelopment, or deprivation" (World Health Organization, 2010; online).

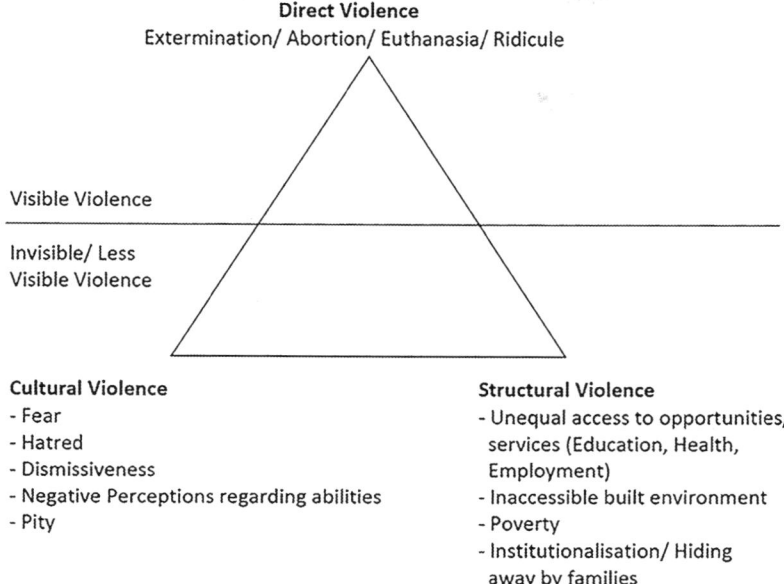

Fig. 2.1 Disability and the triangle of violence. Source: adapted from Galtung (1990)

As can be seen in Fig. 2.1, this violence can range from more visible and direct forms of violence, such as the deliberate killing of babies and children with a disability in countries such as Ghana (Kassah et al., 2012) to less visible and less direct forms of violence including negative attitudes towards pwds (Livneh, 1982), an inaccessible environment (Banda-Chalwe et al., 2014) or social structures that prevent access to key forms of social capital such as education and employment (Brittain et al., 2020). For a more detailed discussion of the impacts of direct, cultural and structural violence upon the lives of pwds see Brittain (2012). The combined effect of direct, cultural and structural violence against pwds is social exclusion.

How disability is defined within a particular society potentially says a lot about how that society perceives disability and pwds. Below is a typical dictionary definition of the term 'disability', which clearly pathologises disability, that is, represents it as biologically situated and produced:

> **Disability,** *n.*—1. A physical incapacity; either congenital or caused by injury, disease, etc., esp. when limiting a person's ability to work.

Definitions of disability such as this form the basis for what constitutes conventional views of disability, which are explored in more detail in the next section. In the following chapters the contributing authors will explain what is meant by disability in their own respective countries.

2.3 Theories and Models to Assist in the Understanding Why 'Disability' Exists

According to Smart (2009) "models of disability define disability, determine which professions serve people with disabilities, and help shape the self-identities of those with disabilities" (p. 3). Theories and models of disability seek to explain in a systemised way the behaviours of both people without disabilities towards pwds and the ways in which pwds interact with the wider society (Llewellyn & Hogan, 2000) in order to try and explain the treatment of pwds and how and why discrimination might occur (Dirth & Branscombe, 2017). However, it is important to understand that no single model or theory of disability can explain all aspects of, or issues pertaining to, disability. It is also important to understand that these models and theories also tend to be based firmly on a Global North or Westernised conception of disability, whereas in the Global South they may take a different approach (Watermeyer et al., 2019). However, given that the focus of this handbook is on European nations, the models and theories outlined would appear to be appropriate in aiding our understanding. In what follows next, a brief explanation is given of six such theories and models—the medical, social, relational, human rights and hybrid or new models of disability (affirmative, embodiment) and ableism.

Medical Model

This is the oldest of the models of disability that emphasises a disability-specific or categorical approach that strengthens and continues the idea that 'disability' is within the person and their individual impairment(s) and is therefore a problem for, and of, the individual with the impairment(s) (Brittain, 2016). Therefore, the general view is that any problems encountered by pwds are the result of *their* physical and/or mental impairments and are independent of the wider sociocultural, physical and political environments. As a result of this perspective, the only rational course of action is to try and correct the perceived problem through medical interventions or cures (World Health Organization, 2002). The underpinning cornerstone for this perspective is the 'normal' body with any impairments being a deviation from this socially constructed perspective of what a 'normal' body should look like and how it should function and, therefore, be deemed abnormal or sub-human and less able, that is, disabled (Reynolds, 2017). This then creates an environment which not only promotes discrimination against pwds, but also devalues their worth as citizens (Scullion, 2010).

Social Model

In an attempt to negate the negative implications of the medical model of disability, an alternative social model of disability emerged from the disability rights movement in the United Kingdom in the mid-1970s (UPIAS, 1976). Morris (1991) claims that from the perspective of the social model if people's attitudes were to change, and there was effective public policy that legislated that environmental barriers should be removed, then many of the problems associated with disability would disappear, for as Brisenden (1986) states:

> Disablement lies in the construction of society, not in the physical condition of the individual. However, this argument is usually rejected precisely because to accept it involves recognising the extent to which we are not merely unfortunate but are directly oppressed by a hostile social environment. (p. 176)

Therefore, the social model highlights and recognises that society is organised in ways designed to exclude pwds based upon deeply rooted prejudices against them emanating from a medical model approach. The social model highlights that these segregating factors (social attitudes and the built environment) have been manufactured by, and naturalised through, a social system designed and governed by a medical model perspective of pwd (Shapiro et al., 2012). What this appears to indicate is that it is a change in underlying attitudes and levels of understanding that are key to changing the situation for pwds. Indeed, it could be argued, from this perspective, that if underlying attitudes and levels of understanding were to change in a positive manner, then the necessary changes in social policy should follow as a natural progression of the new situation and many of the problems associated with disability would disappear (Shakespeare & Watson, 2002).

Relational Model

In contrast to the medical and social models, Thomas (2007) claims that the relational model, sometimes also called the biosocial model, considers lived experience, psycho-emotional wellbeing, social oppression, impairment and the body as simultaneously biological, cultural and social. Previously, authors such as Imrie (1997) and Birkenbach (1990) had argued that both the medical and social models are inherently weak because they overlook or deny the interactional character of disablement. However, both authors do acknowledge the difficulties of trying to locate disablement in a relationship between a medical and a functional problem and the social responses to it, as they claim the concept of disability requires. Birkenbach (1990) argues that the social model must recognise that there is a physical state that prevents pwds being afforded equal opportunities and treatment, in that their very physical differences mean that society has to react to them, and their various needs in a way different from the way it reacts to the same needs of the rest of society. As an example of this, French (1993) rejects the idea that her visual impairment generates disabilities that are wholly socially created, commenting that her impairment (blindness) disables her from recognising people and makes her "unable to read non-verbal cues or emit them correctly" (p. 17). The relational model therefore introduces 'impairment effects', which refer to restrictions in activity in the lives of pwds arising directly from their impairments. However, impacts such as these can spread beyond any restrictions caused just by biology (e.g. chronic pain) to the social arena resulting in social and psycho-emotional oppression caused by negative attitudes to disability. The relational model therefore highlights how pwds can be socially oppressed, even when environmental barriers are absent, and how their emotional wellbeing can be undermined during interactions with the wider society without a disability in ways that may limit their options for participation (Smith, 2013).

Human Rights Model

Berghs et al. (2019) claim that a model of disability "should be a means to change society (and its collective values), in addition to upholding the human dignity of disabled people's lives in every aspect of society" (p. 1037). According to Degener (2017) the human rights model argues that society should acknowledge the value of all persons based on their inherent human worth, rather than basing a person's value on what they are perceived to be able to contribute to society. Smith and Bundon (2018) claim that this model concerns itself with a wide raft of human rights issues with its interconnected concerns for political, civil, economic and cultural rights seen as underpinning a broad roadmap for change. It is this approach that underpinned the drawing up of the United Nations Convention on the Rights of Persons with Disabilities (UNCRPD) (United Nations, 2006), which according to Misener and Darcy (2014) is designed to make society a more just place for pwds to participate through the adoption of eight principles. These are: (1) respect for inherent dignity, individual autonomy including the freedom to make one's own choices and independence of persons; (2) non-discrimination; (3) full and effective participation and inclusion in society; (4) respect for difference and acceptance of pwds as part of human diversity and humanity; (5) equality of opportunity; (6) accessibility; (7) equality between men and women; and (8) respect for the evolving capacities of children with disabilities and the right of children with disabilities to preserve their identities (Misener & Darcy, 2014, p. 3; United Nations, 2006).

Affirmative Model

The medical and social models of disability are underpinned by the idea that to have a disability is a 'tragedy' as both models posit pwds as being victims of either biological or societal circumstances and are underpinned by the idea that pwds want to be just like their peers without disabilities, even where this would require a complete rejection of their identity as pwds (Abrams & Adkins, 2020). The affirmative model, which arose out of disability culture, considers such models to be disabling in and of themselves and proposes an oppositional approach based on a 'non-tragic' view of disability, by shifting the focus to a celebration of diversity (French & Swain, 2004). In doing so, it acknowledges the positive identities that pwds have and embraces their rights to be the way they are, that is 'equal but different' (French & Swain, 2004, p.38).

Biopsychosocial Model

Another model is the biopsychosocial model, developed in 2002 by the WHO under the name International Classification of Functioning, Disability and Health framework (ICF) (World Health Organization, 2002). The ICF combines the medical and the social model of disability and adds the individual perspective. The model is explained in more detail in the section 'Disability in this handbook' (see Sect. 2.5), as we borrow our understanding of 'disability' for this handbook from this model.

Ableism

In terms of disability studies, the concept of ableism is perhaps the newest addition to the researchers' armoury and has, according to Loja et al. (2013), been the subject of extensive research focused on the way pwds are treated within the wider society. Ableism builds upon the medical and social models of disability, but can also be applied to other marginalised groups such as women, ethnic minorities and the LBGTQ+ community, allowing for intersectional research. With respect to pwds Wolbring (2012) claims that "ableism describes prejudicial attitudes and discriminatory behaviours toward persons with a disability" (p. 78) that are related to one's understanding of the ability and the rights and benefits afforded to persons deemed 'normal'. Ableism is therefore closely connected with the idea of norms and normalcy, and the resultant imposition of normative values for maintaining the power of one group over another, in that those who best fit the construed norms uphold power over those who diverge from them (Brittain et al., 2020). Ableism therefore may lead to pwds being devalued within the society in which they live, leading to segregation, social isolation and social policies that may limit opportunities for their full societal participation. This occurs as a result of a combination of the ableist attitudes that nearly all people within society are socialised into, albeit to varying degrees (OHRC, n.d.), and an inaccessible environment that is often built only with those who embody the normative values of the dominant group in mind (Nourry, 2018). These two, combined with the strong links between ableism and capitalism (c.f. Oliver & Barnes, 2012), underpin the economic, structural and psycho-emotional oppression encountered on an almost daily basis by many pwds.

Disableism

Goodley (2014) differentiates between ableism and disableism, although in practice they are closely linked. According to Goodley ableism emphasises discrimination based upon ability and in favour of people without disabilities, whereas disablism emphasises discrimination against pwds based upon "a failure to fit the capitalist imperative" (p. xi) whereby pwds are considered unproductive members of society. The role of the social oppression highlighted above is therefore to both benefit those closely associated with the desired normative values and to marginalise those that differ from them through social closure, which Patillo (2008) claims are the establishment and sustenance of boundaries formed by the group that dominates a particular field in an effort to keep out potential newcomers. In terms of access to sport and physical activity Brittain et al. (2020) highlight how ableism might be used by people without disabilities to exclude some pwds from sports participation in order to keep the benefits of access to this social arena to themselves through a process known as opportunity hoarding. According to Brar (2016), "opportunity hoarding is a deliberate process by which social closure enables the dominant group to disproportionately amass the available rewards in a particular field, thereby strengthening and entrenching their dominant position within that field" (p.66). One of the ways this occurs is through a process known as 'internalised ableism'.

Internalised Ableism

Based on this almost ubiquitous perception of disability as a pathological issue leading to a digression from a socially expected physical norm, both people without and with a disability within society are encouraged, through numerous sources, to internalise many of the perceptions of disability embedded within an ableist approach to disability. Consequently, despite challenges to this perception by disability activists via the social model of disability, it appears to some pwds that the causes of many of their problems lie within them and their own impairments (Brittain & Beacom, 2016). This leads to what Campbell (2009) calls 'internalised ableism'. Within an ableist perspective, the existence of disability is often merely tolerated rather than celebrated as a component of human diversity, and internalised ableism commonly forces some pwds to assimilate ableist norms by assuming an identity other than their own (Campbell, 2008), which relates to a rejection of their disabled identity as highlighted by Abrams and Adkins (2020) in the description of the affirmative model above.

2.4 Language and Disability

According to Wilson and Martin (2018) which model or theory of disability that is applied within a particular culture, particularly in a policy context, will have implications for equality and inclusion, because it will affect the language used in relation to disability. Language is, at its most simple, just a series of words or characters. It is the meanings attached by humans to these words or characters that make language relevant. One function of language is communication, but in communicating humans also, more often than not, convey the underlying meaning behind the words or characters used. It is also claimed that language plays a key role in politics, domination and control (Brittain, 2016). The meanings attached to the words or characters used are socially constructed within the social or cultural group within which an individual grows up and develops. Therefore, there can be major differences in the perceived meanings of words such as 'disability', 'disabled' and even what constitutes 'sport', dependent upon the social and cultural group within which an individual learns their proscribed meanings. However, as some social groups and cultures within a given society are more powerful or have more influence than others one set of meanings for these words may gain dominance, even over those meanings proscribed by the group they refer to. According to Goodley (2014) language and definitions of disability can even be used as a form of social closure citing the case of the UK where austerity budgets led to a severe narrowing of neoliberal definitions of disability in order to restrict access to state benefits. Therefore, how a country defines disability can have major repercussions for who is deemed 'disabled' within a particular country and who then has access to support and services.

'Disabled Person' or 'Person with a Disability'?

One of the ways in which language differences regularly arises is in whether people with impairments should be described as 'disabled people' or 'people or persons with a disability'. For instance, the Canadian government has advocated a 'person first' approach whereby the emphasis is on being a person first and foremost, and having a disability second. However, many people with impairments claim that disability is not actually part of who they are, but something imposed externally by society (McColl, 2019). According to Equality Training (n.d. online):

> disabled people use the term 'impairment' to talk about their medical condition or diagnosis or description of their functioning. On the other hand, 'disability' describes the social effects of impairment. 'Disability' is not a description of a personal characteristic. A disabled person is not a 'person with a disability' as the person does not own the disability in the way that you might be 'a person with brown hair'. (p 1)

The use of 'disabled person' is strongly associated with the social model of disability, highlighting the externally imposed nature of 'disability', that is, a person can have an impairment without it necessarily disabling them. Despite this, as the various chapters of this handbook will highlight, preferences for the use of 'disabled person' or 'person with a disability' still vary widely from country to country and even within countries, and as a consequence also at the European level.

Able-Bodied or Non-Disabled?

According to the Cambridge Dictionary the term 'able-bodied' refers to "people who are healthy and have no illness, injury, or condition that makes it difficult to do the things that other people do" (Cambridge Dictionary Online, 2021). Samantha Renke, an actor with a disability and activist, claims that some members of the disability community oppose the use of this term because "it implies that all people with disabilities lack 'able bodies' and completely ignores invisible disabilities, such as Dyslexia or Asperger's—you can be disabled and have a fully 'able' body" (Renke, 2020), and secondly, it implies that pwds do not have the ability to use their bodies well. These are just two examples from many that highlight how language use and perceived meanings of words or phrases can make people feel either included or excluded from the wider society.

2.5 Disability in This Handbook

Throughout the handbook the reader will notice various terms used to refer to disability. In Chap. 1, we used 'persons with a disability', as we wanted to stress, bearing the UNCRPD in mind, that every person is valued primarily for who he/she/x is and is not judged purely for having a disorder or impairment. As mentioned above, we recognise the possibility that different meanings can be assigned to the terms in the respective countries that are part of this handbook.

For the overall meaning of disability for this handbook we rely on the definitions used by the United Nations and the World Health Organization. According to the UNCRPD, pwds include those who have long-term physical, mental, intellectual or sensory impairments which, in interaction with various attitudinal and environmental barriers, may hinder their full and effective participation in society on an equal basis with others. The UNCRPD recognises disability as an evolving concept (United Nations, 2006). This definition is in line with the ICF (World Health Organization, 2002). The ICF is the WHO's framework for health and disability, and internationally it serves as the conceptual basis for the definition, measurement and policy formulation for health and disability. The ICF is a tool to measure people's level of functioning in society, no matter the reason for their impairment(s). It acknowledges that every human being can experience a decrease in health and thereby experience some form of disability. "This is not something that happens to only a minority of humanity. ICF thus 'mainstreams' the experience of disability and recognises it as a universal human experience" (Kostanjsek, 2011; p. 5). The

ICF combines both the medical and the social model of disability (supra) and adds the individual perspective. According to the ICF, disability is an interaction between bodily features, personal factors and contextual factors. The ICF model is a biopsychosocial model which captures human functioning at three levels:

1. Biological aspects (body functions and structures, e.g. arms and legs). For instance, if a person cannot move his/her/x legs, he/she/x experiences a limitation in functioning at the body function level.
2. Individual aspects (human action or activity and what a person is (still or not) able to do). For instance, if a person has difficulty in walking, he/she/x experiences a limitation in the execution of a specific activity.
3. Social aspects (a person's ability to participate in all aspects of society, e.g. work, family, sport, etc.). For instance, if a person cannot participate in sport because of environmental barriers (e.g. inaccessible transport or sport facilities), then he/she/x is restricted at the participation level. See Fig. 2.2 for an illustration of the model.

The ICF recognises the influence of various factors on human functioning. These factors include the person's health condition (disease or disorder), (internal) personal factors (e.g. gender, age, education and income, personality or coping strategy) and (external) environmental factors (physical and social environment, such as a person's house, the presence of tools/aids/assistive devices, social attitudes, friends, legal and social structures, architectural characteristics). These factors can positively or negatively impact a person's functioning. For example, the proximity of an adapted sports complex can contribute to a pwds' capability to exercise. On the other hand, a negative perception or image among sport club members about pwds can create an unwelcoming atmosphere at the club for pwds, thereby

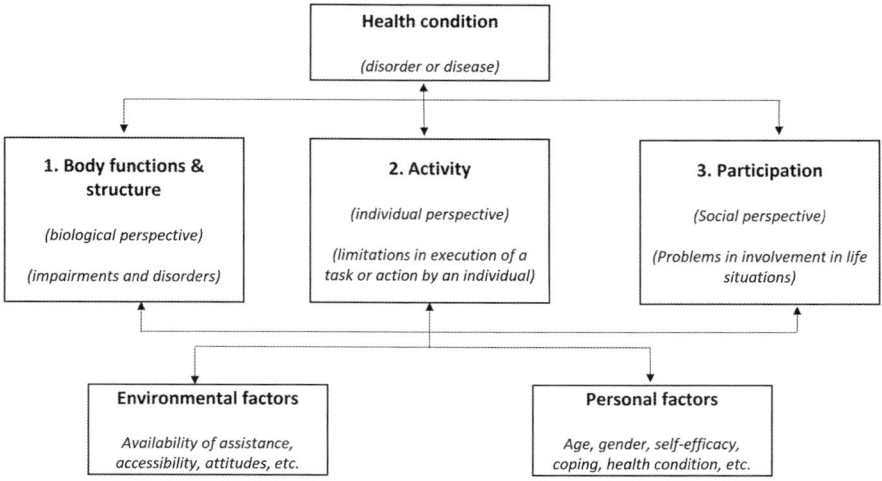

Fig. 2.2 The ICF model for disability. Source: adapted from World Health Organization (2002)

hindering their participation in sport. The ICF clearly demonstrates the complex relationship between a disorder/impairment and external and personal factors. Limitations are often caused by one or more disorders and participation problems are often due to one or more limitations. It is also possible that someone has an impairment, for example missing one hand, but does not experience any limitations in the performance of certain activities, such as jogging. For example, a person may have mobility problems, but may not experience hindered social participation because of the availability of adapted transport. Furthermore, participation in sport may contribute to the physical fitness of a pwd, and thereby enhance his/her/x participation in other domains of social life. According to Kostanjsek (2011), the ICF brought the concepts of the above-mentioned models "into a comprehensive whole of multiple dimensions of human functioning synthesizing biological, psychological, social and environmental aspects" (p. 11).

Relevance to the Handbook

The ICF framework is relevant to this handbook because contributing authors describe, among other things, the manner and the extent to which pwds participate in sport and recreational physical activity (PA) in their respective countries. Sports participation can be considered a human activity in which pwds can be hindered by their specific limitation or disorder, personal factors such as anxiety and aspects in the external (sports) environment, such as inaccessible transport, accommodations or sport clubs. To make a proper cross-national comparison, it is important to align terminology and define what is meant in this book by pwds. Therefore, in this book, for practical reasons and with the risk of excluding certain groups, we choose to refer to pwds as persons with impairments or disorders in mental and/or physical functions (see Fig. 2.3). In disability sport, these groups are more or less the target populations, as will be shown in the country-specific chapters of this handbook. Under mental functions, we distinguish between intellectual (understanding, learning, e.g., Intelligence Quotient less than 70/75) and psychosocial functions (e.g. hyperactivity/concentration, autistic spectrum disorder). People with chronic disorders or diseases are excluded from our focus. However, this is a challenging principle to adhere to, as a chronic condition can, but does not necessarily always, lead to a physical limitation. People with multiple sclerosis, for example, may end up using a wheelchair as a result of neural function deterioration, which then influences their participation in sport and PA. So, there is an inherent overlap between physical disabilities and chronic disorders/diseases.

The ICF clearly indicates that health conditions and personal factors may influence a person's ability to execute tasks or actions (activity) and to be involved in society (participation). This allows for valuable comparisons between levels of sports participation of people with specific disabilities and sociodemographic variables, such as age and gender. In the country-specific chapters (Chaps. 3–21) authors will describe sports participation levels for pwds (provided data is available) and

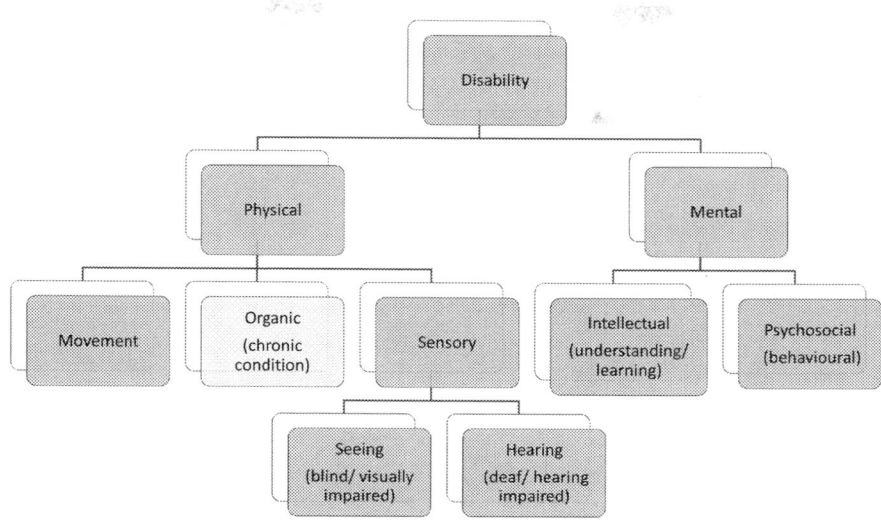

Fig. 2.3 Classification of disabilities in the handbook. Source: adapted from Von Heijden-Brinkman et al. (2013)

give details with regard to used indicators and methods. The indicator used to measure disability will determine whether respondents in surveys report having a disability as defined above. It is expected/anticipated that indicators used in surveys or in registration data to determine whether a group/person/respondent has a disability (per type and severity) will differ between and even within countries. We aim to overcome this possible limitation in Chap. 3, as in that chapter a cross-national comparative analysis is performed from a pan-European perspective.

Furthermore, the ICF recognises the influence of environmental factors on activity and participation levels of pwds and recognises that specific interventions may be necessary to remove barriers in society. Therefore, this handbook pays special attention to the policy systems of disability sport in the respective countries, to see whether existing policies and structures (can) stimulate access to sport for pwds. In this sense, we may consider the policy system for disability sport and its characteristics as the necessary input that first leads to throughputs (regulations, support, interventions, etc.), then outputs (delivery of sport activities in clubs) and finally to the intended outcome of higher sport participation levels by pwds. Besides the policy system, authors will also pay attention to the barriers (and facilitators) experienced by pwds to participate in sport in their country.

To sum up: in this book, pwds are referred to as persons with impairments or disorders in mental and/or physical functions. For readability, in this handbook we prefer to use the term 'disability' and 'persons with a disability or with disabilities' instead of disorders or impairments, but we leave room for contributing authors to align with local parlance in regard to this concept. In the ICF, the term 'handicap' or 'disability' refers to the social aspects of human functioning. Having a disability is not so much a characteristic of the individual, as it is caused by circumstances in society. Society must then ensure the optimal participation of people with impairments or disorders and activity limitations in social life. Social changes, including in sport, are necessary to make this possible. Furthermore, we prefer to use person first language as much as possible, as we recognise, bearing the UNCRPD in mind, that every person is valued primarily for who he/she/x is/are and not judged purely for having a disorder or impairment.

2.6 How Many People Have a Disability?

It is not exactly known how many people globally and in the European region live with some form of disability. For that we have to rely on estimates, mostly based on population surveys or censuses. As mentioned in the introduction to this handbook, it is estimated that about 15% of the world's population (i.e. one billion people) lives with some form of disability. This estimate, carried out by the WHO and World Bank in 2011, was based on a first ever review of large data sources (WHO & The World Bank, 2011).

Measuring Disability Is Difficult

The WHO and the World Bank (2011), as well as the UN (2019), stress that measuring disability is not an easy task, since disability is a complex multidimensional experience. "It is the combination of limitations in functioning across multiple domains (e.g. walking, seeing), each on a spectrum, from little or no disabilities to severe disabilities, either within a particular domain or across multiple domains" (United Nations, 2019; p. 21). Since domains of functioning are on a continuum, the UN argues in its 'Flagship report on disability and development' that in order to be able to determine the prevalence of disability some threshold level of functioning needs to be established to distinguish between 'persons with disabilities' and 'persons without disabilities' (United Nations, 2019). The WHO and the World Bank (2011) and the UN (2019) found that countries do not define disability uniformly, and use their own indicators and data collections on the basis of their specific policy needs. Censuses and surveys take varying approaches to measuring disability, leading to different rates of disability, between and even within countries. For instance, the WHO and the World Bank (2011) found that countries reporting a low disability prevalence rate tend to collect disability data through censuses or use measures that are focused exclusively on a narrow choice of impairments, whereas countries that report higher disability prevalence tend to collect their data through surveys and apply a measurement approach that records activity limitations and participation restrictions. Moreover, prevalence rates will be higher if institutionalised populations are included in a survey. Prevalence rates will also be different comparing data based on 'self-reported' and 'measured' aspects of disability. Additional problems arise when measuring disability in children. Proxy responders in surveys, parents or caregivers may not be able to represent the experience of the child (WHO & World Bank, 2011).

According to the UN, the growing attention of the international community and governments to addressing the rights of pwds and to mainstreaming disability into national development agendas has included an increase in national efforts to collect data on disability. The UNCRPD mandates state parties to collect such data. Furthermore, the ICF, advocated by the WHO as a conceptual model to standardised measurement of the multidimensional aspects of disability, is believed to represent a breakthrough for collecting data on disability (United Nations, 2019). The UN observes that national disability statistics are increasingly available, partly due to the growing number of countries that collect disability data in censuses. Moreover, the UN notices that a number of organisations have been working on methodologies to improve the quality of disability statistics worldwide (United Nations, 2019).

The WHO helps countries to collect data on disability and functioning through the Model Disability Survey (MDS) (WHO & The World Bank, 2017). The MDS operationalises the ICF model of disability. The purpose of the MDS is to collect data about all dimensions of disability: information about impairments, activity limitations, participation restrictions and the environmental factors that facilitate or hinder full participation. The module about functioning in MDS asks questions about respondents' overall problems in daily life. It covers problems with mobility, hand and arm use, self-care, seeing, hearing, pain, sleep and energy, breathing, affect, interpersonal relationships, handling stress, communication, cognition, household tasks, community and citizenship participation, caring for others, work and schooling. Respondents answer how much of a problem they experience on a scale from 1 to 5 (1 means no problem and 5 means extreme problems) (WHO & The World Bank, 2017). With MDS four categories of disabilities can be measured: sensory, mental, intellectual and physical disability (World Health Organization, 2022). In 2016, a brief MDS module was developed that is appropriate for integration in existing and regularly implemented household surveys, such as labour force or living standards and expenditure surveys (United Nations, 2019).

Another instrument the UN describes in the 'flagship report' (2019) is the short set of the Washington Group on Disability Statistics (WG). In 2001, the WG was set up by the United Nations Statistical Commission to facilitate the measurement of disability and cross-national comparison of data on disability. The WG developed a series of question sets on disability, based on the ICF, as well as, in collaboration with the United Nations Children's Fund (UNICEF), a child functioning module to identify children with functional difficulties. These sets can be added to censuses or surveys. The short set (WG-SS) covers six questions about functional domains or basic actions, namely: seeing, hearing, mobility, cognition, self-care and communication. Each question has four types of response: no difficulty, some difficulty, a lot of difficulty and unable to do it at all. This allows for the calculation of estimates for the level of functioning within each domain or among different combinations of domains (The Washington Group on Disability Statistics, 2022; United Nations, 2019).

Despite these initiatives the UN stresses the need to further increase the availability of data on disability and continue building capacity in countries to collect these data. Data on the prevalence of disability for the European region is presented in neither the World Report on Disability (WHO & The World Bank, 2011) nor in the UN 'flagship report' (United Nations, 2019). The WHO Regional Office for Europe (2022) estimates that in Member States of the WHO European Region, six to ten out of every 100 people live with a disability. In total, an estimated 135 million people in Europe live with a disability.

Unfortunately, the above-mentioned reports do not pay attention to data on sport participation disaggregated by disability. Both indicators (sport participation and disability) would need to be included in population surveys in order to be able to measure participation levels by different types and severity of disability. As mentioned in Chap. 1, around the globe and in Europe, in particular, uniform data that enables cross-national comparisons of sport participation by pwds is mostly lacking. In Chap. 3 we will present sport participation rates of the population in the European Union (EU) disaggregated by disability (based on the question in the Special Eurobarometer on sport regarding whether a respondent experiences barriers towards sport participation because of a disability) (European Commission, 2018).

Disability in Europe

Eurostat presents data on disability for countries in the European Region using the Global Activity Limitation Indicator (GALI, Eurostat, n.d.). GALI is used for observing limitations in activities people usually do because of one or more health problems. The limitation should have lasted for at least the past six months. Three answer categories are possible: 'severely limited', 'limited but not severely' or 'not limited at all'. GALI aligns with the activity or individual level of the ICF model (see Fig. 2.2).

GALI survey respondents are asked to report whether they perceive activity limitations due to any health problem (by self-reporting) using one single question. GALI is used yearly in the European Statistics of Income and Living Conditions (EU-SILC) survey. The statistical population consists of all persons living in private households in participating European countries, aged sixteen years and over. EU-SILC contains a small module on health, composed of three variables on health status, called the Minimum European Health Module (MEHM), one of which is the GALI, next to self-perceived health and chronic morbidity (people having a long-standing illness or health problem) (Eurostat, n.d.).

According to the SILC survey carried out throughout most European countries, on average a quarter of the population in the EU (27 countries from 2020) experiences moderate (17.5%) to severe (7.4%) limitations in the execution of daily activities as a result of health problems (hereafter long-standing limitations, Eurostat, 2022a). Figure 2.4 shows the variety in the extent to which populations in European countries involved in this handbook experience long-standing limitations.

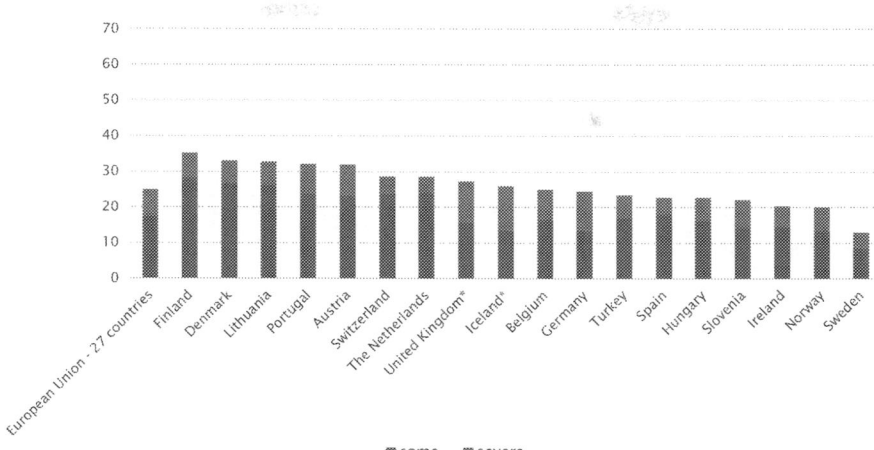

Fig. 2.4 Self-reported long-term limitations in daily activities due to health problems, population 16 years and older, population EU-27 countries and participating countries in the handbook (% share of population, 2020). *United Kingdom and Iceland data from 2018. For practical reasons Northern Ireland is regarded as a separate unit in the handbook. In the EU-data, Northern Ireland will be regarded part of the UK and therefore is missing in the figure. Source: Eurostat (2022a) (HLTH_SILC_12)

Self-perceived long-standing limitations in 2020 seem relatively lower in Sweden, Norway and Ireland, but relatively higher in Finland, Austria, Portugal, Lithuania and the Netherlands. Eurostat explains in a factsheet that in the EU men are less likely than women to report long-standing activity limitations (Eurostat, 2022b). Furthermore, people in higher age groups tend to report some or severe long-standing limitations more than those in lower age groups. And prevalence of self-reported long-standing limitations is highest in the lowest income quintile group and decreases progressively as income increases. Higher educated people are also less likely to report long-standing limitations (Eurostat, 2022b).

Another indicator for which Eurostat presents data concerns functional and activity limitations, used in the second wave of the European Health Interview Survey (EHIS). This survey was conducted between 2013 and 2015 among persons aged fifteen years and over in private households. The survey included questions for the evaluation of the health state of the population, which among others referred to the main physical and sensory functional limitations (e.g. related to vision, hearing or walking). Answer categories were 'none', 'moderate', 'severe' (including not able at all) (Eurostat, 2021, 2022b). On average, 36.7% of the EU-27 population aged fifteen and over reported (moderate or severe) physical or sensory limitations. A total of 26.8% of the respective population reported moderate functional limitations and another 9.9% reported severe functional limitations (see Fig. 2.5). It shows that at national level shares of the population that experience functional limitations differ, ranging from 19.5% in Cyprus (not in figure) to 60.2% in Finland. From the countries participating in the handbook, severe functional limitations were most

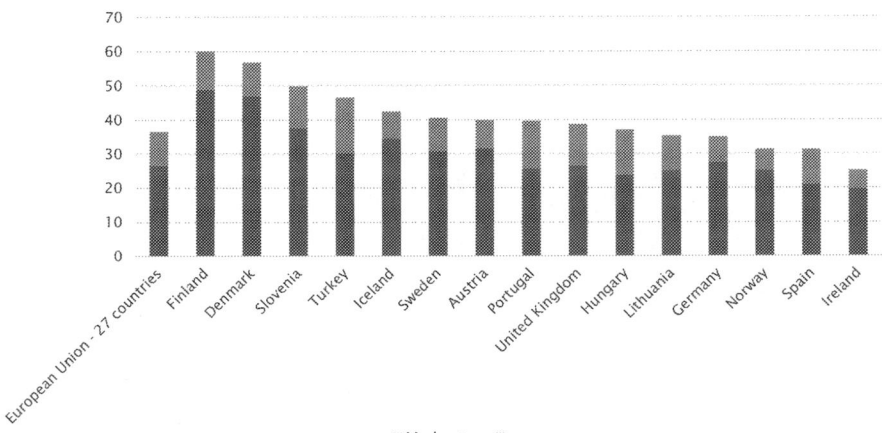

Fig. 2.5 Distribution of persons aged 15 years and older with physical and sensory functional activity limitations, population EU-27 countries and participating countries in the handbook (% share of population, 2014). Data not available for the Netherlands, Belgium and Switzerland. For practical reasons Northern Ireland is regarded as a separate unit in the handbook. In the EU-data, Northern Ireland will be regarded part of the UK and therefore is missing in the figure. Source: Eurostat (2021) (HLTH_EHIS_PL1E)

prevalent in Turkey, Portugal, Hungary, Slovenia and the United Kingdom (at least 12% of the reference population) (see Fig. 2.5). Women were more likely than men, older people more likely than younger people and persons with lower education levels more likely than persons from higher education levels to report physical and sensory limitations (not in figure, Eurostat, 2022b).

All of the above indicators presented by Eurostat are derived from self-reported data. This means that they are, to a certain extent, affected by respondents' subjective perception as well as by their social and cultural background (Eurostat, 2022b). In the country-specific chapters authors will present data on disability prevalence that is available in their respective countries. The reader will notice that these data are likely to deviate from the data presented here.

2.7 What Is Meant by Disability Sport?

Sport

Depending on the context, sport is defined differently. According to Coakley (2015) defining sport in official terms and choosing what type of activity qualifies as sport is an important process in organisations, but also in communities and societies. Being classified as an official sport gives special status to an activity. It is likely to increase participation levels or funding and community support, says Coakley. For instance, in the international sport arena of federations, sport is defined more strictly or exclusively compared to how individuals or societies at large define sport (Le Clair, 2011). Activities are included and excluded as sports at the Olympic and Paralympic Games (e.g. cricket is not an Olympic sport, ice skating is, while cricket in itself is considered a sport by individuals in a non-Olympic setting). Walking is considered a sport in Scandinavian countries and participants see themselves as sportspersons (Coakley, 2015). Sport regarded as an end in itself is defined more strictly than sport regarded as a means for social inclusion. In research, it is useful to operationalise sport with specific indicators in order to determine participation levels in certain populations. It is not the intention of this handbook to find a conclusive definition of sport or to make a statement about what kind of activities are in or out, but to define sport in such a way that it fits in with the daily practice of participation in sport by pwds. The definition used in the European Sports Charter (Council of Europe, 2021) could align well with that daily practice, as it defines sport in the context of Sport for All, in which we are interested for this handbook. Sport is defined as "all forms of physical activity which, through casual or organised participation, are aimed at maintaining or improving physical fitness and mental well-being, forming social relationships or obtaining results in competition at all levels" (Council of Europe, 2021; p. 4). The Council of Europe considers sport as a social, educational and cultural activity based on voluntary choice and expects sport to make contributions to personal wellbeing (physical and mental) and social development. Furthermore, the development of sport is inclusive and access to sport considered a human right (Council of Europe, 2021). Other official definitions put focus on certain elements of competitive or organised sport (see Coakley, 2015; Le Clair, 2011). This has implications, according to Coakley (2015). When emphasis is laid on rules and competitions or high performance, many people will be excluded from participation. Coakley argues that "when sport is defined to include a wide range of physical activities that are played for pleasure and integrated into local expressions of social life, physical activity rates will be high and overall health benefits are likely" (2015; p. 8). In this handbook too, we wish to include recreational and grassroots activities with the inclusion of pwds in sport in mind. Following Coakley (2015; p. 8), sports can be seen as social constructions: "parts of the social world that are created by people as they interact with one another under particular social, political and economic conditions". This means that, for instance, in the various countries that are part of this handbook different decisions could have been made by what is understood as sport for pwds, leading to their inclusion or exclusion.

With regard to the term "all forms of physical activity" as mentioned in the definition of the Council of Europe, the editors do not include physical activities such as gardening or functional cycling and walking to and from public transport, work and school or household chores. The definition of Scheerder (2003) would better fit our understanding of sport. Scheerder's definition conforms to a democratic vision of sport participation: "active participation in physical exercise activities in a sportive context, practiced during leisure time, and without a merely utilitarian character" (Scheerder, 2003; p. 13). Following the previous discussion the editors do not intend to define sport too strictly in advance, as this would leave the contributing authors little room describing country-specific interpretations.

'Disability Sport' or 'Sport for Persons with a Disability'?

In this handbook, an extra dimension is added to the concept of sport, because we deal with sport intended for, organised or practiced by pwds. Sport and PA may well have a different meaning and content for pwds than for persons without a disability in the respective countries. This might bring changes to the scope and definition of the general concept of sport. It is anticipated that the concept of 'disability sport' will be defined more precisely through the cross-national comparison based on the country-specific chapters in this handbook. Different terms can be used to describe what we call disability sport, for example, see 'disabled sport', 'sport for the disabled', 'adapted sport', 'disability sport', sport practiced by pwds', and so on. The term 'disability sport' or 'disabled sport' may imply that we mean sport that has been designed for or is specially practiced by (a selected group of) pwds (e.g. goalball for persons with visual impairment), when in reality pwd also practice 'traditional' sports that have been modified or adapted to include pwds (e.g. wheelchair tennis, tandem cycling) as well as sports that require little or no modifications to allow pwds to participate (see DePauw & Gavron, 2005). For this handbook we prefer to use the terms 'disability sport' and 'sport for/by pwds' interchangeably. 'Disabled sport' is not preferred, because sport itself cannot be disabled and 'sport for the disabled' does not utilise person first language (see DePauw & Gavron, 2005). In this handbook we explain 'disability sport' in two ways: by referring to the sport and PA activity itself and to the policy and organisational landscape or system that delivers, supports or promotes participation in sport by pwd. Both dimensions are the subject of analysis in this handbook.

Sport Activities As argued above, the decisions regarding what is called sport and in this case disability sport might differ according to the social context. Therefore, as with the activities, we define 'disability sport' broadly. When it comes to inclusion in sport for pwds, Kiuppis (2018), as well as Misener and Darcy (2014), refer to the inclusion spectrum. This model was first introduced by Black in the late 1990s and modified several times since then to provide practitioners with different methods of supporting inclusion in sport (see Black, 2011, 2020; Black & Williamsen, 2011; Stevenson, 2009). The idea is that participation in sport can occur across a continuum of possibilities and all forms should be valued equally. Inclusion is about having the possibility to choose what activity, where, how and with whom a pwd wants to be involved and about taking responsibility for providing that range of choices (see Kiuppis, 2018; Misener & Darcy, 2014). Following the ideas of the inclusion spectrum, all sorts of sport and recreational physical activities can be part of our concept. The inclusion spectrum seems to combine three ways of providing for inclusion: by choosing how (what kind of activities), with whom (social setting) and where and when (organisational setting) sport is provided.

For example, it may concern sport activities that are open for everyone to participate without adaptions or modifications (e.g. a community run where all individuals participate according to their own ability at the same time on the same course, also called a fully integrated or inclusive activity) (see Misener & Darcy, 2014); sport activities that are slightly or more strongly adapted or modified to allow for the participation of pwds (e.g. adaptations in rules, equipment, group size, composition of group (see wheelchair basketball or sitting volleyball)); and sport activities that are designed especially for (a selected group of) pwds (e.g. goalball, murder ball, race running (also called separate or alternate activities)).

The social setting may vary as well: individuals with a specific type of disability play/train together (e.g. a group of athletes with intellectual impairment, called ability groups); persons with various disabilities play/train together; persons with a disability play/train together with individuals without a disability (full inclusion).

Furthermore participation in sport may vary by organisational setting: pwds have their own (separate/segregated) sport clubs or environments (e.g. a deaf sport club); pwds participate in a separate team/group in a 'traditional' sport club and access it in their own way (e.g. wheelchair basketball division at a mainstream basketball club, also called parallel integration, see Christiaens & Brittain, 2021); pwd participate in the same activity, group or team together with persons without a disability in a traditional non-disabled sport club or environment (also called full inclusion, see Christiaens & Brittain, 2021, see also Black, 2020; Kiuppis, 2018: Misener & Darcy, 2014). The term reverse integration is used to refer to settings and activities where athletes without disabilities are included in disability sport together with their peers with a disability. For instance, in wheelchair basketball athletes without disabilities can play in competitions (see Kiuppis, 2018). Relevant for our handbook is that all forms may appear to be relevant in the country-specific contexts and options are not excluded prior to that analysis.

2.8 How Inclusive Is Sport for Persons with a Disability?

Perhaps one of the key issues in trying to connect disability, sport and inclusion is what is actually meant by the term and concept of 'inclusion'. What should inclusion look like in practice? One of the key problems with the inclusion agenda is that policymakers rarely, if ever, define what they mean by 'inclusion'. This leaves the way open for those on the ground who are responsible for interpreting and operationalising policy recommendations with an enormous amount of wiggle room in interpreting inclusion a way that suits their needs (i.e. minimal disruption and effort), rather than in a way that suits those it is designed to 'include' (i.e. pwds).

What Do We Mean by Inclusion?

At its most basic, inclusion is the state of being included or having the opportunity to take part. However, in reality, it is far more complicated than that, as inclusion entails diverse ideas and values about equality, equity, fairness and distributive justice and how to best achieve these things (Brittain, 2016b). An example of equality in a sporting context might be as simple as the notion that everyone in a team gets the same shirt to wear (of exactly the same size). In this way, no one can claim to have been treated differently. Yet, in reality, the shirt may actually only fit a small number of the team members. What is lacking from this view of equality is a sense of equity and fairness. If all team members are given the same shirt, but in a size that suits each individual member of the team then it can be claimed that everyone has been included in an equal and equitable manner. However, fairness is not just about everyone getting the same thing. In the end, it is about all people getting what they need in order to try and achieve their own life-goals, as well as those common to the society they live in. True inclusion, therefore, is about valuing all individuals, giving equal access and opportunity to all, and removing discrimination and other barriers to involvement. The larger goal is to ensure that all people feel a sense of belonging, as well as feeling respected and valued for who they are (Miller & Katz, 2002).

Differing Interpretations of Inclusion

By failing to make it clear what is actually meant by 'inclusion', the International Paralympic Committee (IPC) and international and national policy makers have unfortunately cleared the path for those who are charged with implementing inclusion policy within society to interpret inclusion in ways that best fit their own needs rather than the needs of pwds (Christiaens, 2018). In terms of sport and disability, one of the key issues is that inclusion is often used as a generic term encompassing all under-represented groups (e.g. age, gender, sexuality as well as disability). In this state of affairs, there is also an overarching assumption that stakeholders know exactly what is meant by inclusion, and as we have argued, there is a great deal of cloudiness and malleability in operationalised understandings.

Yet, these understandings undergird important questions about sport and disability, such as who should be considered to be included (e.g. only those with mild disabilities who can achieve standards set by those in society without disabilities or all pwds, including those with severe disabilities), what inclusion actually looks like in practice and foundational debates about whether inclusion is more about access to opportunity rather than placement within a setting primarily for those without disabilities. As a result, answers to questions such as these remain elusive. According to Christiaens (2018), it is the answer to these questions that guide the operationalisation of inclusion in the field of sport and disability.

2.9 How Do We Define the System of Disability Sport?

As for the system of disability sport or sport for/by pwds, all previously mentioned forms will be provided for by agents in the policy and organisational landscape. In that regard too, the handbook takes a broad approach to disability sport. It captures, in our understanding, all forms of sport organised or provided by the 'traditional' sport agents (sport federations and sport clubs); commercial, public-private or social (sport) clubs (e.g. fitness or swimming locations, including sport for all and/or therapeutic settings); and the informal or non-organised sport setting where individuals participate in sport by themselves or in private groups with varying composition. When we refer to 'traditional' sport agents, in the first instance federations and clubs that have been established for athletes without disabilities are what we are referring to. As mentioned earlier, pwds participate within this traditional setting. The policy of integrating the responsibility for sport provision for pwds into these sports organisations is called 'mainstreaming' (Kitchin et al., 2019; Kitchin & Howe, 2014). According to the WHO, mainstreaming in general refers to the process by which governments and other stakeholders ensure that pwds participate equally with others in any activity and service intended for the general public. For that to happen, barriers to participation need to be identified and removed, possibly requiring changes to laws, policies, institutions and environments. But this does not mean the focus is solely on 'mainstream' sport settings.

Disability sport also covers 'para sports' and related organisations. Para sports include all sports that can be practiced in the Paralympic context of training and competing at national and international levels. But outside the Paralympic sphere there are numerous (disability) sports that are contested competitively on a national and international stage and enjoyed mainly on a participatory or merely recreational level in community centres, backyards or sport clubs (Hums & Pate, 2018). So, disability sport as a system comprises the organisational infrastructure around the Paralympic Movement,[1] as well as that around mainstream sports and governing bodies outside this system. It includes the elite level and the grassroots level. The Paralympic Movement and other elite sport systems, such as the Deaflympics, INAS (International Federation for Athletes with an Intellectual Impairment), CPISRA (Cerebral Palsy International Sports and Recreation Association), IWAS (International Wheelchair and Amputee Sports Association) and IBSA (International Blind Sports Association) may influence the promotion of sport participation of pwds at the grassroots level. Elite sport benefits from a strong talent pool at the recreational level, and there may be a strong connection between the bottom and top end of the so-called sport pyramid. Recreational sport for pwd may have originated from competitions for wounded/injured soldiers, which contributed to the inclusion

---

[1] The Paralympic movement is considered, by Brittain and Beacom (2018), as the infrastructure around the International Paralympic committee with its attendant governance and development organisations, National Paralympic Committees, emerging Para sport federations and organising committees for regional and international competitions including the Paralympic Games.

of pwds in sport over time (Brittain & Beacom, 2018). It may also be possible that a country has a Paralympic Movement, whilst disability sport at a grassroots level is not yet fully developed. This book will present sport for pwds at different participation levels, taking the grassroots level as a starting point, and including the elite level when appropriate and/or of relevance. Furthermore, it is anticipated that the scope of the disability sport system is broader than only sports-related organisations. Sports can be delivered in other settings, as mentioned earlier, such as schools, health care, communities, fitness centres and so on. Contributing authors are encouraged to analyse the disability sport system in their respective countries taking into account all of these different options.

In Fig. 2.6 a preliminary version of a conceptual model for 'disability sport' is presented. It has been discussed and shared with the contributing authors beforehand (Van Lindert et al., 2020). The figure is based on the Long-Term Athletes Development model (LTAD) adjusted by the Canadian Sport for Life for training athletes with a physical disability. The model is used by various Canadian sport organisations for persons with various types of disability, for example, Special Olympics Canada or Canadian Blind Sports (Higgs & Legg, n.d.; Higgs et al., 2019; Canadian Sports Centre, n.d.; see also Misener & Darcy, 2014). It makes use of different developmental stages an individual (mostly by age) goes through to become a lifelong sports participant/athlete. Through the LTAD, pwds can train to achieve

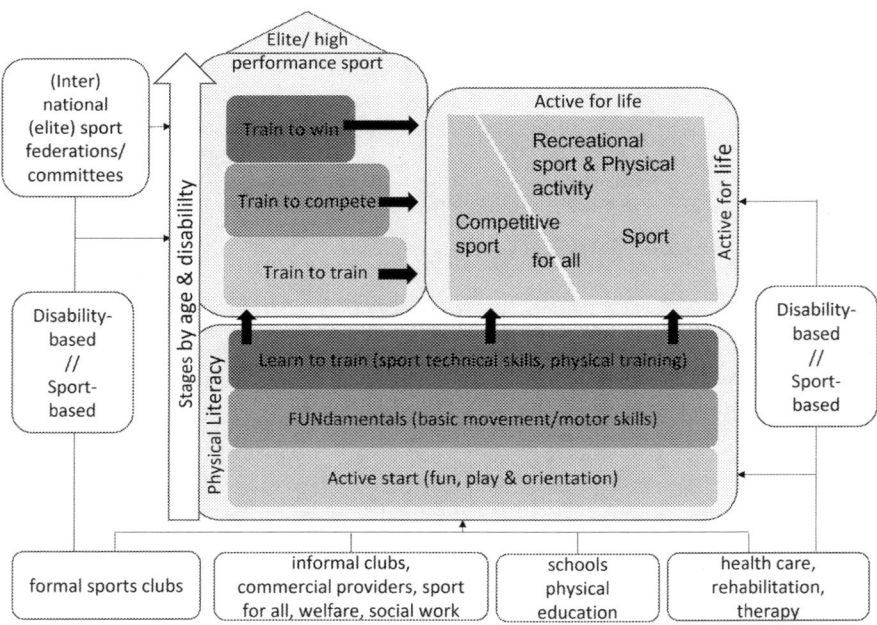

Fig. 2.6 Preliminary model for disability sport in the handbook. Source: adapted from LTAD model for athletes with a disability (Higgs & Legg, n.d.; Higgs et al., 2019) and the Church model of sports (Scheerder et al., 2011)

excellence in high performance or can choose to pursue healthy lifelong physical activity. There are seven basic steps that apply to all athletes, with and without disabilities: (1) active start, (2) FUNdamentals, (3) learn to train, (4) train to train, (5) train to compete, (6) train to win and (7) active for life. The LTAD aligns with the concept of 'physical literacy', where a person learns basic motor skills and skills needed to become active in sport through fun, play and training (the first three stages of LTAD, see also Whitehead, 2010). Children learn these skills at school or in sports clubs at a recreational level. When a person acquires a disability later on in life it may happen that he/she/x will have to become physically literate again because he/she/x has/have to adjust to the new situation. This is a period of great change for the person. Pwds may need to make a new start (stage 1) and should learn or re-learn basic movement and sport skills. The pwd may not be aware of the sporting opportunities that are (still) left for them. The stage of 'awareness' has therefore been added to the LTAD. The stages of 'first contact/recruitment' has been added too and linked to the second stage of LTAD (FUNdamentals). It is important to create a welcoming atmosphere and positive first experiences for athletes with a disability in order to make the first approach to sport easier (Canadian Sports Centres, n.d.; Higgs et al., 2019).

The model in Fig. 2.6 is also inspired by the so-called church model proposed by Scheerder et al. (2011), that presents a whole system of different sport models next to the traditional pyramid model. The pyramid model follows the 'competitive' logic from competitive sport at the bottom of the pyramid, to high level competitive sport and at the top end of the pyramid to elite sport, or in the context of organisations from sports clubs to regional, national and at the top end European sport federations. However, in the church model and in Fig. 2.6 other sport forms (recreational sport, Sport for All, grassroots level sport, etc.) are also taken into account. Relevant to our book is that within the country-specific chapters, authors were asked to describe the structure of their sport system for disability sport and to look beyond the pyramid system of sport. The model can help identify what kind of agents are responsible or involved in organising/providing sport opportunities for pwds.

To conclude, for the purpose of this handbook, we have defined disability sport or sport for/by pwds broadly as the system that delivers, supports and promotes participation in sport and PA in a sporting context by pwds at all levels, both mainstream and adapted, sport-based and disability-based, at a grassroots and recreational level (fun, orientation, fun and learn to train), competitive level (training for competitions) and elite sports level (training to win), as well as the infrastructure that supports these practices. The main focus of the handbook however will be on the systems that support or promote sport participation of pwds at a grassroots or Sport for All level.

References

Abrams, T., & Adkins, B. (2020). Tragic affirmation: Disability beyond optimism and pessimism. *Journal of Medical Humanities, 43*, 117–128. https://doi.org/10.1007/s10912-020-09612-y

Banda-Chalwe, M., Nitz, J. C., & de Jonge, D. (2014). Impact of inaccessible spaces on community participation of people with mobility limitations in Zambia. *African Journal of Disability, 3*(1), 33–49.

Berghs, M., Atkin, K., Hatton, C., & Thomas, C. (2019). Do disabled people need a stronger social model: A social model of human rights? *Disability & Society, 34*(7–8), 1034–1039.

Birkenbach, J. (1990). *Physical disability and social policy*. University of Toronto Press.

Black, K. (2011). Coaching disabled children. In I. Stafford (Ed.), *Coaching children in sport*. Routledge.

Black, K. (2020). *The inclusion spectrum incorporating STEP*. The Inclusion Club.

Black, K., & Williamsen, D. (2011). Designing inclusive physical activities and games. In A. Cereijo Roibás, W. Stamatakis, & K. Black (Eds.), *Design for sport* (1st ed., pp. 195–224). Routledge. https://doi.org/10.4324/9781315258140

Brar, V. (2016). Using Bourdieu's theory of practice to understand academic under achievement among inner-city students in British Columbia: A conceptual study. Unpublished PhD thesis, Simon Fraser University.

Brisenden, S. (1986). Independent living and the medical model of disability. *Disability, Handicap & Society, 1*(2), 173–178.

Brittain, I. (2012). The Paralympic Games as a force for peaceful coexistence. *Sport in Society, 15*(6), 855–868.

Brittain, I. (2014). *From Stoke Mandeville to Sochi: A history of the summer and winter Paralympic Games*. Common Ground Publishing.

Brittain, I. (2016). *The Paralympic Games explained* (2nd ed.). Routledge.

Brittain, I. (2016b). Olympism in action: Inclusion of persons with disabilities through sport activities. In Proceedings of the international Olympic Academy 56th session for young participants, International Olympic Academy, Greece (pp. 149–160).

Brittain, I., & Beacom, A. (2016). Leveraging the London 2012 Paralympic Games: What legacy for people with disabilities? *Journal of Sport and Social Issues, 40*(6), 499–521.

Brittain, I., & Beacom, A. (Eds.). (2018). *The Palgrave handbook of paralympic studies*. Palgrave Macmillan. https://link.springer.com/book/10.1057/978-1-137-47901-3

Brittain, I., Biscaia, R., & Gerard, S. (2020). Ableism as a regulator of social practice and people with disabilities' self-determination to participate in sport and physical activity. *Leisure Studies, 39*(2), 209–224.

Cambridge dictionary online. (2021). Able-bodied. Retrieved from: https://dictionary.cambridge.org/dictionary/english/able-bodied

Campbell, F. (2008). Exploring internalized ableism using critical race theory. *Disability & Society, 23*(2), 151–162.

Campbell, F. (2009). *Contours of ableism: The production of disability and abledness*. Palgrave Macmillan.

Canadian Sports Centres. (n.d.). No accidental champions poster. Retrieved May 2, 2022, from http://canadianblindsports.ca/wp-content/uploads/2013/01/No-Accidental-Champions-Poster.pdf

Christiaens, M. (2018). Towards mainstreaming: A principle – practice gap in the UK sports sector. Unpublished PhD Thesis. Available from: https://curve.coventry.ac.uk/open/items/90fff1fa-cca3-48cf-81e3-f11551f63978/1/

Christiaens, M., & Brittain, I. (2021). The complexities of implementing inclusion policies for disabled people in UK non-disabled voluntary community sports clubs. *European Sport Management Quarterly*, 1–21. https://doi.org/10.1080/16184742.2021.1955942

Coakley, J. (2015). *Sports in society: Issues and controversies* (11th ed.). McGraw-Hill Education.

Council of Europe. (2021). Revised European sports charter. In *Council of Europe*. Council of Europe. https://wcd.coe.int/ViewDoc.jsp?Ref=Rec(92)13&Sector=secCM&Language=lan English&Ver=rev&BackColorInternet=9999CC&BackColorIntranet=FFBB55&Back ColorLogged=FFAC75

Degener, T. (2017). A new human rights model of disability. In V. Della Fina, R. Cera, & G. Palmisano (Eds.), *The United Nations convention on the rights of persons with disabilities* (pp. 41–59). Springer.

DePauw, K. P., & Gavron, S. J. (2005). *Disability sport* (2nd ed.). Human Kinetics. https://books.google.ch/books/about/Disability_Sport.html?id=BPsqAoFtG-sC&redir_esc=y

Dirth, T. P., & Branscombe, N. R. (2017). Disability models affect disability policy support through awareness of structural discrimination. *Journal of Social Issues, 73*(2), 413–442.

Equality Training. (n.d.). The art of respectful language. Retrieved from: http://www.equalitytraining.co.uk/images/news/language_of_respect.pdf

European Commission. (2018). *Eurobarometer: Sport and physical activity. Special Eurobarometer 472*. European Commission.

Eurostat. (2021). Physical and sensory functional limitations by sex, age and educational attainment level. HLTH_EHIS_PL1E. https://ec.europa.eu/eurostat/databrowser/view/hlth_ehis_pl1e/default/table?lang=en

Eurostat. (2022a). Self-perceived long-standing limitations in usual activities due to health problem by sex, age and income quintile. HLTH_SILC_12. https://ec.europa.eu/eurostat/databrowser/view/hlth_silc_12/default/table?lang=en

Eurostat. (2022b). Functional and activity limitations statistics. Eurostat statistics explained. https://ec.europa.eu/eurostat/statistics-explained/index.php?title=Functional_and_activity_limitations_statistics

Eurostat. (n.d.). Health variables of EU-SILC. https://ec.europa.eu/eurostat/cache/metadata/en/hlth_silc_01_esms.htm

French, S. (1993). Disability, impairment, or somewhere in between. In J. Swain, V. Finkelstein, S. French, & M. Oliver (Eds.), *Disabling barriers – enabling environments* (pp. 17–25). Open University.

French, S., & Swain, J. (2004). Whose tragedy? Towards a personal non-tragedy view of disability. In S. French & J. Swain (Eds.), *Disabling barriers - enabling environments* (pp. 34–40). Sage.

Galtung, J. (1990). Cultural violence. *The Journal of Peace Research, 27*(3), 290–302.

Goodley, D. (2014). *Dis/ability studies: Theorising disablism and ableism*. Routledge.

Guttmann, L. (1952). On the way to an international sports movement for the paralysed. *The Cord, 5*(3), 7–23.

Guttmann, L. (1976). *Textbook of sport for the disabled*. HM and M Publishers.

Higgs, C., & Legg, D. (n.d.). *Special report. Canadian sport for life for athletes with a disability*. Canadian Sport for Life. https://www.specialolympicsns.ca/wp-content/uploads/2016/02/Special-Report.pdf?c8e1f5

Higgs, C., Way, R., Harber, V., Jurbala, P., & Balyi, I. (2019). *Long-term development in sport and physical activity 3.0*. Canadian Sport for Life. https://doi.org/10.4324/9781003195153-8

Hums, M. A., & Pate, J. R. (2018). The International Paralympic Committee as a governing body. In I. Brittain & A. Beacom (Eds.), *The Palgrave handbook of paralympic studies* (pp. 173–196). Palgrave Macmillan.

Imrie, R. (1997). Rethinking the relationships between disability, rehabilitation, and society. *Disability and Rehabilitation, 19*(7), 263–271.

Kassah, A. K., Kassah, B. L. L., & Agbota, T. K. (2012). Abuse of disabled children in Ghana. *Disability & Society, 27*(5), 689–701.

Kitchin, P., & Howe, P. (2014). The mainstreaming of disability cricket in England and Wales: Integration 'one game' at a time. *Sport Management Review, 17*(February), 65–77. https://doi.org/10.1016/J.SMR.2013.05.003

Kitchin, P., Peile, C., & Lowther, J. (2019). Mobilizing capacity to achieve the mainstreaming of disability sport. *Managing Sport and Leisure, 24*(6), 424–444. https://doi.org/10.1080/23750472.2019.1684839

Kiuppis, F. (2018). Inclusion in sport: Disability and participation. In *Sport in society* (Vol. 21, Issue 1, pp. 4–21). Routledge. https://doi.org/10.1080/17430437.2016.1225882.

Kostanjsek, N. (2011). Use of the International Classification of Functioning, Disability and Health (ICF) as a conceptual framework and common language for disability statistics and health information systems. *BMC Public Health, 11*(SUPPL. 4), S3. https://doi.org/10.1186/1471-2458-11-S4-S3

Le Clair, J. M. (2011). Global organizational change in sport and the shifting meaning of disability. *Sport in Society, 14*(9), 1072–1093. https://doi.org/10.1080/17430437.2011.614765

Livneh, H. (1982). On the origins of negative attitudes toward people with disabilities. *Rehabilitation Literature, 43*, 338–347.

Llewellyn, A., & Hogan, K. (2000). The use and abuse of models of disability. *Disability & Society, 15*(1), 157–165.

Loja, E., Costa, M. E., Hughes, B., & Menezes, I. (2013). Disability, embodiment and ableism: Stories of resistance. *Disability & Society, 28*(2), 190–203.

McColl, A. (2019). Should I say 'disabled person' or 'person with a disability'? Retrieved from: https://theconversation.com/should-i-say-disabled-person-or-person-with-a-disability-113618

Miller, F. A., & Katz, J. H. (2002). *Inclusion breakthrough: Unleashing the real power of diversity*. Berrett-Koehler Publishers.

Misener, L., & Darcy, S. (2014). Managing disability sport: From athletes with disabilities to inclusive organisational perspectives. *Sport Management Review, 17*(1), 1–7. https://doi.org/10.1016/j.smr.2013.12.003

Morris, J. (1991). *Pride against prejudice: Transforming attitudes to disability*. The Women's Press Ltd.

Nourry, O. (2018). How Ableism leads to inaccessibility. Retrieved from https://www.24a11y.com/2018/how-ableism-leads-to-inaccessibility/

OHRC (Ontario Human Rights Commission). (n.d.). Ableism, negative attitudes, stereotypes and stigma. Retrieved from http://www.ohrc.on.ca/en/policy-preventing-discrimination-based-mental-health-disabilities-andaddictions/5-ableism-negative-attitudes-stereotypes-and-stigma

Oliver, M., & Barnes, C. (2012). *The new politics of disablement*. Palgrave Macmillan.

Patillo, M. (2008). Race, class, and neighborhoods. In A. Lareau & D. Conley (Eds.), *Social class: How does it work?* (pp. 264–292). Russell Sage.

Renke, S. (2020, July 14). We might argue over how to talk about disability but it's a debate worth having. Retrieved from: https://metro.co.uk/2020/07/14/disability-language-debate-12987662/

Reynolds, J. M. (2017). "I'd rather be dead than disabled"—The ableist conflation and the meanings of disability. *Review of Communication, 17*(3), 149–163.

Scheerder, J. (2003). Level playing fields? Social stratification in leisure-time sports participation from a social change perspective. Unpublished doctoral thesis, KU Leuven.

Scheerder, J., Vandermeerschen, H., Van Tuyckom, C., Hoekman, R., Breedveld, K. & Vos, S. (2011). Understanding the game: sport participation in Europe. Facts, reflections and recommendations. In *Sport policy and management studies* (Vol. 10). University of Leuven/Research Unit of Social Kinesiology & Sport Management.

Scullion, P. A. (2010). Models of disability: Their influence in nursing and potential role in challenging discrimination. *Journal of Advanced Nursing, 66*(3), 697–707.

Shakespeare, T., & Watson, N. (2002). The social model of disability: An outdated ideology? *Research in Social Science and Disability, 2*, 9–28.

Shapiro, D., Pitts, B., Hums, M., & Calloway, J. (2012). Infusing disability sport into the sport management curriculum. *Sport Management International Journal, 8*(1), 101–118.

Smart, J. F. (2009). The power of models of disability. *Journal of Rehabilitation, 75*(2), 3–11.

Smith, B. (2013). Sporting spinal cord injuries, social relations, and rehabilitation narratives: An ethnographic creative non-fiction of becoming disabled through sport. *Sociology of Sport Journal, 30*(2), 132–152.

Smith, B., & Bundon, A. (2018). Disability models: Explaining and understanding disability sport in different ways. In I. Brittain & A. Beacom (Eds.), *The Palgrave handbook of paralympic studies* (pp. 15–34). Palgrave Macmillan.

Stevenson, P. (2009). The pedagogy of inclusive youth sport: Working towards real solutions. In H. Fitzgerald (Ed.), *Disability and youth sport*. Routledge.

The Washington Group on Disability Statistics. (2022). WG short set on functioning (WG-SS). https://www.washingtongroup-disability.com/question-sets/wg-short-set-on-functioning-wg-ss/

Thomas, C. (2007). *Sociologies of disability and illness: Contested ideas in disability studies and medical sociology*. Palgrave Macmillan.

United Nations. (2006). United Nations Convention on the rights of persons with disabilities. Available from: https://www.un.org/development/desa/disabilities/convention-on-the-rights-of-persons-with-disabilities.html

United Nations. (2019). *Disability and development report. Realizing the sustainable development goals by, for and with persons with disabilities*. United Nations.

UPIAS (Union of Physically Impaired Against Segregation). (1976). *Fundamental principles of disability*. UPIAS.

Van Lindert, C., Scheerder, J., & Brittain, I. (2020). *Instructions to write a country-specific chapter (internal document)*. Mulier Institute.

Von Heijden-Brinkman, A., Van den Dool, R., Van Lindert, C., & Breedveld, K. (2013). (On) beperkt sportief 2013: Monitor sport- en beweegdeelname van mensen met een handicap. https://www.mulierinstituut.nl/publicaties/12543/onbeperkt-sportief-2013/

Watermeyer, B., McKenzie, J., & Swartz, L. (Eds.). (2019). *The Palgrave handbook of disability and citizenship in the global south*. Springer.

Whitehead, M. (2010). *Physical literacy throughout the life course*. Routledge. https://doi.org/10.4324/9780203881903

Wilson, L., & Martin, N. (2018). Models of disability affect language: Implications for disability, equality and inclusivity practice. *The Journal of Inclusive Practice in Further and Higher Education, 10*(1), 4–19.

Wolbring, G. (2012). Expanding ableism: Taking down the Ghettoization of impact of disability studies scholars. *Societies, 2*(3), 75–83.

World Health Organization. (2002). *Towards a common language for functioning, disability and health*. ICF. https://www.who.int/publications/m/item/icf-beginner-s-guide-towards-a-common-language-for-functioning-disability-and-health

World Health Organization. (2010). Definition and typology of violence. http://www.who.int/violenceprevention/approach/definition/en/index.html

World Health Organization. (2022). How is disability conceptualized in the MDS? https://www.who.int/multi-media/details/how-is-disability-conceptualized-in-the-mds

World Health Organization & The World Bank. (2011). *World report on disability*. World Health Organization. https://www.who.int/teams/noncommunicable-diseases/sensory-functions-disability-and-rehabilitation/world-report-on-disability

World Health Organization & The World Bank. (2017). *Model disability survey (MDS) survey manual*. World Health Organization. https://www.who.int/publications/i/item/9789241512862

World Health Organization Regional Office for Europe. (2022). Facts on disability.. https://www.who.int/europe/news-room/fact-sheets/item/disability.

Chapter 3
Participation in Sport and Physical Activity Amongst People with a Disability: A Pan-European Comparative Approach

Jeroen Scheerder, Kobe Helsen, Caroline van Lindert, and Ian Brittain

3.1 Introduction

Previous sports participation studies have indicated that so-called harmonised data surveys are of indispensables value to make both cross-national and cross-temporal comparisons (see f.i. Scheerder & Helsen, 2020; Scheerder et al., 2011, 2020; Van Tuyckom et al., 2010). However, accurate data that allow for comparisons between countries on the one hand and/or across different time intervals on the other mostly are disparate, scarce or even not existing at a European level, let alone at an international level. As a consequence, it is hard to make precise comparisons between different countries concerning, amongst other things, the level and organisational context of sports participation, or the popularity of specific sports practices. Seemingly, as can be noted from the following country-specific chapters, most countries rely on national sports participation data collected by means of different methods and standards (see also Chap. 23 in which the various methods used for measuring participation in disability sport are summarised). One of the key

---

J. Scheerder (✉)
Department of Movement Sciences, KU Leuven, Leuven, Belgium

Policy Research Centre on Sports on behalf of the Flemish Government, Leuven, Belgium
e-mail: jeroen.scheerder@kuleuven.be

K. Helsen
Department of Movement Sciences, KU Leuven, Leuven, Belgium

C. van Lindert
Mulier Institute, Utrecht, The Netherlands
e-mail: c.vanlindert@mulierinstituut.nl

I. Brittain
Centre for Business in Society, Coventry University, Coventry, UK
e-mail: aa8550@coventry.ac.uk

advantages of using national sports participation data lies in the fact that country-specific features and cultures can be taken into account while gathering a wealth of data. Nevertheless, in terms of validity and reliability, methodological issues arise as this kind of data can hardly be used for comparisons between different countries due to dissimilarities in definitions, categorisations, operationalisations and so on (Scheerder et al., 2011).

Parallel to the country-specific approach used in the following country-specific chapters, in this chapter a cross-national method as described by Scheerder et al. (2011) will be applied to gain insight into patterns of both active participation in physical activity and (club-organised) sport amongst people with a disability. In contradiction to national surveys based on country-specific data, for the cross-national approach harmonised data collection based on a homogenised questionnaire is required. Indeed, if available, cross-national surveys offer a good alternative to make pan-European comparisons. Although in this case, usually, less comprehensive and less detailed data are at one's disposal, the advantage of the usage of cross-national surveys lies in the similarity in terms of methods and standards used in the research. Therefore, the cross-national, harmonised approach is more likely to meet criteria in terms of both validity and comparability (Scheerder et al., 2020). Definitely, the harmonisation of definitions and formulations in questionnaires optimises an accurate comparison between countries.

Previous studies presenting pan-European sports participation findings based on harmonised and standardised surveys can be found, amongst others, in Claeys (1982a, 1982b), Helsen and Scheerder (2020a, 2020b, 2021), Nagel et al. (2020), Scheerder and Helsen (2020), Scheerder et al. (2020) and UK Sport (1999). It should also be noted, however, that these kinds of studies either include only a limited number of countries and/or do not necessarily report on sports participation amongst people with a disability. Therefore, in order to overcome these gaps, it is appropriate to make use of data stemming from harmonised pan-European or international surveys in which sport-related questions are included. Examples of such general pan-European or international surveys are the *Eurobarometer Survey* (EB, see European Commission, 2004, 2010, 2014, 2018), the *European Health Interview Survey* (EHIS, see Eurostat, 2021b, 2021c), the *European Social Survey* (ESS, see ESS, 2021), the *European Union Statistics on Income and Living Conditions* (EU-SILC, see Eurostat, 2021d, 2021g), the *European Values Study* (EVS, see GESIS/Leibniz Institute for the Social Sciences, 2021a), the *Harmonised European Time Use Surveys* (HETUS, see Eurostat, 2021e, 2021j), the *Household Budget Survey* (HBS, see Eurostat, 2021a, 2021f), the *International Social Survey Programme* (ISSP, see GESIS/Leibniz Institute for the Social Sciences, 2021b, 2021c), the *International Trade in Sporting Goods* (SPRT_TRD, see Eurostat, 2021h) and so on. Concerning the EHIS and the EU-SILC surveys we also refer to Chap. 2 since these studies have also been referred to regarding the prevalence of disability in European countries.

3.2 Material and Methods

In this chapter, most of the analyses rely on fully harmonised data, collected in the framework of the previously mentioned Eurobarometer survey (EB). The reason why we opt for the EB is multi-fold. First, the EB allows for analysing participation in sport and/or physical activity amongst people with a disability. This is not necessarily the case for all of the pan-European or international surveys listed above. Second, the EB consists of data that are collected in all of the (former) EU member states, including the UK. Third, different time intervals are available in the EB. More precisely, comparisons can be made between three separate measurements (see below). This will enable us to compare data throughout a time-span of almost ten years. Fourth, the EB spans a wide age range, including EU citizens aged fifteen years and older. Fifth, the available data not only address active participation in sport (and/or physical activity) in general, but also provide more specific information on sports participation amongst members of a sports club and/or a fitness centre. All of these points can be considered as an added value that other studies do not provide.

Along with the Eurobarometer instrument, two of the other pan-European surveys that we referred to in the introduction contain data regarding the sporting and physical activity behaviour amongst people with a disability. More specifically, it concerns the *European Health Interview Survey* (EHIS) and the *European Social Survey* (ESS). However, the EHIS and ESS databases show some limitations that are not present in the EB data. For instance, with regard to the EHIS surveys, the available data refer to two different periods of time, namely 2006–2009 on the one hand and 2013–2015 on the other. Thus, data are not related to one specific year of measurement as several years for each measurement are considered. In addition, a comparison throughout time can only be made between these two periods of measurement, which makes it difficult to draw firm conclusions, at least from a time-trend perspective. Moreover, the 2006–2009 EHIS survey only includes data concerning the fifteen EU member states at the time. With regard to the ESS, data for only one measurement are available, implying that no time-trend analysis can be performed. Also, the ESS data refer to 2014, and only include twenty European countries, amongst which are two non-EU countries (i.e. Norway and Switzerland).

Making use of EB survey material, however, also means that we have to deal with some limitations. First, compared to national surveys, the EB is less suitable for in-depth analyses at the (sub)national level due to the lower number of cases per country (ranging from around 500 respondents for Cyprus, Luxembourg and Malta to at least 1000 respondents for all of the other (former) EU member states). For more in-depth analyses, again, we refer to the following country-specific chapters in this book. Second, no findings on children will be reported as the EB surveys used in this chapter are conducted amongst subjects fifteen years of age and older. Third, proper interpretation of results can prove difficult as specific social and cultural contexts might cause dissimilar connotations of similar concepts in different countries, even within the European Union. Fourth, as will be explained below, a well-defined description of the concept of 'disability' lacks in the EB surveys that are used. For more details concerning the EB instrument, its material and the methodology applied, we refer to the European Commission (2010, 2014, 2018).

In the EB surveys, data on participation in sport, as well as participation in physical activity, are available for 2004, 2009, 2013 and 2017 (see European Commission, 2004, 2010, 2014, 2018). However, only the 2009, 2013 and 2017 Special Eurobarometer studies are of relevance here since they allow for analyses regarding people with a disability. In order to be able to make such analyses with regard to people with a disability, the 2009, 2013 and 2017 EB surveys provide information on disability by means of the following research questions:

- *From the following reasons, what is currently preventing you the most from practicing sport more regularly?* (Question used in the EB of 2009; only one answer possible)
- *What are the main reasons currently preventing you from practicing sport more regularly?* (Question used in the EBs of 2013 and 2017; multiple answers possible)

One of the possible answers to this question was 'a disability or illness prevents you from doing sport'.[1] As the EB surveys do not provide other information on the disability status of the respondents, we decided to use this specific question to determine whether a respondent can be categorised as a person with a disability or not. It is clear that, based on this information, full accuracy cannot be guaranteed as persons with a disability can perfectly answer the above question by ignoring that disability or illness may prevent them from being sports active. A person with a disability can feel not be hindered by his/her/x disability to practice sport more regularly. We can therefore assume that we probably are dealing with a systematic underestimation of the number of people with a disability. On the other hand, in this context, 'illness' can be understood as having a chronic disease rather than a short sickness preventing someone to partake in sport, because the question concerned relates to practicing sport more regularly. In order to be able to participate in sport on a more regular basis, one can be supposed not to suffer from a long-lasting illness. However, this depends on the illness and its severity. People with a chronic illness can be perfectly able to participate in sport, even on a more regular basis than is the case for people with a disability. According to the 2009, 2013 and 2017 EB surveys, 14.7%, 13.4% and 14.3% of the respondents, respectively, are classified as 'persons with a disability or illness *that prevents them from practicing sport more*

---

[1] Apart from the disability/illness-related answer, also the following answers, amongst others, were listed: 'you do not have the time', 'it is too expensive', 'you do not like competitive activities', 'there are not suitable sports infrastructures close to where you live', 'you do not have friends to do sports with' and so on. Respondents could also answer 'other' or 'don't know'. In the 2009 EB questionnaire only one answer could be provided, whereas in the 2013 and 2017 EB questionnaires multiple answers were possible. This can lead to different outcomes since disability might be a problem, but not necessarily is considered by respondents as the most important reason for preventing them from practicing sport.

regularly'. These figures seem to stay consistent over time as well as to fit fairly with the ones referred to in Chap. 2, amongst which are the numbers provided by the World Health Organization (WHO).[2]

As, so far, no other similar pan-European data on active participation in sport and physical activity for people with a disability are available, at present, we consider the EB data to give the best possible and most up to date indication of the sports participation situation amongst people with a disability in the different (former) member states of the European Union. This is especially the case when it comes to making a cross-national comparison from a time-trend perspective. This implies, however, that non-EU member states, like Norway and Switzerland, are not included as far as the EB data are concerned. On the other hand, and as stressed before, the EB data allow not only for comparisons between different EU member states, but also for comparisons over different time intervals (supra).

To define whether a respondent is actively participating in sport, the following research question from the EB survey is used:

– *How often do you exercise or play sport?*

Respondents were able to provide their answer by means of different frequency categories.[3] Those who did not indicate 'never' or 'don't know'[4] are classified as being an active sports participant. Thus, we do not differentiate between frequency levels in our analyses. Furthermore, in order to discern the number of club-organised sports participants as well as the number of fitness participants, the following research question is posed:

– *Are you a member of any of the following clubs where you participate in sport or recreational physical activity?*

For this question, multiple answers were possible.[5] When one indicated 'sports club', the individual is classified as being a club-organised sports participant.[6] When one indicated 'health or fitness centre', the individual is classified as being a fitness

---

[2] The EHIS and EU-SILC data, however, show higher rates for moderate disability and lower rates for severe disability. This can be due to different operationalisations and methods used (see Chap. 2).

[3] Possible answers included the following categories: (i) 5 times a week or more; (ii) 3–4 times a week; (iii) 1–2 times a week; (iv) 1–3 times a month; (v) less often; (vi) never; (vii) don't know.

[4] More specifically, respondents who indicated 'don't know' were classified as missing.

[5] The possible answers included the following categories: (i) health or fitness centre; (ii) sports club; (iii) socio-cultural club that includes sport in its activities (e.g. employees' club, youth club, school- and university-related club); (iv) other; (v) no, not a member of any club; (vi) don't know.

[6] Note that for the current analyses respondents answering 'socio-cultural club that includes sport in its activities' are not considered as club-organised sports participants. In their study, however, Scheerder et al. (2020) did consider both people being sports active in a sports club and people being sports active in a socio-cultural association as club-organised sports participants. However, we do report the results for both participation in a 'sports club' and in a 'sociocultural association', on the one hand, and participation in a 'sports club' and/or a 'sociocultural association', being a combined variable, on the other hand (see Tables 3.2 and 3.3).

participant. The results for participating in a socio-cultural association are presented separately (see Tables 3.2 and 3.3).

The EB surveys not only allow for analyses regarding active sport practice, they also contain data related to participation in physical activity. Here, the following research question is used:

– *And how often do you engage in other physical activity such as cycling from one place to another, dancing, gardening and so on? By 'other physical activity' we mean physical activity for recreational or non-sport-related reasons.*[7]

Different frequency categories were provided to the respondents.[8] Respondents who did not answer 'never' or 'don't know'[9] are defined as being physically active. As is the case for participation in sport (supra), we do not differentiate between frequency levels in our analyses.

Analyses in this chapter will be performed with regard to different modes of participation, namely (i) participation in physical activity, (ii) participation in sport, (iii) participation in a sports club, (iv) participation in a socio-cultural association providing sports activities and (v) participation in a fitness centre. Results will be presented in general, but also in relation to the respondents' social background, including sex, age and education, for both 'people with a disability' and people 'without a disability', or at least people who did (not) indicate that disability or illness is a reason to be prevented from practicing sport (supra). With regard to the designations of 'people with a disability' and 'people without a disability', we want to make clear that we use these terms from a practical point of view to enable empirical analyses between the two groups of (non-)participants. The split between these two categories is purely operational, and therefore does not involve any further assessment or connotation. For use of the term 'people with a disability' we also refer to Chap. 2 in which this issue is discussed in more detail. Because the results presented in this chapter are based on secondary analyses, references to the original and/or secondary sources are included, at the bottom of the respective figure or table. Concerning the calculations made, weight coefficients provided in the original databases are applied. For more details on the weighting procedure, we refer to European Commission (2010, 2014, 2018).

Together with the aforementioned opportunities, there is another added value related to the Eurobarometer Survey as it not only allows for comparing data between several time intervals and between different EU member states, but between significant clusters of countries as well. More precisely, the results of our analyses will be presented at the European level in general and at the level of the different countries, but also at the level of predefined geographical clusters within the

---

[7] In the 2009 EB questionnaire a slightly different question was posed, namely: *And how often do you engage in a physical activity outside sport such as cycling or walking from a place to another, dancing, gardening and so on?*

[8] Possible answers included the following categories: (i) 5 times a week or more; (ii) 3–4 times a week; (iii) 1–2 times a week; (iv) 1–3 times a month; (v) less often; (vi) never; (vii) don't know.

[9] More specifically, respondents who indicated 'don't know' were classified as missing.

Table 3.1 Classification of (former) EU member states (N = 28) according to their geographical location

Northern Europe	North Eastern Europe	South Eastern Europe	Southern Europe	Central Europe	Western Europe
Denmark	Estonia	Bulgaria	Cyprus	Austria	Ireland
Finland	Latvia	Croatia	Greece	Belgium	United Kingdom
Sweden	Lithuania	Hungary	Italy	Czechia	
	Poland	Romania	Malta	France	
		Slovakia	Portugal	Germany	
		Slovenia	Spain	Luxembourg	
				The Netherlands	

European Union. As regards the latter, a geographical classification of all (former) EU member states has already been developed in earlier studies (see Scheerder et al., 2020; Scheerder & Helsen, 2020) and can be applied in this chapter too. In this way, we will be able to investigate whether differences in participation in sport occur between different geographical parts of the European Union. For this, a classification containing six geographical clusters or regions is used. Rather than relying on any existing typology or taking political and cultural (dis)similarities into account, the geographical location of each EU member state is considered, primarily for pragmatic reasons. This results in a classification of (former) EU member states that is presented in Table 3.1. Although this classification is rather pragmatic, it is clear that it corresponds, to a certain degree, to Esping-Andersen's (1990) classic typology of welfare states and its further development by other authors. In his classic, Esping-Andersen (1990) differentiates between (i) universalist welfare states (Northern Europe), (ii) liberal welfare states (Western Europe), (iii) corporate welfare states (Central Europe), (iv) Mediterranean welfare states (Southern Europe) and (v) so-called post-communist welfare states (Eastern Europe).

Lastly, in the present chapter and complementary to the EB data, we will also make use of material collected in the framework of the SIVSCE project (see Elmose-Østerlund & Ibsen, 2016; Nagel et al., 2020). SIVSCE stands for 'Social Inclusion and Volunteering in Sports Clubs in Europe'. It concerns a cross-national research project executed in 2015[10] on behalf of the European Commission (see also following country-specific chapters and Chap. 23). This study sought to collect, analyse and discuss comparable data on sports clubs across ten European countries, including Belgium (Flanders), Denmark, England, Germany, Hungary, the Netherlands, Norway, Poland, Spain and Switzerland. Some of the findings from this study relate to people with a disability, and therefore can be considered as being of added value

---

[10] The SIVSCE research project consisted of two online sub-studies, one related to sports clubs and the other related to members and volunteers active in sports clubs (Elmose-Østerlund & Ibsen, 2016; Nagel et al., 2020). The sports club survey was conducted in 2015 among 35,790 sports clubs covering the ten participating European countries. The survey among the members and volunteers of the sports clubs was executed in 2016. It reached out to over 13,000 members and volunteers belonging to 642 sports clubs in the respective European countries.

to this chapter, hence their insertion where possible and appropriate. The data concerned deal with aspects of social integration. More specifically, the SIVSCE results will be presented with regard to the representation of people with a disability amongst the members of a sports club, as well as the share of clubs that have special initiatives aimed towards the promotion of sports participation amongst people with a disability.

3.3 Results

In this section the outcomes based on our secondary analyses of the EB survey material are reported. Additionally, as indicated, some extra analyses based on the data from the SIVSCE research project will be included too. First, we focus on the results with regard to participation in physical activity, (club-organised) sport and fitness. Here, findings are presented from both a pan-European and time-trend perspective. Thereafter, specific outcomes at national and regional level are presented. For this, we will make use, amongst others, of radar charts. These diagrams will make it easier to visually identify whether geographical differences between EU member states occur. Finally, the results regarding participation in different modes of physical activity and sport are shown, according to three social background characteristics—that is, sex, age and educational level.

Participation in Physical Activity, (Club-organised) Sport and Fitness

According to the 2017 EB survey, 43% of persons with a disability aged fifteen and over are physically active (Table 3.2). In 2009 and 2013 this number equals 72% and 52%, respectively. People without a disability have higher scores for each of these three measurements, but here, too, a decrease in physical activity level can be detected (Table 3.3). It is remarkable that the amount of people being physically active has significantly diminished during the past decade, both amongst people with and without a disability. The sharp drop between 2009 and 2013 can possibly be attributed to a difference in formulation of the respective question that is used in the 2009 questionnaire versus the 2013 and 2017 questionnaires (supra). Nevertheless, it can be stated that the level of physical activity has clearly reduced between 2009 and 2017, in particular amongst people with a disability (minus 29% versus minus 19% amongst people without a disability). Even if we take the same (number of) countries—being 27 EU member states, including the UK, but excluding Croatia[11]—the analyses show a similar trend as described above (EU27 outcomes for 2013 and 2017 are presented between brackets in Tables 3.2 and 3.3). A

---

[11] Croatia joined the European Union in 2013. Therefore, no results regarding this country are available for 2009. Or in other words, the EU27 member states include all EU28 member states, excluding Croatia being the country that most recently joined the EU, but including the UK since the UK was a member state of the EU till it left the EU due to the Brexit which took place in January 2020.

Table 3.2 Participation in physical activity, (club-organised) sport and fitness in (former) EU27/EU28 member states amongst people with a disability or illness aged 15 and over (2009–2017), percentages of total population

	2009 EU27	2013 EU28 (EU27)	2017 EU28 (EU27)	X^2
Physical activity	72.4[a]	52.2[b] (52.1[b])	43.2[c] (43.2[c])	662.360*** (655.399***)
Sports participation	34.8[a]	36.0[a] (35.9[a])	27.6[b] (27.7[b])	70.417*** (66.325***)
Participation in a sports club	5.4[a]	6.0[a] (6.0[a])	4.0[b] (4.1[b])	16.130*** (14.733**)
Participation in a socio-cultural association	4.7[a]	3.0[b] (3.0[b])	2.5[b] (2.5[b])	29.468*** (28.695***)
Participation in a club(sports club + socio-cultural association)	9.2[a]	8.7[a] (8.7[a])	6.5[b] (6.5[b])	20.364*** (19.459***)
Participation in a fitness centre	3.0[a]	5.4[b] (5.4[b])	4.3[b] (4.3[b])	25.723*** (25.348***)

[a,b,c] *** $p<0.001$; ** $p<0.01$; * $p<0.05$
Note1: Numbers with a different superscript differ significantly from one another
Note2: EU27 outcomes for 2013 and 2017 are presented between brackets
Source: Authors' own calculations, based on Eurobarometer data (European Commission, 2010, 2014, 2018)

Table 3.3 Participation in physical activity, (club-organised) sport and fitness in (former) EU27/EU28 member states amongst people without a disability or illness aged 15 and over (2009–2017), percentages of total population

	2009 EU27	2013 EU28 (EU27)	2017 EU28 (EU27)	X^2
Physical activity	87.2[a]	72.6[b] (72.5[b])	68.1[c] (68.1[c])	2293.050*** (2274.282***)
Sports participation	62.3[a]	61.4[a] (61.3[a])	58.3[b] (58.4[b])	82.626*** (74.272***)
Participation in a sports club	11.5[a]	13.2[b] (13.2[b])	12.9[b] (13.0[b])	32.114*** (33.243***)
Participation in a socio-cultural association	3.7[a]	3.1[b] (3.1[b])	3.4[a,b] (3.4[a,b])	11.824** (11.646**)
Participation in a club(sports club + socio-cultural association)	14.7[a]	15.8[b] (15.8[b])	15.8[b] (15.8[b])	12.117** (13.011**)
Participation in a fitness centre	9.1[a]	11.5[b] (11.6[b])	11.8[b] (11.9[b])	100.905*** (103.013***)

[a,b,c] *** $p<0.001$; ** $p<0.01$; * $p<0.05$
Note1: Numbers with a different superscript differ significantly from one another
Note2: EU27 outcomes for 2013 and 2017 are presented between brackets
Source: Authors' own calculations, based on Eurobarometer data (European Commission, 2010, 2014, 2018)

decrease over the past years as is the case for being physically active, both amongst people with and without a disability, can be noted as well when it comes to the evolution of the level of participation in (club-organised) sports, as has also been reported by Scheerder et al. (2020: 320–322) and Scheerder and Helsen (2020: 46–47). On the other hand, participation in fitness seems to have significantly gained in popularity, at least between 2009 and 2017 but not between 2013 and 2017, again both amongst people with and without a disability. However, it is clear to what extent both groups differ in terms of participation: in 2017, only 4% amongst people with a disability actively engages in fitness, whereas this percentage equals almost 12% amongst people without a disability.

Participation in (Club-organised) Sport and Fitness at National and Regional Level

When we take a closer look and interpret the 2017 data for people with a disability at the level of the EU member states, one can see that high sports participation scores can be detected for countries such as Sweden (77%), Finland (71%) and Denmark (61%), and that countries like, amongst others, Greece (5%), Bulgaria (9%) and Italy (10%), on the other hand, show very low percentages (see Fig. 3.1). For their part, Lithuania (30%), Austria (26%) and Latvia (26%) position themselves in the middle group. From this picture, it can be deduced that a geographical pattern can be discerned. This becomes even more clear when we present the data in a reduced way, according to geographical location based on the classification presented in Table 3.1 (supra). More precisely, from Fig. 3.2 we learn that, in particular, Northern Europe is head and shoulders above the other regions in Europe when considering sports participation amongst people with a disability. This is somewhat remarkable since the difference between Northern Europe on the one hand and Central and Western Europe on the other is less obvious when it comes to sports participation amongst people without a disability. Or formulated in other words, it appears that the sports participation gap between people with versus without a disability is much smaller in countries from Northern Europe, compared to countries in all of the other European regions. Actually, this difference in levels of sports participation is the highest in countries from Central and Western Europe, since these countries, compared to countries from North Eastern, South Eastern and Southern Europe, show rather high sports participation scores for people without a disability.

Cross-regional analyses can be performed not only for sports participation in general, but, more particularly, also with regard to participation in a sports club and in a fitness centre. Figures 3.3 and 3.4 show that both sports club participation and fitness participation score relatively high amongst people with a disability in Northern Europe, compared to other regions in Europe, in particular North Eastern Europe, South Eastern Europe and Southern Europe, as evidenced by the irregular shape of a peak towards the top of Figs. 3.3 and 3.4. Thus, again, a geographical pattern can be detected as well for participation in club-organised sport and participation in fitness. Countries belonging to the Northern Europe region are clearly on top, in terms of their position on the (club-organised) sport and fitness participation

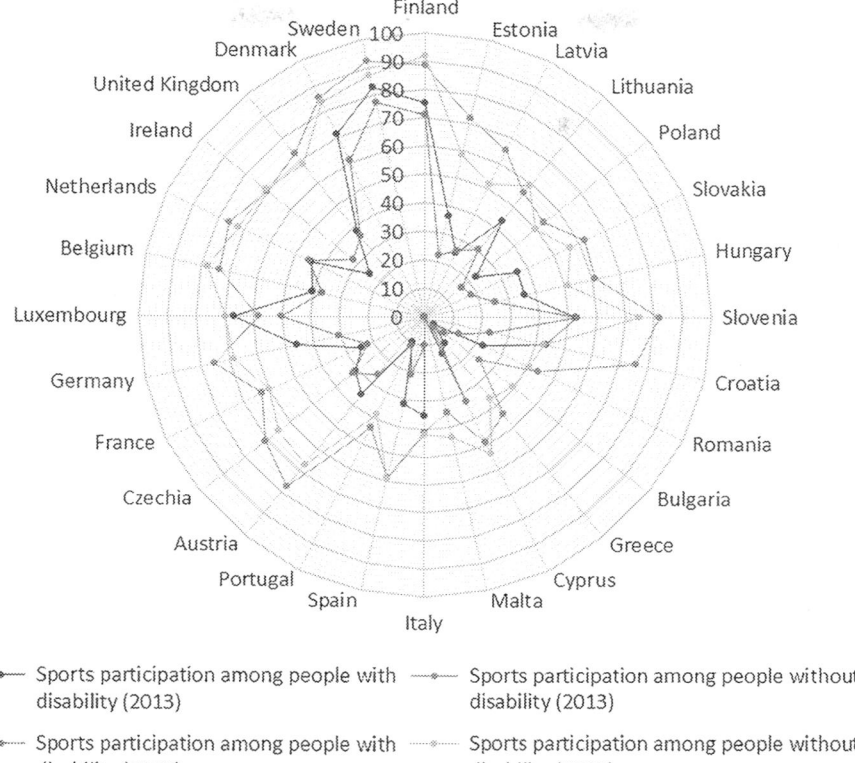

Fig. 3.1 Sports participation in (former) EU28 member states amongst people with and without a disability or illness aged 15 and over according to country (2013–2017), percentages of total population. *Note*: Due to a low number of cases in at least one of the two EB data sets (less than 50 respondents with disability in the respective country), the numbers of Estonia, Latvia, Lithuania, Slovakia, Slovenia, Croatia, Cyprus, Malta, Luxembourg and Ireland need to be treated with caution. *Source*: Authors' own calculations, based on Eurobarometer data (European Commission, 2014, 2018)

ladder, while countries from Eastern and Southern Europe clearly rank lower and countries from Western and Central Europe position themselves between these regions. Similar geographical and regional patterns show up for the participation levels regarding people without a disability.

The above insights regarding the participation in a sports club amongst people with a disability, based on Eurobarometer data for 2013 and 2017, can be confirmed when we have a look at the findings from the SIVSCE research project held in 2015 in ten European countries (supra). In the SIVSCE project, the question was raised to what extent different population groups are represented in sports clubs, including people with a disability. The results show that people with a disability are more strongly represented amongst the members and volunteers of sports clubs belonging to Northern, Western and Central European countries, while this seems to be less the case for sports clubs in Eastern and Southern European countries

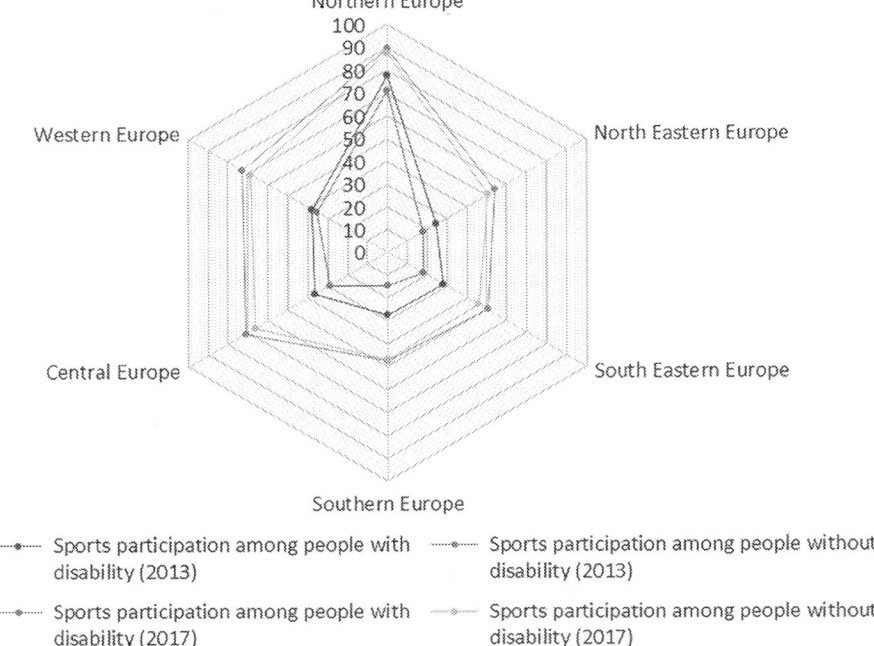

Fig. 3.2 Sports participation in (former) EU28 member states amongst people with and without a disability or illness aged 15 and over according to region (2013–2017), percentages of total population. Source: Authors' own calculations, based on Eurobarometer data (European Commission, 2014, 2018)

(Fig. 3.5). However, as a Central European, albeit non-EU27 country, Switzerland takes a somewhat isolated if exceptional position, as seven out of ten Swiss sports clubs appear to indicate that they do not reach out to people with a disability at all. In contrast, in countries such as England, Germany and Norway, sports clubs are more likely to be successful in this regard, as seven in ten of them have at least a certain representation of people with a disability amongst their members and volunteers. Countries in which people with a disability are more likely not to be represented by a majority of the sports clubs also seem to score highly for not or underrepresenting other groups in society, like people with a migration background and elderly (65+ years of age). For instance, in Poland, and to a somewhat lesser degree also in Belgium (Flanders), Hungary and Spain, more than 30% of the sports clubs appear to have no representation at all of specific population groups, namely people with a disability, people with a migration background and elderly people (Fig. 3.6). Yet, it should be noted that this does not necessarily concern the same sports clubs. Of course, by making such cross-national analyses, one also has to take into consideration the country-related specificities in terms of the social, cultural and economic situation.

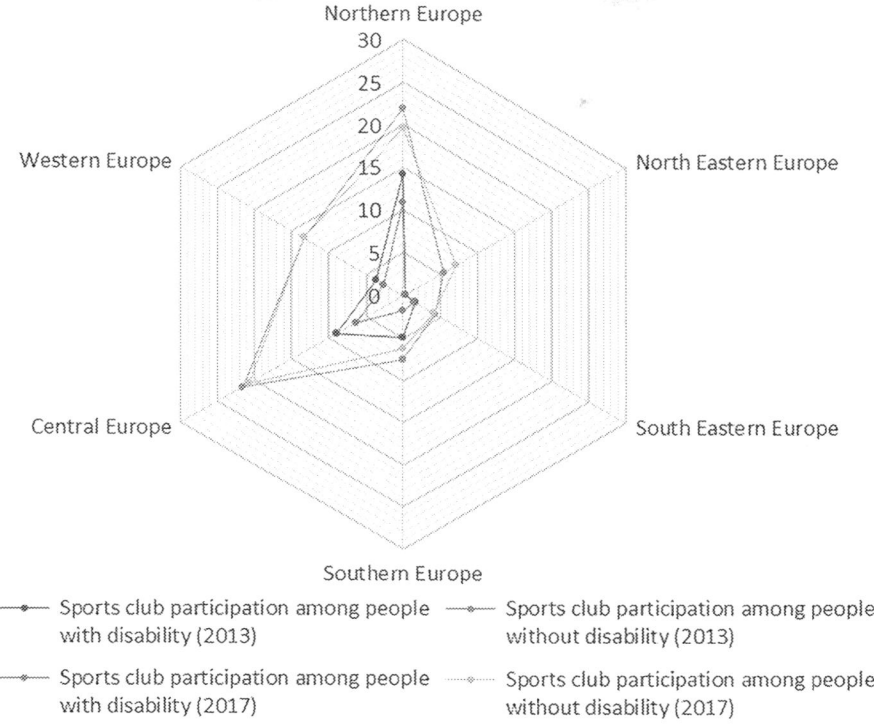

Fig. 3.3 Participation in a sports club in (former) EU28 member states amongst people with and without a disability or illness aged 15 and over according to region (2013–2017), percentages of total population. Source: Authors' own calculations, based on Eurobarometer data (European Commission, 2014, 2018)

Still based on the data of the SIVSCE research project, we are also able to analyse whether sports clubs take special initiatives for specific population groups. Figure 3.7 shows that sports clubs in different European countries significantly differ on this matter. In Hungary, four out of ten sports clubs indicate to have such initiatives with regard to people with a disability, whereas on the other side of the spectrum, in Denmark, only one in ten sports clubs appears to do so. Moreover, it seems that, geographically seen, we get an opposite picture compared to the analysis regarding the (non-)representation of people with a disability amongst the members and volunteers of sports clubs (see Figs. 3.5 and 3.6). More precisely, we learn from Fig. 3.7 that sports clubs in Eastern and Southern Europe seem to do better when it comes to providing special initiatives towards people with a disability, than is the case for sports clubs in Northern, Western and Central Europe. At first sight, this may be interpreted as somewhat surprising as the last group of countries perform significantly better in terms of participation in sports clubs amongst people with a disability, as we have demonstrated previously (see Fig. 3.3). However, one could also reason that sports clubs in Eastern and Southern Europe need to take such

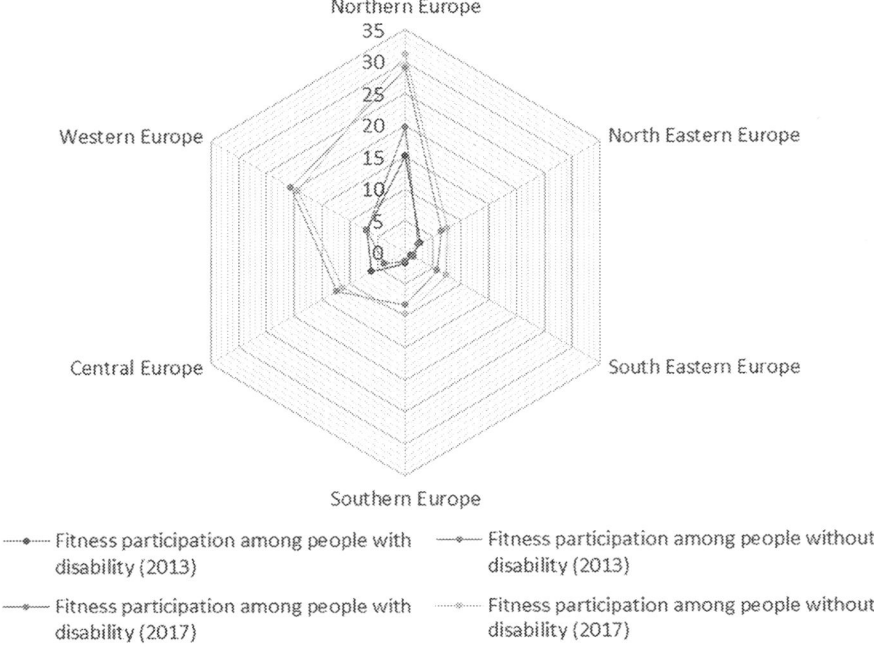

Fig. 3.4 Participation in a fitness centre in (former) EU28 member states amongst people with and without a disability or illness aged 15 and over according to region (2013–2017), percentages of total population. *Source*: Authors' own calculations, based on Eurobarometer data (European Commission, 2014, 2018)

action towards people with a disability, precisely because they are more likely to underperform in attracting this population group, at least in comparison with sports clubs from, in particular, Northern European countries. This tends to be the chicken-and-egg paradox as it is not clear whether you need special programmes (cause) to reach out to a certain target group, or whether you initiate special programmes (effect) to keep a specific group of participants on board. The truth is probably in between, implying that both approaches are necessary.

Participation in Different Modes of Physical Activity and Sport According to Some Social Background Characteristics

Studies generally demonstrate that sports participation is socially stratified. More precisely, previous comparative research at a European level has shown that active involvement in leisure-time physical activity and sport remarkably differs in terms of, amongst others, sex, age and socio-economic status (see Hartmann-Tews, 2006; Helsen & Scheerder, 2020a, 2021; Moreno-Llamas et al., 2020; Scheerder & Helsen, 2020; Van Tuyckom & Scheerder, 2008, 2010a, 2010b). However, it is less known whether such patterns of social stratification also exist in the active participation in

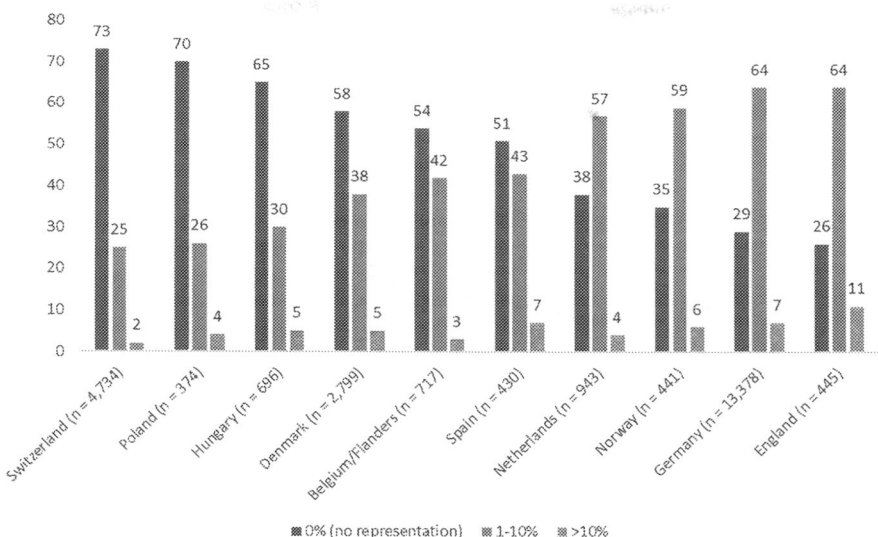

Fig. 3.5 Representation of people with a disability in sports clubs from ten European countries (2015), percentages of total number of sports clubs. *Note:* Numbers between brackets below the bars in the figure concern the number of people with a disability for each specific country. *Source:* Authors' own calculations, based on Nagel et al. (2020)

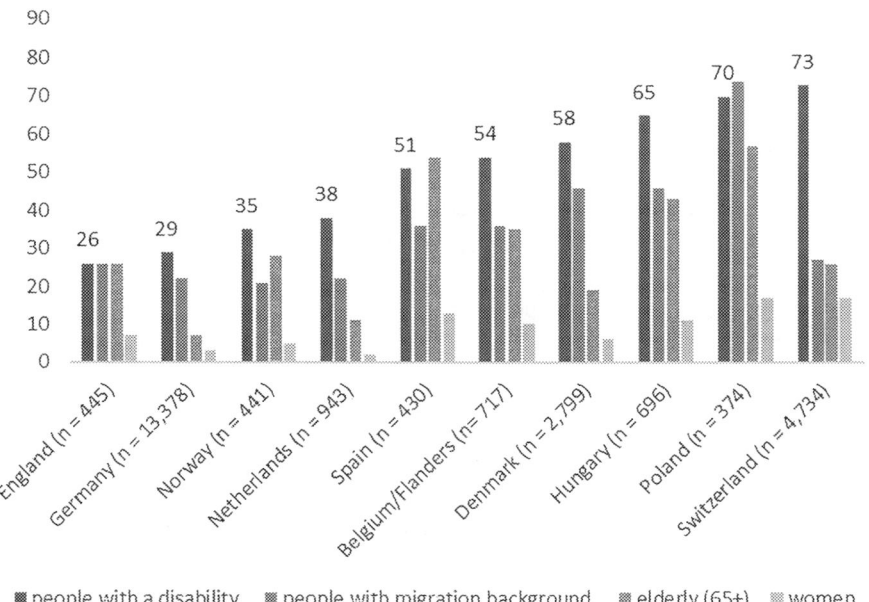

Fig. 3.6 Non-representation of specific population groups in sports clubs from ten European countries (2015), percentages of total number of sports clubs. *Note1:* Numbers between brackets below the bars in the figure concern the number of people with a disability for each specific country. *Note2:* For readability reasons, only the percentages related to people with a disability are shown. *Source:* Authors' own calculations, based on Nagel et al. (2020)

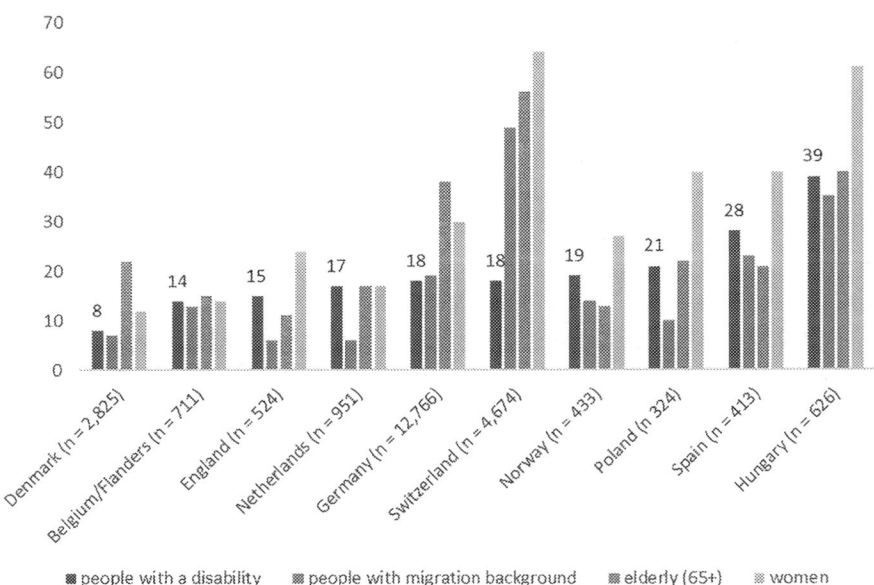

Fig. 3.7 Number of sports clubs with special initiatives for specific population groups in ten European countries (2015), percentages of total number of sports clubs. *Note1:* Numbers between brackets below the bars in the figure concern the number of people with a disability for each specific country. *Note2:* For readability reasons, only the percentages related to people with a disability are shown. *Source:* Authors' own calculations, based on Nagel et al. (2020)

physical activity and sport amongst people with a disability, in particular from a cross-national, time-trend perspective. Here, again, the Eurobarometer surveys are of help, as these data allow for analysing participation in physical activity and sport based on social background characteristics, such as sex, age and education.

The results presented in Tables 3.4 and 3.5 indicate that, indeed, a socially stratified pattern concerning different modes of participation in physical activity and sport can be detected, both amongst people with and without a disability. More specifically, it appears that men participate more than women when it comes to taking part in physical activity and (club-organised) sport. For fitness participation, however, the difference between the two sexes is much smaller, non-existent or even in favour of women. These outcomes go for people with and without a disability, across the 2009–2017 timespan. In terms of age, people aged 55 years and over systematically score lower on participation in physical activity, (club-organised) sport as well as fitness, compared to people aged 15–54 years, both amongst people with a disability and people without a disability. Moreover, the youngest, aged 15–24 years, stand head and shoulders above the other age groups, again amongst people with and without a disability. With regard to educational status, the findings indicate that, generally, people who are still studying, and, to a somewhat lesser degree, also higher educated people, perform significantly better for participation in physical activity, (club-organised) sport and fitness, in comparison to low and middle educated people. This outcome applies, again, for people with a disability as well as people without a disability.

Table 3.4 Physical activity (PA), overall sports participation and sports participation in different organisational settings in (former) EU27/EU28 member states amongst people with a disability or illness aged 15 and over according to background characteristics (2009–2017), percentages of total population

	2009 (EU27)					2013 (EU28)						2017 (EU28)					
	PA	Sport	Sports club	Sociocult	Club	PA	Fitness	Sociocult	Club	Sport	Sports club	PA	Fitness	Sociocult	Club	Sport	Sports club
Total	72.4	34.8	5.4	4.7	9.2	52.2	3.0	3.0	9.2	36.0	6.0	43.2	5.4	3.0	8.7	27.6	4.0
Sex																	
Men	76.7	39.4	9.4	5.1	12.8	56.9	3.7	3.0	12.8	38.8	8.3	47.7	5.2	3.5	10.8	30.6	5.3
Women	69.1	31.2	2.4	4.4	6.3	48.6	2.5	3.0	6.3	33.9	4.3	39.9	5.6	1.8	7.1	25.4	3.2
Age																	
15–24 years	81.8	67.8	21.0	7.0	21.0	70.3	10.6	8.2	21.0	75.7	12.8	66.7	20.9	7.0	19.6	53.9	3.1
25–39 years	88.9	63.6	11.9	7.1	18.6	72.1	4.9	4.9	18.6	53.9	11.8	60.1	12.1	3.7	14.1	52.0	9.8
40–54 years	82.5	47.8	6.2	3.7	8.9	65.6	4.5	2.1	8.9	49.0	9.2	51.6	7.2	3.4	11.1	38.4	5.3
55 years and over	68.1	27.4	3.8	4.6	7.7	44.7	2.1	2.7	7.7	27.6	4.0	38.4	3.1	2.0	6.7	21.4	3.2
Education																	
Low	67.0	22.0	2.5	4.1	5.8	39.9	1.4	2.5	5.8	21.5	3.0	28.7	2.5	2.0	5.5	16.0	1.9
Middle	74.9	38.7	6.5	4.0	9.8	52.4	2.9	1.8	9.8	36.8	4.7	46.9	3.8	2.5	6.5	26.7	3.8
High	83.8	58.6	9.7	8.4	16.2	70.6	6.7	4.7	16.2	54.6	11.8	61.1	10.9	3.6	16.1	45.4	8.5
Still studying	83.1	73.1	19.7	1.4	19.7	81.9	11.3	16.8	19.7	77.7	23.4	63.5	29.8	4.7	33.7	65.9	2.4

Note1: EU27 member states include all EU28 member states except for Croatia being the most recent country that joined the European Union in 2013
Note2: 'sociocult' = socio-cultural association that offers, amongst others, sports activities
Note3: 'club' = combination of two organisational settings (i.e. sports club and socio-cultural association that offers, amongst others, sports activities)
Source: Authors' own calculations, based on Eurobarometer data (European Commission, 2010, 2014, 2018)

Table 3.5 Physical activity (PA), overall sports participation and sports participation in different organisational settings in (former) EU27/EU28 member states amongst people without a disability or illness aged 15 and over according to background characteristics (2009–2017), percentages of total population

	2009 (EU27)						2013 (EU28)						2017 (EU28)					
	PA	Sport	Sports club	Sociocult	Club	Fitness	PA	Sport	Sports club	Sociocult	Club	Fitness	PA	Sport	Sports club	Sociocult	Club	Fitness
Total	87.2	62.3	11.5	3.7	14.7	9.1	72.6	61.4	13.2	3.1	15.8	11.5	68.1	58.3	12.9	3.4	15.8	11.8
Sex																		
Men	88.3	66.6	15.0	4.2	18.4	8.7	76.0	66.3	17.5	3.0	20.0	11.0	72.3	64.6	17.3	3.7	20.2	11.6
Women	86.1	58.2	8.2	3.3	11.2	9.4	69.4	56.8	9.0	3.3	11.8	12.0	64.0	52.2	8.7	3.1	11.5	12.0
Age																		
15–24 years	92.7	81.4	17.8	4.5	21.0	13.0	79.8	81.5	21.7	5.5	26.0	18.3	75.2	76.7	21.1	5.4	25.8	18.8
25–39 years	88.9	69.3	12.1	3.0	14.8	13.3	75.9	68.2	12.1	2.7	14.4	14.8	71.2	65.4	13.0	2.7	15.4	15.4
40–54 years	88.0	61.4	11.2	3.2	14.1	8.1	73.2	59.8	12.9	2.0	14.4	9.9	69.0	57.3	12.6	2.2	14.3	10.5
55 years and over	81.3	45.0	7.5	4.6	11.7	3.4	65.3	46.2	9.9	3.3	12.9	6.4	61.7	45.4	9.4	3.9	12.8	7.0
Education																		
Low	78.9	37.3	6.1	3.6	9.4	2.6	53.0	35.0	5.7	2.2	7.8	4.4	48.1	31.6	5.8	2.0	7.6	4.4
Middle	87.7	61.2	10.1	3.6	13.5	7.9	72.4	57.6	11.1	2.1	12.9	9.9	65.2	51.6	9.3	2.5	11.4	9.0
High	91.9	76.0	15.4	3.8	18.5	13.4	81.6	74.9	16.8	3.7	20.0	15.9	77.9	71.4	17.6	3.8	20.8	16.3
Still studying	93.0	86.5	20.2	4.6	23.3	14.9	83.3	87.4	25.4	7.2	31.0	19.1	79.4	84.2	23.8	7.7	30.4	20.9

Note1: EU27 member states include all EU28 member states except for Croatia being the most recent country that joined the European Union in 2013
Note2: 'sociocult' = socio-cultural association that offers, amongst others, sports activities
Note3: 'club' = combination of two organisational settings (i.e. sports club and socio-cultural association that offers, amongst others, sports activities)
Source: Authors' own calculations, based on Eurobarometer data (European Commission, 2010, 2014, 2018)

So, we may state that participatory differences between different social groups amongst people with a disability are very much similar to the social discrepancies that are registered amongst people without a disability. Social determinants such as sex, age and educational level thus impact the level of physical activity, (club-organised) sports participation and fitness participation amongst people with a disability. Moreover, no obvious shift can be noticed between the three time intervals, indicating that a process of democratisation did not occur during the past decade. Or formulated in other words, social inequality seems to persist amongst people with a disability, as regards participation in physical activity and different forms of sports behaviour.

Speaking in terms of social inequality, the EB data also make it possible to analyse, for the EU member states, the association between income inequality and the level of sports participation. In order to measure income inequality, the ratio is calculated between the poorest 20% in the population of a given country on the one hand and the richest 20% on the other. In EU member states such as Belgium, Czechia and Denmark, the gap between these two income groups equals about four, while in Bulgaria, Lithuania and Spain this ratio is between seven and eight (see Fig. 3.8). This

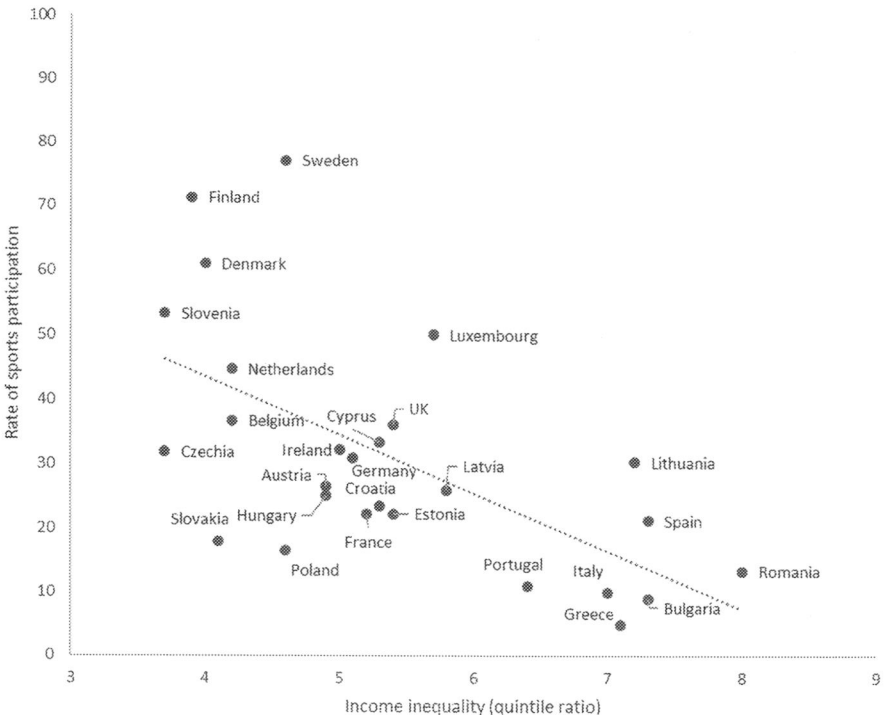

Fig. 3.8 Association between income inequality (2010–2017, quintile ratios) and rate of sports participation amongst people with a disability 15 years of age and over (2017) in EU27 (due to a lack of data, Malta cannot be included in this dispersion diagram) countries. *Note:* $r_{Pearson} = -0.62$ ($p<0.01$). *Source*: Authors' own calculations, based on European Commission (2018) and UNDP (2020)

implies that more equal societies can be clearly distinguished from more unequal societies within the European Union (see also OECD, 2017). It has been shown that people living in unequal societies, and thus societies with a larger income gap, are at higher risk of becoming physically and sports inactive (Pabayo et al., 2017; Scheerder & Helsen, 2020, see also Wilkinson & Pickett, 2009). Therefore, the question can be raised whether this association also occurs in people with a disability. From the scatterplot presented in Fig. 3.8, we learn that a significant relationship exists between income inequality and the rate of sports participation amongst people with a disability. More precisely, as has already been shown in Figs. 3.1 and 3.2, it can be noted that people with a disability from countries in Northern Europe, such as Denmark, Finland and Sweden, are more likely to partake in sports compared to their counterparts from other countries in Europe. However, the former concern more equal societies, while the latter are more unequal societies, especially countries in Southern and South-Eastern Europe. Thus, complementary to the geographical differences described earlier in this chapter, it is clear that levels of sports participation can also be associated with disparities in income inequality at state level.

3.4 Conclusion

In this chapter, it was our aim to present findings with regard to participation in physical activity and different modes of sports practice by people with a disability. Complementary to the results already presented in the previous country-specific chapters, the outcomes in the current chapter are based on secondary analyses of available pan-European data. More specifically, we were able to rely on data collected in the framework of the Eurobarometer surveys on participation in physical activity, (club-organised) sport and fitness (European Commission, 2010, 2014, 2018), complemented by data from the SIVSCE research project (Elmose-Østerlund & Ibsen, 2016; Nagel et al., 2020). These data sets allow for both cross-national and cross-temporal analyses. The reported findings indicate that, compared to people without a disability, people with a disability significantly underperform when it comes to active participation in physical activity, (club-organised) sport and fitness. However, as is the case with people without a disability, rates of participation in physical activity and sport are declining over time. In addition, clear geographical patterns have been shown to exist, implying that people with a disability from Northern European countries are more likely to be physically and sports active. This geographical difference also goes for club-organised sport and participation in fitness. In Northern but also Western and Central European countries, it appears that more sports clubs have people with a disability amongst their members and volunteers than in other European regions. On the other hand, we have shown that sports clubs in Eastern and Southern Europe seem to do better when it comes to providing special initiatives for people with a disability. Finally, our results indicate that social differences occur between different groups of people with a disability, especially regarding participation in physical activity and (club-organised) sport. More specifically, sex, age and educational level seem to be determining factors. Since these disparities do not diminish throughout time, it is clear that a process of democratisation has not yet taken place. Women, elderly and lower educated people with a disability are more likely to be physically and sports inactive than their respective counterparts, namely men, youngsters and higher educated people with a disability.

The geographical and social differences that have been reported in this chapter indicate that more efforts are needed to offer people with a disability more and better opportunities to partake in physical activity and (club-organised) sports activities. In 1975, the *European Sport for All Charter* was launched by all European ministers responsible for sport at the time (COE, 1976). Article 1 of this charter clearly stipulates that every individual shall have the right to participate in sport. About one decade later, in 1986, the Sport for All Charter was supplemented by the *European Charter on Sport for All: Disabled Persons* (COE, 1986). Here, it was recommended that governments of all European member states should orientate their policies so that people with a disability may have adequate opportunities to take part in recreational physical activities, which would not only improve their physical fitness and mental well-being, but which would also encourage social communication (COE, 1986). Despite almost fifty years of Sport for All policies and campaigns, at a national and European level, significant inequalities still persist. The empirical evidence provided in this chapter, in addition to the findings reported in the previous chapters, urges further policy action, preferably coordinated at the supranational level but in close partnership with national and local actors from both the profit and non-profit sectors (see also Chap. 23).

Some limitations, however, need to be taken into consideration. Firstly, there is a lack of accurate and comparable data as regards the participation in physical activity and (club-organised) sports activities amongst people with a disability. For the analyses included in this chapter, we had to rely on data from the 2009, 2013 and 2017 EB databases. Though the EB survey can be considered a relevant tool, in the EB sport-related surveys, a variable is missing to assess whether respondents have a physical and/or intellectual disability or not. As explained at the beginning of the chapter, we had to make use of an indirect variable for our analyses, which may lead to an underestimation of the number of people with a disability. Also, the operationalisation of participation in physical activity has changed slightly over time, which makes it less easy to accurately compare outcomes between different time intervals.

Secondly, participation data collected by means of long-lasting surveys are scarce, not only at a pan-European but also at a country level, and particularly regarding the participation in physical activity and sports practices by people with a disability. Parallel to the need for cross-temporal data, it is of importance to collect data from a comparative, pan-European perspective too. After all, harmonised participation data, both cross-nationally and cross-temporally, are highly needed to identify participation trends and possible policy gaps. Based on insights that can be gained from these data, policy-makers will be able to develop and implement empirically evidenced policy programmes to promote and facilitate participation, not only for those who already enjoy many opportunities, but primarily for those who need the benefits of being physically and sports active the most.

References

Claeys, U. (1982a). *Rationalising sports policies. Sport in European society: A transnational survey into participation and motivation*. Council of Europe/Committee for the Development of Sport.

Claeys, U. (1982b). *Rationalising sports policies. Sport in European society: A transnational survey into participation and motivation (Technical Supplement)*. Council of Europe/Committee for the Development of Sport.

COE. (1976). *The European sport for all charter*. Council of Europe/Committee of Ministers.

COE. (1986). *The European charter on sport for all. Disabled persons*. Council of Europe/Committee of Ministers.

Elmose-Østerlund, K. & Ibsen, B., in cooperation with Breuer, C., Feiler, S., Llopis-Goig, R., Nagel, S., Nichols, G., Perényi, S., Piątkowska, M., Scheerder, J., Seippel, Ø., Steinbach, D. & Van der Werff, H. (2016). *Social inclusion and volunteering in sports clubs in Europe. Introduction to the project*. University of Southern Denmark/Centre for Sports, Health & Civil Society.

Esping-Andersen, G. (1990). *The three worlds of welfare capitalism*. Polity.

ESS. (2021). European Social Survey (ESS). Data and documentation. Retrieved May 15, 2021, from https://www.europeansocialsurvey.org/data/

European Commission. (2004). *The citizens of the European Union and sport (Special Eurobarometer 213/Wave EB62.0)*. European Commission/Directorate-General for Education & Culture.

European Commission. (2010). *Sport and physical activity (Special Eurobarometer 334/Wave EB72.3)*. European Commission/Directorate-General for Education & Culture.

European Commission. (2014). *Sport and physical activity (Special Eurobarometer 412/Wave EB80.2)*. European Commission/Directorate-General for Education & Culture.

European Commission. (2018). *Sport and physical activity (Special Eurobarometer 472/Wave EB88.4)*. European Commission/Directorate-General for Education, Youth, Sport & Culture.

Eurostat. (2021a). Consumption expenditure of private households (HBS). Retrieved May 15, 2021, from https://ec.europa.eu/eurostat/cache/metadata/en/hbs_esms.htm

Eurostat. (2021b). European Health Interview Survey (EHIS). Retrieved May 15, 2021, from https://ec.europa.eu/eurostat/cache/metadata/en/hlth_det_esms.htm

Eurostat. (2021c). Eurostat: Your key to European statistics. European Health Interview Survey (EHIS). Retrieved May 15, 2021, from https://ec.europa.eu/eurostat/web/microdata/european-health-interview-survey

Eurostat. (2021d). Eurostat: Your key to European statistics. European Union statistics on income and living conditions (EU-SILC). Retrieved May 15, 2021, from https://ec.europa.eu/eurostat/web/microdata/european-union-statistics-on-income-and-living-conditions

Eurostat. (2021e). Eurostat: Your key to European statistics. Harmonised European Time Use Surveys (HETUS). Retrieved May 15, 2021, from https://ec.europa.eu/eurostat/web/products-manuals-and-guidelines/-/KS-RA-08-014

Eurostat. (2021f). Eurostat: your key to European statistics. Household Budget Survey (HBS). Retrieved May 15, 2021, from https://ec.europa.eu/eurostat/web/microdata/household-budget-survey

Eurostat. (2021g). Income and living conditions (ILC). Retrieved May 15, 2021, from https://ec.europa.eu/eurostat/cache/metadata/en/ilc_esms.htm

Eurostat. (2021h). International Trade in Sporting Goods (SPRT_TRD). Retrieved May 15, 2021, from https://ec.europa.eu/eurostat/cache/metadata/en/sprt_trd_esms.htm

Eurostat. (2021j). Time Use Survey (TUS). Retrieved May 15, 2021, from https://ec.europa.eu/eurostat/cache/metadata/en/tus_esms.htm

GESIS/Leibniz Institute for the Social Sciences. (2021a). European Values Study (EVS). Retrieved May 15, 2021, from https://www.gesis.org/en/services/finding-and-accessing-data/european-values-study

GESIS/Leibniz Institute for the Social Sciences. (2021b). International Social Survey Programme (ISSP). Leisure Time and Sports – ISSP 2007 (ZA4850). Retrieved May 15, 2021, from https://dbk.gesis.org/dbksearch/sdesc2.asp?no=4850&search=issp%202007&search2=&field=all&field2=&DB=e&tab=0&notabs=&nf=1&af=&ll=10

GESIS/Leibniz Institute for the Social Sciences. (2021c). International Social Survey Programme (ISSP). Citizenship II – ISSP 2014 (ZA6670). Retrieved May 15, 2021, from https://dbk.gesis.org/dbksearch/sdesc2.asp?ll=10&notabs=&af=&nf=&search=&search2=&db=e&no=6670

Hartmann-Tews, I. (2006). Social stratification in sport and sport policy in the European Union. *European Journal for Sport & Society, 3*(2), 109–124.

Helsen, K., & Scheerder, J. (2020a). Fitness(-related) trends within and between countries. Towards a fit (in) Europe? In J. Scheerder, H. Vehmas, & K. Helsen (Eds.), *The rise and size of the fitness industry in Europe. Fit for the future?* (pp. 389–436). Palgrave Macmillan.

Helsen, K. & Scheerder, J., with the cooperation of Alexandris, K. & Hover, P. (2020b). Flemish running events in international perspective: participant profile, motivation and attitudes. Results based on the European RUN for HEALTH project. In *Sport policy & management studies* (Vol. 72). KU Leuven/Policy in Sports & Physical Activity Research Group. https://gbiomed.kuleuven.be/english/research/50000737/groups/policy-in-sports-physical-activity-research-group/bms-studies/bms72-spm.pdf

Helsen, K. & Scheerder, J. (2021). Sports participation, physical (in)activity and overweight in the European Union. A comparative study based on pan-European data 2002–2017. In *Sport policy & management studies* (Vol. 67). KU Leuven/Policy in Sports & Physical Activity Research Group. https://gbiomed.kuleuven.be/english/research/50000737/groups/policy-in-sports-physical-activity-research-group/bms-studies/bms67.pdf

Moreno-Llamas, A., García-Mayor, J., & De la Cruz-Sánchez, E. (2020). Physical activity barriers according to social stratification in Europe. *International Journal of Public Health, 65*, 1477–1484.

Nagel, S., Elmose-Østerlund, K., Ibsen, B. & Scheerder, J. (Eds.). (2020). Functions of sports clubs in European societies. A cross-national comparative study. In *Sports economics, management & policy* (Vol. 13). Springer.

OECD. (2017). *Understanding the socio-economic divide in Europe (Background Report)*. OECD Centre for Opportunity & Equality.

Pabayo, R., Fuller, D., Lee, E. Y., Horino, M., & Kawachi, I. (2017). State-level income inequality and meeting physical activity guidelines. Differential associations amongst US men and women. *Journal of Public Health, 40*(2), 229–236.

Scheerder, J., & Helsen, K. (2020). The weight of numbers. Prevalence of overweight, sedentary behaviour and sport/fitness participation from a comparative pan-European perspective. In J. Scheerder, H. Vehmas, & K. Helsen (Eds.), *The rise and size of the fitness industry in Europe. Fit for the future?* (pp. 33–72). Palgrave Macmillan.

Scheerder, J., Helsen, K., Elmose-Østerlund, K., & Nagel, S. (2020). Exploring pan-European similarities and differences in club-organised sports. A cross-national and cross-temporal comparison. In S. Nagel, K. Elmose-Østerlund, B. Ibsen, & J. Scheerder (Eds.), *Functions of sports clubs in European societies. A cross-national comparative study* (Sports economics, management & policy) (Vol. 13, pp. 315–344). Springer.

Scheerder, J., Vandermeerschen, H., Van Tuyckom, C., Hoekman, R., Breedveld, K. & Vos, S. (2011). Understanding the game: sports participation in Europe. Facts, reflections and recommendations. In *Sport policy & management studies* (Vol. 10). University of Leuven/Research Unit of Social Kinesiology & Sport Management. https://gbiomed.kuleuven.be/english/research/50000737/groups/policy-in-sports-physical-activity-research-group/bms-studies/bms10-spm.pdf

UNDP. (2020). United Nations Development Programme. Human development reports: income inequality, quintile ratio. Retrieved December 16, 2021, from http://hdr.undp.org/en/indicators/135106#

UK Sport. (1999). *COMPASS: Sports participation in Europe. A project seeking the co-ordinated monitoring of participation in sport in Europe*. UK Sport.

Van Tuyckom, C., & Scheerder, J. (2010a). A multilevel analysis of social stratification patterns of leisure-time physical activity amongst Europeans. *Science & Sports, 25*(6), 304–311.

Van Tuyckom, C., & Scheerder, J. (2010b). Sport for All? Insight into stratification and compensation mechanisms of sporting activity in the EU-27. *Sport, Education & Society, 15*(4), 495–512.

Van Tuyckom, C., & Scheerder, J. (2008). Sport for All? Social stratification of recreational sport activities in the EU-27. *Kinesiologia Slovenica, 14*(2), 54–63.

Van Tuyckom, C., Scheerder, J., & Bracke, P. (2010). Gender and age inequalities in regular sports participation. A cross-national study of 25 European countries. *Journal of Sports Sciences, 28*(10), 1077–1084.

Wilkinson, R., & Pickett, K. (2009). *The spirit level. Why more equal societies almost always do better*. Allen Lane.

Chapter 4
Denmark: Disability Sports Policy at Arm's Length

Christian Røj Voldby and Karsten Elmose-Østerlund

4.1 Introduction

In Denmark, there are numerous projects, policies, initiatives and programmes advocating or creating opportunities for both children and adults with disabilities to participate in sport. Furthermore, there are several forms of social services and support that may also influence participation in sport. While some are explicitly aimed at increasing sports participation, most are not. In this chapter, we will outline the policies and structures that may influence participation in disability sport in Denmark. Furthermore, we present sports participation levels and compare people with disabilities to people without disabilities. The findings and conclusions in our chapter are based on previous research and reports that draw on national surveys, as well as disability-specific studies; document analysis of relevant documents from culture, education, social services and health policies (e.g. law texts and official guidelines for service delivery); and interviews with representatives from national interest groups. Though our chapter mainly utilises existing data, we offer new insights into disability sport in Denmark by merging the existing information into a coherent narrative.

C. R. Voldby (✉)
Research Unit for Active Living, Department of Sports Science and Clinical Biomechanics, University of Southern Denmark, Odense, Denmark
e-mail: cvoldby@health.sdu.dk

K. Elmose-Østerlund
Centre for Sports, Health and Civil Society, Research Unit for Active Living, Department of Sports Science and Clinical Biomechanics, University of Southern Denmark, Odense, Denmark
e-mail: kosterlund@health.sdu.dk

4.2 Country Profile

Characteristics of Denmark

Table 4.1 provides some key facts and statistics about Denmark. Denmark is considered a universalist welfare state and as such has a high level of redistribution and welfare rights. The system of governance in Denmark is a parliamentary democracy. At the national level, the legislative body is the parliament with 179 elected members. Denmark consists of five regions and 98 municipalities that are governed by elected councils. Most of the health, education and social service legislature is administered and implemented at the local level. The vast majority of Danes live in urban areas supported by a relatively high standard of living and a well-developed social welfare services. These include unemployment benefits, and (mostly) free education and health care.

Sport in Denmark

From 1945 up until the 1970s, there was a significant increase in the amount of governmental support for sports participation. However, no significant political involvement and steering followed (Ibsen et al., 2015). The aims and priorities of sports policy have not changed much over time, and organised sport in Denmark is still characterised by great independence from the state, while at the same time being an integral part of the Danish welfare model. The two primary pillars of support remain the allocation of profits from the national lottery to NSOs at the national

Table 4.1 Facts and statistics for Denmark

Population[1]	5,843,347
Area (km^2)[2]	42,947
Density (inhabitants/km^2)	136
Urbanisation (urban population as % of total population)[3]	88
Political organisation	Parliamentary constitutional monarchy
Structure of the state	Unitary
Number of regions	5
Number of municipalities	98
GDP per capita (US dollars)[4]	60,213
Number of official languages	1
EU membership	Since 1972
Welfare model	Universalist

Sources: [1]Statistics Denmark (2021b); [2]Statistics Denmark (2021a); [3]The World Bank (2021b); [4]The World Bank (2021a)

level and municipal subsidies for sports clubs. The latter takes the form of providing sports facilities free of charge or for a small fee, and an amount paid to clubs based on their membership numbers (typically for members aged 25 or under) (Ibsen & Elmose-Østerlund, 2016).

Historically, both participation in and the organisation of sport have been heavily influenced by the rise of popular movements, in particular the gymnastics movement and the sports movement. The gymnastics movement was primarily tied to rural areas, and one of the three major national sports organisations (NSOs) in Denmark, the Danish Gymnastics and Sports Association (DGI, Danske Gymnastik-og Idrætsforeninger), can be traced back to this movement. Another movement, the sports movement, which was primarily popular in urban areas and, at least to begin with, among the bourgeois, formed the beginning of the Sports Confederation of Denmark (DIF, Danmarks Idrætsforbund) (Ibsen & Eichberg, 2012). A third NSO is the Danish Association of Company Sports (DFIF, Dansk Firmaidrætsforbund), which organises sports clubs associated with Danish companies. Most sports clubs in Denmark are members of DIF, DGI or both, while DFIF is considered a smaller and more specialised organisation.

Table 4.2 provides a picture of the sport profile of Denmark. As can be seen, the primary economic support for the organisation of sports comes through local municipalities, who fund the construction, maintenance and operation of sports facilities. The national sports budget, which stems from national lottery funds, is predominantly allocated to the three NSOs (DIF, DGI and DFIF).

Table 4.2 Sport profile for Denmark

Government authority responsible for sport	Ministry of Culture
Membership of sports club, children (7–15 years) (% of population)[1]	86
Membership of sports club, adults (16+ years) (% of population)[1]	39
Membership of fitness or health centre, children (7–15 years) (% of population)[1]	22
Membership of fitness or health centre, adults (16+ years) (% of population)[1]	25
Membership of socio-cultural club that includes sport in its activities (e.g. employees' club, youth club, school- and university-related club) (% of population)[2]	8
Sport participation, at least once a week (% of population)[2]	63
Number of national sport federations (member organisations of DIF)[3]	62
Number of sport clubs in total (estimated 2006)[4]	16,000
Number of sport clubs that are registered members of an NSO (2020)[5]	11,534
Number of sport club members in clubs that are registered members of an NSO (2020)[5]	2,536,619
National budget for sport (EUR millions)	129
National budget for sport federations (DIF, DGI & DFIF) (EUR millions)	85
Local budget for sport (EUR millions)	660
Share of economic value of volunteers in sport in the GDP (%)[6]	0.56

Sources: [1]Pilgaard and Rask (2016); [2]European Commission (2018); [3]Sports Confederation of Denmark (2021); [4]Ibsen (2006); [5]Tofft-Jørgensen and Gottlieb (2020); [6]GHK (2010)

Regarding participation in sport, the latest national survey estimates that 86% of children aged 7–15 years and 61% of adults aged 16 years or older are 'usually' active in sports. Concretely, the respondents were asked: 'Do you usually participate in exercise/sports?' and were able to respond with 'Yes'; 'Yes, but not at the moment' or 'No'. The percentages reported include only the respondents who reported 'Yes'.

In the Eurobarometer survey, the percentage of adult Danes that are active in sports at least once a week is estimated at 63%. These figures place Denmark among the countries in Europe with the highest level of sports participation. Since the first national sports participation surveys were conducted in the 1960s, the sports participation rate among Danes has increased, however it seems to have stagnated at the current level during the past decade (Pilgaard & Rask, 2016).

Among children, the dominant organisational form for sport is sports clubs. In total, 86% of Danish children have participated regularly in at least one sports activity in a sports club within the last year. A total of 47% have done self-organised sport (outside any organised setting), while 22% have done sport in a commercial fitness centre or other private offering. Among adults, the dominant way to do sport is self-organised (62%) followed by sports clubs (39%) and commercial fitness centres or other private offerings (25%) (Pilgaard & Rask, 2016). Thus, the organisation of sport in Denmark is characterised by a great diversity with both non-profit and for-profit organisations playing a central role.

Disability in Denmark

There is no official and universally accepted definition of disability in Denmark (Danish Disability Council, 2005). However, following the Danish ratification of the UN Convention on the Rights of Persons with Disabilities in 2009 (United Nations, 2006), the social model of disability has seen increased use when organisations and legislators define disability. The acknowledgement, that 'disability results from the interaction between persons with impairments and attitudinal and environmental barriers that hinders their full and effective participation in society on an equal basis with others' (United Nations, 2006) is therefore—at least on paper—a guiding principle in both governmental and grassroot work.

An adequate picture of society's attitude towards people with disabilities remains difficult to capture. A recent study indicates that there is a high level of acceptance of people with disabilities in both workplaces and education (Bøgelund et al., 2015). Furthermore, a number of different organisations are working to protect the rights of people with disabilities. A number of laws and policies focus on availability and accessibility, either directly, such as the 'Act on Social Services' (Ministry of Social Affairs and the Interior, 2015), or integrated into other areas, such as special school provisions in the 'Education Law' (Ministry of Children and Education, 2020), and the priority of disability sports in certain areas of the 'Leisure and Recreation Act' (Ministry of Culture, 2015). Even so, 40% of those who report that they have a

Table 4.3 Facts and statistics on disability in Denmark regarding the adult population, aged 16–64 years (estimated % of population, n=20,386)

	%
No disability	69
Minor physical disability or chronic health problem	17
Major physical disability or chronic health problem	10
Minor mental disability	6
Major mental disability	3
Both physical and mental disability	6

Source: Amilon et al. (2017)

major mental/intellectual disability have experienced discrimination because of their disability. The same is true for 24% of those who report they have a major physical disability. The discrimination stems mostly from experiences in work or education, with family and friends, or when meeting strangers. Interestingly, only 1% have experienced discrimination from other people in the context of associations, including sports clubs (Amilon et al., 2017).

Various measures of disability have been used when surveying the prevalence of disability. Table 4.3 presents the results from a national survey conducted among adults aged 16–64 years (Amilon et al., 2017). Among adults, 31% responded that they had a disability (Table 4.3). Out of these, most respondents identified themselves as having 'a minor or major physical disability or chronic health problem'. It is worth mentioning that the definition of disability in the survey was broad and it includes 'chronic health problems' such as arthritis, stress and similar conditions. Among children, the most prevalent disabilities are mental disabilities (reported by 43% of those with a disability) followed by physical disabilities (reported by 18%) and chronic diseases (reported by 17%) (Disabled People's Organisations Denmark, 2016). It should be mentioned that there are a number of methodological limitations to both surveys. Most notably, the data on children is based on a survey distributed exclusively and directly to parents that are members of disability organisations. Nevertheless, the surveys provide an indication of how many people are living with a disability and of which type.

Emergence or Rise of Disability Sport in Denmark

The beginning of the twentieth century and the introduction of the welfare state resulted in the first stand-alone law securing insurance and support for people with disabilities (at this time, the term invalidity was used), in 1921. As political attention increased, the 'National Association of the Crippled and Maimed' was founded in

1925. The name was changed to 'National Organisation of Cripples' in 1948 and again in 1988 to 'Disabled People's Organisations Denmark'. However, the term disability was used several years earlier, when the 'Danish Disabled Sports Association' (DHIF) was founded in 1971 to promote participation in sports for people with a disability. The organisation changed name in 2016 to 'Parasport Denmark' and is today considered the primary organiser of sports clubs with programmes for disabled people (both mainstream sports clubs with special programmes and disability sports clubs exclusively focusing on disability sport). While systematic registration of membership clubs has proved difficult, the number of membership clubs seems to have slowly increased from 392 in 2009 to 461 in 2018 (Parasport Denmark, 2018).

Parasport Denmark remains one of the primary organisations influencing the organisation of disability sports in Denmark. It is important to also describe the numerous other influential governmental and non-governmental agents. In the next section, we will illustrate how these different agents attempt to influence and promote sports for people with a disability.

4.3 The Disability Sport System

Structure of Disability Sport

Figure 4.1 illustrates both the various agents that influence disability sport and the relationships between them. The most influential financial and structural relationships have been illustrated in the model. In the following, we will describe how the different actors influence the field of disability sport and how they cooperate.

Governmental Agents

As is true for the mainstream sports policy, the Ministry of Culture is a key agent in the disability sports landscape as they govern the distribution of funds from the national lottery. The funds are primarily distributed to the two largest NSOs, Sports Confederation of Denmark (DIF, Danmarks Idrætsforbund) and Danish Gymnastics and Sports Association (DGI, Danske Gymnastik-og Idrætsforeninger). DIF and DGI are key agents in terms of organising disability sports, and we will discuss their role in depth later in this section.

Historically, at the governmental level, most of the disability services and support were organised at the regional level. However, in 2006 the responsibility was transferred to local municipalities. There are therefore no regional actors explicitly linked to the organisation of disability sports. The Ministry of Health and its regional health departments are mentioned in the model, as they indirectly influence disability sport participation through financing and governance of a number of relevant

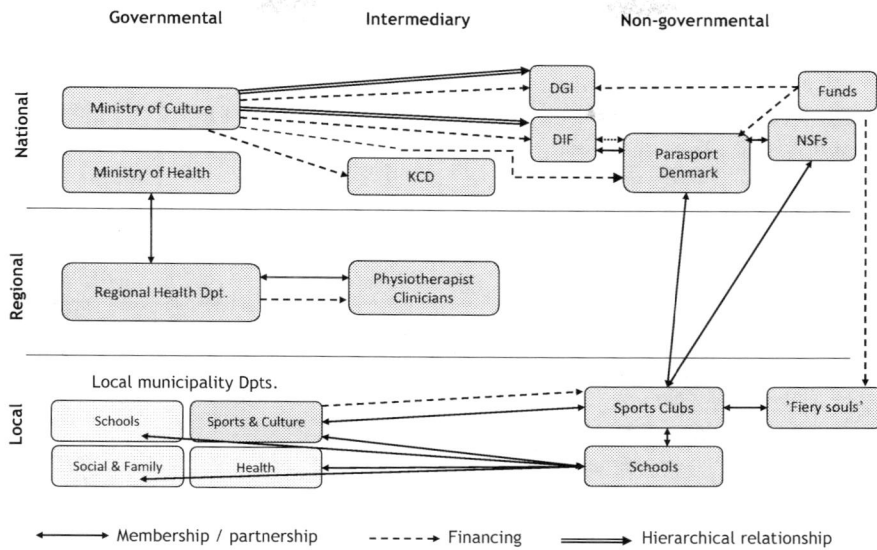

Fig. 4.1 Disability sport framework for Denmark. Abbreviations used: KCD (Knowledge Centre on Disability); DGI (Danish Gymnastics and Sports Association); DIF (Sports Confederation of Denmark); NSFs (National Sports Federations)

regional health services (e.g. specialised equipment). Although this chapter does not focus on the effects of health service delivery, we will briefly touch upon the influence of the regional health services later in the section when discussing the role of physiotherapists and clinicians.

While the national governmental agents are responsible for legislature and policy at a national level, and therefore the grand narrative and direction of disability sports policy, the local municipalities are responsible for actually enforcing and implementing the legislature. Furthermore, in extension of the national policy, these local departments formulate their own local policies.

Each municipality differs in the way they organise their governance, but we identify three key areas that are highly relevant to disability sport participation. It is important to note that our description here will be that of a typically organised municipality, but there are numerous organisational differences across the 98 municipalities. In most municipalities, a 'Sport and Culture Department' is the most explicitly influential agent at the local level. Typically, they administer and distribute access to all local sport facilities. According to the 'Leisure and Recreation Act' (Ministry of Culture, 2015), disability sport activities which require a specific facility must be prioritised above mainstream sport when allocating access to this specific facility. In other words, mainstream sport should not occupy specific facilities that are necessary for disability sport. The Sport and Culture Department also allocates economic support for sports clubs based on their total number of members (under the age of 25). In some municipalities, the sum is increased for sports club members with disabilities.

Another relevant department is the 'Social and Family Services Department' where allocation of social services such as transport and adaptive equipment is administrated. The allocation of such services relies on the 'Principle of Compensation', dictating that compensation must be given, so that people with disabilities can overcome barriers for equal participation in society. This principle is integral to all social service delivery in Denmark, and each municipality carries the responsibility for this. As a consequence, municipalities must work to provide a wide range of support (e.g. logistic, economic, social and medical) in order for people with disabilities to participate in society. This also includes sports participation. Thus, the Social and Family Services Department becomes a very important actor in terms of reducing or even eliminating barriers to participation in disability sports (e.g. in terms of transportation and equipment).

Furthermore, the 'Sector Responsibility Principle' applies to all the different governmental actors. This principle demands that all actors work towards inclusion and equal access for everyone (including persons with disabilities). For example, this means that the Sport and Culture Department is responsible for ensuring adequate accessibility to sports facilities, just like the 'School department' is responsible for ensuring inclusivity in physical education. There is, however, no controlling agent, and the different departments are each responsible for evaluating and following up on the level of inclusion and equal access. The work to ensure inclusion and equal access is therefore spread across the various departments. As a consequence, it is uncommon for municipalities to have dedicated departments working for equal access and rights for persons with disabilities across different arenas.

Intermediate Agents

One intermediate actor, the 'Knowledge Centre on Disability' (KCD), is found at the national level. Before changing their name in 2019, they were known as the 'Knowledge Centre on Disability Sports'. While their goal has been broadened, they still focus on producing knowledge, documenting best practice and advising other actors about adapted physical activity and participation in sports. They are funded partly by the Ministry of Culture and the Ministry of Danish Agency for Labour Market and Recruitment. The KCD can be consulted ad hoc by anyone working within the field of disability sports. They therefore work together with a wide range of governmental and non-governmental actors.

While the influence on sports participation is arguably limited, it is worth mentioning that treatment by physiotherapists is financed at the regional level. This is especially relevant for people with a physical disability, as they rely heavily on treatment from physiotherapists to maintain and develop vital motor functions. Clinicians and general practitioners are often gatekeepers for various types of social services or support and their clinical assessments are necessary when applying for different types of assistance (e.g. specialised equipment and transport). While these services are often not directly linked to disability sports, they may play a crucial role in terms of participation in sports.

Non-governmental Agents

The two large NSOs, DGI and DIF, differ in their internal organisation, but both work to promote sports participation (e.g. by offering sports club development programmes, by managing tournaments and by supporting the national sports federations (NSFs)). DGI has their own department, 'DGI Inclusion', that carries out projects focusing on inclusion in sports, while DIF funnels funds to disability sports through 'Parasport Denmark'. DGI Inclusion is a project-focused department working broadly with inclusion (also for at-risk groups), mostly together with local agents (e.g. schools and sports clubs) (DGI, 2021). Parasport Denmark is an umbrella organisation working together with NSFs, sports clubs and municipalities to help promote disability sport. While most of their membership clubs are disability sports clubs, they also work together with mainstream sports clubs through partnerships (e.g. the 'Paralympics' and development of special education for coaches and instructors). They also organise and manage tournaments in various disability sports (e.g. boccia and goalball).

At a national level, Parasport Denmark remains the biggest and most influential agent. Mainly because the very purpose of the organisation is the promotion of disability sports, but also because the 'National Paralympic Committee' is organised under Parasport Denmark. Some NSFs are, of their own accord, working actively with disability sport either by promoting parasport disciplines related to their own discipline (e.g. the 'Danish Table Tennis Association' promoting para-table tennis), integrating disability sport in the education of coaches and instructors or developing inclusive sport programmes. However, the focus on such initiatives varies heavily when comparing different NSFs. Parasport Denmark has recently changed their strategy to focus more on collaboration with other NSFs. Parasport Denmark is primarily funded through DIF, but they do raise money from various benefactors and foundations.

Parasport Denmark is steered by DIF through a framework agreement, which stipulates the strategic objectives of the organisation, while at the same time providing a set amount of economic resources. While Parasport Denmark must align their work with the strategic directions of the framework agreement, they operate with a relatively high degree of autonomy. In other words, the goals are set, but the approach and methods are undetermined.

The most influential non-governmental agents at the local level are the sports clubs themselves. Sports clubs are key agents, as they provide an arena in which people with disabilities can participate in sport. Either in teams exclusively for persons with disabilities or integrated into mainstream sports. Sports clubs solely for people with disabilities are almost exclusively organised under Parasport Denmark. At the same time, some mainstream sports clubs have teams aimed at people with disabilities (e.g. a handball club with a team for children with CP). These clubs are most often members of the relevant sports federation (e.g. the Danish Handball Association) while at the same time they often become members of Parasport Denmark. Finally, it is worth mentioning that many people with disabilities are integrated in mainstream sports clubs on their own initiative, without the formation of specific teams for people with disabilities. Clearly, this form of integration is most common among people with less severe disabilities (Østerlund et al., 2014).

It varies heavily how much the sports clubs work towards inclusion of people with disabilities. One explanation could be that initiatives often emerge locally, and as a result of a set of circumstances rather than a specific strategy. Many initiatives for people with disabilities are initiated either by people with a disability themselves, or parents of children with a disability, and therefore emerge seemingly randomly across both mainstream and disability sports clubs.

Sometimes, such initiatives are organised outside of regular sports club settings, initiated by one or more highly devoted volunteers. These volunteers are often very passionate about a specific topic or group and work very actively in their local community. Some initiatives focus on a specific cause or group rather than a specific sports activity. Other initiatives stem from a wish to participate in a specific sports activity. Such initiatives will often be associated with or originate from sports clubs.

In Denmark, we have several devoted volunteers who have received public attention for their disability sport projects. For example, the 'Happiness League', a handball league for children with Downs Syndrome, run by a former professional handball athlete, has inspired multiple local handball clubs across the country to create teams for children with disabilities. These projects sometimes transform into grassroot movements and provide many people with disabilities with the possibility of participating in sport. This is the case for the 'Team Twin Association', which currently has eight local departments across the country. The association received substantial support after the founders, two twin brothers (one of whom has cerebral palsy), finished an official Ironman distance together. Associations like these are not necessarily linked to sports clubs, but many do work together with sports clubs in order to get access to sports facilities and other resources.

Steering of Disability Sport

Relationships

As can be seen in Fig. 4.1, the disability sport framework is characterised by relatively few hierarchical relationships, and only at the national level between the Ministry of Culture and the two large NSOs—DIF and DGI. And even in this case, the NSOs have large autonomy to act and achieve the goals within the framework agreements between the Ministry of Culture and each NSO. Apart from this, the relationships mainly take the form of memberships, partnerships and/or financial relationships, and most often the relationships leave significant room for interpretation and action among the implementing actors. It thus seems relevant to describe

4 Denmark: Disability Sports Policy at Arm's Length

the steering of disability sport as 'Disability sports policy at arm's length', which is also the title of this chapter.

Legislative Framework

Based on our description of the disability sport system in Denmark, it may already be evident that disability sport is not explicitly steered through legislation at the national level. While social services and general welfare are heavily steered through legislation, the same cannot be said about disability sport. The most relevant piece of legislation for sports participation is arguably the 'Leisure and Recreation Act' (Ministry of Culture, 2015). While the law does contain certain possibilities for increased support for persons with disabilities in sports activities, it does not directly stipulate how and if local administrations should work to include persons with disabilities in sports activities.

It is worth mentioning that the more general 'Act on Social Services' (Ministry of Social Affairs and the Interior, 2015) has potential influence when it comes to sport participation for people with disabilities. The Act on Social Services provides a set of rights for persons with disabilities that, for some people, help make participation in sports possible. The Act on Social Services is mostly implemented at the local level, as municipalities provide special taxi transportation, adaptive equipment, personal helpers or financial support. All of these services are provided based on the Act on Social Services. The Act on Social Services is arguably the single most relevant piece of legislation in terms of securing rights and equality for people with a disability. While some paragraphs of the Act may indirectly influence participation in sport, one paragraph is noteworthy: section 104 specifically requires the municipality to offer activities (e.g. sports) that are suitable for persons with disabilities (Ministry of Social Affairs and the Interior, 2015). This provides the rationale for and justifies a lot of the programmes that municipalities are carrying out in practice with the aim of facilitating participation in sport.

Additionally, other governmental policies and practice in sectors such as health, education and culture must adhere to four key principles (Danish Disability Council, 2005): The *Principle of Equality* states that all governmental actors must work towards equal rights for persons with or without disabilities. The *Principle of Sector Responsibility* decentralises the responsibility to each subsection of public administration. In short, each actor is responsible for securing equal access. The *Principle of Compensation* states that the government must provide aid and support in order for people with disabilities to participate in society. Lastly, the *Principle of Solidarity* requires service and support to mainly be financed by general taxation. These four principles are the foundations of the disability policy in any field, but are mostly discussed in the context of social and welfare policy. While these four principles are not directly written into the legislature, they are—historically and practically—very closely tied to the Act on Social Services (Ministry of Social Affairs and the Interior, 2015).

Policy Framework

The primary governmental source of influence can be found in the three-year framework agreements that are set up between the Ministry of Culture and both large NSOs, DIF and DGI. These framework agreements include strategic directions and goals, while at the same time determining the financial framework for each organisation. The formulation of goals and visions in the framework agreements is based on a consensus-oriented process with negotiations between the Ministry of Culture and the NSOs. Furthermore, the goals are traditionally formulated very broadly and therefore leave the NSOs with a relatively high degree of autonomy.

In the latest iteration of the agreements with DIF and DGI, a stand-alone strategic focus on disability sports was added. This means that both DGI and DIF must actively work to promote disability sports through partnerships with NSFs, network groups, coach/volunteer education and other projects. The framework agreements were originally set to cover the period from 2015 to 2018. They have since been prolonged to also cover 2019 and 2020. As of today, no new framework agreements have been signed. Together with a strategic goal of establishing better collaboration with municipalities, this constitutes the core of the policy focus on disability sports.

The aim of recruiting more people with disabilities into sport is pursued mostly at the local level, together with sports clubs and other local actors. Several different initiatives and programmes are therefore being carried out across the country, often run by consultants from either DGI or Parasport Denmark. Parasport Denmark also runs two national projects, 'Superinductor' and 'How Difficult Can it Be?'. While the first is a 'matchmaking program', where consultants from Parasport Denmark seek out people with disabilities and match them with sports clubs, the latter is a national promotion campaign featuring posters and advertisements on TV. The objective of more collaboration with local governments is pursued through different project groups in selected municipalities, driven by regional consultants from both DGI and Parasport Denmark.

The framework agreements remain the most overt and direct channel for the government to influence the organisation of disability sport. It is worth mentioning that, indirectly, the government may influence disability sports through legislation that dictates the strategy and practice of municipalities in fields such as social welfare, transportation, culture and sport. However, historically not much has changed in terms of disability sports policy. 'Sport for All' remains the key policy objective and focuses on the inclusion of people with disabilities, migrants and socially disadvantaged groups.

Financial, Governance and Managerial Support

Financial Support

As has been described earlier, Parasport Denmark is the central agent promoting participation in disability sport. While there are other regional or local initiatives, Parasport Denmark may be considered the main provider of managerial support for sports clubs and other programmes and projects working with disability sport. While there are other sources of financial support (sponsorships and commercial activities), Parasport Denmark relies heavily on the financial support stemming from: 1) their allocation of the lottery funds (~ EUR 740.000) and 2) a specific allocation of funds directly from the Ministry of Culture (~EUR 1.4 million) (Parasport Denmark, 2019).

The main financial support for sports clubs at a local level stems from municipalities (local government). There is almost no direct—or indirect—financial support from the state at a national level. At the local level however, the local administrations provide financial support for sports club based on the number of members under the age of 25. They also provide and maintain local sports facilities in accordance with the 'Leisure and Recreation Act' (Ministry of Culture, 2015).

Governance and Management Support

As mentioned earlier, the NSOs receive funds from the state through the Ministry of Culture, which steers the NSOs through framework agreements. There are no other types of direct and formalised managerial support available specifically for the NSOs or NSFs. This further cements the large degree of decentralisation (often referred to as the 'arm's length principle') allowing sports organisations to act autonomously.

Level of Integration or Inclusion

It is difficult to assess the level of integration or inclusion of people with disabilities in Danish society in general, and in sport specifically. The latter question will be treated in the next section regarding the sports participation of people with disabilities. More generally, it is worth once again highlighting the 'Act on Social Services' (Ministry of Social Affairs and the Interior, 2015), which awards concrete rights to people with disabilities. However, the figures noted earlier—that 40% of those who report they have a major mental/intellectual disability and 24% of those who report they have a major physical disability have experienced discrimination because of their disability (Amilon et al., 2017)—point to continuous challenges with integration and inclusion of people with disabilities in Danish society.

4.4 Sport Participation by People with Disabilities

Monitoring and Evaluation

The national survey on sports participation by Pilgaard and Rask (2016) referred to previously in this chapter has not differentiated levels of sports participation according to disability. However, in 2012 and 2016, the 'Survey of Health, Impairment and Living Conditions in Denmark' (SHILD) collected data on participation in sport and physical activity and differentiated this according to disability (including both physical and mental disabilities). The data was collected by a mixture of online surveys and telephone interviews among large representative samples of the Danish population (in 2012: N = 18,957; in 2016: N = 22,771) (Amilon et al., 2017; Damgaard et al., 2013).

A limitation of the data is that the data collection methods are likely to have excluded some groups from participating in the survey. These include people with severe physical or mental disabilities, who are not able to reply to self-administered surveys or to provide meaningful answers on the phone when unassisted. Thus, these groups are likely to be underrepresented in the samples, which should be taken into account when reading the results (Østerlund et al., 2014). However, the data are still well-suited to providing a representative picture of the participation in sports and physical activity among the Danish population, and comparing participation trends among people with disabilities to those for people without disabilities.

Sport Participation

In Denmark, as in many other countries, sport participation among people with disabilities is lower than that of the total population. In this section, we will describe how participation levels vary between different types of disabilities and organisational forms.

The differentiation according to disability applied in the surveys distinguishes between three disability categories: physical disability, chronic health problem and mental disability. Within these three categories, the respondents have assessed whether they rated their disability as 'minor' or 'major'. In the presentation of the results from the 2016 survey, physical disability and chronic health problem have been merged into one category: 'physical disability and chronic health problem'.

In the 2016 survey, only one question was included regarding sport and physical activity. The respondents were asked to report how many days per week they did sport or were physically active for at least 30 minutes (see Fig. 4.2). From Fig. 4.2 it becomes apparent that people with disabilities are generally less physically active than people without a disability, illustrated by the fact that the group of inactive or modestly active people (0–1 days per week) is bigger in all four disability groups compared to the group without a disability. The figure also shows that inactivity is

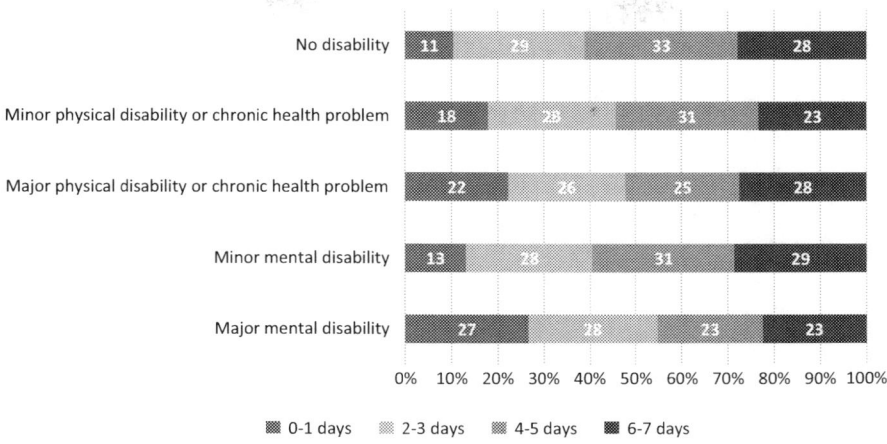

Fig. 4.2 Number of days per week the respondents do sport or are physically active for at least 30 minutes, grouped by type and severity of the disability (%, n = 20,451). Source: Amilon et al. (2017)

most common among people who classify their disability as 'major', irrespective of whether it is a physical disability, chronic health problem or mental disability.

In conclusion, the type and severity of a disability seem to play a significant role for participation in sport and physical activity. At the same time, the percentage distributions inform us that a high proportion of people with a major physical disability, health problem or mental disability are regularly active in sports or physical activity. Thus, many people with a disability manage to fit in sport or physical activity in their everyday lives.

Since the 2016 survey did not differentiate sports participation according to different organisational settings, we rely on data from the 2012 survey for this information. In this survey, the respondents were asked to report whether they were active in sport or exercise in (1) any form or organisation, (2) a sports club, (3) a fitness centre and (4) self-organised (outside any organised setting) (see Fig. 4.2). Figure 4.3 shows that the highest sports participation rates can be found among people without a disability, regardless of the organised setting. Furthermore, the severity of the disability seems to play an important role for the participation rates regardless of the organised setting. They are consistently lower for people with major disabilities.

The distributions in Fig. 4.3 also reveal interesting differences in participation according to the organisational setting. Generally, it seems that people with disabilities participate less in sports club settings compared to other organisational forms. Around three in ten people with a major disability (of any form) do sport in a fitness centre, while this is the case for around two in ten in sports clubs. Statistical regression analysis conducted with the same data further supports this finding, in the sense that the negative effect of the three forms of disability is bigger for sports club

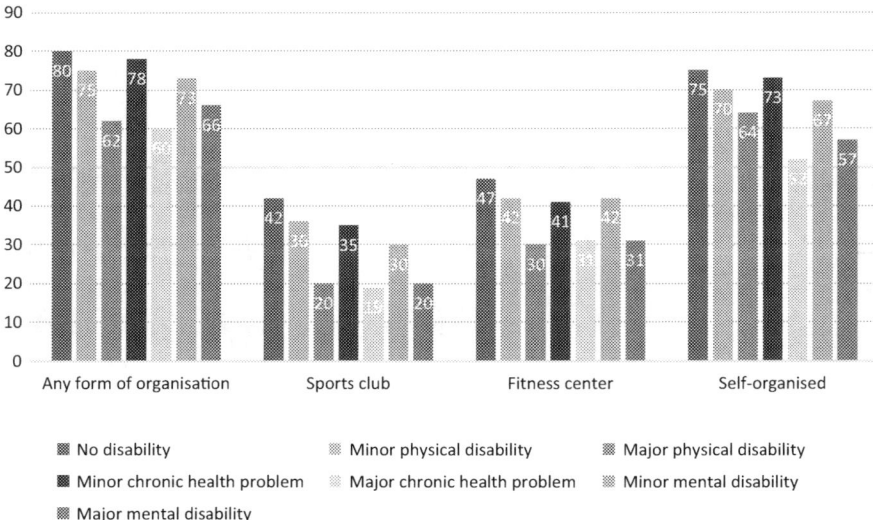

Fig. 4.3 Whether the respondents are active in sport or exercise in general and in any of the three organisational forms: sports club, fitness centre or self-organised, grouped by type and severity of the disability (%, n = 18,957). Source: Østerlund et al. (2014)

participation than for participation in any of the other organised settings (Østerlund et al., 2014).

The same regression analysis also shows that the negative effects from having a disability on sports participation in general, and in the three organisational settings, are reinforced when combined with certain socio-demographic characteristics. The negative effects of having a disability seem to be amplified by: being male, being elderly, having a short-term education, being unemployed and having a low income (Østerlund et al., 2014).

In conclusion, having a disability seems to have a negative effect on sports participation. A negative effect that seems to be strongest in the context of participation in sports clubs. This may be explained by the (often) non-flexible setting of sports clubs (e.g. specific cultural traditions, many people and noise) making participation difficult for people with certain disabilities. While self-organised activities tend to be more flexible and can be adapted to fit specific needs.

A Closer Look at the Sports Clubs

A recent cross-European research project, 'Social integration and Volunteering in Sports Clubs in Europe' (SIVSCE), allows us to more closely examine the structure of sports clubs and their work with integration of people with disabilities. In the project, survey data was collected both at the club level (with the participation of

3631 Danish sports clubs) and at the member level (with the participation of 3163 members from 36 sports clubs) (Elmose-Østerlund et al., 2017).

At the club level, the results showed that a majority of Danish sports clubs (58%) estimated having no members with a disability (physical or mental) in their membership, while 38% of the clubs estimated that people with disabilities made up 1–10% of their membership. A small proportion of the clubs (1%) could be regarded as disability sports clubs in which more than 75% of the members had some form of disability. The clubs were also asked if they had targeted initiatives aimed at integrating people with disabilities in their membership. Less than one in ten Danish clubs (8%) reported having such initiatives (Breuer et al., 2017).

A likely interpretation of the club level results is that although most sports clubs, at least in principle, are open to all who want to participate, few clubs have a specific focus on integrating specific 'target groups' such as people with disabilities. This is also likely to partly explain why a majority of the surveyed Danish sports clubs report having no members with a disability.

At the member level, Fig. 4.4 shows how almost one in five members (19%) in Danish sports clubs reports having some form of disability, of which the most common was a 'physical disability' (11%) followed by a 'chronic illness' (7%) and a hearing impairment (3%).

Among the 19% of members with some form of disability, close to three out of four (73%) reported that their disability did not restrict them in any way from doing the sport of their choice. Thus, it can be assumed that many of these members had less severe disabilities. This can perhaps help explain why only 3% of the members with a disability reported only doing sport in a group that was devoted to people

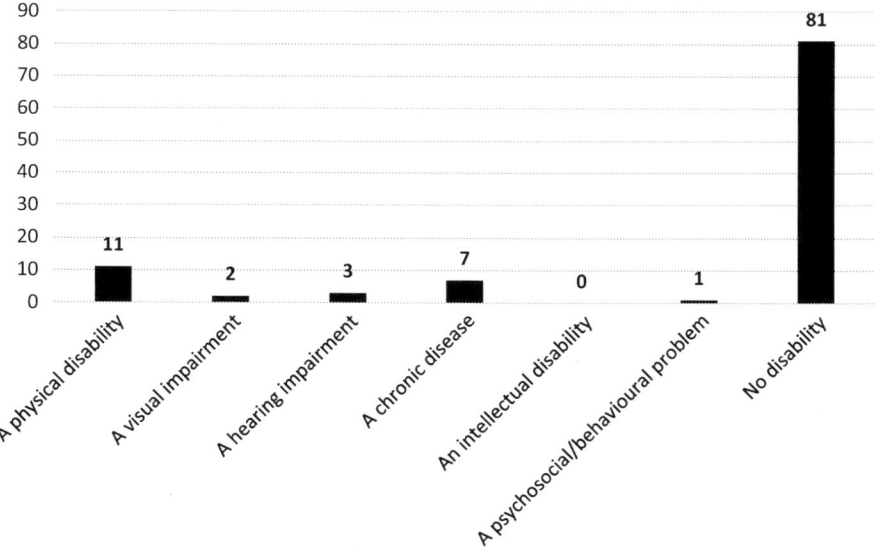

Fig. 4.4 The distribution of sports club members according to whether they have a disability and which disability (%, n = 3163). Source: van der Roest et al. (2017)

with disabilities. Of the remaining 97%, 33% reported doing sport both in a group devoted to people with disabilities and in an inclusive group comprising people with and without disabilities, while the remaining 64% only did sport in an inclusive group (van der Roest et al., 2017).

The member level results can be interpreted positively in the sense that they illustrate that many people with some form of disability are integrated in sports clubs. Furthermore, the results indicate that the vast majority of people with disabilities that are members of sports clubs do sport in inclusive teams/groups (consisting of people with and without disabilities) rather than segregated teams/groups (consisting of people with disabilities only). This could be interpreted as a positive finding, since integration in inclusive groups is often considered an ideal form of integration.

However, the results also show that people with severe disabilities are underrepresented in sports clubs. Because this group is underrepresented in sports clubs and in the survey, the data collected among sports club members could lead us to conclude that people with disabilities are mainly integrated into sports clubs in inclusive groups. However, this conclusion might not apply to the group of people with severe disabilities, who are less likely to be able to fit into inclusive groups within sports clubs. Thus, the results mainly concern the integration of people with less severe disabilities and are not likely to be representative for people with disabilities in general.

Barriers and Facilitators

The barriers to and facilitators of sports participation have been described extensively in the international literature (e.g. Shields et al., 2012). These studies indicate that there are a wide range of personal and environmental factors influencing participation. This is also true in Denmark, but to the knowledge of the authors of this chapter, no large-scale and systematic study of barriers and facilitators has been carried out in the Danish context.

Barriers

However, a list of barriers was developed by two of the primary interest groups: Parasport Denmark and the Knowledge Centre on Disability (KCD) (Ministry of Culture, 2009). The list is based on the two organisations' work and experience with trying to increase participation and inclusion in disability sport:

- A shortage of mainstream sports offers that are accessible to people with disabilities, particularly in sports clubs
- A shortage of adapted sports offers targeted at people with severe disabilities

- A shortage of educated coaches and instructors that are equipped to cater for people with diverse disabilities
- A shortage of specialised equipment in sports clubs that allows for people with severe disabilities to do sport
- A shortage of transport offers to and from sports offers that are accessible to people with disabilities
- Problems related to accessibility at sports facilities for people with physical disabilities
- Economic struggles of people with disabilities due to disability-related expenses
- A lack of coordination and cooperation between sports and disability organisations
- A lack of acceptance from society towards the sports participation of people with disabilities

The list of barriers points towards a need for better quality, quantity or logistical (transportation, accessibility, economic) structures related to sports offers in general. It is also worth noting that while the described barriers may reflect the interests of Parasport Denmark and KCD, they do emphasise the importance of the quality and quantity of accessible programmes in sports clubs.

Facilitators

The authors of this chapter were not able to identify any documents from a specific Danish context that address the facilitators for participation of people with disabilities in sport.

4.5 Conclusion

In this chapter, we have offered new insights into disability sport in Denmark by merging the existing information into a coherent narrative. In many ways, the headline of this chapter 'Disability sports policy at arm's length' sums up well how disability sport is promoted in a Danish context. 'Sport for all' is a stated goal for sports policy, but the concrete and binding policies to promote sports among various underrepresented groups in sport are more or less absent. This includes people with disabilities, who are significantly less active in sport in general, and voluntary organised sport in particular, than people without disabilities.

In many ways, the political steering regarding disability sport resembles the general model of political steering regarding voluntary organised sport, which is built on a foundation of trust. The policymakers trust the relevant organisations (NSOs, sports clubs) to work for the inclusion of people with disabilities, and do not feel the urge to set specific goals for these organisations to meet or have their integration efforts evaluated against. Recently, a stand-alone strategic focus on disability sports was added to the framework agreements between the Ministry of Culture and the two large NSOs, DIF and DGI, but without any specific goals for the organisations to meet. Whether this 'arm's length principle' from the policy makers towards the policy implementers helps to promote or hinder—or has no effect on—the inclusion of people with disabilities in organised sport is an open question. However, given that the Danish sports system relies on the same 'arm's length principle' and has one of the highest sports participation rates in Europe, it is not clear that more detailed political steering (e.g. by the use of more 'targeted subsidies' for the inclusion of people with disabilities) would have a positive effect on the participation of people with disabilities in voluntary organised sport.

A positive finding regarding the participation of people with disabilities in sport is that though the rates of participation are generally lower among people with disabilities, and decrease with the severity of the disability, many people with disabilities are regularly active in physical activity and sport. One could call this 'silent inclusion', in the sense that people with disabilities identify suitable sports activities that are accessible to them inside and/or outside organised settings. As such, many activities and sports initiatives are realised 'bottom-up' by engaged volunteers or professionals, who are often not driven by political agendas, but by personal commitment. More support for and resources devoted to such initiatives could possibly help foster integration of underrepresented population groups in sport, including people with disabilities.

Finally, it should be mentioned that in this chapter the effects of the COVID-19 pandemic on the sports participation of people with disabilities could not be taken into account, as no data on the effect of COVID-19 lockdowns in Denmark were available specifically for people with disabilities. However, so far it seems that the lockdown has had diverse effects, such as changes in activity choices and either more or less sports activity. The long-term effects of the pandemic are still to be evaluated.

References

Amilon, A., Bojsen, L. B., Østergaard, S. V., & Rasmussen, A. H. (2017). *Personer med Handicap. Hverdagsliv og levevilkår 2016*. VIVE – The Danish Center for Social Science Research.

Bøgelund, M., Nielsen, A., Jensen, H. H., & Hagelund, L. (2015). *Befolkningens holdninger og handlinger i relation til personer med handicap*. National Board of Appeal & Danish Disability Council.

Breuer, C., Feiler, S., Llopis-Goig, R., Elmose-Østerlund, K., et al. (2017). *Characteristics of European sports clubs. A comparison of the structure, management, voluntary work and social integration among sports clubs across ten European countries*. Centre for Sports, Health and Civil Society, University of Southern Denmark.

Damgaard, M., Steffensen, T., & Bengtsson, S. (2013). Hverdagsliv og levevilkår for mennesker med funktionsnedsættelse. : SFI – Det nationale forskningscenter for velfærd.

Danish Disability Council. (2005). Dansk Handicappolitiks Grundprincipper. Retrieved December 10, 2020, from https://dch.dk/sites/dch.dk/files/media/document/Dansk%20Handicappolitiks%20Grundprincipper%20handicaptilg%C3%A6ngelig.pdf

DGI. (2021). *DGI Inklusion*. Retrieved May 19, 2021, from https://www.dgi.dk/samarbejd/om-vores-fokusomraader/programomraader/dgi-inklusion

Disabled People's Organisations Denmark. (2016). *DH Temperaturmåling: Inklusion af børn med handicap i den almindelige undervisning*. Retrieved May 19, 2021, from https://handicap.dk/arbejder-vi-for/vidensbank/dhs-inklusionsundersoegelse-2016

Elmose-Østerlund, K., Ibsen, B., Nagel, S., Scheerder, J., Breuer, C., Claes, E., et al. (2017). *Explaining similarities and differences between European sports clubs. An overview of the main similarities and differences between sports clubs in ten European countries and the potential explanations*. Centre for Sports, Health and Civil Society, University of Southern Denmark.

European Commission. (2018). *Special Eurobarometer 472. Sport and physical activity*. TNS Opinion & Social.

GHK. (2010). *Volunteering in the European Union. Final report submitted by GHK*. Educational, Audiovisual & Culture Executive Agency (EAC-EA) and Directorate General Education and Culture (DG EAC). Retrieved May 19, 2021, from https://ec.europa.eu/citizenship/pdf/doc1018_en.pdf

Ibsen, B. (2006). *Foreningsidrætten i Danmark: udvikling og udfordringer*. Danish Institute for Sports Studies.

Ibsen, B., & Eichberg, H. (2012). Dansk idrætspolitik – mellem frivillighed og statslig styring. In H. Eichberg (Ed.), *Idrætspolitik i komparativ belysning - national og international*. University Press of Southern Denmark.

Ibsen, B., & Elmose-Østerlund, K. (2016). Country summaries – Denmark. In B. Ibsen, G. Nichols, & K. Elmose-Østerlund (Eds.), *Sports Club Policies in Europe: A comparison of the public policy context and historical origins of sports clubs across ten European countries*. Centre for Sports, Health and Civil Society, University of Southern Denmark.

Ibsen, B., Østerlund, K., & Laub, T. (2015). Sport clubs in Denmark. In C. Breuer, R. Hoekman, S. Nagel, & H. van der Werff (Eds.), *Sport clubs in Europe* (Sports economics, management and policy) (Vol. 12). Springer.

Ministry of Children and Education. (2020). *Education law*. Retrieved December 10, 2020, from https://www.retsinformation.dk/eli/lta/2020/1396

Ministry of Culture. (2009). *Idræt for alle. Breddeidrætsudvalgets rapport – baggrund og analyse*. Ministry of Culture.

Ministry of Culture. (2015). *The act on non-formal education and democratic voluntary activity*. Retrieved December 10, 2020, from https://epale.ec.europa.eu/sites/default/files/the_act_on_non-formal_education_and_democratic_voluntary_activity.pdf

Ministry of Social Affairs and the Interior. (2015). *Consolidation act on social services*. Retrieved December 10, 2020, from https://www.english.sm.dk/media/14900/consolidation-act-on-social-services.pdf

Østerlund, K., Ryding, K., & Jespersen, E. (2014). *Idræt, fritid og helbred for mennesker med funktionsnedsættelse*. Department of Sports Science and Clinical Biomechanics, University of Southern Denmark.

Parasport Denmark. (2018). *Annual Report Parasport Danmark 2018*. Retrieved September 1, 2020, from https://magasin.parasport.dk/vrigemagasiner/Parasport_Danmark_Beretning/parasport-danmark-beretning-2018/?page=4

Parasport Denmark. (2019). *Annual Report Parasport Danmark 2019*. Retrieved September 1, 2020, from https://parasport.dk/media/3475/2019_aarsregnskab_parasport_danmark.pdf

Pilgaard, M., & Rask, S. (2016). *Danskernes motions- og sportsvaner 2016*. Danish Institute for Sports Studies.

Shields, N., Synnot, J. S., & Barr, M. (2012). Perceived barriers and facilitators to physical activity for children with disability: A systematic review. *British Journal of Sports Medicine, 46*(14), 989–997.

Sports Confederation of Denmark. (2021). *The federations*. Retrieved May 19, 2021, from https://www.dif.dk/en/forbund

Statistics Denmark. (2021a). Area. Retrieved May 19, 2021, from https://www.dst.dk/en/Statistik/emner/geografi-miljoe-og-energi/areal/areal

Statistics Denmark. (2021b). Population in Denmark. Retrieved May 19, 2021, from https://www.dst.dk/en/Statistik/emner/befolkning-og-valg/befolkning-og-befolkningsfremskrivning/folketal

The World Bank. (2021a). GDP per capita (current US$) - Denmark. Retrieved May 19, 2021, from https://data.worldbank.org/indicator/NY.GDP.PCAP.CD?locations=DK

The World Bank. (2021b). Urban population (% of total population) – Denmark. Retrieved May 19, 2021, from https://data.worldbank.org/indicator/SP.URB.TOTL.IN.ZS?locations=DK

Tofft-Jørgensen, L., & Gottlieb, P. (2020). *Idrætten i tal 2019*. Sports Confederation of Denmark. Retrieved May 19, 2021, from https://www.dif.dk/da/politik/vi-er/medlemstal

United Nations. (2006). Convention on the Rights of Persons with Disabilities (CRPD). Retrieved May 19, 2021, from https://www.un.org/development/desa/disabilities/convention-on-the-rights-of-persons-with-disabilities/convention-on-the-rights-of-persons-with-disabilities-2.html

Van der Roest, J.-W., Van der Werff, H., Elmose-Østerlund, K., Albrecht, J., Breuer, C., Claes, E., et al. (2017). *Involvement and commitment of members and volunteers in European sports clubs. A comparison of the affiliation, voluntary work, social integration and characteristics of members and volunteers in sports clubs across ten European countries.* Centre for Sports, Health and Civil Society, University of Southern Denmark.

Chapter 5
Finland: Facts Behind the Long and Complicated Process of Disability Inclusion in Sports

Kati Lehtonen and Aija Saari

5.1 Introduction

This chapter will provide an in-depth view of the key disability sports organisations and their roles in the Finnish landscape. The Ministry of Education and Culture (OKM, Opetus-ja kulttuuriministeriö), which funds national sport policies, is the largest public organisation. Public and third sector organisations create policies and programmes which are then implemented together with several sports organisations and municipalities at different levels from local to national. The double strategy approach in sports services for persons with disabilities means keeping up traditional disability sports while working for and with increased inclusion in the mainstream setting. In many sports, disability sports are already integrated into National Sport Federations' (NSF) structures and policies. However, the level and broadness of this development vary, and the process towards inclusion is still ongoing.

K. Lehtonen (✉)
Jamk University of Applied Sciences, Jyväskylä, Finland
e-mail: Kati.Lehtonen@jamk.fi

A. Saari
Finnish Paralympic Committee, Helsinki, Finland
e-mail: aija.saari@paralympia.fi

© The Author(s), under exclusive license to Springer Nature Switzerland AG 2023
C. van Lindert et al. (eds.), *The Palgrave Handbook of Disability Sport in Europe*, https://doi.org/10.1007/978-3-031-21759-3_5

5.2 Country Profile

Characteristics of Finland

Finland is one of the Nordic countries representing the ideal type of Nordic welfare state. In a broad framework, Finland features the cornerstones of the Nordic model: equality and universality. In addition, the state has a strong role in organising social services and education (Alestalo, 2010). Because of its history as part of the Swedish kingdom for approximately 700 years and the Grand Duchy of Russia for more than 100 years, it is different compared to other Nordic countries. Finland gained its full independence in 1917. Today the number of inhabitants is over 5.5 million.

The population density is low compared to other European countries. However, urbanisation is increasing and the population is centralised around the main cities. For example, more than 20% of the Finnish population live in the capital city Helsinki and its neighbourhood municipalities: the Helsinki urban area. Education, as well as children and adolescents, is at the core of the Finnish welfare state ethos. Finnish children and adolescents have been among the top scorers in the Programme for International Students Assessment, PISA (OECD, 2018), and the educational system has been seen as a Finnish export product (OKM, 2019). Moreover, Finland has the world's highest level of human capital, consisting of education and health, which is considered to be an important determinant of economic growth (Lim et al., 2018) (Table 5.1).

Sport in Finland

There are around 10,000 Finnish sports clubs and 69% of the population participates in sport at least once a week. The characteristics of the Nordic sport model typically include sports organisations based on volunteerism and democratic

Table 5.1 Facts and statistics of Finland

Population (number of inhabitants)	5,518,000
Area (km^2)	338,445
Density (inhabitants/km^2)	18.1
Urbanisation rate (%)	85.4
Political organisation	Parliamentary democracy
Structure of the state	Unitary
Number of provinces	18
Number of municipalities	310
GDP per capita (US Dollars)	42,340
Number of official languages	2 (Finnish and Swedish)
EU membership	1995
Welfare model	Nordic model

Sources: Tilastokeskus (2019), Eurostat (2017) and Kuntaliitto (2019)

decision-making structures. Both the model and the whole sport system are different in Finland compared to the other Nordic countries (Lehtonen, 2017b; Lehtonen & Mäkinen, 2020). What sets Finland apart is that the state has a strong role as a coordinator of sport, especially in regard to funding. The state's sport budget consists of the revenues of the national lottery and betting proceeds. The total amount of the annual budget for sport is approximately 150 M€. The Ministry of Education and Culture (OKM) is responsible for administrating the distribution of subsidies for sports. However, because the sports organisations are also strongly involved in implementing sport policy, the Finnish system is regarded as a mixed model between state and sports organisations (Henry, 2009; Lehtonen & Mäkinen, 2020).

According to the Sports Act (390/2015), the municipalities are responsible but not forced to allocate institutional subsidies to mainstream sports clubs and other local-level associations. The number of sports clubs having grants from the municipalities is approximately 4700 (Koski, 2013), less than half of the total number of Finnish sports clubs.

During the past few years, the governance model of the Finnish sport system has been under construction and several national-level non-governmental organisations have been unified. These structural changes have been the major sport policy issue of the 2010s (Lehtonen, 2017a). The High-Performance Unit (HUY, Huippu-urheiluyksikkö) was established within the Finnish Olympic Committee (OK, Olympiakomitea) in 2013, and five years later the whole organisation was re-organised. The idealistic proposal has been to move towards a centralised, non-governmental structure and to merge both sport for all and elite sport actions into the agenda of one organisation, namely the Olympic Committee (Mäkinen et al., 2019). Along with these structural changes during the 2010s, disability sports federations also re-organised themselves (see Sect. 5.3).

At the governmental level, the new governing model is based on networks of national policy programmes aiming to increase physical activity at the local level. Because education as well as children and youth have been the main ethos of the Finnish welfare state, policy programmes have also mainly focused on school environments and local policy network practices. One of these programmes is Finnish Schools on the Move, the main aim of which is to increase pupils' physical activity during their school days and develop a more active and pleasant overall operating culture in comprehensive schools (Lehtonen & Laine, 2020). By doing this, across the wider spectrum, the sport system has adopted forms and mechanisms of New Public Governance, which is the current paradigm in public sector administration (cf. Grix & Phillpots, 2011; Lehtonen, 2017a; Lehtonen & Laine, 2020) (Table 5.2).

Disability in Finland

Finnish disability politics aims to define disability as a condition which forms in interaction between the individual and obstacles in society. This is an ongoing process from medical model thinking towards social model and human rights practices,

Table 5.2 Sport profile of Finland

Government authority responsible for sport	Ministry of Education and Culture
Membership sport club (% of population)	13
Membership fitness or health centre (% of population)	14
Membership socio-cultural club that includes sport in its activities (e.g. employees' club, youth club, school- and university-related club) (% of population)	6
Sport participation, at least once a week (% of population)	69
Number of national sport federations	70
Number of sport clubs	10,000
Number of sport club members	1.1 million
National budget for sport (€ × 1,000,000)	167
National budget for sport federations (€ × 1000)	22,686
Local budget for sport (€ × 1,000,000)	730
Share of economic value of volunteers in sport in the GDP (%)	0.5–1.0

Sources: EC (2010, 2018), OKM (2018) and Mäkinen et al. (2015)

and it changes the way of portraying and defining disability, with consequences in both terminology and data collection. However, person-first language translates poorly into Finnish, causing long, complicated or, in the context of physical activity, even paradoxical concepts, such as 'a person with an impairment of movement in moving'. Consequently, concepts such as disability sport and disabled athletes or participants are still used parallel to 'parasport' and respectively 'para-athlete' (Table 5.3).

The National Institute of Health and Welfare (THL) has responsibility to collect data related to disability. THL mainly relies on registers and population surveys as its key data resources. Concerning disability statistics, the trend is to approach disability from the perspective of reduced functional capacity. Population surveys use a battery of questions based on the ICF Framework (International Classification of Functioning, Disability and Health) created by the Washington Group on Disability Statistics.[1] Questions about functional capacity also make it possible to identify persons who experience different limitations and compare their situation with the rest of the population (Nurmi-Koikkalainen et al., 2020).

The most reliable data on the prevalence of disabilities of Finnish citizens comes from the FinSote study (see Table 5.4). Approximately half a million Finns (14%) are estimated to have severe difficulties in seeing, hearing, moving or cognition (Sainio et al., 2019).

---

[1] The Washington Group on Disability Statistics is working under the auspices of the UN Statistical Commission. The main purpose of the WG is the promotion and coordination of international cooperation in generating statistics on disability suitable for censuses and national surveys. Its major objective is to provide basic information on disability that is comparable worldwide.

Table 5.3 Changes of disability sports terminology from 1980 until today, from Finnish to English

1980	Today
Invalidi/vammainen [invalid/handicapped/disabled]	Henkilö, jolla on ~ vamma [Person with a disability]
Vammainen/pitkäaikaissairas [Disabled/long term ill]	Henkilö, jolla on liikkumisen tai toimimisen rajoite/toimintarajoitteinen henkilö [Person with an activity or mobility impairment]
Vammainen lapsi/oppilas [Disabled children, pupil]	Erityistä tukea tarvitseva lapsi/oppilas [Children/pupil with special needs]
Vammaisurheilu [Disability sports]	Vammaisurheilu/paraurheilu [Disability sports/parasports]
Vammaisurheilija [Disabled athlete/Athlete with a disability]	Vammaisurheilija/paraurheilija/Special Olympics-urheilija/elinsiirtourheilija [Athlete with a disability/para-athlete, Special Olympics -athlete, athlete with transplantation]
Erityisryhmien liikunta [Physical activity for special groups]	Soveltava liikunta [Adapted physical activity]
Erityisryhmäläinen, erityisliikkuja [Special person]	Erityisryhmiin kuuluva henkilö [Adaptive participant]

Source: Saari (2011b)

Table 5.4 Statistics on activity limitation (disability) in Finland, % of population, 20 years or older, based on FinSote 2017–2018 (n = 26,405)

1. Difficulty[a] to walk half a km (mobility impairment)	5.8
2. Difficulty[a] to read the text in the newspaper (seeing impairment)	2.2
3. Difficulty[a] to hear a conversation between several persons (hearing impairment)	2.8
4. Difficulty[b] in remembering	2.8
5. Difficulty[b] to concentrate	4
6. Difficulty[b] to learn	4.8
Any activity limitation (disability), 1–6	**13.7**

Source: Sainio et al. (2019)
[a]Self-evaluation: major difficulty, cannot do at all
[b]Self-evaluation: poor or very poor

Emergence of Disability Sport in Finland

The history of disability sports in Finland can be divided into four phases of development: the early stage (1920–1960), the period of organisational development (1960–1980), the period of stabilisation (1980–2000) and the new millennium with increased integration from 2000 until today (Kummu, 2007; Saari & Kummu, 2009). Figure 5.1 summarises these phases from the viewpoint of sports associations for persons with disabilities.

The Finnish Deaf Sports Federation (SKUL, Suomen Kuurojen Urheiluliitto, earlier: The Finnish Athletic Association of the Deaf) was established in 1920.

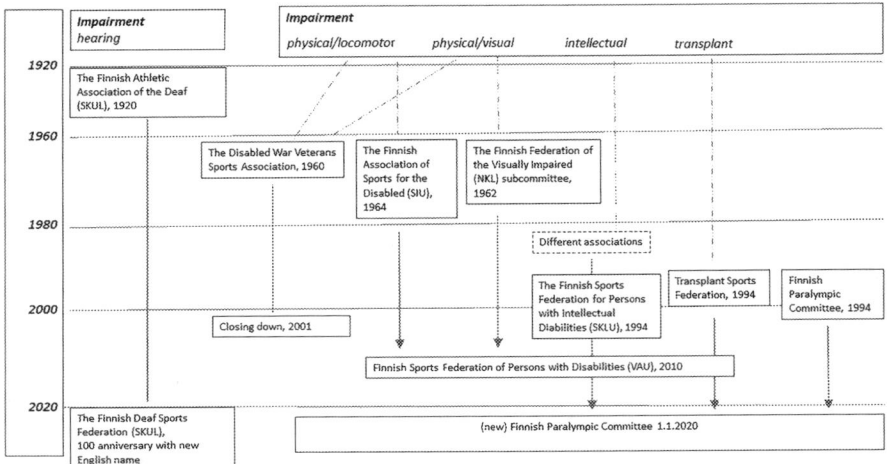

Fig. 5.1 The birth and re-structure of various disability sports associations in Finland

Sports activities for people injured in war (earlier: war invalids and the war blind) started soon after the Second World War in the late 1940s. Disability sports were practised on a modest scale, mostly under the purview of rehabilitation institutes and disability organisations.

In the 1960s, the government started to support disability sport through subsidies. As a consequence, several disability-specific sports federations were established: in 1960 the Disabled War Veterans Sports Association (Sotainvalidien Urheiluliitto), in 1962 a sports committee under the Federation of the Visually Impaired (NKL, Näkövammaisten Keskusliitto) and in 1964 the Finnish Association of Sports for the Disabled (SIU, Suomen Invalidien Urheiluliitto). The latter took responsibility for coordinating Paralympic activities. Sports for persons with intellectual disability started under the Association for Intellectual Disabilities (KVL) in the late 1960s (Kummu, 2007; Myllykoski & Vasara, 1989).

Finland got its first Sports Act in 1980. The law gave disability sports more equal status in Finnish physical culture. Promotion of adapted physical activity and provision of accessible sporting facilities became part of welfare state policy. Several new organisations were established in 1994, such as The Finnish Paralympic Society (today: Finnish Paralympic Committee), the Finnish Adapted Physical Activity Federation (SoveLi) and the Transplant Sports Federation. Moreover, sports activities for people with intellectual disabilities were united under a new organisation in 1994, the Finnish Association of Sports for Intellectual Disabilities (SKLU, Suomen Kehitysvammaisten Liikunta ja Urheilu), which also took responsibility for the newly launched Special Olympics activity (Kummu, 2007; Saari & Kummu, 2009).

The new era started at the beginning of the millennium. Co-operation between national disability-specific sports federations became stronger. In 2010, the national disability sports federations for persons with physical disabilities (SIU and NKL), intellectual disabilities (SKLU) and transplants merged under a new umbrella federation, the Finnish Sports Federation of Persons with Disabilities (VAU, Suomen Vammaisurheilu ja -liikunta). It took another ten years until the next step, namely the unification of the VAU and the (old) Finnish Paralympic Committee on 1 January 2020. Today the new Paralympic Committee is the largest non-governmental disability sports organisation in Finland. It has more than 20 employees, and 203 local disability associations, 61 local sports clubs and 17 Paralympic sports governing NSFs as members.

Since the millennium there has been much effort and progress made towards inclusion. The popularity of Paralympic sports has grown hand in hand with increased visibility and success. Since 1999, elite athletes with a disability have been given athlete grants. Disability sport integration process started in 2002 (see Level of Inclusion). The Finnish broadcasting company YLE started to invest in promoting the visibility of disability sports in the beginning of 2000s. In terms of increased cooperation, the Espoo 2005 Athletics Open European Championships organised in connection with a major mainstream sports event, the World Athletics Championships in Helsinki, was the national turning point. The election of wheelchair racer Leo-Pekka Tähti as Athlete of The Year 2016 was an important sign of equal recognition of elite athletes with a disability.

5.3 The Disability Sport System

Structure of Disability Sports (Fig. 5.2)

Governmental Agents

The structure of the Finnish disability sport system consists of several independent actors from different societal sectors. However, as described in Sect. 5.2, the state has a guiding role. At the national level, the OKM (Ministry of Education and Culture) guides sport policy, its legislation and financing and sports facility construction. The National Sports Council (VLN, Valtion liikuntaneuvosto) is a panel of experts assisting the ministry. The council is politically elected and appointed by the government for the duration of the parliamentary term. It is called upon to address major issues related to sports and physical activity and, in particular, evaluate the impact of the government's actions in the field of sports and physical activity. The council's three sections are supposed to handle issues related to adapted physical activity and disability sport, but usually these issues belong to the Section for Non-discrimination, Equality and Sustainable Development.

The regional state administrative agencies distribute some of the subsidies and act as links between national and local-level sport policy practices. At the local level, 310 municipalities offer sports services for their residents, including people with disabilities. Within the municipalities there are approximately 100 adapted physical activity (APA) instructors, who organise local health-enhancing APA services for residents. This unique Finnish system is a result of various developmental

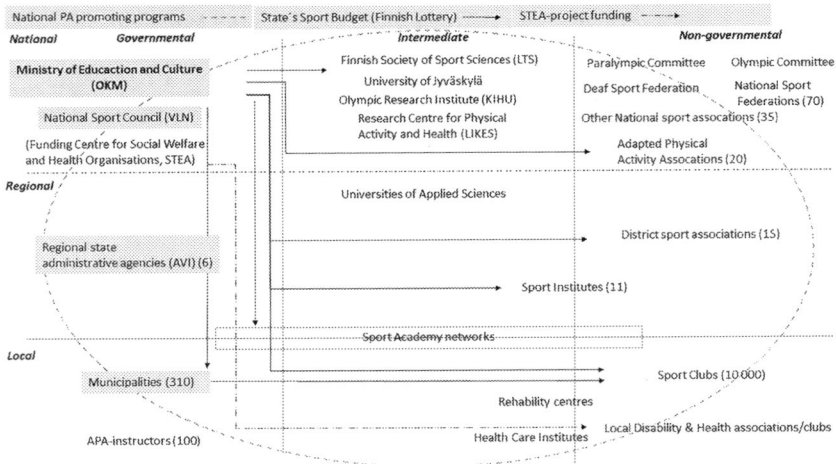

Fig. 5.2 The structure of the Finnish disability sports landscape. Arrows are showing financial relationships

steps, such as the successful development projects of the Finnish Society of Sports Sciences (LTS, Liikuntatieteellinen Seura), starting in the late 1960s, which led to the establishment of the first APA Committee in the Ministry of Education and Culture in 1980–1981. The ministry drafted an amendment to the Sports Act in 1983, according to which municipalities with populations of over 10,000 may hire an APA instructor subsidised by the government. The guiding idea was that APA instructors provided by the local sport system would supplement the supply of disability sports federations. Today they are financed by the municipalities and serve as important links between the public and the voluntary field, as well as between disability-specific and mainstream services (Kaurala & Väärälä, 2010). The network of municipal APA instructors is coordinated by the Paralympic Committee.

Intermediate Agents

The Finnish Society of Sports Sciences (LTS) has an important role between the ministry, federations, municipalities and universities. The LTS organised the first APA seminar in 1969. A national APA congress has been organised every four years since 1986. By maintaining APA networks, collecting national recommendations on APA and organising nationwide APA seminars, it offers meeting places and development platforms for researchers and professionals. The LTS also keeps up an English website on APA (LTS, 2020).

The University of Jyväskylä, other universities of applied sciences and vocational institutes from the fields of health, sports, leisure and rehabilitation are part of the APA networks. In most universities, APA content is embedded in universities' curricula both in theory and practice. For instance, since 2016, over 1200 students all over Finland have received study credits by acting as personal buddies (PAPAI) for children and youths with a disability, assisting them in finding a sporting hobby (Paralympiakomitea, 2020a).

From the elite sport perspective, sport academy networks at the local, regional and intermediate levels cross-cut the sectors from governmental to non-governmental. Academies consist of a diverse group of actors such as municipalities, sports clubs, sports institutes, sports federations and schools. Currently there are 21 academies across Finland promoting goal-oriented training and studying for young athletes, including para-athletes. There are 86 para-athletes at sports academies and the number is rising (Paananen, 2020).

In the area of research, the KIHU Olympic Research Institute and LIKES Research Centre for Physical Activity and Health are the most important actors. The former is focused on elite sports research including para-athletes. Their contribution to Paralympic sport lies mainly in performing physiological tests and a few development projects. LIKES focuses on a physically active life. It conducts and publishes research, provides expert information for decision-making and coordinates development projects and large national action programmes, such as School on the Move.

Non-governmental Agents

The Olympic Committee (OK, Olympiakomitea) currently has no activities around people with a disability. However, its High-Performance Unit is responsible for the selection of and sending the team to the Paralympics. Other non-governmental actors that provide sports for people with a disability include the National Sports Federations (NSF) (70), other National Sports Associations (35) and Sports District Organisations (15) (see Level of Inclusion).

The Paralympic Committee and the Finnish Deaf Sports Federation (SKUL, Suomen Kuurojen Urheiluliitto) have the traditional role of organising and governing sports, physical activity and recreation for their members. They are members of the OK, but still independent, and get their funding directly from the ministry in the same way as other sports organisations. The 100-year-old SKUL is responsible for the sport and physical activity of the deaf and hearing-impaired persons with its 13 member clubs. Until recently deaf sports have not been actively involved in disability sports integration processes. After moving to same office infrastructure in 2018 co-operation between Olympic Committee, Paralympic Committee and NSFs has increased.

Since the merger of the VAU and National Paralympic Committee in the beginning of January 2020 (see Sect. 5.2, Emergence of disability sport in Finland), the new Paralympic Committee is responsible for the sporting and physical activity of people with physical, visual and intellectual impairments and those who have undergone organ transplantation or are in dialysis treatment. It also serves as the national sports federation for disability-specific sports (goalball, boccia, wheelchair rugby and showdown) and for disability sports which have not yet been integrated, such as chess and shooting for the visually impaired, para ice hockey, electric wheelchair hockey, para powerlifting and seven-a-side soccer. Special Olympics Finland is also under the Paralympic Committee's umbrella. The Paralympic Committee runs several recreation and leisure projects and programmes. For instance, there are five regional centres renting adaptive equipment and various accessibility and outdoor programmes (Paralympiakomitea, 2020d.)

Approximately 1000–1500 mainstream sports clubs organise activities for persons with disabilities, which represents 10–15% of the total number of Finnish sports clubs (Saari, 2015b). In addition, there are a large number (around 1500) of disability-specific local clubs and non-profit associations which have a dual role as disability policy advocates and promoters of health-enhancing physical activity for their members. Most of these national non-profit associations are members of the Finnish Adapted Physical Activity Federation (SoveLi). SoveLi promotes health-enhancing physical activity with its 20 member organisations and their local member clubs (approximately 1000) in the field of public health, disability and physical activity.

There are 11 sports institutes (training centres), all of which have services for people with disabilities. In addition, approximately five institutes have more specific training programmes or they organise events for athletes with disabilities. For instance, the Pajulahti Sports Institute serves as the Olympic and Paralympic training centre, Vuokatti Sports Institute has organised several international games in paraskiing and Kisakallio Sport Institute in some team sports, such as paracurling.

Steering of Disability Sport

Legislative Framework

The Finnish Constitution (731/1999) is the basis of all legislation and exercise of government power. It details the fundamental rules, values and principles of Finnish democracy. The Sports Act (390/2015), the Act on Equality between Women and Men (609/1986, amendments 915/2016) and the Non-discrimination Act (1325/2014) state that everyone is equally entitled to participate in sports and physical activity at all levels and chosen roles. Moreover, the United Nations Convention on the Rights of Persons with Disabilities (CRPD), which was ratified in Finland in 2016 (2016), and especially its Article 30, stresses the importance of choice. The Land Use and Building Act (132/1999, amendment 222/2003) and the government regulation on accessibility (241/2017) give guidelines for building accessible sports facilities. The greatest challenge is provided by the old Disability Services and Assistance Act (380/1987) which regulates transportation, personal assistance and special aids. The new Disability Services Act enters into force in 2023, but the application practices of the new Act will be established no sooner than 2025 (Nurmi-Koikkalainen et al., 2020).

Policy Framework

Disability sport has developed hand-in-hand with adapted physical activity (APA) policies and practices. APA is an academic field of study, a profession (see Sect. 5.3, Governmental Agents) and a service delivery or adapted activities for persons with disabilities or hindrances in participation. Disability sport refers to sport designed for, and practiced by, people or athletes with disabilities. Inclusion policy adopted by disability sport federations has brought these two fields together.

The Sports Act, and its amendments in 1984, was a turning point for disability sport and APA (Kaurala & Väärälä, 2010) (see Governmental and Intermediate Agents). In current state policy, inclusion is both the goal and means for the health and wellbeing of the population. Consequently, sport and physical activity are seen as tools to strengthen civil society and inclusion. Provision of equal access to sport for people with disabilities is a crucial part of the policy objectives and programmes of the VLN. However, the disability movement has had only little interest in sports and physical activity. For instance, in the Finnish Disability Forum's survey for the CRPD parallel report (Vesala & Vartio, 2019), access to sports and physical activity plays only a small role.

Financial, Governance and Managerial Support

Financial Framework

The responsible administrator of disability sport on the governmental level is the OKM, Ministry of Education and Culture. It is in charge of distributing the state's sport subsidies to all national-level sports associations, including the Paralympic Committee, district sports associations, sports institutes and sports academies. The only notable exception is the High-Performance Unit, which forwards some state's subsidies directly to NSFs for the development of elite Paralympic sports. During recent years, the total amount of these subsidies has been around 5–6 million euros annually. In 2020 almost €400,000 was targeted at elite Paralympic sports (Olympiakomitea, 2020).

In 2020, the amount of institutional subsidies to perform basic tasks for non-governmental national actors such as sports associations organising activities around disability sport or APA was €2.9 million. There is no follow-up on the financial value of disability sports-related work in national sports federations, but some estimations can be given. In 2013 (Saari, 2015a), 28 mainstream sports federations (out of 70) provided information on working months consumed for disability sports, the value of this being approximately €400,000. Today the value of the disability sport-related work of national sports federations is probably closer to one million euro, but no facts are available.

The financial value of APA or disability sport in non-governmental local-level organisations, such as mainstream sports clubs and public health associations, is even harder to estimate, because they are subsidised directly from the municipalities and may also receive money from other sources such as the ministry, the EU and companies. Since 2013, OKM has allocated project subsidies for local sports clubs' various development projects of approximately €3–5 million, for 300–400 sports clubs annually. In 2019, 25% of them reported disability sport as one of their development targets (Oja et al., 2020). Municipalities also organise APA resources by themselves. In 2017, municipalities targeted resources for APA of between 8–9.5 million euro (Ala-Vähälä, 2018).

Local practitioners, coaches and persons with a disability can apply for grants from private foundations administrated by the Paralympic Committee or other disability organisations (Paralympiakomitea, 2020c). The purpose of these grants is to support persons with disabilities in participating in conferences and sports-related visiting tours, as well starting a hobby. However, the economic value of this is small, approximately €150,000 per year.

Governance and Management Support

When a mainstream sports federation, sports club or other service provider takes over responsibility for disability sport or launches new services for persons with a disability, they often need support. The Paralympic Committee organises grassroots events and try-out programmes which serve as platforms for NSFs to present their sports and meet persons with disabilities. In addition, personnel from the Paralympic Committee act as inclusion consultants on accessibility, adaptive equipment, equality and non-discrimination planning, classification knowhow, competition arrangements and other disability-specific issues. Moreover, web training in APA and disability sport is open to all and free of charge (Paralympiakomitea, 2020e).

Level of Inclusion

In this paper the concept of integration refers to the disability sport integration process and transfer of disability sports, athletes with disabilities and programmes into mainstream sport federations. Inclusion is the ultimate goal of these actions and processes and it refers to equal participation opportunities, sense of belonging and being welcomed.

There were two kinds of projects, financed by the OKM: those which had elite-level parasports transfer into the mainstream federation as the goal (integration) and those that worked on wider inclusion and participation of persons with disabilities. An example of the former was the Finnish Paralympic Committee's integration project during 2005–2007 and of the latter, the Sports for All Children project (2002–2008), which focused on developing inclusive training for instructors and coaches which was further developed in the Open for All Sports programme (2006–2010) (Saari, 2015a).

The status of the inclusion of NSFs has been evaluated three times since 2011. In 2011, out of 12 NSFs which were in charge of Paralympic sports, many reported success in competitions, but challenges in finance and attitudes. They also reported a lack of support for local sports clubs and problems in the recruitment of new athletes (Saari, 2011a). In 2014, out of 70 respondents 38 NSFs had at least some responsibility for disability sports, but there was varied commitment, magnitude and dimensions. Some prioritised elite-level Paralympians and were not keen on taking full responsibility, whilst others tried to cover the whole spectrum from grassroots and recreation to Special Olympics and elite-level parasports. The most successful NSFs have a long history with persons with disabilities. For instance judo and equestrian sports have worked with athletes with disability since the 1980s. The swimming federation took responsibility for disability swimming (today: para-swimming) among the first sports federations in the early 2000s (Saari, 2015a).

The inclusion development received an extra boost in 2015, when the OKM ordered a prerequisite to have equality and non-discrimination strategy documents before being given funding. These strategy documents were collected and analysed in 2018 from a disability sports perspective. Out of 117 documents the majority (86%) mentioned the word disability, disability sports or adapted physical activity, and 84% of documents had concrete plans, programmes or practices, such as accessibility improvements or special programmes for persons with disabilities. Only a small minority (13%) seemed to realise that equal opportunities in sports mean equality not only as a participant or an athlete, but also as a coach or an employee (Saari & Sipilä, 2018).

Local-level surveys for sport clubs show a slight increase in disability sport or inclusive activities. In 2014 (Saari, 2015b), out of 326 respondents 160 (49%) reported having one or more members with a disability, in a total of 41 sports. In a recent survey with 334 respondents the number was 177 (62%) (Saari, 2020). In the Paralympic Committee's sports-finder website called Löydä oma seura, which is a platform for sports clubs and other sports providers has 440 advertisers (Paralympiakomitea, 2020b). Number of sport clubs which organise disability sport or adapted activities is expected to increase with the help of newly launched Avoimet ovet [Open doors] project, which will focus on consulting sports clubs with special issues connected to persons with disabilities' participation in sports.

Barriers and Facilitators of the Disability Sport System and Policy

The independency of actors working in different sectors in the Finnish sport system is a complex question in the frame of system and policy practices. The OKM, which is in charge of funding sports, has not felt the need to create common strategic goals for disability sport and APA, nor to progressively steer the development of inclusion. However, the mixed system has given OKM the opportunity to launch new policy programmes, for example, for schools, and in that way act over the national sports federations. Therefore, the system based on networks and the mixed sport model is flexible and able to better modify its practices and take in the divergent actors which are needed to improve disability sports practices and policies (cf. Lehtonen & Laine, 2020).

At the moment Finland is developing the production of welfare state services such as education and social and health care as a response to growing expenses. Annual social and health care expenses represent more than 47% of municipalities' overall expenses (Kuntaliitto, 2019). Moreover, Finland is ageing rapidly, and, as we know, the risk for disabilities grows with age. According to predictions by Finnish Statistics (Tilastokeskus, 2020) it is estimated that 40.2% of the population over 64 years old will be living in sparsely populated municipalities where the population number is under 2000 in 2040 compared to cities and urban areas (population over 100,000), where the share of the population over 64 years will be only 22%. Many of these ageing and sparsely populated municipalities are located in rural areas. This geographical and age group-based polarisation challenges smaller municipalities' capacity to offer equal services for people with disabilities. In addition, most development projects in APA take place in the largest municipalities (Rikala, 2015). Thus, some policy actions have stimulated geographical polarisation and also inequality for people with disabilities.

One local-level barrier is also the strong autonomy of municipalities. For example, the Sports Act gives Finnish sport its overall framework including equality and non-discrimination, but the law is non-compulsory. This gives municipalities a great deal of freedom when discussing the implementation of the Sports Act. Consequently, persons with disabilities and their sports services are often deprioritised in those municipalities which suffer from ageing and economic problems.

To provide opportunities for persons with disabilities local sport clubs need more trained coaches and instructors, financial support and consultation (Saari, 2015b). Many of the municipals' APA instructors are retiring and their vacancies are often merged into broader fields of health and welfare, which leaves less time for matters of sport and adapted physical activity. Moreover, climate change is setting new challenges for winter sports and Finland's long geographic distances set difficulties. If a person has a disability, commuting is hardly ever a true option.

From the viewpoint of governance, legislation is one of the most important facilitators in disability sports (see Sect. 5.3). For instance, the revision of Sports Act in 2015 contains more equality aspects than ever before. In addition, the Non-discrimination Act (2015) and the Act of Equality between Men and Women (2016) made OKM emphasise these aspects more broadly in sport policy (see Level of Integration and Inclusion). The emphasis on equal access has had practical implications also in those guidelines concerning sports facilities. State subsidies are granted only if accessibility is taken into consideration. This means that an accessibility audit must be conducted in project applications that handle the rebuilding of old facilities. In cases of new building construction projects, an accessibility evaluation document has to be provided (Valtion liikuntaneuvosto, 2014). Guidebooks and knowhow are available for architects and facility constructors, such as those on accessible indoor sports facilities (Kilpelä & VAU, 2013). In addition, the ratification of CRPD in 2016 has given OKM responsibility for following the implementation of the convention in sports and physical activity which, in turn, may in the future result in more equal services for persons with disability.

At a practical level, the Finnish sport system benefits from the nation's small size, long APA history and high-quality university and vocational education for future professionals. Finnish APA professionals are well-connected both nationally and internationally. They keenly follow new innovations and openly share their ideas. Persons with disabilities are represented in most committees and programmes. The ministry's financing system is stable and the general guidelines for various beneficiaries are relatively transparent.

The success and visibility of Paralympic athletes have had a huge impact on public and media attitudes towards parasport and also disability sport in general. Increased visibility has made parasport more appealing to co-operation partners and sponsors. Interest in other disability sports movements, such as the Special Olympics, has also grown.

5.4 Sport Participation by People with Disabilities

Monitoring and Evaluation

The VLN has the obligation to supervise and evaluate the success of sport policy and the impact of the government's actions in the field of sports and physical activity. In addition, the CRPD Article 31–Statistics and data collection states that parties should undertake to collect appropriate information, including statistical data, concerning the participation of persons with disabilities.

The VLN has, for instance, published a report on National Sport Federation's status on disability sports and adapted physical activity (Saari, 2015a) (see Level of Integration and Inclusion) and a status report on the state's role in the promotion of disability sport and APA (Pyykkönen & Rikala, 2018). In addition, the VLN has published a report every four years since 2000 following the development of APA in municipalities, which shows that municipalities are the largest service provider of APA (Ala-Vähälä, 2018). The number of APA groups organised by municipalities is some 10,000–12,000 per year, with approximately 150,000 individual participants. The VLN reports have been used to give guidance on the state's sports strategy and financing policy.

Surveys and studies related to the sports participation of Finnish persons with disabilities are scarce. However, Finland's first initial report on the implementation of the CRPD published by the Ministry for Foreign Affairs in 2019 has a short summary of the OKM's actions towards increased participation of persons with disabilities in recreation, leisure and sport (pp. 61–62). Moreover, the Finnish Disability Forum is preparing a parallel report for the United Nations about the CRPD's implementation and how it has affected the lives of persons with disabilities. The parallel report is based on a survey in 2018, targeted at persons with disabilities and conducted in co-operation with the Human Rights Centre and disability federations (Vesala & Vartio, 2019). The report is due to be published in 2020.

One problem in data collection is the ambiguous and changing rhetoric around the key concepts, such as disability, integration and inclusion. Various actors may have different understandings of inclusion, or, with the intention of being inclusive, they may forget to operationalise it from the point of view of persons with disabilities. For instance, in the large-scale state-led Finnish Schools on the Move programme the main concepts were the 'equality' and 'involvement' of all pupils. When the programme was later evaluated, the data did not give an opportunity to evaluate how pupils with disabilities were involved in programmes compared to other pupils or their physical activity levels before or after the programme (Valtion liikuntaneuvosto, 2019).

In specific disability sport programmes, operationalisation of the inclusion concept can be even more complicated. For some, inclusion is getting into traditional disability-focused activities, separate services and maintaining special knowhow owned by the minority in question, whilst for others it is a process having access to the mainstream, and abandoning disability-focused services and stigmatising labels. It can be both, as stated in the CRPD Article 30. The dual approach (see Saari, 2011b, 2015a; Pyykkönen & Rikala, 2018) respects the processual nature of inclusion and the voices of persons with disabilities and, consequently, may provide more in-depth information to be used in sport policy and programming.

Sport Participation

There is practically no data on the participation levels in sports of Finnish adults with disabilities. Most surveys and studies related to the sports participation of persons with disabilities focus on children and adolescents. The LIITU Survey (2019) is a regular survey of children and young people aged 7–15. Data collection is undertaken every second year and disability is studied through the Washington Group on Disability Statistics (WG). In 2018, the size of the sample was 7132 (72% response rate). Disability is linked to lower physical activity and participation levels. Children and young people with disabilities are less likely to engage in the recommended amount of physical activity than others. Compared to non-disabled pupils, pupils with disabilities are less active during outside recess, far less likely to take part in organised sports activities and less likely to keep to the recommended two-hour limit for daily screen time. Young people aged 11–15 with disabilities participate in sports club activities less (45%) than their able-bodied peers (61%).

The School Health Promotion study (SHP) of Finnish adolescents was a large study of 14–19-year-olds in 2017. In Ng, Sainio and Sit's (2019) report, the data were grouped into physiological and cognitive disabilities through the WG disability statistics and split into active and inactive adolescents based on the PA's recommendations. Approximately 10% of males ($n = 6385$) and 17% of females ($n = 11,107$) reported at least one functional difficulty, and the estimated prevalence of disability among adolescents between 14–19 years old in Finland was 13.5%. Fewer adolescents with disabilities took part in daily PA, especially among those with cognitive disabilities. Males were typically more physically active than females and the levels of PA fell more sharply between the ages of 11 and 16 years among females compared to males. There were fewer active adolescents with walking difficulties, memory difficulties, learning difficulties, concentrating difficulties or general cognitive difficulties than their peers without disabilities. The degree of lowered PA varies depending on functional disabilities, with adolescents with walking difficulties the least active.

The Youth Leisure Time study is regularly repeatable and targeted at children and young people aged 7–29. Children and young people with disabilities was an extra thematic part of the survey in 2019 (Hakanen et al., 2019). The age group in the detached sample was 7–17, but the size of the sample was small ($n = 164$). According to the report, 45% of children and youths without disability (age 7–17 years) are physically active for at least 60 minutes per day every weekday. Among children and youths with disabilities it is only 21%. Boys with disabilities are more physically active (49%) than girls (31%). Physical activity tends to drop with age. In the 7–12 years age group, 26% of children with disabilities are physically active for at least 60 minutes per day every weekday, while the proportion in 13–17-year-olds is 14%. The report also indicates that children and youth with disabilities participate more in organised sport than are active independently in their leisure time: 42% of 13–17-year-olds with disabilities take part in organised sport and 28% are physically active independently. Out of non-disabled children and youths, 49% are physically active independently.

In sport participation research of children and adolescents with disabilities there are certain limitations and challenges. Firstly, there is a lack of objective measures. Self-reported measures often exclude those with severe disabilities or who have difficulties in reading or writing. Special schools or classes are often excluded from school-based surveys. Understanding what physical activity or sports participation is can be challenging for respondents with disabilities. Moreover, different ways of questioning on disability or long-term illness make it hard to make comparisons between various studies. The questions of the WG on Disability Statistics have rapidly spread into surveys, but they are still in the development phase. For instance in the School Health Promotion study, the original WG module was intended for parents or caregivers to respond to and the researcher had to modify the items for adolescents (Ng et al., 2019). In addition, the measure used for walking difficulties may not be the best indicator for a person with physical impairment or using a wheelchair. However, there are some promising research initiatives. For instance the TUTKA (Participation of pupils with disabilities and long-term illnesses in surveys of physical activity behaviour) project is currently developing accessible and easy-to-read questionnaires to apply in special schools (Pikkupeura et al., 2020).

Barriers and Facilitators of Sport Participation from the Individual Point of View

Barriers to sports participation can be divided into internal and external factors. For young people with a disability, internal factors include feelings of loneliness, fear of being bullied, lack of self-confidence, lack of time, lack of money, lack of knowledge of suitable sporting opportunities and health conditions. The external barriers are lack of suitable sporting opportunities, lack of accessible and safe spaces to do sports, lack of skilled coaches, leaders or assistants, the financial expense of hobbies and transportation problems. The barriers are similar with adults and the elderly, but with adults poor education, lack of time and tiredness play a greater role. The ageing population faces more problems with health, pain and safety (Pyykkönen & Rikala, 2018, p. 29). In addition, according to Hakanen et al. (2019), children and youth with disabilities living in the countryside participate less in sporting hobbies. The most active ones live in the larger cities. However, there is lack of research about hindrances and facilitators of sport participation of persons with disabilities.

One of the most promising recent approaches is the PAPAI-model. The PAPAI is a personal coach or buddy who helps a participant with disabilities to find a suitable hobby and overcome most common barriers. Since 2017, approximately 900 children and youths with disabilities have gone through the try-out period organised by students, who receive study credits by acting as a PAPAI. The success rate is close to 50% both in finding a hobby and increasing self-reported physical activity levels (Paralympiakomitea, 2020a).

5.5 Conclusion

In Finland there is a relatively good knowledge base on disability sports history and policies. Disability sports and adapted physical activities have traditionally been organised only in separate settings and based on diagnoses and disability. At the early stage, persons with disabilities were not able to participate in mainstream sports services due to inaccessible facilities, lack of knowledge or negative attitudes. Segregation was justified by (re)habitational goals, peer support and empowerment. Persons with disabilities started to organise their own events and competitions such as the Paralympics, Special Olympics, Transplant Sports and Deaf Sports. This was the only way to get an opportunity to participate in sports or have fair competition.

There is a lack of knowledge with regard to the sports participation of Finnish people with disabilities. The largest gaps concern adults, their physical activity (PA) levels, if they are members of local sports clubs and what are their hindrances and facilitators in doing sports. To fill in the gaps, there are three options. We can try to get more out of existing registers, add new questions to general physical activity surveys and programme evaluations or launch new research concerning physical activity and the sports participation of persons with disabilities. In each option, it is important to define key concepts such as impairment and disability, physical activity and participation in a solid and consistent way to provide reliable and comparable data.

Sports are not separated from society. There has been a shift from the special and segregated towards the mainstream. The inclusive change is most visible in school settings, where the number of special schools has diminished. The majority of elite athletes with a disability are already members in their sport-specific sports clubs and federations, and most disability sports are organised by their sport-specific federations. In addition, disability sports federations have gone through several unification processes. The ongoing change sets challenges for evaluators and governing bodies. For instance, some organisations may have been working inclusively for thirty years, whilst others are just at the beginning. Evaluation is a tool to provide important information for knowledge-based decision-making.

The autonomy of actors and the mixed overall sport system have been both barriers and facilitators of Finnish disability sports development. The state as a main responsible agent of Finnish sport policy and financing has been a good 'back rest' for disability sport: negotiations are organised only between state and disability sports organisations without other intermediate actors. This has increased the trust between single actors in the disability sport system and the state. The state can act as a strong source of the legitimation of inclusion processes. Accordingly, the autonomy and independence of actors can be a barrier to achieving common goals and acting together. To maintain the balance between single interests and national disability sport policy, more attention should be focused on common goal-setting and composing mutually shared policy actions.

References

Act on Disability Services and Assistance. (380/1987). Retrieved August 6, 2020, from https://www.finlex.fi/fi/laki/ajantasa/1987/19870380
Act on Equality between Women and Men. (609/1986). Retrieved August 6, 2020, from https://www.finlex.fi/fi/laki/ajantasa/1986/19860609
Ala-Vähälä, T. (2018). *Soveltavan liikunnan tilanne kunnissa* [The status of adapted physical activity in municipalities]. Valtion liikuntaneuvoston julkaisuja 3/2018. Opetus- ja kulttuuriministeriö & Valtion liikuntaneuvosto.
Alestalo, M. (2010). Pohjoismainen malli ja Suomi [The Nordic model and Finland]. *Sosiologia, 47*(4), 300–309.
Convention on the Rights of Persons with Disabilities, CRPD. (27/2016). Retrieved August 16, 2020, from https://www.finlex.fi/fi/sopimukset/sopsteksti/2016/20160027/20160027_2
EC (European Commission). (2010). *Volunteering in the European Union*. Final Report submitted by GHK. European Commission. Retrieved March 6, 2020, from https://ec.europa.eu/citizenship/pdf/doc1018_en.pdf
EC (European Commission). (2018). *Special Eurobarometer sport and physical activity*. Special Eurobarometer 472 – Wave EB88.4 – TNS Opinion & Social. European Commission.
Eurostat. (2017). *Population density*. Retrieved March 5, 2020, from https://ec.europa.eu/eurostat/tgm/table.do?tab=table&init=1&language=en&pcode=tps00003&plugin=1

Government Regulation on Accessibility [Valtioneuvoston asetus rakennuksen esteettömyydestä]. (241/2017). Retrieved November 26, 2020, from https://www.finlex.fi/fi/laki/alkup/2017/20170241

Grix, J., & Phillpots, L. (2011). Revisiting the 'governance narrative': 'Asymmetrical network governance' and the deviant case of the sports policy sector. *Public Policy and Administration, 26*(1), 3–19.

Hakanen, T., Myllyniemi, S., & Salasuo, M. (2019). *Takuulla liikuntaa. Kyselytutkimus toimintarajoitteisten lasten ja nuorten liikunnan harrastamisesta ja vapaa-ajasta* [Physical activity guaranteed. Survey of participation in physical activity and sport and the leisure time of children and young people with disabilities]. Nuorisotutkimusverkoston/Nuorisotutkimusseuran verkkojulkaisuja 142, Valtion liikuntaneuvoston julkaisuja 2019:5 & Valtion nuorisoneuvoston julkaisuja nro 62. Retrieved November 26, 2020, from https://www.liikuntaneuvosto.fi/wp-content/uploads/2019/09/Takuulla_liikuntaa_Verkkojulkaisu_020619.pdf

Henry, I. (2009). European models of sport: Governance, organizational change and sports policy in the EU. *Hitotsubashi Journal of Arts and Sciences, 50*, 41–52.

Kaurala, O., & Väärälä, A. (2010). *Erityisestä kaikille avoimeen liikuntaan – suomalaisen erityisliikunnan juuret ja kehittyminen* [From special to open for all physical activity – roots and development of Finnish adapted physical activity]. Tutkimuksia 1/2010. University of Jyväskylä, liikuntatieteiden laitos

Kilpelä, N., & VAU. (2013). *Esteettömät sisäliikuntatilat* [Accessible indoor sporting facilities]. Opetus- ja kulttuuriministeriö. Liikuntapaikkajulkaisu 106. Rakennustieto Oy.

Koski, P. (2013). Liikunta- ja urheiluseuroja koskeva tietopohja ja sen kehittäminen. In Valtion liikuntaneuvosto (Ed.), *Liikunnan kansalaistoiminnan tietopohja. Valtion liikuntaneuvoston julkaisuja 6/2013*. Opetus- ja kulttuuriministeriö & Valtion liikuntaneuvosto.

Kummu, L. (2007). *Kummajaisesta huippu-urheiluksi. Suomen vammaisurheilun historia 1960–2005* [The history of Finnish disabled sport]. University of Jyväskylä.

Kuntaliitto. (2019). *Number of Finnish municipalities*. Retrieved March 6, 2020, from https://www.kuntaliitto.fi/tilastot-ja-julkaisut/kaupunkien-ja-kuntien-lukumaarat-ja-vaestotiedot

Land Use and Building Act. (132/1999, amendment 222/2003). Retrieved August 16, 2020, from https://www.finlex.fi/fi/laki/ajantasa/1999/19990132?search%5Btype%5D=pika&search%5Bpika%5D=maank%C3%A4ytt%C3%B6

Lehtonen, K. (2017a). *Muuttuvat rakenteet – Staattiset verkostot. Suomalaisen liikunta- ja urheilujärjestelmän rakenteelliset muutokset 2008-2015* [Changing structures – static networks. The Finnish sport system's structural changes in 2008–2015]. [Academic Dissertation, Liikunnan ja kansanterveyden julkaisuja 331, LIKES-tutkimuskeskus].

Lehtonen, K. (2017b). Building of the legitimacy of a sports organisation in a hybridised operating environment – Case Finland. *European Journal for Sport and Society, 14*(2), 166–181.

Lehtonen, K., & Laine, K. (2020). Creating new sport policy – The case of the Finnish Schools on the Move program. In M. B. Tin, F. Telseth, J. O. Tangen, & R. Giulianotti (Eds.), *The Nordic model and physical culture* (pp. 21–35). Routledge.

Lehtonen, K., & Mäkinen, J. (2020). The Finnish sport system in transition: From a mixed model back to the Nordic sport movement? In M. B. Tin, F. Telseth, J. O. Tangen, & R. Giulianotti (Eds.), *The Nordic model and physical culture* (pp. 117–130). Routledge.

LIITU Survey. (2019). Lasten ja nuorten liikuntakäyttäytyminen Suomessa -tutkimus. In: S. Kokko & L. Martin (Eds.), *Valtion liikuntaneuvoston julkaisuja 2019:1*. Valtion liikuntaneuvosto.

Lim, S. S., Updike, R. L., Kaldjian, A. S., Barber, R. M., Cowling, K., York, H., Friedman, J., Xu, R., Whisnant, J. L., Taylor, J. H., Leever, T. A., Roman, Y., Bryant, M. F., Dieleman, J., Gakidou, E., & Murray, C. J. L. (2018). Measuring human capital: A systematic analysis of 195 countries and territories. *Lancet, 392*(10154), 1217–1234.

LTS, Liikuntatieteellinen Seura. (2020). *Adapted physical activity*. Retrieved August 10, 2020, from https://www.sportscience.fi/adapted-physical-activity.html

Mäkinen, J., Aarresola, O., Frantsi, J., Laine, K., Lehtonen, K., Lämsä, J., Saari, A., & Vihinen, T. (2015). *Liikuntajärjestöjen arvioinnin kehittäminen ja lajiliittokysely* [Developing an evaluation of sport organisations]. KIHU.
Mäkinen, J., Lämsä, J., & Lehtonen, K. (2019). The structural changes of Finnish sports policy networks, 1989–2017. *International Journal of Sport Policy and Politics, 11*(4), 561–583.
Myllykoski, M., & Vasara, V. (1989). *Suomen Invalidien Urheiluliitto 1964-1989* [History of Finnish Association of Sports for the Disabled (SIU) 1964-1989]. SIU.
Ng, K., Sainio, P., & Sit, C. (2019). Physical activity of adolescents with and without disabilities from a complete enumeration study (n = 128,803): School Health Promotion Study 2017. *International Journal of Environmental Research and Public Health, 16*(17), 31–56. https://doi.org/10.3390/ijerph16173156
Non-discrimination Act. (1325/2014). Retrieved August 16, 2020, from https://www.finlex.fi/fi/laki/ajantasa/2014/20141325?search%5Btype%5D=pika&search%5Bpika%5D=yhdenvertaisuuslaki
Nurmi-Koikkalainen, P., Toikka, I., Muuri, A., & Sivula, S. (Eds.). (2020). Roadmap for Systematic Data Collection in Services for People with Disabilities. Finnish Institute for Health and Welfare (THL). Discussion paper 18/2020. 43 p. ISBN 978-952-343-491-2 (online publication). Retrieved November 23, 2020, from http://urn.fi/URN:ISBN:978-952-343-491-2
OECD. (2018). *Pisa 2015: Results in focus.* OECD. Retrieved January 5, 2020, from http://www.oecd.org/pisa/pisa-2015-results-in-focus.pdf
Oja, S., Turunen, M., Inkinen, V., Turpeinen, S., & Lehtonen, K. (2020). *Seuratukihakemusten arviointi 2019.* Seurantaraportti [Evaluation of the state's sports club subsidies]. LIKES-tutkimuskeskus. Retrieved March 3, 2020, from https://www.likes.fi/filebank/2876-Seuratuki2019.pdf
OKM (Ministry of Education and Culture). (2018). *Liikuntatoimi tilastojen valossa* [Basic statistics of Finnish sport]. Opetus- ja kulttuuriministeriö. Retrieved January 12, 2020, from http://julkaisut.valtioneuvosto.fi/bitstream/handle/10024/161346/OKM_2018_41_Liikuntatoimi_tilastojen_valossa.pdf
OKM (Ministry of Education and Culture). (2019). *A brief report on Finnish education exporting* [online]. Ministry of Education and Culture. Retrieved February 18, 2020, from https://minedu.fi/artikkeli/-/asset_publisher/opetusministeri-sanni-grahn-laasosen-koulutusvientimatkalla-15-uutta-sopimusta-ja-yhteistyoavausta
Olympiakomitea. (2020). *Huippu-urheilutuet* [Subsidies for elite sport]. Retrieved June 9, 2020, from https://www.olympiakomitea.fi/huippu-urheilu/huippuvaiheen-ohjelma/valmennuksen-tukijarjestelma/
Paananen, A. (2020). *Olympiakomitea, yhteenveto urheiluakatemioiden ilmoittamista tunnusluvuista OKM kehittämisavustuksen haussa 2019* [Sport academies: Basic statistics and summary]. KIHU.
Paralympiakomitea. (2020a). *Valtti-ohjelma* [The PAPAI programme]. Retrieved February 19, 2020, from https://www.paralympia.fi/liikunta/lapset-ja-nuoret/valtti/in-english
Paralympiakomitea. (2020b). *Löydä oma seura -palvelu* [Find your own hobby service]. Retrieved March 5, 2020, from https://www.paralympia.fi/palvelut/loyda-oma-seura
Paralympiakomitea. (2020c). *Apurahat ja tuet* [Grants and financial support]. Retrieved February 19, 2020, from https://www.paralympia.fi/palvelut/apurahat-ja-tuet
Paralympiakomitea. (2020d). *Perustietoa Paralympiakomiteasta* [Basics of Finnish Paralympic Committee]. Retrieved August 5, 2020, from https://www.paralympia.fi/paralympiakomitea/yleisesti-paralympiakomiteasta
Paralympiakomitea. (2020e). Verkkokoulutus [Web course]. Retrieved August 10, 2020, from https://www.paralympia.fi/verkkokoulutus
Pikkupeura, V., Asunta, P., Villberg, J., & Rintala, P. (2020). Tukea tarvitsevien lasten vapaa-ajan liikunta-aktiivisuus, ohjatun liikunnan harrastaminen ja liikunnan esteet. *Liikunta & Tiede, 57*(1), 62–69.

Pyykkönen, T., & Rikala, S. (2018). *Valtio soveltavan liikunnan ja vammaisurheilun edistäjänä* [The state as a contributor of adapted physical activity and disability sport]. Valtion liikuntaneuvoston julkaisuja 4/2018. Opetus- ja kulttuuriministeriö & Valtion liikuntaneuvosto.

Rikala, S. (2015). *Kohti yhdenvertaisia kuntien liikuntapalveluita. Erityisliikuntaa kuntiin 2013–2015-hankkeen loppuraportti* [Towards equal sports services in municipalities]. Liikuntatieteellisen Seuran tutkimuksia ja selvityksiä nro 12.

Saari, A. (2011a). *Kaikille avoimen liikuntakulttuurin esteet ja nosteet. Väliraportti liikunta- ja urheilujärjestöjen integraation prosesseista* [Inclusive sports culture, hindrances and promoters]. Suomen Vammaisurheilu ja -liikunta VAU ry. Retrieved March 5, 2020, from https://www.paralympia.fi/images/tiedostot/Raportit/kaikille_avoimen_liikuntakulttuurin_esteet_ja_nosteet_2011.pdf

Saari, A. (2011b). *Inkluusion nosteen ja esteet liikuntakulttuurissa. Tavoitteena kaikille avoin liikunnallinen iltapäivätoiminta* [Promotors and hindrances of inclusion in sports and physical activity- aiming at open-for-all after-school activities] [Dissertation, Studies in Sport, Physical Education and Health, University of Jyväskylä].

Saari, A. (2015a). *Vammaisurheilu ja erityisliikunta lajiliitoissa* [Disability sports and adapted physical activity in National Sports Federations]. Valtion liikuntaneuvoston julkaisuja 1/2015. Opetus- ja kulttuuriministeriö & Valtion liikuntaneuvosto.

Saari, A. (2015b). *Erityisliikunta ja vammaisurheilu seuroissa* [Adapted physical activity and disability sports in sport clubs]. Suomen Vammaisurheilu ja -liikunta VAU ry. Retrieved March 5, 2020, from https://www.paralympia.fi/images/tiedostot/ladattavat-tiedostot/vammaisurheilujaerityisliikuntaseuroissa2015-1.pdf

Saari, A. (2020). *Avoimet ovet -kysely urheiluseuroille* [Open doors survey for sport clubs]. Preliminary results, non-published report. Finnish Paralympic Committee, 24.11.2020.

Saari, A. & Kummu, L. (2009) *Vammaisurheilun historianäyttelyn tekstit ja kuvat englanniksi* [Disability sports exhibition texts and photos in English]. Retrieved February 29, 2020, from https://www.paralympia.fi/palvelut/materiaalit/vammaisurheilu-suomessa-historianayttely

Saari, A., & Sipilä, V. (2018). *Vammaisuus, terveydentila ja toimintakyky liikuntajärjestöjen yhdenvertaisuussuunnitelmissa* [Disability, health condittition and functional ability in non-discrimination planning of national sport federations]. Suomen Vammaisurheilu ja -liikunta VAU ry. Retrieved March 5, 2020, from https://www.paralympia.fi/images/tiedostot/Raportit/yhdenvertaisuusraportti-1.pdf

Sainio, P., Parikka, S., Pentala-Nikulainen, O., Ahola, S., Aalto, A.-M., Muuri, A., Nurmi-Koikkalainen, P., Martelin, T., Koskela, T. & Koskinen, S. (2019). Toimintarajoitteisten ihmisten kokemuksia terveyspalveluista [Experiences of health services by persons with functional difficulties]. In: L. Kestilä & S. Karvonen (Eds.), *Suomalaisten hyvinvointi 2018* (pp. 246–264). Terveyden ja hyvinvoinnin laitos. Retrieved November 23, 2020, from http://urn.fi/URN:ISBN:978-952-343-256-7

Sports Act. (390/2015). Retrieved February 19, 2020, from https://www.finlex.fi/fi/laki/alkup/2015/20150390

The Finnish Convention. (731/1999). Retrieved November 20, 2020, from https://finlex.fi/fi/laki/ajantasa/1999/19990731?search%5Btype%5D=pika&search%5Bpika%5D=perustuslaki

Tilastokeskus. (2019). *Suomi lukuina 2019* [Finland in numbers in 2019]. Retrieved March 6, 2020, from http://www.stat.fi/tup/julkaisut/tiedostot/julkaisuluettelo/yyti_sul_201900_2019_21459_net.pdf

Tilastokeskus. (2020). *Yli 64-vuotiaat kunnittain -tilasto* [Statistics: The number of 64-year-olds per municipality]. Retrieved February 19, 2020, from https://www.stat.fi/tup/alueonline/k_vaesto.html

Valtion liikuntaneuvosto. (2014). *Liikuntapaikkarakentamisen suunta-asiakirja* [Guidelines for sports facility construction]. Valtion liikuntaneuvoston julkaisuja 2014:4. Opetus- ja kulttuuriministeriö & Valtion liikuntaneuvosto.

Valtion liikuntaneuvosto. (2019). *Liikkuva koulu -ohjelman kärkihankekauden 2015–2018 ulkoinen arviointi* [Evaluation of the Finnish Schools on the Move programme]. Valtion liikuntaneuvoston julkaisuja 2019:4. Opetus- ja kulttuuriministeriö & Valtion liikuntaneuvosto.

Vesala, H., & Vartio, E. (2019). *Miten vammaisten ihmisten oikeudet toteutuvat Suomessa? Vammaisfoorumin vuonna 2018 toteuttaman kyselyn tulokset taulukkomuodossa* [The Finnish Disability Forum's first evaluation report on CRPD]. Retrieved February 29, 2020, from https://vammaisfoorumi.fi/wp-content/uploads/2019/10/VFKyselyn-perusraportti2019_2.pdf

Chapter 6
Disability and Sport in Iceland

Ingi Þór Einarsson and Vidar Halldorsson

6.1 Introduction

This chapter will provide an overview of sport for people with disabilities in Iceland. The official history of disability sport in Iceland is short but has distinctiveness. Disability sport in Iceland emerged from within Iceland's mainstream non-disabled sports association in the 1970s. This means that disability sport in Iceland was, from the beginning, fully integrated into the Icelandic sports association. However, from the start, most of the actual training and competitions took place in segregated settings. Even though inclusion and integration are more common today than ever before, disability sport in Iceland is still mostly in segregated settings. There is no official policy to date existing to increase inclusion for people with disabilities in mainstream sport. What furthermore makes disability sport in Iceland somewhat unique is that there has never been any discrimination between different disabilities. For instance, the Special Olympics and the Paralympic office are the same in Iceland. Disability sport is further widely acknowledged in Iceland's general culture, where, for instance, the top-level athletes are well known, especially concerning the Olympics and the Paralympics every four years. Icelandic athletes with disabilities have thus been prominent in the competition for the prestigious sportsperson of the year award, and Kristín Rós Hákonardóttir, a disabled swimmer, has been inducted into the Icelandic Sports Hall of Fame—one of only 19 Icelandic athletes.

I. Þ. Einarsson (✉)
Reykjavik University, Sport Science Department, Reykjavik, Iceland
e-mail: ingithore@ru.is

V. Halldorsson
University of Iceland, Department of Sociology, Anthropology and Folkloristics, Reykjavik, Iceland
e-mail: vidarh@hi.is

6.2 Country Profile

Characteristics of Iceland

Iceland is one of the Nordic nations, including Denmark, Finland, Norway, and Sweden, but it is the smallest in population with only 360,000 inhabitants. Geographically, Iceland is situated on a 103,000 km^2 island in the North Atlantic and is the most sparsely populated country in Europe. Around two-thirds of the population live in the capital area on the west coast of Iceland, and the rest live mostly in seaside villages and towns around the country. Iceland became independent from the rule of the Danish monarchy in 1918 and became a republic in 1944. The Icelanders have historically been characterised as homogeneous in terms of race, class, and religion (Skaptadottir & Loftsdottir, 2009). Today's Iceland is an affluent society and can be characterised by social democracy and a strong market economy (Table 6.1).

The central values of the Nordic nations have been noted to be: equality, individual freedom, human rights, and democratic decision making (Esping-Andersen, 1990). In this regard, Iceland follows the Nordic ideology that a good society should foster emancipated and empowered individuals that enjoy freedom, equality, and financial security (Thorlindsson & Halldorsson, 2019). Thus, the "Nordic model" refers to a democratic welfare regime, where the state redistributes resources to secure financial independence for all citizens. Along with the other Nordic nations, Iceland usually scores highly on scales in international comparisons for welfare, equality, and happiness (Andersen & Björkman, 2017). The Nordic welfare state also attempts to reconcile the often-contradictory values of freedom and equality by safeguarding individual rights by law and social policy. Scholars have argued that values such as personal freedom, empowerment, emancipation, and even achievement are part of the culture that characterises the Nordic model (Esping-Andersen, 1990; Tomasson, 1980). Iceland is a part of the European Economic Area at the international level, and Iceland is a member of NATO even though Iceland does not have an army.

Table 6.1 Facts and statistics about Iceland

Population (number of inhabitants)	360,000
Area (km^2)	103,000
Density (inhabitants/km^2)	3.5
Urbanisation rate (%)	94
Political organisation	Unitary parliamentary republic
Structure of the state	Unitary
Number of provinces	8
Number of municipalities	72
GDP per capita (US Dollars)	58,370
Number of official languages	Icelandic
EU membership	No
Welfare model	Nordic

Source: Statistics Iceland (Statice.is, 2020)

Sport in Iceland

Iceland has a rich history of sports and is often referred to as *a sporting nation* (Halldorsson, 2017). This history of sports in Iceland can be traced back to the Saga Age (around 930–1262). The Icelandic sagas describe how the Icelandic Vikings took part in many sports-like activities. Thorlindsson and Halldorsson (2019) have argued that the foundations and characteristics of modern Icelandic sports originate from the Saga Age. One of their arguments is that sports were not limited to a privileged class of aristocrats nor a particular leisure class in the Saga Age, as was common elsewhere (see Guttmann, 1978). Instead, sports were a normal part of the Icelanders' lifestyles, like the other Nordic countries, and this built the foundation of the Nordic sports-for-all model (Green et al., 2019; Thorlindsson & Halldorsson, 2019; Tin et al., 2019).

The social organisation of sports in Iceland, and the culture of Icelandic sports, is primarily based on a sports-for-all philosophy, where the locally based sports clubs—which have hegemony in the Icelandic sports scene—are intended to serve all children and adolescents within their local neighbourhoods. The local clubs provide formal training, in many sports, for children from 4 years of age up to adulthood, when people mostly continue their participation more informally. The sports clubs are community based and owned but to a large degree sponsored by the municipalities. The municipalities mostly run the sports clubs with the help of volunteers. Further, participation fees are supposed to cover coaches' salaries. The municipalities predominantly invest resources in youth sports rather than elite sports because of the sports club's societal importance for integrating children and adolescents into society (Halldorsson, 2019b). According to recent Eurostat surveys, Iceland has, proportionally, the highest public financial support for sports and leisure in Europe (Eurostat, 2020). The Icelandic Sports Model does not distinguish between recreational and competitive sports, as most other countries do in their sports model (Halldorsson, 2019a, 2020). The two perceived ideologies—most often perceived as opposites that do not mix, which indicate the "either/or" ideology—combine into a single sports model in Iceland. A parallel emphasis is put on both participation in sport and performance in sport. This mixed system is a key distinctive feature of the Icelandic Sports Model. The model has two main aims in the local sports clubs: (1) to foster the positive personal development of children and adolescents through sport and (2) to develop competitive athletes for sports competition—all within the same formal community sports club organisation (Halldorsson, 2019b, 2020).

All formal sports clubs in Iceland are members of *The National Olympic and Sport Association of Iceland* (ÍSÍ). ÍSÍ is a national association of regional district/sport unions and national federations. The association is funded by the state and is the formal representative of Icelandic sports internationally. The state's sports policy aims to offer all people the opportunity to take part in the sports they choose, for pleasure, health, or for pursuing an athletic career. ÍSÍ is the highest authority for voluntary sports activities in Iceland, and over 100,000 people are registered participants in the Icelandic sports clubs, which represents almost one-third of the Icelandic population (ÍSÍ, 2020). The commercial sports sector in Iceland is slowly growing. However, it can be argued that the formal sports club system has hegemony in the Icelandic sports scene in terms of participation in sports and general status (Halldorsson, 2019a). There are 33 sports federations under the umbrella of ÍSÍ; one of them is *The Icelandic Paralympic Sport Federation* (ÍF) (Table 6.2).

The available figures for participation in formal sport in Iceland are among the highest in the world, where over 90% of all children and adolescents in Iceland practice sports within sports clubs sometime in their youth (Halldorsson, 2019a). Participation is highest among 11–12-year-olds, where between 85 and 90% of children practice formal sports at least once a week, but declines with age, where the percentage is around 60% among 15-year-olds (Halldorsson, 2019a). Football is by far the most popular sport, followed by golf, gymnastics, equestrianism, team handball, and basketball (Halldorsson, 2019a). Sports are further part of the school curriculum in the form of physical education classes, where all children are socialised into sports from beginning school at the age of six. Sports are further popular pastimes in Iceland, where the Icelanders are believed to be generally active in physical exercise and have a great interest in watching sports as well (Halldorsson, 2020; Kuper & Szimansky, 2014). However, recent reliable data on the Icelanders' physical activity, in general, is scarce. A survey from 2019, for instance, shows that around 70% of Icelanders who lived in the capital area (age 16–67) undertook regular physical exercise at least once a week (ISI, 2020), and the percentage of adults

Table 6.2 Sport profile of Iceland

Government authority responsible for sport	Ministry of Education, Science, and Culture
Membership sport club (%)	29
Membership fitness or health centre (%)	N/A[a]
Membership socio-cultural club that includes sport in its activities (e.g. employees' club, youth club, school- and university-related club) (%)	N/A
Sport participation, at least once a week (%)	N/A
Number of national sport federations	33
Number of sport clubs	418
Number of sport club members	199,188[b]
National budget for sport (€ × 1,000,000)	4.5
National budget for sport federations (€ × 1000)	661
Local budget for sport (€ × 1,000,000)	N/A
Share of economic value of volunteers in sport in the GDP (%)	N/A

Source: The Icelandic Sport and Olympic Association (ISI, 2020)
[a]N/A not available
[b]Note that some participants practice more than one sport within ÍSÍ clubs

that walked or biked to work at least three times a week was around 20% in 2014 (Halldorsson, 2014). Some figures further estimate that about 75% of senior citizens undertook sport or physical activity at least once a week (Guðmundsson & Sturludóttir, 2017). Thus, it can be argued that the Icelanders are generally physically active, although data on the general sports participation and physical activity of the Icelandic population is scarce.

Finally, Iceland has been recognised as a "hot-spot" in sports, particularly in team sports (Halldorsson, 2017; McGinn, 2021). Icelandic national teams have attracted international attention for being the smallest nation to qualify for major sports competitions such as World and European Championships and Olympic Games in sports such as football, team handball, and basketball (Halldorsson, 2017). It has been argued that the fundamental reason for this success of Icelandic sports lies within the social, structural, and cultural organisation of Icelandic sports, which deposit resources and emphasise youth sports (participation sports) rather than elite sports (performance sports) (Halldorsson, 2017, 2019a, 2019b). Whereas participation sports are intended to foster friendships and highlight the joy of playing for the sake of playing, usually within the local community, performance sports are result-oriented and work to produce future elite athletes, often within specific and professional sporting environments. Interestingly, Iceland has been doing well on both accounts in recent years. The sports model in Iceland is meant to serve both those who just want to play sports for fun and those who have ambitions of pursuing a sporting career. Furthermore, Iceland does not host professional sports leagues. The top sports leagues in Icelandic sports, such as in football, handball, and basketball, can be characterised to some extent as semi-professional (Halldorsson, 2019a).

Disability in Iceland

Defining disability is a complex task. It has been problematic to gain a consensus on the definition, and the definition of disability is continuously changing (Watson, 2019; Löve et al., 2018; Ingólfsdóttir et al., 2018). Iceland is not a member of the European Union and therefore stands outside of some European regulations regarding individuals with disabilities. Iceland has a vague national plan concerning the education of people with disabilities (whether physical or mental), but not regarding other vital issues such as employment—which is practically non-existent. Furthermore, there are no anti-discrimination laws regarding people with disabilities in Iceland.

The problem of defining disability and the lack of quantifiable international targets for Icelanders regarding people with disabilities has somewhat hindered a thorough and holistic account of disability in Iceland. This has further left the organisation of disability issues in many different hands, leading to a complex structure of the issues of persons with a disability. The data on disability in Iceland are scarce and scattered, providing only a part of the whole picture, making the issues of persons with disabilities in Iceland asynchronous and ambiguous (Löve et al., 2018; Ingólfsdóttir et al., 2018).

However, Iceland recently ratified the UN Convention on the Rights of Persons with Disabilities (CRPD) and intends to pass legislation regarding persons with disabilities' rights. With the proposed bill, Iceland would synchronise its public organisation for persons with disabilities with the UN's larger organisation regulation regarding education and employment of people with disabilities.

There does not exist any official statistics about how many persons have a disability in Iceland. The prevalence of disability in Iceland can only be somewhat reasoned by the numbers from the national social insurance agency (Tryggingastofnun Ríkisins, 2020). The annual report from 2019 states that just under 20,000 persons receive benefits for some disability. That means that around 5% of the Icelandic nation receives financial benefits from the state because of disability. Further, 35,000 persons received a pension because of older age, and 3000 persons received financial assistance for rehabilitation (Tryggingastofnun Ríkisins, 2020).

The Emergence of Disability Sport in Iceland

The official history of disability sport in Iceland is not long but is unique in many ways. The first steps of organised sport for people with disabilities were initiated from within the mainstream sport association of Iceland, The Icelandic Sport and Olympic Association of Iceland (ÍSÍ). In 1972, members of ÍSÍ started to pay attention to the sport for people with disabilities, or rather focus on the lack thereof in Iceland. A committee was formed in late 1972 to improve access and open up the sports community in Iceland for people with disabilities. The committee also started to structure training and competition rules and regulations for individuals with disabilities. The committee collaborated with the National Association of the Disabled in Iceland (Sjálfsbjörg) to form The Sports Association for People with Disabilities, ÍF. The ideology of building a specific programme for disabled sport in Iceland came by chance, as it was mainly due to a friendship of Sigurður Magnússon (then the head of distribution of ÍSÍ) and Dr. Ludwig Guttmann. Thus the initial ideology of sport for people with disabilities in Iceland was under the influence of sports for the disabled in England. In most countries, sports for the disabled were at that time, however, organised by general national associations of people with disabilities, but not by formal sports organisations such as was the case in Iceland (Sigurpálsson, 2012, p. 193).

In the beginning, the focus of sports for people with disabilities in the Icelandic sports clubs was on sports such as swimming, weightlifting, table tennis, and archery, partly under Guttman's influence and partly because the facilities for those sports were available for people with disabilities at the time. However, those sports were not the most popular sports in Iceland at the time. Rather they were considered convenient sports for people with disabilities. In 1974, the first official sport club, ÍFR, focusing only on people with physical disabilities, was established in Reykjavik. In 1981 a sports club focusing only on people with intellectual disabilities was established (ÖSP). In 1984, there were nine sports clubs across Iceland focused only on people with disabilities. The Icelandic Paralympic Sport Federation, ÍF, was formally established in 1979 and was as of then a full member of ÍSÍ as one of the sports federations in ÍSÍ. All sports clubs that focus on sport for people with disabilities are automatically members of ÍF, as well as all sports clubs that have any athletes with disabilities training with them. From the beginning, all types of disabilities were under the supervision of ÍF (physically impaired, intellectually impaired, visually impaired, and hearing impaired). For a few years, people with hearing impairments formed their own specific sports organisation in Iceland but were always in close cooperation with ÍF and have now again fully merged into ÍF. There was never any discrimination between the physically impaired and intellectually impaired in the formal organisation for sport for people with disabilities in Iceland. When the International Paralympic Committee (IPC) was established in 1989, Iceland was among the founders, and in the same year, ÍF joined the Special Olympics organisation officially (ifsport.is, 2020).

6.3 The Disability Sport System in Iceland

Structure of Disability Sport

The Organisation of Disability Sport in Iceland

The organisation of formal sports for people with disability in Iceland is complex. The responsibility for those sports rests on various governmental institutions and sports associations (see Fig. 6.1).

Governmental Agents

At the national level, the Ministry of Education, Science, and Culture is responsible for laws about sport in Iceland. Further, the Ministry of Social Affairs also impacts sports activity for persons with disabilities, more specifically. Both these ministries then hand the responsibility for sports organisations to ÍSÍ. Additionally, ÍSÍ then hands it over to ÍF to organise all sport for persons with disabilities.

The municipalities do not by themselves organise and host any sports activity directly. Instead, the municipalities provide support for the community-owned and community-based sports clubs. However, the municipalities own and run most sports facilities like sports halls and swimming pools in Iceland. Those facilities are often used by schools in the morning, for physical education lessons, as well as for senior citizens who can utilise the facilities like fitness centres but are then open for the sports clubs to use in the afternoons.

It is mandatory to do ten years of an elementary school in Iceland. During those ten years, each student is required to do a minimum of three classes per week in physical education (PE). These school sports are governed by educational law,

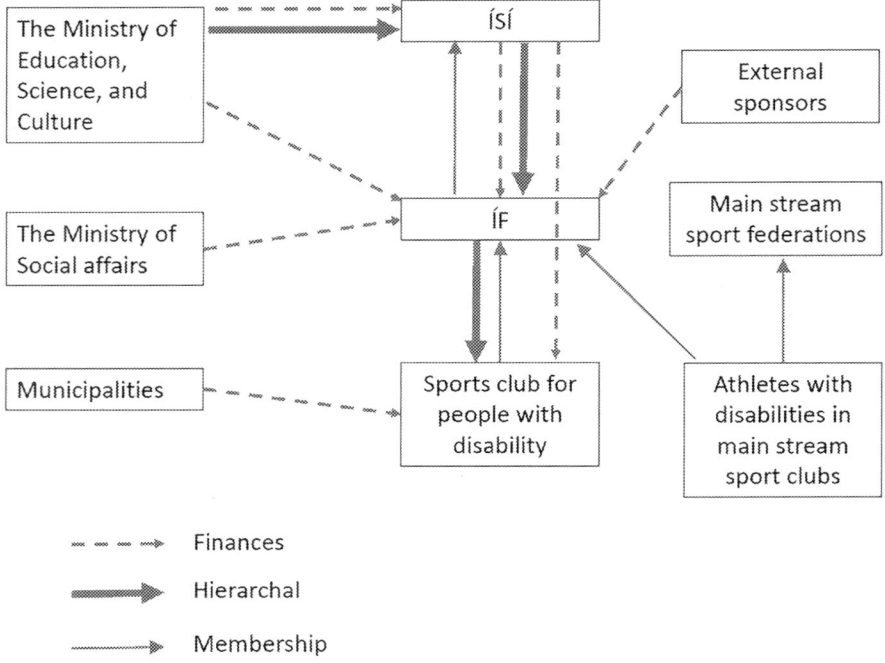

Fig. 6.1 The overall structure of disability sport in Iceland

which also comes from the parliament through the Ministry of Education, Science, and Culture. The PE lessons include all kinds of sport and physical activity and emphasise compulsory swimming lessons. This extends to both public and private schools. In this respect, it is important to note that there are public swimming pools in all towns and neighbourhoods in Iceland, most providing access for individuals with disabilities. The local swimming pools are trendy among the locals and are considered an important part of the Icelanders' public health. In the past, many children with disabilities attended special schools. In those schools, well-trained PE teachers could give the children a positive experience of sport and physical activity at an early age. Now the special schools are getting fewer and fewer in Iceland, and children with disabilities are, as much as possible, integrated into the mainstream school system. However, in the beginning, the Icelandic mainstream schools did not possess the infrastructure, in terms of facilities or experts in adapted physical activity (APA) teaching, to service their students with disabilities to a full extent. However, the universities responded quickly and increased the weight of APA training in the training of PE students. Some schools, especially the special schools for children with disabilities, do much more PE and sports classes than the minimum requirements. The general school system in Iceland plays a vital role in the early experience of sport in the life of many children with disabilities, even more so in the special schools for children with disabilities than in the mainstream schools.

Non-governmental Agents

It is predominantly the responsibility of ÍSÍ, ÍF, and sports clubs to organise all sports activities, whether for non-disabled people or people with disabilities in Iceland. From the beginning, sports for persons with disabilities were organised along with other competitive sports in Iceland. ÍF was, therefore, subject to the same professional standards in sports facilities and coaching (Sigurpálsson, 2012, p. 193). The distinctiveness of ÍF, compared to other sports federations in Iceland, where each federation is representative for only one sport, is that ÍF organises many sports. ÍF is often referred to as "little ÍSÍ" because of their multi-sports role. The relationship between ÍF and other sports federations in Iceland has been fruitful. Many athletes with disabilities often compete in competitions organised by other sports federations or mainstream sports clubs. For example, swimmers with disabilities who train solely with a swimming club focusing on persons with disabilities can always compete at competitions set up for non-disabled swimmers if they meet the qualification requirements. They then become a member of both federations, the Swimming Federation and ÍF. Similarly, a swimmer with a disability who only trains with a mainstream swimming club can always come and compete in competitions that ÍF hosts, and then they also become a member of both federations. Thus, this system provides athletes with disabilities with increased opportunities to practice and compete in both contexts, depending on their ability and ambition.

ÍF organises championships in sports such as archery, boccia, swimming, table tennis, track and field, and weightlifting, often cooperating with the other sports federations. This cooperation is done to give both groups of athletes exposure to each other and use the facility and workforce more effectively. The sports clubs themselves usually organise smaller grassroots competitions. Those smaller grassroots competitions often have a Special Olympics format, where no classification is needed, but athletes are blended based on previous results. Besides the sports mentioned above, bowling, football, gymnastics, and winter sports are also practiced, to some extent, among the athletes with disabilities in the Icelandic sports clubs (Sigurpálsson, 2012, p. 192).

Unified sports for non-disabled people and people with disabilities, such as football and golf, are growing in Iceland, both as training and competition. More sports are planning to open up for that option in the future. ÍF and the corresponding sports federation organise these unified events, usually by two or more sports clubs, some focusing on sport for the disabled and some mainstream clubs. ÍF also hosts a big summer sports camp for children with disabilities of all ages. These sports camps are all about healthy living with a focus on physical activity and a healthy diet. Further, ÍF organises many grassroots events every year often in cooperation with local sports clubs, to give children with disabilities a positive first experience in sports. Many of these events adopt their ideology from the Special Olympics, for instance, the Young Athletes programme that is now running in a few kindergartens in Iceland in cooperation with ÍF.

The private sector further provides some opportunities for the practice of sports or physical fitness. These opportunities are not well documented in Iceland. The fitness centres are open to people with disabilities. However, it is not recorded how well the fitness centres can facilitate people with disabilities or how many persons with disabilities use fitness centres regularly, or to what extent.

Steering of Disability Sport

Legislative Framework

It is the Ministry of Education, Science, and Culture that is responsible for national legislation regarding sport in Iceland. All changes in these laws need to be approved by the Icelandic parliament. There is only one main set of sports laws in Iceland (Íþróttalög. 1998) that covers all organised sport levels from youth to the elite level, including sport for individuals with a disability. The Ministry of Education, Science, and Culture then hands it to ÍSÍ to implement the sports law (see Fig. 6.1). ÍSÍ has its own general rules, regulations, and bylaws, mostly initiated by the international Olympic movement, as well as the national sport organisation of the other Nordic nations, that must fit in the framework of the federal laws coming from the Ministry. Each sport federation (football, swimming, judo, etc.) then has its own rules, regulations, and bylaws, initiated by the international sports federations, that must fit within the structure of ÍSÍ. One of those federations is ÍF, responsible for all organised sport for individuals with disabilities in Iceland. The laws, regulations, and bylaws of ÍF have to fit into the structure of ÍSÍ—as with other sports federations—but there is a second set of laws that ÍF must have in mind. The Ministry of Social Affairs is responsible for laws regarding the general rights of persons with disabilities. Therefore, ÍF must always update its rules and regulations according to changes in those laws, as well as through the laws of the Ministry of Education, Science, and Culture. It has sometimes proven difficult to combine strict competition rules with the general rights of persons with disabilities in Iceland. For example, the newly passed law about user-driven personal assistance does not comply with what IPC allows the national teams to bring to the Paralympic Games.

ISI has an annual meeting every year where the sport rules and regulations are discussed, debated, and changed if deemed necessary. ISI then further leaves it to ÍF's annual general assembly to further discuss the rules and regulations on sport for persons with disabilities in Iceland.

Policy Framework

At the governmental level, there is a working group directly under the Minister of Education, Science, and Culture that makes up the policy for sport in Iceland a few years in advance. In the last working group that published its sports policy for Iceland in 2019, one person was politically appointed, and other members were experts from various sectors in the Icelandic sports community, but none was a specialist in sport for disabled people. The sports policy does not include anything specific about athletes with disabilities in particular. The sports policy is meant to work for all athletes equally.

At the non-governmental level, ÍF has policies about many different sectors of their work. These policies are usually designed by experts in sports and then put forward for discussion and approval at the general assembly, which is held every year.

Financial, Governance, and Managerial Support

Financial Framework

ÍF has, from the beginning, received national public funds from four primary public sources. Firstly, ÍF is partly financed by ÍSÍ, which distributes funds by law from the Ministry of Education, Science, and Culture (which includes funds from the state lottery). Secondly, due to ÍF's unique position among the sports federations, it is also funded directly by the Ministry of Education, Science, and Culture to promote sports for people with disabilities in particular. Thirdly, there are laws that state the rights of persons with disabilities that the Ministry of Social Affairs implements. Since ÍF is responsible for all organised sport for individuals with disabilities, these laws also play a role for ÍF. It means that often ÍF gets extra funding from the Ministry of Social Affairs in cases where ÍF is taking on tasks where ÍF needs to ensure the participants' rights beyond what they are required to do by the general sport's laws. Therefore, the funding from the Ministry of Social Affairs is often to ensure direct access to facilities and sometimes for specialised equipment that individuals with disabilities must have to do sport safely. Further, ÍF also receives funds from sponsors in the private market. Strong companies have for years sponsored ÍF, and in 2019 nearly 30% of the total funding (1 million euros) for ÍF came from the private sector (Ársskýrsla ÍF).

On the local level, the sports clubs in Iceland are financially supported by the municipalities, as mentioned above. The sports clubs are part of sports unions in their communities, which provide the sports clubs with various essential resources. In general, the contribution of the municipalities towards the Icelandic sport clubs is estimated to be around 40 times higher than that received from the state, which mostly relates to building and maintaining sport facilities, employing some basic staff for the clubs, and subsidising participation fees for children and adolescents in the sport clubs—which they do due to the public health benefits of the massive formal sport participation of the youngsters (see Halldorsson, 2019b; Þórlindsson et al., 2015). The municipalities further support individuals with disabilities more directly with free transport to and from sports practices and paying for personal assistants.

Up to the year, 2002 ÍF had its own high-performance fund that would financially help elite athletes with a disability train and compete in their sport. As of the year 2003, the high-performance disability fund merged with the ÍSÍ high-performance fund, and as of that time, athletes with disabilities have had the same opportunities to receive financial assistance from that fund as all other high-performance athletes in Iceland.

Governance and Management Support

As mentioned above, Iceland does not host a professional sports system. Thus, the organisation of sports in Iceland is based on non-profit organisations. It is a community sports culture, with community-owned and community-based sports clubs intended for everyone. The Icelandic sports system is therefore highly dependent on work from volunteers for much of its programme. Thus, parents and other enthusiasts do much of the work in sports organisations and in sports clubs. Some argue that this organisation of sports in Iceland would not be possible without the substantial work that volunteers have done in Icelandic sports through the decades (Gísladóttir, 2006; Þórlindsson et al., 2015). Exact figures on the role of volunteers in Icelandic sports are missing, but general studies show that over 10% of the Icelandic population do volunteer work, many of them in the sports clubs (Hrafnsdóttir et al., 2014). However, in recent years Icelandic sports have moved towards increased professionalism with more professional infrastructure, including paid personnel, educated coaches, and the establishment of a semi-professional sports league in the most popular sports (Halldorsson, 2017).

Level of Integration or Inclusion

At the higher organisation level, disability sport in Iceland is fully integrated into the sports society. ÍF is a full member of ÍSÍ and has been from the time it was founded. There is still no official policy or pressure to dissolve ÍF like some nations have done now and let the sport for athletes with disabilities be integrated into each sport federation. There are always discussions about where in the system the sport for persons with disabilities fits best. At the moment (in 2020), most people agree that the current system fits Iceland better than moving the sport for individuals with disabilities into the other sports federations. The cooperation between ÍF and other sports federations has, however, been increasing over the last few years.

At the level of the athletes themselves, Iceland is however still very much on the segregation level. The special sports clubs for athletes with a disability are still strong and well organised. Most athletes with a disability who participate in organised sport do so with these exclusive clubs for athletes with disabilities. For a long time, this system has been accepted in Iceland as the system that best benefits both the non-disabled and the disabled participants in sports. However, mainstream sports clubs have always been open and willing to accept high-level athletes with a disability, especially athletes with a disability that has a relatively low impact on their sports performance. For example, all athletes with amputation and intellectual disabilities who have competed in the Paralympic Games for Iceland have almost exclusively done the bulk of their training with mainstream sports clubs. Athletes with mild CP and visual impairment competing in the Paralympics have also mostly come from mainstream sports clubs. Still, athletes with a higher level of CP and spinal cord injuries have mostly come from sports clubs that focus on athletes with disabilities. There are probably many reasons why disabled athletes with a relatively low impact on their sports performance are more likely to join the mainstream sports clubs rather than stay solely in sports clubs for people with disabilities than those with a more severe disability. One reason is probably due to the fact that most coaches in the mainstream clubs have not had the knowledge and training to coach and take care of people with severe disabilities, which requires special handling and technique that may differ from their work with more abled participants. Another reason could be that mainstream sports clubs lack facilities and equipment to service people with severe disabilities.

However, athletes with disabilities and their families and the universities responsible for most of the training of coaches, sports teachers, and sports administrators have placed a stronger motion to increase the integration among athletes with disabilities into the mainstream sports clubs at the grassroots level. There is no clear official policy from the Ministry to increase sports inclusion among athletes with disabilities in Iceland to date. Still, with better-educated coaches and better facilities, more athletes with disabilities have the option to take part in sport in integrated settings. However, this integration is only applicable in sports where the mainstream sports clubs offer sports training, which is convenient and popular among people with disabilities. In Iceland, Boccia is, for instance, the most popular sport among athletes with disabilities. Boccia is, however, only practiced in sports clubs that are focusing on persons with disabilities and is not practiced in the mainstream sports clubs. A few mainstream sports clubs (swimming, gymnastics, skating, athletics) have opted for an inclusion strategy to offer special groups for athletes with disabilities within their club. This opens up the possibilities for athletes with disabilities to move more easily from inclusion into integration.

6.4 Sport Participation by People with Disability

Monitoring and Evaluation

Generally, data on the sport participation of people with disabilities in Iceland is limited. However, registered members in the sports clubs for people with disabilities are well known, and ÍF monitors those numbers every year. However, the main problem of collecting thorough data on people with disabilities is that the numbers of people with disabilities are not easily accessible in Iceland due to general data protection regulation (GDPR).

Sport Participation

There are usually around 1000 active members in the sports clubs that are only focusing on people with disabilities in Iceland taking part in at least competitive sport ÍF offers each year, either in the spirit of Special Olympics or the Paralympics (Isi.is, 2020).

In 2014 there was extensive research conducted among children with disabilities in Reykjavik, the capital of Iceland. Every child that was in a special school or with special needs in a physical activity (PA) class in the mainstream school system was offered the chance to participate, and around 70% accepted participation. The papers that followed only published data from children with intellectual impairments due to statistical reasons. Published data shows that 33% of children with intellectual impairment in the age of 6–16 years participated in sports training twice or more each week (Einarsson et al., 2015a). Unpublished data from the same survey indicates 63% of children with all disabilities regularly participate in an organised sport activity, and 41% practice two to three times each week, and only 9% practice more than three times each week. The same numbers for non-disabled children at the same age are 4% for once or fewer each week, 38% for two to three practices each week, and 38% for more than three-sport practices each week. It was further noticed in the survey that children with a disability seemed to favour more low-intensity individual sports like boccia and swimming, while children in the mainstream sport preferred more football and other team sports that often require more intensity.

When children and adolescents in Iceland and their families were asked if they thought their physical activity (PA) was sufficient, around 75% thought it was. It was also noted that there is a firm correlation between the perceived physical activity and the directly measured activity (Einarsson et al., 2016). However, when the same age group and their families with disabilities were asked if they felt their physical activity (PA) was enough, 61% thought their PA was sufficient. In comparison, measured PA showed less than 10% achieved the recommended time in moderate to vigorous physical activity (MVPA). This large difference between objectively and subjectively measured PA indicates that children with disabilities (and their families) overestimate their PA. This lack of knowledge and understanding of PA among the children with ID, especially about the importance of time spent in MVPA, may also play a large role in the low sport participation rate among the children with disabilities.

Barriers and Facilitators

There are various barriers and facilitators that are known in terms of sport participation for people with disabilities in Iceland, physical, practical, and mental.

Barriers

Firstly, sport in Iceland is primarily run by local sports clubs that are very competitive both within the club itself and between the clubs. The local sports clubs' success often affects the community's social morale (Halldórsson, 2020; Thorlindsson et al., 2012). This emphasis on performance is also partly evident within many sports clubs that are focusing on people with disabilities. Thus, it is important for many of the bigger clubs that focus on people with disabilities to get their athletes into the national team, and many clubs have an active high-performance strategy in place. When children in Iceland were asked why they took part in organised sport, both children with disabilities and non-disabled children agreed that it was very important to be with friends and having fun. However, 95% of non-disabled children also said that one of the reasons they took part in the sport was to stay fit or improve in the sport, but only 68% of the children with disabilities agreed with those statements (Einarsson et al., 2015b). This goal and performance strategy of many of the clubs might therefore be a barrier to participation. The fact that boccia is by far the biggest sport for the individual with a disability over the age of 30 years and that many of the participants mainly take part for social reasons further points to this as a barrier for participation.

Second, the sports clubs that focus especially on persons with disabilities only offer a limited number of different sports. This is due to the scarcity of participants with disabilities. For example, a few attempts have been made to start sports like wheelchair basketball and goalball, but these attempts have not been successful due to the lack of participants. Therefore, persons with disabilities have fewer options to find the sport they like to practice compared to their non-disabled peers. It was observed in a survey done by ÍF and the University of Reykjavik in 2018 that few mainstream sports clubs (10%) in Iceland do provide special sports training for people with disabilities. However, most of them (95%) claim that their doors are open to all who are willing to practice. Again it has to be pointed out that the local clubs' competitiveness might not appeal to many persons with disabilities.

Thirdly, people with disabilities' opportunities to practice sports outside of the capital area are even more limited than in the capital area. Even though most disabled individuals in Iceland live in an urban setting, many smaller communities outside of the capital and surroundings are so small that there is only a handful of individuals with disabilities. It is, therefore, difficult to create a sustainable structure around sport for individuals with disabilities. There are, however, several clubs around the country that offer formal sport participation for people with disabilities but with even fewer options for different sports than in the capital area.

Fourth, it can also be a barrier that necessary equipment such as specialised wheelchairs or other high-tech equipment are not readily available. From interviews with participants or their families, it has come through that the sport the person with a disability is doing was not their first choice. The first choice was not an option because of the high cost of equipment (Kynningardagur, Y.A.P. 2016). It is not clear who should pay for that equipment in the Icelandic sport system.

And finally, one of the biggest barriers in making the sport for persons with disabilities more integrated is that sometimes the individual with a disability who wants to take part in a sports practice needs special assistance. Many communities in Iceland give children with disabilities personal assistance for free for a few hours a month. Some families have elected to use that assistance to help their children at sports practices. However, the hours that the aid is available is rarely enough to cover all the sports practices, and many families claim the lack of assistance as one of the biggest barriers to take part in more sport practices.

Facilitators

On the other hand, recent trends have, in many ways, facilitated sport practice by people with disabilities. Firstly, although some of the older sports facilities are not easily accessible for all individuals, they are getting fewer and fewer after laws were passed that all public buildings must be accessible for all persons. Iceland is an affluent and modern society, and most sport facilities are new and with good access for all people regardless of any disability.

Secondly, the biggest and most active sports clubs for individuals with disabilities are centralised in the capital area. This centralisation creates longer distances to and from sport practices, which is a known barrier for sport participation among children with disabilities (Hutzler & Korsensky, 2010). To compensate for this, most bigger communities in Iceland have organised a transport system for individuals with disabilities, which can help them get to and from sports facilities when they are going to participate in organised sport exercises. This service is free of charge for persons with disabilities and enables more people to participate in sports.

Third, often the sports clubs have higher demands for time slots than are available at the facilities. When that happens, the community's administration allocates each club a time slot in the sports facilities. It can happen that the clubs will not get the time they want, and that can be seen as a barrier to participation, but at least the clubs for individuals with a disability are more or less at the same place in the pecking order as the mainstream clubs.

ÍSÍ, ÍF, and the universities are working on a plan to get more local mainstream sports clubs to be willing and able to offer individuals with disabilities opportunities to participate in sports. ÍSÍ and ÍF are together encouraging the mainstream clubs to advertise their programme to understand that it is for all individuals. The universities are as well putting more focus on adapted physical activity in future PE teachers' and coaches' training.

6.5 Conclusion

This chapter has highlighted how the structure of sport for people with disabilities in Iceland is mainly dependent on the mainstream sport system in Iceland. Historically, Iceland has been considered a sporting nation with good results internationally in individual sport and team sport. This sport success comes despite there being no full professional sports in Iceland, as ÍSÍ fosters both elite and grassroots sports within the same system. The same applies to sport for people with disabilities in Iceland. ÍF is responsible for all sport for people with disabilities in Iceland, from grassroots to Icelandic championships in all sports and sending participants to Special Olympics and Paralympics. This emphasis on the performance side of the sport for people with disabilities has led to considerable achievements of Icelandic athletes in disability sport in international competition and the further recognition of disability sport in Iceland. Iceland has thus had multiple winners at the Paralympic games and always sends many athletes to the Special Olympics games. On the other hand, data on children with disabilities in Iceland shows that the sport's competitiveness is not as attractive to children with disabilities as to other children. It can thus be argued that the focus on the competition part of the sports for people with disabilities is one of the reasons why relatively fewer people with disabilities take part in organised sport in Iceland than people without disabilities.

From the beginning of disability sport in Iceland, there has been a strong sports club structure focusing only on people with disabilities. This means that the sports structure for people with disabilities in Iceland has mainly been in segregated or integrated settings. With a population of only 360,000, there are not so many athletes with a disability. Sports events in Iceland for people with disabilities are, however, often surprisingly large in numbers of participants, often reaching over 100 competitors with various disabilities. Visually impaired athletes compete next to spinal cord injuries and amputees and intellectually impaired athletes in these sporting events. However, team sports for people with disabilities have often been challenging to maintain because of the low number of participants.

It has been one of the biggest strengths of ÍF that the federation has from the beginning included all disabilities in their sports programme, and there has never been discrimination between the different disabilities. The unification within the system has been an essential part of the sports structure for people with disabilities in Iceland. Currently, almost all mainstream sports clubs in Iceland are open to the inclusion of people with disabilities in their programme, even though there is no official policy in Iceland to move sport for people with disabilities into inclusion settings. With better trained and educated coaches, it is expected that the number of disabled athletes that choose to practice their sport in inclusion settings will rise in the next few years, marking the future for disability sport in Iceland.

References

Andersen, L. A., & Björkman, T. (2017). *The Nordic secret: A European story of beauty and freedom.* Fri Tanke.

Einarsson, I., Johannsson, E., Daly, D., & Arngrimsson, S. A. (2016). Physical activity during school and after school among youth with and without intellectual disability. *Research in Developmental Disabilities, 56,* 60–70.

Einarsson, I., Olafsson, A., Hinriksdottir, G., Johannsson, E., Daly, D., & Arngrimsson, S. A. (2015a). Differences in physical activity among youth with and without intellectual disability. *Medicine and Science in Sports and Exercise, 47,* 411–418.

Einarsson, I. T., Johannsson, E., Daly, D., & Arngrimsson, S. A. (2015b, May). [Physical activity and physical condition of Icelandic primary and secondary school children with intellectual disability]. *Laeknabladid, 101*(5), 243–248. https://doi.org/10.17992/lbl.2015.05.25. PMID: 26019126.

Esping-Andersen, G. (1990). *The three worlds of welfare capitalism.* Princeton University Press.

Eurostat. (2020). Employment in sport by educational attainment level. Eurostat. https://ec.europa.eu/eurostat/web/products-datasets/-/sprt_emp_edu

Gísladóttir, Þ. L. (2006). *Hagrænt gildi íþrótta í íslensku nútímasamfélagi* [Unpublished MA Dissertation, Bifrost University].

Guðmundsson, H., & Sturludóttir, G. J. (2017). Greining á högum og líðan aldraðra á Íslandi 2016. [The lives of the elderly in Iceland in 2016]. Reykjavik: Félagsvísindastofnun Háskóla Íslands.

Green, K., Sigurjónsson, T., & Skille, E. (Eds.). (2019). *Sport in Scandinavia and the Nordic countries.* Routledge.

Guttmann, A. (1978). *From Ritual to Record: The Nature of Modern Sports.* Columbia University Press. http://www.jstor.org/stable/10.7312/gutt13340

Halldorsson, V. (2014). Íþróttaþátttaka íslenskra ungmenna: Þróun íþróttaþátttöku og greining á félagslegum áhrifaþáttum. *Netla – veftímarit um uppeldi og menntun.* https://doi.org/10.1177/1012690220912415

Halldorsson, V. (2017). *Sport in Iceland: How small nations achieve international success.* Routledge.

Halldorsson, V. (2019a). Sports participation in Iceland. In K. Green, T. Sigurjónsson, & E. Skille (Eds.), *Sport in Scandinavia and the Nordic countries* (pp. 87–107). Routledge.

Halldorsson, V. (2019b). The *Black Swan* of elite football: The case of Iceland. *Soccer and Society, 21*(7), 711–724.

Halldorsson, V. (2020). National sport success and the emergent social atmosphere: The case of Iceland. *International Review for the Sociology of Sport.* https://doi.org/10.1177/1012690220912415

Hrafnsdóttir, S., Jónsdóttir, G. A., & Kristmundsson, Ó. H. (2014). Þátttaka í sjálfboðaliðastarfi á Íslandi. *Stjórnmál & Stjórnsýsla, 10*(2), 427–444.

Hutzler, Y., & Korsensky, O. (2010). Motivational correlates of physical activity in persons with an intellectual disability: A systematic literature review. *Journal of Intellectual Disability Research, 54,* 767–786.

Ifsport.is. (2020). *Upplýsingar um Íþróttasamband Fatlaðra.* https://www.ifsport.is/page/upplysingar

Ingólfsdóttir, J. G., Jóhannsdóttir, Th., & Traustadóttir, R. (2018). Working relationally to promote user-participation in welfare services for young disabled children and their families in Iceland. *Nordic Welfare Research, Special Issues on User Participation, 3*(1), 33–46.

ISI. (2020). Tölfræði Íþróttahreyfingarinnar 2013. Íþrótta- og Ólympíusamband Íslands. https://www.isi.is/um-isi/utgafa/tolfraedi/

Íþróttalög. (1998). *Íþróttalög no. 64/1998.* https://www.althingi.is/lagas/nuna/1998064.html

Kuper, S., & Szimansky, S. (2014). *Soccernomics.* HarperSport.

Kynningardagur, Y. A. P. (2016). *Hvati,* (1), 18.

Löve, L., Traustadóttir, R., & Rice, J. (2018). Achieving disability equality: Empowering disabled people to take the lead. *Social Inclusion: Special Issue on Disability Equality, 6*(1), 1–8. https://doi.org/10.17645/si.v6i1.1180

McGinn, M. (2021). *Against the elements: The eruption of Icelandic football*. Pitch Publishing.

Sigurpálsson, B. V. (2012). Mesti sigurinn felst í þátttökunni. In S. J. Lúðvíksson (Ed.), *Íþróttabókin: ÍSÍ – Saga og samfélag í 100 ár* (pp. 190–196). Íþrótta- og Ólympíusamband Íslands.

Skaptadottir, U. D., & Loftsdottir, K. (2009). Cultivating culture? Images of Iceland, globalization and multicultural society. In S. Jakobsson (Ed.), *Images of the North: Histories – Identities – Ideas* (pp. 205–216). Rodopi.

Statice.is. (2020). https://www.statista.com/statistics/455834/urbanization-in-iceland/

Thorlindsson, T., & Halldorsson, V. (2019). The roots of Icelandic physical culture and sport in the Saga Age. In M. Tin, F. Telseth, J. O. Tangen, & R. Giulianotti (Eds.), *The Nordic model and physical culture* (pp. 101–116). Routledge.

Thorlindsson, T., Valdimarsdottir, M., & Jonsson, S. H. (2012). Community social structure, social capital and adolescent smoking: A multi-level analysis. *Health & Place, 18*, 796–804.

Þórlindsson, Þ., Halldorsson, V., Hallgrímsson, J. H., Lárusson, D., & Geirs, D. P. (2015). *Íþróttir á Íslandi: Umfang og hagræn áhrif*. [The scope and economic impact of sports in Iceland]. Reykjavík: Félagsvísindastofnun Háskóla Íslands.

Tin, M., Telseth, F., Tangen, J. O., & Giulianotti, R. (2019). *The Nordic model and physical culture*. Routledge.

Tomasson, Richard F. (1980). *The First New Society*. University of Minnesota Press.

Tryggingastofnun. (2020). *Ársskýrsla tryggingastofnunar 2019*. https://www.tr.is/tryggingastofnun/tr-i-tolum/arsskyrslur

Watson, N., Roulstone, A., & Thomas, C. (eds.) (2019). *Routledge Handbook of Disability Studies*. London: Routledge.

Chapter 7
Norway

Marit Sørensen and Nina Kahrs

7.1 Introduction

Since 2007 Norway has had an inclusive model for disability sport (now termed para sport) in their main sport organisation, The Norwegian Olympic and Paralympic Committee and Confederation of Sports (NIF). This means that all sport federations and regional organisations have the responsibility for offering their sport to individuals with a disability on equal terms with others.

This chapter describes the country, general sport and its organisation and some facts about disability, using public sources of documents and statistics. Norway is not a full member of the EU, and did not therefore provide data for the 2017 Eurobarometer on Sport and Physical Activity.

Further, this chapter describes the process of integration of the former disability sport organisations into the mainstream non-disabled sport organisations and presents some experiences from that process. Here sources are utilised and cited from formal evaluations and research reports. In addition, in order to update the knowledge, we carried out interviews with a panel consisting of four employees in NIF with a long experience of the integration process, as well as six former and presently active athletes with extensive organisational experience in the NIF.

With thanks to NIF (Norwegian Olympic and Paralympic Committee and Confederation of Sports) and advisor for para sport, Mette M. Berg.

M. Sørensen (✉) · N. Kahrs
The Norwegian School of Sport Sciences, Oslo, Norway
e-mail: marit.sorensen@nih.no; nina.kahrs@broadpark.no

© The Author(s), under exclusive license to Springer Nature Switzerland AG 2023
C. van Lindert et al. (eds.), *The Palgrave Handbook of Disability Sport in Europe*, https://doi.org/10.1007/978-3-031-21759-3_7

7.2 Country Profile

Characteristics of Norway

Norway is a long and partly narrow country, stretching from approximately 58 to 71 degrees north and approximately 7 to 31 degrees east. In addition comes Spitsbergen, The Bouvet Island and Jan Mayn further north (Store, norske leksikon (The Great Norwegian Encyclopedia), 2020). It borders with Sweden, Finland and Russia in the east, and has a long coastline to the Atlantic Sea in the west. It is a mountainous country with many fjords. The majority of the population live in the eastern and southern part. Oslo, situated in the south east, is the capital. There are also population concentrations around the towns Bergen in the west, Trondheim in the middle of the country and Tromsø in the north (Table 7.1).

After World War 2, for most of the time up until 2013 Norway was led by the labour movement, which aimed to restore the country and develop it into a modern welfare state. There is a low unemployment rate, free health care and education, and it has been a relatively egalitarian society with a high standard of living for most of its inhabitants (Store Norske Leksikon (Great Norwegian Encyclopedia), 2020).

From being a poor country in the past, Norway has developed into a rich country with a GDP ranking number 4 in the world in 2018. The reason is mainly due to petroleum and natural gas, but it is also rich in hydro-power, seafood and fresh water (Store Norske Leksikon (Great Norwegian Encyclopedia), 2020). The previous government, a coalition between conservative and centrum parties, has been criticised for cutting down on welfare goods for individuals with illness and disabilities (NRK-The Norwegian Broadcasting Corporation, 2018).

Table 7.1 Facts and statistics of Norway

Population, June 2020 [a]	5,374,000
Area (km^2) [b]	385,203
Length from southeast to northeast (miles) [b]	1100
Coastline with fiords (km) [b]	25,148
Coastline without fiords (km) [b]	2552
Urbanisation rate 2018 (%) [c]	83
Political organisation [b]	Parliamentary constitutional monarchy
Number of counties (2020) [b]	11
Number of municipalities (2020) [b]	356
GDP per capita (2019, euro) [d]	69,530
Number of official languages	2
EU membership	EØS

Sources: [a] Statistisk Sentralbyrå (Statistics Norway) (2018); [b] Store Norsk Leksikon (Great Norwegian Encyclopedia) (2020); [c] Central Intelligence Agency (CIA) (2018); [d] FN sambandet Norge (United Nations Association of Norway)

Norway has a history of first being a part of Denmark, then later in a union with Sweden before it gained independence in 1905 as a constitutional monarchy. The process leading to the independence has given Norwegians a proud sense of identity coloured by the national romantic movement of the nineteenth century. Most Norwegians take pride in considered being democratic, humble and respectful, and consider modesty a virtue, but at the same time a modern society constantly changing. Around 80% of the inhabitants are ethnic Norwegians (Central Intelligence Agency (CIA), 2018).

Officially Norway has a policy of making participation and independence possible for all (Regjeringen (The government), 2003a, 2003b). Money is made available for people with disability, for example, for individual user assistance from the government, but it is not earmarked. Because the main responsibility for such arrangements rests on the municipality, the result is very different practices depending on where in the country you live (The Norwegian Federation of Organisations of Disabled People (FFO), 2019; Oslo Economics, 2020).

Sport in Norway

The objective of the national sports policy is to ensure that people have access to a broad range of local sports activities, whether organised by membership-based sports clubs or independently. The value and effect of playing sport for both health and social inclusion are the primary reason why the state provides funding for sporting activities (Regjeringen (The government), 2020). The main partner for the government to achieve this aim is the main organiser of sport activities, both top-level sport, recreational sport as well as children's sport, namely the Norwegian Olympic and Paralympic Committee Norwegian and Confederation of Sports (NIF). NIF is the largest voluntary organisation in the country (Store Norske Leksikon (The Great Norwegian Encyclopedia), 2020).

The Norwegian Confederation of Sports (Norges idrettsforbund, NIF) was established in 1946, and at the same time The Ministry for Church and Education (Kirke-og undervisnings-departementet) established a department for sport, later called the department for youth and sport (Statens ungdoms-og idrettskontor (STUI) (Store Norske Leksikon (The Great Norwegian Encyclopedia), 2020). As of 2006, the name of the sport organisation changed to The Norwegian Confederation of Sports and Olympic and Paralympic Committee (still shortened as NIF). The organisation of NIF today and its associations with some international organisations are shown in Fig. 7.1. It is a membership-based voluntary organisation with a central administrative unit, a confederation of 55 individual sport federations and a unit of 11 regional organisations (NIF, 2022a). The NIF is an independent organisation which receives funding from the Ministry through various channels, through which the Ministry influences how the money is spent (Kulturdepartementet (Ministry of Culture, 2012)). Sport councils were organised by NIF in around 370 municipalities, consisting of representatives from all local sport clubs that are members of NIF (Waldahl, 2009), the number being reduced to 328 in 2022 (NIF, 2022a). They are

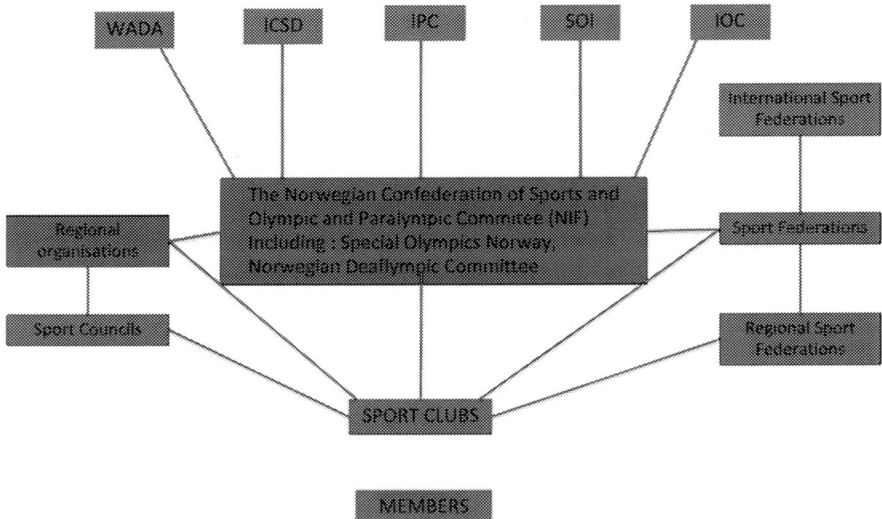

Fig. 7.1 The organisation of The Norwegian Confederation of Sports and Olympic and Paralympic Committee (NIF, 2019a)

responsible for collaboration with the municipalities, and also distribute the money from the ministry to local activities (Local Activity Means, LAM).

In addition, there are commercial fitness and health centres as well as organisers of outdoor life and hiking, such as The Norwegian Trekking Association (DnT). Several of these are organised in Friluftslivets Fellesorgansisasjon (The Common organisation for Outdoor life) (FRIFO), that has close relations to NIF.

Sport Profile and Levels of Participation

The Norwegian Olympic and Paralympic Committee and Confederation of Sports (NIF) is the largest voluntary organisation in the country. Approximately 90% of Norwegian children have at one stage in their life taken part in activities organised by one of the organisational levels of the NIF (Bakken, 2017) (Table 7.2).

Disability in Norway

Disability tends to be defined in slightly different ways in different contexts, making giving exact numbers a challenge. As a general term, disability has been replaced by the term "reduced functional ability", defined as "loss of, injury to, or deviant function in a body part or one of the body's psychological, physiological or biological functions" (BufDir (The Norwegian Directorate for Children, Youth and Family Affairs), 2020).

Table 7.2 Sport profile of Norway

Government authority responsible for sport	Ministry of Culture
Membership sport clubs % of population (2018) [a]	36
Memberships fitness clubs/health centres % (2017) [b]	33
Physical Activity participation once a week % (2018) [a]	80%
Number of national sport federations (2019) [c]	55
Number of sport clubs (2020) [d]	11,000
Number of Sport club members (2020) [c]	Ca. 2,100,000
National budget for sport total 2020 (million euro [e]) [d]	280,422,982
National budget for sport federations 2020 (million euro [e]) [d]	2,606,800
Central and regional budget for sport 2020 (million euro [e]) [d]	12,691,000
Share of economic value of volunteers in sport (of the GDP %) (2017) [f]	Ca. 1.17%

Sources: [a] SSB (Statistics Norway) (2018); [b] Van der Roest et al. (2017); [c] NIF (2019a); [d] Regjeringen (The government) (2020); [e] 1 NOK = 0.098 euro; [f] Fladmoe et al. (2018)

The official policy and attitude towards individuals with a disability are based on the UN Convention on the Rights of Persons with Disabilities (UNCRP) signed in 2007, and ratified in 2013, and are to create an inclusive society for all (Bufdir, 2018). This is ensured through several laws and regulations, many of which were combined into a comprehensive law relating to equality and a prohibition against discrimination (Equality and Anti-Discrimination Act) combining several former separate laws (Ministry of Culture, 2019). An anti-discrimination "ombud" and tribunal has also been established. Accessibility is regulated through several laws and regulations about universal design, such as the law of planning and building (Kommunal-og Moderniseringsdepartementet (Ministry of Local Government and Modernisation), 2008), and regulations for buildings and outdoor areas such as technical regulation, TEK-17 (Direktoratet for byggkvalitet (Directorate for building quality), 2017). A specific regulation for universal design within information technology came into effect at the start of 2021 (Kommunal-og Moderniseringsdepartementet (Ministry of Local Government and Modernisation), 2019). In the educational system, all children, including those with disabilities, are supposed to receive education "adapted to the abilities and aptitude of the individual pupil" (Utdanning-og forsknings departementet (Ministry of Education and Research), 1998). Individuals with a disability may get assistive aids for everyday life through NAV (The Norwegian Labour and Welfare Administration) and also support for special training and activity equipment. However, equipment especially for sport competitions is not covered (Oslo Economics, 2020). There are also several possibilities for support to transport, support for a car or different types of travel. According to the law of health and care services §3-2, all municipalities should be able to offer "support contacts", that is, individuals paid by the municipality for supporting individuals with a disability in social and physical activities in order to have a meaningful life (Helsenorge, 2019). Those with longstanding and large needs for assistance also have a right to get

"Brukerstyrt Personlig Assistance" (user directed personal assistance) after certain criteria.

In Norway, there are legal restrictions in registration of individuals with a disability. There are therefore large variations in methodology for prevalence estimates, and some of them vary by as much as 2%. However, as an overall estimate, around 17.6% of the population between 15 and 66 years have some kind of a disability (all in all just above 900,000 persons), 4% more women than men (Statistisk sentralbyrå (SSB) (Statistic Norway, 2018). Self-reported long-term limitations in daily activities due to health problems were given by in all 16.4% of the population 16 years and older in 2016 (Eurostat, 2017). In 2017, a total of 325,900 people received disability pensions: 189,300 women and 136,600 men. This represents almost 10% of the population aged 18–67. Among the pension recipients up to the age of 35, men outnumber women slightly, but the majority of women increases in each subsequent age group (SSB, 2018) (Table 7.3).

Emergence and Rise of Disability Sport in Norway

The first organisation for disability sport in Norway was The Oslo Sport Club for the Deaf in 1892. After The World Organisation of sport for the deaf was established in 1924, The Norwegian Deaf-Sport Organisation was formed in 1925. The first sports clubs for people with visual impairments were formed in the 1940s. Before 1960 sport for individuals with a disability was mainly activities in special schools or institutions (Mathisen, 1972). Organised sport for individuals with a disability in general was initiated by the leader of the state's youth and sport office (Statens ungdoms- og idrettskontor, STUI), Rolf Hofmo, at the end of the 1950s through Bedriftsidretten (Corporate sport), but it was not until 1971 that The Norwegian Sport Federation for the Disabled (Handicapidrettsforbundet) was formed as an

Table 7.3 Disability in Norway: estimates by type of disability. NB! This is not a complete overview of all disabilities

Type of disability within the 17.6% (ca. 900,000)	N
Mental illness [a,b]	Ca. 360,000
Locomotor disabilities [c]	197,000
Hearing impairments [c]	31,415
Diagnosed	8000
Visual impairments [d]	320,000
Blind	9300
Developmental disorders [e]	Ca. 25,000
Diagnose codes from ICPC2 [c] (International Classification of Primary Care)	146,350

[a] There has never been an organisation for sport for people with mental illness, even if a project tried to include this in the 1990s (Vanebo, 2002)
Sources: [b] Statistics Norway (2018); [c] Karlsen et al. (2019); [d] Skogli et al. (2019); [e] National Competence Unit for Developmental Disorders (2019)

independent federation of sport in the Norwegian Olympic and Paralympic Committee and Confederation of Sport (NIF).

In 1996 NIF decided to start a process in order to integrate disability sport into the mainstream non-disabled sport federations. It was initiated by the Norwegian Sport Organisation for the Disabled (Handicapidrettsforbundet) and supported by the Ministry. Before 1996, disability sport was organised as follows:

The Norwegian Sport Organisation for the Disabled (Handicapidrettsforbundet) was a separate federation within NIF with its own regional bodies. They elected their own leaders centrally and regionally and had their own representatives in the governing body (The General Assembly). They were members of several international organisations for various groups, and International Paralympic Committee from 1989.

Deaf Sport started internationally already in 1924 with "Silent Games" in Paris. Norwegian Deaf Sport Organisation was a separate organisation only associated with NIF before 1997.

Sports for Developmental/intellectual disabilities had their own committee in NIF before 1997. There has never been an organisation for sport for people with mental illness, even if a project tried to include this in the 1990s (Vanebo, 2002).

The first step in the integration process was to merge the different disability organisations into one. The new disability sport organisation was formed in 1997 and called The Norwegian Federation of Sport for Disabled (NFI).

During the ten years (1997–2007) NIF, through The Norwegian Disability Sport Federation (NFI), worked to ensure that all the sport federations prepared for taking over the responsibility to organise their sport including for individuals with a disability. In 2007 The Norwegian Disability Sport Federation (NFI) was dissolved, and all sport organisations were given the responsibility as intended, and all disability sport organisations were merged into the specific sport federations. Norges Fler-idretts Forbund (Multi-sports Federation) was established in order to take care of sports such as boccia and carpet curling that had no existing federation from before, and it included Friskis and Svettis, an exercise organisation. The development can be illustrated on the timeline in Fig. 7.2.

7.3 The Disability Sport Within the System

Structure of Disability Sport

Governmental Agents

The Ministry of Culture has the overall responsibility for the administration of profits generated by Norsk Tipping AS (Norway's national lottery and gaming provider) for investment in sporting activities. The Ministry influences how their policy is carried out through the ways they earmark and channel their funding (see Fig. 7.4). Various administrative tasks associated with the channelling of funding into sports

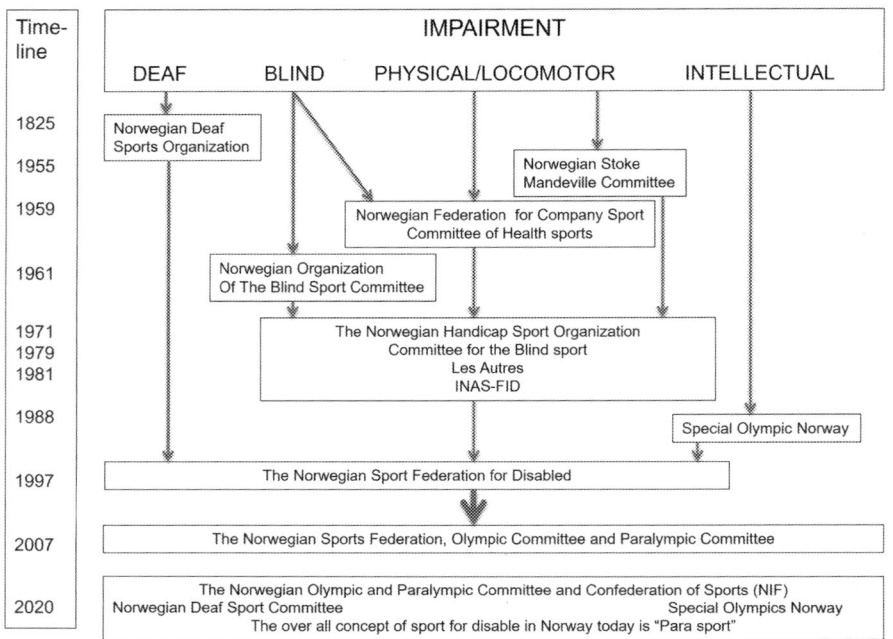

Fig. 7.2 Timeline of the development of disability sport in Norway

facilities and physical activity have been delegated from the Ministry of Culture to municipalities and county authorities (Regjeringen (The Government), 2003a). The Ministry of Education and Integration also supports educational activities within the sport organisations when they fulfil criteria in the Adult Education Act (NIF, 2019a).

Intermediate Agents

The regional organisations employ consultants for disability sport (see Fig. 7.1). They serve as support and help for regional and local sports clubs in establishing activities for individuals with disabilities and recruitment to these activities. The Norwegian Labour and Welfare Administration (NAV) administers funds for technical aids and equipment for leisure time activities in the counties and municipalities. The majority of municipalities have sport councils (idrettsråd), that among their responsibilities should make sure there are activity possibilities for all (Waldahl, 2009). The sport councils also have the responsibility to distribute earmarked funding for Local Activity Means (LAM) from the Ministry of Culture through NIF. All local sport clubs arranging activities for children and youth can apply, and the number of active members with a disability is among the criteria to receive such support. For 2020 NIF received 34.913 million NOK/36,456,000 Euros to distribute for

LAM from the Ministry of Culture (NIF, 2020a, see Figure 4). As part of the public health care services, Healthy Life Centres (HCL, Frisklivssentraler) exist in the majority of municipalities (263 in 2018) according to Statistics Norway (2018), and some of these have established collaboration with the local sport organisations.

Non-governmental Agents

The Norwegian Olympic and Paralympic Committee and Confederation of Sport (NIF) is the largest grant recipient from the ministry and is the state's most important activity partner (Regjeringen (The government), 2003b). All 55 regular sport federations have the responsibility to organise their sport for individuals with a disability. Several of the sport federations employ their own disability sport consultant. There are also several non-governmental organisations (NGOs) such as The VI Foundation (Stiftelsen VI), The Gjensidige foundation, the foundation Sparebankstiftelsen, The Damm Foundation to mention a few, that in various ways provide funding for activity initiatives also for individuals with a disability. Ridderrenet is an NGO that arranges an annual winter sport festival for individuals with a disability at Beitostølen, assisted by the military. They offer IPC classification and this is therefore an area of recruitment to disability sport.

In Norway, The Norwegian Olympic and Paralympic Committee and Confederation of Sport (NIF) has developed a model that includes disability sport in their mainstream non-disabled sports federations and regional organisations, as described. The central organisation (NIF) has employees that work specifically for disability sport including the Paralympic Committee, the Committee for Deaf Sport and Special Olympics. From 2007 there was no longer a Disability Sports Organisation. The individual sport federations and regional organisations have the responsibility for organising sports also for those with a disability, but there are still some specialised clubs at local levels, such as the sport club HODR for individuals with visual impairments (Gåsemyr et al., 2019). All sport federations have the responsibility to organise their sport also for individuals with a disability, and the new multi-sport federation is open for all. The structure is illustrated in Fig. 7.3.

Secondary Agents

There are several rehabilitation centres that serve as a recruiting arena for disability sport. A few have physical activity and sport as their main focus, such as Beitostølen Health Sport Centre and Valnesfjord Health Sport Centre, and others are actively promoting physical activity and sport in addition to other forms of rehabilitation, such as The Cato centre and Sunnaas Rehabilitation hospitals. The Norwegian School of Sport Sciences educates coaches and has para sport as part of their coach education. Also, all first year students spend one week during the winter season as assistants at Ridderrennet. They receive lessons about disability sport as part of the preparation for this event (NIH, 2017).

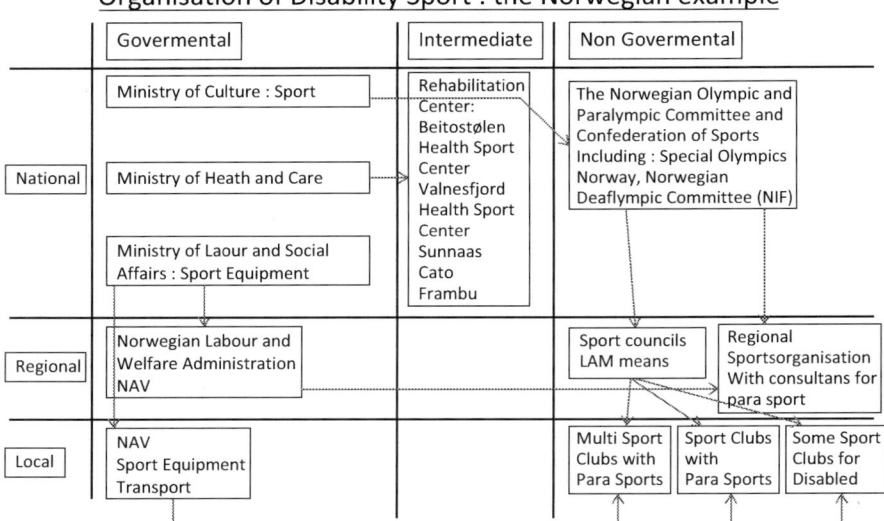

Fig. 7.3 Organisation of disability sport in Norway

Steering of Disability Sport

The Norwegian Olympic and Paralympic Committee and Confederation of Sports (NIF) have the responsibility for voluntary organised sport. Their highest authority is the general assembly (Idrettstinget). The general assembly consists of representatives from the sport federations and the regional organisations. The 55 sport federations have the responsibility to organise their sport for members with a disability. Several of them have employed their own disability sport consultants. However, NIF and the regional organisations are supposed to support the federations and coordinate the work with the necessary competence. In addition to the Paralympic Committee in NIF, there are now two full-time and one half-time employees in the central organisation of NIF, with a special responsibility to follow up the sport federations and regions in their work with individuals with a disability. They also have the main responsibility for classification, the function as general secretary for Deaf Sport and as head office for Special Olympics Norway. Further, eleven regional disability sport consultants are employed by the regional organisations and work in the regions with recruitment and advice at the regional and local level (NIF, 2019a).

Relationships

The Ministry of Culture is responsible for the policy areas of culture, equality and discrimination, copyright, the media, sport and the voluntary sector. The Ministry also has overarching responsibility for the state lotteries run by Norsk Tipping and for regulating gaming and lotteries run by private organisations (Regjeringen (The Government), 2020). The main activity partner is The Norwegian Olympic and Paralympic Committee and Confederation of Sport (NIF). In addition to providing a basic sum, money for top-level sport, recreational sport, federations and regional organisations, the Ministry earmark some of the money going through NIF for specific purposes, such as Local Activity Means (LAM) targeting children and youth (see Fig. 7.4). Various administrative tasks associated with the channelling of funding into sports facilities and physical activity have been delegated to municipalities and county authorities.

Legislative Framework

The official Norwegian policy is based on the CRPD, aimed at creating an inclusive society for all. The rights of individuals with a disability are protected by several laws and regulations, such as The Equality and Anti-discrimination Law of 2007 (Barne – og likestillingsdepartementet (Ministry for Children and Equality), 2019), as an example. Within education all children are supposed to receive education adapted to their individual needs since 1976 (Utdannings-og forskningsdepartementet (Ministry for Education and Research), 1998). Within organised sport NIF have their own set of laws and regulations, among them regulations about children's sport, but no specific laws or regulations for disability sport other than what the

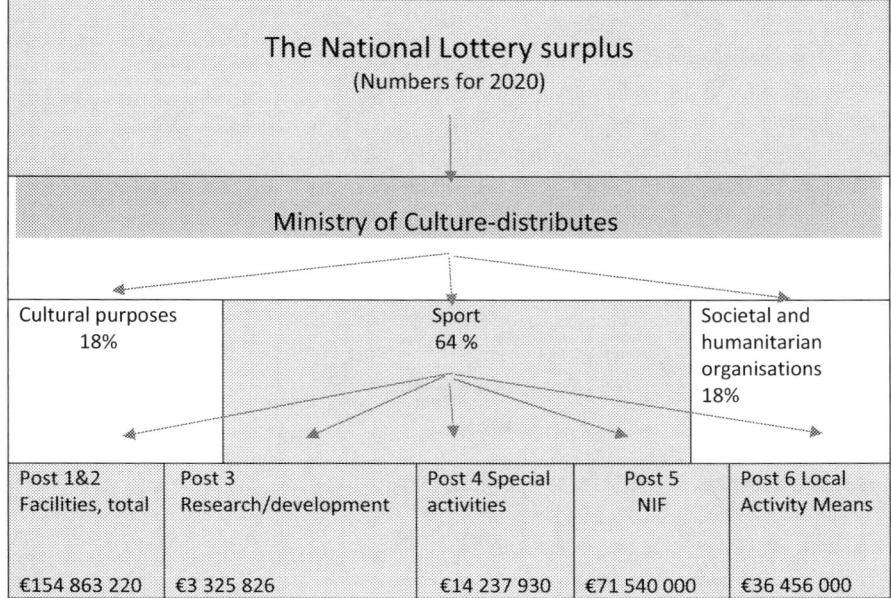

Fig. 7.4 How finances from the National Lottery surplus were distributed for 2020 (NIF, 2020c)

International Paralympic Organisation (IPC) have established for classification in competitive sport.

Policy Framework

The government's sport policy is summed up in the vision "Sport and physical activity for all". The objective of this sports policy is to ensure that people have access to a broad range of local sports activities, whether organised by membership-based sports clubs or independently (Regjeringen, 2019). The government has developed a plan for inclusion of people with disability for the period 2020–2030, the aim of the plan is "Et samfunn for alle" (A society for all) (Barne – og likestillingsdepartementet (Ministry for Children and Equality), 2018).

As the main activity partner, NIF is an important agent for fulfilling the policy of the government. They therefore receive considerable funding (see Fig. 7.4), but also contribute heavily with a large amount of voluntary work and other ways of financing their activities (sponsorships, etc.). NIF works out their own strategy and policy for their activity, and the general assembly (Idrettstinget) is the highest authority to sanction these (NIF's langtidsplan og strategidokumenter, 2019). However, the process to integrate disability sport into the mainstream non-disabled sports federations was discussed with and supported by the ministry at the time (Sørensen et al., 1999).

Financial, Governance and Managerial Support

Within the total grant dedicated to sport-related purposes (Fig. 7.4), the Ministry of Culture provides a basic financial support to the NIF (see Table 7.4).

According to a recent report from Oslo Economics (2020), 13.1 million NOK (1,283,800 euros) went from post 5.1 to para sport (disability sport) in 2017. Post 5.2 to the sport federations represent the largest contribution to para sport (21.1 million NOK/2,067,800 euros) in 2017. Based on certain criteria (e.g. activity and other results), it is given as an integration grant for the federations to develop their

Table 7.4 Distribution of grants from the Ministry of Culture (post 5) within NIF

Post on budget	NOK (million)	Euro (million)
5.1 Basic support NIF centrally and regionally	129,500,000	12,691,000
5.2 Basic support to the sport federations	266,000,000	26,068,000
5.3 Children, youth and recreational sport	171,500,000	16,807,000
5.4 Top-level sport	163,000,000	15,974,000
Total	730,000,000	71,154,000

Source: NIF (2020c)
Approximately 5,490,000 euro will go to disability sport (1 NOK = 0.098 euro)

sport for individuals with disabilities. Post 5.3 is dedicated to children, youth and recreational sport, and is also distributed based on result criteria. In 2017, 7.8 million NOK/764,400 euros were granted to the sport federations. There has been a positive increase in financial support for disability top-level sport. The total funding to the Paralympic Committee has gone from 18 million NOK (1,764,000 euros) in 2007 to 61 million NOK (5,978,000 euros) in 2019. NIF is a membership-based organisation, and a considerable portion of the financial base at the local level is the membership fees as well as income from sport events and voluntary work. In addition, para sport also has sponsorships and support from other public funds and from various foundations such as Sparebankstiftelsen (DNB), Stiftelsen Dam, Gjensidigestiftelsen and a foundation named VI (us) (NIF, 2019c).

7.4 Sport Participation

As mentioned earlier in this chapter, there are restrictions on registration of individuals with disabilities that makes monitoring sport participation of persons with disabilities difficult. Therefore we only have either number of clubs or activities that report number of members with a disability, apart from individuals competing at a paralympic level (Dale, 2019).

Paralympic Top-Level Sport

According to Dale (2019), two trends have represented challenges for the Norwegian top-level para sport, and that is difficulties with recruitment, and increased competition from other nations who have given higher priority to para sport on a high level. However, recent new earmarked funds have created new opportunities (Fig. 7.5).

General Disability Sport Participation

In Norway, registration of persons based on information about their health or disability is generally not allowed in order to protect the privacy of the individual. The sport organisations can therefore only count the total number of members with a disability. Therefore, the numbers of actual members with a disability in the following are estimates based on reports from clubs and regions (NIF, 2019b). This is not a sport-specific problem, and Statistics Norway has started a project in order to improve our knowledge base (Dale, 2019) (Figs. 7.6 and 7.7).

The basis for the registration of members in the Norwegian Olympic and Paralympic Committee and Confederation of Sports are the groups in the regional organisations taking part in sports competitions and who are members in the various activities. Because only numbers and not individuals are counted, it has been a

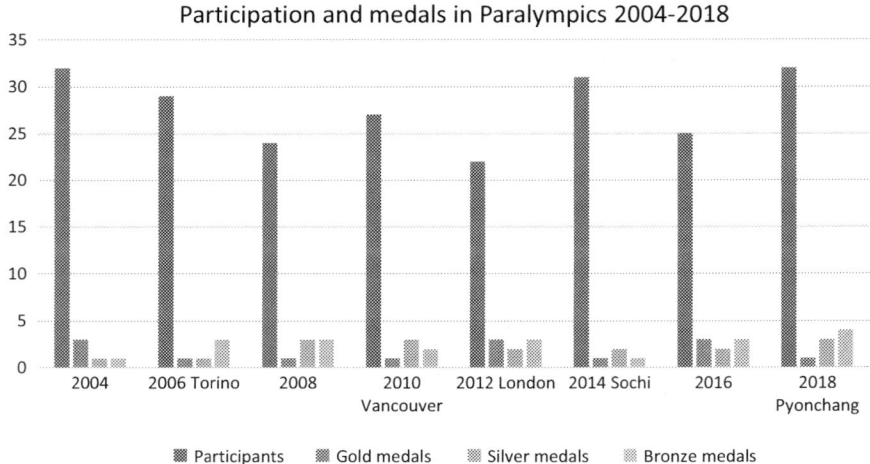

Fig. 7.5 Participation and medals in summer and winter Paralympic games from 2004 to 2018

Fig. 7.6 Numbers of members active in para sport (NIF, 2020a)

problem that the same member may be counted several times if they participate in more than one type of activity or sport, so that the numbers are somewhat uncertain. On the other hand, several of the regional activities are not counted among the number of active members because it is not counted in the numbers from the sport federations. The numbers reported from the Sport Federations can still give some idea about what are the most popular sports among those with a disability (see Table 7.5).

Some of the smaller federations may have only a few para sport participants, but of the 55 sport federations there is now only one federation (The Casting Federation) reporting no para sport members. It has been a relatively stable number of active members with a disability since 2016. The increase seems to be in particular among children and youths, but there are challenges in getting specific and reliable data (Dale, 2019). Also, it is still not known how the Covid pandemic have influenced sport participation and club memberships.

The Social Inclusion and volunteering in sports clubs in Europe (SIVCE) project registered how many of members and volunteers in samples of European sports

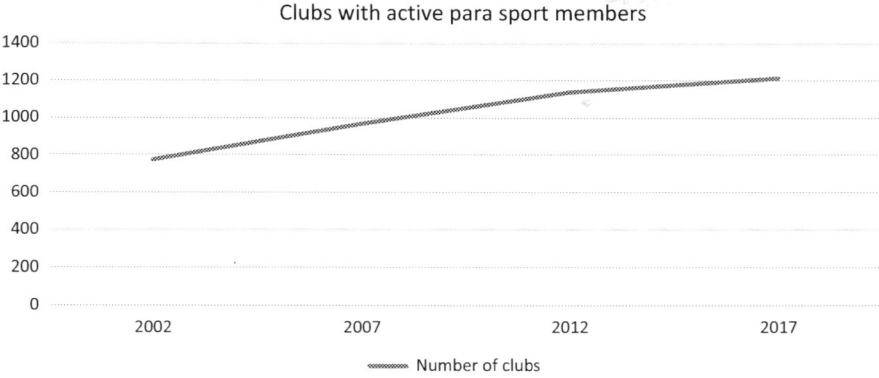

Fig. 7.7 Clubs with active para sport members from 2002 to 2017 (Dale, 2019)

Table 7.5 Number of para sport members within the 15 most popular sports 2019

Sport	Numbers active in para sport
Football	2031
Multisport	1344
Handball	1332
Swimming	928
Athletics	547
Dancing	496
Bandy	461
Gymnastics	392
All sport/sport school	325
Skiing	300
Equestrian	283
Golf	258
Climbing	253
Shooting	178
Martial arts	145

Source: NIF (2020a)

clubs reported to have a disability (Van der Roest et al., 2017). For Norway, 88% of the sample of 30 clubs reported no disability, 4% reported a physical disability, 4% a sensory disability, 6% a chronic disease, 1% a psychosocial/behavioural problem and less than 1% an intellectual disability (one person may have reported more than one type of disability). Five per cent practiced sport in a group consisting of people with disability only, 53% practiced sport in groups consisting of people without a disability and 32% did both. The project also gave more detailed information about how disability and health problems restricted them in the sport setting (Van der Roest et al., 2017). It is therefore still worth noticing that the number of persons with disabilities engaged in organised sport is still lower than for the general population (Oslo Economics, 2020).

7.5 The Integration Process

The process called "The integration process", starting in 1996 in order to prepare for today's organisation of Norwegian sport, was monitored and evaluated from 1996 until 2003 by a research team from The Norwegian School of Sport Sciences, led by associate professors Marit Sørensen and Nina Kahrs (Sørensen & Kahrs, 2006). The following reports were delivered: status report in 1999, based on document analyses, questionnaires to all sport federations, regional organisations, representatives to the general assembly in 1997, as well as interviews with employees in NIF centrally and the sports federations; an evaluation report in 4 parts+ synopsis, 2003; status check with the federations in 2008; and a book chapter (Sørensen & Kahrs, 2011). Also in 2008, a report on equality and diversity in Norwegian sport was published by the ombud for equality and inclusion, supporting several of the issues pointed out in the evaluations (Fasting et al., 2008). The main content and numbers below are, however, taken from the most recent status report by Dale in 2019, and Oslo Economics in 2020, as well as the interviews from 2020, described in the introduction. It is however interesting that some of the challenges pointed out early in the process have turned out to remain difficult to solve over the years.

Level of Inclusion

There was already from early on in the process a reasonable consensus that the process to integrate disability sport into the general sport federations has resulted in more positive attitudes and willingness to include individuals with disabilities (Sørensen & Kahrs, 2011). The quality and magnitude and accessibility of actual possibilities within the different sports vary considerably. This is due to several factors; size and resources in the sports federations, which sports are the more suitable for the different individuals with their disability, and available competence within the organisation. There is no easy scale to measure how well integrated individuals with a disability are, but in the evaluation of the process we tried to describe what factors had to be in place in an organisation in order to be called "truly inclusive" (Sørensen & Kahrs, 2006). We used these factors for a rough evaluation of how far the various sport federations, regional and local clubs had come in their process of integration/inclusion (Sørensen & Kahrs, 2006). As could be expected, there were great variations between various sports and regions. It is important to remember that such processes take time (Fig. 7.8).

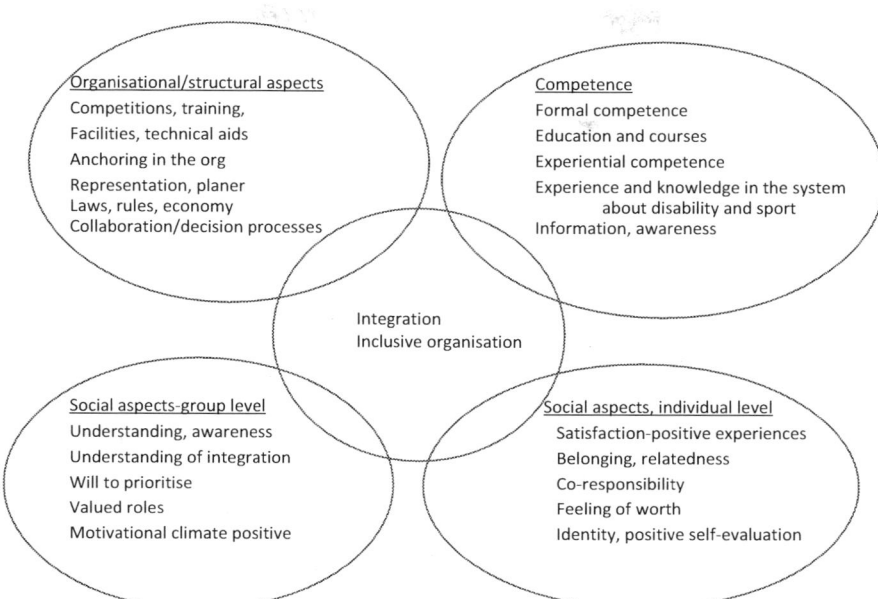

Fig. 7.8 Factors that need to be in place for integration (Sørensen et al., 1999)

New Terminology

From 2017, NIF decided to change the many terms used within disability sport into the umbrella term "para sport". On their web page they explain that para sport is not limited to Paralympic sport, but means parallel forms of regular sports, adapted to various disabilities, but of equal value (NIF, 2019a). This interpretation will be used further in this chapter.

Experiences with the Integration Process

According to Dale (2019) the process of integrating disability sport into the mainstream non-disabled sport federations has overall been successful and fulfilled the intentions. It has been a positive development of activity opportunities in more sports, more variations and several solutions in creating suitable activities. This may be reflected in the overview of the number of para sport members to be found within the different sport federations (see Table 7.5).

Already early in the process positive attitudes and willingness to include individuals with a disability in all levels of the organisation appeared to exist (Sørensen et al., 2003), and this seems to have continued to develop positively (Dale, 2019). There has been a positive increase in financial support for Paralympic sport, as mentioned above. The federation for multisports has been successful, and has a high percentage of members with a disability (NIF, 2020a).

Knowledge and competence about disability sport have been pointed out as an important issue from the start, both centrally and locally in the organisation (Sørensen et al., 2003). Centrally, NIF has kept a unit of two and a half positions in 2020. They have the responsibility for following up the money provided for para sport, to lead the network of regional para sport consultants, work with and support the sport federations, development of competence about para sport, work with and coordinate classification, coordinate the committees for Deaf Sport and Special Olympics and try to influence general policy. The Norwegian School of Sport Sciences has a one year course in APA (Adapted Physical Activity), and offered for some years a specialisation in disability sport within their coaching bachelor degree, and this is still a topic within their coach education (NIH, 2017).

Para sport is meant to be included in the coach education of most sport federations, and it is a challenge to disseminate competence out into the regional and local parts of the organisation (Kahrs, 2006). There seems to be large variations between the federations as to how well this is taken care of, but no exact data exist about this today. There are also initiatives to improve the education of coaches in para sport at the Olympic/Paralympic training centre. The regional consultants have been considered important from early on. The responsibility for their employment has been shifted from the central organisation to the regional, a shift that has been said to give positive effects in the regional and local organisations (Dale, 2019).

For many years Norwegian sport used the slogan "Sport for all". Today the official aim of the NIF is formulated to be "Sport enjoyment for all", and a new strategic plan for disability sport (para sport) for 2022–2027 was launched in February 2022 with the title "One sport – equal opportunities" (NIF, 2022b).

Gains of the Inclusive Model

Questionnaires and interviews of para sport athletes in the early phases of the integration process (Sørensen & Kahrs, 2011) pointed out the main positive experiences to be that it is a positive signal in itself that persons with a disability are members on the same terms as others. Further that there are more possibilities, more sports to choose from and that the sports federations increase their competence about disability sport. It is clear that the support for top-level para athletes has improved, and that there are more and stronger demands to sport events.

In summing up what is reported in Dale (2019) and the interviews in 2020, which means ca. 10–12 years after the new organisation was finally established, some of the same issues can still be recognised. There seems to be reasonable consensus about the following.

All in all the Norwegian sport organisations take more and a more active responsibility for disability sport/para sport. In spite of some local or regional variations, there seems to be more engagement from other agents in society such as foundations, for example, VI (US), and the collaboration with the public support through NAV for activity aids has been extended to individuals older than 26 years.

There is more diversity in types of sports available for individuals with a disability (around 60 sport possibilities), among them more sports that appeal to the young and that they can do with friends without disability, for example, climbing, snowboard.

Even if there are still difficulties with registration, there seems to be an increase in number of sports clubs having one (or more) members with a disability, but the numbers are not totally verifiable. There are for instance some initiatives that are not counted in the registration system, for example, regional low threshold all activity groups.

Elite para sport has never been better off financially. Some say the situation is approaching that of regular elite sport, but there is some disagreement as to how close it is. For the elite the quality of coaching has improved, but there are also more demands in order to be enrolled as an elite para athlete. It is now more usual that para sport is part of larger sport events with their own classes, for example, in Norwegian Championships in some sports.

The Olympic Training Centre has started up regional "tasting arrangements" where newcomers may try out sports together with elite athletes. This initiative is considered to be very positive. There are some differences between disability groups as to how much they have gained through the integration process, especially those with developmental/intellectual disabilities seem to have benefited.

Barriers

Recruitment to para sport is still a considerable challenge. This is due to several factors. The general higher level of integration in our society and educational system provides less role models and people in a similar situation to learn from in the same way that the former special schools and institutions did, because they were good breeding grounds for disability sport. The regional consultants are important in the work to build networks and contacts in this respect (Sørensen & Kahrs, 2011; Dale, 2019). In addition, there seems to be a lack of general public strategies and initiatives that contribute to contact and distribution of information to parents and children as well as adults with disabilities. It is reported that participation for some is hindered by existing organisation of possibilities for transport, activity aids and guides/assistants/interpreters, but there is local variation (Sørensen & Kahrs, 2011; Oslo Economics, 2020).

No longer having their own organisations and representatives in both the central and regional organisations had formally reduced democratic representation and visibility for people with a disability as a group (Sørensen & Kahrs, 2011). It was an ambition from the start that the sports councils should ensure representation from individuals with a disability, but this seems not to have become a reality in all regions. However, there is so far no concrete data about this.

The integrated organisational model in NIF created some problems for the sport for individuals with hearing disabilities, in particular as to representation in the International Deaf Sport Organisations. The International Committee of Sport for the Deaf (ICSD) demanded that representatives to the organisation had to have a hearing impairment. If not, there were threats to exclude Norwegian deaf athletes from international competitions. A Norwegian Deaf Sports Committee was therefore formed, and there are eight clubs for Deaf Sport (NIF, 2020b).

Lack of knowledge and competence about disability sport and adaptation of sport is still a barrier for parasport athletes. This can be seen in the difference between the federations with and without dedicated consultants in how well they are able to support their clubs (Dale, 2019). There are large variations between both sports federations and regions in how well they have developed parasport, and also among the municipalities in how well the support systems and funding possibilities for children and youth with disabilities are utilised, resulting in differences in possibilities for participation (Dale, 2019; Oslo Economics, 2020).

The active athletes in the early phases of the process reported that the most important that was lost in the process was that it is sometimes felt psychologically tough and lonely to be the only athlete with a disability, and that they did not always feel welcome, especially when it happened that they literally were forgotten—both in invitations and at actual events (Sørensen & Kahrs, 2011). It was also pointed out that their sport achievements were not well understood in relation to the classification system, and that those with the least need for help and support were given priority, while those in need for extensive adaptions and support lost. They also reported a feeling that disability sport was losing its characteristics and that there were few disability sport events left.

According to the most recent reports, some of the same issues seem to still be present (Dale, 2019; Oslo Economics, 2020). Some are also supported by the interviews we made in 2020. The main points include that many of the existing social milieus within disability sport have disappeared and that the individuals with a disability are more scattered. Some think it was easier to get started with sport before when there were disability sports groups to get started in. There seems to be an agreement that those with the largest needs for support and adaptions have benefitted less than those who need less adaptations and support. It is easier and demands less to engage those with less practical demands, and the costs and the need for special competence increase with more support demands for the individual clubs.

Those who do not want to engage in competitive sport, but only want to exercise, keep fit or take part for the social aspect, have lost opportunities. Also, as a sub group of the population, those with disabilities have lost systematic representation in the sport organisation. Even if there are examples of elite-level athletes combining their career with some work in the organisations, or work there after their careers, the group no longer has their own delegates to the general assembly or the regional assemblies. The intention to ensure representation in the local sport councils does not seem to have been fulfilled. There is large variation in how well the councils operate in general, and it may be difficult to find local candidates, but there does not seem to be any formal requirements for such representation in any part of the organisation. So far there is no available data on this issue.

There are large variations in how well the responsibility is handled, both between the individual sport federations and in the regions. In the districts it is difficult to arrange team sports due to large geographical distribution.

7.6 Conclusion

Since 2007 Norway has organisationally included disability sport (now termed para sport) in their regular sport organisations within The Norwegian Olympic and Paralympic Committee and Confederation of Sports (NIF). This means that all sport federations and regional sport organisations have the responsibility to offer their activities to individuals with disabilities on equal terms with others. The process was developed through various stages with a ten year preparatory period before the organisations for disability sport were dissolved. The process has been evaluated and the progress been reported on several occasions, the latest report came in 2020. For the purpose of this book, interviews were conducted in September 2020. Ten people with extensive experience from the process as employees at various levels of the organisation, active para sport athletes and individuals who combine those two roles were interviewed. There seems to be reasonable consensus that the inclusive organisational model is here to stay, and that establishing it is a long process where patience is needed. There are many gains: The Norwegian Olympic and Paralympic Committee and Confederation of Sports, as a whole, taking more responsibility for disability sport; a clearly better organisation of elite para sport; and more sports available, in particular for children and youth among the most important.

There are also some losses described, and we have tried to sum up some take home messages of challenges to be aware of for others who might try this type of organisation of disability sport.

Inclusion is not ensured with an organisational model alone—it needs constant work with the social aspects and competence development, financially and practically! Sport activities suitably adapted to the individuals are necessary. Recruitment demands constant attention and initiatives. Special initiatives for groups of individuals with disability may be an important step on the road to inclusion! Take care of and stimulate good, existing milieus! More overarching strategies for the collaboration between the sport organisations and the central and regional public authorities are needed, and strategic information must be used in order to convince potential participants in para sport. There should also be a focus on recreational activities, and not only on competitive sport.

Leaders of the various parts of the organisation must show that inclusion is taken seriously and show the way and let finances follow. Especially dedicated people (ildsjeler) and active profiled athletes are still an important force in the work. In addition it may seem as if local initiatives with local ambassadeurs are important. Ensure democratic representation in the organisation at level with gender, ethnic minorities and so on. Actions in order to increase participation in para sport must be carried out at all levels of the organisation.

References

Bakken, A. (2017). Ungdata 2017 (Youth data). NOVA rapport 10/17.
Barne – og likestillingsdepartementet (Ministry of Children and Equality). (2018). *Et samfunn for alle* (A society for all). En strategiplan (A strategy plan) for 2020 – 2030. Oslo.
Barne – og likestillingsdepartementet (Ministry for Children and Equality). (2019). *Et samfunn for alle. Regjeringens strategi for likestilling av mennesker med funksjonsnedsettelser 2020 – 2030* [A society for all. The strategy of the government for equality of persons with a disability 2020-2030]. Ministry for Children and Equality.
BufDir (The Norwegian Directorate for Children, Youth and Family Affairs). (2020). Retrieved September 10, 2020, from https://bufdir.no/en
Bufdir (The Norwegian Directory for Children, Youth and Family Affairs). (2018). Retrieved February 22, 2020, from https://bufdir.no
Central Intelligence Agency (CIA). (2018). *The world Factbook.* Retrieved September 9, 2020, from https://www.cia.gov/library/publications/the-world-factbook/geos/no.html
Dale, Ø. (2019). *Paraidretten. Situasjonsbeskrivelse av norsk idretts tilrettelegging av idrett for mennesker med nedsatt funksjonsevne* [The para sport. A situational description of Norwegian Sport's work for sport for individuals with disability]. The Norwegian Confederation of Sports.
Direktoratet for byggkvalitet (Directory for building quality). (2017). *Building regulations TEK 17.* Retrieved September 10, 2020, from https://dibk.no.byggereglene/byggteknisk-forskrift-tek17.
Eurostat. (2017). Eu SILC Survey.
Fasting, K., Sand, T. S., Sisjord, M. K., Thoresen, T., & Beyer Broch, T. (2008). *Likestilling og mangfold i norsk idrett* [Equality and diversity in Norwegian Sport]. Likestillings- og integreringsombudet.
Fladmoe, A., Sivesind, K. H., & Arnesen, D. (2018). *Oppdaterte tall om frivillig innsats Rapport 2* [Updated numbers on voluntary contributions]. Center for Research on Civil Society and Voluntary Sector.
Funksjonshemmedes Fellesorganisasjon (FFO) (The Norwegian Federation of Organisations of Disabled People). (2019). Retrieved January 23, 2020, from https://www.ffo.no/Tema/gi-meg-fem/.
Gåsemyr, J., Johnsen, J., & Halbo, L. (Eds.). (2019). *Idrett og Friluftsliv for synshemmede 1969 – 2019, Hodr idrettslag gjennom 50 år.* ISBN: 978-82-303-4378-4.
Helsenorge (Health Norway). (2019). Støttekontakt (Support contact). Retrieved December 18, 2020, from https://www.helsenorge.no/hjelpetilbud-i-kommunene/stottekontakt/
Kahrs, N. (2006). *Funksjonshemmedes idrett og integreringsprosessen 10 år etter. En situasjonsrapport* [Disability sport and the integration process 10 years after. A situation report]. Norges Handikapforbund, Øst.
Karlsen, H. T., Wettergreen J., & Jensen A. (2019). *Utredning av ny levekårsstatistikk for personer med funksjonsnedsettelse* [Investigation of new statistics for the living conditions of disabled persons]. SSB Notater 2019/42, 27.
Kommunal- og Moderniseringsdepartementet (Ministry of Local Government and Modernisation). (2008). *Lov om plan og bygging* [Law about planning and building]. Retrieved September 10, 2020, from https://lovdata.No/dokument/NLE/LOV-2008-06-27-71
Kommunal- og Moderniseringsdepartementet (Ministry of Local Government and Modernisation). (2019).
Kulturdepartementet (Ministry of Culture). (2012). *Den norske idrettsmodellen* [The Norwegian Sports model]. Stortingsmelding (White paper) 26, 2011–2012.
Kulturdepartementet (Ministry of Culture). (2019). *Lov om likestilling og forbud mot diskriminering* [Equality and Anti-Discrimination Act]. Retrieved September 10, 2020, from https://lovdata.No/dokument/LOV-2019-06-21-57
Mathisen, G. (1972). *Historie. B-kurs kompendiet.* NHIF.

Nasjonalt kompetansemiljø for utviklingshemming (National Competence service for developmental disorders). (2019). Retrieved September 12, 2020, from https://naku.no/utviklingshemming-mennesket-og-diagnosen/

NIF (Norges Idrettsforbund - The Norwegian Confederation of Sports and Olympic and Paralympic Committee). (2019a). *Om NIF (about NIF)*. Retrieved September 12, 2020, from https://www.idrettsforbundet.no/om-nif

NIF (Norges Idrettsforbund - The Norwegian Confederation of Sports and Olympic and Paralympic Committee). (2019b). *Nøkkeltall – rapport 2018* [Key figures - Report 2018]. Norges idrettsforbund.

NIF (Norges Idrettsforbund - The Norwegian Confederation of Sports and Olympic and Paralympic Committee). (2019c). *Idretten vil – langtidsplaner for 2019-2023* [What sport wants- long term plans for 2019-2023]. Retrieved September 23, 2020, from https://www.idrettsforbundet.no/contentassets/8149372c5d4d439cb1b34fc1625032f0/idretten-vil_langtidsplan-for-norsk-idrett-2019-2023_lr.pdf

NIF (Norges Idrettsforbund - The Norwegian Confederation of Sports and Olympic and Paralympic Committee). (2020a). *Felles samordnet registrering paraidrett 14-19* [Common coordinated registration para sport 2014-2019]. NIF.

NIF (Norges Idrettsforbund - The Norwegian Confederation of Sports and Olympic and Paralympic Committee). (2020b). *Norges døveidrettsutvalg* [Norwegian Deaf Sport Committee]. Retrieved September 25, 2020, from https://www.doveidrett.no

NIF (Norges Idrettsforbund - The Norwegian Confederation of Sports and Olympic and Paralympic Committee). (2020c). *Spillemidler – rapport 2019* [Report on use of means from lottery 2019]. Norges idrettsforbund.

NIF (Norges idrettsforbund - The Norwegian Confederation of Sports and Olympic and Paralympic Committee). (2022a). Retrieved May 25, 2022, from https://www.idrettsforbundet.no/om-nif

NIF (Norges idrettsforbund - The Norwegian Confederation of Sports and Olympic and Paralympic Committee). (2022b). *En idrett- like muligheter. Para-strategi for norsk idrett 2022 – 2027* [One sport - equal opportunities. Para-strategy for Norwegian sport 2022-2027]. Retrieved February 11, 2022, from https://www.paraidrett.no/siteassets/dokumenter/diverse/parastrategien-nif.pdf

NIH (Norges idrettshøgskole - The Norwegian School of Sort Sciences). (2017). *Studiehåndbok (Studyhandbook) 2017-2018*. Norges idrettshøgskole.

NRK (The Norwegian Broadcasting Corporation). (2018). Retrieved June 15, 2020, from http://www.nrk.no/norge/regjeringen.foreslaar-kutt-til-multi-handikappede_-glutensyke-og-inkontinente_1.14239215

Oslo Economics. (2020). *Idrett for mennesker med funksjonsnedsettelser* [Sport for people with disability]. OE-rapport 2020-57. Oslo Economics.

Regjeringen (The government). (2003a). Retrieved February 23, 2020, from https://www.regjeringen.no/no/dokumenter/stmeld-nr-40-2002-2003-/id197129/?ch=1

Regjeringen (The government). (2003b). Retrieved February 27, 2020, from https://www.regjeringen.no/en/topics/culture-sports-and-non-profit-work/innsiktsartikler/sports-policy/id2001187/

Regjeringen (The government). (2019). Public Health Report- a good life in a safe society. White Paper No. 19 (2018–2019).

Regjeringen (The government). (2020). The distribution of means to sport purposes. Retrieved September 12, 2020, from https://www.regjeringen.no/contentassets/bea6418f69404de4ba0baa79192fbcbb/prm-34-20-vedlegg-hovedfordelingen-av-spillemidler-til-idrettsformal.pdf

Skogli, E., Stokke, O. M., & Myklebust, A. (2019). *Rapport om øyehelse i Norge* [Report on eye-health in Norway]. Menon publikasjon 57/2019.

Sørensen, M., & Kahrs, N. (2006). Integration of disability sport in the Norwegian sport organizations: Lessons learned. *Adapted Physical Activity Quarterly, 23*, 184–202.

Sørensen, M., & Kahrs, N. (2011). En idrett for alle? (A sport for all?) In V. Hanstad et al. (Eds.), *Norsk idrett- indre spenning og ytre press* (Norwegian Sport, inner tension and outward pressure). Akilles.

Sørensen, M., Kahrs, N., Aadland, I. L., Bjelland, L. A., Garden, J. H., Johnsen, J., Moors, D., & Pensgaard, A. M. (1999). *Evaluation of the integration process in Norwegian Sport*. English summary of report 1. The Norwegian School of Sport Sciences.

Sørensen, M., Kahrs, N., Aamodt, I. L., & Strand, G. H. (2003). *Evaluering av integreringsprosessen I norsk idrett* [Evaluation of the integration process in Norwegian Sports]. Report, part 2. The Norwegian School of Sport Sciences.

Statistisk Sentralbyrå (Statistics Norway). (2018). Retrieved September 11, 2020, from https://www.ssb.no/nasjonalregnskap-og-konjunkturer/artikler-og-publikasjoner/frivillige-utforte-142000-arsverk/

Store Norske Leksikon (The Great Norwegian Ecyclopedia). (2020). Retrieved August 10, 2020, from https://snl.no/Norge

Utdannings- og forskningsdepartementet (Ministry for Education and Research). (1998). Retrieved September 20, 2020, from https://lovdata.no/dokument/NL/Lov1998-07-17-61

Van der Roest, J. W., van der Werff, H., & Elmose-Østerlund, K. (2017). *Involvement and commitment of members and volunteers in European sports clubs*. SIVSCE report, University of Southern Denmark.

Vanebo, K. (2002). *Økt fysisk aktivitet i psykiatrien. Sluttrapport* [Increased physical activity in psychiatry - final report]. Norges idrettsforbund.

Waldahl, R. H. (2009). *Samspill mellom idrett og kommuner: idrettsrådene* [Interplay between sport and the municipalities through the sports councils] (p. 6). Institute for Societal Research, Report 2009.

Chapter 8
Beyond Inclusion: Opportunity Structures in Sports for All in Sweden

Kim Wickman and Linda Torége

8.1 Introduction

In light of an ongoing organisational change towards inclusion of PWD in the Swedish Sports Confederation (RF, Riksidrottsförbundet), this chapter identifies and discusses opportunity structures for sports participation in Sweden by describing how national and regional authority policies can contribute to the sports infrastructure for diversity. For a change at the grassroots level, the entire organisation requires changes. We use the term *opportunity structures* to emphasise the ability to create an environment that offers something new and vitalising for all, not explicitly for PWD. According to our approach, policies are understood as roadmaps for the opportunities and obligations that key stakeholders have to follow when it comes to developing sports towards and beyond inclusion. Further, we reflect on the current organisational change in the RF, which involves the inclusion of all sports currently governed by the Swedish Parasport Federation, into a National Sports Federation (Specialidrottsförbund). An National Sports Federation is the national governing body of a specific sport in Sweden, for example, the Swedish Football Federation, the Swedish Gymnastics Federation and the Swedish Athletic Federation. However, there has never been a razor-sharp line between sports for athletes with or without labels. Throughout history, athletes have always sought the best conditions for training and competition in various sports. This also applies to PWD, albeit to a limited extent. In this chapter, we discuss the key structural and historical conditions in Sweden and address the knowledge gaps and unanswered questions that warrant

---

K. Wickman (✉)
Department of Education, Umeå University, Umeå, Sweden
e-mail: kim.wickman@umu.se

L. Torége
Parasport Development Manager, The Swedish Parasport Federation, Stockholm, Sweden
e-mail: linda.torege@parasport.se

further research. This chapter informs policy and practice aimed at enhancing PWDs' access to sport and physical activity and associated social and environmental inclusion. The insights presented can be used to inform existing and future sports-based programmes and interventions to strengthen their conceptual foundation, design, processes, equity and impact.

8.2 Country Profile

Characteristics of Sweden

The capital of Sweden is Stockholm. Sweden is a constitutional monarchy and a parliamentary democracy. The political power lies with the parliament (Riksdag) and government (Regering). The monarch has only ceremonial functions, and the Parliament has 349 members in a single chamber. Sweden has three levels of domestic government: national, regional and local. However, the European level has become increasingly important since Sweden joined the European Union (EU) in 1995. The government consists of a prime minister and 22 ministers and is the driving force in the process of legislative change, thereby influencing the development of Swedish society. The government rules Sweden by implementing the decisions of the Parliament and by formulating new laws or law amendments on which the Parliament decides (Riksdagen, 2020).

Of around 10 million (0.13% of the world's population) people who live in Sweden, about two million are under the age of 18, and 85% live in cities. Over the last few decades, Sweden has received many immigrants, receiving 163,000 asylum seekers in 2015. Of those, 114,000 arrived during September–December, and 70,000 were children. In the same year, 35,000 children unaccompanied by a custodial parent sought asylum, of whom 26,000 arrived during the last four months of the year (SOU, 2017, p. 12). Approximately 19% of Swedes are born in another country, while about one in five children in Sweden has a family with roots in another country (SCB, 2020a). These extraordinary circumstances had relevance to the inclusion process of PWD in sport. Owing to the impact of the large number of asylum seekers, the integration process of immigrants had to be prioritised by the Swedish government and the RF was assigned to support this process (Table 8.1).

Sport in Sweden

Some sports federations in Sweden are over a hundred years old, while others are recently formed. Regardless of age, they offer a wide variety of sports, including individual- or team sports and different activites during the summer and winter (Riksidrottsförbundet, 2016). The RF was established in 1903 as the primary institution for voluntarily organised sports in Sweden and is commonly referred to as the

Table 8.1 Facts and statistics of Sweden

Population	10,348,730
Area	449,964 km²
Density (inhabitants/km²)	25.4
Urbanisation rate (%)	1.05
Political organisation	Parliamentary democracy
Structure of state	Unitary
Number of provinces/political regions	21
Number of municipalities	290
GDP per capita (US Dollar)	55,767
Number of official languages	1 (5)[a]
EU membership	1995
Welfare model	Nordic model

Source: SCB (2020a)
[a]Swedish is the official language, and there are five minority languages recognised by the parliament of Sweden (SCB, 2020b; UN Statistics Division, 2020; UN Department of Economics and Social Affairs, 2020)

Swedish sports movement. The RF holds a strong position in Swedish society and is trusted by the government to administer Swedish sport towards the government's established objectives regarding civic education, public health, growth and entertainment (Karp et al., 2016). The Swedish sports movement is a system of sport delivery based solely on voluntary organisations that are autonomous from but dependent on the national, regional and local governmental authorities in the Swedish political system. In the Scandinavian countries, sport is organised by voluntary, member-based, non-profit and democratically structured sports clubs. Furthermore, there is a high degree of public funding for sport in these countries (Bergsgard & Norberg, 2010; Stenling & Sam, 2020). The government's role has traditionally been limited to decisions on the extent of funding and overarching goals for it, while the RF has the mandate to decide how to reach these goals.

The RF received its first government grant in 1913 (Norberg, 2004) and has since been receiving granted permanent annual state subsidies for sporting activities as the main provider of nationwide sport and on all levels, from the recreational to the elite level. Based on a common understanding between the RF and the government, corporatism and collaboration, or an 'implicit contract' (Norberg, 2011, p. 319), have been established, which has enabled the government to control its expenditure and the RF to preserve its self-determination in a corporative collaboration (Fahlén et al., 2015; Karp et al., 2016; Norberg, 2011). The RF's main tasks include representing the voluntary and membership-based club sports in communication with authorities, officials and the society; administering and distributing government funds to affiliated organisations; stimulating sports development and research; coordinating social and ethical issues; leading and coordinating antidoping work; coordinating international cooperation; protecting sports' historical legacy; and acting as the government authority for the 55 upper secondary elite sport schools with some 1200 students in 30 sports (Leif Thorstenson, personal communication, 12 March, 2021).

As demonstrated in Table 8.2, row three, there are no data available according to membership in fitness clubs or health centres because they are kept from public subsidies for political reasons since, in most cases, they are privately owned companies driven by profit (Fahlen & Ferry, 2019). According to Eurobarometer (2017), 44% of the Swedish respondents answered that they use fitness clubs for recreational purposes. However, this is an indication of membership in fitness clubs and does not give a clear picture of the entire population in Sweden or of PWD.

The Swedish Research Council for Sport Science (2020) has been assigned the task of initiating, coordinating and supporting sports research, providing information and being responsible for monitoring state aid to sports, and creating conditions that facilitate collaboration between researchers at universities and colleagues and other key stakeholders in the field. Additionally, the Swedish Research Council for Sport Science is the only organisation in the field of sport and physical activity in the country with the requisite expertise and experience for both research and the monitoring of state aid. The organisation works closely with the RF and the National Sports Federations. Operations of the Swedish Research Council for Sport Science are financed partly by the Ministry of Culture through the RF and the Ministry of Education and Research. A large proportion of the Swedish Research Council for Sport Science's revenues is used for research funding (Swedish Research Council for Sport Science, 2020). In Sweden and the rest of Europe, Sport for All refers to children's and adults' accessibility to practise competitive sports for fitness and recreational reasons. Denmark, Norway and Sweden (as in this case) have Sport for All as their main policy goal for sports (Skille, 2011). These countries also have among the highest participation rates in Europe (Fig. 8.1).

Each National Sports Federation has its own board of directors, which makes the ultimate decisions for the federation. Every second year, the National Sports

Table 8.2 Sport profile of Sweden

Government authority responsible for sports	Department of Culture
Membership sport club (% of the population)	32.8%
Membership fitness or health centre (% of the population)	No information available
Sport participation, at least once a week (% of the population)	64%
Number of special sports federations	72
Number of sport clubs	18,000
Number of sport club members	3,149,000
National budget for sport	180 million euros
National budget for sport federations[a]	Approx. 53.8 million euros
Share of economic value of volunteers in sports in the GDP (2014)	3.32%
Local budget for sports	No information available

Sources: Riksidrottsförbundet (2020a) and Segnestam Larsson and Wagndal (2018)
[a]The RF disseminates funds from 180 million euros to sport federations for organisational and activity support

8 Beyond Inclusion: Opportunity Structures in Sports for All in Sweden

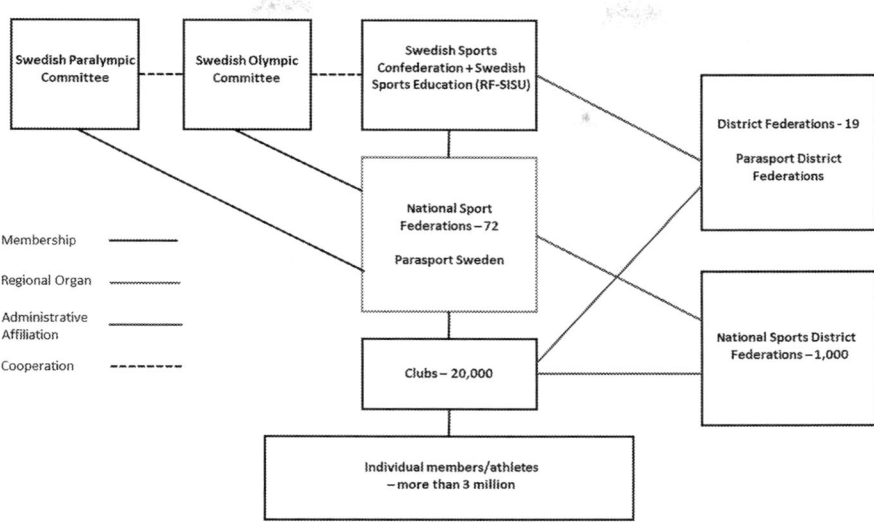

Fig. 8.1 The Swedish Sport organisation (The Federation of Deaf Sport is one of 72 special sports federations)

Federations meet at the biennial general meeting (RIM, Riksidrottsmöte), where they choose a board of directors/national sports council that governs the RF between the RIMs. Each of the 19 RF's districts has its own board but no power to vote at the RIM. Approximately three million of Sweden's total population is estimated to be involved in organised sports in Sweden, either as an athlete or as a voluntary non-profit worker (Stenling & Sam, 2017), making it by far the largest popular movement in Sweden that is considered to contribute to several positive social effects (Wickman, 2017).

The defining character of and main organising principle for contemporary club sports in Sweden is that of individuals forming and/or taking part as members of voluntary and membership-based sports clubs. The RF is the umbrella organisation for the 72 National Sports Federations organised in what is called the Nordic model, which means that it is run as an independent people's movement. Like many other models of sports organisations, the RF is primarily financed by the state and municipalities (cf. Fahlén et al., 2015; Fahrner & Klenk, 2018). About 18,000 non-profit clubs, with 650,000 voluntary leaders, form the basis of the Swedish sports movement. The clubs are members of the 72 National Sport Federations, depending on the sporting activities offered. The 72 National Sport Federations organise more than 250 different sports. These fererations, together with the 19 sports districts in Sweden, support and assist sports clubs in the chosen district. The umbrella organisation, the RF, has a monopoly on all federation sports in Sweden. The National Sports Federations are entitled to follow the statutes of the RF, the Antidoping Charter and the rules against illegal betting in sport (Riksidrottsförbundet, 2020b), while forming their own.

The member organisation of the International Paralympic Committee in Sweden is the Swedish Parasport Federation, which operates in the same manner and in close partnership with the National Olympic Committee in Sweden (Svenska Parasportförbundet, 2020a).

Disability in Sweden

The question of what is meant by disability and impairment (see Table 8.3 for translation) and the interaction between these terms is multifaceted. Five somewhat different ways of looking at impairment and disability are presented in Swedish disability research: an individual (Danermark, 2005; Priestley, 1998), a cultural (Corker & Shakespeare, 2002), a social (Thomas, 2004), a relational (Hjelmquist et al., 1994) and a biopsychosocial perspective (World Health Organization, 2001). The biopsychosocial model is an interdisciplinary model that looks at the interconnection between biology, psychology and socio-environmental factors and is the model that mainly influences the Swedish Parasport Federation's standpoint and value system. Disability organisations, state and county governments and foundations are all included among the funders of research, and the question of interplay between the environment and the individual is central to Swedish disability research.

Estimations suggest that the number of PWD in general in Sweden is between 1.3 and 1.8 million, which is between 12% and 18% of the total population (FUNKA, 2020). However, any exact figure of the prevalence of disability across nations is difficult to estimate due to different definitions of disabilities and because registers are not always accessible (Grönvik, 2009; Mont, 2007). International legal agreements, such as the UN Declaration on Human Rights and the Declaration on the Rights of the Child, are examples of two important international legal agreements. The responsibility of fulfilling and exercising international law rests with the Swedish government. In 2018, 74,000 people (40% women) made 111,400 contributions according to the Act concerning Support and Service to Persons with Certain Functional Disabilities (LSS, Lag om stöd och service till vissa funktionshindrade).

Table 8.3 Changes of disability sports terminology from 1980 until today, from Swedish to English

Handikappad	Handicapped
Funktionshindrad	Disabled
Utvecklingsstörd	Intellectual impaired
Person med intellektuell funktionsnedsättning	Person with intellectual disability
Parasportare	Para-athlete
Idrottare med funktionsnedsättning	Athlete with disability
Handikappidrottsförbundet	The Handicap Sport Federation (1969–2015)
Parasportförbundet	The Parasport Federation (from 2015)

The majority of the interventions were granted to people aged 23–64 years (Socialstyrelsen, 2020). The UN's Standard Rules on the Equalisation of Opportunities for PWD (2020) is a cornerstone of Swedish disability policy. The Swedish government ratified the UN Convention on the Rights of PWD in 2008. Unlike the standard rules, the convention is legally binding. As a result, Sweden has committed to ensuring that national legislation does not discriminate against PWD. The RF seeks to ensure that all its activities are in agreement with the international legal agreements that the government signs (Riksidrottsförbundet, 2008). The LSS is an important prerequisite for PWD to be involved in society at large but also in sports. The LSS enables education, work, and income and is a bridge to social inclusion. The intention of LSS is to contribute to increased autonomy and empowerment and to enable an active life for PWD.

Emergence of Disability Sports in Sweden

Disability sports were organised in 1962 by the Swedish Disability Federation (De Handikappades Riksförbund, DHR), a national association for persons with physical disabilities (Lundquist Wanneberg, 2017; Wickman, 2017). In 1969, the government report 'Sports for All' cited the importance of disability sports. In the same year, the Swedish Parasport Federation (it changed its name in 2015 from the Swedish Sports Organisation for the Disabled; Svenska Handikappidrottsförbundet, SHIF) was founded and became one of 72 National Sports Federations within the RF. Even before the inception of the disability sports organisation, disability organisations and sport organisations discussed, over 15 years, where the disability sports organisation should best be placed (Wickman, 2017). The discussion was whether to organise it under the umbrella of the RF or the organisation for persons with physical disabilities 'the Swedish Disability Federation', today called the DHR (Delaktighet, Handlingskraft och Rörelsefrihet). According to current knowledge, the government was not involved in how sports for PWD were to be organised (Fig. 8.2).

Since 1969, the Swedish Parasport Federation has administered sports for persons with physical, visual and intellectual disabilities. Through collective mobilisation, the federation is an central player when it comes to influencing power, enforcing change and raising awareness of issues that are important to make sports more equitable and accessible. Swedish Deaf Sports have been practiced in Sweden since the early 1890s. The Swedish Deaf Sports Federation was founded in 1913 and is the world's second oldest sports federation for deafness. It received status as a member of the RF in 1995 but is not a member of the Swedish Parasport Federation.

In connection with the RF's highest decision-making body (RIM), the sports 'parliament', the Swedish Parasport Federation decided to establish a long-term sustainable strategy for the inclusion of sports administered by the Swedish Parasport Federation, but which could have their homes in various National Sports Federations. The reason for this proposal was an organisational review of Swedish

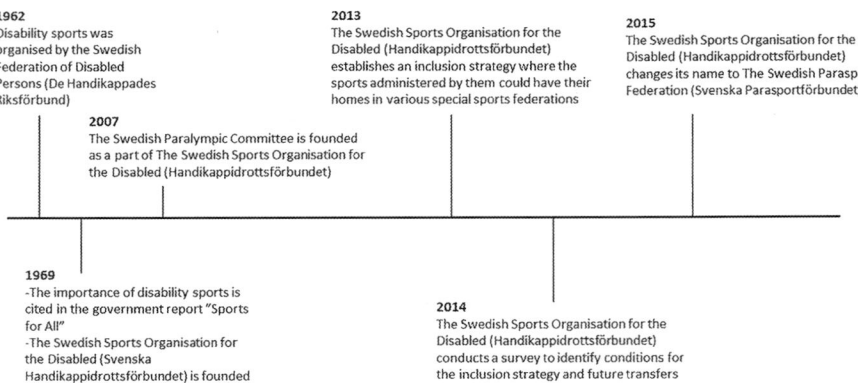

Fig. 8.2 The emergence of parasport in Sweden

sports that was conducted to investigate its structure and financial flows to create higher efficiency (Nivert & Lervik, 2008). The model was the Norwegian Sports Confederation and Olympic Committee, and the inclusion process that took place between 2002 and 2008 (Sørensen & Kahrs, 2006, 2011). The organisational review contained a proposal that advocated the dismantling of the Swedish Parasport Federation and the inclusion of athletes with disabilities in National Sports Federations. Further, in 2014, the Swedish Parasport Federation conducted a survey among all the existing sports in the Swedish Parasport Federation to identify the conditions for inclusion and then drew up action plans for collaboration and the future transfer and inclusion of sports from the Swedish Parasport Federation to the National Sports Federations. When the inclusion of the 18 sports began, four sports had already been formally included in their mainstream sports federations since 2013: swimming, table tennis, judo and powerlifting.

8.3 The Disability Sport System

Structure of Disability Sports

With approximately three million members in nearly 20,000 non-profit local sports clubs, the RF is the country's largest popular movement (Riksidrottsförbundet, 2020a). In Sweden, while almost everyone is, at some point in their lives, an active member of a sports club, relatively few children and adults with disabilities take part in sports temporarily or on a regular basis. The reasons for this disparity include a range of individual, social and environmental factors that have been recognised in several studies and reports. For example, for athletes with disabilities, few opportunities are present in the design and access to being physically active (cf. Geidne & Jerlinder, 2016; Kristén et al., 2002; Wickman, 2017), and as a result, the chance for PWD to develop confidence and skills in sport and physical activity is limited

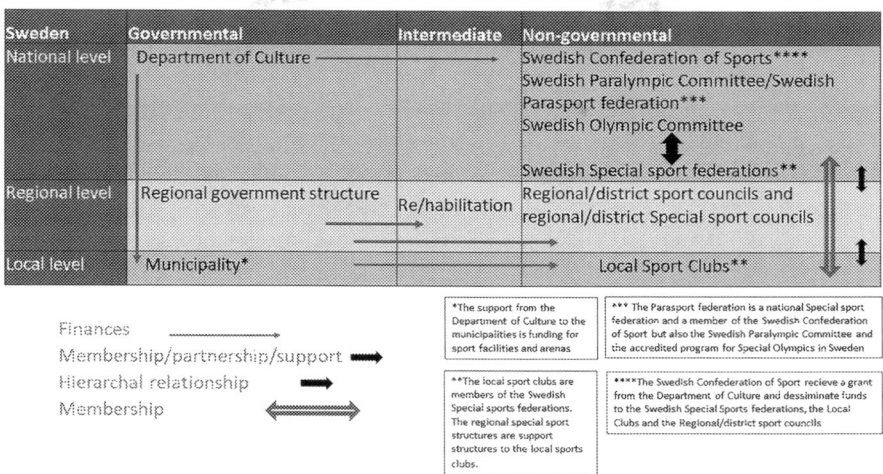

Fig. 8.3 The funding and co-dependency of the national, regional and local sports between the different geographical levels of the governmental, intermediate and non-governmental levels of sport in Sweden

(Geidne & Jerlinder, 2016; Hodge & Runswick-Cole, 2013; Wickman, 2017). This phenomenon has also been highlighted in several international studies in the field of disability sport (cf. DePauw & Gavron, 2005; Fay, 2011; Misener & Darcy, 2014; Darcy et al., 2020). In Sweden, this structural inequality is evident at both the recreational and elite levels, as PWD typically have fewer opportunities to participate in organised sports compared to non labelled persons (cf. Geidne & Jerlinder, 2016; Wickman, 2017).

In Sweden, parasports are sports played by PWD, including physical, visual and intellectual disabilities. Some parasports are variations on existing able-bodied sports, while others such as goalball, wheelchair rugby and electric wheelchair floor hockey have been specifically created for PWD and do not have an able-bodied equivalent. At a competitive level, disability sports classifications are applied to allow people of varying abilities to face similar opposition. Today, most of Sweden's modern indoor facilities have adapted premises, which means good accessibility for PWD. Many places offer leadership training and try-out days in sports, with a special focus on the intended target group (Fig. 8.3).

Governmental Agents

As mentioned in the first part of the chapter, the parliament of Sweden is the legislative power and decides upon laws that the regional or municipal political structures will interpret at their level of governance. The regional level will determine and run, for example, support through rehabilitation and access to assistive devices. The municipalities determine the type and amount of assistance a PWD can receive, including care units and special schools for pupils with intellectual disabilities.

The national governmental agency for sports in Sweden is the Department of Culture. The government's role has traditionally been limited to decisions on the extent of funding and overarching goals for it, while the RF has the mandate to decide how to reach these goals. The low degree of conflict and the relationship between the sports movement and Swedish authorities are generally ascribed to the 'Swedish model' and 'a typical feature of Swedish welfare politics'. The registered number of members and the activities that the local sport clubs run mark a base for the municipalities to support the local sport clubs. Most of the sports facilities, both indoor and outdoor, are municipality-owned and often part of a school. The municipalities have the responsibility for transport for PWD, which can often determine whether an para-athlete can take part in the weekly sport session or a competition.

Intermediate Agents

The welfare model in Sweden mandates that the political regions in Sweden be responsible for healthcare. The regional political structure has the overall responsibility for rehabilitation access to adapted equipment and other support systems for different disability groups. Therefore, the regional authorities have an intermediate role to play regarding disability sports in Sweden.

Non-governmental Agents

In the Scandinavian countries, sport is organised by voluntary, member-based, non-profit and democratically structured sports clubs. Sports clubs are the main implementers of sports in Sweden (Toftegaard Støckel et al., 2010). Further, there is a relatively high degree of public funding for sport in these countries (Bergsgard & Norberg, 2010). The RF holds a strong position in Swedish society and is trusted by the government to administer Swedish sport towards the government's established objectives regarding civic education, public health, growth and entertainment (Karp et al., 2016). Since Sweden is an elongated country and population differences between north and south, it affects the range of parasport. In the south, where the population density is generally high, there are greater opportunities for more sports and, above all, more team sports and opportunities for tournaments for PWD than in the north. Above all, these are major differences between sparsely populated areas and large cities. However, in the north, where the winter is longer, there is a greater range of winter sports such as cross-country skiing and downhill skiing for PWD. One such example is The Total Ski School. Totalskidskolan is a ski school that welcomes all skiers with a permanent disability—visual, physical or intellectual. Totalskidskolan located in Åre in Northern Sweden and is a non-profit organisation. The RF, their members, the National Sports Federations and their member clubs all play a role in policy development. However, gyms and health/fitness clubs do not for organisational and political reasons.

Secondary Agents

In Sweden, there are right-based civil society organisations that represent the PWD, for example, the Swedish disability movement, DHR (Delaktighet, Handlingskraft och Rörelsefrihet) and Swedish Association of Local Authorities and Regions (SKR, Sveriges Kommuner och Regioner). These organisations have partnerships with the Swedish Parasport Federation for policy change, for example, during the annual National Almedalen Week. Almedalen Week is a democratic meeting when a range of actors in the public, private and non-profit sector, together with political representatives and the media, meet for a week in Visby on Gotland to discuss political issues, for example, in regard to disability, physical and social inclusion and accessibility on different levels in society (Henrik Hjelmberg, personal communication, July 2, 2020). These organisations are non-governmental but can, in contrast to the Swedish Parasport Federation (Svenska Parasportförbundet, 2021a), limit and indirectly impact the policy decision, according to Parasport, for example, through organised seminars, debates and dialogues with politicians such as at Almedalen, or through podcasts such as Paradalen, a FaceTime video dialogue during 2020 (Svenska Parasportförbundet, 2021b). Parasport Sweden has its own political programme, which was updated in 2020, and creates the basis of the work throughout the organisation.

Over the years, the Swedish Federation of the Visually Disabled (SRF) has cooperated with the Swedish Parasport Federation. Together the two organisations work for an increased active life for PWD (Henrik Hjelmberg, personal communication, July 2, 2020). SKR affects policy on all levels for the benefit of the citizens in Sweden therefore they are an important organisation to keep a continuous dialogue with concerning policy (Henrik Hjelmberg, personal communication, July 2, 2020). The Swedish National Association for People with Intellectual Disability (FUB, Förbundet för personer med utvecklingsstörning/intellektuell funktionsnedsättning) works with people with intellectual disabilities on local, regional and national levels. The Swedish Parasport Federation cooperates with the FUB to develop Special Olympics activities in Sweden (Henrik Hjelmberg, personal communication, July 2, 2020).

Steering of Disability Sports

The Department of Culture gives RF the mandate to be the main policymaker and to disseminate financial funds based on the policies (Bergsgard & Norberg, 2010). The Swedish Parasport Federation is a member of RF as well as the International Paralympic Committee and several other international Parasport-related organisations. To be a member of the RF, certain criteria must be fulfilled by the member federation. The federation must have a minimum number of members and member clubs and must run one or more sports. The member clubs in the federation determine the governance of the federation through a democratic model. The respective National Sports Federation reports facts to the RF based on the membership

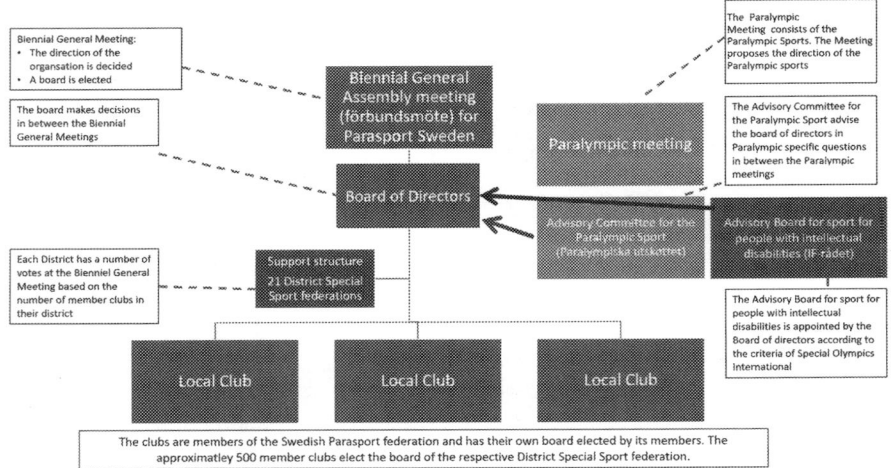

Fig. 8.4 The governance model of the Swedish Parasport Federation

criteria annually to enable a prolonged membership. During the RIM meeting every second ear, the RF takes up new member federations and has the power to exclude members who no longer fit the criteria as members of the RF (Fig. 8.4).

The Swedish Parasport Federation and the Swedish Paralympic Committee are made up of local member clubs. The number of members in the clubs determines how many votes the clubs have at the annual general meeting in the respective 21 districts under the umbrella of the Swedish Parasports Federation. The number of clubs in the respective district makes up the number of votes at the National Parasport Federation's biennial general meetings where policies, strategies and the national board are elected to steer the federation and the Swedish Paralympic Committee for the following two years. The national board of directors comprises seven members and one chairperson/president. The Swedish Parasport Federation acts as the Swedish Paralympic Committee. To steer the Paralympic Committee, a Paralympic Meeting is held biennially for all Swedish National Sports Federations with Paralympic Sports in Sweden. The Paralympic Meeting suggests the direction the Swedish Paralympic Sports should take in the following two years. The advisory committee (*utskott*) advises the national board of directors of the Swedish Parasport Federation on questions concerning Paralympic-related questions, such as delegation to the Paralympics and membership in the International Paralympic Committee (IPC).

Relationships

The relationships and policy framework—such as the RF statutes, strategies and values in sport—have been described in the following sections: Sport in Sweden, Structure of Disability Sports and Steering of Disability Sports.

Legislative Framework

Several Swedish laws regulated service and support to PWD such as the Swedish Social Services Act (Socialtjänstlagen, SoL), the Swedish Local Government Act (Kommunallagen, KL) and the Act concerning Support and Service for Persons with Certain Functional Impairments (Lagen om stöd och service till vissa funktionshindrade, LSS). These acts give PWD the right to support to help them participate in society. The LSS was enforced in 1994. It is a human rights law designed to offer persons with extensive disabilities greater opportunities to lead independent lives and to ensure that they have equal living conditions and enjoy full participation in community life. The law gives PWD the right to personal assistance, a form of support that is mostly funded by taxes. The amount of help they receive is determined by the extent of their disabilities. People not covered by the support offered can seek assistance from their local council/municipality under the Social Services Act. In 2009, the Discrimination Act was introduced in Sweden to strengthen the legal protection of the individual and to help victims of discrimination obtain and redress financial compensation. The purpose of the Act is to combat discrimination and promote equal rights and opportunities regardless of sex, transgender identity or expression, ethnicity, religion or other beliefs, functional impairment, sexual orientation or age and is divided into two parts:

1. The proactive part of the law imposes a duty to take positive action and concerns working life and the educational system.
2. The reactive part of the law deals with the prohibition of discrimination in working life, in the educational system and in other areas of society.

National Policy Framework

In 1999, the Swedish Parliament (*Sveriges Riksdag*) decided that the national policy on sports should consist of three main pillars that should guide the grants given to the Swedish Confederation of Sport (SOU, 2008).

1. Sports shall increase public health.
2. The organised sport must be ethical, democratic, free and autonomous—ensure sport for all—no discrimination in regards to the seven discrimination groups.
3. Elite sport is an important national entertainment sector.

Two parliamentary decisions, the first in 1999 and the second in 2009, create the foundation for yearly governmental grants to the RF. In 2008, the government evaluated the Swedish sport policy. The evaluation did not result in a change to the policy, but the rights of the child were emphasised.

Every year, the government sends a regulation letter to the RF with a yearly grant based on the three sport policy pillars. In the regulation letter for 2021, the RF was given an extra grant of an additional four million euros for the implementation of a physical literacy project in schools in Sweden (Regleringsbrev, 2020). This special venture follows other additional grants where the government gives the RF the task of delivering on objectives set by the government in power.

Regional Sports Policy and Support for Sports for PWD

The different political regional councils administer support to the sports fraternity according to the 19 political regions/counties. Governmental regions operate differently. The governmental regions sometimes use the RF district/regional sports offices to disburse money to the special sports district/regional offices for, for example, football and parasport. Sometimes, the regional National Sports Federations receive funding directly from governmental regional offices. Across Sweden there are examples of development centres for PWD, for example, the regional and local development and competence centres in Östersund in the north (Östersund Kommun, 2020), Eskilstuna in central Sweden (Eskilstuna kommun, 2020) and Malmö in the south (Malmö stad, 2020). These development centres cooperate with RF and in some cases with different Swedish Universities in the development of training, competition and equipment with regard to Parasport.

Financial, Governance and Managerial Support

Financial Framework

As described above in the section about the Swedish sports system, there is a relatively high degree of public funding for sports in Sweden (Bergsgard & Norberg, 2010). Since 1913, the RF has received government grants (Norberg, 2004). In 2020, the National Government granted the RF nearly five billion SEK (approximately 420,000,000 euros) to disseminate to the National Sports Federation, direct to the clubs and, for example, to research (Riksidrottsförbundet, 2020b, 2020c). The RIM in 2017 gave the RF the task of critically examining the way the financial support was disseminated to the National Sports Federations to enable a high degree of results according to the strategies decided and the government goals for the funding. During the RIM in 2019, it was decided that a portion of the governmental grant should be disseminated to the National Sports Federations that run Parasports. In 2020, a grant totalling 20 million SEK (approximately 2,000,000 euros) was divided based on certain criteria to 27 National Sports Federations. This was the first time this had occurred.

Local sports clubs receive funding based on the activities they report in the local activity (LOK) support system. To avoid false reporting, the RF conducts spot checks. The local clubs register their activities in five different groups: girls versus boys aged 7–12 years, 13–16 years, 17–20 years, 21–25 years and 26 and older. According to sport leaders and PWD, they are not gender divided. There are certain rules linked to this support system—such as the size of the group, the length of minutes the activity must be held for and the number of coaches per group (Riksidrottsförbundet, 2020d).

The definition of athletes with disabilities has been discussed, and the current data do not provide a correct figure. The General Data Protection Regulation (GDPR) is very strict, and sports clubs are not allowed to gather, store or use data that are not strictly relevant for the clubs' daily programmes. Although there is state support through LOK, the main funding for local sports clubs' activities comes from municipalities and members of the clubs. According to statistics from the RF, 1559 clubs have registered five or more activities for PWD in the LOK support system in 2019. Of those clubs, 199 were members of the Swedish Parasport Federation and 17 were members of the Swedish Deaf Sport Federation. In total, there were nearly 20,000 registered local sports clubs in the LOK support system in 2018 (Leif Thorstenson, personal communication, 12 March, 2021).

According to a report from the RF (Arnoldsson, 2019), the government allocated 264 million SEK to the RF in 2015 for work on the 2015–2018 initiative for working with asylum seekers and newcomers who recently received a residence permit in Sweden. A total of 3240 such projects were implemented during the period by sports associations in 279 municipalities. The activities within the projects gathered just over one million participants. The districts also invested in education and training initiatives aimed at both the target group and members of local sports clubs in general, as well as internal skills development. Notably, the report does not focus on new arrivals with disabilities. The 2030 Development Agenda (UN, 2006) recognises the importance of empowering people in vulnerable situations, including for example PWD and refugees. As global attention to intersectionality issues has been increasing, it is essential to enhance the link between disability and migration to overcome barriers of exclusion. The broad spectra of sport experiences and language backgrounds among new arrivals with disabilities are a fact and a reality that must be met with professionalism and knowledge, a capacity that requires resources, adaptations and long-term investments probably far above what was in the plan when the inclusion process of Parasport was initiated in Sweden.

Governance and Management Support

The municipalities around Sweden own the most indoor and outdoor sports facilities. The clubs rent the facilities for their programmes at a low cost or no cost at all. The municipalities also support with direct grants and, sometimes, funding for projects. The amount differs from municipality to municipality. The members of the club pay a membership fee and a training fee. The training fee can differ from nothing up to several thousand Swedish kronor (SEK) for a season. The government offers governance and managerial support to the sport fraternity in Sweden, but there are local variations. RF offers support to the National Sports Federations, mainly in line with moving the federations towards implementation of Strategy 2025 (described in more detail below). The National Sports Federation can also get support in certain development or organisational processes. Depending on what sports they offer, the clubs are members of the National Sports Federation, and the federations support the clubs with capacity building, such as referees and coaching education, and they administer local and regional league systems, such as football leagues, at different competitive levels/competitions. The Swedish Sports district offices also offer capacity building and club development initiatives and processes (SISU idrottsutbildarna, 2020a). The National Sports Federation and the RF's district offices also offer governance support for special and Regional Sports Federation. The Swedish Parasport Federation supports other National Sports Federation by including sports from the Swedish Parasport Federation to the receiving federation. During a transition period, the Swedish Parasport Federation acts as a hub for parasport competence in Sweden due to its unique experience in sports in Sweden and its regional structure running Parasport in the country (Riksidrottsförbundet, 2020e).

Level of Integration or Inclusion

'Strategy 2025 – A Strong Parasport in Sweden' (The Swedish Parasport Federation, 2020a) is the collective name for the Swedish Parasport Federation's strategic work to be completed in 2025. The changing process is now in motion and is composed of 14 of the initial 18 National Sports Federation. Table tennis, swimming, powerlifting and judo have already been handed over (Svenska Parasportförbundet, 2020b). In the long term, the organisational change in RF means that the Swedish Parasport Federation will also change according to needs and circumstances.

During the RF RIM in May 2017, the RF decided that the current 'Strategy 2025' was to be divided into five development pathways. One of the pathways is 'inclusive sport for all'. Inclusion means that the same opportunities should be available to all members of the RF irrespective of their ability, background, age, gender, wealth or place of residence. One of the key principles of the organisational change towards the inclusion of sport is that according to RF's 'Strategy 2025', PWD should, in a broader inclusion perspective, have equal opportunities to undertake different sports on all levels (from recreational to elite) and should be afforded similar opportunities as those enjoyed by their able-bodied peers. In practice, this means that the National Sports Federations are encouraged to play a more significant role in expanding their programmes and services to include PWD. According to previous research (Sørensen & Kahrs, 2006), fulfilling the objective of an integrated sports organisation is not without risks and efforts—especially when it comes to persons with severe disabilities, who need extra support and adjustments. When comparing PWD (especially persons with severe disabilities) with non labelled peers, they face a considerably greater risk of dropping out of sports, becoming early leavers from training and competitions and remaining in activities that are difficult to include in any of the existing National Sports Federation (e.g. goalball and wheelchair rugby). Currently, these sports have no National Sports Federation that conducts sports like the parasport in question. However, the intention is that all sports governed by the Swedish Parasport Federation should be included in a National Sports Federation in the future. The main target group of the RF and the government has been to include people with different backgrounds (regarding country/ethnic group), as well as girls and women. In 2020 the RF, through cooperation with the Swedish Parasport Federation, initiated generic parasport coaching education and added information on its website concerning inclusion of PWD for the first time (SISU Idrottsutbildarna, 2020b).

As the RF has made the decision that PWD should be able to enjoy equal opportunities to their nonlabelled peers, it has emphasised its responsibility: administer sports for non labelled persons. In 2020, 27 of the 72 sport federations were funded through the RF to develop and support parasport in Sweden. According to Strategy 2025, all the National Sports Federations should be proactive and work towards inclusion. The funds were disseminated for the first time in 2020 to support the development of adapted sports environments (Riksidrottsförbundet, 2020f).

An important notification is that the Swedish Deaf Sports Federation, Svenska Dövidrottsförbundet (SDI), is not a part of the Swedish Parasport Federation. It was founded on November 6, 1913, and is the joint promotional and administrative body for all organised deaf sports in Sweden. The SDI is a member of the RF and the Swedish Confederation of Sport Education (SISU) and is the highest authority of regional deaf leagues and sports clubs organised in regional Deaf Sports Divisions. The Swedish Deaf Sports Federation is a special category organisation that encompasses many different sports. It is like a miniature RF (SDI, 2020).

8.4 Sports Participation by PWD

Monitoring and Evaluation

Although the Swedish research community has addressed problems in RF, such as poor recruitment from underrepresented groups (cf. Kulturdepartementet, 2011; Karp et al., 2016), many researchers who study different aspects of implementation and change in RF have found that there is one dominant logic—the logic of competition and ranking—that imbues all sports practices in Sweden regardless of the activity's aim (Eliasson, 2009; Engström, 1999; Fahlén & Aggestål, 2011; Fahlén & Karp, 2010; Sjöblom & Fahlén, 2010; Stenling & Fahlén, 2009). The body of knowledge concerning the sports movement's ongoing attempts in Sweden to increase accessibility has highlighted several explanations for the limited range of fitness and recreation activities for PWD (Geidne & Jerlinder, 2016; Kristén et al., 2002; Wickman, 2017). For example, difficulties in transforming accessibility projects into permanent activities due to organisational resistance to change have been identified. These results point towards organisational frames that limit both accessibility to the sports clubs and the range of the activities within the clubs. These results are well in line with the extensive research on sports policy implementation, which has shown that local sports clubs are rather resistant to external change initiatives (Fahlén et al., 2015) and that ideals formulated on a political level have little impact on everyday practice in sports clubs (Sjöblom & Fahlén, 2010; Skille, 2010; Stenling & Fahlén, 2016). Scholars have described these structures as solid and, consequently, hard to change (cf. Skille, 2010; Stenling & Fahlén, 2009). What has been noted in previous research is that if insufficient resources are made available for the removal of barriers in the environment, this can be regarded as an expression of the oppression of certain people. Similar ideas are expressed in the proposition 'From Patient to Citizen' (1999/2000, p. 79). The Swedish government does not specifically invest in the evaluation of sport programmes for parasports and does not monitor programmes, as that task has been given to the RF, which is responsible for monitoring the implementation of programmes run by its member organisations (Karp et al., 2016).

Sport Participation

In educational research on inclusion, several scholars have emphasised that the process of labelling pupils as deviant in itself works against inclusion (cf. Slee, 2011). Such an assumption should also apply to sport. Although sport, unlike school, is voluntary, there are similarities in the way of understanding inclusion. Categories such as PWD tend to explain disability as something rooted in the individual. These categorisations, in turn, will then be tied to the organisation of the sport system, where special support and resources will be provided on the basis of such individualising categorisations (cf. Haug, 2014). A key aspect of the notion of inclusive sport is that difficulties to practice sport in a certain 'able-bodied way' should not be viewed as generically rooted in individual deficits. Instead, the sport system should strive to adapt its practices of development and learning so that all athletes can attend. Such an ideology, however, presumes a change in how disability is conceived of and categorised (Tegtmejer et al., 2021).

In Sweden there is no available data regarding frequency, type of sport and who is participating where in parasport. The LOK support system referred to in the previous section, which describes the financial framework, is the only tool that gives an indication of the number of activities during one year for PWD under the umbrella of the RF. It is important to note that the definition of a PWD in the LOK support system includes people with a neuropsychiatric disorder, which means that the information is misleading in the sense that not only physical, intellectual and visual impairments are included in the statistics. In order for follow-up of the inclusion process to be possible, transparency is required on how adjustments and decisions on support take place, both within a specific sports context and within the sports movement in general.

Barriers and Facilitators

Barriers

The barriers PWD encounter involve many societal domains, including family life, social participation, contacts with welfare agencies, school, work and sport. Even if their right to live in society on the same basis as others is stipulated in the United Nations Convention on the Rights of PWD, they face discrimination and are not given the same opportunities to participate fully in society (WHO, 2011). In a new study (Nordlund et al., 2022) the aim was to identify any distinction in expectations between the Para-athletes versus stakeholders. The results indicate some factors that can enable or prevent successful inclusion in sport organisations. For instance, the respondents expected that inclusion could facilitate people with and without a label to perform sports together and act as role models to each other. The respondents also thought that recruitment into sports activities would increase after the organisational change. The economy was the area of most concern for the respondents; they believed that participation in sports was likely to increase after inclusion and that the costs would also adapt the sport environment for PWD. Regarding facilities, there was a less clear pattern. Some were concerned about a lack of accessible facilities and equipment, while others were unconcerned. The tendency was that athletes were slightly less worried about resources, while stakeholders were slightly more optimistic about future participation in sports among PWD (Nordlund et al., 2022).

Facilitators

At the individual level, PWD can receive support and help to apply for individual adapted sports aids via an LSS administrator, a social worker or a trainer or coach in the local sports club. This aid will be owned by the individual. At the group level, stakeholders in the local sports club or sports district can apply for funding to purchase adapted sports aids for their participants to use. The aid will be owned by the club or district. At the system level, the RF in general and the Swedish Parasport Federation in particular conduct advocacy work to change policies for equal sport participation.

8.5 Conclusion

In this chapter, we have critically synthesised what is known about Parasport in Sweden and identified key issues and directions for the ongoing organisational change towards inclusion in the RF. Much has happened in the last half century since the Swedish Parasport Federation became part of the RF. Many roadblocks have been identified and removed. Most of Sweden's modern indoor facilities today have adapted premises, which means good accessibility for PWD. In many places, leadership training and try-out days in sports are offered, with a special focus on acceptance for diversity. As this chapter has shown, the Swedish sports movement has the knowledge and overall experience of sports for children, young people and adults with disabilities; therefore, it is a good pathfinder and explorer of new opportunities in creating meaningful, socially relevant and sustainable sport policies. The question that remains is whether the inclusive process in the RF will be successful in creating a context in which different stakeholders and athletes interact and shape the field of (para) sport in innovative ways so that it will be accessible for all. Knowledge sharing and learning processes across the RF on a vertical and horizontal level will be of importance to give special financial support on an environmental and individual level to increase accessibility and participation on equal terms in the future.

It is important to have a shared understanding of how such development can be created. Practice-based, collaborative studies between academia and sports organisations is one way to find different research-based improvement and strategies to inclusion depending on the challenges and needs that exist in sport. The main responsibility for the development environment lies with the sports movement, but what form it takes will depend on the closeness of the relationships and collaborations between the RF, the Swedish Parasport Federation and the National Sports Federations. As such partnerships evolve, they can become increasingly integrated, adding to their value for parasport-athletes' development. Finally, there is no 'one-size-fits-all' approach to understanding the relationship between sport, disability and inclusion. Most importantly, the critical aspects emphasised in this chapter stress the need for practice-based research anchored in scientific knowledge and proven experience to better achieve the inclusion goals. Long-term planning is required and also to work systematically. Researchers and leaders and decision makers within and outside the sports organisation need to prioritise work on collaborative learning and create conditions within the organisation that allow all stakeholders to develop the inclusive environment together. These efforts are necessary to ensure that all athletes get access to the sport environment they are entitled to.

Acknowledgements This study is part of a project headed by Lotta Vikström, which has received funding from the European Research Council under the European Union's Horizon 2020 research and innovation programme (Grant Agreement No. 647125, 'DISLIFE Liveable Disabilities: Life courses and opportunity structures across time', 2016–2021). This study is also part of a project led by Kim Wickman (Equal Conditions in Sweden's Largest Popular Movement—Success Factors for Increased Inclusion in the Field of Sports) and financed by the Forte Foundation (*Forskningsrådet för hälsa, arbetsliv och välfärd,* Forte 2018-01759). We would like to thank Malin Andersson, who assisted us with the layout of the figures.

Declaration of Conflicting Interests The author(s) declare no potential conflicts of interest with respect to the research, authorship and/or publication of this chapter.

References

Arnoldsson, J. (2019). *Idrott för nyanlända 2015–2018 En rapport om verksamhet, uppföljning och forskning inom satsningen. Sports for new arrivals 2015–2018* [A report on activities, follow-up and research within the initiative]. Riksidrottsförbundet. Retrieved January 16, 2021, from https://www.rf.se/globalassets/jamtland-harjedalens-if/dokument/integration/sammanfattning-idrott-for-nyanlanda-och-asylsokande-2015-2016.pdf

Bergsgard, N. A., & Norberg, J. R. (2010). Sports policy and politics—The Scandinavian way. *Sport in Society, 13*(4), 567–582. https://doi.org/10.1080/17430431003616191

Corker, M., & Shakespeare, T. (2002). *Disability/postmodernism. Embodying disability theory*. Continuum.

Danermark, B. (Ed.). (2005). *Sociologiska perspektiv på funktionshinder och handikapp* [Sociological perspectives on disability and handicap]. Studentlitteratur.

Darcy, S., Ollerton, J., & Grabowski, S. (2020). "Why Can't I Play?": Transdisciplinary learnings for children with disability's sport participation. *Social Inclusion, 8*(3), 209–223. https://doi.org/10.17645/si.v8i3.2750

DePauw, K. P., & Gavron, S. J. (2005). *Disability sport* (2nd ed.). Human Kinetics.

Eliasson, I. (2009). *I skilda idrottsvärldar. Barn, ledare och föräldrar i flick- och pojkfotboll* [In different sports worlds. Children, leaders and parents of girls and boys soccer]. [Doctoral dissertation, Umeå University]. http://urn.kb.se/resolve?urn=urn:nbn:se:umu:diva-22378

Engström, L.-M. (1999). *Idrott som social markör* [Sport as a social marker]. HLS Förlag.

Eskilstuna kommun. (2020). *Idrottspolitisk plan för Eskilstuna kommunkoncern 2016-2021* [Sportspolitical plan for Eskilstuna municipality 2016-2021]. https://www.eskilstuna.se/download/18.2480b83e1619376f0d02b862/1519301245932/Idrottspolitisk%20plan%20för%20Eskilstuna%20kommunkoncern%202016-2021.pdf

Eurobarometer. (2017). *Special Eurobarometer 472: Sport and physical activity*. Retrieved December 16, 2020, from https://data.europa.eu/euodp/en/data/dataset/S2164_88_4_472_ENG

Fahlén, J., & Karp, S. (2010). Access denied: the new 'Sports for all'-programme in Sweden and the reinforcement of the 'Sports performance' logic. *Sport & EU Review, 2*(1), 3–22.

Fahlén, J., & Aggestål, A. (2011). Ambitioner mot traditioner. Föreningsidrottens vidgade ansvar [Ambitions versus traditions. Club sports widened responsibility]. *Svensk idrottsforskning, 1*, 24–28.

Fahlén, J., Eliasson, I., & Wickman, K. (2015). Resisting self-regulation: An analysis of sport policy programme making and implementation in Sweden. *International Journal of Sport Policy and Politics, 7*(3), 391–406. https://doi.org/10.1080/19406940.2014.925954

Fahlen, J., & Ferry, M. (2019). Sports participation in Sweden. In K. Green, T. Sigurjónsson, & E. Å. Skille (Eds.), *Sport in Scandinavia and the Nordic countries* (pp. 136–171). Routledge.

Fahrner, M., & Klenk, C. (2018). Multilevel policy implementation: exploring organisational coordination—the case of the German Swimming Federation's national training framework implementation, *10*(3), 549–566. https://doi.org/10.1080/19406940.2018.1447499

Fay, T. (2011). Disability in sport it's our time: From the sidelines to the frontlines (Title IX-B). *Journal of Intercollegiate Sport, 4*(1), 63–94. https://doi.org/10.1123/jis.4.1.63

Funka. (2020). Retrieved September 3, 2020, from http://www.funka.com/design-for-alla/tillganglighet/statistik/

Geidne, S., & Jerlinder, K. (2016). How sports clubs include children and adolescents with disabilities in their activities. A systematic search of peer-reviewed articles. *Sport Science Review, XXV*(1–2), 29–52.

Grönvik, L. (2009). Defining disability: Effects of disability concepts on research outcome. *International Journal of Social Research Methodology, 12*, 1–18.

Haug, P. (2014). The practices of dealing with children with special needs in school: A Norwegian perspective. *Behavioural and Emotional Difficulties, 19*(3), 296–310.

Hjelmquist, E., Rönnberg, J., & Söder, M. (1994). *Svensk forskning om handikapp: En översikt med social- och beteendevetenskapliga perspektiv* [Swedish research on handicap: An overview from a social and behavioural science perspective]. Socialvetenskapliga Forskningsrådet.

Hodge, N., & Runswick-Cole, K. (2013). 'They never pass me the ball': Exposing ableism through the leisure experiences of disabled children, young people and their families. *Children's Geographies, 11*(3), 311–325.

Karp, S., Fahlén, J., & Löfgren, K. (2016). More of the same instead of qualitative leaps – A study of inertia in the Swedish sports system. *European Journal for Sport and Society, 11*(3), 301–320. https://doi.org/10.1080/16138171.2014.11687946

Kristén, L., Patriksson, G., & Fridlund, B. (2002). Conceptions of children and adolescents with physical disabilities about their participation in a sports programme. *European Physical Education Review, 8*(2), 139–156.

Kulturdepartementet. (2011). *Regeringsbeslut 15* [Government decision 15]. Kulturdepartementet.

Lundquist Wanneberg, P. (2017). Sport, disability and women: A study of organised Swedish disability sport in 1969-2012. *Polish Journal of Sport and Tourism, 24*(4), 213–220. https://doi.org/10.1515/pjst-2017-0020

Malmö stad. (2020). *Tillsammans för ett öppet och tryggare Malmö* [Together for an open and safe Malmö]. https://motenmedborgarportal.malmo.se/welcome-sv/namnder-styrelser/kommunfullmaktige/mote-2019-11-20/agenda/budget-2020-med-plan-for-2021-2022-version-191106pdf?downloadMode=open

Misener, L., & Darcy, S. (2014). Managing disability sport: From athletes with disabilities to inclusive organizational perspectives. *Sport Management Review, 17*(1), 1–7.

Mont, D. (2007). Measuring health and disability. *Lancet, 369*(9573), 1658–1663.

Nivert, M., & Lervik, K. (2008). *Organisationsöversikt av svensk idrott. [Organizational overview of Swedish sports]*. Stockholm: Andre & Hol.

Norberg, J. R. (2004). *Idrottens väg till folkhemmet—studier i statlig idrottspolitik 1913-1970* [Sport's road to the welfare state—Studies in Swedish government policy towards sport, 1913–1970]. SISU Idrottsböcker.

Norberg, J. R. (2011). A contract reconsidered? Changes in the Swedish state's relation to the sports movement. *International Journal of Sport Policy and Politics, 3*(3), 311–325.

Nordlund, M., Wickman, K., Vikström, L., & Karp, S. (2022). Equal abilities - The Swedish Parasport Federation and the inclusion process. *Scandinavian Sport Studies Forum, 13*, III–129.

Östersund Kommun. (2020). *Rörelse för alla* [Movement for all]. Retrieved February 20, 2020, from https://ostersund.se/kommun-och-politik/tillganglighet-mangfald-och-jamstalldhet/rorelse-for-alla%2D%2D-parasport.html

Priestley, M. (1998). Constructions and creations: Idealism, materialism and disability theory. *Disability & Society, 13*(1), 75–94.

Regleringsbrev. (2020). *Regleringsbrev för budgetåret 2021 avseende anslag 13:1 inom utgiftsområde 17 kultur, medier, trossamfund och fritid* [Regulation letter for the budget year 2021 concerning 13:1 within financial section 17 Culture, media, religious associations and leisure]. Retrieved March 11, 2021, from https://www.esv.se/Statsliggaren/Regleringsbrev?rbid=21363

Riksdagen. (2020). *Minutes of the declaration of the Swedish government*. Retrieved August 10, 2020, from https://www.riksdagen.se/sv/dokument-lagar/dokument/protokoll/protokoll-20181940-mandagen-den-21-januari_H60940

Riksidrottsförbundet [The Swedish Sport Confederation]. (2008). *Swedish sport – international policy*. Riksidrottsförbundet.

Riksidrottsförbundet [The Swedish Sport Confederation]. (2016). *Sport – A good start in life*. https://www.rf.se/contentassets/8fa3fca8b54b4b5f8bd2aa05cb3ce533/idrott%2D%2D-en-bra-start-i-livet.pdf

Riksidrottsförbundet [The Swedish Sport Confederation]. (2020a). *Idrottsrörelsen i siffror* [The Sports movement in numbers]. Riksidrottsförbundet.

Riksidrottsförbundet [The Swedish Sport Confederation]. (2020b). *RF:s Stadgar I lydelse efter RF-stämman 2019* [The Swedish Sports Confederation statutes in line with decision at the Bienniel General Meeting in 2019]. https://www.rf.se/globalassets/riksidrottsforbundet/nya-dokument/nya-dokumentbanken/stadgar-och-regelverk/rfs-stadgar-2020-01-01.pdf

Riksidrottsförbundet [The Swedish Sport Confederation]. (2020c). *Bilaga 1 Organisationsstöd SF 2020-2021 till utl 3d* [Appendix 1 Organisational monetary support to Special Sport Federations

(SF) 2020-2021]. https://www.rf.se/globalassets/riksidrottsforbundet/nya-dokument/mediearkiv/bidrag-och-stod/tilldelade-stod/organisationsstod-sf/organisationsstod-sf-2020-2021.pdf?w=900&h=900

Riksidrottsförbundet [The Swedish Sport Confederation]. (2020d) [Grants and financial support to local sports clubs LOK support system rules and forms]. https://www.rf.se/globalassets/riksidrottsforbundet/nya-dokument/mediearkiv/bidrag-och-stod/lok-regler-och-blanketter/lokstodsforeskrifter-from-20200101.pdf

Riksidrottsförbundet [The Swedish Sport Confederation]. (2020e). *Uppdragsersättning Parasportförbundet* [Grant for Assignment to The Swedish Parasport Federation]. https://www.rf.se/globalassets/riksidrottsforbundet/nya-dokument/mediearkiv/bidrag-och-stod/tilldelade-stod/regelverk/uppdragsersattning-parasportforbundet.pdf?w=900&h=900

Riksidrottsförbundet [The Swedish Sport Confederation]. (2020f). *Bilaga 4 Verksamhetsstöd SF paraidrott 2020-2021 till utl 3 d* [Activity programme support Special Sport Federations (SF) for parasport 2020-2021]. https://www.rf.se/globalassets/riksidrottsforbundet/nya-dokument/mediearkiv/bidrag-och-stod/tilldelade-stod/verksamhetsstod-sf/verksamhetsstod-sf-paraidrott-2020-2021.pdf?w=900&h=900

SCB Statistiska Centralbyrån. (2020a). *Utrikes födda i Sverige* [Statistics in Sweden]. Retrieved April 16, 2020, from https://www.scb.se/hitta-statistik/sverige-i-siffror/manniskorna-i-sverige/utrikes-fodda/?showRelatedFacts=False&showRelatedArticles=True

SCB Statistiska Centralbyrån. (2020b). *Statistikdatabasen* [Statistics in Sweden]. Retrieved August 11, 2020, from www.statistikdatabasen.scb.se

Segnestam Larsson, O., & Wagndal, M. (2018). *Det frivilliga arbetet i Sverige som del av BNP* [Volunteer work in Sweden as part of GDP]. http://esh.diva-portal.org/smash/get/diva2:1270696/FULLTEXT02.pdf

SISU idrottsutbildarna. (2020a). *Vi arbetar med föreningsutveckling* [We work with club development]. Retrieved September 23, 2020, from https://www.sisuidrottsutbildarna.se/Viarbetarmed/foreningsutveckling/

SISU idrottsutbildarna. (2020b). *Inkluderande ledarskap för att möta idrottare med funktionsnedsättning* [Inclusive leadership to meet athletes with disability]. Retrieved September 23, 2020, from https://utbildning.sisuidrottsbocker.se/moduler/portal-for-moduler/pw/inkluderande-ledarskap-for-att-mota-idrottare-med-funktionsnedsattning/

Sjöblom, P., & Fahlén, J. (2010). The survival of the fittest: Intensification, totalization andhomogenization in Swedish competitive sport. *Sport in Society: Cultures, Commerce, Media, Politics, 13*(4), 704–717. https://doi.org/10.1080/17430431003616514

Skille, E. Å. (2010). Competitiveness and health: The work of sport clubs as seen by sport clubs representatives—A Norwegian case study. *International Review for the Sociology of Sport, 45*(1), 73–85.

Skille, E. Å. (2011). The conventions of sport club: Enabling and constraining the implementation of social goods through sport. *Sport, Education and Society, 16*(2), 241–253.

Slee, R. (2011). *The irregular school. Exclusion, schooling, and inclusive education*. Routledge.

Socialstyrelsen. (2020). Lägesrapport 2020. 2020-3-6686 [National Board of Health and Welfare]. Insatser och stöd till personer med funktionsnedsättning, 2020 [Initiatives and support for people with disabilities, 2020]. Retrieved January 23, 2021, from https://www.socialstyrelsen.se/globalassets/sharepoint-dokument/artikelkatalog/ovrigt/2020-3-6686.pdf

Sørensen, M., & Kahrs, N. (2006). Integration of disability sport in the Norwegian sport organizations: Lessons learned. *Adapted Physical Activity Quarterly, 23*(2), 184–202.

Sørensen, M., & Kahrs, N. (2011). En idrett for alle? Erfaring med integrering av personer med funksjonsnedsettelser i norsk idrett. In D. V. Hanstad (Ed.), *Norsk Idrett. Indre spenning og yttre press* (pp. 337–353). Fagbokforlaget.

SOU. (2008). *Föreningsfostran och tävlingsfostran. En utvärdering av statens stöd till idrotten* [Association fostering and competition fostering. An evaluation of the state's support to sport]. Fritze.

SOU. (2017). *Att ta emot människor på flykt: Sverige hösten 2015* [To receive people on flight: Sweden autumn 2015]. Fritzes offentliga publikationer.

Stenling, C., & Fahlén, J. (2009). The order of logics in Swedish sport – Feeding the hungry beast of result orientation and commercialization. *European Journal for Sport and Society, 6*, 29–42.

Stenling, C., & Fahlén, J. (2016). Same same, but different? Exploring the organizational identities of Swedish voluntary sport: Possible implications of sport clubs' self-identification for the role as implementers of policy objectives. *International Review for the Sociology of Sport, 51*, 867–883. https://doi.org/10.1177/1012690214557103

Stenling, C., & Sam, M. P. (2017). Tensions and contradictions in sport's quest for legitimacy as a political actor: The politics of Swedish public sport policy hearings. *International Journal of Sport Policy and Politics, 9*(4), 691–705. https://doi.org/10.1080/19406940.2017.1348382

Stenling, C., & Sam, M. P. (2020). Sport advocacy: The art of persuasion and its by-products. *Sociology of Sport Journal, Human Kinetics, 37*(4), 319–327. https://doi.org/10.1123/ssj.2019-0047

Svenska Dövidrottsförbundet (SDI). (2020). Retrieved April 16, 2020, from https://www.svenskdovidrott.se/English

Svenska Parasportförbundet. (2020a). *Strategi 2025 - En stark parasport i Sverige* [A strong parasport in Sweden]. Retrieved April 20, 2020, from https://www.parasport.nu/Strategi2025

Svenska Parasportförbundet. (2020b). *Om Parasportförbundet Sverige* [About the Swedish Parasport Federation]. Retrieved August 24, 2020, from https://www.parasport.nu/forbundsinfo/omparasportforbundet/

Svenska Parasportförbundet. (2021a). Retrieved February 22, 2021, from https://www.facebook.com/watch/?v=705638713557004

Svenska Parasportförbundet. (2021b). *Parasportpolitsika Programmet* [The Parasport Political Programme]. https://www.parasport.nu/globalassets/svenska-parasportforbundet-och-sveriges-paralympiska-kommitte-svenska-parasportforbundet/dokument/blandat/parasportpolitiskt-program-2020%2D%2D-2021.pdf

Swedish Research Council for Sport Science. (2020). Retrieved August 10, 2020, from https://centrumforidrottsforskning.se/en/

Tegtmejer, T., Hjörne, E., & Säljö, R. (2021). 'The ADHD diagnosis has been thrown out': Exploring the dilemmas of diagnosing children in a school for all. *International Journal of Inclusive Education., 25*(6), 671–685. https://doi.org/10.1080/13603116.2019.1569733

Thomas, C. (2004). How is disability understood? An examination of sociological approaches. *Disability and Society, 19*, 569–583.

Toftegaard Støckel, J., Strandbu, Å., Solenes, O., Jørgensen, P., & Fransson, K. (2010). Sport for children and youth in the Scandinavian countries. *Sport in Society, 13*(4), 625–664.

United Nations. (2006). *Convention on the Rights of Persons with Disabilities*. Accessed March 2023.

UN Department of Economic and Social Affairs. (2020). *Population dynamics: World Urbanization Prospects 2018*. Retrieved August 11, 2020, from https://population.un.org/wup/DataQuery/

UN Statistics Division. (2020). Retrieved August 11, 2020, from https://unstats.un.org/home/

Wickman, K. (2017). Idrott och funktionsnedsättning – i spänningsfältet mellan stabilitet och samhällsomvandling [Sport and disability – In the field of tension between stability and social transformation]. In J. Faskunger & P. Sjöblom (Eds.), *Idrottens samhällsnytta. En vetenskaplig översikt av idrottsrörelsen mervärde för individ och samhälle* [Sport's social benefit. A scientific overview of the sports movement added value for the individual and society] (pp. 131–143). Riksidrottsförbundet.

World Health Organization. (2001). *International classification of functioning, disability and health: ICF*. World Health Organization.

World Health Organization. (2011). *World report on disability*. World Health Organization & World Bank.

Chapter 9
Ireland

Catherine Carty and Paul Kitchin

9.1 Introduction

This chapter will provide an in-depth view of sport for people living with disability in the Republic of Ireland from policy to practice levels. The predominant stakeholders governing access to sport for people with disability include the Department of Tourism, Culture, Arts, Gaeltacht, Sport and Media; Sport Ireland; Cara-Sport Inclusion Ireland; Paralympics Ireland; National Governing Bodies of Sport (both mainstream and disability focused); local sports partnerships; as well as the Department of Health and Department of Education and Skills Department of Children, Equality, Disability, Integration and Youth; the Higher Education Sector and their respective partner agencies. Current sport policy for those living with disability stems mainly from the National Sports Policy 2018–2027, Sport Ireland Statement of Strategy 2018–2022, the National Physical Activity Plan for Ireland 2016 and the Sport Ireland Policy on Participation in Sport by People with Disabilities, 2019. Paralympics Ireland supports elite athletes, while Cara-Sport Inclusion Ireland advocates for and builds capacity for the inclusion of people living with disability in sport through the lifespan. A network of Sports Inclusion Disability Officers (SIDOs) based in local sports partnerships operates across the country to support the participation of people with disabilities in sport. Ireland is home to a UNESCO Chair in Inclusive Sport that supports global to local policy development and implementation. This chapter describes Ireland, outlining how sport for people living with disability grew in the country and where it now stands, who supports the

---

C. Carty (✉)
Munster Technological University (MTU), Munster, Ireland
e-mail: Catherine.carty@mtu.ie

P. Kitchin
Ulster University, Coleraine, UK
e-mail: pj.kitchin@ulster.ac.uk

delivery of disability sport and data collection methods. Concluding remarks will point to successes and considerations for addressing the gradient in sports participation that still exists between those living with and without disability in Ireland.

9.2 Country Profile

Characteristics of the Republic of Ireland (ROI)

The island of Ireland is the third largest island in Europe and is home to two governmental jurisdictions namely the Republic of Ireland and Northern Ireland (see Chap. 10) which is part of the United Kingdom. The Republic of Ireland is a parliamentary democracy with a population of 4,761,865, 13.5% of whom report living with disability (Central Statistics Office, 2017a) (Table 9.1). Irish and English are the first and second official languages respectively, and Irish Sign Language (ISL) is the official language for the deaf community. Labour force participation sits at 61.4% (CSO, 2017a). Ireland hosts five of the top ten companies on Forbes' list of The World's Most Innovative Companies (IDA, 2019). It is the fastest growing Eurozone economy, while also being the youngest and one of the most educated (IDA, 2019).

Ireland sits at 16th place in the World Happiness Report 2019 (Helliwell et al., 2019). It ranks third out of 189 countries in the United Nations Human Ranking Index 2019 (United Nations Development Programme, 2019) which acknowledges that inequalities "hurt economies, wastefully preventing people from reaching their full potential at work and in life" (UNDP, 2019, p. 1). In contrast the Disability Federation of Ireland indicated that Ireland is the worst place in western Europe to have a disability (McCarthy, 2020). Highlighting EU Statistics on Income and Living Conditions (EU-SILC) 2018, McCarthy points to the decline in investment in a growing sector operating at pre-2008 levels of funding with 36.8% of people with disabilities experiencing poverty and social exclusion (Eurostat, 2020). With such polarising positions in these international rankings Ireland's performance in the domain of sport for people with disabilities is surely of interest.

Sport in Ireland

The Department of Tourism, Culture, Arts, Gaeltacht,[1] Sport and Media and its statutory agent, Sport Ireland, govern Irish sport. The National Sports Policy (2018–2027) refers to having adapted the Council of Europe definition of sport where "sport means all forms of physical activity which, through casual or organised participation, aims at expressing or improving physical fitness and mental

---

[1] Regions where the Irish language is the main spoken language of the population.

Table 9.1 Fact and statistics of Ireland Republic

Population (number of inhabitants)[a]	4,761,865
Area (km²)	84,421
Density (inhabitants/km²)[b]	70
Urbanisation rate (%)[c]	62.95
Political organisation	Parliamentary democracy
Structure of the state	Constitutional republic
Number of provinces	4
Number of municipal districts[b]	95
GDP per capita (US Dollars)[d]	66,763,735
Number of official languages	3[e]
EU Membership	Since 1973
Welfare model[f]	Nordic, Continental European and Anglo-Saxon

Source: [a]Central Statistics Office (2017a, b); [b]Local Government Information Unit (n.d.); [c]Statista (2020); [d]World Bank (2018); [e]This includes Irish as the first official language, English as the second and Irish Sign Language as the official language for and of the deaf community; [f]NESC (2005)

wellbeing, forming social relationships or obtaining results in competition at all levels" (Council of Europe, as cited in Government of Ireland, 2018, p. 10). The adaption relates to definitions outlined in the Sport Ireland Act 2015 as cited in the National Sport Policy (Government of Ireland, 2018) that distinguishes between recreational and competitive sport:

> 'recreational sport' means "all forms of physical activity which, through casual or regular participation, aim at—(a) expressing or improving physical fitness and mental wellbeing, and (b) forming social relationships;" and "'competitive sport' means "all forms of physical activity which, through organised participation, aim at—(a) expressing or improving physical fitness, and (b) obtaining improved results in competition at all levels. (Sport Ireland Act, as cited in Government of Ireland, 2018, p. 10)

Active travel is excluded, while physical education is included given its connection to physical fitness, mental wellbeing, the formation of social relationships and as an important enabler of lifelong engagement. The intersection of sport with other sectors is also given due consideration in defining sport in the national policy and influences understanding of and stakeholders involved in disability sport. There are many cross-government policies and stakeholders involved in the delivery of sport and physical activity nationally and locally. There are 65 National Governing Bodies of Sport (NGBs) and 29 local sports partnerships who receive financial support from Sport Ireland and for whom the Federation of Irish Sport is the representative organisation (Federation of Irish Sport, 2020).

Sport Ireland, through the National Sport Monitor tracks progress and trends. The 2019 mid-term report shows the trend towards individual sports increases while social sports participation remains strong. The top five activities are personal exercise (16%), swimming (8%), running (7%), cycling (4%) and dancing (3%) (Sport Ireland, 2019a). Volunteering is an important part of the sport ecosystem. A total of

875,000 people report volunteering, gaining satisfaction from their participation (79%) whilst also feeling appreciated (82%). The mental health impact is also monitored and those who are highly active report higher levels of wellbeing (Sport Ireland, 2019a). Under the National Sports Policy the government committed to doubling the funding of sport by 2027. Considering COVID-19 it is hope that this commitment will be honoured and indeed expanded to address mental and physical health consequences. Table 9.2 presents a profile of sport in Ireland.

The Department of Health and the Department of Tourism, Culture, Arts, Gaeltacht, Sport and Media have joint responsibility for physical activity, co-leading the National Physical Activity Plan implementation group. The Health Service Executive (HSE) delivers services to the public. Healthy Ireland is a government-led initiative to support the cross-community development of physical and mental health and wellbeing. Under the Healthy Ireland Framework 2013–2025, the National Physical Activity Plan was developed and launched in 2016. Partnership approaches across government and civil society are used to implement both polices (Department of Health, 2013; Healthy Ireland, 2016). Both initiatives support inclusive approaches to service delivery as evident in the sport policies above.

Sport Ireland and the network of 29 local sports partnerships (LSPs) operating as partnerships between sport, health and education are critical agents in supporting the delivery of the National Sports Policy as well as the National Physical Activity Plan and the Healthy Ireland Framework. HSE health promotion and physical activity teams (where available) at local levels are also critical in supporting this collaboration (O'Keefe & Casey, 2019). LSPs have a remit in relation to disability inclusion and a Sports Inclusion Disability Officer in each to serve to address the inequity in access.

Table 9.2 Sport profile of Ireland up to 2020/21 Republic of Ireland

Government authority responsible for sport	Department of Tourism, Culture, Arts, Gaeltacht, Sport and Media/ Sport Ireland
Membership sport club (%) [a]	35
Membership fitness or health centre (%) [a]	15
Membership socio-cultural club that includes sport in its activities (e.g. employees' club, youth club, school- and university-related club) (%) [a]	45
Sport participation, at least once a week (%) [a]	43 (Eurobarometer 19% p. 96)
Number of national sport federations [b]	76 (35 all Island, incl NI)
Number of sport clubs [b]	12,000
Number of sport club members (%) [c]	43
National budget for sport (€ × 1,000,000) [d]	114.5
National budget for sport federations (€ × 1000) [e]	13,800
Local budget for sport (€ × 1,000,000) [f]	7291
Share of economic value of volunteers in sport in the GDP (%) [b]	€1.1 billion per annum
COVID-19 Budget for Sport (€ × 1,000,000) [e]	70.0

Sources: [a]Sport Ireland (2019); [b]Federation of Irish Sport (2020); [c]Sport Ireland (2020b); [d]Sport Ireland (2017b, 2020a); [e]Sport Ireland (2020c); [f]Sport Ireland (2019b)

Disability in Ireland

Legally the Equal Status Act 2000 sets out the definition of disability as

> (a) the total or partial absence of a person's bodily or mental functions, including the absence of a part of a person's body, (b) the presence in the body of organisms causing, or likely to cause, chronic disease or illness, (c) the malfunction, malformation or disfigurement of a part of a person's body, (d) a condition or malfunction which results in a person learning differently from a person without the condition or malfunction, or (e) a condition, disease or illness which affects a person's thought processes, perception of reality, emotions or judgement or which results in disturbed behaviour. (Government of Ireland, 2000, pp. 5–6)

Terminology and the prevailing understanding of disability in Ireland align with that used among UN agencies and conventions, where people with disabilities "include those who have long-term physical, mental, intellectual or sensory impairments which in interaction with various barriers may hinder their full and effective participation in society on an equal basis with others" (United Nations, 2006, p. 4). This aligns with the World Health Organization's (WHO) International Classification of Functioning Disability and Health (ICF) (2013) or biopsychosocial model, while Ireland also embraces a human rights model as advocated by the Office of the High Commissioner of Human Rights (n.d.), albeit this understanding is most prevalent at an official level, in official documents and in academia. On the ground in communities, terminology and understanding vary and many terms are used including people with disabilities and disabled people, for example, people with autism, autistic people, s/he is autistic. The general population and media remain somewhat unsure and sometimes cautious around use of terminology in the area of disability. Thankfully some terminologies, historically common, now recognised as inappropriate, offensive or derogatory have been parked in history.

The National Disability Authority is an independent statutory body that advises government on matters pertaining to disability, accessibility and universal design in Ireland. While the National Disability Inclusion Strategy 2017–2021 (NDIS) represents a whole-of-government approach to improving the lives of persons living with disability. Ireland was the last country in Europe to ratify CRPD in 2018.

In the 2016 census, 643,131 people (13.5%) reported living with disability, with 87% reporting good or very good health. The 2016 disability figure is an 8% increase in the 2011 figure, due to the increased population over 65. Of those under 20, 6.7% reported living with disability, in the 70–74 age group this rose to 27.5%, increasing to 49.5% among those aged 75+ (Central Statistics Office, 2017a). Further statistics on disability in Ireland are presented in Tables 9.3 and 9.4.

The questions on disability in the Census were developed in 2011 following consultations with stakeholders, and they will remain the same for the 2021 census.

Table 9.3 Statistics on disability in Ireland (aged <1 to 85+) in 2016

	%	Count
Prevalence of population who stated they had a disability [a]	13.5	643,131
Prevalence of moderate/severe physical disabilities (movement) [b]	11.4	
Prevalence of substantially limited basic physical activity [b]	5.5	262,818
Prevalence of blindness or serious vision impairment [a]	1.2	54,810
Prevalence of deafness or serious hearing impairment [a]	2.2	103,676
Prevalence of intellectual disabilities [a]	1.4	66,611
Prevalence of psychological or emotional condition [a]	2.6	123,515
Prevalence of difficulty learning, remembering or concentrating [a]	3.3	156,968
Prevalence of difficulty connected with pain, breathing or other chronic illnesses [a]	6.2	296,783

Sources: [a]Central Statistics Office (2017a); [b] Eurostat (2020)

Table 9.4 Population (number) by difficulty in tasks of daily living, Census Year 2016

	Count
Difficulty in dressing, bathing or getting around inside the home	140,366
Difficulty in going outside home alone	184,945
Difficulty in working or attending school/college	210,639
Difficulty in participating in other activities (leisure, transport)	229,397
Total disabilities	1,830,528

Central Statistics Office (2018)

Two questions aligned with ICF, addressed disability and a positive response to either question resulted in being classified as living with a disability, see Tables 9.3 and 9.4 (Central Statistics Office, 2017a).

The National Disability Inclusion Strategy 2017–2021 sets out key actions including those of relevance to the sports sector. It expresses "a vision of an Irish society in which people with disabilities enjoy equal rights and opportunities to participate in social and cultural life, can work if they want to do so, have choice and control over how they live their lives, and can reach their full potential" (Department of Justice and Equality, 2017, p. 2).

Emergence or Rise of Disability Sport in Ireland

Disability sport National Governing Bodies and other agencies have been operational in Ireland since the 1960s (see Table 9.5).

A few key events in the early 2000s catalysed developments at a steady pace up to the present time. Disability sport in Ireland accelerated at pace following Irish successes at Paralympic Games and hosting the Special Olympics World Games in 2003. This event in particular laid a positive marker on the impact of disability sport on the lives of people with intellectual disabilities, their families and all of society.

Table 9.5 Early disability sport organisations in Ireland by year of establishment

Irish Wheelchair Association Sport[a]	1960
Special Olympics Ireland[a]	1978
Cerebral Palsy Sport Ireland[b]	1978
Irish Disabled Sailing Association	1980
Irish Blind Sport[a]	1989
Irish Deaf Sport Association[a]	1986
Paralympic Council of Ireland[a]	1987
Spinal Injury Ireland	1993
Riding for the Disabled [c]	Early 1990s

Source: [a]National Disability Authority (2005); [b]Cerebral Palsy Sport Ireland (n.d.); [c]Para Equestrian Ireland (n.d.)

The event unified the country and the high level of media exposure brought significant political attention to disability sport and it is hard to segregate this entirely with what followed as commitments, legislation and funding to act for better provision (RTE, 2014). The Education for Persons with Special Educational Needs Act, 2004, provided for inclusive education as per a child's best interest (Government of Ireland, 2004). The Disability Act 2005 paved the way for further developments, including the mainstreaming of disability services across government policy including sport and its intersecting departments, especially justice, education and health (Government of Ireland, 2005).

In 2005, a timely report on Promoting the Participation of People with Disabilities in Physical Activity and Sport in Ireland was published (National Disability Authority, 2005). The UN had declared 2005 as the International Year of Sport and Physical Education, and preparations for article 30 of the Convention on the Rights of Persons with Disabilities relating to sport were in train. The report was co-created with people with disabilities, addressing many of the elements that would be needed to effectively provide for those with disabilities in sport and physical activity. A range of socioecological factors were explored, and four key recommendations emerged (see Table 9.6).

By 2005 several other national agencies and stakeholders were laying the foundations for progress. Sport Ireland (formerly Irish Sports Council) and Munster Technological University (formerly Institute of Technology Tralee) held the first National Adapted Physical Activity Conference in 2003. The ideas of a National Adapted Physical Activity Centre, now Cara-Sport Inclusion Ireland, and a regional network of Sport Inclusion Disability Officers (SIDOs) emerged. The second conference, in 2005, moved towards "Getting it Right, the foundations of systemic coordinated delivery". In 2007, Cara was established as a collaboration between Sport Ireland and the Munster Technological University (MTU) with the role of increasing participation number, providing education and training and supporting organisations to be disability inclusive. Later (2017) Cara was designated as the agency to support Sport Ireland in its policy commitments related to sports participation. In 2008 twenty local sports partnerships (LSPs) appointed SIDOs (Sport

Table 9.6 Recommendations for promoting the participation of people with disabilities in physical activity and sport in Ireland (2005)

1. Develop a national framework for inclusive physical activity and sport
2. Aligned leadership with above with national, regional and local strategies
3. Inclusive strategies for increasing participation and quality experiences
4. Education and training

Source: National Disability Authority (2005)

Ireland, n.d.-c). All 29 LSPs now have a remit in to provide opportunities for people with disabilities in sport, with the support of 29 SIDOs.

9.3 The Disability Sport System

Structure of Disability Sport

A complex web of interconnections exists across the sport ecosystem in Ireland. Multiple policies stemming from different government departments are implemented with the support of a variety of statutory and non-statutory agencies. Partnership approaches to the implementation of policy and strategy objectives are common. Financing pathways also cross paths with different government departments contributing to the funding of both physical activity and sport. From national government to devolved local authorities, funding is distributed across the ecosystem, with respect to the roles and responsibilities of the recipient organisations (see Table 9.7).

Governmental Agents

The predominant government agents in the sport and disability sport system in Ireland are the Department of Tourism, Culture, Arts, Gaeltacht, Sport and Media and its statutory agency Sport Ireland. They drive the National Sports Policy 2018–2027 with a Sports Leadership Group comprising representatives from allied government departments, Sport Ireland, the wider sports sector, local government and the leisure sector among others. This emphasises the cross-sectoral nature of sport and endeavours to bring cohesion to the collective agenda (Government of Ireland, 2018).

Physical activity is under the joint responsibility of the Departments of Health and the Department of Tourism, Culture, Arts, Gaeltacht, Sport and Media. The National Physical Activity Plan implementation group also includes the Department of Education, the Department of Children, Equality, Disability Integration and Youth, the Department of Housing Local Government and Heritage, the Department

Table 9.7 Disability sport framework for Ireland

Ireland	Governmental	Intermediate	Non-Governmental	
National	Dept. of Tourism, Culture, Arts, Gaeltacht, Sport and Media	Sport Ireland	Cara- Sport Inclusion Ireland	
	Dept. of Health	Sport Northern Ireland	Paralympics Ireland	Federation of Irish Sport
		Health Service Executive	NGBs Disability Sport	NGBs Sport
	Dept. of Education	Healthy Ireland		
	National Physical Activity Plan Implementation Group		Ireland Active	UNESCO Chair
Regional		Community Healthcare Organisations	Higher & Further Education	Regional NGBs e.g. special olympics
Local	Local Authorities	Local Sports Partnerships	Sport Inclusion Disability Officers / Programmes	Schools
		Health Service Physical Activity and Health Promotion teams	Disability Service Providers	Community Sport and Physical Activity Hubs
			Sports Clubs	Sport Centres

Financing - - - - -> Membership/partnership <====> Hierarchical relationship ====>

of Rural and Community Development, the Health Service Executive, Sport Ireland and the academic sector.

Significant synergies exist between plans and policies originating from sport and those from health. The government departments and their statutory agents emphasise the need for partnership approaches at national and local levels and the important role played by intermediate, non-governmental agents. Local authorities are important stakeholders in delivering sport at local levels. Local sport partnerships bring together local authorities, local health agents and local education agents in coordinating and delivering on policies at local authority level. Each local sport partnership has a sport disability inclusion officer (see below).

Intermediate Agents

Sport Ireland, Healthy Ireland and the Health Service Executive (HSE) are the key intermediate agents operating in Ireland. They have statutory remits to deliver on national policy and to monitor progress. They distribute national funding to sporting bodies to deliver recreational and elite sport services for people with disabilities.

Sport Ireland works with and funds 65 non-governmental National Governing Bodies of Sport (NGBs). Four NGBs (Deaf Sports Ireland, Special Olympics Ireland, Vision Sport Ireland (all three are all Island (ROI & NI) and Irish Wheelchair Association Sport (ROI only)) cater exclusively for people with disabilities. A further 23 NGBs have diversity and inclusion officers and have capacity and capability to include people with disabilities in their programmes. Ireland has a network of local sports partnerships (LSPs) operating at the local levels to support the delivery of national policy and strategy locally. The Federation of Irish Sport is the membership body representing over 100 NGBs and LSPs. Beyond NGBs, Sport Ireland engages with a further 18 sports organisations who also receive funding to support the delivery of the strategy. They provide support at a local level via local sports partnerships (Sport Ireland, 2018).

The Health Service Executives are also key partners in the delivery of services via the local sports partnership network across the country. The 29 local sports partnerships span nine community healthcare organisations. Nationally and locally the partnerships between sport and health are critical for advocacy, funding and policy implementation. Both Sport Ireland and the HSE have dedicated funding lines to support the participation of people with disabilities in sport (O'Keefe & Casey, 2019).

Non-governmental Agents

Sport Ireland designates Cara-Sport Inclusion Ireland and Paralympics Ireland to support delivery of national objectives (Sports Ireland, 2019) pertaining to the inclusion of people living with disability in Ireland from recreational to elite level. Paralympics Ireland focuses solely on supporting high-performance athletes living with disability to achieve success in elite sport. Cara-Sport Inclusion Ireland as the agency to support the implementation of Sport Ireland's policy commitments has a broad remit that extends across sport, education and health domains. Cara also receives funding from the health sector and corporate sponsorship.

Ireland has a network of 29 local sports partnerships (LSPs) and Sports Inclusion Disability Officers (SIDOs) and/or programmes. They receive grants from Sport Ireland to support the engagement of people with disabilities (Sports Ireland, 2019). Both NGBs and SIDOs are supported by Cara through education and training. In addition, Health Promotion and Physical Activity Officers working within HSE structures support the provision of physical activity independently and alongside the LSPs. Multiple other organisations support the delivery of services at local levels including the National Disability Authority, the National Council for the Blind, Enable Ireland, Inclusion Ireland, Disability Federation of Ireland and Ireland Active members. In addition, through the services of Sport Ireland Institute, Sport Ireland Coaching and Sport Ireland National Sports Campus further opportunities for people with disabilities at high performance and participation levels are facilitated. Ireland Active is the representative body of public and private leisure facilities in Ireland; they also advocate for inclusive provision across their network.

Higher education programmes, through their adapted physical activity programmes, work placements, community service programmes and volunteering initiatives are a significant facilitator of sport for people with disabilities. These outreach activities sometimes operate based on referrals through the health system and otherwise as partnerships with local disability groups and disability sport groups. Across community centres, health clubs, outdoor education centres, golf clubs, residential care centres, disability service organisations, many organisations are delivering programming opportunities in sport for people with disabilities.

While most children living with disability in Ireland are in mainstream schools, the Irish Special Schools Sports Council (ISSSC) voluntarily provides sports activities in 30 schools for 3500 pupils with mild general learning disabilities; sports include Athletics, Basketball, Gaelic[2] games IRFU Tag Rugby, Orienteering, Quiz and Soccer. Other agencies include Active School Flag, the COPE foundation, the Crann Centre, Siel Bieu, St Michaels House.

Steering of Disability Sport

Relationships

The government departments with responsibility for sport and health and their statutory agencies are the drivers; they have central responsibility for policy while delivery responsibility is devolved to the local level through a hierarchical arrangement with local agencies. All policies emphasise the critical importance of working in partnership for the delivery of key objectives in relation to disability sport. Furthermore, they emphasise the central role of people with disabilities in shaping policy and practice.

With interconnected objectives, the National Sports Policy informs the Sport Ireland Strategy and the Sport Ireland Policy on Participation in Sport by People with Disabilities which in turn designates Cara-Sport Inclusion Ireland as the support agency to assist in the implementation of Sport Ireland's policy participation commitments. It references Paralympics Ireland as the lead agency for high-performance athletes living with disability.

Cara's Strategy 2019–2021 emphasises the importance of partnerships, nationally and locally (Cara, 2019).

Governing bodies of sport for people with disabilities and mainstream NGBs also drive opportunities inclusion. A Disability Sport Organisation Network Forum was set up in 2020 to facilitate joint advocacy from the sector, highlighted during the COVID-19 pandemic; it is currently ad hoc but moving to formalise its structures. Health sector policies and staff also drive opportunities albeit to a lesser extent in terms of human and financial resources.

Legislative Framework

The Sport Ireland Act 2015 tasks Sport Ireland with the administration and development of sport in Ireland. As with its predecessor the Irish Sports Council Act 1999, it does not explicitly reference disability although it does task Sport Ireland with developing strategies for increasing participation and coordinating strategy implementation (Government of Ireland, 1999, 2015). The Irish Equality and Human

---

[2] Irish National Sports, run by the Gaelic Athletic Association (GAA).

Rights Commission (IHREC) Act 2014 charges the Commission with raising awareness around human rights, protecting and promoting rights and elimination of discrimination. It oversees enforcement and compliance with the Equal Status Act 2000–2012 which addresses discrimination on the grounds of disability, including failure to provide a service to accommodate the needs of a person with a disability (Government of Ireland, 2014). Four human rights instruments ratified by Ireland between 1989 and 2018 explicitly reference sport, the Convention on the Rights of Persons with Disabilities, the Convention on the Rights of the Child, the Convention on the Elimination of all forms of Discrimination Against Women and the International Covenant of Economic, Social and Cultural Rights. While the Irish Constitution does not assume international agreements such as these are part of state law, Irish Courts have attached pervasive authority to international human rights instruments (IHREC, n.d.). The Disability (Miscellaneous Provisions) Bill 2016 was drafted to give more legislative protections aligned with the 2018 ratification of the Convention on the Rights of Persons with Disabilities (CRPD) and nominated the Irish Human Rights and Equality Commission (IHREC) to promote, protect and monitor its implementation. However in January 2020 the Bill lapsed as the government was dissolved (Government of Ireland, 2020). Given the explicit reference to sport in CRPD this is regrettable, the formation of a new government may see this bill taken forward.

Policy Framework

A myriad of related policies across government impact on overall provision, for succinctness the key policies in sport and health are the focus here. With reference to disability sport the National Sports Policy 2018–2027 lists as one of the seven core values "Promotes inclusion; Sport must be welcoming and inclusive, offering appropriate opportunities for participation and improvement to all. We will promote inclusion to deliver our desired outcomes with a focus on addressing social, disability, gender, ethnic and other gradients" (Government of Ireland, 2018, p. 19). Sport Ireland's Statement of Strategy (2018–2022) outlines how it will support national policy implementation and cites lifelong and inclusive sport as the first of three pillars in its strategy (Sport Ireland, 2018). Doubling down on this prioritisation of inclusivity, Sport Ireland launched its Policy on Participation in Sport by People with Disabilities (Sports Ireland, 2019) which sets out a number of actions to advance disability inclusion across the sport ecosystem.

Some physical activity opportunities are delivered by the Health Service Executive and partners through the implementation of the Healthy Ireland Framework and the National Physical Activity Plan (NPAP) 2016. The Framework envisions an Ireland "where everyone can enjoy physical and mental health and wellbeing to their full potential" and seeks to "Increase by 20% the proportion of population undertaking regular physical activity across each life stage" (Department of Health, 2013, p. 34) through a whole of government whole of society approach. The National Physical Activity Plan (NPAP) wants to see a "particular focus on disadvantaged areas, people with disabilities, older people, and those who are otherwise socially excluded" (Healthy Ireland, 2016, p. 27). It outlines one specific action to "develop guidelines, support materials and referral pathways to promote physical activity for organisations providing mental health services and disability services" (Healthy Ireland, 2016, p. 37) in partnership with the Department of Health, Mental Health Commission, Cara, National Disability Authority and Sport Ireland. The Healthy Eating Active Living (HEAL) Policy Priority Programme was established in late 2016 to coordinate and lead activity across health services, to ensure implementation of the NPAP. However, it appears that less than 10% of interventions target or include those with disabilities (O'Keefe & Casey, 2019). Supervised by healthcare professionals, many classes are targeted at those recovering from surgery or illness or are designed to reverse frailty in early stages/prevent falls, if those with chronic conditions and underlying conditions are included the figure is higher (Mansergh, 2020).

Financial, Governance and Managerial Support

Financial Framework

Funding of the disability sport sector stems predominantly from core government funding, dormant account funding allocation and corporate sponsorship. Much of the budget allocations stem from Sport Ireland managed streams, while additional funding and benefit in kind, via contributions to the local sport partnerships and Sport Inclusion Disability Officer programmes, also stem from the health sector. It is primarily delivered nationally, via local government mechanisms, LSPs or Community Health Organisations, Local Community Development Committees and Children & Young Peoples Service Committees.

In Ireland, in addition to core allocation from government, sport benefits from a dormant accounts fund whereby funds sitting in credit institutions in Ireland that have been inactive for 15 years are distributed across nine government departments including sport. Sport Ireland applies for and administers funding under this scheme. Disability is one of three areas prioritised. Sport Ireland manages funding streams aligned with its strategic objectives and government policy on sport. It has four funding streams and in 2019 it allocated €12.845 million to NGBs, €8.46 million to high-performance sport, €1.934 million to the International Carding Scheme and €7.291 million to the local sports partnerships (Sport Ireland, 2019b). Disability sport allocations are outlined in Tables 9.8 and 9.9. Three of the four disability-specific NGBs are all island and receive funding in Northern Ireland, via sport and health routes. Most sport bodies benefited from an increase in funding in 2020. Tables 9.8 and 9.9 provide an overview of disability sport funding.

The Healthy Ireland Fund supports the delivery of Healthy Ireland Framework and policies under its umbrella including the NPAP. It was allocated €5 million per annum in 2017–2019, €6 million in 2020 and €10 million in 2021. Some

Table 9.8 Disability NGBs and LSPs supported directly by Sport Ireland in 2020

LSPs SIDO/non-SIDO	€916,000
Deaf Sports Ireland	€65,000
Vision Sports Ireland	€48,000
Irish Wheelchair Association	€285,000
Special Olympics Ireland	€1,400,000
Paralympics Ireland	€1,300,000
Cara-Sport Inclusion Ireland €130,000 (dormant accounts €180,000) [b]	

Source: Sport Ireland (2019b, 2020b)

Table 9.9 Key 2019 Sport Ireland funding of sport for people with disabilities

Total ongoing investment via core, dormant accounts and women in sport grants	€5,720,000
• Beneficiaries LSPs, NGBs, Paralympics, athletes, Cara and other agencies	
Women in sport funding for disability initiatives	€60,000
• Beneficiaries IWA-Sport, Deaf Sports, Paralympics Ireland and Cara	
National Governing Body (NGB) disability funding from dormant accounts	€1,585,000
• Dormant accounts funding: Disability Sports Projects	€328,000
High-Performance (HP) Paralympics Ireland	€1,714,000
• Supported para athletes under the International Carding Scheme	€548,000
Local sports partnerships for SIDOs	€101,500
Sports Inclusion Disability Capital (from dormant accounts)	€200,000
Cara Core Funding and dormant accounts 2019	€270,000

Source: Sport Ireland (2019b, 2020b) and Lettis (2020)

projects are delivered in collaboration with Sport Ireland. In 2017, €1.35 million was distributed, €54,000 of which went to Special Olympics. In 2017, €3.8 million Healthy Ireland funding went to Local Community Development Committees, Children & Young Peoples Service Committees administered within the local authority structures. HSE funding to LSPs in 2017 was €600,000 representing a small part of their overall budget. Funding for disability-focused initiatives from HSE grant supports is under 10% (O'Keefe & Casey, 2019). Corporate sponsorship and fundraising are also important parts of the disability sport financial framework, contributing up to 50% of overall funding needs at all levels (Paralympics Ireland, 2019). In the case of the all island Special Olympics non-government funding contributed 62% of funding needs (Nolan, 2020).

Governance and Management Support

Sport Ireland oversees the Governance Code for Sport. All NGBs and LSPs need to adopt the code by 2021. This stems from the National Sports Policy Action 31 and will ensure appropriate governance in Irish sport.

To support effective implementation and improvement, the Sport Ireland Organisational Development and Change Unit provides a comprehensive range of mentoring, networking, management and leadership services, interventions and training opportunities (Sport Ireland, n.d.-b). One of Cara's objectives is to strengthen organisational leadership and governance (Cara, 2019) in the period up to 2021.

The Sport Ireland National Governing Body Unit supports regular dialogue with the NGBs and advises on governance, change management, strategic planning and procedural issues and compliance (Sport Ireland, n.d.-a). Of relevance also is the Sport Ireland Strategic Planning, Evaluation and Knowledge (SPEAK) system to support and monitor the activities of the LSPs. While the Service Provider Governance System is the national IT system used by the HSE to provide real time information on the Section 38 and 39 Grants for physical activity and LSPs.

Level of Integration or Inclusion

Sport Ireland seeks to provide for people with disabilities through mainstream and disability-specific provision (Sports Ireland, 2019). Every LSP has responsibility to deliver on this. The SIDO network and programme across the country support people with disabilities to find activities aligned with their needs and interests. As stated in the Cara Strategy it advocates choice across from fully segregated to fully integrated activities (Cara, 2019) in line with the CRPD. Cara provides supports to NGBs and LSPs seeking to provide greater levels of integration. Twenty three of 60 mainstream NGBs have dedicated diversity and inclusion officers. The three largest mainstream NGBs in the country have dedicated staff, committees and/or frameworks to support their disability inclusion work, namely the Gaelic Athletic Association (GAA), Irish Rugby Football Union (IRFU) and the Football Association of Ireland (FAI). The Sports Inclusion Disability Charter further demonstrates the movement towards better integration. Many mainstream NGBs and their clubs are increasing their work with people with disabilities as evidenced through Sport Ireland funding to mainstream sport bodies for disability programmes and integration activities.

9.4 Sport Participation by People with Disabilities

Monitoring and Evaluation

The Irish Sports Monitor is the main vehicle Sport Ireland use to track progress towards targets set in the National Sports Policy. Surveys are conducted via telephone and the interim report for 2019 presents data from 4255 interviews. Data on disability participation is gathered as part of the assessment of social gradients in sports participation. Congruent with other countries, participation data is not at a level that enables international comparison from the perspective of disability inclusion. Ireland reports on physical activity thought the WHO countryfiles, the international Children's PA report card in 2014, add the Health Behaviour in Schoolage Children (HBSC) study. Sport Irelands strategy does indicate an action calling for more data:

> Include disability issues in sport and physical activity in our research programme and liaise with the disability sector and other relevant agencies (for example, Central Statistics Office) to ensure that participation in sport and physical activity by people with disabilities is regularly monitored and reported on and is evidence based. (Sports Ireland, 2019, p. 8)

In 2018 the first all island collaborative research study looking at participation in sport, physical activity and physical education among children aged 10 to 18 was conducted. The Children's Sport Participation and Physical Activity Study 2018 involved 6651 children from 86 schools in Ireland and 29 in Northern Ireland. The Child Functioning Module questionnaire was used to assess disability status (Woods et al., 2018). In terms of meeting the physical activity guidelines CSPPA 2018 found no differences at primary or post primary school level between children with and without disabilities. As only 13% of children met the guidelines nationally, it is possible that the instrument was not sensitive enough to capture difference at a statistically significant level. However of serious policy concern in community sport reporting was the gradient in active participation and sports club membership found to exist by disability status which increased substantially in the post primary school years (Woods et al., 2018).

Sport Participation

Sport Ireland has been actively seeking to address disability gradients in sport, physical activity and sedentary behaviour for many years. The Irish Sports Monitor (ISM) has been operational since 2007 (Lunn et al., 2007) and by 2017 data gathered led the ISM to acknowledge an urgent need to address gradients in participation around disability (Ipsos MRBI and Irish Sports Council, 2014; Sport Ireland, 2017a; Sport Ireland & Ipsos MRBI, 2015). Social gradients in participation are monitored across age, disability, level of education and socio-economic status. Between 2017 and 2019 there has been a 2% improvement in the gradient relating to the participation of those reporting long-term health problem, illness or disability (33%) and those unaffected by these matters (49%). Overall in 2019, 33% of those with a long-term illness or disability report participating regularly in sport, while 61% regularly walk for recreation (Sport Ireland, 2019a).

Table 9.10 consolidates participation in sport by disability and long-term illness versus the general population from 2013–2019 ISM reports. As the report noted in 2015 and worth restating, some activities have similar participation levels, that is, swimming, dancing, weights, yoga and Pilates regardless of ability while team

Table 9.10 Irish sports monitor participation %, 2013–2019

	ISM 2013 [a] (n = 9390)			ISM 2015 [b] (n = 8540)			ISM 2017 [c] (n = 8482)			ISM 2019 [d] (n = 8504)		
	Total population (%)	Long term illness/ disability (%)	Long term illness/ disability that prevents sports participation (%)		Those with an illness or disability	Those with no illness or disability		Total population (%)	Long term illness/ disability (%)	Long term illness/ disability that prevents sports participation (%)		Those with an illness or disability	Those with no illness or disability
Exercise	12.2	8.6	6.4	Exercise	8.5	13.4	Exercise	13.7	9.4	7.8	Exercise	11.0	17.0
Swim	9.4	9.6	9.1	Swim	7.8	8.7	Run	8.2	2	1.2	Swim	9.0	9.0
Run	8.5	3.0	1.9	Run	2.3	7.2	Swim	8	8.4	8.4	Cycle	4.0	5.0
Cycle	5.9	4.4	4.5	Cycle	2.9	5.7	Cycle	5.5	3.7	3.4	Yoga	3.0	3.0
Soccer	5.9	2.1	1.5	Soccer	1.6	4.8	Soccer	4.8	3.6	2.1	Run	2.0	8.0
Dance	4.3	3.4	3.3	Dance	3.2	2.8	Dance	3	3.5	2.2	Soccer	2.0	4.0
Golf	3.3	2	1.6	Golf	1.4	2.7	Golf	2.7	1.7	0.9	Dance	2.0	3.0
Weights	2.9	2.2	2.2	Gaelic Football	0.6	2.4	Weights	2.3	2.4	2.2	Weights	2.0	2.0
Gaelic Football	2.6	1.0	0.8	Yoga	1.8	2.1	Gaelic Football	2	0.7	0.1	Pilates	1.0	2.0
Rugby	1.4	0.5	–	Weights	1.6	1.5	Yoga	1.5	1.7	1.6	Golf	1.0	3.0
				Pilates	0.8	1.3	Pilates	1.4	1.3	1.3	Gaelic Football	n/r [e]	2.0
				Hurling/ Camogie	0.6	1.2	Hurling/ Camogie	1.2	0.2	0.2	Hurling/ Camogie	n/r [e]	1.0
							Rugby	1.1	0.4	0.2			

Source: [a]Ipsos MRBI and Irish Sports Council (2014); [b]Sport Ireland & Ipsos MRBI (2015); [c]Sport Ireland (2017a); [d]Sport Ireland (2019a); [e]not recorded; Emphasis: comparison of persons with and without disability.

sports and running show considerable variance depending on ability levels. The monitor records sports participated in over the previous seven days. It is administered across the year to capture seasonal variation.

Despite people living with disabilities having similar motivations for participation as people without disabilities (namely health and fitness, spending time with friends and family and controlling weight) results point to a participation gradient in both physical activity participation and sedentary behaviour, with those with disabilities being less active and reporting more sedentary behaviour (Sport Ireland, 2019c). Those with long-term illness or disability are twice as likely to report sedentary behaviour than those without such illness or disability. This further underscores the need to address disability as a priority area as referenced in 2017 (Sport Ireland, 2017a). The 2017 ISM results for social participation among those with a long-term illness or disability found that while people with disability have lower club membership, 22.9% versus 37.1%, the gradient for attending events (14.5% v 19.7%) or volunteering (7% v 11.8%) is lower, demonstrating interest in involvement in sport. Physical activity opportunities vary and include organisations part-sponsored by the Health Service Executive (HSE), such as Parkrun or ExWell, Staying Fit for the Future that are run by HSE health promotion directly.

Barriers and Facilitators

The most recent national study on barriers and facilitators was conducted by Cara-Sport Inclusion Ireland as part of the I'm In Too, campaign. Throughout 2019 and 2020, 140 people across 22 counties living with disability and parents of children with disabilities were interviewed or participated in focus groups. They explored barriers to, facilitators of and impact of sport in their lives. The results informed a co-created Sport Inclusion Disability Charter to be signed by sporting organisations, calling for openness and understanding, trained staff and volunteers, inclusive activities, accessible facilities and inclusive promotion (Cara, n.d.). Detailed research outputs of I'm In Too are currently being compiled.

Barriers

Prior to the above, a comprehensive study among adults and children living with disability and parents of children living with disabilities that surveyed, through interview and focus groups, the barriers to participation in physical activity and sport was conducted by the National Disability Authority (NDA) in 2005. Open questions related to environmental factors were asked about the reasons for participating/not participating in physical exercise and sport, and the barriers and incentives to participation. This preceded the establishment of the SIDO programme within LSPs and the Cara Centre as well as more widespread funding of disability sport NGBs as well as mainstream NGBs seeking to operate more inclusively. The

Table 9.11 Barriers to participation in physical activity and sport by people with disabilities in Ireland

Poor physical education (PE) provision in schools
Negative school experiences
Low expectations from teachers' families and peers
Lack of knowledge of what is available
Lack of information and expertise
Poor community facilities and lack of access to facilities and programmes
Ad hoc structures and approaches
Transport difficulties
Lack of coverage of a wide range of sports in the media
Lack of experience of the benefits of physical activity
Untrained staff and lack of accessible facilities
Lack of companions who can facilitate access to facilities and programmes when required
Inadequate sponsorship and coaching
Lack of a culture of general participation in physical exercise and sport in Ireland

Source: National Disability Authority (2005)

Table 9.12 Facilitators of participation in physical activity by people with disabilities in Ireland

Stronger leadership
Improved and inclusive community facilities including playgrounds
The provision of adequate PE and physical activity experiences in the school and in the community
Adequate and accessible information services
Comprehensive education, training and coaching programmes that provide PE teachers, coaches, trainers and managers with the required inclusive PE, sport and physical activity training and expertise

Source: National Disability Authority (2005)

NDA identified that coordinated and concerted efforts would be needed to address these broad ranging barriers (see Table 9.11).

Facilitators

The study also addressed facilitators, and these are listed in Table 9.12.

9.5 Conclusion

Ireland has been progressively advancing opportunities in and through sport for those living with disabilities for over 60 years, with accelerated intentional government-led action evident since the mid-2000s. In particular, Special Olympics World Games 2003 had a formative role in stimulating public awareness and Irish political action with regard to the persons living with disability including in and through sport. A dedicated national centre, Cara-Sport Inclusion Ireland, and a network of NGBs and LSPs with Sport Inclusion Disability Officers support the multiple agencies, sports organisations and volunteers that strive to deliver better opportunities for people with disabilities in and through sport through the lifespan. At elite level Ireland has participated in every summer Paralympic Games since 1960 and Paralympics Ireland continues to grow in terms of reach and success. The mainstreaming of disability inclusion into all prevocational programmes advocated by the National Disability Authority in 2005 is not yet commonplace. While progress had been made many other barriers and facilitators identified in 2005 remain outstanding and have been reiterated though the I'm In Too initiative. Purposeful actions towards universal practice in a whole of society approach should be considered to take the agenda forward at scale. The complex web of interconnecting policies linked with sport needs unification and coordination from the individual level through to the societal/community level actions, including through better data and monitoring.

Monitoring data on people living with disability in sport pertains predominantly to individual participation as opposed to employment, leadership and other outcomes of interest in human rights and sustainable development contexts. Future data could be disaggregated to identify inequity within the heterogeneous domain of disability (e.g. intellectual disability, deaf-blind) and across areas of intersectional concern, such as women and girls living with disability, ethnic minorities including travellers with disability and the LGBTQI community living with disability. Disaggregated data obtained on engagement in sport should align with physical activity guidelines for health. Much data gathered is currently based on national methodologies. Aligning with international activities such as human rights reporting or sports-based reporting on the Sustainable Development Goals would enable broader understanding of outcomes, international comparison, benchmarking and insights. This could help to shape and inform results-based management in national policy and practice. Aligning indicators and mechanisms for surveillance, that embrace enough disaggregation, utilised at the country level by the WHO, with those that could report on human rights and SDGs could represent a coherent path forward.

Partnership approaches to the development and delivery of associated sports-related policies and strategies to impact improved opportunities for people living with disability are very evident. Likewise, funding stems from varied government sources as well as being subsidised by corporate finance and fundraising. The majority of funding is administered by Sport Ireland (*€111 million overall budget in 2018*), with smaller allocations coming through health budgets despite the well-reported significant impact of disability sport on health outcomes, population health and prevention. Intention to ensure the active involvement of those with disability in shaping policy development and implementation is very evident in policy. However, how this plays out in practice across the board in all policy areas is less evident, although the I'm In Too initiative and resultant Charter took that intention to full circle. Developments in other aspects of disability provision and investment in

Ireland may lag behind sport. Creating the ideal ecosystem for engagement in sport through the lifespan requires a whole of government and whole of society approach that touches on many systems and policies well beyond sport.

References

Cara. (2019). *Cara Strategy 2019-2021*. https://caracentre.ie/cara-about-us/
Cara. (n.d.). *Sport Inclusion Disability Charter*. https://caracentre.ie/sport-inclusion-disability-charter/
Central Statistics Office. (2017a). *Census 2016*. Retrieved January 10, 2020, from Census 2016 website: https://www.cso.ie/en/releasesandpublications/ep/p-cp9hdc/p8hdc/p9tod/
Central Statistics Office. (2017b). *Census 2016 Summary Results – Part 1* (Vol. 414). https://www.cso.ie/en/media/csoie/newsevents/documents/pressreleases/2017/prCensussummarypart1.pdf
Central Statistics Office. (2018). *Statbank*. Retrieved April 22, 2020, from https://statbank.cso.ie/px/pxeirestat/Statire/SelectVarVal/saveselections.asp
Cerebral Palsy Sport Ireland. (n.d.). *Cerebral Palsy Sport Ireland*. Retrieved April 21, 2020, from https://www.facebook.com/pg/Cerebral-Palsy-Sport-Ireland-122108847871612/about/?ref=page_internal
Department of Health. (2013). A framework for improved health and wellbeing 2013 – 2025. *Department of Health*. https://doi.org/http://www.dohc.ie/publications/Healthy_Ireland_Framework.html
Department of Justice and Equality. (2017). *National Disability Inclusion Strategy 2017-2021*.
European Commission. (2018). *Special Eurobarometer 471 Report Fairness, inequality and intergenerational mobility Fieldwork December 2017 Publication Survey requested by the European Commission, Special Eurobarometer 471 Report*. https://doi.org/10.2766/483047
Eurostat. (2020). *People at risk of poverty or social exclusion by level of activity limitation, sex and age Source of data: Eurostat*. https://appsso.eurostat.ec.europa.eu/nui/show.do?dataset=hlth_dpe010&lang=en
Federation of Irish Sport. (2020). *Federation of Irish Sport*. Retrieved January 10, 2020, from https://www.irishsport.ie/about/
Government of Ireland. (1999). *Irish Sports Council Act* (6).
Government of Ireland. (2000). *Equal Status Act, 2000*.
Government of Ireland. (2004). *Education for Persons with Special Educational Needs Act*. Pub. L. No. 30, Education for Persons with Special Educational Needs Act 1.
Government of Ireland. (2005). *Disability Act 2005*.
Government of Ireland. (2014). *Irish Human Rights and Equality Commission Act 2014*. Www.Irishstatutebook.Ie §.
Government of Ireland. (2015). *Sport Ireland Act*. Pub. L. No. 15.
Government of Ireland. (2018). National Sports Policy 2018 – 2027. *Department of Transport, Tourism and Sport*, 1-106. www.dttas.gov.ie
Government of Ireland. (2020). *Disability (Miscellaneous Provisions) Bill 2016 – No. 119 of 2016 – Houses of the Oireachtas*. Retrieved April 30, 2020, from https://www.oireachtas.ie/en/bills/bill/2016/119/
Healthy Ireland. (2016). *Get Ireland Active! National Physical Activity Plan for Ireland*. (48). https://www.hse.ie/eng/about/who/healthwellbeing/our-priority-programmes/heal/heal-docs/get-ireland-active-national-physical-activity-plan-for-ireland.pdf
Helliwell, J. F., Layard, R., & Sachs, J. D. (2019). *World Happiness Report 2019*. http://worldhappiness.report/
IDA. (2019). *Facts About Ireland*. https://www.idaireland.com/newsroom/publications/ida_facts_about_ireland_2019

IHREC. (n.d.). *Human Rights Law in Ireland - IHREC - Irish Human Rights and Equality Commission*. Retrieved April 30, 2020, from https://www.ihrec.ie/your-rights/human-rights-law-ireland/

Ipsos MRBI and Irish Sports Council. (2014). *Irish Sports Monitor 2013 Annual Report. 2011* (except 2010). http://www.irishsportscouncil.ie/Research/Irish-Sports-Monitor-Annual-Report-2013/

Lettis, M. (2020). Sport Ireland Research Review Communication 12th May 2020. Archived Material.

Local Government Information Unit. (n.d.). Local government facts and figures: Ireland. *LGIU*. Retrieved December 4, 2019, from https://lgiu.org/local-government-facts-and-figures-ireland/

Lunn, P., Layte, R., & Watson, D. (2007). The Irish Sports Monitor. *First Annual Report*, 1–60. http://www.esri.ie/news_events/latest_press_releases/irish_sports_council_publ/index.xml

Mansergh, F. (2020). Healthy Ireland Research Review Communication 6th November 2020. Archived Material.

McCarthy, J. (2020, January 9). Joanne McCarthy: Ireland worst country in western Europe to have a disability. *The Irish Times*. https://www.irishtimes.com/opinion/joanne-mccarthy-ireland-worst-country-in-western-europe-to-have-a-disability-1.4134074

National Disability Authority. (2005). Promoting the Participation of People with Disabilities in Physical Activity and Sport in Ireland. In *National Disability Authority*.

NESC. (2005). *The Developmental Welfare State*. Dublin: National Economic and Social Council.

Nolan, G. (2020). Special Olympics Ireland, Research Review Communication, 15th October 2020. Archived Material.

O'Keefe, B., & Casey, C. (2019). *Active for Health: Report of the Working Group to Support Development of Outcomes Strategy for HSE Funding and Work with Local Sports Partnerships*. www.coventry.gov.uk/beactivebehealthy

Office of the High Commissioner of Human Rights. (n.d.). *Office of the High Commissioner of Human Rights*. Retrieved April 22, 2020, from https://www.ohchr.org/EN/Issues/Disability/Pages/DisabilityIndex.aspx

Para Equestrian Ireland. (n.d.). Retrieved April 21, 2020, from http://paraequestrianireland.com/index.php/about-us/

Paralympics Ireland. (2019). Success Takes More Strategic Plan 2019-2025. In *Strategic Plan 2019-2025*. https://static1.squarespace.com/static/56a0f3870e4c11ce96649329/t/5ca4bca4f4e1fcd633c015bb/1554300083130/Paralympics+Ireland_Strategic_Report_Digital_Download_Version.pdf

RTE. (2014). *Special Olympics 2003 - Ten Years On*. https://www.rte.ie/sport/cricket/2013/0621/457994-special-olympics-2003-ten-years-on/

Sport Ireland. (2017a). *Irish Sports Monitor 2017 Annual Report*. www.sportireland.com

Sport Ireland. (2017b). *Sport Ireland Annual Report 2017*.

Sport Ireland. (2018). *Sport Ireland Statement of Strategy 2018-2022*. https://doi.org/10.17352/2455-8702.000013

Sport Ireland. (2019a). *Irish Sports Monitor 2019*. www.sportireland.ie/research

Sport Ireland. (2019b). *Sport Investment 2018*. 1–12.

Sport Ireland. (2019c). *Sport Investment 2019*. https://www.sportireland.ie/sites/default/files/2019-10/invest19_updated-final.pdf

Sport Ireland. (2020a). *Local Sports Partnerships Annual Report 2019*. Retrieved December 16, 2020, from https://www.sportireland.ie/sites/default/files/media/document/2020-06/2019-lsp-annual-report_1.pdf

Sport Ireland. (2020b). *Sport Ireland Sport Investment 2020*. Retrieved December 16, 2020, from https://www.sportireland.ie/sites/default/files/2020-01/invest_final.pdf

Sport Ireland. (2020c). Sport Ireland welcomes Budget 2021 allocation. *Sport Ireland*. Retrieved December 16, 2020, from https://www.sportireland.ie/news/sport-ireland-welcomes-budget-2021-allocation#:~:text=The%20funding%20announced%20by%20the,announced%20in%20the%20coming%20weeks.

Sport Ireland. (n.d.-a). NGB overview. *Sport Ireland*. Retrieved May 1, 2020, from https://www.sportireland.ie/national-governing-bodies/ngb-overview

Sport Ireland. (n.d.-b). Organisational development & change. *Sport Ireland*. Retrieved April 30, 2020, from https://www.sportireland.ie/organisational-development-change

Sport Ireland. (n.d.-c). *Sports Inclusion Disability Programme*. Retrieved April 20, 2020, from https://www.sportireland.ie/news/sports-inclusion-disability-programme

Sport Ireland, & Ipsos MRBI. (2015). *Irish Sports Monitor: 2015 Annual Report*. 74. http://www.sportireland.ie/Research/Irish-Sports-Monitor-Annual-Report-2015/Irish-Sports-Monitor-Annual-Report-2015.pdf

Sports Ireland. (2019). *Sport Ireland Policy on participation in sport by people with disabilities*. https://www.sportireland.ie/sites/default/files/2019-11/sport-ireland-policy-on-participation-in-sport-by-people-with-disabilities.pdf

Statista. (2020). Ireland - urbanization 2008-2018. *Statista*. Retrieved May 5, 2020, from https://www.statista.com/statistics/455844/urbanization-in-ireland/

UNDP. (2019). *Inequalities in Human Development in the 21st Century Palau Introduction. Briefing note for countries on the 2019 Human Development Report*. http://hdr.undp.org/en/data

United Nations. (2006). *The United Nations Convention on the Rights of Persons with Disabilities and Optional Protocol*.

United Nations Development Programme. (2019). *Human Development Report 2019. Beyond income, beyond averages, beyond today: Inequalities in human development in the 21st century*. https://doi.org/10.18356/b80ebada-en

Woods, C. B., Powell, C., Saunders, J. A., O'Brien, W., Murphy, M. H., Duff, C., Farmer, O., Johnston, A., Connolly, S., Belton S., & Belton, S. (2018). *The children's sport participation and physical activity study 2018 (CSPPA 2018)*. 1–108.

World Bank. (2018). GDP per capita (current LCU) – Ireland. *Data*. Retrieved May 5, 2020, from https://data.worldbank.org/indicator/NY.GDP.PCAP.CN?locations=IE

World Health Organisation. (2013). How to use the ICF: A practical manual for using the International Classification of Functioning, Disability and Health (ICF). Exposure draft for comment. In *How to use the ICF: A practical manual for using the International Classification of Functioning, Disability and Health (ICF). Exposure draft for comment*. https://doi.org/10.1016/j.dhjo.2015.03.002

Chapter 10
Northern Ireland: Disability Sport in a Shared Space

Paul Kitchin and Catherine Carty

10.1 Introduction

This chapter will provide an in-depth view of sport for people with disabilities in Northern Ireland (NI) from policy to practice levels. The predominant stakeholders governing access to sport for people with disabilities include the Department of Communities (DoC), Sport Northern Ireland, National and Provincial Governing Bodies of Sport (both mainstream and disability focused), Local Councils, Disability Sport NI, Paralympics GB & Ireland, as well as the Higher Education Sector and their partner agencies. Current disability sport policy stems mainly from the Sport Matters: The Northern Ireland Strategy for Sport and Physical Recreation, 2009–2019 and Active Living: No Limits 2016–2021. Across Northern Ireland, a number of agencies support delivery of policies at regional and local levels. Support is given to regional/local disability sport inclusion staff to support such agencies. This chapter on Northern Ireland will outline the ecosystem of sport for people with disabilities, disaggregated participation, moderating factors for participation, as well as the instruments and methods used in data collection. A focus will be placed on the facilitators and barriers that impact sport participation in this region. Concluding remarks will point to successes and considerations for addressing the gradient that still exists between those with and without disability in Northern Ireland.

P. Kitchin (✉)
Ulster University, Belfast, UK
e-mail: pj.kitchin@ulster.ac.uk

C. Carty
Muster Technological University, Kerry, Ireland
e-mail: Catherine.carty@ittralee.ie

10.2 Country Profile

Characteristics of Northern Ireland

Northern Ireland (NI) comprises just over 17% of the island of Ireland and is characterised by uplands and low mountains. NI is one of the three devolved regions within the UK. As a devolved region of the UK, it shares commonalities with Wales and Scotland in the devolution of legislative powers, but in sport it operates a hybrid governance system with multiple sports belonging to both the UK and Ireland and in some cases Northern Ireland itself. Given this unique and nuanced circumstance, it requires a separate analysis.

The NI Assembly and (Stormont) Executive are examples of a political system based on ensuring all communities have a role in power-sharing, termed a consociational democracy and which provides government stability. This type of government roughly ensures that each major community group is adequately represented by its elites in parliament. The Legislative Assembly consists of 90 elected members from 18 parliamentary constituencies, and policy is implemented through a 'programme for government'.

NI has a population of approximately 1.9 million people which comprises 2.8% of the UK or 39% of the total population on the island of Ireland. The population is ageing as 16% of its citizens are aged 65 and over and are 98.28% white, with approximately 1% Asian or Asian British, 0.2% Black or Black British and approximately 0.5% from other ethnic groups. The religious affiliation of the population includes two significantly large groups, 48% Protestant or brought up protestant and 45% Catholic or brought up Catholic (NISRA, 2011).

NI is the smallest economic area of the UK and has a GDP of €43.6 billion. The primary industries in the region are arable and pastoral farming, fishing, quarrying and forestry. Population density varies across the region, with average density recorded at 137.90 people per square mile, ranging from 2535.7 in Belfast to 40.8 in Fermanagh and Omagh, giving the region about 20% of the density of the UK and approximately 80% the density of the Republic of Ireland (ROI) (NISRA, 2011) (Table 10.1).

Sport in Northern Ireland

Sport is one of the major cultural past-times in Northern Ireland. Due to the history of the region, sport has been developed upon community lines, which has led to a fairly unique situation in Europe. The Northern Irish government is involved in sport through its DoC, which amongst its remit covers sport and recreation (see Table 10.2). Sport Northern Ireland (Sport NI) is responsible for implementing the region's sport strategy 'Sport Matters: The Northern Ireland Strategy for Sport and Physical Recreation, 2009–2019' (Sport NI, 2009) that defines sport as "all forms

Table 10.1 Facts and statistics of Northern Ireland

Population (number of inhabitants)[a]	1,881,641
Area (km^2)	1430
Density (inhabitants/km^2)[a]	134
Urbanisation rate (%)[b]	63
Political organisation	Consociational democracy
Structure of the state	Statelet
Number of counties	6
Number of local government districts	11
Number of official languages	1
EU membership	1974–2020
Welfare model	Welfare state

[a]NISRA (2011)
[b]Macauley (2017)

Table 10.2 Sport profile of Northern Ireland 2019

Government authority responsible for sport	Department of Communities/Sport Northern Ireland
Membership sport club (%)[a]	23
Membership fitness or health centre (%)[a]	15
Sport participation, at least once a month (%)[a]	56
Number of national sport federations	60 (35 all Island, including ROI)
Number of sport clubs	3000
Percentage of sport club members (%)[b]	24
Regional budget for sport (€ × 1,000,000)[c]	35
Regional budget for sport federations (€ × 1000)	–
Local budget for sport (€ × 1,000,000)[c]	203
Per capita sport spending (€)	132.22
COVID-19 Sport Sustainability Fund (€m)[d]	25

[a]Donnelly (2011)
[b]Statista (2020)
[c]Ferguson (2020)
[d]Sport NI (2020a)

of physical activity which through casual or organised participation, aim at expressing or improving physical fitness and mental wellbeing, forming social relationships, or obtaining results in competition at all levels" (Sport NI, 2009, p. 4).

Participation can be difficult to determine because of the variety of ways that it is measured. For instance, the rate of general adult participation in physical activity recommended by the Chief Medical Officer (CMO) is 35% (30 minutes of moderate intensity activities on at least five days per week) (Donnelly, 2011). However, when the question asks those who participated in *sport* at least once in the previous 12 months, the figure rises to 56% and this figure has been consistent between 50% in 2007 and 56% in 2019 (DoC, 2019a; Sport NI, 2015). In terms of participation, around 23% of people in NI are members of sport clubs and of these just under half are members of health and fitness clubs. Of all club members, around 20% are members of more than one club (Sport NI, 2012).

Disability in Northern Ireland

The terms 'people with disabilities' and 'disabled people' are both used in Northern Ireland; the former is more socially acceptable, but the latter conforms to the social model of disability used across the UK. In Northern Ireland the Disability Discrimination Order (DDO) 2006 is operational, and within this act disability is defined as "a physical or mental impairment which has a substantial and long-term adverse effect on a person's ability to carry out normal day-to-day activities" (Equality Commission for Northern Ireland, 2007, p. 2). The policy that was driving action for people with disabilities was "A strategy to improve the lives of people with disabilities—2012 to 2015" published by the DoC and extended until March 2017 when government at Stormont was suspended.

NI collects statistical information on disability according to general activity limitation indicators (GALI) and specific impairment types. Of the daytime population estimates, there are 1,775,187 people in NI and the self-reported health ratings are included in Table 10.3. Most people rate their health as very good or good, while 15% rate their health as fair. About 4% claim bad health and 1% of the population claim they experience very bad health (see Table 10.3). Of these groups (20% of the population) claim that day-to-day activities are either limited a little (8.5%) or limited a lot (11.5%).

Of a population of 1,810,863, 20.6% reported that their day-to-day activities were limited because of a long-standing health problem or disability (NISRA, 2011). Two households in every five have at least one individual with a long-standing health problem or disability, with urban and town areas reporting higher figures. Census 2011 respondents identified with experiencing a range of impairments. The most frequently reported impairments are identified in Table 10.4.

Table 10.3 All population figures: general health

General health claimed as	Population	
	Count	%
Very good	847,832	48
Good	564,239	32
Fair	263,422	15
Bad	78,573	4
Very bad	21,121	1
Total	75	100

Source: NISRA (2011))

Table 10.4 Statistics on disability in Northern Ireland

Prevalence of population who stated they had a disability (% of population)	**20.6**
Prevalence of moderate/severe physical disabilities (movement) (% of population)	19
Prevalence of substantially limited basic physical activity (% of population)	17
Prevalence of blindness or serious vision impairment (% of population)	3
Prevalence of deafness or serious hearing impairment (% of population)	8
Prevalence of intellectual disabilities (% of population)	4[a]
Prevalence of psychological or emotional condition (% of population)	10
Prevalence of difficulty learning, remembering or concentrating	3
Prevalence of difficulty connected with pain, breathing or other chronic illnesses (% of population)	25
Other	11

Source: NISRA (2011)
[a] A possible cause of the high prevalence of intellectual disabilities as a percentage of the population is the broad definition used in Census 2011. The question asked: **Do you have any of the following conditions which have lasted, or are expected to last, at least 12 months?**
• A learning difficulty, an intellectual difficulty, or a social or behavioural difficulty
This question has been reformed for the Census 2021 into
• An intellectual or learning disability (e.g. Down syndrome)
• A learning difficulty (e.g. dyslexia)
Which may lead to a lower percentage as seen in other comparable countries

People with a disability are less likely to participate in Northern Irish society than non-disabled people. In sport, people with a disability are roughly half as likely to participate in sport as non-disabled people (DoC, 2019c; Donnelly, 2011).

Emergence of Disability Sport in Northern Ireland

There is little published on the history of disability sport, but practices emerged across Northern Ireland throughout the late twentieth century through local clubs and community associations with the first national disability sport event being the Special Olympics Ireland Games in Belfast in 1986. Disability sport emerged through informal opportunities provided by local councils and not-for-profits for people with disabilities to take part in sport and recreation. Organisations such as the Royal Institute for the Blind in NI, Action on Hearing Loss and Special Olympics Ireland had independently coordinated efforts of these informal groups/clubs to provide activities for people with disabilities. Disability Sport Northern Ireland (Disability Sport NI) was established in 1998 as a company limited by guarantee. Disability Sport NI's aim is the tackling of the underrepresentation of people with disabilities in sport. Disability Sport NI focuses on working with Sport NI, the national governing bodies (NGBs), local government and sports clubs to develop more opportunities for people with disabilities, but also plays an important role in upskilling and capacity building the NI sport's workplace in disability awareness and coaching (Disability Sport NI, 2019).

10.3 The Disability Sport System

Structure of Disability Sport

The organisation of sport in this region is complex. There are mixed governance arrangements in this region, explained as a "complex bi-partite governance system" (Liston et al., 2013, p. 344) with sport organised on either an all-Ireland basis, a UK-basis or as the six UK counties of Northern Ireland. For example, the following organisations also have a stake in sport within this region, "the Irish Sports Council (ISC), the Irish Institute of Sport (IIS), sports coach United Kingdom (scUK, which is funded through a combination of charity, Sport England and UK Sport monies); non-governmental groups such as Coaching Ireland (CI), the British Olympic Association (BOA), the Olympic Council of Ireland (OCI), the Paralympic Council of Ireland (PCI); [and] voluntary-run national associations such as the Northern Ireland Commonwealth Games Council" (Liston et al., 2013, p. 345).

Governmental Agents

The NI Executive is responsible for governing the region, and within its departments, sport falls under the remit of the DoC with school sport funded by the Department of Education. The DoC is the largest of the Executive Departments and has a number of responsibilities, including benefits and pensions, housing, regeneration, museums and libraries, arts and culture, local government, and the voluntary and community sector, which all arguably intersect with the responsibility for sport and physical activity across Northern Ireland. The DoC is responsible for 15 non-departmental public bodies (NDPB), including Sport NI in Fig. 10.1, which assist the DoC in delivering its sport-related work.

Using a combination of the NI 'block grant' (the money provided for devolved administration by the UK Westminster government) and lottery funds, the DOC

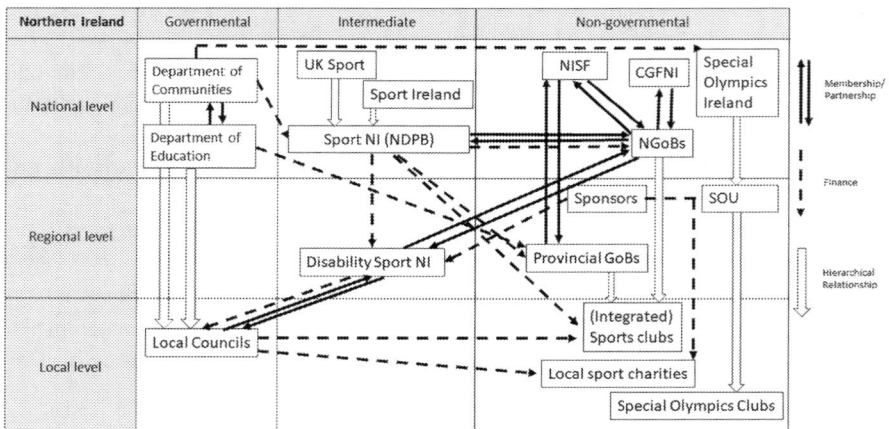

Fig. 10.1 Disability sport framework for NI

directly funds Sport NI and some local councils to deliver sport. However, little direction is provided by the DoC about where the funds should be invested and the programming and training opportunities are left to the discretion of Sport NI and local government sport and physical activity departments.

At the local level, local councils are major providers of sporting infrastructure and also a funder of sports development. At this local level, greater decision-making exists to prioritise the development of disability sport, and this is through the funding of inclusive clubs and/or the creation of accessible facilities. They are part-funder of the Disability Sport Hubs that operate across NI and are located at 11 selected district leisure centres.

Intermediary Agents

At an intermediate level the picture is complex as explained previously. Athletes and sports clubs within the region can be allied to Irish, Northern Irish or UK-wide governing bodies, making three intermediate actors relevant—UK Sport, Sport Ireland and Sport NI. Details of Sport Ireland are contained in the Republic of Ireland chapter. The non-departmental public body responsible for sport is Sport NI. Their vision is: Northern Ireland: renowned as a place where people enjoy, engage and excel in sport (Sport NI, 2020b). Their objectives are threefold: to increase and support the number of people adopting and sustaining a sporting lifestyle; to increase and support the number of people to reach their sporting goals through a structured environment; and to help more Northern Ireland athletes to win at the highest level.

Operating across the region is Disability Sport NI which is a registered charity aiming to increase the health and well-being of people with disabilities through sport. Sport NI and Disability Sport NI worked in partnership with the Northern Irish branch of Disability Action to develop the most current disability sport and physical activity policy, 'Active Living: No Limits 2021' (Sport NI, 2016). UK Sport and Sport Ireland policies also operate within NI for athletes when elite para-athletes interact with international para-sport competitions.

Non-governmental Agents

The Northern Ireland Sports Forum (NISF) and the Commonwealth Games Federation NI (CGFNI) operate at this national level to assist in developing awareness of disability sport opportunities. The NISF is a lobbying and advocacy group for the governing bodies of sport that operates in Northern Ireland akin to the Activity Alliance in the UK or the Irish Federation for Sport in ROI.

Since the publication of a Disability Mainstreaming (Sport) Policy in 2006, a number of national and regional governing bodies have integrated participation and competition opportunities for disability sport. The results of this have been mixed, as there was no pressure placed on organisations that did not do this. The policy allowed the provision of segregated opportunities based on the lack of resources available to sports organisations. This policy also informs both programming and staffing responsibilities that attempt to foster participation from local club levels

(Kitchin et al., 2019). Local sport clubs provide a number of inclusive/integrated or segregated sporting opportunities for people with disabilities to get involved in sport.

Secondary Agents

Within NI, there exist 'special schools' to provide special education to meet the needs of young people with disabilities which are funded by the Department of Education. In 2019/2020, 19.3% (67,254) of all pupils had special educational needs. To determine this need, and whether students attend a mainstream school or a special school, pupils are assessed by the Department of Education and issued a statement. In this same year 30.2% of these pupils were then educated in a special school (Department of Education, 2020). A number of sports organisations (for instance, the Gaelic Athletic Association and the Irish Football Association) target these special schools and some residential care units to ensure their grassroots activities are reaching the appropriate market.

Steering of Disability Sport

Relationships

The DoC has a direct financial, partnership and hierarchal relationship with local councils across Northern Ireland. While each local council can raise its own revenue through commercial and residential rates, the DoC can extend government grants to support additional projects, such as £15 million of £38 million in 2011 to support the development of the Bangor Aurora—the region's sole London Olympic and Paralympic Legacy project that also acts as a Disability Sport Hub.

UK Sport and Sport Ireland work in partnership with Sport NI to support elite athletes in training and competition. While funds are dedicated to supporting these athletes, they are distributed by Sport NI. Sport NI supports Disability Sport NI through a financial and partnership relationship where support for elite Paralympic athletes and the development of disability sport are the remit of the latter. Disability Sport NI also works in partnership with national and provincial NGBs providing inclusive training to their staff and volunteers (Disability Sport NI, 2019).

Non-governmental organisations have myriad relationships. The major ones are the financial relationships between the national and provincial GBs and Sport NI. This financial relationship is dependent upon the development of sport plans that address the KPIs of the national sport strategy. Although this relationship is often considered hierarchal, it resembles a partnership as Sport NI is also accountable for the performance of the NGBs against their business plan.

Legislative Framework

Northern Ireland has three key pieces of legislation governing disability that impact the disability sport sector: the Disability Discrimination Order (DDO) 2006, Special Educational Needs (SEN) and Disability Order 2005 and Sections 49a and 75 of the NI Act 1998. The Disability Discrimination Order ensures that employers and service providers cannot discriminate on the grounds of disability, which encompasses facilities for sport participation. The Order does not cover disability discrimination in education, and as such the SEN and Disability Order 2005 ensures reasonable adjustments are made in all levels of education, including inclusive physical education. Section 49a of the Act requires the DoC to promote positive attitudes towards disabled people and encourage participation by disabled people in public life. Article 75 of NI Act provides a legal obligation on public authorities to promote equality of opportunity between, amongst other things, persons with a disability and persons without. Indeed Lenahan suggests that "it is simply not acceptable (or indeed legal) for Government, of whatever the level, to neglect matters of disability sports equality. There is a legal duty for Government to promote equality of opportunity in sport" (Lenahan, 2019, online). Research supported by the Equality Commission has found that the participation of people with disabilities in public life has not increased in the recent past and, despite these guidelines in place, the situation is "worrying" (Banks et al., 2015, p. 10).

Policy Framework

In NI, specific policies and strategic documents regarding the development and the management of disability sport are few, but the current strategy for encouraging participation is the Active Living: No Limits (2016–2021) strategy, which focuses on improving the health and well-being of people with disabilities in NI. The strength of the current strategy is the buy-in from a range of stakeholders in sport and outside sport, such as the NI Executive and Disability Action, an NI charity working to promote, protect and uphold the human rights of people with disabilities. Because of this, it is aligned specifically to the overarching sport strategy for NI (Sport Matters), but also contributes to targets established by the NI Executive's strategy 'to improve the lives of people with disabilities (2012–2017)', and their Active Ageing Strategy (2016–2021), as well as the Department of Health's Physical and Sensory Disability Strategy and Action Plan (2012–2017).

Examples of disability sport programming include the following initiatives: Active Clubs, Active Sport Awards, Active Inclusion and Active Living: No Limits 2021 Action Plan. The latter aims to "improve the health and wellbeing of people with disabilities in Northern Ireland through participation in sport and active recreation. The Plan has the support of the Northern Ireland (NI) Executive across all its Departments, and was launched alongside an announcement of investment to provide specialist sports equipment as part of development of eleven disability sports hubs across NI".

Financial, Governance and Managerial Support

Financial Framework

Funding for mainstream sport comes from a variety of sources, the largest of these being local councils across the region, then lottery funding—that allocated to Sport NI and that which is not. Funding for sport also comes from government departments, Peace funding from the EU and funding for further and higher education (Ferguson et al., 2019). In recent times investment in disability sport has increased by nearly 45% between 2006 and 2012 (Donnelly, 2011). Sport NI claims this has resulted in increased opportunities, although Sport NI tempers this with the admission that the most notable advances are in the areas of elite performance (Kitchin et al., 2019; Sport NI, 2013). The need to boost grassroots disability sport participation in the region is stark. As indicated in Table 10.5, people with disabilities in

Table 10.5 SAPAS 2010 key performance indicator (KPI) results

KPI	Item	Description	General population	PWD
1	Physical activity	The proportion of adults participating in at least 30 minutes of at least moderate intensity activities **per day** (which can be made up of bouts of at least 10 minutes) on at least five days in the last seven days. This definition is derived from the Chief Medical Officer's recommendation with regard to physical activity	35%	23%
2	Sport participation	The proportion of adults participating in sporting activities of at least moderate intensity in the last seven days (for at least 30 minutes in duration)	37%	19%
3	Club membership	The proportion of adults having been a member of at least one club in which they can participate in sport or physical activity in the last four weeks	23%	13%
4	Competitions	The proportion of sports participants having taken part in at least one organised sporting competition in the last 12 months	22%	12%
5	Coaching	The proportion of sports participants having received coaching in the last 12 months	18%	10%
6	Volunteering	The proportion of adults having carried out any sports voluntary work without receiving any payment except to cover expenses in the last 12 months. This includes, for example, helping to run an event, raising money, providing transport, coaching or mentoring but not the time spent solely supporting family members	9%	7%
7	Live sporting events	The proportion of adults having attended at least one live sporting event in Northern Ireland in the last 12 months	37%	24%
8	Satisfaction with sports provision	The proportion of adults satisfied with sports provision in their local area	62%	53%

Source: Kitchin and Crossin (2018) adapted from Donnelly (2011)

Northern Ireland experience lower participation rates and experience lower quality of service in every key performance indicator (KPI) of the national strategy.

Most funding for disability sport comes from external sources to the clubs. Local councils, Disability Sport NI, the governing bodies and sponsors directly fund disability sport, but most of these draw their funds from the DoC or Sport NI. In 2019, Disability Sport NI generated over €1.2 million and expended just over €1 million. Their key income sources were Sport NI core, capital and project grants (est. over 70%) and other sources of income (just under the remaining 30%). Their major outgoings went on equipment (20%), sport and club development (29%), participation and competition (32%) and other expenses at the remaining 20% (Disability Sport NI, 2019).

In 2011, Sport NI coordinated the funding of Special Olympics Ulster (SOU) to the tune of £2.3 million over four years, which was renewed in 2016. These funds were derived from five government departments which saw that the work that SOU does align with their responsibilities for the programme of government. The most recent funding figures suggest that SOU receives over £600,000 per annum split between the DoC and the Departments of Health and Education (DoC, 2019b).

Within mainstream governing bodies, such as the Ulster Gaelic Athletic Association, subsidies are provided to support the development and competition of their wheelchair hurling and Gaelic football for athletes with learning difficulties. Private funds can be sources also, either through commercial sponsorship, an example of which is the Progressive Building Society and their support of the Disability Sport Hubs around NI, or through donations and other small funding sources.

Some programmes (and their funding amounts) have been tailored for specific target groups. Recent examples include those for Deaf Sport NI—Developing Deaf People (£6000) and the NI Primary School 5 Star Sports Challenge (£45,000). The first project sought to enable deaf children, young people and adults to participate in a range of sports programmes, delivered by qualified deaf sport coaches. The aim was for deaf people to take their first steps into joining a deaf sports club or a mainstream sports club after completion. The second programme delivered awareness raising, education and participation opportunities to promote the benefits of sport, address commonly held negative beliefs about people with disabilities and encourage active involvement in mainstream sport (Sport NI, 2015).

Governance and Management Support

For grassroots sporting opportunities, the current system of Disability Sport Hubs is managed in partnership between Disability Sport NI and staff at the local leisure centres and sponsored by Progressive Building Society (Progressive Building Society, 2019). This coordination of facility and programming personnel ensures that the distributed hubs are utilising equipment and maximising participant numbers. Within the Special Olympics, the Ulster branch, while funding is provided by departments of the NI Executive, governance is supported through Special Olympics Ireland and its wider international network.

Within some local sporting clubs that are integrated sports clubs (usually a partnership or merger between a disability sports club and a mainstream sports club), strategic management support is provided by the governing body in conjunction with Disability Sport NI that can deliver a range of learning and development courses.

Disability Sport NI develops and provides a range of training and educational services which aim to create a more inclusive sports system. Their courses are divided into four sections including courses such as Sports Leaders Awards, which promote disability inclusion within sport, and team building opportunities for people of all backgrounds to try disability sport. These courses are evaluated and address the KPIs outlined in Sport Northern Ireland's Disability Action Plan. Disability Sport NI has the flexibility to assist with increasing inclusion training for sports organisations when the latter is in receipt of targeted government funds to develop disability sport, creating extra capacity in the sport system (Kitchin et al., 2019).

Level of Integration and Inclusion

Efforts at direct intervention from the DoC to national and provincial governing bodies have resulted in mixed results at increasing opportunities through sport (Kitchin et al., 2019). The original policy on mainstreaming (integration) was the Disability Mainstreaming Policy (DMP), which was launched in 2006. The policy included no definition of mainstreaming and permitted organisations to offer integrated experiences or offer a segregated service (which the policy calls a twin-track approach). This policy encouraged all sports organisations in NI to adopt five priorities: (1) to promote disability sport; (2) to provide equitable access to participation opportunities for PWD; (3) to offer full consultation in future sport policy; (4) to develop programmes and policies that are targeted to specific needs; and (5) to take positive actions to redress the historical marginalisation of persons with a disability (Sport NI, 2006). While this was a starting point for making the organised sport more accessible, the widening physical activity agenda conceptualises activity occurring in many more domains than just sport.

At present, the Disability Sport Hubs are attempting to increase participation by localising these opportunities within every local government area through leisure centres rather than solely organised sport. Integration is still at a rudimentary level across NI, but the growth between 2000 and 2020 of sporting opportunities has been significant, with the DoC, governing bodies, Ulster Special Olympics and Disability Sport NI responsible for much recent development.

Opportunities are increasing, but are not as prevalent as non-disabled participation opportunities. The funding from commercial sources, such as the Progressive Building Society, has enabled dedicated staff to assist in this development. However, the Special Olympics and some local sport charities have led the way from as early as the late 1990s, with Belfast Lough Sailability an example of a charity offering inclusive sailing for people with a disability. Most recently, the Irish Football

Association has created an Inclusive Clubs Initiative that aligned standalone disability football clubs with partnerships or mergers with mainstream football clubs (Kitchin & Crossin, 2018).

10.4 Sport Participation by People with Disabilities

Monitoring and Evaluation

The government measures sporting participation of the population through the Continuous Household Survey (CHS), which contains questions on the experience of sport in NI (DoC, 2019c). In the strategy for sport in NI (Sport NI, 2009)—Sport Matters—there were 26 targets, yet only 1 of these provided specifics for disability sport:

> [Physical Activity Target 10] By 2019, to deliver at least a six percentage points increase in participation rates in sport and physical recreation among people with a disability (from the 2013 baseline). (Sport NI, 2015, p. 11)

This provides a basic baseline and ongoing monitoring, and due to S49a and S75 of the NI Act (1998), data is available for people with a disability. The Northern Ireland Adult Sport and Physical Activity Survey (SAPAS; see Donnelly, 2011) was commissioned by Sport NI to provide statistically robust data on participation, club membership, volunteering, coaching attitudes to sport and spectating amongst a representative sample of Northern Ireland adults (aged 16 years and over) in order to reliably enhance the understanding of sport and physical activity patterns and determinants across the population. Unfortunately, despite the high quality and quantity of information that was collected during SAPAS, the survey has not been recommissioned. As such much of this chapter draws on data from 2011 as little outside the CHS is regularly recorded at a national level.

In 2011 Sport NI published the survey's results noting that 23% of people with a disability participated in physical activity (5 × 30 min) and that 19% participated in sport (Donnelly, 2011), which differed somewhat from the CHS that reported 32% participating in sport (DoC, 2019c). Irrespective of which figures are chosen, these figures demonstrate a significant gap with commensurate participant rates for non-disabled people (37% and 59% respectively). The data is, however, limited by its creation of one generic category—people with disabilities (see below)—and therefore, figures for the diversity of disability are lacking.

Sport NI also collects data for its ongoing reporting to the DoC with respect to the expectations required in the NI Act (1998) on equality. All organisations that receive public funding are required by the Equality Commission for NI to complete an Equality and Good Relations Duties report specifically addressing Section 75 of the NI Act 1998 and Equality Scheme and Section 49A of the Disability Discrimination Act 1995 and Disability Action Plan. The reports measure outputs, such as participation numbers and targeted funding, but do little to address outcomes from these interventions.

The main methods of data collection were by survey. SAPAS was carried out in conjunction with Ipsos/Mori, while the CHS is carried out by the Northern Ireland Statistic and Research Agency.

The SAPAS survey was designed in partnership with stakeholders from sport and physical activity professions. The definition of disability in this research is "those who have a long-standing disability, infirmity or illness. This includes problems due to age" (Donnelly, 2011, p. 102), while a sport participant was defined as "an adult who participated in any sport (regardless of duration and intensity) in the last 12 months" (ibid., p. 101). However, sport was only one of the four domains in which physical activity was measured. A three-stage sample design was implemented using electoral wards as a primary sampling unit, a random sample of output areas, and then a random sample of postcodes for contact. An overall response rate of 55% was recorded. According to Donnelly (2011), a total of 4653 interviews were conducted between 23 July 2009 and 10 August 2010.

The CHS has been operating since 1983 and collects data to provide a regular source of information on a wide range of issues relevant to Northern Ireland. In relation to adult sport, it asks six questions relating to sport participation, club membership, benefits from sport and spectating. Similar to SAPAS, this is also carried out via computer-aided personal interviews. The 2018–2019 survey included 5736 respondents conducted between April 2017 and March 2018 (DoC, 2019c).

Sport Participation

Before detailing the nuances of sports participation for people with disabilities within this region in sport, Table 10.5 highlights that people with disabilities trail behind the non-disabled population in every key performance indicator in the national sport strategy; in most areas they are half as likely to participate in active sport and physical activities (Kitchin et al., 2019; Donnelly, 2011).

Participation

From a series of government publications (DCAL, 2013; DoC, 2016; Hull, 2014) the participation of people with disabilities in sport can be characterised as marginal. Recent data from the CHS is gained by asking slightly different questions about sport than those asked in SAPAS. As a result the 2018–2019 CHS records monthly (24–49% non-disabled) and yearly (35% and 64%) participation figures higher than what is recorded in SAPAS (DoC, 2019c). One advantage of the CHS over the SAPAS results is that they provide trend data. Weekly participation figures for people with a disability stood at 16% in 2009–2010, through 21% in 2012–2013 (when the PA10 baseline was set), and have risen to 30% in 2018–2019, which implies that Sport NI is on track to satisfy the one KPI set in Sport Matters (Sport NI, 2009). While demonstrating one picture of sport participation these figures are only for those aged 16+, information at junior levels is lacking.

According to Woods et al. (2018), the participation rate of young people with disabilities is behind their non-disabled participants in many indicators. Overall, 22 of non-disabled young people compared to 7% of young people with disabilities achieved the recommended physical activity guidelines (of at least 60 minutes of moderate-to-vigorous physical activity every day). Participation in sport within primary schools was 67% for non-disabled youth compared to 54% of young people with disabilities and at post-primary schools the results indicated 51% and 41% respectively. In summary, disability status was a key factor impacting the participation of young people in sport and physical activity.

Frequency

Digging further into the details, only the SAPAS report has specific details on the frequency of activity. It reports that the average session was 46 minutes, yet 49% of people with disabilities take no part in physical activity at all (compared to 20% without a disability). For those that do, weekly participation equals 19% for sport participation (for at least 30 minutes in duration) which is significantly less active than non-disabled people across all age ranges. The average time per week spent on sport was 46 minutes, less than the 87 minutes enjoyed by non-disabled people. Of those who did participate 12% were involved in sport one or two days per week, 5% were involved three to four days per week and 2% were involved five or more days per week. Donnelly (2011) does highlight that people with disabilities were older than average (55 years) and that participation declines with age.

Type of Sport

The main activities engaged in by people with a disability over the past seven days included walking (5.4%), swimming or diving (5.1%), exercise bike or other exercise machines (4.3%), golf, pitch and putt (3.0%), and dance (2.9%). It should be noted that these are mainly individual pursuits as there is no need for social interaction in many of these activities.

Club Membership

The membership figure for people with disabilities stands at 13% as opposed to 23% for the non-disabled population (Donnelly, 2011) and 14% and 24% from the CHS (DoC, 2019c). There is currently no register of disability sport clubs in NI and, therefore, differentiating between mainstream and disability sport membership is not possible.

Participation in competitions is again much lower than average among people with disabilities (12%) as opposed to 22% for non-disabled people (Donnelly, 2011). The gap between people with disabilities and the non-disabled population remains wide across different age groups (16–29 years: 8% compared to 31%;

30–49 years: 13% compared to 20%; and 50+ years: 12% compared to 20%). As yet, there is no data available to show what percentage of this participation is in mainstream/inclusive or segregated sporting opportunities.

The SAPAS report found that 7% of people with a disability volunteer in sporting clubs. While below the 9% average of the total adult population, a higher proportion of young and middle-aged people with disabilities volunteer than the non-disabled population (16–29-year-olds: 15% compared to 9% without a disability; and 30–49-year-olds: 16% compared to 11%) (Donnelly, 2011). As Donnelly suggests, disabled people between 16 and 49 are more likely to volunteer than their peers without a disability.

Other Sport Contexts

Opportunities exist outside of the mainstream club structure. The Disability Sport Hubs are mentioned above, but to specifically target young people with a disability there are programmes delivered by the national and provincial bodies of sport, in partnership with Disability Sport NI, in schools across Northern Ireland. Those that target the 'special school' system do so through fun days, structured weekly sessions that can take place at schools, or at local clubs that offer facilities as part of their Club Equality policies.

Both Special Olympics Ulster and the charity Mencap run learning disability football programmes that are not mainstreamed. The Irish Football Association, however, has a dedicated disability football strategy (IFA, 2016) that assists in coordinating the variety of contexts in which football is delivered.

Despite the focus on sports clubs and schools, the most relevant domain for people with disabilities to do physical activity is at home (157 minutes of at least moderate physical activity per week on average) (Sport NI, 2015).

Comparison with Participation of General Population

As alluded to above, in all areas of activity measurement—whether by SAPAS or more recently the CHS—people with disabilities lag behind the general population within Northern Ireland, with the noted exception of volunteering within clubs.

Barriers and Facilitators

Barriers

Like facilitators, there are also a series of barriers that people with disabilities encounter when taking part in sport in NI. Research has examined multiple barriers to people with disabilities' participation in sport (Darcy et al., 2017), and while these barriers can be explored here, it is limited by the lack of diversity in the data. SAPAS can account for disability with gender, age and social class, but as with the CHS the definition used to define disability is all encompassing and, therefore, examining by disability type is not currently possible.

The major barriers offered by people with disabilities themselves are injury and illness from their disability (60%) and increasing age (20%) (Sport NI, 2015). Data is available on satisfaction with sport provision across NI, with 53% of people with disabilities being satisfied while 24% are dissatisfied. These figures contrast with the greater satisfaction and lower dissatisfaction of all respondents (Donnelly, 2011).

A major barrier that the district disability sport hubs are attempting to alleviate is the urban/rural divide in NI. Rural community isolation has been a factor in preventing the aged and people with disabilities from accessing a range of community services, including sport (Gallagher et al., 2011; Warburton et al., 2016). These issues are significant as they commonly involve transport constraints and pass extra responsibilities onto family and friends. Gallagher et al. (2011) recommended that disability awareness training in these communities, transport operators and their local government could ease some of these restrictions.

Facilitators

There are a number of facilitators that already encourage participation in sport. Firstly, a clear plan through Active Living: No Limits 2016–2021 establishes a set of targets and affords responsibilities. That the plan is produced by a Steering Group that contains sport and non-sport disabled people's organisations ensures that it is grounded in the lived experience of people with disabilities. Second, Donnelly (2011) reports that the key motivations among people with disabilities are enjoyment (59%) and keeping fit (46%) and around one in five people with disabilities uses sport to assist in their dealing with injury/disability.

In terms of making participation easier, Donnelly (2011) suggests that facility proximity (24%), cheaper prices (19%) and people to go with (17%) would benefit users. Additionally people with disabilities feel that improved access (6% compared to 4% among the general public) and receiving support for specific needs (6% compared to 2%) are slightly more relevant for increasing participation (Donnelly, 2011).

10.5 Conclusion

The purpose of this chapter has been to provide an in-depth view of sport for people with disabilities in Northern Ireland. The characteristics of the region, its sporting system and the relationships between key organisations have been outlined. In addition to this an overview of the participation levels of people with disabilities in sport has been presented, replete with information on how this data is collected and the prevailing barriers and facilitators of sport.

The development of the disability sport infrastructure has been extensive over the past decade. The focus on increasing participation—as set by a KPI in Sport Matters—has seen responses to this by many mainstream and disability sports organisations, the Irish Football Association and Special Olympics Ireland being prominent examples of each. The quantitative nature of participation targets has meant that the majority of organisations report outputs in terms of the number of people with disabilities involved, or the number of training courses run, or the amount of funds invested.

However, despite these successes, questions remain. To what extent has this disability sporting infrastructure in NI considered the implications of the UNESCO (2017) Kazan Action Plan for the availability and accessibility of place? Of the people with disabilities who play sport, what is the nature of their disability/impairment? NI lacks data on the diversity of those who identify as people with disabilities as there is no breakdown by disability type. Where are the opportunities to play sport for people with disabilities? There is no single database of sports clubs that offer mainstream and/or integrated sporting opportunities for people with disabilities. How effective has our investment in disability sport been so far? At present there is no mechanism to assess the value of this increase in participation. Further details breaking down the funds given to governing bodies to delivery sport would enable a clearer picture to emerge.

There is also a lack of ambition in sport system targets—as exposed by Sport Matters—and this is not all the fault of Sport NI or Disability Sport NI, but rather in part the system of governance in the region. For Sport NI the fact that one-fifth of sport participants are people with disabilities and have only one dedicated KPI (notably they are included in more generic ones that *can* benefit all participants), but further KPIs focusing on retention or elite performance that move away from output measurements could be worthy of consideration. More significantly, sport in this region needs to increase the regularity in which participation and involvement statistics are calculated. While a regular measure of reporting, the limitations of the CMS are that the survey is very broad and further iterations of SAPAS are needed.

Future research should set out to contribute to addressing the questions raised above, particularly in understanding the diversity of disability sport and examining and detailing the club infrastructure for disability sport. Research, however, should be carried out in conjunction with people with disabilities and ideally in partnership with a range of disabled people's organisations and sports organisations—both mainstream and disability sport.

References

Banks, G., Hamilton, E., & Rooney, F. (2015). *Inequalities in participation in public life in Northern Ireland*. Ipsos MORI.

Darcy, S., Lock, D., & Taylor, T. (2017). Enabling inclusive sport participation: Effects of disability and support needs on constraints to sport participation. *Leisure Sciences, 39*(1), 20–41.

DCAL/Department for Arts, Culture and Leisure. (2013). *Young people and sport in Northern Ireland*. Available at https://data.gov.uk/dataset/4cd43174-e527-4f17-980c-320eaba0acbd/young-people-and-sport-in-northern-ireland

Department of Education. (2020). *Special education needs: 2019–2020 key statistics*. Accessed at: https://www.education-ni.gov.uk/sites/default/files/publications/education/Special%20Educational%20Needs%202019-2020.pdf

Disability Sport NI/Disability Sport Northern Ireland. (2019). *Annual report: April 2018–March 2019*. Disability Sport NI.

DoC. (2016). *Experience of Sport and physical activity in Northern Ireland*. : Department of Communities. Available at: https://www.communities-ni.gov.uk/sites/default/files/publications/communities/experience-of-sport-and-physical-activity-in-northern-ireland-201516.pdf.

DoC. (2019a). *Experience of Sport in Northern Ireland. Findings from the continuous household survey 2018/19*. Department of Communities. Available at: https://www.communities-ni.gov.uk/system/files/publications/communities/experience-sport-northern-ireland-201819.pdf

DoC. (2019b). *Ministers launch Special Olympics Ireland Winter Games*. Available at: https://www.communities-ni.gov.uk/news/ministers-launch-special-olympics-ireland-winter-games

Donnelly, P. (2011). *The Northern Ireland adult sport and physical activity survey 2010*. Sport Northern Ireland.

Equality Commission for Northern Ireland. (2007). *Definition of disability*. Equality Commission for Northern Ireland.

Ferguson, K. (2020). *An analysis of the management process in sport for development projects in Northern Ireland*. Unpublished PhD thesis. Ulster University.

Ferguson, K., Hassan, D., & Kitchin, P. J. (2019). Sport and underachievement among protestant youth in Northern Ireland: A boxing club case study. *International Journal of Sport Policy and Politics, 10*(3), 579–596.

Gallagher, B. A. M., Hart, P. M., O'Brien, C., Stevenson, M. R., & Jackson, A. J. (2011). Mobility and access to transport issues as experienced by people with vision impairment living in urban and rural Ireland. *Disability and Rehabilitation, 33*(12), 979–988.

Hull, D. (2014). *Provision for Sport for those with a Disability*. NI Assembly Research and Information Centre. Available at: http://www.niassembly.gov.uk/globalassets/documents/raise/publications/2014/culture_arts_leisure/14214.pdf

IFA/Irish Football Association. (2016). *Irish FA disability strategic plan, 2016–2020*. Available at: https://www.irishfa.com/media/7489/disability-strategy-booklet-a4.pdf

Kitchin, P. J., & Crossin, A. (2018). Understanding which dimensions of organisational capacity support the vertical integration of disability football clubs. *Managing Sport and Leisure, 22*(1–2), 28–47.

Kitchin, P. J., Peile, C., & Lowther, J. (2019). Mobilizing capacity to achieve the mainstreaming of disability sport. *Managing Sport and Leisure, 24*(6), 424–444.

Lenahan, P. (2019). *Legal and sporting obligation to promote equality of opportunity among people with disability*. The Irish News. Available at http://www.irishnews.com/paywall/tsb/irishnews/irishnews/irishnews//sport/2019/07/27/news/legal-and-sporting-obligation-to-promote-equality-of-opportunity-among-people-with-disability-paul-lenehan-1671615/content.html

Liston, K. K., Gregg, R., & Lowther, J. (2013). Elite sports policy and coaching at the coalface. *International Journal of Sport Policy and Politics, 5*(3), 341–362.

Macauley, C. (2017). People in Northern Ireland's rural areas 'are happier'. *British Broadcasting Corporation*. Available at https://www.bbc.co.uk/news/uk-northern-ireland-41397806.

NISRA. (2011). *Census 2011*. Available at https://www.nisra.gov.uk/statistics/census/2011-census

Progressive Building Society. (2019). Progressive Building Society confirms three-year sponsorship with Disability Sport NI. Available at: https://theprogressive.com/your-society/latest-news/2019/may/progressive-building-society-confirms-three-year-sponsorship-with-disability-sport-ni

Sport NI. (2006). *Mainstreaming disability sport*. Sport Northern Ireland.

Sport NI. (2009). *Sport matters: The Northern Ireland strategy for Sport and physical recreation, 2009–2019*. Belfast.

Sport NI. (2012). *Corporate Plan, 2012–2015*. Available at: http://www.sportni.net/sportni/wp-content/uploads/2013/03/SNICorporatePlan201215.pdf

Sport NI. (2013). *Disability sport action plan 2012–2015*. Available at: http://equalityinsport.org/wp-content/uploads/2015/12/Sport-NI-Disability-Action-Plan-2012-2015.pdf

Sport NI. (2015). *Draft corporate plan 2015–2020: Equality impact assessment*. Available at http://www.sportni.net/sportni/wp-content/uploads/2013/03/Sport-NI-EQIA-Corporate-Plan-2015-2020-Final-for-Section-75-Consultation.pdf

Sport NI. (2016). *Active living: No limits*. 2016–2020. Available at: http://www.sportni.net/sportni/wp-content/uploads/2016/10/Active-Living-No-Limits-Action-Plan-2016-2021.pdf

Sport NI. (2020a). *Sport sustainability fund*. Available at http://www.sportni.net/funding/our-funding-programmes/sports-sustainability-fund/

Sport NI. (2020b). *About us*. Available at http://www.sportni.net/about-us/

Statista. (2020). Share of sport club members in Northern Ireland from 2009/2010 to 2018/2019. Available at https://www.statista.com/statistics/554717/members-of-at-least-one-sports-club-organization-northern-ireland/

UNESCO. (2017). *Kazan action plan*. Available at: https://en.unesco.org/mineps6/kazan-action-plan

Warburton, J., Scharf, T., & Walsh, K. (2016). Flying under the radar? Risks of social exclusion for older people in rural communities in Australia, Ireland and Northern Ireland. *Sociologia Ruralis, 57*(4), 459–480. https://doi.org/10.1111/SORU.12129

Woods, C. B., Powell, C., Saunders, J. A., O'Brien, W., Murphy, M. H., Duff, C., … Belton, S. (2018). *The children's sport participation and physical activity study 2018* (CSPPA 2018), pp. 1–108.

Chapter 11
United Kingdom: An Inclusionary Approach to Sport

Matej Christiaens, Ian Brittain, and Christopher Brown

11.1 Introduction

The sport system in the United Kingdom (UK) differs in several areas from other countries' organisation and political regulations of sport. In the UK, sport is a devolved issue that is dealt with by the home countries with some overlap with the national government for elite sport provision. Furthermore, the UK has adopted an inclusive approach to the organisation and regulation of sport which makes it difficult to separate disability sport structures from the non-disabled sport structure. The overall sport system in the UK and its home countries (excluding Northern Ireland; see Chap. 10) is discussed in this context with significant emphasis on how this relates to disability sport provision. The chapter draws on data from the literature, policy documents and research conducted by the authors which included surveys and interviews with stakeholders.

M. Christiaens (✉)
Liverpool Business School, Liverpool John Moores University, Merseyside, UK
e-mail: m.m.christiaens@ljmu.ac.uk

I. Brittain
Centre for Business in Society, Coventry University, Coventry, UK
e-mail: aa8550@coventry.ac.uk

C. Brown
Department of Psychology, Sport and Geography, University of Hertfordshire, Hatfield, UK

11.2 Country Profile

Characteristics of the UK

The United Kingdom of Great Britain and Northern Ireland (UK) has comprised of four home countries (nations) since 1921: England, Scotland and Wales (which collectively make up Great Britain), and Northern Ireland (Fig. 11.1). As Northern Ireland is covered elsewhere in this book, it might seem straightforward to just cover Great Britain. However, the UK is a complex state that saw an important change in 1999 when devolved powers were awarded to the home countries: Scotland, Wales and Northern Ireland, while England remains the only home country that has no devolved powers and is ruled by the UK government. Furthermore, as Great Britain has no legislative powers, it remains important to discuss the UK rather than Great Britain in this chapter.

Devolution is important as it gave greater powers to the devolved nations for the development of sport. However, this also makes the UK a complex country with various levels of decision-making and fragmented responsibilities for the provision of sport. While joining the European Union in 1973 had a significant impact on the provision of sport, the UK left the European Union on 31 January 2020. The implications of Brexit on sport provision in the UK is uncertain, and it has renewed calls for an independence referendum in Scotland while also reigniting talks about a united Ireland.

Today, the UK can be described as an ageing multicultural society. While 13% of the population belongs to an ethnic minority (Crouch & Minhas, 2017),

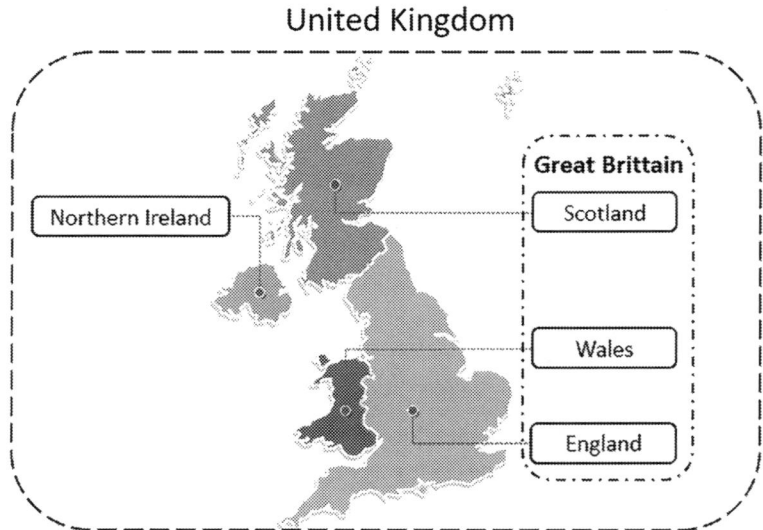

Fig. 11.1 Map of the UK

multiculturalism is more an English phenomenon than it is a UK one because the majority of ethnic minorities live in England and more precisely in the inner city areas of the former industrial cities. The largest minority groups are from countries of the former British Empire such as Pakistan and India. Similar to most European countries, the UK is seeing an ageing population, with 18% of the population aged 65 years and over (Office for National Statistics, 2019a) and this is projected to increase to 24.8% of the population by 2050. Those aged 85 years and over, the fastest growing segment, are projected to make up 5% of the population by 2050 (Office for National Statistics, 2019a). As life expectancy is steadily increasing and the likelihood of becoming disabled increases with age, the time people spend in poor health has also increased (Office for National Statistics, 2019a). These trends, coupled with a slow annual growth rate of 0.5%, will have significant implications for the sports delivery system in the UK. Table 11.1 shows some of the key facts and characteristics of the UK.

Sport in the UK

As sport is a devolved issue in the UK, sports participation is measured separately by each nation. This results in some comparison issues, as each sport organisation responsible for this has adopted different measures. The biggest differences are found in terms of sport frequency (e.g. once a week in England compared to once in the last four weeks in Scotland), duration of activity and the activities included (there is a growing trend to include walking). Additionally, abrupt changes in methodology[1] have taken place within England (2016–2017) that resulted in a massive increase in sport participation from 36% to 75% in the same year. This makes any comparison within the UK or with other countries in the EU difficult. Despite these differences and changes to methodologies, it could be argued that sport participation in the UK has remained fairly stable between 2007 and 2019 (Christiaens, 2018). Furthermore, it is clear that disabled people (DP) have a lower sport participation rate throughout the UK. A sports profile for the UK can be found in Table 11.2.

Since others have dealt with mainstream sport policy in greater detail elsewhere (e.g. Bergsgard et al., 2007; Coghlan & Webb, 2003; Collins, 2010; Green & Houlihan, 2005; Houlihan, 2005; Houlihan & Lindsey, 2013), Table 11.3 provides a short summary of the sport development policies in the UK. This overview illustrates that the government's approach to the funding of sport has not changed much since the 1960s with a prioritisation of elite success and school sport over community sport with intermittent focus on underperforming groups and social inclusion (e.g. sport for DP). However, there was a significant shift in the sport structures when the Sport's Review Group decided in 1989 that a shift was necessary from disability sport clubs towards the inclusion of DP in non-disabled sport clubs (Minister for Sport's Review Group, 1989). The Sport's Review Group expected national governing bodies of sport (NGBs)

---

[1] The changes to methodology include a broadening of the definition of what constitutes physical activity and a loosening of the timeframe in which people need to be active and for how long.

Table 11.1 Facts and characteristics of the UK

	UK	England	Wales	Scotland
Population (number of inhabitants)	66,435,600	55,977,178	3,138,631	5,438,100
Area (km^2)	243,600	130,420	20,735	80,077
Density (inhabitants/km^2)	275	429	151	67.9
Urbanisation rate (%)	83.1	/	/	83
Structure of the state	Unitary state with devolution	Personal union	Personal union	Personal union
Political organisation	Parliamentary constitutional monarchy	Devolution to local authorities	Devolution parliamentary democracy	Devolution parliamentary democracy
Number of provinces (regions)[a]	12	9	5	8
Number of municipalities	408	343	22	32
GDP per capita (euro)	32,710	36,318	22,900	29,300
Number of official languages	1	2[b]	2[c]	4[d]
EU membership	1973–2020			
Welfare model	Anglo-Saxon model/liberal welfare state system			

Sources: Eurostat (2018); ONS (2019b, 2019c); World Bank (2018); edited by Christiaens, M.
[a]The regions in the UK are made up of 9 English regions + Scotland, Wales and Ireland. However, the nations of Wales and Scotland recognise their own regions
[b]English and Cornish
[c]English and Welsh
[d]English, Gaelic, Scottish and British Sign Language

and other mainstream agencies to provide DP with the same opportunities for participating in sport as non-disabled people enjoyed. It was their belief disability sport organisations did not have the resources to do so adequately. As a result, the government takes an "inclusive" approach to sport which makes it hard to separate mainstream sport from disability sport policy.

Disability in the UK

In the UK, the Equality Act 2010 (EqA 2010) defines disability. According to the EqA 2010, a person is disabled if they have a physical or mental impairment and if the impairment has a substantial and long-term (12 months or more) adverse effect on their ability to carry out normal day-to-day activities (Great Britain Parliament, 2010). People with certain severe or progressive diseases are also covered by the Act, but these are not systematically counted within the "core disabled" population.

11 United Kingdom: An Inclusionary Approach to Sport

Table 11.2 Sport profile of the UK

	UK	England	Wales	Scotland
Government authority responsible for sport	Department for digital, culture, media and sport (DCMS)	DCMS	Welsh government	Scottish government
Membership sport club (%)	11	/	57 (age 7–16) 27 (age 15+)	/
Membership fitness or health centre (%)	15.6	19.9	12.8	15.3
Sport participation (%)	/	77.7[a]	32[b]	80[c]
Sport participation of DP (%)	/	59 (adults)[a] 66 (children)[a]	23[b]	39[c]
Sport participation non-disabled (%)	/	81.5[a]	41[b]	87[c]
Number of national sport federations (NGBs)[d]	89	111	93	97
Number of sport clubs	151,000	72,117	3775	13,000
Number of fitness facilities	7239	5994	382	655
Number of sport club members	7.3 m	1.8 m	/	787,362
National budget for sport (€ × 1,000,000)	2947	/	/	1.3
National budget for sport federations (€ × 1000)	/	/	/	/
Local budget for sport (€ × 1,000,000)	480[e]	345.1[e]	191.2[f]	207[g]
Economic value of volunteers in sport	/	£2.7bn	/	/
Economic contribution of sport	£39bn	/	/	/

Sources: Active Lives (2020); Allison (2002); Department for Culture Media and Sport (2019); European Commission (2018); LeisureDB (2019); National Governing Body CEO Forum (2015); Office for National Statistics (2018, 2019b, 2019d); Scottish Government (2019); SIRC (2013); Sport England (2012a, 2018, 2019a, 2019b, n.d.); Sport Wales (2018, 2020); Sportscotland (2019a); StatsWales (2019); Welsh Government (2020); edited by Christiaens, M.
[a]Sport participation at least two times in the last 28 days
[b]Sport participation three times or more per week
[c]Sport participation at least once in the last 28 days
[d]In the UK, NGBs are the equivalent of national sport federations. Furthermore, as sport is a devolved issue, it is the home country's sport council that is responsible for recognition of NGBs. This explains the difference in the number of NGBs across the home countries
[e]This figure is only for sport
[f]This figure is a sum for libraries, culture, heritage, sport and recreation
[g]This figure is a sum for sport facilities and other recreational activities and sport spending

Table 11.3 Sport priorities in the UK

Date	Sport priority
1960–1982	Development of sport facilities
1982–1991	Focus on sports for all/the disadvantaged
1992–1997	Establishment of National Lottery to fund sport and a shift of funding towards school and elite participation
1998–2005	Funding shifts to social inclusion, sport for all and equality
2005–2012	The UK won the bid to host the Olympic and Paralympic Games; funding shifts to elite participation
2012–2015	Funding shifts to creating an active, healthy lifestyle and inclusion and equality
2015–present	Funding shifts away from the NGBs and towards physical activity

Adapted from Christiaens (2018)

Following the definition of disability provided by the EqA 2010, the prevalence of disability in the UK is about 21% (see Table 11.4). However, there are significant regional discrepancies which can partially be explained by the link between disability and age, education and socio-economic status (Blackburn et al., 2010; Braithwaite & Mont, 2009). For example, children show a disability prevalence of 8%, while almost half (45%) of 65+ (pension age) have a disability. There are also differences between the nations, with England (20%) having the lowest prevalence of disability compared to Scotland (23%) and Wales (25%), but even within these regions, there are significant differences, for example, within England itself the North East region which is one of the poorest (21.6%) had the highest percentage of activity limitations and London which has a significant lower mean age (14.2%) the lowest (Office for National Statistics, 2014). Regarding terminology used in the UK, the government provides a helpful guide on inclusive language. This guide is created to provide a framework for both businesses and individuals to normalise social interactions. Besides giving some general advice such as: "Avoid medical labels", "Use positive descriptors" and "address disabled people [sic] in the same way as you talk to everyone else", the government has created a list of words to use and avoid, see Table 11.5.

Emergence and Rise of Disability Sport in the UK

Historically, DP had limited opportunities for organised sport (DePauw & Gavron, 2005) and there is little evidence of organised sport for DP prior to World War II (WWII) (Brittain, 2012). People with hearing impairments were the first group to have access to sport and to formalise sport participation in clubs. The earliest known and established sport club for DP was the Glasgow Deaf and Dumb Football Club established in 1872 (Le Clair, 2012).

The World Wars of the twentieth century greatly influenced society's view of disabilities and brought rehabilitation to the foreground (Huber, 1984). Ludwig Guttmann, Director of the Spinal Unit at Stoke Mandeville hospital, was key in the

11 United Kingdom: An Inclusionary Approach to Sport

Table 11.4 Disability prevalence in the UK

	UK	England	Wales	Scotland
Prevalence of disabilities, total (% of population)	21	20	25	23
Prevalence of disabilities, total (% of children)	8			
Prevalence of disabilities, total (% of 18–65)	18			
Prevalence of disabilities, total (% 65+)	44			
Prevalence of disabilities, total (% of males/females)	19/22			
Prevalence of moderate/severe physical disabilities (movement) (% of DP)	49			
Prevalence of moderate/severe seeing disabilities (% of DP)	12			
Prevalence of moderate/severe hearing disabilities (% of DP)	14			
Prevalence of intellectual disabilities (mental health) (% of DP)	25			
Prevalence of psycho-social (behavioural) disabilities (% of DP)	9			
Prevalence of intellectual disabilities (stamina/breathing/fatigue) (% of DP)	37			
Prevalence of intellectual disabilities (dexterity) (% of DP)	26			
Prevalence of intellectual disabilities (memory) (% of DP)	16			
Prevalence of intellectual disabilities (learning) (% of DP)	13			

Source: Department for Work and Pensions (2019)

Table 11.5 Disability terminology

Avoid	Use
(the) handicapped, (the) disabled	Disabled (people)
Afflicted by, suffers from, victim of	Has [name of condition or impairment]
Confined to a wheelchair, wheelchair-bound	Wheelchair user
Mentally handicapped, mentally defective, retarded, subnormal	With a learning disability (singular), with learning disabilities (plural)
Cripple, invalid	Disabled person
Spastic	Person with cerebral palsy
Able-bodied	Non-disabled
Mental patient, insane, mad	Person with a mental health condition
Deaf and dumb; deaf mute	Deaf, user of British sign language (BSL), person with a hearing impairment
The blind	People with visual impairments; blind people; blind and partially sighted people
An epileptic, diabetic, depressive and so on	Person with epilepsy, diabetes, depression or someone who has epilepsy, diabetes, depression
Dwarf; midget	Someone with restricted growth or short stature
Fits, spells, attacks	Seizures

Source: Office for Disability Issues (2020)

development of disability sport as he recognised the physiological and psychological values of sport within rehabilitation (McCann, 1996). He was the first to introduce sport as part of a rehabilitation programme and would later organise the Stoke Mandeville Games (Brittain, 2012). The Stoke Mandeville Games were a great success and have transformed into the second largest multi-sport event in the world, the Paralympic Games.

With such an achievement it is easy to forget that Guttmann was at the forefront of another important development in the UK. He was a key influence in the development of disability sport structures in the UK. In 1948, as a result of the Stoke Mandeville Games, Guttmann established the British Paraplegic Sports Society (BPSS) (DePauw & Gavron, 2005). In an attempt to manage the plethora of organisations emerging, Guttmann founded an umbrella organisation, the British Sports Association for the Disabled (BSAD) in 1961 (Thomas, 2008). BSAD was later restructured into three regional organisations: the Activity Alliance in England, Scottish Disability Sport and Disability Sport Wales.

Over the years, the strategic responsibility for disability sport has shifted towards the sport councils (the arm's length bodies responsible for mainstream sport) as well as an increasing emphasis and responsibility for the NGBs. Yet, the evidence suggests that disability sport remains at best loosely and differentially integrated into mainstream sport. While there is commitment from the national disability sport organisations (NDSOs) towards the inclusion of disability sport, in practice this is a lot harder to achieve and greatly depends on the willingness of the mainstream NGBs.

11.3 The Disability Sport System

Historically, the role of the central government has been interwoven into the sporting landscape, but as a result of devolution, there has been a noticeable shift from a strong, hierarchical government to governance through networks and partnerships (Rhodes, 1990; Skelcher, 2000). This shift in governmental structure has caused power erosion and weakened the state's ability to deliver policy (Bevir & Rhodes, 2006, 2008; Skelcher, 2000). This has resulted in the creation of non-departmental public bodies that operate at an "arm's length" from the government. This led to the creation of "sport councils" that have executive, administrative, commercial and regulatory functions. However, while this assures their independence, they are almost completely funded by the government and are accountable to it. The creation of such a myriad of multi-agency policy delivery leads to confusion and overlap between the various organisations, bodies and councils involved in policy delivery (Phillpots et al., 2010). This historical development has led to increased fragmentation and complexity of the sport structures in the UK, with a government that is reluctant to intervene in matters of sport. Figure 11.2 provides an overview of the (disability) sport system in the UK in terms of its structure and sport funding.

11 United Kingdom: An Inclusionary Approach to Sport

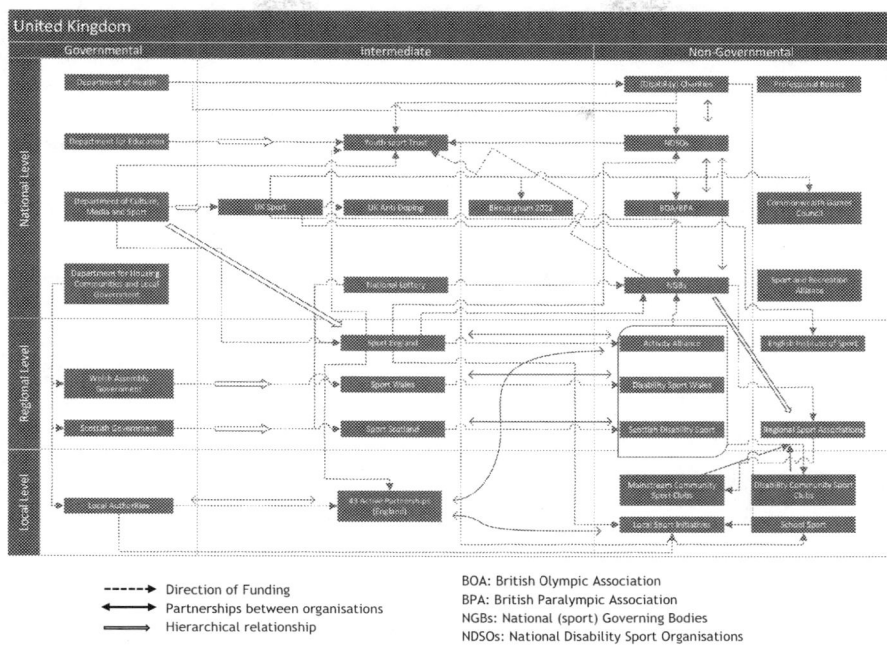

Fig. 11.2 The (disability) sport structure in the UK

Structure of Disability Sport

As a consequence of the Sport's Review Group in 1989, a gradual shift is noticeable away from a dispersed and fragmented disability sport structure towards the inclusion of disability sport within non-disabled sport provision. This was borne out of a belief that disability sport organisations did not have the means or the resources to provide adequate sporting opportunities. As such, NGBs and other mainstream agencies were expected to provide the same opportunities for DP that non-disabled people enjoy. This development has blended mainstream and disability sport structures, which makes it largely impossible to distinguish between them.

Sport in the UK is structured around two competing ideologies, "sport for all" and elite sport. While elite sport is mainly a national responsibility of the Department of Digital, Culture, Media and Sport (DCMS), community sport is a devolved matter for the regional governments (i.e. the Welsh Assembly government, the Scottish government and the DCMS for England). Both elite sport and community sport are led by sport councils that work in partnership with the regional disability sport federations (Activity Alliance, Disability Sport Wales and Scottish Disability Sport). Here we discuss the governmental, intermediate and non-governmental agents in the UK.

Governmental Agents

Sport in the UK is very much a *multi-departmental* responsibility, with various departments contributing to the overall strategy and funding of sport. For instance, the Department for Housing, Communities and Local Government sets budgets for the devolved governments which, in turn, use part of this funding to support their regional sport councils. On the other hand, the Department for Education supports school sport through the Youth Sport Trust, while the Department of Health has a crucial role in funding (disability) charities, involved in supporting sport activities, and funding National Disability Sport Organisations (NDSOs), which provide and support sporting opportunities for specific impairment groups (see Table 11.6). As a result, the governing of sport is grounded in the principles of independence, partnerships and collaborations between actors at all levels.

Local authorities play a central role in the provision of community sport and recreation facilities. Local city town councils enable a huge range of leisure activities and sport to happen. They also have an important role in facilitating and supporting partnerships in the sport sector. Some of the key priorities of the local councils are to remove barriers to participation, improve the local sport delivery system, and invest and maintain sport facilities. However, there is no legal requirement for local authorities to provide facilities or sporting activities.

Intermediate Agents

Sport in the UK is largely organised through the arm's length principle. The sport councils (UK Sport, Sport England, Sport Wales and Sport Scotland) and the Youth Sport Trust (YTS) work together to influence sport policy but also to fulfil the vision set by the government through a shared goal of maximising sporting success in all

Table 11.6 National disability sport organisations (NDSOs) in the UK

Organisation	Role
British Blind Sport	Provides blind and partially sighted people with opportunities to participate in sport and physical activity
Cerebral Palsy (CP) Sport	Supports people with cerebral palsy to reach their full potential through sport and active recreation
Dwarf Sports Association (DSA) UK	Promotes and provides regular sporting opportunities for people with dwarfism and restricted growth
LimbPower	Supports amputees and people with limb impairments to find the right sport or leisure activity for their needs and ability
Mencap	Promotes sport opportunities for people with a learning disability
Special Olympics Great Britain	Provides year-round sports programme for children and adults with learning (intellectual) disabilities
UK Deaf Sport	Encourages people who are deaf and hard of hearing to participate, enjoy and excel at sport
WheelPower	Provides opportunities, facilities and equipment to support DP to participate in sport and lead healthy active lives

Source: Activity Alliance (2020b)

its forms (Sport England, 2016b). Each organisation has its own area of responsibility and targets within the sport landscape and these will now be explored further.

UK Sport is responsible for elite sporting success in the UK. They work closely together with the British Olympic and Paralympic Associations (BOA/BPA), the Commonwealth Games Council, the English Institute of Sport and the National Governing Bodies (NGBs). The primary role of UK Sport is to strategically invest National Lottery and Exchequer (direct government funding) income to maximise the performance of the athletes in the Olympic and Paralympic Games and the global events which precede them (Cushion et al., 2010). They operate two streams of funding, central funding for NGBs and direct athlete funding. However, athletes with disabilities remain less frequently funded compared to non-disabled athletes, with only 25% of the 1125 athletes in receipt of direct funding (UK Sport, 2019). This is a direct result of their funding criteria that only fund DP who are perceived to have a strong potential to win a gold medal at the Paralympic Games compared to being a medallist at the Olympic Games.[2]

The regional sport councils, such as Sport England, Sport Wales and Sport Scotland, are responsible for the community sport system in the UK. They are also responsible for strategically investing lottery and Exchequer income to sustain and increase sport participation levels and to increase equality in the sport sector. The main investment streams are NGBs, facilities and stand-alone sport projects. It is important to note here that funding is awarded in accordance with the strategic objectives, which tend to change every four years. All regional sport councils have inclusion expectations written into their current strategy and link, at least to some extent, funding to inclusive objectives (Sport England, 2016a; Sport Wales, 2019; Sportscotland, 2019b).

Youth Sport Trust (YST) is a key organisation with a focus on sport for young people through a school sport delivery system. To achieve this aim, YST focuses on the delivery of quality physical education, satellite sport clubs for after school delivery, and to help schools open their facilities during weekends, holidays and after school hours. Furthermore, since the Warnock report in 1978, the government has encouraged the integration of DP into mainstream schools, making school sport an integral part of DP lives.

Non-governmental Agents

The sport organisations and sport clubs, many being not-for-profit charitable entities, play a pivotal role in the delivery of sport across the sector. At a *national level* the British Paralympic Association (BPA) and the Commonwealth Games Council work closely together with the NGBs in the delivery of elite sporting success. Their role is seen as identifying talent, supporting performance development and delivering competitive success for athletes with disabilities.

---

[2] Band A—medalists at Olympic Games or Senior World Championships or gold medalists at Paralympic Games or Senior World Championships. up to £28,000 pa. Band B—a minimum of a top eight finish at Olympic Games or Senior World Championships or medalists at Paralympic Games or Senior World Championships up to £21,500 pa.

The *national governing bodies* are the UK equivalent of sport federations elsewhere in Europe. NGBs represent a specific sport or sometimes combine multiple sports that are closely affiliated. They are responsible for managing their sport in terms of administration, coaching, mass participation, elite sporting success and, in the last 30 years, increasing responsibility for the delivery of sport for DP. In the UK there is no single recognised legal structure for NGBs. Therefore, they exist in a range of legal forms, including incorporated association, limited company, community interest company, trust, and charitable incorporated organisation. While NGBs are independent entities, the majority of their funding comes from either the sport councils or the national lottery. As a result, they are in a power-dependence relationship in which they are held accountable, based on key indicators linked to the governmental sport strategy. To be eligible for funding, NGBs need to gain recognition from the regional sport councils. In essence, the NGBs fulfil a central role in the sport landscape in which they are being pulled in all directions, often with competing objectives.

The *National Disability Sport Organisations* have a key role in the delivery of sport for DP. They are organised around specific impairments and seek to provide advice, support and opportunities for people within these impairment groups. Their mission is to improve the quality of life for DP through sport and physical recreation. They offer a low barrier entrance to sport through the organisation of events and work actively across the sport landscape to advocate and support disability sport provision. Additionally, they provide knowledge, information and experience to NGBs and other organisations in the sport landscape.

UK Coaching is a charitable organisation tasked with the professionalisation of the sport landscape through the development and implementation of a world-leading coaching system. Competent coaches are key in the delivery of (inclusive) sport for DP and their experience within sport is often dependent upon the competences of their coach (Christiaens, 2018). UK Coaching has recognised this gap and has attempted to make coach education more inclusive in addition to organising workshops focused on coaching DP.

Disability Sport Federations (DSFs) operate at a regional level (Activity Alliance, Disability Sport Wales and Scottish Disability Sport) and strive towards a society where DP are just as likely to be active as non-disabled people. They have a difficult past, as they were supposed to be the umbrella organisation for disability sport (including NDSOs) in their regions but ended up alienating organisations within the disability sport landscape due to funding priorities from the sports council (Thomas, 2003). However, it seems that the DSFs have evolved into knowledge institutions with meaningful partnerships across the sport landscape. They are a key partner of the sport councils and are an important voice in shaping sport policy and a funding partner in terms of sport delivery for DP.

At a *local level*, the UK sport sector is characterised by a plethora of voluntary *community sport clubs*. The UK sports system has more small, single-sport clubs than any other country in Europe except France (Harris et al., 2009). These sport clubs are often managed and run by volunteers and have a unique culture that is directly influenced by the values and motives of their volunteers. As a result of the voluntary nature of their involvement, their obligations and loyalty lie with the club rather than with government policy. This independence is further enhanced by the way funding is allocated in the UK, from the centre to NGBs, while rarely making its way to the sport clubs. It makes it possible for sport clubs to decide for themselves and, if deemed necessary, to resist or oppose other actors such as central government, the sport council and their NGB. This highlights one of the biggest difficulties of sports development in the UK as sport clubs are found to ignore central sport policy and focus on their own survival (Harris et al., 2009; May et al., 2013). This has been one of the major barriers in terms of translating the inclusionary vision of sport from the central government, sport council and NGBs into practice (Christiaens, 2018).

Steering of Disability Sport

Legislative Framework

Compared to other European countries that have a civil law system, the UK operates under a common law system. Common law is not codified and heavily relies on judicial precedents which are binding. As such it would be possible to refer to the law system as "case law". While it is impossible to discuss and cover the full extent of case law in this chapter, focus will be given to government legislation affecting the sports landscape in the UK.

In terms of sport, the UK government has adopted a non-interventionist approach to sport and, in contrast to some European countries, there is no general law of sport. Sport bodies are treated as autonomous independent organisations that have a tradition of self-regulation through their international federations and the Court of Arbitration for Sport (CAS). However, there are important pieces of legislation, coming from other areas, that impact sport. Additionally, while scarce, there has been direct state intervention by means of legislation and/or other regulatory mechanisms. This interference includes issues of public safety and order at sports events (e.g. following the Hillsborough disaster of 1989); the legal rights of the participants (e.g. discrimination); commercial decisions in relation to sport (e.g. Hosting of the Olympic and Paralympic Games in 2012); and protecting the integrity of the sport (e.g. match fixing, corruption and doping).

For DP seeking to engage in sport or physical activity, the Equality Act 2010 (EqA 2010) is the most important piece of legislation. This act defines disability and makes it unlawful for service providers to treat DP less favourably because of their disability. Service providers (e.g. sport clubs) must make "reasonable adjustments" to the way they provide their services by removing the barriers preventing DP from accessing them. However, there is fierce criticism of the vague and ambiguous language (Goodley, 2014; Lockwood et al., 2012) and, in practice, this has often led to an understanding of inclusion as the removal of physical barriers (Christiaens & Brittain, 2021).

In addition, disability benefits are critical in enabling some DP to be active. Without such support, some would be unable to afford travel and pay for exercise and/or specialist equipment. Disability benefits are regulated through the Welfare

Table 11.7 Additional laws and regulations in the UK

Legislation	Explanation
National Lottery Act 2006	Regulates how the profits of games of chance are distributed in the UK (sport and charities are amongst the main recipients)
Safeguarding of Vulnerable Groups Act 2006	Requires a disclosure and barring service check for any individual involved with children or vulnerable people (e.g. coaches of DP)
Employment Rights Act 1996	It deals with rights that most employees can get when they work, including unfair dismissal (e.g. dismissal based on discriminatory grounds)
Broadcasting Act 1996	Makes specific provision for the "listing" of events, meaning that they are events that enjoy a measure of protection as they are considered of national interest (e.g. the Paralympic Games)
UN Convention on the Rights of Persons with Disabilities (CRPD) 2006	The UK is a signatory of the CRPD 2006, which makes provision for DP to participate in sport and physical activity and has incorporated this in the EqA 2010

Sources: https://www.legislation.gov.uk/; https://www.ohchr.org/

Reform Act 2012 which saw the introduction of universal credit and the Social Security (Personal Independence Payment [PIP]) Regulations 2013. Further relevant laws and regulations can be found in Table 11.7.

Policy Framework

As community sport is a devolved issue in the UK, this section will discuss the policy framework for the devolved nations separately. This discussion will focus on the two most important entities in creating, influencing and implementing sport policy: the government and the sport councils which have a responsibility for both mainstream and disability sport. However, it must be noted that the sport councils work closely with the disability sport federations in creating their sport strategy.

In *England* the DCMS is responsible for setting out the government strategy for community sport and does so through its publication *Sporting Future: A New Strategy for an Active Nation* in 2015. This strategy was highly influenced by the government being displeased with the sport participation figures, which have shown a decrease since the Olympic and Paralympic Games in 2012 (UK Government, 2013, 2014a, 2014b, 2015). This highlighted the need for a "new" approach to sport through the identification of five desirable outcomes which are physical well-being, mental well-being, individual development, social and community development, and economic development. However, the broad government strategy has not changed with a continuous focus on elite sport and increasing sport participation, as indicated in this strategy:

> For more than a decade, the government's policy on sport has been to get more people participating in sport and to win more Olympic and Paralympic medals. Both of these are valuable, and will remain part of this new strategy. (Department for Culture Media and Sport, 2015, p. 16)

The new strategy has renewed interest in underperforming groups, recognising the participation gap of DP (who are twice as likely to be inactive as non-disabled) and the elderly, showing the intersectionality between these groups. This strategy does bring a number of new elements. It emphasises a move away from funding the active population in an attempt to make them more active, towards funding focused on the inactive population. It broadened the remit of Sport England so that it became responsible for sport outside school from the age of 5 rather than 14, believing that a person's attitude towards sport is shaped before they even reach the age of 14.

It also emphasises the role of Sport England in realising the objectives as outlined in this strategy. Accordingly, Sport England's strategy, as outlined in the publication of *Towards an Active Nation: Strategy 2016–2021*, emphasises the aim of increasing sport participation, particularly in relation to under-represented groups including DP. Furthermore, they are trialling a new approach towards engaging DP within sport. They partnered up with a mental health charity, Mind, which had over 36,000 formerly inactive people taking part in physical activity. This clearly shows the intent of Sport England to work closely with charities and non-sport organisations to meet its targets. Additionally, there is a focus on more local delivery, and they are piloting local physical activity strategies in a number of selected geographic areas.

In *Scotland*, the government have aligned their strategy with the World Health Organization's (WHO) *Global Action Plan on Physical Activity 2018–2030: More Active People for a Healthier World*. The government has outlined their strategy in *A More Active Scotland: Scotland's Physical Activity Delivery Plan 2018*. A first key point in this strategy is the high emphasis the government puts on promoting walking as recreation but also as part of active travel. The government has created a specific strategy, *Let's Get Scotland Walking—The National Walking Strategy 2014*, and works with Paths for All to fulfil this ambition. Secondly, there is a desire to address barriers faced by groups at risk of inactivity through supporting opportunities for DP. This is supported by *A Fairer Scotland for Disabled People 2016* which created an action plan for sport participation amongst other areas. This is strongly supported by SportScotland which has a strong commitment to inclusion that underpins all desired outcomes of their strategy *Sport for Life: A Vision for Sport in Scotland 2019*. Core to their strategy is making sport more accessible for people who do not take part and aims to achieve this through working together across and beyond sport partners.

The Welsh government created an ambitious 20-year plan, *Climbing Higher 2005*, to tackle inactivity in *Wales*. This is the first and only government strategy for sport in Wales since it has become a devolved matter. Climbing higher sets out a clear, radical and inclusive vision for the future of sport and active recreation in Wales for the next 20 years. The essence of this strategy is to maximise the contribution that sport and active recreation can make to well-being in Wales across its many dimensions. This ambitious plan spans across areas of health, economy, culture, society, environment and Wales on the world stage. It is clear that this strategy focuses on "sport for good" in addition to a focus on elite sporting success and hosting major sporting events. To achieve its goals, the Welsh government and SportWales are focusing on investment in facilities.

Since the devolution of public health from the National Health Service (NHS) to local authorities in 2013, many local councils have taken the opportunity to integrate physical activity into public health policy as part of a wider shift from a system that treats ill-health to one that promotes well-being. As part of a nationwide shift towards engaging non-sporting partners, there are calls for working with health providers. Through physical activity referral programmes, the local governments hope to support and engage the inactive population in physical activity. This approach follows advice from the National Institute for Health and Care Excellence (NICE) which recommends that those working in primary care should identify adults who are not meeting the UK physical activity guidelines. Those on the physical activity referral programme receive discounted access to professional coaches and physical activity group sessions.

Financial, Governance and Managerial Support

Financial Framework

Sport is a major contributor to the UK economy, contributing around 2.1% of the gross value added (GVA) (see Table 11.8) and 1.2 m jobs or 3.7% of all jobs in the UK (SIRC, 2017b). The Olympic and Paralympic sector (not including sports such as football and golf for which the Games are not considered to be the pinnacle of their sport) provide more than half of sport-related economic activity with a GVA of £18.9 bn with the summer Olympic sports generating £16.1 bn (85%) of this GVA and Paralympic sport contributing £2 bn with wheelchair basketball alone being worth £42 m to the country (SIRC, 2017a). The GVA is largely following the pattern of participation (or demand) among sports. For this reason, the sector is driven by Athletics, Swimming and Cycling which have the highest engagement rates.

The contribution of sport-related economic activity highlights the importance of investing in the sport sector. As the UK has integrated disability provision within the mainstream structures, it is often difficult to separate the funding streams for disability sport from sport for non-disabled people. This is further complicated as the revenue streams for sport organisations are varied and dependent on the type of organisation. While arm's length organisations are almost fully funded directly or indirectly by the government (e.g. Sport England and Activity Alliance), funding for the voluntary

Table 11.8 The economic importance of sport in the UK

	Gross value added		Employment		Consumer expenditure	
	£m	%	000's	%	£m	%
UK (2016)	£37,300	2.1	1200	3.7	29,207	2.9
Scotland (2016)	2749	2.1	64.8	2.7	2669	3
Wales (2016/17)	1191	2.2	29.7	2.1	637	2.3
England (2010)	20,300	1.9	441	1.8	17,384	2.3

Sources: SIRC (2013, 2017a, 2018a, 2018b; edited by Christiaens, M.)

sector (the community sport club level) shows more mixed revenue streams and comes through donations, grants, public sector contracts or trading income. For NGBs, much depends on the funding priorities of the sport councils. For example, in England, 46 sports were funded between 2013 and 2017 with a total value of £493 m (Sport England, 2013). However, the newly proposed funding cycle 2017–2021 will cut the amount of NGBs funded to 25 sports with a total value of only £102 m. As for the provision of disability sport opportunities, voluntary community sport clubs can often apply for grants that are offered by the sport councils, the NDSOs, sport federations and disability charities. These grants are often limited in nature and cover a specific investment (e.g. purchase of equipment and a specific inclusive programme).

Local authorities have traditionally been a big investor in the sport landscape contributing over £1 bn in funding year on year through complex multi-departmental funding streams. However, since the 2008 financial crisis, austerity has hit the local authorities and the third sector economy hard and continues to dominate government policy. Austerity is "a form of voluntary deflation in which the economy adjusts through the reduction of wages, prices, and public spending to restore competitiveness, which is (supposedly) best achieved by cutting the state's budget, debts, and deficits" (Blyth, 2013, p. 2). The Department for Communities and Local Government responsible for funding local authorities has seen overall funding cut by 51% between 2010 and 2015 (Parnell et al., 2015). A further 56% reduction in funding was planned between 2015 and 2020 (HM Treasury, 2015) and 168 councils did not receive any grant funding from 2019 onwards while having to contribute to the central government instead (Local Government Association, 2018).

One of the groups most affected by austerity is DP. Arguably, public spending cuts disproportionately focus on the poorest members of society (Blyth, 2013; Duffy, 2013). In addition to a direct reduction in social benefits, it is estimated that reforms to disability benefits will result in 1.25 million people losing some if not all of their disability benefits (Beatty & Fothergill, 2015). This is compounded by a reduction of investment in the tertiary sector, such as disability charities, on which so many DP rely for (sport) services.

DP are further disadvantaged as austerity has resulted in funding uncertainty and budget cuts for sport, leisure and physical activity (Local Government Association, 2018; Parnell et al., 2015; Widdop et al., 2018). This has resulted in a reduction by two-thirds over the last decade on council-run sports facilities which are often frequented by DP. Furthermore, spending on sports development and community recreation which often focuses on inclusion and vulnerable groups has fallen 64% to £93 million in 2018 (Ellson, 2019).

Governance and Management Support

The UK government has seen the professionalisation of sport as key to the realisation of its sport strategy. This has resulted in political commitment to strive towards excellence through the professionalisation of sport structures in the UK (Department for Culture, Media and Sport, 2001, 2008, 2012, 2015). This has focused on two areas in particular: improving and establishing good governance, and professionalising the workforce with a specific focus on coaching.

To support this, Sport England and UK Sport have developed a Code for Sports Governance that will apply to all organisations within the UK, in addition to the governance frameworks of the other sport councils. While these codes have traditionally been voluntary, the new Code for Sports Governance details a mandatory set of requirements for organisations seeking government funding (Sport England & UK Sport, 2016). However, it is not only funding which could be hit if authorities do not comply with the code. The government could also take other punitive measures—including the withdrawal of the support sporting bodies need when bidding to host major events. One of the big pillars of the governance code is improving diversity throughout the organisation as sport organisations should better reflect the public it serves.

The UK coaching system is built on volunteerism, accounting for 78% of the coaching body (Sports Coach UK, 2011) and relies heavily on the "goodwill" of these volunteers (Taylor & Garratt, 2008). Coaching has seen significant investment over the years (e.g. investment of £16 million as part of the Olympic and Paralympic Legacy goals), while other initiatives, such as Sportivate, focused on inspiring young people to become a coach (Sport England, 2012b). In recent years, sport coaching has seen diverse projects to increase coaching competences in coaching DP. Disability Sport Wales has introduced a Disability Inclusion Training (UKDIT) course to support the professional development and upskilling/learning of sports professionals, coaches and volunteers. Coaching UK runs various continuing professional development (CPD) workshops focused on disability inclusion training and the Activity Alliance has partnered up with supermarket chain, Sainsbury, to deliver Sainsbury's Inclusive PE Training Programme. These programmes are much needed as DP experience a lack of skills and knowledge amongst coaches, which has a negative impact on their well-being and sport participation (Christiaens, 2018). Furthermore, coaches are increasingly asking athletes to pay for their services with DP most often targeted under the presumption that they require more effort and/or are more time consuming to coach or in need of one-to-one coaching (Christiaens, 2018).

Lastly, in the UK, DP are keen volunteers with 47% currently engaged in volunteering which is higher than the non-disabled population (34%) (English Federation of Disability Sport, 2017). However, DP are more likely to have a negative experience and perceive barriers to volunteering. Indeed, DP are still confronted with negative and discrimative experience while volunteering which often results in demished confidence and self-worth and when placed in its historical context results in internalised social attitudes preventing DP from seeking volunteering opportunities (Kappelides & Jennifer, 2019). Moreover, DP predominantly volunteer in disability-related organisations and in local community groups and not so often in sport (English Federation of Disability Sport, 2017), as illustrated during the 2012 London Olympic and Paralympic Games where, despite an effort of the organisors, volunteers with a disability accounted for only 5% of all volunteers (Darcy et al., 2014).

Level of Integration or Inclusion

In 1989 the UK abandoned the separation of sport provision for DP. As a result, the sport structures were reformed to integrate disability sport delivery. Indeed, the sport councils and NGBs are now responsible for the delivery of sport for DP. However, the UK remains characterised by ableist structures which is evidenced by the approach to and perceived importance of disability by some NGBs who still prioritise non-disabled sport over sport for DP (Brittain & Beacom, 2016; Christiaens & Brittain, 2021). This is despite most NGBs being in receipt of Sport England funding to provide for DP. Furthermore, the power and funding structures in the UK mean that the voluntary community sport clubs have much freedom and independency often resulting in tension and rebellious tendencies against (inclusive) policy from above. It is then perhaps not surprising that only 1% of sport club membership is a DP (Christiaens, 2018) and that DP remain the largest underperforming group when it comes to sport participation, which will be elaborated on in the next section.

11.4 Sport Participation by Disabled People

Monitoring and Evaluation

The physical activity and sports participation of DP aged 16+ is monitored by Sport England's Active Lives Adult survey (Sport England, n.d.). For children and young DP (5–16-year-olds), physical activity and sports participation is assessed by Sport England's Active Lives Children and Young People survey (Sport England, n.d.). The surveys monitor and evaluate physical activity and sport participation of young people and adults in England, in line with the government's Sporting Future strategy (Sport England, n.d.). The Active Lives surveys are national surveys conducted by market research company, Ipsos MORI, which manages the data collection and analysis process on behalf of Sport England (Ipsos MORI, 2019a, 2019b).

Active Lives Adult

The survey sample is randomly selected from the Royal Mail's Postal Address File. Online completion is encouraged, but paper versions of the survey are available to respondents. Of the 177,876 people that completed the 2018/2019 survey, 5.8% self-identified as having a limiting disability or long-standing impairment. In this survey, sport participation is defined as having participated twice in the last 28 days.

Active Lives Children and Young People

The survey sample randomly selects schools listed on the Department for Education's list (Ipsos MORI, 2019a). Special schools, schools specifically providing education opportunities for children with special educational needs or disability, were excluded from the sample (Ipsos MORI, 2019a). Physical activity and sport participation data for children and young DP were only available to primary, secondary or independent schools with pupils identifying as having a disability.

A total of 109,503 schools completed the survey. Data on the number of children and young DP that completed the survey was not available. In this survey, three measures are used to represent physical activity: less active (less than an average of 30 minutes a day), fairly active (an average of 30–59 minutes a day) and active (60+ minutes a day).

Sport Participation

The data discussed in this section focuses on Active Lives data from England. Sport participation of DP from Wales,[3] Scotland[4] and Northern Ireland[5] presents a similar picture of a participation gap between DP and non-disabled people. The Active Lives data in England is the most comprehensive dataset. Therefore, this will be the focus of the remainder of this section.

Sport Participation (Adults Aged 16+)

DP (41%) are more inactive than non-disabled (20%) (Sport England, 2019b). Inactivity increases with the number of impairments an individual has. For example, 31% of people with one impairment are inactive compared to just under half (49%) of individuals with three or more impairments (Sport England, 2019b). The sport participation of DP is low compared to the rest of the population. Just 18% of DP participated in sport at least twice in the last 28 days, compared to 39% of non-disabled people (Active Lives Online, 2020).

Since the first round of data gathering for Active Lives Adult in November 2015/2016, DP participating in sporting activities at least once in the last year has increased from 36.8% to 41.8% in November 2018/2019 (Sport England, 2020).

---

[3] Please see National Survey for Wales 2018–19: Sport and Active Lifestyles—State of the Nation Report for further information. The report is available from: https://www.sport.wales/content-vault/sport-and-active-lifestyles-survey/

[4] Please see Disability and Sport report for further information. The report is available from: https://sportscotland.org.uk/media/2592/learning-note-disability-and-sport.pdf

[5] Please see Experience of Sport in Northern Ireland 2018/19' report for further information. The report is available from: https://www.statista.com/statistics/535077/sport-participation-northern-ireland-uk/

When reviewing increased levels of sporting activity across the same time period, the data has remained fairly stable. In November 2015/2016, 18.8% of DP participated in sporting activities at least twice in the last 28 days compared to 18.9% in November 2018/2019 (Sport England, 2020).) Brown and Pappous (2018a), in their analysis of sport participation since the 2012 Paralympic Games, found DP sport participation peaked a year after the 2012 Paralympics, but subsequently declined in 2016 to levels just above sport participation rates recorded in 2005.

Sport Participation (Children and Young People Aged 5–16)

A smaller participation gap exists between DP and non-disabled children and young people compared to adults aged 16+. Children and young DP are more inactive as they get older (34% for ages 11–16) compared to their early years (22% for ages 5–7) (Sport England, 2019a). This is a similar picture for non-disabled children and young people (31% for ages 11–16; 17% for ages 5–7) (Sport England, 2019a). In the past 12 months, levels of inactivity for children and young DP decreased for those aged 7–16 by approximately 4.1% (Sport England, 2019a). It is unclear why a decrease occurred and more data is needed before any meaningful trends or conclusions can be inferred from the data.

Sport Participation by Sport Type (Adults Aged 16+)

According to data from the Active Lives Adult survey, fitness class activities (9.4%) are the most frequently participated activity by DP, regardless of impairment type. Swimming and cycling (7.3%) are amongst the most popular activities for DP (Active Lives Online, 2020). While cycling is popular across the spectrum of impairment quantity, swimming is more popular for individuals with two or more impairments. The difference in popularity between sporting activities is small and therefore the order of importance should be viewed with caution. DP participate in a range of individual sports (such as swimming [7.3%], cycling [7.3%] and running [5.8%], more often than team sports [2.5%]).

Sport Participation by Region (Adults Aged 16+)

The UK has one of the widest income gaps, and inequality has been found to reduce the likelihood of participation in sport (Collins, 2010). Regional participation in sport and physical activity by DP is consistent with wealth distribution across the country. The South East and South West regions have the highest median total household wealth in Great Britain, whereas the North East region has the lowest (Active Lives Online, 2020). Similarly, participation of DP in sport and physical activity at least twice in the past 28 days is highest in the South East (67.7%) and South West (65.6%) regions, but lowest in the North East (58.5%).

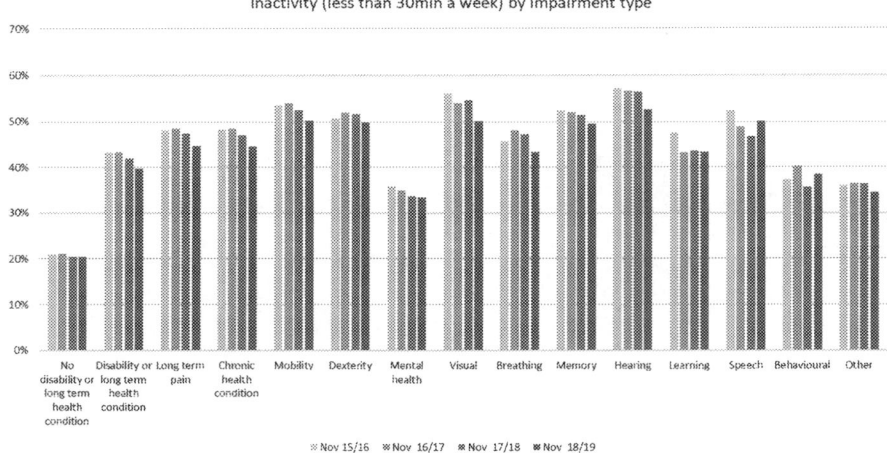

Fig. 11.3 Inactivity by impairment type. Source: adapted from Active Lives Online, 2020

Sport Participation by Impairment (Adults Aged 16+)

Individuals with behavioural impairments (23%) participate in sport the most (Active Lives Online, 2020). People with impairments listed as other[6] (22.9%), mental health (21.9%), learning (21.6%) and speech (21.6%) comprise the top five impairment types for sport participation at least twice in the past 28 days in England (Active Lives Online, 2020). People with hearing (12%) and visual (12.5%) impairments participate in sport the least (Active Lives Online, 2020). See Fig. 11.3 for an overview of inactivity by impairment.

Sport Participation by Club Membership (Adults Aged 16+)

The disparity between the sport participation of DP and non-disabled people is even steeper when looking at participation in club associations. Data from the Active Lives Survey (Active Lives Online, 2020) shows that of those who are active, 44.8% of non-disabled people participate in club associations compared to 29.4% of DP. However, when looking at club membership of non-disabled sport clubs, which are now required to deliver equal services to DP, data from athletics and swimming show that only 1% of club membership is formed by DP (Christiaens, 2018).

---

[6] Sport England defines this impairment category as people without the following impairment types: behavioural, mental health, learning, speech, long-term pain, dexterity, breathing, chronic health condition, mobility, memory, visual and hearing (Sport England, 2016).

Barriers and Facilitators

Barriers

Research has found ableism to be a significant constraining factor in the sport participation of DP in the UK. Brittain, Biscaia and Gérard (Brittain et al., 2020) claim ableism creates internalised oppression limiting the ability of DP to access sporting opportunities, due to a denial of accumulation of social, economic and cultural capitals and the ability to self-determine. The ableist environment of the UK sporting system is evident by many sporting opportunities failing to promote the social benefits of sport participation, instead promulgating the normative notions of competitiveness and body ideals (Ives et al., 2019). Ableism appears to play a key role in the understanding of inclusion and how it is operationalised in different sport clubs and organisations, resulting in placing a DP in an existing non-disabled environment while this rarely leads to inclusive outcomes (Christiaens and Brittain, 2021). Furthermore, a number of sporting organisations lack experience and knowledge in providing sport participation opportunities for DP, stemming from a failure to consider disability as a consumer market worth focusing on (Brown & Pappous, 2018a; Christiaens, 2018; Johnson, 2019). Indeed, a perceived lack of appropriate sporting opportunities and awareness of sport provision can constrain some individuals from participating in sport (Brown, 2019). A lack of awareness of opportunities can stem from inaccessible or inefficient communication channels being used by providers (Activity Alliance, 2020a; Christiaens, 2018; Ives et al., 2019), indicative of an ableist mindset within organisations.

The systematic reduction in welfare and public services available to DP in the UK has been a significant barrier to sport participation. Austerity measures implemented by the UK Coalition government and the Conservative party had a detrimental impact on the physical, social and mental health of some DP (Brittain & Beacom, 2016; Cross, 2013). The combination of negative and prejudiced characterisations of DP in the UK media (Crow, 2014; Briant et al., 2013), austerity measures and the mobility component of PIP have prompted some DP to fear losing welfare benefits if seen to be active (Activity Alliance, 2020a; Brown & Pappous, 2018a, 2018b; Christiaens, 2018; Johnson & Spring, 2018). Nearly half of the people in Johnson and Spring's (2018) study were worried about participating in physical activity as they believed this would make them look more mobile and thus "less disabled" than they actually are. This in turn could lead to a reduction in their disability benefits and, in essence, punish them for participating in sport and physical activity (Brown & Pappous, 2018a; Christiaens, 2018; Johnson & Spring, 2018).

Facilitators

Research has emphasised the importance of activities prioritising fun and enjoyment as a facilitator for increasing sport participation (Ives et al., 2019; Sport England & English Federation of Disability Sport, 2016). Indeed, communications from trusted sources, such as medical professionals or disability organisations, may be more effective if the social benefits of sport are championed rather than medical benefits (Sport England & English Federation of Disability Sport, 2016). In addition to positioning sport participation around fun and enjoyment, it is important that organisations provide sufficient information about the activity. This can help reduce potential anxiety about what to expect when attending the opportunity (Sport England & English Federation of Disability Sport, 2016). Information about activities can include, but are not limited to, activity-related imagery, videos and written communications which, if delivered through trusted communication channels, can help reduce unease about participation in sport (Sport England & English Federation of Disability Sport, 2016). It is important that DP have a choice of suitable sport participation opportunities (Brown, 2019; Christiaens, 2018; Ives et al., 2019; Sport England & English Federation of Disability Sport, 2016). Inclusive sport sessions are a popular option for sport participation (Activity Alliance, 2020a), and providers who have been successful in engaging DP in sport generally have knowledge and experience of inclusive sport (Johnson, 2019). Notwithstanding the preference for inclusive sport, organisations that provide increased sporting options for DP in the form of impairment-specific sessions are important too (Sport England & English Federation of Disability Sport, 2016). Impairment-specific sessions may be particularly appealing to DP who might be uncomfortable participating with non-disabled people because of perceived competency deficits or lack of confidence. In sum, the best way to facilitate sport participation for DP would seem to be to provide a compelling sporting offer, through diversity of choice and information.

11.5 Conclusion

As demonstrated throughout this chapter, the UK disability sport system is highly complex and fragmented as a result of devolution. With integrated sport structures, the UK is unique within Europe. However, as this chapter has shown, this has not necessarily translated into bridging the disparity between physical activity of DP and non-disabled people. Moreover, despite NGBs having to deliver for DP, their sport participation remains disturbingly low in non-disabled community sport clubs.

While the process of inclusion started in 1989, this was largely based on a voluntary approach that did not change much in practice. It is only much more recently, with the introduction of the EqA in 2010 and the adoption of coercion methods by the government, that the sport sector started to introduce significant change. The overall objectives of the government have not changed much over the years and have focused on elite performance on the world stage and increasing physical activity with a changing focus on target groups. The government, who operates through its arm's length sport councils, is increasingly looking to NGBs and other sports organisations to deliver its policy objectives. However, community sport clubs feel detached from their NGBs and unpersuaded by the government to deliver against their objectives. This is not surprising as community sport clubs, contrary to their

NGBs, are financially independent from the government and rely heavily on volunteers who have very different motivations than those of the government.

The sport sector in the UK is looking ahead to uncertain times. First of all, despite the government claiming an end to austerity, this is unlikely to have a direct impact on the sport sector. On the contrary, the sport sector has not recovered from previously imposed austerity measures. Moreover, with dwindling local budgets and local council debts spiralling out of control, sport provision through local councils is looking at gloomy times. Secondly, the implications of Brexit on sport have not been fully assessed yet, but it is almost certain this will impact in a number of ways. Lastly, the outbreak of COVID-19 has brought many aspects of social life to a halt with many sporting events being cancelled and sport clubs closing their doors as they are seen as a highly contagious environment. The financial and social impact of COVID-19 on the sport sector is uncertain at this point. Furthermore, the Coronavirus Act 2020 further curtails the rights of DP and, in England, the 2020 Act relaxes the rules and standards for social care services, suspending the Care Act 2014 to the extent that they constitute a violation of DP's most basic human rights (Human Rights Watch, 2020). With the pandemic increasing in severity, the National Healthcare System (NHS) has adopted a controversial "scoring system" to decide who receives critical care and who does not. This scale is based on the "Clinical Frailty Scale" and treats DP as a "sub-class" of the population putting DP at risk of treatment (Boyd, 2020; Ryan, 2020). There have also been stories reported where DP are pressured into signing "do not resuscitate" forms and stories of "do not resuscitate" orders where "learning disabilities" or "Down's syndrome" have been given as the reason (Ryan, 2020). This evidences the ongoing structural and institutionalised ableism within British society.

To conclude, despite an inclusive approach to the sport structures in the UK, it remains a struggle for DP to engage in physical activity and sport. The sport participation levels have stagnated and not much has changed between 2007 and 2019. The sport sector remains dominated by an ableist culture that makes it difficult and/or unpleasant for DP to engage within the non-disabled sport landscape that is supposed to cater for them. Furthermore, changes to disability benefits have some DP scared of engaging in physical activity despite the clear benefits physical activity has for DP.

References

Active Lives Online. (2020). *Welcome to active lives online*. https://activelives.sportengland.org/.
Activity Alliance. (2020a). *Annual disability and activity survey 2019/20*.
Activity Alliance. (2020b). *National disability sport organisations*. http://www.activityalliance.org.uk/together/ndsos.
Allison, M. (2002). Sports Clubs in Scotland Summary (Issue 10).
Beatty, C., & Fothergill, S. (2015). Disability benefits in an age of austerity. *Social Policy and Administration, 49*(2), 161–181. https://doi.org/10.1111/spol.12117
Bergsgard, N., Houlihan, B., Mangset, P., Nødland, S., & Rommetvedt, H. (2007). *Sport policy: A Comparative analysis of stability and change*. Elsevier Ltd.

Bevir, M., & Rhodes, R. (2006). *Governance stories*. Routledge.

Bevir, M., & Rhodes, R. (2008). The differentiated polity as narrative. *British Journal of Politics and International Relations, 10*(4), 729–734. https://doi.org/10.1111/j.1467-856X.2008.00325.x

Blackburn, C. M., Spencer, N. J., & Read, J. M. (2010). Prevalence of childhood disability and the characteristics and circumstances of disabled children in the UK: Secondary analysis of the family resources survey. *BMC Pediatrics, 10*, 21. https://doi.org/10.1186/1471-2431-10-21

Blyth, M. (2013). *Austerity: The history of a dangerous idea*. Oxford University Press.

Boyd, C. (2020). *Fury over NHS "coronavirus scoring system" which treats learning disability patients like a "sub-class of the population."* Daily Mail. https://www.dailymail.co.uk/news/article-8214689/Fury-NHS-coronavirus-scoring-discriminates-against-learning-disability-patient.html.

Braithwaite, J., & Mont, D. (2009). Disability and poverty: A survey of World Bank poverty assessments and implications. *Alter, 3*(3), 219–232. https://doi.org/10.1016/j.alter.2008.10.002

Briant, E., Watson, N., & Philo, G. (2013). Reporting Disability in the Age of Austerity: The Changing Face of Media Representation of Disability and Disabled People in the United Kingdom and the Creation of New 'Folk Devils'. *Disability & Society 28*(6): 874–889. https://doi.org/10.1080/09687599.2013.813837

Brittain, I. (2012). *From stoke Mandeville to Sochi*. Common Ground Publishing.

Brittain, I., & Beacom, A. (2016). Leveraging the London 2012 Paralympic Games: What legacy for disabled people? *Journal of Sport & Social Issues, 40*(6), 499–521. https://doi.org/10.1177/0193723516655580

Brittain, I., Biscaia, R., & Gérard, S. (2020). Ableism as a regulator of social practice and disabled peoples' self-determination to participate in sport and physical activity. *Leisure Studies, 39*(2), 209–224. https://doi.org/10.1080/02614367.2019.1694569

Brown, C. (2019). *"I still think we've got mountains to climb": Evaluating the grassroots sport participation legacy of the London 2012 Paralympic Games for disabled people in England* [University of Kent]. https://doi.org/10.1002/cb.1444/abstract

Brown, C., & Pappous, A. (Sakis). (2018a). "The legacy element… It just felt more woolly": Exploring the reasons for the decline in people with disabilities' sport participation in England 5 years after the London 2012 Paralympic Games. *Journal of Sport and Social Issues 42*(5), 343–368. https://doi.org/10.1177/0193723518781237

Brown, C., & Pappous, A. (Sakis). (2018b). The organisational performance of national disability sport organisations during a time of austerity: A resource dependence theory perspective. *International Journal of Sport Policy, 10*(1), 63–78. https://doi.org/10.1080/19406940.2017.1381635

Cavanagh, J., Bartram, T., Meacham, H., Bigby, C., Oakman, J., & Fossey, E. (2017). Supporting workers with disabilities: A scoping review of the role of human resource management in contemporary organisations. *Asia Pacific Journal of Human Resources, 55*: 6–43. https://doi.org/10.1111/1744-7941.12111

Christiaens, M., & Brittain, I. (2021). The complexities of implementing inclusion policies for disabled people in UK non-disabled voluntary community sports clubs. *European Sport Management Quarterly*. https://doi.org/10.1080/16184742.2021.1955942

Christiaens, M., (2018). *Towards mainstreaming: A principle – practice gap in the UK sports sector (Unpublished doctoral dissertation)* [Coventry University]. http://curve.coventry.ac.uk/open/items/90fff1fa-cca3-48cf-81e3-f11551f63978/1/

Coghlan, J., & Webb, I. (2003). *Sport and British politics since 1960*. Routledge.

Collins, M. (2010). From 'sport for good' to 'sport for sport's sake' – not a good move for sports development in England? *International Journal of Sport Policy and Politics, 2*(3), 367–379. https://doi.org/10.1080/19406940.2010.519342

Cross, M. (2013). Demonised, impoverished and now forced into isolation: The fate of disabled people under austerity. *Disability & Society, 28*(5), 719–723. https://doi.org/10.1080/09687599.2013.808087

Crouch, J., & Minhas, P. (2017). *Interpreting in the 21 century*.

Crow, L. (2014). Scroungers and superhumans: Images of disability from the summer of 2012: A visual inquiry. *Journal of Visual Culture,13*(2), 168–181. https://doi.org/10.1177/1470412914529109

Cushion, C., Nelson, L., Armour, K., Lyle, J., Jones, R., Sandford, R., & O'Callaghan, C. (2010). *Coach learning and development: A review of literature.*

Darcy, S., Dickson, T. J., & Benson, A. M. (2014). London 2012 Olympic and Paralympic Games: Including volunteers with disabilities—A podium performance?. *Event Management, 18*(4), 431–446. https://doi.org/10.3727/152599514X14143427352157

Department for Culture Media and Sport. (2001). *A sporting future for all: The Government's plan for Sport.* https://www.sportdevelopment.org.uk/index.php/subjects/48-policy/73-a-sporting-future-for-all.

Department for Culture Media and Sport. (2008). *Playing to win: A new era for sport.* DCMS.

Department for Culture Media and Sport. (2012). *Creating a sporting habit for life: A new youth sport strategy.* http://www.cabdirect.org/abstracts/20123185861.html.

Department for Culture Media and Sport. (2015). *Sporting future: A new strategy for an active nation.* https://www.gov.uk/government/uploads/system/uploads/attachment_data/file/486622/Sporting_Future_ACCESSIBLE.pdf.

Department for Culture Media and Sport. (2019). *Annual report and accounts for the year ended 31 March 2019.*

Department for Work & Pensions. (2019). *Family Resources Survey 2017/2018: Disability Database.*

DePauw, K., & Gavron, S. (2005). *Disability Sport* (2nd ed.). Human Kinetics.

Duffy, S. (2013). *Counting the cuts.*

Ellson, A. (2019). Leisure centres close as spending on council-run sports facilities plunges. *The Times.* https://www.thetimes.co.uk/article/leisure-centres-close-as-spending-on-council-run-sports-facilities-plunges-6tqg7gxmb.

English Federation of Disability Sport. (2017). *Encouraging more disabled people to volunteer in sport.*

European Commission. (2018). Sport and physical activity. In *Special Eurobarometer* (Vol. 472). https://doi.org/10.2766/483047

Eurostat. (2018). *Regional Innovation Monitor: United Kingdom.* https://ec.europa.eu/growth/tools-databases/regional-innovation-monitor/region/united-kingdom

Goodley, D. (2014). *Dis/ability studies: Theorising disablism and ableism.* Routledge.

Great Britain Parliament. (2010). Equality Act 2010 (Vol. C15). http://www.legislation.gov.uk/ukpga/2010/15/contents

Green, M., & Houlihan, B. (2005). *Elite Sport development: Policy learning and political priorities.* Routledge.

Harris, S., Mori, K., & Collins, M. (2009). Great expectations: Voluntary sports clubs and their role in delivering national policy for English sport. *VOLUNTAS: International Journal of Voluntary and Nonprofit Organizations, 20*(4), 405–423. https://doi.org/10.1007/s11266-009-9095-y

HM Treasury. (2015). *Spending review and autumn statement 2015.* https://www.gov.uk/government/news/spending-review-and-autumn-statement-2015-key-announcements.

Houlihan, B. (2005). Public sector Sport policy: Developing a framework for analysis. *International Review for the Sociology of Sport, 40*(2), 163–185. https://doi.org/10.1177/1012690205057193

Houlihan, B., & Lindsey, I. (2013). Sport policy in Britain. In B. Houlihan & I. Lindsey (Eds.), *Sport policy in Britain.* Routledge. https://doi.org/10.4324/9780203094273

Huber, C. (1984). An overview and perspective on disabled sport: Past, present, future. *Rehabilitation World, 8*, 8–11.

Human Rights Watch. (2020). *UK: COVID-19 law puts rights of people with disabilities at risk.* https://www.hrw.org/news/2020/03/26/uk-covid-19-law-puts-rights-people-disabilities-risk.

Ipsos MORI. (2019a). Active lives children and young people survey 2018/2019 year 2 technical note: September 18–July 19.

Ipsos MORI. (2019b). Active lives survey 2018/2019 year 4 technical note: May 18–May 19. http://www.ipsos-mori.com/terms.

Ives, B., Clayton, B., Brittain, I., & Mackintosh, C. (2019). 'I'll always find a perfectly justified reason for not doing it': challenges for disability sport and physical activity in the United Kingdom. *Sport in Society, 0*(0), 1–19. https://doi.org/10.1080/17430437.2019.1703683

Johnson, E. (2019). *Delivering activity to disabled people: The workforce perception gap.* http://www.activityalliance.org.uk/assets/000/002/641/Activity_Alliance_Deliverer_Perceptions_Research_Report_Final_Accessible_PDF_report_original.pdf?1548778930.

Johnson, E., & Spring, E. (2018). *The activity trap: Disabled people's fear of being active.*

Kappelides, P., & Spoor, J. (2019). Managing sport volunteers with a disability: Human resource management implications. *Sport Management Review, 22*(5), 694–707. https://doi.org/10.1016/j.smr.2018.10.004

Le Clair, J. (2012). *Disability in the global Sport arena: A sporting chance.* Routledge.

LeisureDB. (2019). *State of the UK fitness & swimming industry.*

Local Government Association. (2018). *LGA budget submission: Autumn 2017.*

Lockwood, G., Henderson, C., & Thornicroft, G. (2012). The equality act 2010 and mental health. *British Journal of Psychiatry, 200*, 182–183. https://doi.org/10.1192/bjp.bp.111.097790

May, T., Harris, S., & Collins, M. (2013). Implementing community sport policy: Understanding the variety of voluntary club types and their attitudes to policy. *International Journal of Sport Policy and Politics, 5*(3), 397–419. https://doi.org/10.1080/19406940.2012.735688

McCann, C. (1996). Sports for the disabled: The evolution from rehabilitation to competitive sport. *British Journal of Sports Medicine, 30*(4), 279–280.

Minister for Sport's Review Group. (1989). *Building on ability: Sport for people with disabilities.*

National Governing Body CEO Forum. (2015). The state of play. *International Journal of Play, 2*(3), 161–162. https://doi.org/10.1080/21594937.2013.853462

Office for Disability Issues. (2020). *Inclusive language: Words to use and avoid when writing about disability.* https://www.gov.uk/government/publications/inclusive-communication/inclusive-language-words-to-use-and-avoid-when-writing-about-disability.

Office for National Statistics. (2014). *2011 census for England and Wales.* http://www.ons.gov.uk/ons/guide-method/census/2011/index.html.

Office for National Statistics. (2018). *Scottish local government financial statistics 2017–2018.*

Office for National Statistics. (2019a). *Living longer: Is age 70 the new age 65?* https://www.ons.gov.uk/peoplepopulationandcommunity/birthsdeathsandmarriages/ageing/articles/livinglongerisage70thenewage65/2019-11-19.

Office for National Statistics. (2019b). *Local authority revenue expenditure and financing England: 2019 to 2020 budget.*

Office for National Statistics. (2019c). *Population estimates.* https://www.ons.gov.uk/peoplepopulationandcommunity/populationandmigration/populationestimates.

Office for National Statistics. (2019d). *Scotland's people annual report 2018.*

Parnell, D., Millward, P., & Spracklen, K. (2015). Sport and austerity in the UK: An insight into Liverpool 2014. *Journal of Policy Research in Tourism, Leisure and Events, 7*(2), 200–203. https://doi.org/10.1080/19407963.2014.968309

Parnell, D., Widdop, P., & King, N. (2015). Local authority cuts loom large over community sport. *Connect Sport.* https://e-space.mmu.ac.uk/620612/.

Phillpots, L., Grix, J., & Quarmby, T. (2010). Centralized grassroots sport policy and "new governance": A case study of county Sports partnerships in the UK - unpacking the paradox. *International Review for the Sociology of Sport, 46*(3), 265–281. https://doi.org/10.1177/1012690210378461

Rhodes, R. (1990). Policy Networks. *Journal of Theoretical Politics, 2*(3), 293–317.

Ryan, F. (2020). It is not only coronavirus that risks infecting society – Our prejudices do, too. *The Guardian.* https://www.theguardian.com/commentisfree/2020/apr/09/nice-guidelines-coronavirus-pandemic-disabled.

Scottish Government. (2019). *Government Expenditure and Revenue in Scotland (GERS): 2018 to 2019.* https://www.gov.scot/publications/government-expenditure-revenue-scotland-gers/pages/5/.

SIRC. (2013). *Economic value of Sport in England: Sport outcomes evidence review report*.
SIRC. (2017a). *The economic importance of Olympic and Paralympic Sport*.
SIRC. (2017b). *UK Sport Satellite Account, 2016 (Provisional)*. http://www.sportsthinktank.com/uploads/uk-sport-satellite-accounts-for-2011-12-july-2015.pdf
SIRC. (2018a). Measuring the social and economic value of sport in Wales. Report 1: Social return on Investment of Sport in Wales 2016/17.
SIRC. (2018b). *The economic importance of Sport in Scotland 1998–2016*.
Skelcher, C. (2000). Changing images of the state: Overloaded, hollowed-out, congested. Public Policy and Administration, 15(3), 3–19. https://doi.org/https://doi.org/10.1177/095207670001500302
Sport England. (2012a). *Higher education Sport participation and satisfaction survey: National Report Year one*.
Sport England. (2012b). *Sport England strategy 2012–17*.
Sport England. (2013). *National Governing Body 2013/17 whole Sport plan investment guidance*.
Sport England. (2016a). *Active people survey 10Q2*.
Sport England. (2016b). *Towards an active nation: Strategy 2016–2021*. https://sportengland-production-files.s3.eu-west-2.amazonaws.com/s3fs-public/sport-england-towards-an-active-nation.pdf.
Sport England. (2018). *Sporting activities and governing bodies recognised by the Sports councils*. https://www.sportengland.org/media/13708/list-of-uk-recognised-ngbs-and-sport-october-2018.pdf.
Sport England. (2019a). *Active lives: Children and young people survey 2018/19*. Sport England, December, 1–34.
Sport England. (2019b). *Active lives adult survey 18/19 report*. https://sportengland-production-files.s3.eu-west-2.amazonaws.com/s3fs-public/2020-01/active-lives-adult-may-18-19-report_1.pdf?ehS5l7YBm3YeLHgNwXLmUSbTZPENafJY.
Sport England. (2020). *Active lives online*. https://activelives.sportengland.org/.
Sport England. (n.d.). *Active Lives*. Retrieved March 2, 2020, from https://www.sportengland.org/know-your-audience/data/active-lives#overview
Sport England, & English Federation of Disability Sport. (2016). *Mapping Disability: Engaging disabled people: the research*.
Sport England, & UK Sport. (2016). *A code for Sports governance*.
Sport Wales. (2018). *Sport Wales: Annual accounts 2016–2017*.
Sport Wales. (2019). *Sport Wales: Business plan*.
Sport Wales. (2020). *Full state of the nation: Report 2018–19*.
Sports Coach UK. (2011). *Sports coaching in the UK III: A statistical analysis of coaches and coaching in the UK*. http://www.sportscoachuk.org/sites/default/files/Sports-Coaching-in-the-UK-III.pdf.
Sportscotland. (2019a). *Playing our part: Summary of progress 2018–19*. https://sportscotland.org.uk/media/5020/sportscotland_playingourpart2019.pdf
Sportscotland. (2019b). *Sport for life: A vision for sport in Scotland*.
StatsWales. (2019). *Budgeted revenue expenditure by authority and service*.
Taylor, B., & Garratt, D. (2008). The professionalisation of sports coaching in the UK: Issues and Conceptualisations. In *Sport. Education and Society*. http://hdl.handle.net/2173/92580
Thomas, N. (2003). Sport and disability. In B. Houlihan (Ed.), *Sport and society. A student introduction* (1st ed., pp. 105–124). SAGE Publications. https://doi.org/10.4135/9781446278833.n10
Thomas, N. (2008). Sport and disability. In B. Houlihan (Ed.), *Sport and society. A student introduction* (2nd ed., pp. 205–229). SAGE Publications.
UK Government. (2013). *Inspired by 2012: The legacy from the London 2012 Olympic and Paralympic Games I* (issue July).
UK Government. (2014a). *Inspired by 2012: The legacy from the London 2012 Olympic and Paralympic Games III* (issue July).
UK Government. (2014b). *The long term vision for the legacy of the London 2012* (issue February).

UK Government. (2015). *Inspired by 2012: The legacy from the London 2012 Olympic and Paralympic Games II* (issue August).
UK Sport. (2019). *The United Kingdom Sports council: Annual report and accounts*.
Welsh Government. (2020). *National Survey for Wales: Results*. https://gov.wales/national-survey-wales-results-viewer.
Widdop, P., King, N., Parnell, D., Cutts, D., & Millward, P. (2018). Austerity, policy and sport participation in England. *International Journal of Sport Policy, 10*(1), 7–24. https://doi.org/10.1080/19406940.2017.1348964
World Bank. (2018). *Country profile: United Kingdom*. https://databank.worldbank.org/views/reports/reportwidget.aspx?Report_Name=CountryProfile&Id=b450fd57&tbar=y&dd=y&inf=n&zm=n&country=GBR.

Chapter 12
Austria: Half Way to Inclusion?

Torsten Wojciechowski and Claudia Stura

12.1 Introduction

This chapter reviews disability sports in Austria, which has a long history. Several international disability sports events have previously been hosted in Austria, including the first Winter Deaflympics Games in 1949, the Winter Paralympics in 1984 and 1988 as well as the Special Olympics World Winter Games in 2017. Disability sports is granted subsidies by federal law. On the federal level, the Ministry for Arts, Culture, Civil Service and Sport is mainly responsible for sports. In addition, disability sports promotion is part of the coalition agreement between the conservative party and the green party during the current period of office (2020–2024).

Several Austrian states have included disability sports promotion in their sports laws, too. Besides the federal level, the regional governments also are responsible for disability sports. Hence, policy programmes concerning disability sports exist on different political levels. In addition, several voluntary sports organisations are responsible for disability sports. While the big organisations are the Austrian Disability Sports Confederation, the Austrian Paralympic Committee and Special Olympics Austria, some sport for all federations also have special divisions for disability sports (Austria has three sport for all federations). In this chapter, we will explore the relationships between all these organisations and their roles in Austrian disability sports and discuss sports participation for people with a disability in Austria.

T. Wojciechowski (✉)
EHiP - Europäische Hochschule für Innovation und Perspektive, Backnang, Germany
e-mail: torsten.wojciechowski@ehip.eu

C. Stura
Fachhochschule Kufstein Tirol, Kufstein, Austria
e-mail: claudia.stura@fh-kufstein.ac.at

12.2 Country Profile

Characteristics of Austria

Large parts of Austria consist of alpine mountains and most parts of Austria are rural areas. The largest city in Austria is Vienna (about 1.9 Mio. citizens). There are five cities in Austria that have between 100,000 and 300,000 inhabitants (Graz, Linz, Salzburg, Innsbruck and Klagenfurt), five cities have between 40,000 and 65,000 inhabitants, and 15 cities have between 20,000 and 40,000 inhabitants.

The Republic of Austria is a federal parliamentary democracy that is described as highly centralised (Erk, 2004). It was established after World War I in 1918 and consists of nine regional states: Burgenland, Carinthia, Lower Austria, Upper Austria, Salzburg, Styria, Tyrol, Vorarlberg and Vienna. After the period of the authoritarian *Ständestaat* (corporate state) from 1934 to 1938 and the Nazi-Regime (1938–1945), the Austrian Republic was re-established in 1945 on the basis of the constitution from 1920. The federal governmental system consists of two political chambers, the stronger *Nationalrat* (the elected first chamber) and the weaker *Bundesrat* (the second chamber that consists of delegates from the nine states). The government is led by a chancellor who gets elected by the members of the *Nationalrat*. The president of the Republic of Austria is elected directly by the people and has mainly a representative function (Fallend, 2013; Storr, 2012). Since 1945, the parties in power have mostly been coalitions of the two major parties (the conservative Austrian People's Party [ÖVP] and the Social Democratic Party [SPÖ]) or a single-party government of one of these parties. In January 2020, the ÖVP formed a coalition—for the first time—with the Austrian Green Party.

Austria's economy is generally well-performing but has recently slowed down. Living standards and subjective well-being in Austria are among the highest across all OECD countries and labour demand has been robust for the previous years. Since many jobs have been filled by migrants or cross-border commuters, recruitment has been difficult and skills mismatch. Hence, structural unemployment is relatively high. Other challenges refer to integrating immigrants, especially low-skilled foreigners, and improving environmental sustainability (OECD, 2019) (Table 12.1).

Table 12.1 Facts and descriptives of Austria

Population (number of inhabitants)[a]	8,858,775
Area (km^2)[a]	83,878
Density (inhabitants/km^2)	106
Urbanisation rate (%)[b]	58
Political organisation	Parliamentary democracy
Structure of the state	Federal
Number of provinces	9
Number of municipalities[c]	2117
GDP per capita (€)[d]	56,889
Number of official languages	1
EU membership	Since 1995
Welfare model	Rhineland

[a]Sozialministerium/BMI (2018)
[b]The World Bank (2018)
[c]Statistik Austria (2020)
[d]OECD (2018)

Sports in Austria

On the federal level, the Ministry of Arts, Culture, Civil Service and Sport is responsible for sports. The *Bundes-Sportförderungsgesetz* (National Law on Sports Promotion) regulates central mechanisms of state sports promotion. At the regional level, the responsibility for sports lies in different ministries. It differs from state to state. All the regional states in Austria have, additionally to the national law, regional laws on sports promotion. The federal minister for sports and the state ministers for sports cooperate through the Conference of Ministers responsible for sport. On the local level, the local municipalities are responsible for sports—some have special departments for sports (e.g. Vienna or Innsbruck). The cities and towns are organised in the Austrian Association of Cities and Towns, which is formed by 252 out of 2100 local authorities—especially the larger ones. This association has a Committee for Sports Affairs.

The voluntary sports system of today's Austria was built on the organisational structures before 1934. Currently, around 60 sport-specific national sports federations exist in Austria—many of them built upon regional federations. Beneath the national federations, three sport-for-all organisations exist: the ASKÖ (*Arbeitsgemeinschaft für Sport und Körperkultur Österreich*), the Austrian Gymnastics and Sports Union (SPORTUNION), and the General Sports Association Austria (*Allgemeiner Sportverband Österreich*, ASVÖ)—all of them have regional affiliates in the Austrian states. The national Olympic sports federations and the national sport-for-all organisations form together the National Olympic Committee of Austria. To coordinate sports nationally, in 1946, the Austrian Sports Organisation (*Österreichische Bundes-Sportorganisation*, BSO) was founded, which is still the umbrella organisation for sports in Austria (Strohmeyer, 1978). Since 2019 the BSO has been operating under the name Sport Austria.

Sport Austria—the Austrian sports organisation—is a non-profit institution, which represents the interests of sports both in Austria and in international organisations (Bundes-Sportorganisation, 2020b). Therefore, Sport Austria is the central platform for coordination and consultation within the Austrian sports system, while the National Olympic Committee (NOC) is in charge of Olympic sports only. In addition to these organisations, several other organisations exist in the Austrian sports system, like the Armed Forces Sports Centres or Austrian Sport Aid (Marschik & Müllner, 2011).

Marschik and Müllner (2011) highlight the strong ties between the sports organisations and politics and point out that after World War I the two big political parties, the conservatives and the social democrats, tried to get power over sports. This resulted in the separation of sports into two politically oriented sports organisations: a conservative Christian-oriented sports organisation and a workers' sports organisation. After World War II, this politically influenced divide went on with the SPORTUNION being ideologically close to the conservative Austrian People's Party and the ASKÖ being ideologically close to the Social Democratic Party of Austria. The ASVÖ, which was founded in 1949, has the objective to separate sports from politics and can be seen as politically neutral (Marschik & Müllner, 2011).

Referring to the framework of Scheerder et al. (2017), the Austrians' general sports governance model centres around the federal level and is based on a co-governance relationship of governmental and non-governmental actors that was formed in the second half of the twentieth century. Due to its welfare policy principles, Austria and many other western European countries' governments increasingly subsidise and interfere in sports (van Bottenburg, 2011). In comparison to the German sports system, the influence of the government on the non-governmental sports organisations is stronger in Austria than in Germany, even though both share common historical roots (van Bottenburg, 2011). Since 2017 the *Bundes-Sport GmbH* (Federal Sports Ltd), which is owned completely by the Republic of Austria, is the responsible intermediary organisation for the financial support of the voluntary sports sector. While sports participation increased in several European countries in previous years, it decreased in Austria and is below the European average, as Eurobarometer data shows. For example, 38% of all respondents in Austria exercise or play sport on a weekly basis, while the European average is 40% (European Union, 2017) (Table 12.2).

Disability in Austria

Traditionally the political discourse about disability in Austria centres around medical aspects (Naue, 2006, 2009). Until 1990, the legal framework was based on laws from 1957 (law on the welfare of war victims, *Kriegsopferversorgungsgesetz*), 1965 (decree of reference rate, *Richtsatzverordnung*; replaced in 2010 by the decree of estimation, *Einschätzungsverordnung*) and 1969 (Austrian Employment Law for Persons with Disabilities, *Behinderteneinstellungsgesetz*). With the Federal Disability Law (*Bundesbehindertengesetz*) from 1990 a first change took place and the formerly used term of *Beschädigte* ("injured" people) was replaced by the term *behinderte Menschen*

Table 12.2 Sports profile of Austria

Government authority responsible for sports	Ministry of Arts, Culture, Civil Service and Sport
Membership sports club (% of population)[a]	13
Membership fitness or health centre (% of population)[a]	16
Membership socio-cultural club that includes sports in its activities (e.g. employees' club, youth club and school- and university-related club) (% of population)[a]	5
Sports participation, at least once a week (% of population)[a]	38
Number of national sports federations[b]	60
Number of sports clubs[b]	14,228
Number of sports club members[b]	2,970,829
National budget for sports (€ × 1,000,000)[c]	130
National budget for sports federations (€ × 1000)[d]	86,576
Local budget for sports (€ × 1,000,000)[e]	563
Share of economic value of volunteers in sports in the GDP (%)[f]	0.82

[a]Special Eurobarometer 472 (2017)
[b]BSO (2019)
[c]BMF (2019)
[d]Austrian Sports (2018)
[e]KDZ (2015)
[f]SportsEconAustria (2019)

(disabled people). In 1992, the *Behindertenkonzept der Bundesregierung* (Disability Plan of the Federal Government) was presented and in 1997 the prohibition of discrimination against persons with disabilities was introduced into the Austrian Constitution (Naue, 2006). In 2006, with the *Bundes-Behindertengleichstellungsgesetz* (Federal Law for the Equality of People with Disabilities) the European Directive 2000/78/EC was implemented in Austria (Schober et al., 2012). In 2008, Austria signed the UN Convention on the Rights of Persons with Disabilities and adjusted their *Bundesbehindertengesetz* (Naue, 2009; Schober et al., 2012). The impact of the European regulations on Austrian disability policy led to a change in the understanding of disability from a strong medical focus to a focus that is more oriented towards human diversity and difference (Naue & Kroll, 2010). In 2012, the National Action Plan on Disability 2012–2020 was presented, which also contains a sub-chapter in regard to sports. In November 2019, the Action Plan was extended until the end of 2021, because developing a new action plan for 2021–2030 has gone along with several coordination problems (18/7 MRV from 31 October 2019). In 2022, the National Action Plan on Disability 2022–2030 was adopted.

In 2015, the Austrian Statistical Authority conducted a survey on disability in Austria. In this survey, the operationalisation of disability was based on the International Classification of Impairments, Disabilities and Handicaps (ICIDH) of the WHO. Based on this survey, nearly one-fifth (18.4%) of the people 15 years and older living in Austria face at least one form of permanent disability (within a range from light to severe disability), while a minimum of 5.2% (385,000 persons) face

Table 12.3 Disability in Austria

Type of disability	Percent
Mobility problems	14.1%
Nervous or psychological impairments	3.7%
Visual impairments	3.0%
Hearing impairments	2.1%
Mental or learning problems	0.8%
Voice and pronunciation problems	0.4%
Disabilities not assigned to a distinct category	5.1%

Source: Bundesministerium für Arbeit, Soziales und Konsumentenschutz (2017)

severe disabilities. The highest proportion is in the area of mobility problems (14.1%), followed by disabilities not assigned to a distinct category (5.1%), nervous or psychological impairments (3.7%), visual impairments (3.0%), hearing impairments (2.1%), mental or learning problems (0.8%), and voice or pronunciation problems (0.4%). Around 0.5% of the Austrian inhabitants, who are 15 years and older, depend on a wheelchair and 0.03% are classified as being blind. About 7.3% of the population reported multiple disabilities. In the age group 60 years and older the proportion of disability is nearly 2.5 times higher than in the age group between 20 and 60 (33.6% to 13.6%) and people with lower education levels are rather handicapped than people with higher education levels (24.6% to 9.3%). Gender differences are small and people not born in Austria are rather not handicapped than people born in Austria (14.1% to 19.3%) (Bundesministerium für Arbeit, Soziales und Konsumentenschutz, 2017) (Table 12.3).

Rise of Disability Sports in Austria

The *Hauptverband für Gehörlosen-Sport in Österreich* (Main Confederation for Deaf Sports in Austria) was the first disability sports association in Austria. It was founded in 1931. Since 1960—after several name changes—it was named *Österreichischer Gehörlosen Sportverband* (Austrian Deaf Sports Confederation, ÖGSV) (Österreichischer Gehörlosen Sportverband, 2020a). Reiter (2009) and Vock (2017)—both referring to Kneissl (1988)—describe three phases in the development of disability sports in Austria, beginning after World War II: the pioneer phase (1945–1973), the "perfection" phase (1974–1987) and the modern phase (since 1988). During the first phase the focus was on war victims. Disabled veterans started to organise sports programmes and competitions for their members, especially blind people and people with amputations. The first Austrian championship for people with disabilities took place in 1947 and the first sports club for people with disabilities was founded in 1948 in Linz. In 1948, the *Österreichische Versehrtensportverband* (ÖVSV, Austrian Invalidity Sports Association) was founded. In 1949, Austria hosted the winter games for deaf people. In 1951, the first formal educational programmes for coaching sports for people with disabilities were established, and since then, a week of sports for people with disabilities is carried out in Austria (Reiter, 2009; Vock, 2017).

The second phase was strongly influenced by the rise of international sports events like the first Winter Paralympic Games in 1976 and led to the internationalisation and professionalisation in the field of disability sports. In addition to war victims, other groups of people with disabilities were included in Austrian disability sports. In 1976, the ÖVSV was accepted as an extraordinary member in the BSO. In 1996, the ÖVSV was accepted as an ordinary member with special assignment by the BSO. The Austrian Paralympic Committee and Special Olympics Austria became ordinary members of the BSO as well. In 1984 and 1988, the Winter Paralympics were hosted in Innsbruck (Österreichischer Behindertensportverband, 2020a; Reiter, 2009; Vock, 2017).

In 1989, the name of the umbrella organisation was changed to *Österreichischer Behindertensportverband* (Austrian Disability Sports Organisation; ÖBSV) and so the focus was no longer on war victims (Österreichischer Behindertensportverband, 2020a; Reiter, 2009; Vock, 2017). In 1993, Special Olympics Austria was founded and the Special Olympics Winter Games were hosted in Schladming in Austria. They were the first winter games outside North America (Special Olympics Österreich, 2020a). In 1994, the Austrian Federation of Adapted Physical Activity (AFAPA) was founded. Its goal was the distribution of the concept of adapted physical activity in Austria (Dinold, 2010). It was closed in 2014. In 1998, the Austrian Paralympic Committee was founded (Österreichisches Paralympisches Committee, 2020b). Since 2003, the ÖBSV is an ordinary member of the BSO (without special assignment). In the same year the right of funding for disability sports was embedded in the Austrian law for sports promotion (Österreichischer Behindertensportverband, 2020a; Reiter, 2009; Vock, 2017) (Fig. 12.1).

12.3 The Disability Sports System

Structure of Disability Sports (Fig. 12.2)

Governmental Agents

In accordance with Article 15 of the Austrian *Bundes-Verfassungsgesetz* (Austrian Federal Constitution Law), the federal states are responsible for sports. Defining responsibility for sports on the basis of Article 77 of the *Bundes-Verfassungsgesetz* the Federal Ministry of Arts, Culture, Civil Service and Sport takes a leading role in sports in Austria and the responsibilities of the different agents are defined in the *Bundes-Sportförderungsgesetz*. The Federal Ministry of Arts, Culture, Civil Service and Sport defines disability sports as a cross-sectional subject and refers to high-performance disability sports as well as equality as major concerns. Equality is implemented through the promotion of the disability sports associations (ÖBSV, ÖPC, SOÖ), the integration of high-performance athletes with disabilities in the

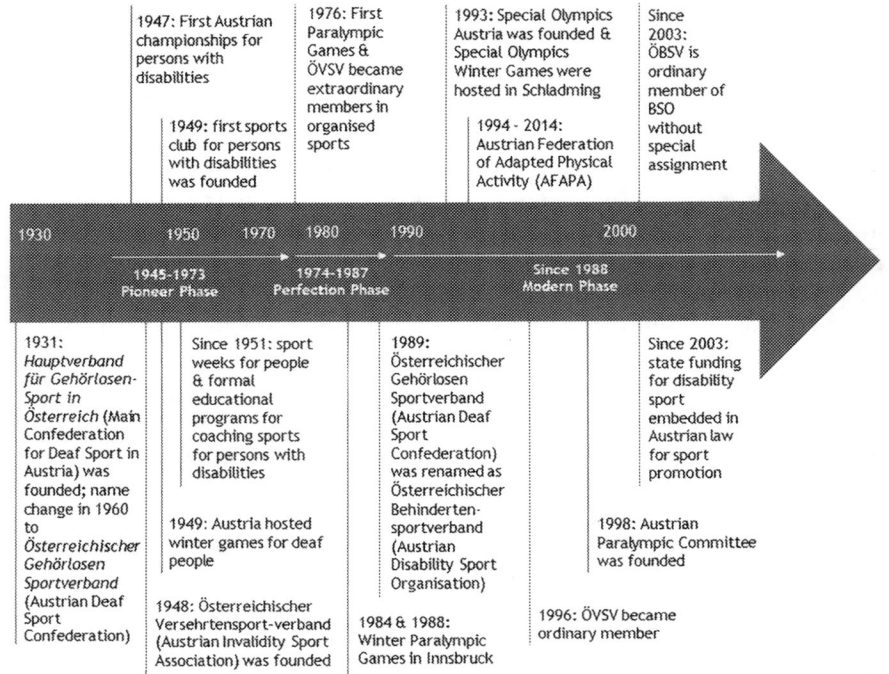

Fig. 12.1 The development of disability sports in Austria

stately subsidy programmes, supported by the *Sporthilfe*, and the integration of athletes with disabilities into sports federations (see below) (Bundesministerium für Kunst, Kultur, öffentlicher Dienst und Sport, 2020). At the state level, ministries that are responsible for several policies, such as sports, also have the responsibility for disability sports. In some states, the governor or the deputy governor is responsible for sports as well as disability sports. To coordinate disability sports between the federal ministry and the state ministries, the conference of ministers responsible for sports was established. On the local level, the municipalities are responsible for sports. The municipalities use the Austrian Association of Cities and Towns to discuss and coordinate their sports-related issues.

Intermediate Agents

In accordance with Scheerder et al. (2017), intermediate agents connect governmental actors and sports federations. In Austria, these intermediate agents are *not* sports confederations. The intermediate agents have different legal forms, ranging from public corporations to non-profit organisations. Four intermediate agents play a central role in the disability sports system at the federal level—primarily in regard to financing disability sports. First, the *Bundes-Sport GmbH*—a public corporation—plays an

12 Austria: Half Way to Inclusion?

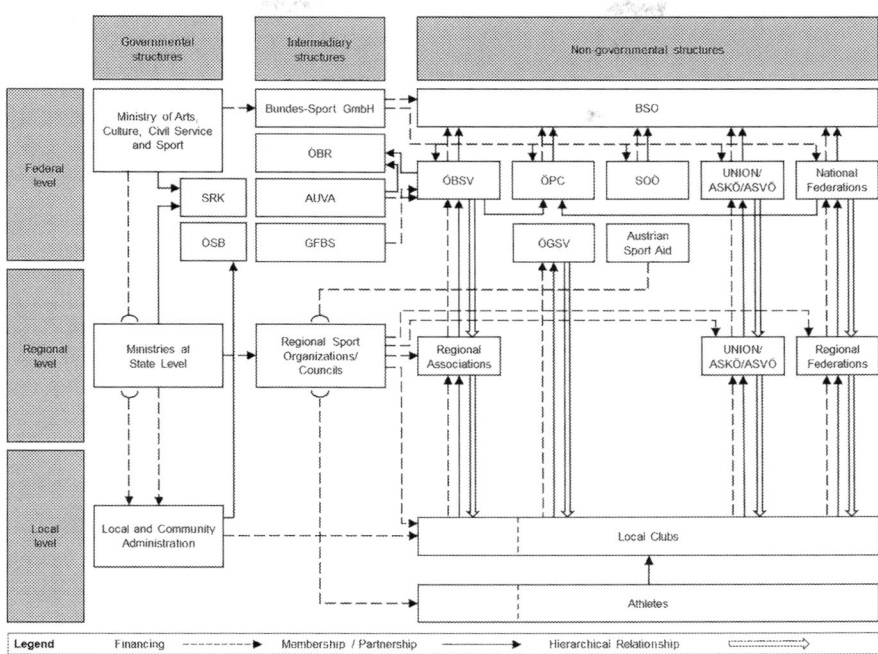

Fig. 12.2 The structure of disability sports in Austria. Notes: *AUVA* General Accident Insurance Institution, *BSO* Austrian Sports Organisation; Bundes-Sport *GmbH* Federal Sports Ltd., *GFBS* Company for the Promotion of Disability Sport, *ÖBR* Austrian Disability Council, *ÖBSV* Austrian Disability Sports Association, *ÖGSV* Austrian Deaf Sports Confederation, *ÖPC* Austrian Paralympic Committee, *ÖSB* Austrian Association of Cities, *SOÖ* Special Olympics Austria, *SRK* Sports Minister Conference

important role. It administrates the money that the federal government grants to the non-state sports organisations based on the *Bundes-Sportförderungsgesetz*. Second, the *Allgemeine Unfallversicherungsanstalt* (General Accident Insurance Institution, AUVA)—a public corporation established on the basis of paragraph 24 of the *Allgemeine Sozialversicherungsgesetz* (Social Security Law)—also funds parts of the organised disability sports system (*Österreichischer Behindertensportverband*, ÖBSV). Third, both, AUVA and ÖBSV, are members of the *Österreichischer Behindertenrat* (Austrian Disability Council), a non-profit lobby organisation for disability interests. Fourth, the *Gesellschaft zur Förderung des Behindertensports* (Company for the Promotion of Disability Sport, GFBS) plays an important role in financing the ÖBSV as a private rights marketer that exclusively manages the sponsoring relationships of the ÖBSV (Österreichischer Behindertensportverband, 2020b, 2020h). The GFBS is a limited liability company with one associate that is a private entity outside the ÖBSV.

At the state level, regional sports organisations/councils act on behalf of the governments in most Austrian states. Their composition and tasks are defined through sports laws at the state level.

Non-governmental Agents

In Austria, there are four disability sports organisations: ÖGSV, ÖBSV, ÖPC and SOÖ. In addition, all federal sport for all associations are voluntary organisations. The ÖGSV promotes high-performance sport for deaf people, sport for all and youth sport. It has 13 clubs as members and is a member of the European Deaf Sports Organisation and the International Committee of Sports for the Deaf (Österreichischer Gehörlosen Sportverband, 2020b, 2020c).

Sport for all, as well as elite sports, is included in the ÖBSV. The confederation has the following goals (§3 of the statutes of the ÖBSV):

- Promotion of sports for adults and young people with disabilities to strengthen their health, to regain and maintain their physical abilities and to promote their active participation, independence and social inclusion
- To promote and support the work of their regional affiliates and local clubs
- To build relationships with national and international disability sports associations and to represent Austrian disability sports nationally and internationally

The ÖBSV is a member of the BSO and the ÖPC and has regional affiliates in all nine Austrians states. Following the goal of inclusive policy, the ÖBSV cooperates with the following 14 sports governing bodies in regard to the development of high-performance disability sports: archery, badminton, billiards, bob and skeleton, canoe, climbing, golf, ice hockey, karate, riding, rowing, sailing, ski and snowboard, table tennis, taekwondo, tennis, triathlon, and wrestling. Another 18 sports are on the future agenda of the ÖBSV in regard to developing cooperation and partnerships (Österreichischer Behindertensportverband, 2020d). In summary, the Austrian sports system seems to be somewhere in between an inclusive sports system that includes people with disabilities into the overall sports system and a twofold sports system that builds on specific disability sports organisations as well as on inclusion of people with disabilities into the overall sports system. The relationship between the mainstream sports federations and the disability sports federations is complex and versatile. This makes it difficult to identify overall cooperation patterns.

Internationally, the ÖBSV is a member of the Cerebral Palsy International Sports and Recreation Association (CPISRA), the International Blind Sports Association (IBSA), the International Sports Federation for Persons with Intellectual Disability (INAS), the International Wheelchair and Amputee Sports Federation (IWAS), the International Wheelchair Basketball Federation (IWBF), the International Wheelchair Rugby Federation (IWRF), the International Federation of CP-Football (IFCPF) and the Federation Internationale De Powerchair Football Association (FIPFA) (Österreichischer Behindertensportverband, 2020f).

The ÖBSV organises sports weeks for people with disabilities each year. Since 2014, it also organises school games for students with disabilities (in the beginning in Vienna only; in 2019 also in Linz). It organises national championships for people with disabilities in several sports and offers inclusive education for sports coaches in different kinds of sports for people with a disability (Österreichischer Behindertensportverband, 2019). To prevent sexual assault, the ÖBSV cooperates with the BSO, the club "100% Sport" (*Österreichisches Zentrum für*

Genderkompetenz im Sport; Austrian centre for gender qualification in sports) and a working group against sexual assault in sports that is organised by the state (Österreichischer Behindertensportverband, 2020c).

The ÖPC was founded in 1998. It is independent from the national Olympic committee and was founded by the ÖBSV with the goal of sending athletes to the Paralympic Games (preamble of the statutes of the ÖPC). Aside the ÖBSV and its regional affiliates, the mainstream Austrian federal sports federations can become members of the ÖPC which supports, promotes and integrates sports for people with a disability (§5 of the statutes of the ÖPC). While the mission of the ÖBSV has a broader scope, the mission of the ÖPC is focused on the promotion of high-performance sport for people with a disability and promotion of the Paralympic movement in Austria (§3 of the statutes of the ÖPC).

SOÖ describes the promotion of sports for people with intellectual disabilities as well as striving for an inclusive society as its main goals. It organises national Special Olympic Games in a two-year cycle and promotes programmes like Special Olympic Unified Sports, or an educational initiative for sports and inclusion in Austrian schools. In addition, it organises different competitions in several kinds of sports and sends athletes to the Special Olympic World Games (Special Olympics Österreich, 2020c).

Secondary Agents

Non-sports organisations like the Austrian General Accident Insurance Institution (AUVA) also offer disability sports programmes in their rehabilitation centres. Their main goal is the rehabilitation of people with disabilities (Allgemeine Unfallversicherung, 2020).

Steering of Disability Sport

Relationships

The relationship between the state and mainstream non-governmental agents can be considered as principal-agent relationships. They are moderated primarily through the *Bundes-Sport GmbH* (BSG) and regional sports organisations/councils. The state defines general goals and rules for the distribution of funding by disability and sports laws while the dissemination of the money is coordinated between the intermediary and the disability sports organisations. On the intermediary level, the mainstream sports organisations play a major role. Different ministries appoint two members to the supervisory board of the BSG—one by the ministry responsible for finance and one by the ministry responsible for sport. Additional members are appointed by the BSO, from which one has to be appointed upon recommendation of the Austrian Olympic Committee (§33 of the *Bundes-Sportförderungsgesetz*). In addition to the supervisory board, the BSG has two other bodies whose members get elected: the commission for sport for all and the commission for high-performance sport. Two members of the commission for sport for all get appointed by the sports ministry and four by the BSO. The same principle is applied to the commission for high-performance sport: two members are appointed by the sports ministry and four by the BSO. From these four BSO members, two have to be elected from the summer Olympic sports federations, one from the winter Olympic sports federations and one from a sports federation that is not Olympic. Members from disability sports organisations can't be appointed or elected to any of these boards (§36–§37 of the *Bundes-Sportförderungsgesetz*).

Similar frameworks exist in nearly all Austrian states. All of them have regional sports organisations/councils that are responsible for the promotion of sports, or they have an advisory role related to the ministry. All of these consist of members from the ministry and the non-state sports organisations. Some of their members are from the state parliament. Only in Tyrol, where the *Landessportrat* (Regional Sports Council) has only an advisory role, one out of 15 members has to come from a regional disability sports organisation.

In summary, this shows that especially on the regional level the disability sports organisations are not very influential. On the federal level, it looks differently, because laws that address the needs of people with disabilities on the federal level provide a legal framework that gives disability sports more attention than on the regional level. This legal framework is addressed in the next section.

Legislative Framework

The legislative framework for disability sports is primarily defined through the *Bundes-Behindertengleichstellungsgesetz* (BGStG) and the *Bundes-Sportförderungsgesetz* (BSFG), sports laws and sports promotion guidelines on the state level, and sports promotion guidelines on the local level.

The goal of the BGStG is to eliminate or to prevent discrimination against people with disabilities and to enable participation and self-determined lifestyles for people with disabilities (§1). Based on this legally defined objective, excluding members of disability sports organisations from the board and the commissions of the BSG needs to be challenged. The law prohibits discrimination against people with disabilities and people that have close relationships with them (§4). Eight of the nine Austrian states have equivalent laws on the state level (in Burgenland an equivalent law is under construction). In the Upper Austrian *Chancengleichheitsgesetz* (law on equal opportunities) the state has the obligation to ensure programmes for the promotion of sports activity for people with disabilities (§17 section 2 no. 5). The BGStG and the other state laws do not address the topic of sports explicitly.

The BSFG defines the inclusion of people with disabilities into sports as one of its 13 goals (§2). It defines the promotion of disability sports and the inclusion of people with disabilities into sports as one of its promotional subjects (§7, §9, §14). The promotional subjects are further defined in §13 section 4 for the ÖPC, §13 section 5 for the ÖBSV and §13 section 6 for SOÖ. The ÖBSV and the federal sports federations have the obligation to work together with each other in regard to disability sports (§20). On the state level, each of the nine Austrians states has a sports law. In six of these sports laws disability sports is addressed explicitly. In Upper Austria and Tyrol the laws define the promotion of sports in all its manifestations—explicitly mentioning disability sports as one of these manifestations (in both laws §1). In Styria equal sports participation irrespective of personal characteristics like age, sex, disabilities and others is defined as an objective (§1). In Burgenland, Carinthia and Lower Austria the promotion of disability sports is defined as one of the promotional tasks. It is important to note that the term *Versehrtensport* (sports for "damaged" people) is still used in Carinthia (§1) and Lower Austria's law (§2) uses the terminological combination of *Versehrten- und Behindertensport* (sports for "damaged" and people with disabilities). The sports laws of Salzburg, Vienna and Vorarlberg do not refer explicitly to disability sports. In the state of Burgenland the sports promotion guidelines offer special funding for the construction or renovation of spectator facilities with a focus on accessibility. In Salzburg, individual promotion of high-performance athletes with disabilities through the Salzburg Sports Aid is regulated via the sports promotion guidelines, but not by law. In the sports promotion guidelines of Vienna (not a law), sports promotion in general as well as promotion of sports events is linked to the integration of disabled sport. In sum, the only state that does not refer to disability sports in its legal framework is Vorarlberg. Although nearly all Austrian regional states refer in some way to the promotion of disability sport, none of the sports laws on a state level refer to the inclusion of people with disabilities into the mainstream sports system like the BSFG does.

At the local level, the municipalities have the ability to define their legal framework for sports promotion through guidelines. Based on a survey with members of the ÖSB, around two-thirds of the municipalities do have such guidelines and around 9% of these guidelines refer to the integration and inclusion of "disadvantaged people"—which may include people with disabilities (Schantl et al., 2014).

Policy Framework

The National Action Plan on Disability 2012–2020 was developed to implement the UN Convention on the Rights of Persons with Disabilities. This programme concludes that disability sports is not included in the overall sports system yet. It defines the following objectives in regard to disability sports: inclusion of disability sports into the overall sports system, establishing accessibility in public spaces, the expansion of sports programmes for people with disabilities, the follow-up of an adopted strategy for improving sports facilities and establishing sports programmes for persons with disabilities outside high-performance sport. The plan includes several specific tasks: promoting disability sports within the scope of health promotion and disease prevention, including interpretations into sign language when giving state funding for sports events, access as a requirement for state funding for building or restoring sports facilities, establishing more media presence for disability sport, a stronger integration of sports and disability sports into the health system, conducting a longitudinal study on the effects of sports on health of people with disabilities, ongoing promotion of KADA (non-profit organisation for the support of athletes after their sporting career), and disability-specific education for teachers of Physical Education (Bundesministerium für Arbeit, Soziales und Konsumentenschutz, 2012). The federal ministry perceives most of these tasks as partly implemented, only the last two tasks as fully implemented (Bundesministerium für Arbeit, Soziales und Konsumentenschutz, 2015). The Austrian National Council of Persons with Disabilities (2013) criticises that the promotion of disability sports is focused mainly on high-performance sport and that due to the lack of an inclusive educational system in Austria, sports activities for children with disabilities are not equally promoted in schools.

The *Nationaler Aktionsplan Bewegung* (National Action Plan for Physical Activity) is also an important policy programme. It highlights the inclusion of people with disabilities in developing multi-division sports clubs (i.e. sports clubs with several types of sport in one club) with a focus on health promotion. It mentions the benefits of sports for people with disabilities several times (Bundesministerium für Landesverteidigung und Sport, 2013).

In addition, the *Regierungsprogramm 2020–2024* (the coalition agreement) between the ÖVP and the Austrian Greens includes the following objectives: the promotion of disability sports, the inclusion of people with disabilities into overall sports and access to sports facilities for athletes with disabilities as well as for spectators with disabilities (Die Neue Volkspartei & Die Grünen, 2019). In coalition agreements of four out of nine states, the promotion of disability sports (Salzburg, Tyrol) or the inclusion of people with disabilities in the overall sports system (Salzburg, Styria, Vienna) is addressed as well.

Financial, Governance and Managerial Support

Financial Framework

Sports in Austria are funded by the state on all political levels. On the federal level, the money comes mainly from gambling based on §20 of the *Glücksspielgesetz* (gambling law). The BSFG explicitly refers to the responsibility of the federal states and the autonomy of the sports organisations (§2). The BSG allocates it to sports organisations on the federal level. However, sports organisations still have to apply for funding from the BSG. The management level of the BSG decides about it, if necessary with approval of its boards.

Based on §5 and §13 of the BSFG, sports organisations with special tasks have to receive 5% of the overall sports funding plus additionally at least €1,110,000. These organisations are the BSO, the Austrian Olympic Committee, the ÖBSV, the ÖPC, and SOÖ. From this money, the ÖBSV can claim 21.25%, the ÖPC 8% and SOÖ 4%. In 2019, €86,000,000 was spent in total via the BSG on sports organisations at the federal level. The ÖBSV received around €1,330,000, the ÖPC around €630,000 and SOÖ around €370,000. In sum, disability sports organisations at the federal level received around €2,330,000 or 2.7% from the total budget of sports funding (data from Bundes-Sport GmbH, 2020) (Table 12.4).

Table 12.4 National funding of Austrian disability sports organisations (2019)

Organisation	Funding
Austrian Disability Sports Organisation (ÖBSV)	€1,330,000
Austrian Paralympic Committee (ÖPC)	€630,000
Special Olympics Austria (SOÖ)	€370,000

Source: Bundes-Sport GmbH (2020)

Additionally, the ÖBSV receives funding from the AUVA and the Company for the Promotion of Disability Sports (GFBS) (Österreichischer Behindertensportverband, 2020b). How much money the ÖBSV gets from these organisations remains unknown. The ÖBSV complains that the shift from inclusion of athletes with disabilities to the general sports federations leads to a decrease in funds for the ÖBSV (Österreichischer Behindertensportverband, 2020b). On the individual level, high-performance athletes with disabilities may receive funding from the Austrian *Sporthilfe* (Sports Aid), which is a non-profit organisation (Sporthilfe, 2020).

On the state level, the regional affiliates of the ÖBSV are funded by the regional states (in many states via their regional sports organisations/councils). How much money the states spend on sports and disability sports is hard to estimate, because this information is only partially available publicly. Fritz et al. (2004) estimate the total amount between €80,000,000 and €119,000,000 for sports from the Austrian federal states in 2000. More recent estimations show higher sums. In 2015, Burgenland spent a total sum of €3,862,600 on sports from which €17,822 (0.46%) was spent on disability sports (Sport Burgenland, 2018). In 2017, Lower Austria spent €20,426,176 on sports from which €98,604 (0.47%) was spent on disability sports, and Tyrol spent €22,280,529 on sports from which €70,400 (0.32%) was spent on disability sports (Amt der Niederösterreichischen Landesregierung, 2018; Landesrechnungshof Tirol, 2018). For 2019, the state of Salzburg planned to spend €4,935,200 on sports from which around €22,000 (0.44%) should have been spent on disability sports (Land Salzburg, 2019). For 2015, the state of Carinthia invested €7,460,000 into sports (Landesrechnungshof Kärnten, 2017); the proportion of money spent on disability sports is unknown. Taking the mean of the sums of these five states, one can estimate a total spending of the Austrian states on sports around €129,720,000. Taking a mean percentage of 0.42% for disability sports, one can estimate a total spending of around €545,000 on disability sports by the Austrian states.

On the local level, Austrian municipalities invest around €560,000,000 each year on sports (Schantl et al., 2014). The proportion of money spent on disability sports is unknown.

Governance and Management Support

Together with the federal and regional associations of the ASKÖ, ASVÖ and SPORTUNION, the BSO offers a certified training programme (free of charge) on a workshop basis in the field of mainstream sports management. Full-time members, as well as voluntary members, of the Austrian sports clubs and regional or national associations/federations are invited to participate in these courses. The participants have to participate in nine mandatory modules (each module takes four hours) and two elective modules (Bundes-Sportorganisation, 2020a). In addition, the SPORTUNION offers management training courses via its academy. The SPORTUNION Academy and the *Deutsche Sportakademie* (German Sports Academy) also jointly offer distance learning programmes for the *Sportbetriebswirt* (sports business economist) and *Sportfachwirt* (sports business administrator) (Deutsche Sportakademie, 2020; SPORTUNION Akademie, 2020). The ASKÖ and the ASVÖ offer some management training activities as well, but fewer in total.

Education and training programmes for coaches are mainly offered by the *Bundessportakademie* (Federal Sports Academy, BSA)—which is a public school in four locations: Graz, Innsbruck, Linz and Vienna. The BSA offers education programmes for mainstream sports instructors, sports coaches, diploma sports coaches and sports teachers on a course base. It also offers a six-semester full-time programme for diploma sports teachers (on school level following level 8). Since 2012, BSA and ÖBSV jointly offer courses about disability sports as part of instructor and coaching education programmes (Bundessportakademie, 2020; Österreichischer Behindertensportverband, 2020e). The regional sports federations organise training courses for their respective sports—some of them in cooperation with the ÖBSV and related to disability sports.

Level of Integration or Inclusion

As described above, people with disabilities have equal access to sports opportunities, facilities and activities by law in Austria. The policy framework targets a better inclusion of people with disabilities into society in general and sports in particular. Several objectives were defined and accomplished more or less. Nevertheless, there is still a long way to go to reach full inclusion. At the moment, it seems that people with disabilities are stuck somewhere in the middle. On the one hand, specific sports organisations like ÖBSV, ÖGSV, ÖPC and SOÖ offer sports for people with disabilities. On the other hand, there is a clear tendency for a better inclusivity of people with disabilities into overall sports. This seems to weaken the power and influence of disability sports organisations and pushes them to cooperate with the overall sports organisations. However, it also puts pressure on the overall sports organisations, because they are expected to include people with disabilities into their overall sports programmes. In order to do that they need to further develop their knowledge and expertise. The education and training programmes of the BSA and the regional sports organisations offer programmes in this field for coaches. This enables coaches in disability sports organisations and in overall sports organisations to further develop their competencies and to deal with this challenge. If the current situation is a transition period that will lead into a more inclusive sports system or if the duality of specific disability sports organisations and overall sports organisations that also include people with disabilities into their daily sports activities remains still unknown. The political initiatives concerning disability sports are twofold. On the one hand, they demand a stronger inclusion of people with disabilities into the overall sports system, and on the other hand, they promote specific disability sports actions and organisations. This may be the result of political struggles about how sports for people with disabilities should be organised.

12.4 Sports Participation by People with Disabilities

Monitoring and Evaluation

There is not much data on sports participation in Austria available—especially in the field of disability sports. As mentioned above, with the National Action Plan on Disability 2012–2020 a longitudinal study of the effects of sports on the health of people with disabilities was planned. The progress report from 2015 mentioned first considerations concerning the design of a long-term study (Bundesministerium für Arbeit, Soziales und Konsumentenschutz, 2015). This seems to be the current status quo. What exists to date is the official statistics from the BSO about club numbers and individual memberships in the ÖBSV on the one hand (please see data below in long-term perspective). On the other hand, some data was generated with the 2014 health study regarding disability and physical activity (see also below).

Sports Participation

Membership in Disability Sports

The BSO publishes membership statistics of their members every year on their homepage. These data go back to 1998 and allow a longitudinal perspective. The statistics contain the club numbers and the individual memberships of the different sports and of special sports like disability sports. This data is matched with the base of the membership reports of the affiliated organisations. These may entail some inaccuracies. One reason may be multiple memberships of individuals that are members of more than one sports club. These individuals are counted multiple times. The other inaccuracy is a content-wise issue, equalling membership with sports participation. This may lead to an over-interpretation of sports participation rates, because passive members are counted, too.

The number of clubs and memberships in disability sports includes the number of clubs and memberships from ÖBSV and ÖGSV. The club number has fluctuated between 83 and 118 over the last 20 years. Considering that the ÖGSV counts 13 clubs to date, most likely, around 10–15% of these clubs are clubs of the ÖGSV and 85–90% of the ÖBSV (Fig. 12.3).

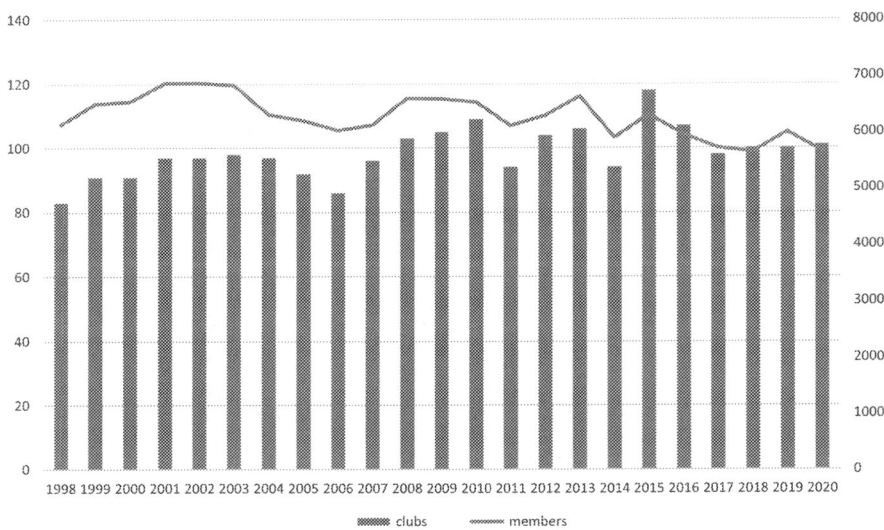

Fig. 12.3 Membership in disability sports in Austria (data from the membership statistics of the BSO; memberships of ÖBSV and ÖGSV). Source: https://www.sportaustria.at/de/ueber-uns/mitglieder/mitgliederstatistik/

The individual memberships in disability sports organisations fluctuate between 5642 in 2018 and 6678 in 2001/2002. Over time, it shows a slight decline. From 1998 until 2020 the membership statistics list explicitly the amount of supportive individual members in disability sports. It shows between 2126 and 2914 supportive non-active members. This means a proportion between 30.9% and 47.5%. This leads to the conclusion that the real sports participation of people with disability in disability sports clubs is around one-third to half smaller than the numbers reported. Based on this data, one can estimate that in relation to the appreciated 385,000 persons with severe disabilities only around 1% participate in organised sports in the ÖBSV or the ÖGSV. There is no data available that shows how this proportion will change when adding the—unknown—number of people with disabilities in SOÖ clubs or in overall sports clubs. However, it may not go up significantly.

If the fluctuations of numbers of clubs and memberships reflect a real fluctuation, or if it is an artefact of the data collection method, remains unknown and, thus, needs further analysis. If the decline in individual membership displays real fluctuation, it is possible that this is an effect of the ongoing inclusion policy that tries to integrate athletes with disabilities into the overall sports system. Nevertheless, this can only be assumed and not be supported by existing data.

The ÖBSV offers a broad spectrum of 34 different sports, including alpine skiing, archery, badminton, basketball, bicycling, billiards, boccia, canoeing, climbing, dancing, ice hockey, fencing, football, goalball, golf, judo, karate, Nordic skiing, riding, rowing, rugby, sailing, shooting, showdown, sitting ball, skittles, swimming, table tennis, taekwondo, tennis, torball, track and field, triathlon and weightlifting (Österreichischer Behindertensportverband, 2020g). The ÖGSV offers 16 different sports for its members: alpine skiing, badminton, beach volleyball, cycling, bowling, futsal, orienteering, running, skittles, snowboard, *Stocksport* (a sport similar to curling), table tennis, tennis, track and field, volleyball and wrestling (Österreichischer Gehörlosensportverband, 2020d). The ÖPC lists the following sports: alpine skiing, archery, badminton, biathlon, bicycling, boccia, canoeing, cross-country skiing, football five-a-side, goalball, ice sledge hockey, judo, riding, rowing, shooting, snowboard, swimming, table tennis, taekwondo, triathlon, track and field, weightlifting, wheelchair basketball, wheelchair curling, wheelchair dancing, wheelchair fencing, wheelchair rugby and wheelchair tennis (Österreichisches Paralympisches Committee, 2020a, 2020c). Special Olympics Austria includes the following sports: alpine skiing, basketball, bicycling, boccia, bowling, dancing, figure skating, floorball, floor hockey, football, golf, judo, motor activities training programmes, Nordic skiing, powerlifting, open water, riding, sailing, sitting volleyball, snowboard, snowshoe tracking, speed skating, *Stocksport*, swimming, table tennis, tennis, track and field, and volleyball (Special Olympics Österreich, 2020b).

Empirical Data on Sports Participation of People with Disabilities

A national health survey called Österreichische Gesundheitsbefragung 2014 (Austrian Health Interview Survey 2014, ATHIS) was conducted by Statistik Austria (the Austrian Statistical Institution). In this survey 15,771 people 15 years and older were interviewed using computer-assisted telephone interviewing (CATI) in combination with an additional written questionnaire. The survey was conducted between October 2013 and June 2015. The questionnaire was based on the European Health Interview Survey (EHIS). The first part of the questionnaire (online survey) contained questions about physical and sensory functional limitations (seeing, hearing, walking) and the second part of the questionnaire (written questionnaire) contained some questions about physical activity and sports (sports, fitness or recreational leisure activities, bicycling and muscle-strengthening activities). The report presents findings on these topics, specifically with regard to age groups and sex (Statistik Austria, 2015). The report does not contain any data on physical activity and sports in relation to physical and sensory functional limitations. The presented findings below were computed with R Studio version 1.2.5033 using the data of ATHIS. The dataset was provided by Statistik Austria. The used items of the survey are presented in the appendix.

Table 12.5 shows the results for sports and physical activity of people with disabilities in their leisure time. All relationships between the analysed forms of disability and sports and physical activity are significant. However, one has to keep in mind that the total numbers of people that are blind or nearly blind ($N = 14$) and hard of hearing or deaf ($N = 7$; $N = 6$) are very low, so that these percentages have to be interpreted very cautiously.

As Table 12.5 shows there is a slight decrease in sports and physical activity for those with some difficulty in seeing and hearing and a stronger decrease for those with a lot of difficulty in these. The relationships are weak (Somers' d between 0.046 and 0.087). For people with difficulty in walking, the decrease is even

Table 12.5 Sports and physical activity of people with disabilities in Austria (minimum 10 minutes/week)

	No difficulty	Some difficulty	A lot of difficulty	Blind or nearly blind/hard of hearing or deaf/can't do it
Difficulty in seeing	74.4% (N = 10,055)	71.1% (N = 1487)	53.8% (N = 78)	57.1% (N = 8)
Difficulty in hearing in quiet rooms	74.3% (N = 11,011)	67.5% (N = 584)	43.4% (N = 33)	42.9% (N = 3)
Difficulty in hearing in noisy rooms	75.2% (N = 8822)	70.7% (N = 2514)	62.4% (N = 290)	33.3% (N = 2)
Difficulty in walking without walking aid	74.9% (N = 11,216)	57.9% (N = 242)	45.4% (N = 108)	50.7% (N = 69)
Difficulty in walking up or down	75.6% (N = 11,071)	54.6% (N = 418)	42.9% (N = 115)	44.3% (N = 31)

Source: Austrian Health Interview Survey 2014 (data provided by Statistik Austria; coding: 1 = yes, 2 = no or less than once a week; p_{all} = 0.000; Somers' $d_{\text{Difficulty in Seeing}}$ = 0.046; Somers' $d_{\text{Difficulty in hearing quiet rooms}}$ = 0.087; Somers' $d_{\text{Difficulty in hearing noisy rooms}}$ = 0.054; Somers' $d_{\text{Difficulty in walking}}$ = 0.218; Somers' $d_{\text{Difficulty in walking up or down}}$ = 0.242)

Table 12.6 Cycling of people with disabilities in Austria (minimum 10 minutes/week)

	No difficulty	Some difficulty	A lot of difficulty	Blind or nearly blind/ hard of hearing or deaf/can't do it
Difficulty in seeing	26.7% (N = 3606)	24.3% (N = 508)	18.6% (N = 27)	21.4% (N = 3)
Difficulty in hearing in quiet rooms	26.5% (N = 3924)	24.1% (N = 209)	14.7% (N = 11)	14.3% (N = 1)
Difficulty in hearing in noisy rooms	26.0% (N = 3048)	27.3% (N = 972)	26.5% (N = 123)	16.7% (N = 1)
Difficulty in walking without walking aid	26.7% (N = 3997)	23.2% (N = 97)	16.4% (N = 39)	9.6% (N = 13)
Difficulty in walking up or down	26.8% (N = 3931)	22.2% (N = 170)	14.6% (N = 39)	8.6% (N = 6)

Source: Austrian Health Interview Survey 2014 (data provided by Statistik Austria; coding: 1 = yes, 2 = no or less than once a week; $p_{\text{Difficulty in seeing}}$ = 0.033; Somers' $d_{\text{Difficulty in seeing}}$ = 0.028; $p_{\text{Difficulty in hearing quiet rooms}}$ = 0.059; Somers' $d_{\text{Difficulty in hearing quiet rooms}}$ = 0.031; $p_{\text{Difficulty in hearing noisy rooms}}$ = 0.377; Somers' $d_{\text{Difficulty in hearing noisy rooms}}$ = −0.012; $p_{\text{Difficulty in walking}}$ = 0.000; Somers' $d_{\text{Difficulty in walking}}$ = 0.079; $p_{\text{Difficulty in walking up or down}}$ = 0.000; Somers' $d_{\text{Difficulty in walking up or down}}$ = 0.074)

stronger in relation to those who have no difficulty compared to those with a lot of difficulty to those with some difficulty. The relationships are medium (Somers' d 0.218–0.242).

Table 12.6 shows the results for cycling of people with disabilities in their leisure time. Again, one has to keep in mind that the total number of people that are blind or nearly blind (N = 14) and hard of hearing or deaf (N = 7; N = 6) are very low so that these percentages have to be interpreted very cautiously.

Table 12.7 Muscle-strengthening activities of people with disabilities in Austria

	No difficulty	Some difficulty	A lot of difficulty	Blind or nearly blind/ hard of hearing or deaf/can't do it
Difficulty in seeing	44.9% (N = 6065)	42.3% (N = 885)	37.2% (N = 54)	28.6% (N = 4)
Difficulty in hearing in quiet rooms	44.8% (N = 6641)	39.9% (N = 345)	26.3% (N = 20)	42.9% (N = 3)
Difficulty in hearing in noisy rooms	45.4% (N = 5321)	42.6% (N = 1515)	36.1% (N = 168)	33.3% (N = 2)
Difficulty in walking without walking aid	44.9% (N = 6731)	35.2% (N = 147)	31.9% (N = 76)	41.9% (N = 57)
Difficulty in walking up or down	45.3% (N = 6648)	32.5% (N = 249)	32.8% (N = 88)	37.1% (N = 26)

Source: Austrian Health Interview Survey 2014 (data provided by Statistik Austria; coding: 1 = yes, 2 = no or less than once a week; $p_{\text{Difficulty in seeing}} = 0.028$; Somers' $d_{\text{Difficulty in seeing}} = 0.029$; $p_{\text{Difficulty in hearing quiet rooms}} = 0.001$; Somers' $d_{\text{Difficulty in hearing quiet rooms}} = 0.058$; $p_{\text{Difficulty in hearing noisy rooms}} = 0.000$; Somers' $d_{\text{Difficulty in hearing noisy rooms}} = 0.035$; $p_{\text{Difficulty in walking}} = 0.000$; Somers' $d_{\text{Difficulty in walking}} = 0.094$; $p_{\text{Difficulty in walking up or down}} = 0.000$; Somers' $d_{\text{Difficulty in walking up or down}} = 0.122$)

As Table 12.6 shows, there is nearly no decrease in cycling for those with some difficulty in seeing and a stronger decrease for those with a lot of difficulty. The relationship is weak (Somers' $d = 0.028$). The results in line two and three of people with difficulty in hearing are not significant. For people with difficulty in walking, again, there is nearly no decrease for those having some difficulty and a stronger decrease for those with a lot of difficulty. The relationships are weak as well (Somers' d 0.74–0.079).

Table 12.7 shows the results for muscle-strengthening of people with disabilities in their leisure time. All relationships between the analysed forms of disability and muscle-strengthening are significant, although one has to keep in mind, again, that the total numbers for the group of persons that are blind or nearly blind ($N = 14$) and hard of hearing or deaf ($N = 7$; $N = 6$) are very low so that these percentages have to be interpreted very cautiously.

As Table 12.7 shows, there is a slight decrease in muscle-strengthening activities for those with some difficulty in seeing and hearing and a stronger decrease for those with a lot of difficulty—especially for those having difficulty hearing in quiet rooms. The relationships are weak (Somers' d between 0.029 and 0.058). For people with difficulty in walking the decrease is, again, even stronger for those having some difficulty in relation to those who have no difficulty compared to those with a lot of difficulty to those with some difficulty. The relationships are weak as well (Somers' d 0.094–0.122).

Because of the scarce empirical research in regard to the participation of people with disabilities, it is not possible to draw substantial conclusions about barriers and facilitators that influence sports participation of people with disabilities.

12.5 Conclusion

In Austria, disability was traditionally viewed from a medical perspective. The developments that took place on the UN and EU level spilled over to Austria and initiated a change in the direction of a social perspective on disability and a more inclusive approach to disability and disability sports. In the 1930s, specific disability sports organisations were developed in Austria and are currently a fixed part of the Austrian sports system. The three largest organisations are members of the BSO and receive state funding from the intermediate *Bundes-Sport GmbH*, guaranteed by law. From a theoretical perspective, the system can be described as a principal-agent system with co-governance between the state and non-governmental sports organisations that are connected through the intermediate *Bundes-Sport* GmbH.

Policy initiatives concerning disability exist that also include tasks in regard to disability sports. These tasks demand a stronger inclusion of people with disabilities into sports in general on the one hand and a promotion of the existing disability sports structures on the other hand. Currently, the Austrian sports system seems to be somewhere in between an inclusive sports system that includes people with disabilities into the overall sports system and a double-structured sports system that builds on specific disability sports organisations as well as on inclusion of people with disabilities into the overall sports system. The future remains unclear, while there seem to be tendencies towards a more inclusive system.

Data on sports participation of people with disabilities in Austria are rare. In the *Nationaler Aktionsplan Behinderung 2012–2020* a longitudinal study aimed to analyse the effects of sports on people with disabilities, but it was not conducted yet. However, the membership statistics of the BSO allow some conclusions about membership of people with disabilities in the Austrian disability sports organisations ÖBSV and ÖGSV. This data suggests that only around 1% of the people with disabilities in Austria participate in specific disability sports organisations. Findings from the Austrian Health Interview Survey 2014 show that people with disabilities participate less in sports activities than people without disabilities and that this gap is increasing with the severity of disability.

Currently, people with disabilities are underrepresented in the Austrian sports system even though the system includes specific sports offers and, as politically claimed, the opportunity for people with disabilities to participate in the overall sports organisations. Due to the lack of specific empirical data on sports participation of people with disabilities, unfortunately, it is not possible to present more detailed information in this regard to date. Hence, more empirical research is needed.

Acknowledgements The authors would like to thank Angela Scalet for her support on the preparation of Fig. 12.1 and Statistik Austria for providing the data of the ATHIS study.

Appendix: ATHIS Items (English Version)

- Question PL2 (difficulty in seeing)

    Respondents wearing glasses:
    Do you have difficulty seeing even when wearing your glasses or contact lenses? Would you say ...
    Respondents not wearing glasses:
    Do you have difficulty seeing? Would you say ...

    1. No difficulty
    2. Some difficulty
    3. A lot of difficulty
    4. Cannot do at all/Unable to do

- Question PL4 (difficulty in hearing in quiet rooms)

    Respondents with hearing aid:
    Do you have difficulty hearing what is said in a conversation with one other person in a quiet room, even when using your hearing aid? Would you say ...
    Respondents without hearing aid:
    Do you have difficulty hearing what is said in a conversation with one other person in a quiet room? Would you say...

    1. No difficulty
    2. Some difficulty
    3. A lot of difficulty
    4. Cannot do at all/Unable to do

- Question PL5 (difficulty in hearing in noisy rooms)

    Respondents with hearing aid:
    Do you have difficulty hearing what is said in a conversation with one other person in a noisier room, even when using your hearing aid? Would you say ...
    Respondents without hearing aid:
    Do you have difficulty hearing what is said in a conversation with one other person in a noisier room? Would you say ...

    1. No difficulty
    2. Some difficulty
    3. A lot of difficulty
    4. Cannot do at all/Unable to do

- Question PL6 (difficulty in walking without walking aid)

    Do you have difficulty walking half a kilometre on level ground without the use of any aid? That would be a distance that one needs between five and ten minutes. Would you say ...

1. No difficulty
2. Some difficulty
3. A lot of difficulty
4. Cannot do at all/Unable to do

- Question PL7 (difficulty walking up and down)

    Do you have difficulty walking up or down 12 steps? Would you say …

    1. No difficulty
    2. Some difficulty
    3. A lot of difficulty
    4. Cannot do at all/Unable to do

- Question PE4 (cycling)

    In a typical week, on how many days do you BICYCLE for at least 10 minutes continuously to get to and from places?

- Question PE6 (physical activity)

    In a typical week, on how many days do you carry out sports, fitness or recreational (leisure) activities for at least 10 minutes continuously?

- Question PE8 (muscle-strengthening activities)

    In a typical week, on how many days do you carry out activities specifically designed to strengthen your muscles? Include all such activities even if you have mentioned them before.

References

Allgemeine Unfallversicherung. (2020). *Behindertensport*. Online: https://www.auva.at/cdsconten t/?contentid=10007.671205&portal=auvaportal, last retrieval: 24.05.2020.

Amt der Niederösterreichischen Landesregierung. (2018). *Sportbericht 2018 Niederösterreich*. Online: http://www.noe.gv.at/noe/Sport/Sportbericht_2018.pdf, last retrieval: 19.05.2020.

Austrian National Council of Persons with Disabilities. (2013). *Alternative report on the implementation of UN convention on the rights of persons with disabilities in Austria*. Online: https://www.behindertenrat.at/wp-content/uploads/2018/07/OEAR-Report_En2013_final_lang.pdf, last retrieval: 13.02.2020.

Austrian Sports. (2018). *Förderungen 2018*. Online: https://www.austrian-sports.at/wp-content/uploads/2019/09/Foerderungen2018v01102018-2.pdf, last retrieval: 13.02.2020.

BMF. (2019). *Bundesvoranschlag 2019*. Online: https://service.bmf.gv.at/BUDGET/Budgets/2018_2019/bfg2019/teilhefte/UG17/UG17_Teilheft_2019.pdf, last retrieval: 13.02.2020.

BSO. (2019). *Mitgliederstatistik per 31.12.2019*. Online: https://www.sportaustria.at/fileadmin/Inhalte/Dokumente/Mitgliedsstatistik/Sport_Austria-Mitgliederstatistik2020.pdf, last retrieval: 13.02.2020.

Bundesministerium für Arbeit, Soziales und Konsumentenschutz. (2012). *Nationaler Aktionsplan Behinderung 2012–2020. Strategie der österreichischen Bundesregierung zur Umsetzung der UN-Behindertenrechtskonvention.* Online: https://broschuerenservice.sozialministerium.at/Home/Download?publicationId=165, last retrieval: 16.05.2020.

Bundesministerium für Arbeit, Soziales und Konsumentenschutz. (2015). *Nationaler Aktionsplan Behinderung Zwischenbilanz 2012–2015.* Online: https://broschuerenservice.sozialministerium.at/Home/Down-load?publicationId=362, last retrieval: 16.05.2020.

Bundesministerium für Arbeit, Soziales und Konsumentenschutz. (2017). *Bericht der Bundesregierung über die Lage der Menschen mit Behinderungen in Österreich 2016.* Online: https://broschuerenservice.sozialministerium.at/Home/Download?publicationId=428, last retrieval: 13.02.2020.

Bundesministerium für Kunst, Kultur, öffentlicher Dienst und Sport. (2020). *Behindertensport.* Online: https://www.bmkoes.gv.at/sport/behindertensport.html, last retrieval: 16.05.2020.

Bundesministerium für Landesverteidigung und Sport. (2013). *Nationaler Aktionsplan Bewegung.* Online: https://broschuerenservice.sozialministerium.at/Home/Download?publicationId=551, last retrieval: 16.05.2020.

Bundes-Sport GmbH. (2020). *Förderstandsveröffentlichung 2019.* Online: https://www.austriansports.at/wp-content/uploads/2020/05/Foerderstandsveroeffentlichung2019.pdf, last retrieval: 12.05.2020.

Bundessportakademie. (2020). *Ausbildungsstruktur.* Online: https://www.bspa.at/organisation/ausbildungsstruktur/, last retrieval: 19.05.2020.

Bundes-Sportorganisation. (2020a). *Sport Austria-Management Zertifikatskurs.* Online: https://www.sportaustria.at/de/schwerpunkte/fortbildungsangebot/sport-austria-management-kurs/, last retrieval: 19.05.2020.

Bundes-Sportorganisation. (2020b). Sport Austria-Management Zertifikatskurs. Online: https://www.sportaustria.at, last retrieval: 07.09.2020.

Deutsche Sportakademie. (2020). *Kooperation mit SPORTUNION-Akademie.* Online: https://www.deutschesportakademie.de/presseitem/4909/kooperation-mit-sportunion-akademie, last retrieval: 19.05.2020.

Die Neue Volkspartei & Die Grünen. (2019). *Aus Verantwortung für Österreich. Regierungsprogramm 2020–2024.* Online: https://www.dieneuevolkspartei.at/Download/Regierungsprogramm_2020.pdf, last retrieval: 19.05.2020.

Dinold, M. (2010). Ansätze und Projekte zu Special Olympics und Bewegungsangebote für Menschen mit mentaler Behinderung in Österreich. In M. Wegner & H.-J. Schulke (Eds.), *Behinderung, Bewegung, Befreiung. Ressourcen und Kompetenzen von Menschen mit geistiger Behinderung* (pp. 90–100). Universität Kiel.

Erk, J. (2004). Austria: A federation without federalism. *Publius: The Journal of Federalism, 34*(1), 1–20.

European Union. (2017). *Special Eurobarometer 472 - Sport and physical activity.* Online: https://ec.europa.eu/commfrontoffice/publicopinion/index.cfm/survey/getsurveydetail/instruments/special/surveyky/2164, last retrieval: 07.09.2020. doi:10.2766/483047.

Fallend, F. (2013). Austria: A federal, a decentralized unitary or a 'hybrid' state? Relations between the welfare state and the federal state after 1945. In J. Loughlin, J. Kincaid, & W. Swenden (Eds.), *Routledge handbook of regionalism and federalism* (pp. 235–247). Taylor and Francis, Routledge.

Fritz, O., Schratzenstaller, M., Smeral, E., & Thöni, E. (2004). Bedeutung und Effekte der öffentlichen Sportförderung. *WIFO Monatsberichte, 9*, 697–707. Online: https://www.wifo.ac.at/jart/prj3/wifo/resources/person_dokument/person_dokument.jart?publikationsid=25256&mime_type=application/pdf, last retrieval: 19.05.2020.

KDZ. (2015). *Kommunale Freizeitinfrastrukturen am Beispiel Sport.* Online: https://www.staedtebund.gv.at/fileadmin/USERDATA/staedtetag/2017/Tagungsunterlagen/AK3_03_2_Schantl_KDZ_Bericht_KommunaleFreizeitinfrastrukturen_Optimized.pdf, last retrieval: 13.02.2020.

Kneissl, O. (1988). 30 Jahre Österreichischer Versehrtensportverband. Basis für den Behindertensportverband der Zukunft. In Ö. Versehrtensportverband (Ed.), *30 Jahre ÖVSV. Rückblick Vorschau* (pp. 11–14). Österreichischer Versehrtensportverband.

Land Salzburg. (2019). *Landesvoranschlag 2019.* Online: https://www.salzburg.gv.at/politik_/Documents/LVA_2019.pdf, last retrieval: 19.05.2020.

Landesrechnungshof Kärnten. (2017). *Sportförderung*. Online: https://www.lrh-ktn.at/images/download/Berichte/LRH-Bericht%20Sportförderung.pdf, last retrieval: 19.05.2020.

Landesrechnungshof Tirol. (2018). *Prüfbericht. Ausgewählte Bereiche der Sportförderungen des Landes Tirol*. : Landesrechnungshof Tirol. Online: https://www.tirol.gv.at/fileadmin/landtag/landesrechnungshof/downloads/berichte/2018/Sportfoerderungen.pdf, last retrieval: 13.05.2020.

Marschik, M., & Müllner, R. (2011). The governance of Austrian sport: History and presence. In C. Sobry (Ed.), *Sports governance in the world: A socio-historic approach* (pp. 69–87). Éditions Le Manuscrit.

Naue, U. (2006). Governing disability in Austria: Reflections on a changing political field. *Disability Studies Quarterly, 26*(2) https://dsq-sds.org/article/view/695/872

Naue, U. (2009). Österreichische Behindertenpolitik im Kontext nationaler Politik und internationaler Diskurse zu Behinderung. *SWS-Rundschau, 49*(3), 274–292.

Naue, U., & Kroll, T. (2010). Bridging policies and practices: Challenges and opportunities for the governance of disability and ageing. *International Journal of Integrated Care, 10*, 1–7. https://doi.org/10.5334/ijic.522

OECD. (2018). *Gross Domestic Product (GDP)*. Online: https://data.oecd.org/gdp/gross-domestic-product-gdp.htm, last retrieval: 13.02.2020.

OECD. (2019). *OECD economic surveys Austria 2019*. Online: http://www.oecd.org/economy/surveys/Austria-2019-OECD-economic-survey-overview.pdf, last retrieval: 03.09.2020.

Österreichischer Behindertensportverband. (2019). *Jahresbericht 2019*. Online: https://obsv.at/fileadmin/user_upload/OBSV_Jahresbericht_2019.pdf, last retrieval: 17.05.2020.

Österreichischer Behindertensportverband. (2020a). *Aufnahme in die Österreichische Bundes-Sportorganisation (BSO)*. Online: https://obsv.at/verband/chronik/aufnahme-in-die-bso/, last retrieval: 12.05.2020.

Österreichischer Behindertensportverband. (2020b). *Finanzierung des ÖBSV*. Online: https://obsv.at/verband/chronik/finanzierung-des-oebsv/, last retrieval: 16.05.2020.

Österreichischer Behindertensportverband. (2020c). *Für Respekt und Sicherheit - und gegen sexualisierte Gewalt*. Online: https://obsv.at/verband/gewaltpraevention/, last retrieval: 17.05.2020.

Österreichischer Behindertensportverband. (2020d). *Inklusionsverantwortung*. Online: https://obsv.at/sport/inklusion/, last retrieval: 17.05.2020.

Österreichischer Behindertensportverband. (2020e). *Inklusives Ausbildungsprogramm*. https://obsv.at/sport/ausbildung/, last retrieval: 19.05.2020.

Österreichischer Behindertensportverband. (2020f). *Mitgliedschaften*. Online: https://obsv.at/verband/mitgliedschaften/, last retrieval: 12.05.2020.

Österreichischer Behindertensportverband. (2020g). *Sportarten*. Online: https://obsv.at/sport/sportarten/, last retrieval: 23.05.2020.

Österreichischer Behindertensportverband. (2020h). *Unterstützen Sie Menschen mit Behinderung*. Online: https://obsv.at/menschen/unterstuetzung/, last retrieval: 16.05.2020.

Österreichischer Gehörlosen Sportverband. (2020a). *Chronik*. Online: https://oegsv.at/chronik/, last retrieval: 20.05.2020.

Österreichischer Gehörlosen Sportverband. (2020b). *Eine Organisation stellt sich vor*. Online: https://oegsv.at/eine-organisation-stellt-sich-vor/, last retrieval: 20.05.2020.

Österreichischer Gehörlosen Sportverband. (2020c). *Mitglieder*. Online: https://oegsv.at/mitglieder/, last retrieval: 20.05.2020.

Österreichischer Gehörlosen Sportverband. (2020d). *Sportbereiche*. Online: https://oegsv.at/, last retrieval: 23.05.2020.

Österreichisches Paralympisches Comittee. (2020a). *Sommersportarten*. Online: https://oepc.at/sport/sommersportarten/, last retrieval: 23.05.2020.

Österreichisches Paralympisches Comittee. (2020b). *Wie alles begann*. Online: https://oepc.at/, last re-trieval: 12.05.2020.

Österreichisches Paralympisches Comittee. (2020c). *Wintersportarten*. Online: https://oepc.at/sport/wintersportarten/, last retrieval: 23.05.2020.

Reiter, F. (2009). *Entwicklung und Verortung des Behindertensports im nationalen Sportraum Österreich*. Diploma Thesis. Vienna: Universität Wien.

Schantl, A., Hochholdinger, N. & Hödl, C. (2014). *Kommunale Sportförderung in Österreich. Status Quo und Perspektiven.* Wien: KDZ. Online: https://www.staedtebund.gv.at/fileadmin/USERDATA/staedtetag/2017/Tagungsunterlagen/AK3_03_3_Schantl_KDZ_KommunaleSportfoerderung_2014_Optimized.pdf, last retrieval: 16.05.2020.

Scheerder, J., Claes, E. & Willem A. (2017). Does it take two to Tango? The Position and Power of National Sport Bodies Compared to Their Public Authorities. In J. Scheerder, A. Willem & E. Claes (eds.) *Sport Policy Systems and Sport Federations: A Cross-National Perspective* (pp. 1–17). London: Palgrave Macmillan.

Schober, C., Sprajcer, S., Horak, C., Klein, T. M., Djukic, B., Soriat, J., Pfeil, W. J., & Mayer, S. (2012). *Evaluierung des Behindertengleichstellungsrechts. Wien: Bundesministerium für Arbeit, Soziales und Konsumentenschutz.* Online: https://broschuerenservice.sozialministerium.at/Home/Download?publi-cationId=200, last retrieval: 06.05.2020.

Sozialministerium/BMI. (2018). *Geografie und Bevölkerung.* Online: https://www.migration.gv.at/de/leben-und-arbeiten-in-oesterreich/oesterreich-stellt-sich-vor/geografie-und-bevoelkerung, last retrieval: 13.02.2020.

Special Eurobarometer 472. (2017). *Special Eurobarometer 472: Sport and physical activity.* Online: https://data.europa.eu/euodp/en/data/dataset/S2164_88_4_472_ENG, last retrieval: 13.02.2020.

Special Olympics Österreich. (2020a). *Geschichte.* Online: https://specialolympics.at/geschichte/, last retrieval: 12.05.2020.

Special Olympics Österreich. (2020b). *Regelwerke der Special Olympics Sportarten zum Downloaden.* https://specialolympics.at/regelwerke/, last retrieval: 23.05.2020.

Special Olympics Österreich. (2020c). *Was wir machen.* Online: https://specialolympics.at/was-wir-machen/, last retrieval: 17.05.2020.

Sport Burgenland. (2018). *Burgenländischer Sportbericht 2016/2017.* Online: http://www.bgld-landtag.at/fileadmin/user_upload/XXI_GP/TO/TO43/TO43_Zahl_21-1015.pdf, last retrieval: 09.05.2020.

Sporthilfe. (2020). *Der Verein.* https://www.sporthilfe.at/ueber-uns/der-verein/, last retrieval: 19.05.2020.

SportsEconAustria. (2019). *Unterschätzter Wirtschaftsfaktor Sport.* Online: https://www.spea.at/wp-content/uploads/2019/04/190408-PK-Sport-und-Wirtschaft-SpEA-HVK-V02.pdf, last retrieval: 13.02.2020.

SPORTUNION Akademie. (2020). *Funktionärskurse.* Online: https://sportunion-akademie.at/content/SPORTUNION_Akademie/funktionaerskurse/, last retrieval: 19.05.2020.

Statistik Austria. (2015). *Österreichische Gesundheitsbefragung 2014. Hauptergebnisse des Austrian Health Interview Survey (ATHIS) und methodische Dokumentation.* Vienna: Bundesministerium für Gesundheit. Online: https://broschuerenservice.sozialministerium.at/Home/Download?publicationId=542, last retrieval: 23.05.2020.

Statistik Austria. (2020). *Gemeinden.* Online: https://www.statistik.at/web_de/klassifikationen/regionale_gliederungen/gemeinden/index.html, last retrieval: 12.02.2020.

Storr, S. (2012). Österreich als Bundesstaat. In I. Härtel (Ed.), *Handbuch Föderalismus - Föderalismus als demokratische Rechtsordnung und Rechtskultur in Deutschland, Europa und der Welt: Band IV: Föderalismus in Europa und der Welt* (pp. 671–695). Springer.

Strohmeyer, H. (1978). Österreich. In H. Ueberhorst (Ed.), *Geschichte der Leibesübungen* (Vol. 5, pp. 285–310). Bartels & Wernitz.

The World Bank. (2018). *Urban population (% of total population) – Austria.* Online: https://data.worldbank.org/indicator/SP.URB.TOTL.IN.ZS?locations=AT&name_desc=false, last retrieval: 13.02.2020.

van Bottenburg, M. (2011). Why are the European and American sports worlds so different? Path dependence in European and American sports history. In A. Tomlinson, C. Young, & R. Holt (Eds.), *Transformation of modern Europe: States, media and markets 1950–2010* (pp. 205–225). Routledge.

Vock, S. (2017). *Leistungsbilanz Österreichischer Athleten/innen bei den Paralympics (Zeitraum 1996–2016).* Diploma Thesis. Vienna: Universität Wien.

List of Laws

Allgemeines Sozialversicherungsgesetz (Austrian social security law). Online.: https://www.ris.bka.gv.at/GeltendeFassung.wxe?Abfrage=Bundesnormen&Gesetzesnummer=10008147

Behinderteneinstellungsgesetz (Austrian Employment Law for Persons with Disabilities). Online.: https://www.ris.bka.gv.at/GeltendeFassung.wxe?Abfrage=Bundesnormen&Gesetzesnummer=10008253

Bundesbehindertengesetz (Federal Disability Law). Online.: https://www.ris.bka.gv.at/GeltendeFassung.wxe?Abfrage=Bundesnormen&Gesetzesnummer=10008713

Bundes-Behindertengleichstellungsgesetz (Federal Law for the Equality of People with Disabilities). Online.: https://www.ris.bka.gv.at/GeltendeFassung.wxe?Abfrage=Bundesnormen&Gesetzesnummer=20004228

Bundes-Sportförderungsgesetz 2017 (National Law on Sports Promotion). Online.: https://www.ris.bka.gv.at/GeltendeFassung.wxe?Abfrage=Bundesnormen&Gesetzesnummer=20009941

Bundes-Verfassungsgesetz (Austrian Federal Constitution Law). Online.: https://www.ris.bka.gv.at/GeltendeFassung.wxe?Abfrage=Bundesnormen&Gesetzesnummer=10000138

Einschätzungsverordnung (decree of estimation). Online.: https://www.ris.bka.gv.at/GeltendeFassung.wxe?Abfrage=Bundesnormen&Gesetzesnummer=20006879

Glücksspielgesetz (gambling law). Online.: https://www.ris.bka.gv.at/GeltendeFassung.wxe?Abfrage=Bundesnormen&Gesetzesnummer=10004611

Kriegsopferversorgungsgesetz (law on the welfare of war victims). Online.: https://www.ris.bka.gv.at/GeltendeFassung.wxe?Abfrage=Bundesnormen&Gesetzesnummer=10008166

Upper Austrian Chancengleichheitsgesetz (law on equal opportunities). Online.: https://www.ris.bka.gv.at/GeltendeFassung.wxe?Abfrage=LROO&Gesetzesnummer=20000514

Chapter 13
Disability Sport in Belgium/Flanders: From a Fragmented Mosaic Towards a More Inclusive Landscape

Debbie Van Biesen and Jeroen Scheerder

13.1 Introduction

In Belgium, sport is governed autonomously by the different communities and regions (see below). The focus of this chapter is on Flanders, that is, the Dutch-speaking part in the north of the country. While the disability sports landscape used to be very fragmented in the past, with many smaller agents, each playing their own specific role, the current policies are supporting the transition towards a more unified structure with a few key agents that use their expertise to optimise the disability sports offer and to work in collaboration with mainstream sports organisations fostering inclusion. The key actor on the governmental level in Flanders is *Sport Vlaanderen*, that is, the public sports administration of the Flemish government, whereas the key actor at the non-governmental side is *G-sport Vlaanderen* (Disability Sport Flanders), that is, the umbrella organisation for disability sport in Flanders, founded in March 2022, as a result of the merging process between the two main actors at that time, that is, *Parantee-Psylos* (i.e. the sports federation responsible for the promotion and organisation of club-organised sport for people with a disability on all levels from initiation to elite competition) and *G-sport Vlaanderen* (i.e. the organisation responsible for increasing

---

D. Van Biesen (✉)
KU Leuven, Department of Rehabilitation Sciences, Research Group for Adapted Physical Activity & Psychomotor Rehabilitation, Leuven, Belgium
e-mail: debbie.vanbiesen@kuleuven.be

J. Scheerder
KU Leuven, Department of Movement Sciences, Leuven, Belgium

Flemish Policy Research Centre on Sports, Leuven, Belgium

Delta Group on Good Governance in Sport, Leuven, Belgium
e-mail: jeroen.scheerder@kuleuven.be

© The Author(s), under exclusive license to Springer Nature Switzerland AG 2023
C. van Lindert et al. (eds.), *The Palgrave Handbook of Disability Sport in Europe*, https://doi.org/10.1007/978-3-031-21759-3_13

awareness and knowledge about disability sport in Flanders). This chapter describes the roles and the relationships between these two key actors, as well as other relevant players in the field. Disability sports policy and organisation in the French-speaking and German-speaking parts of Belgium will also be discussed, albeit briefly since less or even no information is available compared to the situation in Flanders. Our chapter is mainly using existing data, most of it retrieved from a large-scale disability sports participation study, funded by the Flemish government and performed in 2018 by both authors of this chapter and their colleagues (Scheerder et al., 2018a, 2018b; Van Biesen et al., 2018). We offer new insights into the organisation of disability sports in Belgium, as it is, to the authors' knowledge, for the very first time in history that the existing data related to this topic is brought together in a coherent narrative.

13.2 Country Profile

Characteristics of Belgium

Belgium is a federal state, structured around a constitutional monarchy. It is a relatively small but densely populated country approximately inhabited by 11.5 million people. Its state structure is rather complicated, since it is composed of two types of federated entities, being regions (i.e. Flemish Region, Walloon Region and Brussels-Capital Region) on the one hand and communities (i.e. Flemish community, French community and German-speaking community) on the other. The country has a federal parliament and a federal government, but the respective communities and regions also have their own legislative and executive bodies. Regional parliaments and governments decide upon place-related matters, such as housing, economy and transportation, while community parliaments and governments are in charge of person-related competences, such as education, healthcare and culture. As part of the cultural sphere, governmental competences with regard to sport, such as the organisation of sport, sport policy planning and the subsidising of non-profit sports governing bodies, are the exclusive responsibility of the three communities (Scheerder & Vos, 2013). As already mentioned, the focus of this chapter is mostly on Flanders, that is, the Dutch-speaking, northern part of Belgium. On the Flemish side, the Flemish Community and Flemish Region are combined into one Flemish federated entity, including the Flemish Parliament and the Flemish government, that decides on all matters in Flanders as well as all matters pertaining to the Dutch-speaking community in the capital of Brussels, including sport-related issues (Scheerder et al., 2011). More detailed facts and statistics regarding Belgium and its communities and regions can be found in Table 13.1.

Table 13.1 Facts and statistics for Belgium, Brussels-Capital Region, Flanders, Wallonia and East Belgium (most recently available data included)

	Belgium	Brussels-Capital Region	Flanders (= Flemish Region)	Wallonia (= Walloon Region)	East Belgium (= German-speaking Community)
Population (number of inhabitants)	11,521,238	1,219,970	6,653,062	3,648,206	77,949
Area (km^2)	30,526	161	13,521	16,844	854
Density (inhabitants/km^2)	377	7577	492	217	91
Urbanisation rate (share of urban population in total population)	98%	NDA	NDA	NDA	NDA
Political organisation	Federal parliamentary constitutional monarchy	NA	NA	NA	NA
State structure	Federal	NA	NA	NA	NA
Number of regions	3	NA	NA	NA	NA
Number of provinces	10	NA	5	5	NA
Number of municipalities	581	19	300	262	9
GDP per capita (euro PPS)	41,546	71,412	42,249	30,236	NDA
Number of official languages	3	2	1	1	1
EU membership	Since 1952	NA	NA	NA	NA
Type of welfare model	Rhineland	NA	NA	NA	NA

Sources: Eurostat (2019); Statbel (2021); Statista (2021); Statistics Flanders (2021); The World Bank (2019)
NA not applicable
NDA no data available

Sport in Belgium

Thanks to its central geopolitical position at the crossroads of different cultures and nation states in Europe, a long-standing, rich and variegated sporting culture exists in Belgium. Before the import of modern sports by the British, traditional games, such as the handball game called *kaatsen* or the bowling game called *beugelen* (closh), were popular, in particular in Flanders (Taks et al., 1999). Many of these folk games originate from mediaeval times. Archery and fencing associations occurred in the oldest Belgian cities and date back to the Middle Ages (Renson, 1976). They can be considered as one of the oldest still-existing sports associations in the world. In Belgium, also the first international sports federation rooted, at the time being the *Fédération Européenne de Gymnastique* (nowadays the *Fédération*

Internationale de Gymnastique, FIG) which was established in 1881 in the city of Liège (Renson, 2006). In 1908 the first university institute in the world where students were able to obtain bachelor's, master's and doctoral degrees in physical education was installed in Belgium, namely at the State University of Ghent (Lenoir et al., 2007). In 1920, the Olympic Games of Antwerp were the first in which the Olympic flag was raised and in which the Olympic oath was pronounced (Renson, 1996). From a managerial perspective, it can be mentioned that many Belgians have become chairman of an international non-profit sports organisation. Moreover, Belgium, so far, is the only country in the world to have provided two presidents of the International Olympic Committee, namely Henri Comte de Baillet-Latour (1925–1942) and Jacques Count Rogge (2001–2013).

Sport has played a remarkable role in the history of Belgium, being both a culturally and politically divided country (Vanreusel et al., 1999). Or put in other words: Belgium's complex political structuration has significantly affected the organisation of sport in Belgium (Scheerder & Vos, 2013; van Poppel et al., 2018). More precisely, most sports governing bodies in Belgium used to be unitary organisations until the late 1970s. Afterwards, in order to make sure that they would still be subsidised by their respective governments, non-profit sports organisations had to split up into two separate wings, namely into an independent Flemish and Walloon federation. To date, almost all sports federations in Belgium are split up in accordance with the communitarian structure of the country, including a separated administration and competition system in Flanders and Wallonia (Scheerder et al., 2015). Thus, it can be stated that sport in Belgium reflects the separated system imposed by the process of political division and constitutional revisions that have taken place during the past half century. In particular this is the case when it comes to public sports policy since the field of sport was one of the first governmental competences over which the communities in Belgium got full authority (Scheerder et al., 2015). As a consequence, since the beginning of the 1970s, each language community in Belgium (i.e. Flemish community, French community and German-speaking community) has its own autonomous sports authority, acting independently and developing a fully separated public sports policy.

On the other hand, sport in Belgium is also used to highlight the alleged unity of the country. For instance, the Belgian Olympic and Interfederal Committee (BOIC) can be considered as a national stronghold, ever since its foundation in 1906. Victories and successful performances at the Olympic and Paralympic Games are therefore strongly embedded in a national and even 'Belgicist' context. Other forms of elite sport, too, are seen as national symbols of Belgian unity. From this perspective, the national basketball, football and hockey teams, among others, are staged to create feelings of national solidarity and unity, albeit most of the time in an ephemeral way (Scheerder et al., 2015; Thibaut, 2000; Vanreusel et al., 1999).

As is the case in most Western European countries, voluntary sports clubs traditionally predominate(d) the leisure-time sports sector in Belgium (Scheerder & Vos, 2013; Taks et al., 1999). Indeed, for a long time, sports clubs held a monopoly in providing sports activities. However, this exclusive position has changed during the past decades. Nowadays, sports activities are provided by a complex mixture of three main types of suppliers, being not only non-profit organisations such as sports clubs, but also commercial and governmental actors. It is estimated that in Belgium somewhat more than 37,000 sports clubs are operative (see Table 13.2). Compared to European standards, Belgium has a dense network of sports clubs as for every 100,000 inhabitants there are on average 323 sports clubs. In Flanders, this number even accounts for 428. Although almost half of the population in Belgium indicates to be sport active at least once a week, only one out of five actively practises sport in a club-organised setting (numbers presented in Table 13.2). At the same time, it

Table 13.2 Sports profile for Belgium, Flanders, Wallonia and East Belgium (most recently available data included)

	Belgium	Flanders	Wallonia	East Belgium
Governmental authority responsible for sport[a]	Ministry of Home Affairs (Football Unit)	Sport Vlaanderen	Administration Générale du Sport (ADEPS)/ Infrasports	Leitverband des Ostbelgischen Sports (LOS)
Membership of sports club, 15+ years (% of population)[b]	16.2%	14.9%	16.3%	NDA
Membership of fitness or health centre, 15+ years (% of population)[b]	9.7%	10.2%	8.4%	NDA
Membership of socio-cultural club that includes sport in its activities (e.g. employees' club, youth club and school- and university-related club), 15+ years (% of population)[b]	5.3%	5.0%	3.5%	NDA
Sports participation, at least once a week (% of adult population)	48.3%[c]	49.9%[d]	NDA	NDA
Number of sports federations (2020)[a]	84 (members of the Belgian Olympic and Interfederal Committee)	71	58	16
Number of sports clubs	*Approx. 37,200*	28,480[e]	*Approx. 8459*	*Approx. 283*
Number of sports clubs that are registered members of an NSO/RSO	*Approx. 30,300*	23,168[e]	6881[f]	230[g]
Number of sports club members in clubs that are registered members of an NSO/RSO	*Approx. 2,108,600*	1,405,165[e]	703,421[h]	NDA
Budget for sport (EUR) (× 1000)	37,999[i]	234,550[i]	114,350[j,k]	NDA

(continued)

Table 13.2 (continued)

	Belgium	Flanders	Wallonia	East Belgium
Budget for sports federations (EUR) (× 1000)	NA	36,316[l]	30,340[m]	NA
Local budget for sport (EUR) (× 1000)	NDA	330,753[n]	297,970[f]	NDA
Share of economic value of volunteers in sport in the GDP (%)	NDA	0.19	NDA	NDA

approx. approximately
NA not applicable
NDA no data available
NSO/RSO national sports organisation/regional sports organisation
[a]Scheerder et al. (2021)
[b]Helsen and Scheerder (2020, 2021)
[c]European Commission (2018)
[d]Scheerder and Thibaut (2021b)
[e]Sport Vlaanderen (2021a)
[f]Adeps (2021a)
[g]Leitverband des Ostbelgischen Sports (2021)
[h]Adeps (2021b)
[i]Sport Vlaanderen (2021b)
[j]Adeps (2021c)
[k]Infrasports (2021)
[l]Sport Vlaanderen (2021c)
[m]Adeps (2021d)
[n]Claes et al. (2017)

can be noted that 10% of the Belgian population (15+ years) is a member of a fitness or health centre. This not only emphasises the popularity of organised fitness but also indicates the growing importance of commercially provided sports activities. Nowadays, running, fitness, recreational walking, tour cycling and recreational cycling are the five most popular sports activities among adults in Flanders (Scheerder & Thibaut, 2021b). Typically club-organised sports, such as tennis and football, still show up in the top ten of most practised sports, but they reach a significantly lower number of people (less than 5% each; Scheerder & Thibaut, 2021b). It is also remarkable that, according to educational status, household income and ethnic background, significant inequalities in levels of active sports involvement still persist among children and adolescents as well as adults (Scheerder & Thibaut, 2021c). Therefore, it can be noticed that despite half a century of Sport for All policies in Flanders/Belgium, patterns of social stratification are still detected, mainly to the detriment of socially vulnerable groups in society (Scheerder & Vandermeerschen, 2016; Scheerder, Vandermeerschen & Breedveld, 2018).

Disability in Belgium

In Belgium, as in many other countries, disability is not always defined the same way, and no consistent terminology is used in the context of disability. Therefore, it is difficult to interpret or compare prevalence data across various sources, depending on the language (community level), age of the participants included (children and/or elderly versus only the active age groups) or context (education, clinical settings, financial agencies, etc.). The most accepted definition (also by the Flemish governmental insurance agencies) is fully in line with the international definitions of the International Classification of Functioning, Disability and Health (ICF), published by the World Health Organization (WHO). The terms 'handicap' and 'impairment' (in Dutch: 'beperking'; in French: 'déficience') are used interchangeably and are defined as any long-term and significant participation problem, due to the interplay between impairments in functions that are mental, psychological, physical and/or sensory in nature, and cause limitations in the performance of activities and personal and external factors. A recent comprehensive review (Scheerder, Vandermeerschen, & Breedveld, 2018) inventoried all existing studies conducted in Belgium related to the prevalence of disability, with the purpose of facilitating the comparison of available data. In summary, based on that inventory, we can say that on average 23% of all Belgian citizens have an illness or impairment (ranging between 10% and 33%), with an estimated average of 12% of Belgians feeling effectively limited in the execution of their daily activities as a result of these health problems. This number falls between the outcomes of the Eurostat Barometer (2017) showing that the self-reported long-term limitations in daily activities in the Belgian population above 16 years old ranges from 8.7% (severe limitation) to 16.1% (some limitations). A similar inventory was produced, based on a comprehensive review of national and international data sources comparing the prevalence between and across various types of disability (Scheerder et al., 2018a). On the basis of that review, the distribution of people with disabilities according to the type of impairment is estimated as represented in Table 13.3.

As the majority of EU countries did, Belgium also signed the *UN Convention on the Rights of Persons with Disabilities* and formally ratified it on 2 July 2009. This was an important step, as it implies that Belgium has the obligation to respect the content of the articles of the Convention, including 'Participation' and 'Full Inclusion' of persons with disabilities as a general principle. In practice, this means that Belgium must adapt its entire legislation (laws, regulations, implementation decrees, etc.) to conform to the 2009 Convention. There are still some areas for improvement on the way to full social inclusion, also in sport, as will be apparent from the remainder of this chapter.

Belgium is a country in transition, and the sports policies at regional levels are in favour to promote full and equal participation of people with disabilities in sport, in particular on club-organisational level. There are, however, no data available yet to support the positive effects of these policies on sports participation of people with disabilities. On the contrary, the majority of people with disabilities report more

Table 13.3 Prevalence of people with disabilities in Flanders/Belgium according to the type of impairment

Type of impairment	Prevalence (%)
Physical (musculoskeletal)	36.5
Visual	8.8
Hearing	7.7
Intellectual	32.1
Mental health disorders, including autism spectrum	14.9

Source: Scheerder et al. (2018a)

sedentary time compared to the general population (Scheerder et al., 2018a). Moreover, significant barriers prevent them from being sufficiently physically active to reach the health norms stipulated by the World Health Organization (WHO, 2019). To illustrate the Belgian situation with a figurative comparison, it can be stated that some obstructions occur on the road towards full inclusion in disability sport. However, it must be stressed that the fragmented landscape of disability sport is in transition and that it has been for a long time.

Emergence and Rise of Disability Sport in Belgium

The history of disability sport in Belgium has similarities with the history of the Paralympics, as both have their origin in a rehabilitation hospital where sport was used as a means for the treatment of injured patients. What the Stoke Mandeville Hospital meant for the history of the Paralympic Games was the Centre for Traumatology and Readaptation at the Brugmann Hospital in Brussels for disability sport in Belgium (De Meyer, 2010). Since 1952, sport was used there as a means of readaptation, with the support of Victor Boin, the then president of the *Belgian Olympic and Interfederal Committee* (BOIC). The idea was picked up by professor Pierre Houssa when visiting the Stoke Mandeville Hospital (Weyters, 2010). Two years later, in 1954, some of their patients took part in an international meeting in Stoke Mandeville (UK). In 1958 a similar meeting was organised in Brussels. The *Belgian Sports Federation for the Disabled* (BSVG) was founded in 1960, with Victor Boin as its first president and Pierre Houssa as one of its vice presidents. According to the new communitarian structure of Belgium (supra), in 1977 it was decided to split the BSVG into the *Dutch-Speaking League of the Belgian Sports Federation for Handicapped People* (BSVG-NL) on the one side and the *French-Speaking Handisport League* (LHF) on the other. These two associations became members of the BSVG. The BSVG itself only retained an umbrella function for the organisation of competitive sport and changed its name to the current name being *Belgian Paralympic Committee* (BPC) in 2001. Until 2003, the BPC secretariat remained housed in the Brugmann Hospital. In 2003, a new accessible building was put into use opposite the BOIC building in Brussels.

For the Dutch-speaking part of Belgium, BSVG-NL was initially oriented dominantly towards sport for people with physical impairments. They adopted the name of *Flemish Disability Sports League* (VLG) in 1987 after a merger in 1983 with the *Flemish Deaf Sports League* (VDSB, nowadays *Dovensport Vlaanderen*) and the *Dutch-Speaking Sports Federation for Visually Handicapped People* (NSVG). The further transition of the disability sports landscape in Flanders continued with a merger of VLG with the *Organisation for After-School Sport in Special Education* (SLOBO) in 1997 and the *Federation for Disability Sport and Outdoor Recreation for People with Intellectual Disability* (NFSOG) in 1999. In 2006, the deaf sports clubs stepped out of VLG. Six years later, in 2012, the organisation adopted the new name of *Parantee* and merged with *Psylos* in 2016 into the sports federation *Parantee-Psylos* (Parantee-Psylos, 2017). At the time of the merger, Psylos was acting as the sports federation for people with mental health disorders, founded in 1971 by the KU Leuven Institute for Physical Education, nowadays Faculty of Movement and Rehabilitation Sciences, in collaboration with 28 psychiatric hospitals.

Until March 2022, Parantee-Psylos was the main agent in the Dutch-speaking part of Belgium with a sports offer for people of all ages, with various types of impairments and health disorders, including physical, intellectual, visual and auditory impairment, autism, mental health issues and chronic health disorders. Parantee-Psylos was recognised and subsidised by the Flemish government as the sports federation responsible for the promotion of disability sport in Flanders and went through another merger process with *G-sport Vlaanderen*, the umbrella organisation responsible to provide support and increase knowledge and awareness about inclusion and disability sport in Flanders (thus no sports provision as such). The process of merger between both organisations was part of the strategy supported by the Flemish government to streamline the previously very fragmented landscape for disability sport throughout the Flemish Region. While in the past many small players were responsible for the expansion of the sports supply for people with a disability, the government encouraged them to join forces into one large disability sports organisation to better tailor the sports offer to the needs and demands of each individual. The process of merger was finalised in March 2022 and the newly created organisation adopted the roles and responsibilities of both previous agents, and the name of the smallest partner in the process, that is, G-sport Vlaanderen.

A few other specific disability sports organisations were not included in the merging process, such as *Special Olympics Belgium* (organiser of the Special Olympic Games yearly for recreational athletes with an intellectual disability), *S-Sport/Recreas* (sports federation providing recreational club-organised sports activities for elderly and people with various types of disabilities) and the *Belgian Deaf Sport Committee* (BDC). This will be further described when we discuss non-governmental agents with regard to disability sports (infra).

As regards the terminology used, 'G-sport' is the preferred and commonly accepted term for disability sport in the Dutch-speaking part of Belgium, whereas 'handisport' is the concept used in the French-speaking part and 'Behindertensport' in the German-speaking part of the country. More precisely, G-sport is defined as doing sport or being physically active by people with a certain type of impairment or disorder (Parantee-Psylos, 2021a). In other words, G-sport aims at reaching people who are hindered by different kinds of barriers to participate with or compete against other people on an equal basis. The impairment can be physical, intellectual, auditory or visual, or it can be a mental health or autism spectrum disorder. These six distinct types are the ones addressed in the most recent G-sport participation survey on which the remainder of this chapter will be based. With the recent legislative adaptation regarding the club-organised sports sector in Flanders (see Decree on Sports Federations, Sport Vlaanderen, 2021d), chronic health disorders (e.g., multiple sclerosis and diabetes) have been added as a seventh type of disorder to target by the G-sport actors, but this offer is only starting to be developed.

13.3 The Disability Sports System in Belgium/Flanders

Structure of Disability Sport

Figure 13.1 illustrates the general structure of disability sport in Belgium, including the various agents and the relations between them. The figure shows a fragmented landscape, due to the different regions each having its own complex structure. This chapter is focusing on the Dutch-speaking part of Belgium, that is, Flanders, where the disability sports system is in transition towards a more unified organisational structure. The situation as depicted in Fig. 13.1, and described underneath, concerns the situation anno 2021.

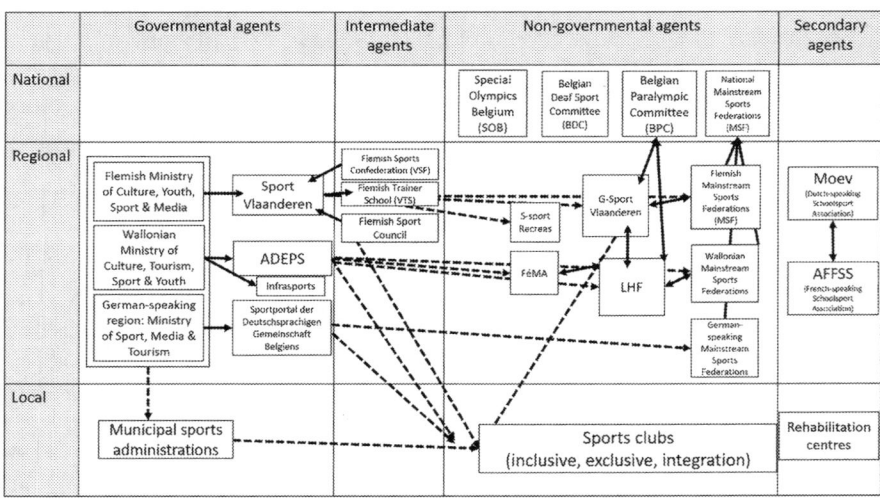

Fig. 13.1 Agents involved in the disability sports landscape in Belgium. Note: dotted arrows indicate financing; full arrows indicate relationship (membership/partnership). Sources: Claes et al. (2017); Scheerder et al. (2011); Scheerder et al. (2021); Scheerder and Vos (2013); Marin-Urquiza et al. (2020)

Governmental Agents

In Flanders, all matters related to sport (including disability sport) are governed by the Ministry of Culture, Youth, Sport and Media, and Sport Vlaanderen in particular (Scheerder et al., 2021). There is no national governmental agency for sports policy in Belgium, except for the *Football Unit* within the Federal Ministry for Home Affairs that deals with security and discrimination issues in sports stadiums. At the (sub)local level, cities and municipalities have the autonomy to take their own initiatives towards disability sport, with the majority of cities and municipalities effectively doing it. Other policy domains, such as Welfare and Equal Rights, play a role in matters related to disability (financial support and allowances for people with disabilities, accessibility of infrastructure, etc.). Within these domains there are some competences that commonly apply to disability and sport, which are therefore also worth mentioning in this context, such as the refunding of adapted sports equipment and the accessibility of sports infrastructure. As the focus in public (sports) policy in Flanders has moved towards more 'inclusivity', sports facilities such as swimming pools and sports halls are considered publicly accessible buildings. Since 2009, owners are obliged to ensure full accessibility when building or renovating sports facilities.

As mentioned previously, Sport Vlaanderen is the sports administration of the Flemish government. The mission of Sport Vlaanderen is to increase lifelong participation in sport for as many as possible of their citizens, including those with disabilities. Sport Vlaanderen is specifically impacting disability sport through the work of consultants, 'named the consultants without barriers'. These consultants are structurally embedded in the organisation and act on the local and regional levels. Sport Vlaanderen and its consultants have a specific role towards G-athletes and G-sports organisations as anchored in 2017 in the Decree on Sports Federations in Flanders (Sport Vlaanderen, 2021d). Their role is to provide financial support to local sports clubs with a structural and regular (i.e. at least on a two-weekly basis) G-sports offer, to provide practical support for clubs that want to start such a G-sport or inclusive offer and to coach organisations how to host inclusive sports events. They also serve as the main contact for the sports services of local municipalities and communities. They play a proactive role, being present as an 'antenna' to detect and remediate any issues these services might face regarding disability sport.

A comparable structure is observed in the French community and the German-speaking community, each having its own government with a Ministry of Sport. As mentioned previously, the regional governments have full autonomy and authority related to the field sport. The organisational counterpart of Sport Vlaanderen in the French community is *ADEPS* (i.e. *Administration Générale du Sport*, previously *Administration d'Education Physique, des Sports & de la Vie en plein aire*) and *Sportportal der Deutschsprachigen Gemeinschaft Belgiens* for the German-speaking community. In the Walloon Region, a specific administrative body, that is, Infrasports, is in charge of policy-making matters related to sports infrastructure.

Intermediate Agents

The most relevant intermediate agents in the disability sports landscape are the *Flemish Sports Confederation* (VSF), the *Flemish Trainer School* (VTS) and the *Flemish Sports Council*. The VSF is the umbrella organisation that takes care of the interests of all sports federations and their members in Flanders. Its role and responsibilities are further highlighted in the section on governance (infra). For the formal education and certification of sports coaches, including the G-sports coaches, the coaching education bodies are responsible. In Flanders, the VTS operates in collaboration with the Flemish sports authority, that is, Sport Vlaanderen, the Flemish universities and the university colleges offering a study programme in movement and sports sciences, as well as the sports federations recognised/subsidised by the Flemish government, in order to achieve this goal. In Wallonia, it is the ADEPS administration itself taking up this role. The Flemish Sports Council consists of experts from the field of (elite) sport. It acts autonomously and provides policy advice for the Flemish government, regarding issues related to sports in Flanders.

Non-governmental Agents

Just as is the case for most of the governmental agents, majority of the non-governmental agents in Belgium act at the regional level. As stated previously, G-sport Vlaanderen is the main non-profit supplier for disability sport in Flanders. It is the only formally recognised and subsidised sports federation for G-athletes of all ages, with various types of impairments and health disorders, including physical, intellectual, visual and auditory impairment, autism, mental health issues and chronic health disorders (supra). The organisation developed in its current form since March 2022, after a decision of the Flemish government in 2021 to revise the Decree on Sports Federations implying consequences for disability sport. To further optimise the G-sports structures, the Flemish government decided to terminate providing financial support for two separate organisations (i.e., Parantee-Psylos and G-sport Vlaanderen). Consequently, the responsibilities of both actors were bundled into one new structurally unified organisation. The newly merged umbrella organisation for disability sport in Flanders adopted the name of its smallest partner, that is, G-sport Vlaanderen. G-sport Vlaanderen has a so-called A to Z offer, including a wide range of para-sports (e.g., boccia, goalball, swimming and power chair hockey) and covering the entire spectrum from initiation to elite sports competition (cfr. Paralympic Games) for 123 G-sports clubs (exclusive offer) reaching 3725 members with a disability and 444 mainstream clubs with an inclusive offer, reaching another 5130 members with a disability. G-sport Vlaanderen took over the bilateral contractual agreements that Parantee-Psylos had with 33 mainstream sports federations (MSF) in Flanders, to support these federations to organise their own inclusive offer. The level of inclusion is on a continuum from limited (G-sport Vlaanderen in charge, supporting the MSF) to full inclusion (MSF in charge with limited support of G-sport Vlaanderen). Apart from the tasks as a disability sports federation, and providing the sports offer, G-sport Vlaanderen is in charge of broader tasks to increase knowledge and awareness in society. These tasks were stated by the 2017 Decree on Sports Federations (Sport Vlaanderen, 2021d) and include:

1. To be a main point of contact for all disability sports agents in Flanders and to support these agents through intensive collaborations
2. To host the portal through which everyone can find his/her way in the disability sports landscape
3. To coordinate the knowledge hub for all themes relevant to disability sports
4. To create awareness in society about disability sports
5. To activate people with disabilities and help them find the offer fitting their needs
6. To grow as a main point of contact to be able to offer all tasks in a highly qualitative way

Another non-governmental agency related to disability sport in Flanders is *S-Sport/Recreas*, which is defined by the Decree on Sports Federations as a multi-sport federation, with a leisure-time club-organised sports offer for the elderly and people with various types of disabilities. A total of 387 G-sports clubs are a member of this federation, with an inclusive or exclusive offer in various sports (basketball, dance, football, etc.).

The main agents in the French-speaking part of Belgium are the *Ligue Handisport Francophone* (LHF) and the *Fédération Multisports Adaptés* (Adapted Multisports Federation, FéMa, 2021). LHF is the sports federation recognised and subsidised by the Wallonia-Brussels government. It can be seen as the French-speaking counterpart of Parantee-Psylos, fulfilling the same roles being supported and funded by the government as the sports federation for disability sport. The goal of the LHF is to allow all people to practise sport, from grass-roots level to elite level. To achieve this objective, the LHF brings together nearly 200 clubs (disability sports clubs and mainstream sports clubs with an inclusive offer combined) in Wallonia and Brussels with more than 30 different sports, ranging from blind football to wheelchair tennis, including basketball, skiing, swimming, track and field, triathlon and so on. LHF and G-sport Vlaanderen are both members of the Belgian Paralympic Committee. FéMA is the French-speaking sports federation for leisure-time sports activities for people with disabilities. The objective of FéMA is to allow these people, whatever their age, to practise at least one sport adapted to their potential. FéMA offers sports activities to anyone with a disability or illness, in Wallonia and Brussels. It brings together more than 100 sports clubs and has nearly 3500 members.

In addition to promoting Sport for All, G-sport Vlaanderen and LHF are also in charge of developing elite sports pathways. More precisely, they supervise athletes who take part in the Paralympic Games, world championships and other international competitions. As such, they both are part of the *Belgian Paralympic Committee* and form the *Paralympic Team Belgium.*

As referred to previously, other organisations on the national level are *Special Olympics Belgium* (SOB) and the *Belgian Deaf Sport Committee* (BDC), each having their own specific role in the disability sports landscape, being responsible for respectively organising a yearly competitive sports event for athletes with intellectual impairment (SOB) and acting as the sports federation for deaf sports clubs and deaf sports competitions (BDC).

Secondary Agents

The main secondary agents playing a role in the disability sports landscape in Belgium are the school sports organisations, the rehabilitation hospitals and the coaching education bodies.

In Flanders, extra-curricular school sport is coordinated by *MOEV* (moev.be) and by the *Association for the French-Speaking Federations for School Sport* (AFFSS, www.sportscolaire.be) in Wallonia. Their aim is to encourage all school-aged children, including those with disabilities, to adopt a healthy and active lifestyle. Therefore, they support school teams in regular education, inclusive education and special schools with the development of their high-quality structured physical exercise and sports policy, embedded in health policy.

The rehabilitation hospitals have an important role in integrating sports in the rehabilitation process to lower the barriers for people who acquire a physical disability for sports and physical activity participation. They focus on increasing the motivation to exercise. In Flanders, a so-called *Start to para-sport* project is currently running across seven rehabilitation hospitals, with para-sport coaches embedded in the hospitals fulfilling the roles to use sports and exercise as a means for the social reintegration of patients during their rehabilitation process (Parantee-Psylos, 2021b). A similar *CAP sur le Sport* project runs in Wallonia, in collaboration with LHF, FéMA and three rehabilitation hospitals (Cap sur le Sport, 2021). Similarly, psychiatric hospitals are key actors for the reintegration of people with mental health disorders in society and in sport. Sport and physical activity are offered as part of their therapy, and some psychiatric centres in Flanders are closely linked to G-sport Vlaanderen (formerly Parantee-Psylos), with their sports clubs having their origin in the therapeutic setting, lowering the barriers for patients and ex-patients to engage and maintain physical activity during and after the acute rehabilitation phase.

Steering of Disability Sport

Relationships

The relationships between relevant agents in the disability sports system in Belgium are depicted in Fig. 13.1, and the nature of their mutual relationships is further described in more detail in the subsequent paragraphs. The complicated political structure of the country leads to a complex network with hierarchical relationships between governmental and non-governmental (disability) sports organisations, bilateral relationships between the organisations with similar roles across the different regions, and intensive relationships, or even past, ongoing or future merger processes between organisations with similar roles within the regions. The latter seems to be particularly the case in Flanders, and this process is steered by the government to simplify the complex disability sports network into a more transparent structure, with the ultimate goal to lower the barrier and promote participation for the end user, being persons with a disability.

Legislative Framework

The government's public policy towards sports federations in Flanders has been expressed in several, subsequent versions of the Decree on Sports Federations (i.e. in 1977, 1999, 2001 and most recently 2017), each of which encompasses a revised sports policy vision (Scheerder et al., 2021). The most recent version of the decree that is currently in place in Flanders was approved in 2016 and installed in January 2017 (Sport Vlaanderen, 2021d). It concerned an update of the previous decree of 2001, with the goal to revise and to make the sports federations better performing, efficient and strong. The funding mechanisms for the entire sports sector are stated in the decree, including the funding procedure for disability sport. In order to rationalise the sports landscape, the 2017 decree mentioned that financial support would only be foreseen for one federation per sport, with disability sport seen as 'one sport'. In return for the (financial) support from the government, each sports federation, including G-sport Vlaanderen for disability sport, needs to submit its policy plan every four years to Sport Vlaanderen. In the policy plan, sports federations have to state their vision and mission and to demonstrate how they will reach the policy goals formulated, their strategy and their work plans, including aspects of quality control. All sports federations receive a minimal basic funding, based on their size (i.e. the number of registered members). Extra funding can be received related to additional goals. As regards mainstream sports federations, this extra funding can be obtained, for instance, for focusing on disability sport and/or inclusion.

Policy Framework

The public sports policy by the Flemish government can be described as a Sports for All policy, implying the government's aim to focus on increased levels of sports participation for all citizens (Scheerder et al., 2021). More specifically, policy actions are oriented towards active promotion of participation in (club-organised) sports and physical activity, with special attention, among others, to extra-curricular sports activities and sports opportunities for people with disabilities. On the one hand, the emphasis is on a stimulating policy-making (i.e. increased levels of participation), whereas on the other hand efforts are made to create a sustainable form of sports policy, for instance, by means of professionalisation and optimisation of the supply and management of sports federations.

Between 1976 and 2015, the Decree on Local Sport stipulated the policy actions cities and municipalities in Flanders had to fulfil in order to receive subsidies from the Flemish government. Based on this decree, since 2008, local authorities were required to prove that they spend attention in their sport policy programmes towards aspects of accessibility and diversity in sport in order to facilitate low-threshold forms of sports participation on the one side and to create equal sports participation opportunities for disadvantaged groups in society on the other (Scheerder et al., 2021). In 2015, however, it was decided to annul the Decree on Local Sports. As a consequence, local authorities gained full autonomy to prepare and implement their sports policy programme. For the financial support, cities and municipalities can partially rely on means from the so-called Municipality Fund ('Gemeentefonds'). Thus, local authorities are free to put their own policy emphasis on one or more disadvantaged groups, for instance, people with disabilities, according to the specific needs and wants of the respective city or municipality. Based on their autonomy, local authorities, however, can also decide not to target any specific group by means of their sports policy programme or even not to pay any policy attention to sport at all.

Support of Disability Sport

Financial Framework

To help ensure a high-quality and sustainable disability sports sector in Flanders, the Flemish government provides public financial support to relevant disability sports actors. The main funding mechanism for disability sport at the regional level in Flanders is based on the Decree on Sports Federations (supra). Referring to figures from 2018 and afterwards (Vlaams Parlement, 2020), in total, a yearly amount of approximately €3900 k is available for club-organised disability sport in Flanders. In 2021, before the merger of G-sport Vlaanderen and Parantee-Psylos, almost half of this budget (46.5%) was paid out to Parantee-Psylos. Most of the remaining part of the budget was spent on G-sports clubs (22%), G-sport Vlaanderen (18.5%), G-sports events (5%), other sports federations that provide sports opportunities for people with disabilities (4.2%), G-sports projects (3%) and other organisations (0.8%). Until that time, financial support could be requested in order to purchase disability-specific sports equipment or to launch a mobility initiative (e.g. organising adapted transport to the sports club) through the G-sport Vlaanderen platform. For their basic funding, local sports clubs and (municipality) schools need to direct themselves to their respective local authority. Depending on the local subsidy regulations and financial means available, local sports clubs and (municipality) schools can apply for financial support in order to, among others, maintain their existing management and supply for people with disabilities, launch new sporting initiatives for people with disabilities and organise sporting events for people with disabilities.

Other funding mechanisms for disability sport are less formalised. They depend on fundraising actions by the actors. For example, Parantee-Psylos generated additional income in 2019 through sponsorship (€25,974), charity (€21,561) and gifts (€3865) (Marin-Urquiza et al., 2020). Another important funding mechanism for Parantee-Psylos/G-sport Vlaanderen (€320,964 in 2019) is through the partnership with *Paralympic Team Belgium*, in collaboration with BPC and LHF. Other G-sports actors also generate additional income through sponsorship, charity and gifts. However, the exact amounts are not publicly available.

Governance and Management Support

When the Flemish government inducted the new version of the Decree on Sports Federations in 2016, four main principles served as a basic framework, namely, (i) rationalisation, (ii) quality improvement, (iii) result orientation and (iv) increase of accountability (Scheerder et al., 2021). As such, the Flemish government aimed for a better performing, more effective and more efficient policy-making regarding the club-organised sports sector in Flanders. Good governance, innovativeness and accessibility, among others, are considered as key objectives. In order to achieve the goals prescribed in the Decree on Sports Federations, the Flemish Sports Confederation (VSF), being the umbrella organisation that takes care of the interests of all sports federations in Flanders, is in charge not only to represent but also to support its member federations concerning legal, administrative, organisational and policy-related issues. Thus, all in all, the direct governance and management support from the Flemish government towards the sports federations in Flanders, including the support for disability sport, is rather limited since it is the Flemish Sports Confederation's responsibility to take up this support towards its members, which themselves have considerable autonomy.

VSF also provides direct management support to local sports clubs, ranging from support regarding legal and administrative issues to management tools to aid clubs, among others, in their strategic planning and financial management. This support service is offered through training sessions and workshops, through the availability of practical tools such as software, manuals and documentation and through an online helpdesk. Apart from VSF, the Flemish Trainer School (VTS) serves as an institution that provides in-service training for staff and coaches enabling them to (further) develop their training and/or management skills and competences.

By means of all these initiatives, the Flemish government (in)directly supports the management and professionalisation of both regional sports federations and local sports clubs, including associations and organisations that offer opportunities for disability sport.

Level of Integration or Inclusion

As in most sectors of society in Belgium (e.g. education, employment, public transportation and media), inclusion and representation of all social groups are supported by laws and decrees. Also in the field of sport such a legal framework is provided. However, full social inclusion and fully equal participation by all citizens are not yet achieved across these sectors (Goethals et al., 2018; Scheerder & Vandermeerschen, 2016; Vandermeerschen et al., 2016). There are still obstacles, of which some link back to what could be described as the 'inclusion paradigm'. The school system, as an example of this paradigm, was traditionally organised in a segregated way in Belgium (mainstream schools versus special needs schools). The top-down decision taken by the Flemish government to support inclusion and to legally reinforce the right of all pupils and students, including those with disabilities, to be enrolled in mainstream education (Onderwijs, 2014), caused considerable opposition, not least from the schools and the teachers as they were not sufficiently prepared or qualified to act inclusively. The lack of teachers' preparation and training is reported as one of the main causes of negative attitudes towards pupils and students with disabilities (Florian & Camedda, 2020).

The paradigm as described before is also observed in the sports sector, where federations and clubs are encouraged and subsidised to work inclusively. This process started in 1999 with the then Decree on Sports Federations that offered incentives for mainstream sports federations (MSF) to provide an inclusive sports programme. As a consequence, there is an increasing number of sports clubs with an offer for athletes with a disability. But, although coach education bodies are gradually progressing towards a more inclusive approach, there is still a lack of qualified trainers with disability-specific knowledge and expertise, which may lead to negative experiences and even drop-out (Burns & Johnston, 2020).

The current sports offer can be categorised across four types of organisational settings. More precisely these types are, respectively, exclusion, segregation, integration and inclusion (see Fig. 13.2). In Flanders, most of the mainstream sports federations (MSFs) moved towards inclusion in collaboration with G-sport Vlaanderen (previously Parantee-Psylos), relying on its specific expertise. Anno 2021, Parantee-Psylos had 33 bilateral contractual agreements with MSFs. During the last 15 years, the number of agreements gradually increased from 10 in 2005 to 19 in 2012 and 26 in 2016 (Parantee-Psylos, 2021c). The level of support and the level of inclusion fluctuate on a continuum from sports federations that ask support from G-sport Vlaanderen to start an inclusive offer (e.g. volleyball) or to organise inclusive training and competition (e.g. swimming and table tennis) to sports federations that are fully responsible for coordinating inclusive training and competition (e.g. basketball, equestrian sports, tennis, and track and field) with limited support from G-sport Vlaanderen. There are currently five MSFs, that is, basketball, football, gymnastics, swimming, and track and field, each counting over 200 persons with a disability among their members.

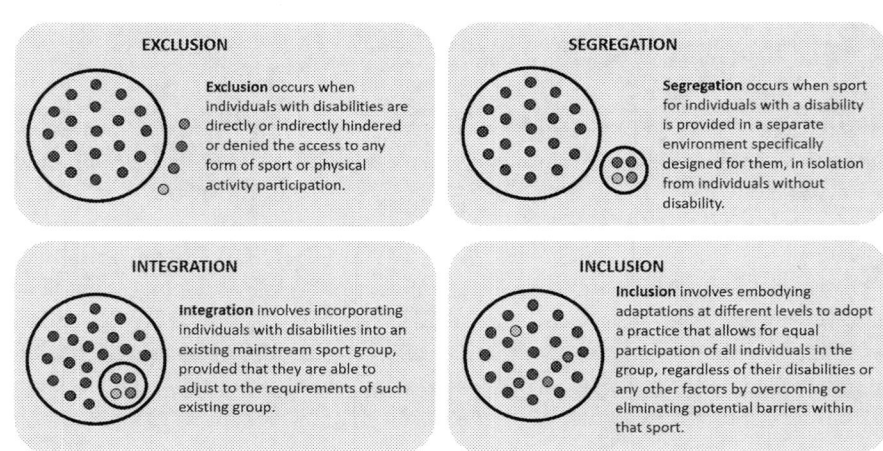

Fig. 13.2 The inclusion continuum. Note: definitions adapted from 'General Comment No. 4' of the UN Convention on the Rights for Persons with Disability (2016) in the context of education. Source: Burns and Johnston (2020)

13.4 Sports Participation by People with Disabilities

Monitoring and Evaluation

Commissioned by G-sport Vlaanderen and with financial support of the Flemish government and Sport Vlaanderen in particular, a large-scale disability sports participation study was conducted in Flanders and the Brussels-Capital Region in 2017. The study was performed by a team of KU Leuven researchers (Scheerder et al., 2018a). The survey aligned with the increasing importance that is given to sport and physical activity in society and, particularly, the growing attention regarding participation opportunities for people with disabilities. It is the first study of its kind on such a large scale, as there is no similar standardised monitoring instrument yet available.

A total sample of 1770 people with disabilities participated in the KU Leuven study. A total number of 215 subjects were removed because the inclusion criteria were not met, that is, having disorders that do not result in limitations of the neuro-muscular skeletal system, such as internal disorders (e.g. heart failure, lung transplants, lung disease, Crohn's disease and kidney failure), cancer (e.g. brain tumour and bone cancer) or extreme fatigue. The remaining sample of 1555 respondents consisted of 878 men (56.5%), 671 women (43.1%) and 6 transgender persons (0.4%). The majority of the respondents had a physical impairment (PI, $n = 710$), followed by intellectual impairment (II, $n = 310$), autism spectrum disorder (ASD, $n = 218$), visual impairment (VI, $n = 127$), mental health disorder (MHD, $n = 105$) and hearing impairment (HI, $n = 85$). The sample consisted of children and young people between 6 and 18 years old (13%, $n = 202$) and adults between 19 and 65 years old (87%, $n = 1353$).

As there is no central registration database for people with disabilities in Belgium, the sample was composed by performing a large-scale recruitment campaign through all possible disability organisations registered throughout the country. The representativeness of the sample was verified and guaranteed based on comparative figures from available national and international participation studies (i.e. the breakdown by type of impairment, age, gender and residence).

Procedure

An online sports participation questionnaire was developed in collaboration with an expert panel and based on relevant existing questionnaires (Scheerder et al., 2013; Theeboom et al., 2015; Vanlandewijck & Van De Vliet, 2004). The definition of sports participation used throughout the study was a broad definition as proposed by Scheerder et al. (2013), that is, physical activity that requires sufficient rate of exertion and takes place in a sportive and/or leisure-time context, without a merely utilitarian character. In this way, it is possible to make a clear distinction between respondents who actively engage in sport versus respondents who do not engage in sport at all during their free time. Along with active participation in sport, the study also examined the frequency of sports practice, and hence we can distinguish three groups of participants, namely, (1) non-participants, (2) occasional or non-regular sports participants (active in sport less than once a week) and (3) regular sports participants (sports activity at least once a week). We note, however, that from a health perspective, the World Health Organization (WHO, 2019) uses different standards than weekly sports practice. Both the type of activity (not just sport but all forms of physical activity, including those with a utilitarian character) and the amount of activity (expressed in minutes/day or minutes/week) that the WHO standard takes into account are different. However, in order to be able to compare the sports behaviour of people with disabilities to general levels and preferences of sports participation among people living in Flanders, the sports participation definition by Scheerder and colleagues was used.

Sports Participation

Frequency

Based on the choices made in the baseline measurement, it is concluded that 35.9% of all people with disabilities in Flanders indicated not having practised any form of sport during the past year (see Table 13.4). We call this group the non-participants (NP). As indicated previously, this group can be identified as being fully sedentary. Conversely, we can say that 64.1% of the respondents had actively taken part in sport in the past year. We call this group the sports participants. We further divide this group into two subgroups. More precisely, the subgroup of regular sports participants (RSP, exercising at least once a week) consists of 51.8% of the total sample, or 80.8% of all sports participants. The group of non-regular sports participants (NRSP) partakes in sport less than once a week and comprises 12.3% of the total sample, or 19.2% of all sports participants. Differences in frequency by type of impairment are depicted in Table 13.4.

Type of Sport

The preferred sports practices are, respectively, swimming, cycling and fitness. Differences across the various impairment groups are shown in Table 13.4. Swimming is by far the most popular sport, as it appears in the top three for every impairment group.

Inclusion in Mainstream Sport

The majority of people with disabilities are active in an inclusive setting (mainstream). About one-third is active in exclusive settings, and another 30% in integration settings. These numbers do not cumulate to 100% because participants can participate in a mixture of organisational contexts.

13 Disability Sport in Belgium/Flanders: From a Fragmented Mosaic Towards a More... 315

Table 13.4 Sports participation of people with disabilities in Flanders

Type of impairment	Frequency (%)*			Sports preference Top-3	Context of regularly active participants				Inclusion continuum		
	RSP	NRSP	NP		Club	Individual	Other*	Fitness	Inclusive	Exclusive	Integration
Physical (n = 710)	36.3	10.6	53.1	Swimming Fitness Hand-bike	**66.3**	**50.0**	7.4	**12.8**	**43.9**	35.1	**39.8**
Visual (n = 127)	55.2	15.0	29.9	Walking Cycling Swimming	**65.7**	**36.8**	**10.0**	**12.9**	**45.7**	43.5	26.1
Hearing (n = 85)	64.8	17.7	17.6	Football Swimming Cycling	**76.4**	45.5	14.5	12.7	**76.2**	33.3	9.5
Intellectual (n = 310)	73.5	11.3	15.2	Swimming Football Track and field	**69.7**	18.9	38.6	9.6	34.0	42.8	**50.9**
Mental health disorder (n = 105)	46.7	13.3	40.0	Walking Swimming Cycling	42.9	42.9	10.2	18.4	**61.9**	38.1	19.0
Autism spectrum disorder (n = 218)	67.0	14.7	18.3	Swimming Running Cycling	**69.2**	34.2	13.0	13.0	**53.5**	26.7	29.7
Total sample (N = 1555)	51.8	12.3	35.9	Swimming Cycling Fitness	**67.0**	36.6	18.1	12.3	**46.1**	36.5	36.9

Source: data derived from Scheerder et al. (2018a)
NP Non-participants
NRSP Non-regular sports participants
RSP Regular sports participants

Club Membership

Most of the sports active participants are members of a sports club (67%). As one-third of the participants indicated being involved in sports individually, this way of participating in sport can be considered as a popular setting too. Fitness and other types of sports activities, such as extra-curricular sport and sport at work, are less popular among people with disabilities.

Sports Participation and Sports Preference According to Demographic Background

In the total sample of people with disabilities, females tend to be less sports active compared to males, with 42% of the females compared to 31% of the males in the NP group. The levels of sports inactivity also appear to augment with increasing age, higher unemployment rates and lower socio-economic status. These findings are consistent over the different impairment categories and in line with other disability sports participation studies found in the literature (cfr. Dairo et al., 2016; Ng et al., 2017).

A novelty by means of the current survey is a unique approach taken to gain insight in the relation between sports preference and social background. Though investigation into social stratification patterns of sports activities practised by different social groups in society has a long-standing tradition in sociological research (see f.i., Scheerder et al., 2002), this kind of analysis, to our knowledge, has not yet been performed with regard to sports participation by people with disabilities. For this, a so-called social status pyramid of sport is set up (Scheerder et al., 2002, 2013; Scheerder & Thibaut, 2021a). In this pyramid different sports activities are ranked according to their social status. For the social status pyramid of disability sports, Scheerder et al. (2018b) calculated a specific index for each sports discipline based on the educational level of the sports participants. As regards the educational background, three categories are discerned, namely, (1) did not complete secondary education, (2) did complete secondary education but no higher education and (3) did complete higher education. Sports activities typically performed by participants with a higher educational level are defined as 'upper-class sports', followed by 'middle-class sports' and 'lower-class sports'. Sports activities in which all social layers equally participate are called 'democratised sports'.

In Fig. 13.3, the social status pyramid of disability sport, as developed by Scheerder et al. (2018b), is presented. It can be seen from this figure that sports activities such as callisthenics, hand-bike, sailing and skiing are mainly practised by upper-class people with disabilities. Middle-class sports activities among people with disabilities are fitness, jogging/running, basketball, table tennis, recreational walking, recreational cycling and tourist cycling, while horse-riding, track and field, karate, football, gymnastics, boccia, judo and netball can be characterised as typically lower-class sports. Swimming, badminton, dancing and petanque, on their turn, are sports activities for which no significant differences between social groups appear and which therefore can be identified as democratised sports. Between the social status pyramid of disability sport on the one hand and the social status

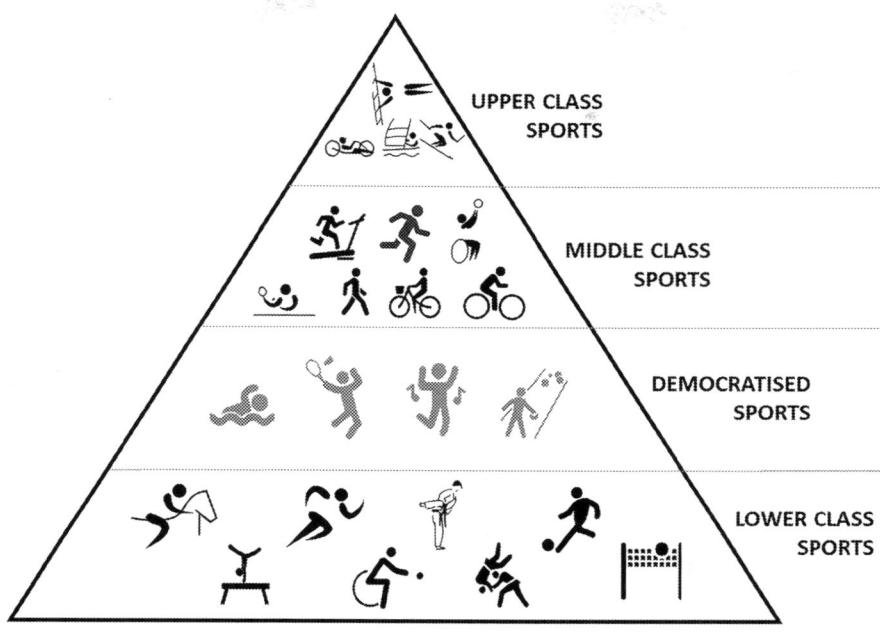

Fig. 13.3 The social status pyramid of disability sport. Source: data derived from Scheerder et al. (2018b)

pyramid of mainstream sport on the other, some remarkable dissimilarities can be noted. According to the findings of Scheerder and Thibaut (2021a), this is the case for callisthenics (middle-class sport), fitness (democratised sport), recreational cycling (democratised sport), swimming (middle-class sport), dancing (lower-class sport), horse-riding (upper-class sport), karate (democratised sport), football (democratised sport) and volleyball (upper-class sport).

From the results presented, the most interesting observations are that horse-riding and track and field are lower-class sports for participants with disabilities, whereas they are to be situated more at the top of the pyramid in mainstream sport. A potential explanation for this might be that horse-riding is frequently used as a therapeutic tool for people with various types of impairments, while for track and field the reason might be that the Flemish Athletics Federation (VAL) takes a leading role in supporting their clubs to implement a more inclusive programme. Historically seen, the VAL was one of the first sports federations to sign a collaborative agreement with Parantee-Psylos. As a result, it now is fully in charge of the disability sports offer and competition.

Sports Participation by People with Disabilities in the French Community and the German-Speaking Community of Belgium

In Wallonia, a recent study was performed by Declerck (2021) to investigate active sports participation among people with disabilities ($N = 510$; 59% female, 41% male). This investigation, however, was limited to people with physical impairments and chronic health disorders including a variety of different pathologies (e.g. musculoskeletal, amputations, spinal cord injury, multiple sclerosis and stroke), covering adults of all ages ranging from 18 to 60 years (65%) and above 60 years (35%). A total of 38% of the sample indicated participating in sports activities, while 62% reported no sports activities of any type. With regard to physical activity participation, 27% of the respondents reported never performing any type of light form of physical activity. The number of non-participants increased with increasing intensity, that is, 46% never performed moderate physical activity and 71% never performed vigorous physical activity (Declerck, 2021). For the German-speaking part of Belgium, no data are available regarding the disability sports participation, at least to the authors' knowledge.

Barriers and Facilitators

Every individual has her/his own motives to become physically active or to live a rather sedentary life. This is also true for people with disabilities. The unique methodology of the sports participation survey conducted in Flanders (supra) provides the opportunity to investigate differences in barriers and facilitators across the various impairment types. The motives appear to be similar across groups, whereas the self-reported barriers were different depending on the type of impairment (Van Biesen et al., 2018). This finding highlights the urgent need for tailored interventions to enhance sports participation by people with disabilities. Or in other words, a one size fits all approach is not recommended.

Barriers

The major barrier is the hindrance by the impairment itself. This is the case for 73% of people with a physical impairment, 69% of people with visual impairments, and 73% of people with autism. Fatigue is the major barrier for 55% of people with mental health disorders (e.g. depression). The high cost is reported as the main barrier for people with hearing impairments (33%), and being too dependent on others for 59% of the people with intellectual impairment. An overview of the three most reported barriers for each impairment group is provided in Table 13.5.

These self-reported barriers on the individual level can be complemented by data from another survey (Marin-Urquiza et al., 2020) that includes the main disability sports agents in Flanders and Wallonia. This survey focuses on the organisation of sport for people with intellectual disabilities across ten European countries. However, for Belgium most of these actors are operating for all types of disabilities, making the data more generalisable. One contact person per organisation was interviewed by means of a semi-structured questionnaire. The organisations report competition with other organisations to acquire funding and to find sponsors and difficulties aligning the activity calendars of the various organisations in order to avoid overlap. Other reported barriers are higher costs to organise activities for people with high support needs (e.g. some people requiring one on one support) and having too many structures in place within one small country. For athletes with

Table 13.5 Self-reported barriers towards sports participation by people with disabilities in Flanders, according to the type of impairment

Type of impairment	N	Most reported barriers	% reported
Physical (musculoskeletal)	710	Impairment hinders	73
		Dependent on others for transport	46
		Dependent on others during sport	43
Visual	127	Impairment hinders	69
		Dependent on others for transport	62
		Dependent on others during sport	51
Hearing	85	Too expensive	33
		Lack of time	31
		Impairment hinders	27
Intellectual	310	Dependent on others for transport	59
		No offer in the community	40
		Impairment hinders	36
Mental health disorders	105	Fatigue (I'm too tired)	55
		Impairment hinders	54
		Worries about what others have to say	41
Autism spectrum disorder	218	Impairment hinders	73
		Dependent on others for transport	44
		Worries about what others have to say	40

Sources: data based on Scheerder et al. (2018a) and Van Biesen et al. (2018)

intellectual disabilities in particular, the organisations report that it is more difficult to include them in mainstream sports clubs because of negative attitudes and lack of knowledge about their disability. The challenges reported by the organisations are to find enough volunteers, accessibility of accommodation, limited mobility of participants, recruiting new members and developing new partnerships.

Self-reported weaknesses by the organisations are the fragmented disability sports landscape, fragmented promotion of activities (through different channels), lack of self-reflection, financial aspect (constantly searching for financial resources), drop-out of volunteers (lack of human resources), lack of knowledge and specialisation about all/different types of disability among the support staff, lack of coordination between structures, dominant focus on the elite level and lack of communication between regions. The self-reported strengths are the contacts with the government, the inclusion process with the mainstream federations, the expertise available within the organisations, the sustainable sports offer and positive attitudes of mainstream sports federations towards social inclusion.

Facilitators

With respect to the motives to become physically active, the two most reported facilitators are similar across all the impairment groups, with 78% of all people with disabilities reporting 'experiencing fun' and 57% reporting 'health benefits'. The third facilitator varies from improving your functional skills (people with physical impairments), spending time with friends (hearing and intellectual impairment), feeling accepted by others (visual impairment and autism) and losing weight (mental health disorders).

13.5 Conclusion

The purpose of this chapter was to review and present the existing knowledge and insights concerning the organisation of disability sport in Belgium. Although Belgium is a rather small country, the complexity of governmental and organisational levels is obvious. In order to enhance clarity and comprehensibility, the focus in this chapter was mainly on Flanders, which is the Dutch-speaking, northern part of the country with about 6.5 million inhabitants. Sport for All is a common goal for sports policy-making in Flanders, and the region has a rich history of policies and legislations in favour of reaching this goal. The baseline of this chapter, for example, 'from a fragmented mosaic towards a more inclusive landscape', concisely summarises the approach taken by the Flemish government to strive towards more inclusion and a more transparent and uniform landscape to organise the sports sector, in particular the disability sports sector. The main actor on the governmental level is Sport Vlaanderen, being the sports governing body of the Flemish government. Disability sports consultants are embedded within Sport Vlaanderen to act on regional, provincial, local and sub-local levels in order to support disability sports initiatives, events and disability sports clubs situated on the inclusion continuum. On a regional level, Sport Vlaanderen works in close collaboration with G-sport Vlaanderen to provide a structural disability sports offer as stated in the Decree on Sports Federations in Flanders. To unify the landscape, governmental decisions forced G-sport Vlaanderen and Parantee-Psylos to merge into this new umbrella organisation for disability sport in Flanders, with an offer for all people of all ages and abilities with any type of impairment or chronic disease.

From the figures presented in this chapter, it can be seen that sports participation is generally lower for people with disabilities compared to the general population, despite a multitude of actions taken by the respective actors with a long history in disability sport. Several barriers can be identified, but one of the main reasons might be the inclusion paradigm, that is, the discrepancy between the top-down enforcement of inclusive policies versus the lack of knowledge and expertise of key stakeholders (e.g. coaches and trainers) to make successful inclusion work. Another reason might be that a 'one size fits all' approach is insufficient to address the needs of the large and diverse population of people with disabilities. Future actions should focus both on educating the support staff and on interventions being more tailored to the individual needs of potential participants, taking into account at least the type and severity of their impairment.

References

Adeps. (2021a). *Etudes et recherches* [Studies and research]. Accessed December 1, 2021, from www.sport-adeps.be.

Adeps. (2021b). *Nombre d'affiliés dans les fédérations sportives reconnues par la FW-B* [Number of members of sports federations recognised by FW-B]. Accessed December 1, 2021, from https://statistiques.cfwb.be/sport/federations-sportives/nombre-daffilies-dans-les-federations-sportives-reconnues-par-la-fw-b/.

Adeps. (2021c). *Répartition du budget 'sport' et de la lutte contre le dopage* [Distribution of the sports budget and of the anti-doping policy]. Accessed December 1, 2021, from https://statistiques.cfwb.be/sport/budget-du-sport/repartition-du-budget-sport-et-de-la-lutte-contre-le-dopage/.

Adeps. (2021d). *Subsides octroyés par la FW-B* [Subsidies awarded by the FW-B]. Accessed December 1, 2021, from https://statistiques.cfwb.be/sport/budget-du-sport/subsides-octroyes-par-la-fw-b/.

Burns, J., & Johnston, M. (2020). *Good practice guide for coaching athletes with intellectual disabilities.* Canterbury: Canterbury Christ Church University. Accessed August 20, 2021, from https://idealproject.org.

Cap sur le Sport. (2021). Accessed September 1, 2021, from https://capsurlesport.org/.

Claes, E., Scheerder, J., Willem, A., & Billiet, S. (2017). Belgium: Flanders. Sport federations and governmental sport bodies. In J. Scheerder, A. Willem, & E. Claes (Eds.), *Sport policy systems and sport federations. A cross-national perspective* (pp. 41–63). Palgrave Macmillan.

Dairo, Y. M., Collett, J., Dawes, H., & Oskrochi, G. R. (2016). Physical activity levels in adults with intellectual disabilities. A systematic review. *Preventive Medicine Reports, 4*, 209–219.

De Meyer, M. (2010). *People in motion. 50 years Belgian paralympic committee 1960–2010.* Roularta Books.

Declerck, L. (2021). *Physical activity level and adaptive sports participation among individuals with a physical disability in French-speaking Belgium* (Unpublished data, with permission of the author).

European Commission. (2018). *Sport and physical activity (Special Eurobarometer 472/Wave EB88.4).* European Commission/Directorate-General for Education, Youth, Sport & Culture.

Eurostat. (2019). *Real GDP per capita.* Accessed July 22, 2019, from https://ec.europa.eu/eurostat/web/main/help/first-visit/tgm.

FéMA. (2021). Accessed September 1, 2021, from https://www.sportadapte.be.

Florian, L., & Camedda, D. (2020). Enhancing teacher education for inclusion. *European Journal of Teacher Education, 43*(1), 4–8.

Goethals, T., Mortelmans, D., & Van Hove, G. (2018). Toward a more balanced representation of disability? A content analysis of disability coverage in the Flemish print media. *Journal of Human Development, Disability & Social Change, 24*(1), 109–120.

Helsen, K., & Scheerder, J. (2020). Fitness(-related) trends within and between countries. Towards a fit (in) Europe? In J. Scheerder, H. Vehmas, & K. Helsen (Eds.), *The rise and size of the fitness industry in Europe. Fit for the future?* (pp. 389–436). Palgrave Macmillan.

Helsen, K., & Scheerder, J. (2021). Sports participation, physical (in)activity and overweight in the European Union. In *A comparative study based on pan-European data 2002–2017 (Sport Policy & Management Studies 67).* KU Leuven/Policy in Sports & Physical Activity Research Group. https://gbiomed.kuleuven.be/english/research/50000737/groups/policy-in-sports-physical-activity-research-group/bms-research-results/results

Infrasports. (2021). *Infrastructures sportives* [Sports infrastructures]. https://infrastructures.wallonie.be/pouvoirs-locaux/infrasports.html. Accessed December 1, 2021.

Leitverband des Ostbelgischen Sports. (2021). *Sportstrukturen in der Deutschsprachigen Gemeinschaft.* Accessed July 9, 2021, from https://ostbelgiensport.be/desktopdefault.aspx/tabid-3214/6004_read-37225/%22%20/h.

Lenoir, M., Tolleneer, J., & Laporte, W. (Eds.). (2007). *100 jaar opleiding lichamelijke opvoeding en bewegingswetenschappen aan de Universiteit Gent [100 years of physical education and movement sciences training at the Ghent University]*. Academia Press.

Marin-Urquiza, A., Kerremans, J., & Van Biesen, D. (2020). How is sport for people with intellectual disabilities organised across Europe: Output from WP2C. Macro level: Review sport organisations, programmes and structures. www.idealproject.org.

Ng, K., Tynjälä, J., Sigmundová, D., Augustine, L., Sentenac, M., Rintala, P., & Inchley, J. (2017). Physical activity among adolescents with long-term illnesses or disabilities in 15 European countries. *Adapted Physical Activity Quarterly, 34*(4), 456–465.

Onderwijs, V. (2014). Grote lijnen van het M-decreet [M-decree key points]. Accessed March 20, 2022, from https://onderwijs.vlaanderen.be/nl/onderwijspersoneel/van-basis-totvolwassenenonderwijs/lespraktijk/je-leerlingen-helpen-en-begeleiden/specifieke-onderwijsbehoeften/grote-lijnen-van-het-m-decreet

Parantee-Psylos. (2017). *Beleidsnota Parantee-Psylos 2017–2020. Historiek* (pg. 12–14) [Policy note Parantee–Psylos 2017–2020. History of the organization (pages 12–14)]. Retrieved from www.parantee-psylos.be/uploads/documents/Luik-I-Beleidsplan-Parantee-Psylos-2017-2020.pdf. Accessed September 1, 2021.

Parantee-Psylos. (2021a). *Wat is G-sport?* [What is disability sport?]. Retrieved from https://www.parantee-psylos.be/wat-is-g-sport. Accessed September 1, 2021.

Parantee-Psylos. (2021b). *G-sport en revalidatie* [Disability sport and rehabilitation]. Retrieved from https://www.parantee-psylos.be/g-sport-en-revalidatie. Accessed September 1, 2021.

Parantee-Psylos. (2021c). *Integratiebeleid* [Policy for integration]. Retrieved from https://www.parantee-psylos.be/integratiebeleid. Accessed September 1, 2021.

Renson, R. (1976). The Flemish archery gilds. From defence mechanisms to sports institution. In R. Renson, P. P. De Nayer, & M. Ostyn (Eds.), *The history, the evolution and the diffusion of sports and games in different cultures (Proceedings of the 4th International HISPA seminar; Leuven; 1975)* (pp. 135–159). BLOSO.

Renson, R. (1996). *The games reborn. The VIIth Olympiad Antwerp 1920*. Pandora.

Renson, R. (2006). *Enflammée par l'Olympisme. Cent ans de Comité Olympique et Interfédéral Belge, 1906–2006*. Roularta.

Scheerder, J., Corthouts, J., Thibaut, E., & Borgers, J. (2021). *Sport. Beleid en participatie in Vlaanderen (Campus Handboek/Management & Bestuur in sport 11) [sport. Policy and participation in Flanders (Management & Governance in sport 11)]*. LannooCampus.

Scheerder, J., Helsen, K., Corthouts, J., Zintz, T., Zeimers, G., & Greimers, D. (2021). *Delta Barometer Goed Bestuur en Innovatie in de Sport. Good Governance & Innovation in Sport Index (GGIS): Resultaten van de GGIS2.0 en vergelijking met de GGIS1.0* [Delta Barometer of Good Governance and Innovation in Sport. Good Governance & Innovation in Sport Index (GGIS): Main results and summary of GGIS1.0 and GGIS2.0] (Beleid & Management in Sport Studies 81). Leuven/Louvain-la-Neuve: KU Leuven/Policy in Sports & Physical Activity Research Group - UCLouvain/Chaire Olympique Henri de Baillet Latour et Jacques Rogge en Management des Organisations Sportives. https://gbiomed.kuleuven.be/english/research/50000737/groups/policy-in-sports-physical-activity-research-group/bms-research-results/results

Scheerder, J., & Thibaut, E. (2021a). *Flemish household study on sports participation 2019. Social status pyramid of sports participation in Flanders according to socio-professional status* (Sport Policy & Management Infographics 106). Leuven: KU Leuven/Policy in Sports & Physical Activity Research Group. https://gbiomed.kuleuven.be/english/research/50000737/groups/policy-in-sports-physical-activity-research-group/bms-research-results/results

Scheerder, J., & Thibaut, E. (2021b). *Studie over de Bewegingsactiviteiten in Vlaanderen (SBV) 1969–2019. Een halve eeuw sportparticipatie in cijfers* [Study on Sport and Physical Activity in Flanders (SSPAF) 1969–2019. Half a century of sports participation in figures] (Beleid & Management in Sport Studies 100). Leuven: KU Leuven/Policy in Sports & Physical Activity Research Group. https://gbiomed.kuleuven.be/english/research/50000737/groups/policy-in-sports-physical-activity-research-group/bms-research-results/results

Scheerder, J., & Thibaut, E. (2021c). *Studie over de Bewegingsactiviteiten in Vlaanderen (SBV) 1969–2019. De sociale gelaagdheid van sportbeoefening* [Study on Sport and Physical activity in Flanders (SSPAF) 1969–2019. Social stratification of sports participation] (Beleid & Management in Sport Studies 101). Leuven: KU Leuven/Policy in Sports & Physical Activity Research Group. https://gbiomed.kuleuven.be/english/research/50000737/groups/policy-in-sports-physical-activity-research-group/bms-research-results/results

Scheerder, J., & Vandermeerschen, H. (2016). Playing an unequal game? Youth sport and social class. In K. Green & A. Smith (Eds.), *Routledge handbook of youth sport (Routledge International Handbooks)* (pp. 265–275). Routledge.

Scheerder, J., Vandermeerschen, H., Borgers, J., Thibaut, E. & Vos, S. (2013). *Vlaanderen sport! Vier decennia sportbeleid en sportparticipatie (Sociaalwetenschappelijk onderzoek naar Bewegen & Sport 5) [Sport in Flanders. Four decades of sports policy and sports participation (Social-scientific research into physical activity & sport 5)]*. Academia Press.

Scheerder, J., Vandermeerschen, H., & Breedveld, K. (2018). Diversity in participation reigns, policy challenges ahead. Sport for all (ages) from a European perspective. In R. A. Dionigi & M. Gard (Eds.), *Sport and physical activity across the lifespan. Critical perspectives* (pp. 45–65). Basingstoke: Palgrave Macmillan. https://doi.org/10.1057/978-1-137-48562-5

Scheerder, J., Vandermeerschen, H., Meganck, J., Seghers, J., & Vos, S. (2015). Sport clubs in Belgium. In C. Breuer, R. Hoekman, S. Nagel, & H. van der Werff (Eds.), *Sport clubs in Europe. A cross-national comparative perspective (Sports Economics, Management & Policy 12)* (pp. 47–67). Springer International Publishing.

Scheerder, J., Vanlandewyck, Y., Van Biesen, D., Cans, E., Lenaerts, L., Meganck, A.-S., & Cornelissen, J. (2018a). *Onderzoek naar de actieve sportdeelname van personen met een beperking in Vlaanderen en het Brussels Hoofdstedelijk Gewest. Een nulmeting* [Disability sport participation study in Flanders and Brussels-Capital Region. A baseline measurement] (Beleid & Management in Sport Studies 47). Leuven: KU Leuven/Policy in Sports & Physical Activity Research Group. https://gbiomed.kuleuven.be/english/research/50000737/groups/policy-in-sports-physical-activity-research-group/bms-research-results/results

Scheerder, J., Vanlandewyck, Y., Van Biesen, D., Cans, E., Lenaerts, L., Meganck, A.-S., & Cornelissen, J. (2018b). Active participation in leisure-time sports among people with different types of disabilities in Flanders (Belgium) (Paper presented at the 15th European Association for Sociology of Sport Conference; Bordeaux; May 23–26, 2018). In N. Delorme (Ed.), *Sport, discriminations and inclusion. Challenges to face (Abstract book of the 15th EASS Conference)* (p. 88). Université de Bordeaux/Faculté Sciences & Techniques des Activités Physiques & Sportives.

Scheerder, J., Vanreusel, B., Taks, M., & Renson, R. (2002). Social sports stratification in Flanders 1969-1999. Intergenerational reproduction of social inequalities? *International Review for the Sociology of Sport, 37*(2), 219–245.

Scheerder, J., & Vos, S. (2013). Belgium: Flanders. In K. Hallmann & K. Petry (Eds.), *Comparative sport development. Systems, participation and public policy (Sports Economics, Management & Policy 8)* (pp. 7–21). New York, NY.

Scheerder, J., Zintz, T., & Delheye, P. (2011). The organisation of sports in Belgium. Between public, economic and social profit. In C. Sobry (Ed.), *Sports governance in the world: A sociohistoric approach. The organisation of sport in Europe: A patch-work of institutions, with few shared points (sport social studies)* (pp. 84–113). Le Manuscrit.

Sport Vlaanderen. (2021a). *Sportclubs* [Sport clubs]. Accessed July 9, 2021, from www.sport.vlaanderen/kennisplatform/thema-sportclubs/.

Sport Vlaanderen. (2021b). *Evolutie budget Sport Vlaanderen periode 2009–2020 (Cijferboek Sport Vlaanderen)* [Evolution of the budget of Sport Vlaanderen 2009–2020]. Accessed December 1, 2021, from https://app.powerbi.com/view?r=eyJrIjoiODg5ZWNhNjEtZjNiMi00YWY2LWIyZmYtMDFmYWUzYTQ5ZjcxIiwidCI6ImNhOWQyZjc5LWMyZDEtNDA2Zi05M2NhLThiOTY0NTNmNGY4ZCIsImMiOjh9.

Sport Vlaanderen. (2021c). *Cijferboek Sport Vlaanderen* [Gradebook Sport Vlaanderen]. Accessed December 1, 2021, from https://app.powerbi.com/view?r=eyJrIjoiODg5ZWNhNjEtZjNiMi00YWY2LWIyZmYtMDFmYWUzYTQ5ZjcxIiwidCI6ImNhOWQyZjc5LWMyZDEtNDA2Zi05M2NhLThiOTY0NTNmNGY4ZCIsImMiOjh9.

Sport Vlaanderen. (2021d). *Sportfederaties. Wettelijk kader* [Sport federations. Legal framework]. Accessed September 1, 2021, from www.sport.vlaanderen/sportfederaties/documenten-en-regelgeving/wettelijk-kader/.

Statbel. (2021). *Structuur van de bevolking* [Demographic composition of the population]. Accessed July 9, 2021, from https://statbel.fgov.be/nl/themas/bevolking/structuur-van-de-bevolking#panel-14.

Statista. (2021). *Gross domestic product (GDP) per capita in Belgium from 2007 to 2019, by region (in euro purchasing power parity)*. Accessed October 17, 2021, from www.statista.com/statistics/525545/gross-domestic-product-gdp-per-capita-in-belgium-by-region/.

Statistics Flanders. (2021). *Gross domestic product per capita*. Accessed July 9, 2021, from https://www.statistiekvlaanderen.be/en/gross-domestic-product-per-capita-0.

Taks, M., Renson, R., & Vanreusel, B. (1999). Organised sport in transition. Development, structure and trends of sports clubs in Belgium. In K. Heinemann (Ed.), *Sport clubs in various European countries (series Club of Cologne 1)* (pp. 183–223). Hofmann.

The World Bank. (2019). *Urban population (% of total population)*. Accessed July 22, 2019, from https://data.worldbank.org/indicator/SP.URB.TOTL.

Theeboom, M., Scheerder, J., Willem, A., Nols, Z., Wittock, H., De Martelaer, K., Clarys, P., De Bosscher, V., Borgers, J., Thibaut, E., Seghers, J., Lefevre, J., De Cocker, K., Haerens, L., De Bourdeaudhuij, I., Cardon, G., & Deforche, B. (2015). Sport en fysieke activiteit [Sport and physical activity]. In J. Lievens, J. Siongers, & H. Waege (Eds.), *Participatie in Vlaanderen 1. Basisgegevens van de Participatiesurvey 2014* (pp. 197–249). Acco.

Thibaut, A. (2000). *Les politiques du sport dans la Belgique fédérale [Sports policy in federal Belgium] (Courrier hebdomadaire du CRISP 2000/18 (1683))*. Centre de Recherche & d'Information Socio-Politique.

Van Biesen, D., Lenaerts, L., Cans, E., Meganck, A. Vanlandewijck, Y., & Scheerder, J. (2018). Barriers and motives towards sport participation across people with various types of impairment in Flanders (Poster presented at the European Conference in Adapted Physical Activity (EUCAPA); Worcester; July 3–5, 2018). Accessed August 20, 2021, from www.eufapa.eu/index.php/eucapa/eucapa-2010.html.

van Poppel, M., Claes, E., & Scheerder, J. (2018). Sport policy in Flanders (Belgium). Country profile. *International Journal of Sport Policy & Politics, 10*(2), 271–285.

Vandermeerschen, H., Vos, S., & Scheerder, J. (2016). Towards level playing fields? A time trend analysis of young people's participation in club-organised sports. *International Review for the Sociology of Sport, 51*(4), 468–484.

Vanlandewijck, Y., & Van De Vliet, P. (2004). *Determinanten van sportgedrag bij personen met een handicap in Vlaanderen (Eindrapport) [Determinants of sports behavior among persons with a disability (Final report)]*. KU Leuven/Faculty of Physical Education & Physiotherapy.

Vanreusel, B., Renson, R., & Tolleneer, J. (1999). Divided sports in a divided Belgium. In J. Sugden & A. Bairner (Eds.), *Sport in divided societies* (pp. 97–111). Meyer & Meyer Sport.

Vlaams Parlement. (2020). *G-sport ondersteuning (Schriftelijke vraag)* [Financial support for disability sports (Written question)]. Accessed April 19, 2022, from https://docs.vlaamsparlement.be/pfile?id=1550761.

Weyters, G. (2010). *Zware klap voor Belgisch Paralympisch Comité* [Sad news for the Belgian Paralympic Committee]. Retrieved from www.sport.be/nl/article.html?Article_ID=440977. Accessed 6 Dec 2021.

World Health Organisation. (2019). *Guidelines on physical activity, sedentary behaviour and sleep for children under 5 years of age*. https://apps.who.int/iris/handle/10665/311664. License: CC BY-NC-SA 3.0 IGO. Accessed 12 July 2021.

Chapter 14
Complexity and Coexistence: Disability Sport in Germany

Jürgen Mittag

14.1 Introduction

In the public perception of Germany, disability sport has so far received only limited attention. Only in the course of major sporting events such as the Paralympics the media and the public briefly have turned their attention to disability sport (Schierl & Bertling, 2007; Knauer-Berg & Bös, 2015). In academic studies, on the other hand, the focus has been primarily on practical investigations and specific thematic focal points, such as questions of competitive sports or school sports (Scheid et al., 2003; Tiemann & Radtke, 2017). Overall, however, little is known about the basic structures and actors of German disability sport (Wegner et al., 2015) and about its history (Wedemeyer-Kolwe, 2010).

In practice, a significant proportion of sport by people with disabilities in Germany continues to take place in specific disability-related sport structures. This is especially true for competitive sports. At the same time, however, integrative approaches have become widely established in German sport, and increasingly inclusive forms are emerging (Niehoff, 2008; Kiuppis & Kurzke-Maasmeier, 2012; Aichele, 2012; Anneken, 2013; Wegner et al., 2015). This is particularly true for mass sports (Knoll & Fessler, 2015) and also for rehabilitation sports (Anneken, 2009; Willig et al., 2010). Institutionally, however, changes have just begun to take place at the structural level. In organisational terms, disability sport in Germany is characterised by a high degree of plurality and differentiation without hierarchical control or coordination. The relationship between the numerous players in German disability sport is characterised more by coexistence than by competition or cooperation.

J. Mittag (✉)
German Sport University Cologne, Institute of European Sport Development and Leisure Studies, Cologne, Germany
e-mail: mittag@dshs-koeln.de

14.2 Country Profile

Characteristics of Germany

Germany is the most populous country in the European Union and also marks—after the European part of Russia—the largest state in Europe. At the end of 2020, around 83.2 million people lived in Germany. Of these, around 21.2 million people have a migration background, which corresponds to a share of 25.4% of the population. Almost half of the immigrants or their descendants are now German citizens. The population density is 233 inhabitants/km^2, displaying a high degree of urbanisation in Germany. In 2019, around 77.4% of the total population lived in cities. Within Germany, there have been significant shifts in the population structure in recent decades. While there was a strong east-west divide in population development until the early 2000s, this trend has waned. Instead, there is now stronger growth in urban regions compared with a shrinking and ageing population in rural areas.

Geographically, Germany is divided into three major landscape zones: the North German Plain, the Central Uplands and the Alpine Foreland with the Alps. Politically, Germany is a federal state with a parliamentary republic as its form of government. The Basic Law (*Grundgesetz*) defines in Article 20 democracy and the welfare state as constitutional principles. Germany is divided into 16 constituent states, officially called Länder (federal states). Three of them—Berlin, Hamburg and Bremen—are city states. Through the Bundesrat, the Länder are represented at federal level and participate in legislation. The Bundestag is the parliament of the Federal Republic of Germany electing the Federal Chancellor. The vertical division of powers between the federal level and the "federated states"—the Länder—leads to a complex system of "political interwovenness" (*Politikverflechtung*).

The German economic system is described as a social market economy that combines business competition with a social balance of interests. The welfare state is based on the principles of solidarity and individual responsibility. In Germany, there is a dense network of social regulations which—in addition to providing security in the event of illness, need for care and old age—also covers the area of disability (Table 14.1).

Sport in Germany

The German sports system is based on at least five core principles (Kurscheidt & Deitersen-Wieber, 2011; Petry & Hallmann, 2013; Breuer et al., 2017; Mittag et al., 2018). The first principle is associational autonomy. It is based on Article 9 of the Basic Law of the Federal Republic of Germany, which guarantees freedom of association. On this basis, gymnastics and sport clubs in Germany organise themselves. At the head of organised sports is the German Olympic Sports Confederation

14 Complexity and Coexistence: Disability Sport in Germany

Table 14.1 Facts and descriptives of Germany

Population (number of inhabitants)	84.3
Area (km²)	353,296
Density (inhabitants/km²)	233
Urbanisation rate (%)ᶜ	77.4
Political organisation	Parliamentary republic
Structure of the state	Federal
Number of provinces	16
Number of municipalities	1839
GDP per capita (US dollars)	46,445.2
Number of official languages	1
EU membership	Since 1952
Welfare model	Rhineland

Source: Statistisches Bundesamt https://www.destatis.de

(Deutscher Olympischer Sportbund, DOSB) with its 100 member organisations, which are made up of 16 regional state sports associations, 66 top sports associations and 18 associations with special tasks. These associations comprise more than 27 million members, largely self-organised in clubs.

Federalism and subsidiarity together form the second principle of German sport (vertical level). In line with the federal structure of the Federal Republic, organised sport is represented at all levels. At the local level, the main actors are the individual clubs. There are currently more than 90,000 gymnastics and sport clubs in Germany. The clubs, in turn, are members of the corresponding local, regional and national associations whose sports they participate in. The main task of the regional state associations is to organise both top-level and mass sports activities. The associations at the national level focus primarily on the goal of determining national champions in various disciplines. They are also responsible for tasks such as finding and promoting talent, organising training courses and setting up and maintaining performance centres.

The third defining principle is the cooperation between the associations and the state (horizontal level). Although there is no legal obligation to support sport at the federal level and sport is only taken into account in the constitutions of the federal states, public authorities are also involved in sport. At the national level, the Ministry of the Interior is primarily responsible for sports; at the regional level, the individual states have different ministerial assignments. In addition, municipal governments and administrations at the local level play a relevant role. Although no formal institutions have been created in sport where representatives of sport organisations and public administrations are formally gathered, there are various informal ties and networks of cooperation. Among the most important is the fact that the financing of sport is essentially shaped by the provision of direct and indirect public funding (Haring, 2010; Thieme & Wadsack, 2013).

Volunteering is the fourth principle of German sport. Around eight million people are involved as volunteers in German sports clubs. The sports sector thus covers the highest rates of voluntary involvement of all sectors of society. As a result, sport is considered as a central actor for self-organised civil society, but also for social coexistence.

A fifth principle of sport in Germany is the coexistence of top-level and recreational sport. On the one hand, Germany is characterised by sustained success in competitive sports. In the perpetual list of medal winners in the Summer Olympics, Germany (including the German Democratic Republic [GDR] and predecessor states) ranks third, and in the list of Winter Olympics, it even tops the list. At the same time, however, the promotion of popular sports has always been an important goal. Accordingly, Germany's population is also characterised by a high level of participation in sports. According to the latest Eurobarometer Sport survey (European Commission, 2017), 62% of all Germans engage in sports at least "rarely", "with some regularity" or "regularly", while only 32% refrain from any kind of physical activity. These figures are well above the average for the member states of the European Union surveyed at that time (Table 14.2).

Disability in Germany

The terms "disabled people" (*behinderte Menschen*) or "people with disabilities" (*Menschen mit Behinderung*) have been used for a long time as general terms in German. Accordingly, considering sport both terms "Behindertensport" and "Sport für Menschen mit Behinderung" are common in Germany. In the general understanding, no distinction is made between "disabled sport" and "disability

Table 14.2 Sport profile of Germany

Government authority responsible for sport	Federal Ministry of Interior (and others at national and regional level)	
Membership sport club (% of population)*		29.21%
Membership fitness or health centre (% of population)*	14.08%	
Membership socio-cultural club that includes sport in its activities (e.g. employees' club, youth club, school- and university related club) (% of population)*		
Sport participation, at least once a week (% of population)*	22.30%	
Number of national sport federations		66
Number of sport clubs		91,000
Number of sport club members		24.3 mio
National budget for sport (€ × 1,000,000)		n/a
National budget for sport federations (€ × 1000)		n/a
Local budget for sport (€ × 1,000,000)		n/a
Share of economic value of volunteers in sport in the GDP (%)		

Source: DOSB (Bestandserhebung 2020ff)

sport". In the course of an increasingly sensitive language, however, the terminology has also in Germany become more differentiated: Based on the academic disability studies, more often a distinction between disability ("Behinderung") and handicapped ("Beeinträchtigung") can be found. While handicap is primarily understood as the physical side, "disability" adds a social dimension. However, in the documents of organised sport, this distinction can hardly be found so far.

In Germany, more than 10 million people live with disabilities, of which about 7.9 million are severely disabled (see Table 14.3). This is a percentage of 9.5 of the population that are severely disabled. Beyond the debates about the social construction of disability (Maschke, 2008), the German definition of disability is based on recommendations of the World Health Organisation (WHO). A disability is defined in German law by the Social Code IX as follows: "People with disabilities are people who have physical, mental, intellectual, or sensory impairments that, in interaction with attitudinal and environmental barriers, are likely to prevent them from participating in society on an equal basis with others for more than six months. An impairment [...] exists if the physical and health condition deviates from the condition typical for the person's age [...]" (own translation according to SGB IX [Sozialgesetzbuch], § 2,1).

In order to be formally recognised as a person with a disability and to establish legal rights, an application must be made to the pension office (*Versorgungsamt*). The severity or the degree of disability (GdB) is determined by this office. This can vary between 20 and 100. It is graduated in steps of ten and is assessed by medical experts upon application. The details are laid down in SGB IX § 152.1 based on the potential of participation in the life of society. If there are changes in health, the degree of disability may change. Persons are considered severely disabled if they have been awarded a degree of disability of at least 50 by the pension offices and have been issued a valid ID card. At the end of 2019, around 7.9 million severely disabled people lived in Germany. Considering the 9.5% share of severely disabled people in the total population of Germany slightly more than half (50.4%) are men, 49.6% are women. Physical disabilities accounted for 59% of severely disabled people. In 25% of cases, the internal organs or organ systems were affected. In 12% of the cases arms and/or legs were restricted in their function, and in a further 11% spine and trunk. In 5% of the cases blindness or visual impairment was present. A share of 4% suffered from hearing loss, balance or speech disorders. Mental or psychological disabilities accounted for 13% of all cases.

The UN Convention on the Rights of Persons with Disabilities has been in force in Germany since 2009, and its implementation has been accompanied by a gradual change in the perception of disability (Waldschmidt & Schneider, 2007; Waldschmidt, 2020). In addition to welfare and rehabilitation measures for people with disabilities, efforts have been made to remove barriers that prevent people from participating in a self-determined way. The concept of inclusion has now been anchored in numerous action plans and mission statements by public and private organisations as well as educational institutions. At the same time, the equal participation of people with disabilities is seen as a cross-cutting task in numerous policy fields. In practice, however, there are clear difficulties in implementing the

Table 14.3 Severely disabled people in Germany by gender and age (*Schwerbehinderung*)

	2007	2009	2011	2013	2015	2017	2019	in %
Total	6,918,172	7,101,682	7,289,173	7,548,965	7,615,560	7,766,573	7,902,960	9.5
Male	3,587,250	3,658,107	3,733,913	3,851,568	3,866,994	3,928,519	3,983,749	9.7
Female	3,330,922	3,443,575	3,555,260	3,697,397	3,748,566	3,838,054	3,919,211	9.3
below 4	14,297	14,275	14,194	13,928	14,703	15,495	17,008	0.5
4 bis 6	14,002	14,336	14,376	14,109	14,626	15,216	17,082	1.1
6 bis 15	91,928	94,708	97,988	99,847	101,493	106,756	114,153	1.7
15 bis 18	39,918	38,250	38,696	41,342	43,128	44,808	45,970	2
18 bis 25	117,157	122,155	123,983	120,515	118,560	121,408	127,187	2
25 bis 35	200,510	210,081	223,679	236,602	245,741	251,261	255,356	2.4
35 bis 45	447,270	417,603	390,234	363,342	345,138	342,298	353,716	3.5
45 bis 55	826,264	874,509	916,329	931,886	910,665	860,586	790,371	6.3
55 bis 60	650,827	674,299	688,194	697,958	712,128	727,492	743,272	11.3
60 bis 62	286,327	331,822	354,317	348,220	341,575	342,530	349,045	15.2
62 bis 65	473,602	446,115	536,489	589,609	575,511	564,522	572,128	17.9
65 and above	3,756,070	3,863,529	3,890,694	4,091,607	4,192,292	4,374,201	4,517,672	25.3
Data: Statistisches Bundesamt								

Source: Statistisches Bundesamt

UNCRPD. The system of specialised institutions for people with disabilities in the form of special schools, residential homes and workshops, which has been established over decades, is considered to be efficient. However, it remains a cleavage to a more self-determined participation of people with disabilities. The ongoing public debates and conflicts among the actors in Germany are not least ignited by the implementation in practice, as problems often become visible when the claim for inclusion meets the everyday worlds of people with disabilities.

Emergence of Disability Sport in Germany

The development of sports for the disabled in Germany can be divided chronologically into five phases (Doll-Tepper, 2008; Wedemeyer-Kolwe, 2011; Innenmoser et al., 2015). The beginnings range from the founding of the first deaf sports club in 1888 in Berlin to the period 1914–1945, marked by two world wars, when the primary focus was on curative measures for war-disabled persons and the restoration of the earning capacity of affected men. In the second phase, from 1950 to 1968, sports for the disabled were also primarily aimed at men, but now had far greater numbers of participants and thus a greater significance than in the interwar period. By the mid-1960s, the German Sports Association for the Disabled that was named "Deutscher Versehrtensportverband" (DVS) had almost 45,000 members. The societal changes at the end of the 1960s were accompanied by a third phase (1969–1990), which was characterised by a fundamental change in disability sport. In the course of this, the leisure dimension and grassroots sports were introduced into disability sport. Further characteristics of this period are the increased inclusion of women and children and the increasing abandonment of the distinction between war and civilian disabled. Consequently, in 1975 the association was renamed the German Disabled Sports Association. In addition, integrative approaches in sport were discussed for the first time in the mid-1970s. Around 1985, another turning point can be identified. The International Year of Disabled Persons, proclaimed by the UN, led to an awakening that also gave new impetus to disability sport. The next phase of sports for the disabled up to about 2008 is characterised by growth and differentiation, which on the one hand is reflected in a health orientation towards rehabilitation sports, but on the other hand is also documented by a growing number of offers for people with intellectual disabilities. The most recent changes since 2009 are due to the implementation of the UN Convention on the Rights of Persons with Disabilities. Overall, major changes in German disability sport can primarily be explained as an expression of the social conditions. The perception and development of disability sports have been shaped not least by the ever-changing interactions with politics, business and organised sports (Schlund, 2017).

14.3 The Disability Sport System

Structure of Disability Sport

With regard to the relationship between state and associations, the structures of disability sport show at first glance some similarities with sport in general. At second glance, on the association side, an even wider range of actors and complexity can be discerned in disability sport at all levels of the system of the Federal Republic of Germany than already exists in the German sport system. Several actors from the social and welfare sector also play an important role here, which is a special feature of sports played by persons with disability in Germany. The involvement of the individual actors varies both vertically across the individual levels of the regional structure of the Federal Republic of Germany and in individual sport areas. Basically, a distinction must be made in disability sport between elite sports, leisure sports and rehabilitation sports. The actual implementation of inclusion ultimately takes place in the clubs and at the municipal level. Here, the diversity is even greater. If one then includes schools and other educational institutions, the diversity almost appears to be confusing. This is all the more true because the relationships between the actors are usually organised in a non-hierarchical way including even funding; memberships and partnerships commonly are not institutionalised, but rather project-related and informal. Against this backdrop Fig. 14.1 avoids indicating specific relationships between the various organisations involved with arrows.

Germany	Public Authorities	Intermediary Bodies	Sport Related Non-Governmental Organisations				Other Agents and Organisations
	Ministries Administrations Legislatures		Associations and Clubs in Non-Disabled Sports		Associations and Clubs in Disabled Sports		
			[territorial-related]	[sports related]	[territorial-related]	[sports and handicap-related]	
National level	Federal Ministry of the Interior [BMI] Other Federal Ministries Sport Committee Bundestag	[Deutsches Institut für Menschen-rechte]	DOSB	National Sports Associations [DFB, DHB, DTB ...]	DBS	National Disabled Sport Associations DGS DBSV SOD DRS	Statutory Accident Insurance [Gesetzliche Unfallversicherung] Health Insurances
Regional level	Ministries (of Sport) of the Bundesländer Sportministerkonferenz Other Regional Ministries Sport Committees Bundesländer	[Informationsstelle für den Sport behinderter Menschen in Deutschland (bis 2019)] [SMK]	Sport Associations at regional level [Landessportbünde]	Regional Sports Associations	Regional Disabled Sports Associations [BRSNW; SBV...]	Regional Disabled Sports Associations	Federal Employment Agency (public) Aktion Mensch (Lottery) Welfare Organisations
Local level	City Governments Heads of Sport Departments Local Administrations Local Councils		Sport Associations at municipal and district level [Stadt- / Kreissportbünde] Non-commercial Sport Clubs	Local Sports Associations	Municipal and district disabled sport Associations Non-commercial	Local Disabled Sports Associations Sport Clubs	Sozialverband Vdk Foundations Public and Private Universities

*N.B.: The German sport system in disability sport is characterised by only limited forms of direct hierarchy and formal control.

Fig. 14.1 The disability sport system in Germany*. *N.B.: the German sport system in disability sport is characterised by only limited forms of direct hierarchy and formal control

Governmental Agents

On the state side, the system of disability sport does not differ fundamentally from the handling of other areas of sports. While the organisation and implementation of disability sport is largely carried out by organised sports and other actors, the state primarily plays a role in setting and promoting the framework at all levels of government. A special feature of disability sport, however, is that the federal government—that is, the national level—plays a particularly active role in disability sport. This is determined by the interest of the federal government in central measures of sport with nationwide reach as well as special sport and socio-political significance. The federal government pursues two key goals: Within the framework of the fundamental promotion of top-class sport, competitive sport for people with disabilities is promoted. In addition, the federal government has set itself the goal of using the integrative effect of sport for the "National Action Plan on Integration" (Bundesministerium für Arbeit und Soziales, 2011) and of further expanding the idea of inclusion in sport in the implementation of the United Nations Convention on the Rights of Persons with Disabilities.

Within the federal government, the Federal Ministry of the Interior ("Bundesministerium des Inneren", BMI) coordinates the federal government's sports policy, which traditionally covers a comprehensive range of sectors. Among the 15 departments of the BMI, which for political reasons has also been responsible for the areas of construction and homeland since 2018, there is also a department for sport. This department is in turn divided into five units, one of which is responsible for sport for people with disabilities. While the federal minister, considering the scope of the ministry, generally hardly sets his own accents in sport policy as well as disability sport, a parliamentary state secretary takes over the political representation of sport. Formally, however, this person is not authorised to issue directives within the ministry, and his or her scope of action depends largely on the backing of the minister. Other institutions are subordinate to the BMI, including the Federal Institute for Sports Science ("Bundesinstitut für Sportwissenschaft", BISp), which promotes and coordinates scientific sports activities.

In addition to the Federal Ministry of the Interior, at least 11 other ministries have partial responsibility for sport as part of their general tasks. The Federal Ministry of Labour and Social Affairs ("Bundesministerium für Arbeit und Soziales", BMAS) plays a special role in the area of disability sport, as it is responsible for promoting sport for the disabled and sport for the disabled in the context of rehabilitation. Since 1981, this ministry has also appointed a federal government representative for the interests of people with disabilities, who is consulted and involved in major decisions. The position was held from 2014 to 2018 by Verena Bentele, a former multiple Paralympic champion in biathlon and cross-country skiing. In addition to these executive actors, the Sport Committee of the Bundestag is also important at the federal level. As the counterpart of the Federal Ministry of the Interior, it deals with similar issues including disability sport. Its activities primarily focus on information, representation and public debates on sport.

In the 16 federal states, disability sport is represented in different institutional settings at the respective state governments. Depending primarily on the party-political composition of the state government, the Ministry of Interior is often responsible for sport and disability sport, but sometimes sport is also linked to family or health policy (Tiemann, 2010). The sport officers (*Sportreferenten*) of the federal states have a central coordinating function. In view of disability politics there are often state representatives for people with disabilities. Regional sport committees also deal with disability sport at the state level. The Conference of Sports Ministers of the Länder ("Sportministerkonferenz", SMK), which met for the first time in 1977, deals with sport matters of supra-regional importance with the aim of forming common opinions and statements. Disability sport and issues of inclusion are regularly on the agenda here.

At the municipal level, disability sport are usually dealt with by heads of department (*Dezernenten*), who are at the top of municipal administrations and politically manage, coordinate and supervise the tasks of sports offices or similarly oriented municipal institutions.

Intermediate Agents

Formal intermediary bodies exist only to a limited extent in German disability sport. As in sport policy in general, the individual institutions mainly work together informally. Nevertheless, committees and institutions have been created at the working level in recent years, in which longer-term cooperation takes place. These include the "AG Inklusion" (Working Group on Inclusion) of the Conference of Sport Ministers, which is concerned with the long-term implementation of inclusion in and through sports. In addition to the states and the federal government, several sports associations, including the "Deutscher Olympischer Sportbund" (DOSB) and the "Deutscher Behindertensportverband" (DBS), also participate in this body. Another intermediary body was the "Informationsstelle für den Sport behinderter Menschen" in Berlin, which operated nationwide. Founded in August 1998, this Information Office was an institution of the Conference of Sport Ministers of the Länder as well as the DOSB and the Free University of Berlin, where it was also institutionally located. Its mission was to improve information on issues and topics related to sports for people of all ages with (different) disabilities throughout Germany. However, these activities were abandoned at the end of 2019.

Non-governmental Agents

Organisational structures for disability sport exist at the national, regional and local levels, but in many cases they have parallel and overlapping structures. Thus, disability sport is dealt with both in the general umbrella organisations of sport (DOSB, state sport associations, city and district sport associations) and in specialised umbrella and professional associations. These can in turn be divided into disability-specific associations and sport-specific associations.

The largest specialised player in disability sport is the "German Disabled Sports Association" (Deutscher Behindertensportverband, DBS), which, as the German umbrella organisation for sport for people with disabilities, also functions as the National Paralympic Committee (NPC) for Germany (Quade, 2015). The DBS is based on 17 state associations, 2 specialised associations and 7 extraordinary organisations. The DBS is itself a member of the DOSB. The roots of the DBS go back to sport-therapeutic offers for the rehabilitation of (war-)injured persons. The DBS has developed a comprehensive training and qualification system for this purpose. In the field of competitive sport, the DBS organises 48 sports, 29 of which are Paralympic. In addition, the German Disabled Sports Youth ("Deutsche Behindertensport Jugend", DBSJ) has been the DBS's own youth organisation since 1985. At the regional level, the DBS is supported by 17 regional associations, such as the North Rhine-Westphalia Association of Sport for the Disabled and Rehabilitation ("Behinderten- und Rehabilitationssportverband Nordrhein-Westfalen", BRSNW) and the Saxon Association of Sport for the Disabled and Rehabilitation ("Sächsischer Behinderten- und Rehabilitationssportverband", SBV). At the local level, there are local disability sport communities (*Behindertensportgemeinschaften*) as well as clubs with departments for disability sport. In total, the DBS has over 643,000 memberships.

Other (umbrella) associations in disability sport are divided according to the type of disability: For athletes with a hearing impairment, there are two different sports associations: the German Deaf Sport Association ("Deutscher Gehörlosen-Sportverband", DGS) for the deaf group and the German Sports Association for the Hard of Hearing ("Deutscher Schwerhörigen Sportverband", DSSV) for the hearing impaired (Schliermann, 2015a, 2015b). The latter is part of the German Federation of the Hard of Hearing, while the much larger DGS (7900 members), which is also the oldest sport association for the disabled, is a member of the DBS as a specialised association. In the DGS 28 sports, including 21 Deaflympic sports, are practised. The German Association for the Blind and Disabled ("Deutscher Blinden- und Sehbehindertenverband", DBSV), which is also a member of the DBS and is primarily active in popular sports, focuses on people with visual impairments. In 1991, Special Olympics Germany ("Special Olympics Deutschland", SOD) was founded with the support of welfare organisations "Caritas" and "Diakonie", the federal association "Lebenshilfe" and the German Association of Disabled Sports. SOD is the offshoot of Special Olympics International as the world's largest sport association for people with intellectual disabilities and multiple disabilities. SOD has 49,100 members and is an extraordinary member of the DBS. The association offers a wide range of sports, but also competitions and competitive forms of play. In addition, SOD organises national games in Germany every two years, alternating between summer and winter games.

An intermediate form of disability-specific and sport-specific orientation is offered by the German Wheelchair Sports Association ("Deutscher Rollstuhl-Sportverband", DRS). It is the umbrella organisation for about 330 sport clubs in about 27 disciplines, including badminton, basketball, archery, fencing, weightlifting, athletics, rugby, swimming, sailing, shooting, sledge ice hockey, tennis, table tennis, winter sports, e-chair sports and wheel field hockey. The activities of the DRS span rehabilitation sport as well as mass and competitive sport. In addition, there are other sport-related associations such as the German Chess Federation for the Blind and Visually Impaired ("Deutscher Blinden- und Sehbehinderten-Schachbund", DBSB) with approximately 300 members.

In sports such as golf, karate and rowing, organisations for people with disabilities are integrated into the general sport associations. As a rule, however, they also have an extraordinary membership in the DBS. Other associations, such as the German Curatorship for Therapeutic Riding ("Deutsches Kuratorium für Therapeutisches Reiten", DKThR), are organisationally linked to the general professional association, such as the German Equestrian Federation in this case. The regional and local substructure of the sport-specific associations varies just as considerably as the range of services offered here.

Secondary Agents

In addition to state and association-related actors, there are a large number of other actors in the field of sport for people with disabilities. Their scope is almost impossible to survey and their involvement is determined not least by the three dimensions of rehabilitation sport, competitive sport and leisure/mass sport for people with disabilities. The German Social Accident Insurance ("Deutsche Gesetzliche Unfallversicherung", DGUV), the umbrella organisation of the commercial employers' liability insurance associations and the accident insurance funds, has an important function. In the German social security system, the statutory accident insurance is one of five compulsory insurances that protect over 70 million people in Germany. It is funded by contributions from employers and the public sector. In addition, sport activities are covered by occupational rehabilitation measures of the Federal Employment Agency ("Bundesagentur für Arbeit"). The DGUV is organised as an association with legal capacity and is primarily active in the areas of prevention and rehabilitation. It supports disability sport and its organisations primarily financially through projects and programmes, but also by funding research.

Another important player is "Aktion Mensch". This organisation was founded in 1964 on the initiative of the Second German Television under the name "Aktion Sorgenkind" and promotes the idea of inclusion primarily through its social lottery, but also through education. The organisation is made up of Germany's six major welfare associations: "Arbeiterwohlfahrt", "Deutscher Caritasverband", "Deutsches Rotes Kreuz", "Diakonisches Werk der Evangelischen Kirche", "Deutscher Paritätischer Wohlfahrtsverband" and the "Zentralwohlfahrtsstelle der Juden in Deutschland". For their part, these welfare associations offer measures and activities in the field of sport for the disabled. However, they also influence the organisation of disability sport through their political activities.

In addition, there are many networks in disability sport with other associations and organisations that deal with disability. Examples include the German Association for Rehabilitation ("Bundesarbeitsgemeinschaft für Rehabilitation", BAR), the German Society for Rheumatology ("Deutsche Gesellschaft für Rheumatologie", DGRh), the German Association for Physiotherapy ("Deutsche Verband für Physiotherapie", ZVK), the German Association of Occupational Therapists ("Deutscher Verband der Ergotherapeuten", DVE) and the German Association for Health Sports and Sports Therapy ("Deutscher Verband für Gesundheitssport und Sporttherapie", DVGS).

An important role is also played by state-, association- and private-based foundations, which are committed to disability sport in various forms and with different financial contributions. The Lower Saxony Lottery Sports Foundation ("Niedersächsische Lotto-Sport-Stiftung"), which was established in 2009 by a resolution of the state government of Lower Saxony, is an example of the state sector. In addition to the German Disabled Sports Association, the founders of the Disabled Sport Foundation ("Stiftung Behindertensport") were the state associations in Bavaria, Lower Saxony and North Rhine-Westphalia. Private foundations include the Gold Kraemer Foundation, founded in 1972 and based in Frechen, where the German Sport Association for the Disabled also has its offices, and the Alexander Otto Sports Foundation, based in Hamburg, which supports local projects in disability sport.

Finally, schools are also important actors in disability sports. Their activities are usually based on the curricula and frameworks of the states that are authoritative in this field. Academics are also involved in shaping disability sport covering both public and, to an increasing extent, private universities, usually organised at the state level. This includes as well German Sport University Cologne that in fact is a university based in North-Rhine Westphalia. Ultimately, if one takes into account the linkages of the actors of the national system of disability sport with those federations from European and international levels, the number of players increases even further.

Steering of Disability Sport

Disability sport in Germany is characterised by a high degree of plurality and differentiation without hierarchical control or coordination. Based on the previous explanations, at least four central groups of actors can be identified: (1) state/public authorities, (2) associations of general sport in Germany, (3) associations specialising in disability sport and (4) other actors, mainly anchored in the different sectors of the social and welfare system as well as the insurance system of the Federal Republic. The degree of complexity is further increased by the fact that numerous—but not all—actors are active at all three levels of the federal structure of Germany. Finally, the activities of the actors also differ according to the three dimensions of competitive sport, rehabilitation sport and leisure sport. In order to explain the interactions and decision-making procedures in the field of sport for the disabled, the concept of governance, which has been discussed in detail in recent years, can be used for Germany. Governance also means the emergence of new non-hierarchical patterns of cooperation between governments and administrations as well as sport organisations and other actors in the field of sports for the disabled. In this process, the formal institutional and organisational autonomy of sport is preserved, and vertical and horizontal networking of the various actors takes place.

Relationships

The relationship between the players in German disability sport is characterised more by coexistence than by competition and cooperation. Lobbying for resources, financial support and public attention does take place to a limited extent. However, this does not happen in the sense of pluralistic antagonism, but rather as a coexistence based on partnership. Among the few available findings on the structural and systematic forms of organisation of disability sport its characterisation as a fragmented, complex and cumbersome structure is shaped by deficient coordination and varying degrees of commitment to disability sport itself. This analysis of the European area can also be applied to Germany (Thomas & Guett, 2014).

Legislative Framework

Sport for the disabled in Germany is based on different legal foundations and regulations. As far as disability sport as a whole is concerned, the Basic Law—without explicitly mentioning sport—makes important general statements: sporting activity is protected by the fundamental right of general freedom of action (Art. 2 (1) GG). Of fundamental importance for disability sport—as for sport in general—is the autonomy of associations, which is based on Article 9 of the Basic Law on freedom of association. In addition, there is the principle of the welfare state, which also covers the area of sport. Special attention for the area of disability deserves the amendment of the Basic Law of 1994 when in Article 3 paragraph 3 the phrase was included that no one may be disadvantaged because of their disability. A key for disability sport as a legal form is that of the non-profit registered association ("nichtwirtschaftlicher Verein", eingetragener Verein) according to § 21ff BGB ("Bürgerliches Gesetzbuch"). In disability sport, too, both the sport associations and the sport clubs are usually legal entities, which as a rule also have the status of non-profit organisations. It is precisely this status that is of central importance for disability sport, as associations recognised as charitable are entitled to certain tax benefits and, on the other hand, are entitled to receive tax-privileged donations.

For the area of inclusion in disability sport, the UN Convention on the Rights of Persons with Disabilities marked a milestone as a treaty under international law. It concretises human rights for the life of disabled people and focuses on an inclusive model of participation. By ratifying the UNCRPD on March 26, 2009, the Federal Republic of Germany not only agreed to report regularly to the United Nations Committee on the Rights of Persons with Disabilities on the measures it has taken to fulfil its obligations under the convention, but also anchored a normative framework that contains indirect legal implications for organised sport (Kiuppis & Kurzke-Maasmeier, 2012). This also involves the state level. On the part of the SMK, a formal decision was made in 2014 to provide greater support to organised sport in intensifying its previous activities in the area of inclusion.

For the area of rehabilitation sport, numerous legal bases from social legislation come into play, which can only be cited here as examples (Anneken & Bungter,

2015): An essential legal basis for the implementation of rehabilitation sport is the Social Code (SGB IX § 64) and the "Framework Agreement on Outpatient Rehabilitation Sport and Functional Training of 1.1.2011", which was concluded by the Federal Working Group for Rehabilitation ("Bundearbeitsgemeinschaft für Rehabilitation", BAR). The services provided by the statutory health insurance funds (*gesetzliche Krankenkassen*) and the pension insurance institutions are based on this agreement. Also relevant is the Child and Youth Welfare Act (Eighth Book of the Social Code—Child and Youth Welfare—SGB VIII). Responsibility for services to children and young people with disabilities is regulated in such a way that integration assistance for intellectually handicapped children and young people is assigned to the law on child and youth welfare. Accordingly, services for mentally and physically disabled children are provided by social welfare. Finally, the Prevention Act (Präventionsgesetz, "Gesetz zur Stärkung der Gesundheitsförderung und der Prävention"), which came into force in 2015, also marks a further important legal framework for disability sport. The mandate formulated here claims to foster health promotion and prevention, in particular to reduce socially induced inequalities in health opportunities, which once again affects disability sport.

Policy Framework

In the past decade, the guiding principle of inclusion has dominated the policy-related implementation of legal requirements and standards in disability sport. In Germany, inclusion is generally understood as the equal coexistence of all people. In shaping inclusion, the focus is on the possibility for all members of a society to participate. In the corresponding sport-related activities, a distinction must be made between national actors on the one hand and associations and clubs on the other. While the national actors usually set the general guidelines in action plans and budget lines, associations set the concrete standards, offer qualifications or training and set up programmes. The actual implementation then takes place at the local level by the clubs.

With this in mind, the German government drew up a National Action Plan in September 2011 after having implemented the UNCRPD. The Federal Ministry of Labour and Social Affairs, as the government focal point, presented the First State Report on August 3, 2011, followed by two more in 2019. The action plan documents all measures with which the federal government is pursuing the development of an inclusive society. The 213 projects and actions also include examples from the world of sport. Particular importance is attached to accessibility. An innovative example of state documentation is offered by the Federal Government Commissioner for the Interests of Disabled Persons. Here, best-practice examples are recorded in an inclusion map and sport offerings are highlighted in particular (Inklusionslandkarte, 2021).

Shortly after the ratification of the CRPD, the DOSB Executive Board made the inclusion of people with disabilities one of the main topics for the next few years (Deutscher Olympischer Sportbund, 2013). Both top sport associations and regional sport associations as well as clubs were supported in the implementation of inclusive pilot projects with model character. One of the DOSB's sustainable projects is called "Qualified for Practice: Inclusion Managers for Nonprofit Sport". The project pursued the goal of establishing 22 jobs for people with disabilities in non-profit sport. The DBS has also developed new offers in the field of inclusion. Particularly noteworthy is the Index for Inclusion in and through Sport, which was developed jointly with experts. The index uses a questionnaire to sensitise sport organisations to the development and expansion of an inclusive sport landscape. While more inclusive offers have been developed in recreational sport, the example of the DBS also shows that inclusion in competitive sport quickly reached its limits (Radtke, 2011, 2018; Radtke & Schäfer, 2019).

Overall, it should be noted that most activities at the policy level are projects. In addition, there are events such as workshops and conferences on disability sport, which, in addition to providing qualifications in view of the considerable diversity and range, primarily serve to promote exchange and networking. Major sporting events are a special case in the fragmented world of disability sport. These are based on close cooperation between state and private actors. The most important major event in the field of sport for the disabled in Germany is the Special Olympics World Games in Berlin in 2023, which are expected to give a further boost to the interest in sport for people with disabilities.

Financial, Governance and Managerial Support

Given the range of public and private actors involved, the different vertical levels involved and the high proportion of project activities, it is not possible to measure the total financial volume of German disability sport. Just as with the general sport funding of the state, the recording of state funding in disability sport alone is a challenge (Haring, 2010; Emrich et al., 2013; Thieme & Wadsack, 2013). Against this background, the following explanations focus on the institutional funding of associations specifically geared to disability sport as well as on the funding of competitive sport.

So far, the funding for disability sport at a regional level, which is more strongly oriented towards mass and leisure sports, has not been systematically summarised. In Bavaria alone, for example, the Bavarian State Ministry of Labour and Social Affairs ("Bayerisches Staatsministerium für Familie, Arbeit und Soziales", StMAS) provides around 1 million euro a year in funding for mass sport for disabled people. The contributions made by local authorities cannot be summarised in an overview either. They play a particularly important role in promoting barrier-free sports and in the construction of sport facilities. Finally, sponsors and private supporters of the associations, such as the "Sparkassen-Finanzgruppe", the largest non-governmental sponsor of German sport, are also left out.

Financial Framework

The Federal Ministry of the Interior supports four associations in disability sport. While the BMI's sport budget remained comparatively stable at a level of just around 130 million euro between 2010 and 2013, it rose to around 140 million euro from 2014 and to 168 million euro in 2016. In 2019, there was another significant boost; 226 million euro were spent on sport by the BMI in that year (Bundesregierung der Bundesrepublik Deutschland, 2014, 2019). These figures include payments to associations, for competitive sport staff and for funding Olympic bases ("Olympiastützpunkte") and federal performance centres ("Bundesleistungszentren"). The associations of disability sport have benefited disproportionately from this increase. While a budget of 5.4 million euro was still available in 2010, funding initially rose slowly to 5.9 million euro by 2013. By 2017, it then increased significantly to 8.0 million euro and even to just over 12 million euro by 2019. This offered disability sport to more than double its governmental funding in a decade. The four associations receiving funding include the German Disabled Sports Association (DBS), the German Sport Association for the Deaf (DGS), Special Olympics Germany (SOD) and the German Chess Federation for the Blind (DBSB). Of this, the DBS received the lion's share with 10.4 million euro in 2019, while 1.0 million euro went to the DGS, 0.7 million euro to SOD and 0.4 million euro to the German Chess Federation for the Blind. The measures supported include funding for competitive sport staff at the administrative offices, the financing of full-time national coaches, support for the participation of German athletes in international competitions at home and abroad, training and assessment courses, the procurement of sport equipment, the promotion of young talents, and health and sport medical care. The promotion of a dual career for athletes with disabilities has also been expanded.

The strategy for these support measures is twofold: In the spirit of inclusion, on the one hand the existing Olympic bases were opened up to top athletes with disabilities. In addition, the Federal Ministry of the Interior supports top sport associations with 150,000 euro in projects if they include athletes with disabilities in international sport events in Germany in the light of inclusive top sports. And the grants for disabled top athletes have been brought into line with those for other top athletes. Now both receive a grant of at least 800 euro a month from the German Sport Aid Foundation.

On the other hand, in light of the specialisation in 2020, the system of specific bases for disability sport has also been upgraded. Instead of the former "Bundesstützpunkt Para Sport", there are now 11 Paralympic training bases in Germany. Another federal support instrument is the offer of a professional position with federal authority. As a result of physical limitations, however, the number of positions with organisations such as the German armed forces is limited.

Governance and Management Support

While the role of the state is primarily that of a financial supporter—and sometimes also a controller—the interaction between associations is more characterised by governance processes revealing non-hierarchical and project-related cooperations. Two examples may illustrate the variations of this cooperation, which comes into play not only in basic but also in project-related coordination and agreement processes. In 2013, for example, the German Olympic Sport Confederation, the German Disabled Sports Association, Special Olympics Germany and the German Sport Association for the Deaf drew up a joint information paper on the origins and objectives of the

UN Convention on the Rights of Persons with Disabilities (cf. DOSB et al., 2013). As a task for non-disability and disability sport organisations, the objective was issued to "develop and implement joint inclusion concepts in order to anchor the idea of self-determined, equal participation in public awareness as well as to strengthen the position of people with disabilities in our society" (ibid., 2).

A concrete project was then formed by the Federal Youth Games ("Bundesjugendspiele"). These were first initiated in the 1950s by the Federal Ministry of the Interior and then by the Federal Ministry for Youth, Family and Health. The compulsory participation for regular schools was based on a resolution of the Standing Conference of the Ministers of Education and Cultural Affairs of the States in 1979. From 2007 onwards, in the course of the inclusion model, a guideline for the participation of pupils with disabilities was developed by the German Disabled Sport Association and the German Disabled Sports Youth in cooperation with the Committee for the Federal Youth Games (in which the DOSB, the German Sport Youth and other professional associations are involved) as well as the Sports Commission of the Standing Conference of the Ministers of Education and Cultural Affairs of the Länder. This was subsequently extended to include competitive sports. The Federal Ministry of the Interior has been promoting the school sport competition "Jugend trainiert für Olympia" (JTFO) for years. As a counterpart to this, the BMI has decided to promote a new nationwide school sports competition for students with disabilities under the title "Jugend trainiert für Paralympics" (JTFP) from 2011. In order to make an active contribution to inclusion, the German Schools Sports Foundation ("Deutsche Schulsportstiftung", DSSS) and the German Disabled Sports Association have reached an agreement aimed at merging the two competitions "Jugend trainiert für Olympia" (JTFO) and "Jugend trainiert für Paralympics" (JTFP).

Level of Integration or Inclusion

A gradual change can be discerned both in general awareness and in the demands of politics and associations: Disability is no longer seen as a deficit, but as a social disadvantage in the sense of a restriction of participation opportunities. And people with disabilities are no longer seen as objects of care, but as self-determined subjects endowed with civil rights. Against this backdrop, it is not enough, according to the prevailing opinion of politicians and associations, to simply create special sports opportunities for people with disabilities—including high-performance sports. As a result, the overall target of bringing together people with and without disabilities through the development and organisation of inclusive sporting activities has been set in various shades. Although there have been attempts at various levels of sport in Germany to bring about equal participation in sports activities for people with disabilities, considerable improvements are still needed before it can be spoken of actual successful inclusion in all areas of German sport, from amateur and recreational to school and professional sport. The current implementation of inclusion ultimately takes place in the clubs. And over there are still considerable differences in the degree of inclusion. These differences can hardly be generalised but are rather subject to individual consideration.

14.4 Sport Participation by People with Disabilities

In recent years, it has been repeatedly criticised that only few data have been collected so far on the level of participation of people with disabilities in organised sport in Germany (Baumann, 2004; Guett et al., 2011). As a result, only a few figures and more general approximations can be presented at the moment. The most concrete data can be taken from the latest participation report of the German Federal Government, which is based on surveys (BMAS, 2016, 2021).

Sport Participation

According to this, around one-third of disabled people practises sport every week, compared to just under 50% of people without disabilities. On the other hand, 55% of disabled people say they never do sport, compared to only 32% of people without disabilities. There are hardly any differences in the sports behaviour of disabled men and women. Similarly, there are hardly any differences in the sports behaviour of people with and without a migration background.

In contrast, there are clear variances in age: Inactivity among disabled people who are between 65 and 79 years old was higher in 2017 (57%) than among disabled people between 18 and 49 years old (46%). The highest participation in sport is found among disabled children and young people. In addition to school sports, 12% of children and adolescents between 3 and 17 have more than four hours of sport a week, 22% between two and four hours and 23% up to two hours of sport (BMAS, 2021, 602ff).

In the data cited, no distinction has been made as to whether disabled people take part in sport in an inclusive or separate setting. However, existing studies have revealed that both forms of sport participation have the potential to contribute to the social integration of people with disabilities (Klenk et al., 2019). On the whole, however, the number of inclusive sporting opportunities is still limited. People with disabilities are underrepresented in general sports clubs. As a result, the demand for the expansion of inclusive sport offerings and barrier-free sport facilities marks a key aspect of the implementation of the UNCRPD.

The membership figures of the German Disabled Sports Association provide indirect information about sport participation from a perspective. Its membership figures have risen continuously since the 1950s. The strongest increases were recorded in the last three decades since the 1990s, when the DBS went from 136,000 members (1990) to 304,500 members (2000) and 531,671 (2010), reaching a peak of 650,986 in 2013. Since then, numbers have declined slightly to 598,661 members in 2020 (Statista, 2020).

Barriers and Facilitators

Studies based on the assessments of experts in disability sport have identified both individual and structural barriers to sport participation (Jaarsma et al., 2014; Ecorys, 2018). Similar aspects have been listed for sport in Germany (Wicker & Breuer, 2014). These individual barriers include personal reasons such as the nature of the disability and the state of health. Structural reasons, on the other hand, include external conditions such as lack of transport, lack of accessibility or basically lack of facilities (Doll-Tepper & Schönherr, 2004). Conversely, fun and health are identified by the experts as the main drivers of personal factors, while social contacts and an appropriate range of sports facilities are identified as central structural supporters for a high level of participation in sport.

The German Disabled Sports Association (DBS) sees the lack of accessible sports facilities and services for people with disabilities as the main reason for the inactivity of people with disabilities. The most recent report of the Federal Government on "Teilhabe" of disabled people also refers to the increased use of digital offers in the field of sport. However, offers and opportunities are so far hardly oriented towards the specific needs and requirements of disabled people (BMAS, 2021, 602, 615).

One of the facilitators in disability sport is the high proportion of volunteers (Dahlmanns, 2015). According to the results of the latest survey on volunteering in Germany, 31 million unpaid people volunteer in their free time in total. The highest percentage of volunteers, 16.3%, can be found in the field of sports. Men still perform such activities at a significantly higher rate than women. On the part of the DBS, reference is generally made to the high level of volunteers in disabled sports. It is stated that in the area of responsibility of the DBS, courses were offered by around 33,000 qualified and licensed exercise leaders and coaches at the end of the 2010s. These are trained and educated in the regional and specialised associations of the DBS in accordance with uniform national guidelines in approximately 700 courses per year.

14.5 Conclusion

Disabled sport in Germany can be functionally divided into three sub-areas: Firstly, it is practised by particularly performance-oriented disabled people as a competitive sport. Secondly, the majority of disabled people who are active in sports do so as recreational sports. And thirdly, it is practised for therapeutic and rehabilitative purposes as rehabilitation sport. Within the framework of these three dimensions, a large scope of different actors is responsible for the organisation of disability sport. Particularly on the side of the associations, disability sport is characterised by a considerable degree of complexity and a juxtaposition of activities. Just in the last few years, in the course of the target of increasingly inclusive sport, significant changes and stronger interactions between the actors can be identified.

Specialised sport clubs for people with disabilities have reoriented themselves and are making now sport-related offers for both people with different types of disabilities as well as people without disabilities. At the same time, sport clubs where previously only non-disabled people were active are offering now access to disabled people (Meier et al., 2016, 2017). However, these processes do not take place to the same extent for all forms of disability. Especially in the case of mental disabilities, the challenges are particularly high. At the same time, some of the reforms are also contested. Especially in the school sector, there are lively and sometimes heated debates about the scope and extent of inclusion (Powell et al., 2008; Hebbel-Seeger et al., 2014; Heyer, 2015; Biermann et al., 2020; Biermann & Powell, 2021; Köpfer et al., 2021). The reforms are not completed yet. For the future, it is to be expected that further changes in disability sport will emerge in the orientation towards the goal of facilitating access to sports facilities, opening up for wider participation and developing a more inclusive range of services. This has become even more relevant after the pandemic since disabled sport in Germany also suffered substantially from the limitations of sport in view of access to facilities, participation in formal activities and a decrease in membership.

References

Aichele, V. (2012). Neu in Bewegung. Das Recht von Menschen mit Behinderungen auf Partizipation im Bereich Sport. In F. Kiuppis & S. Kurzke-Maasmeier (Eds.), *Sport im Spiegel der UN-Behindertenrechtskonvention. Interdisziplinäre Zugänge und politische Positionen* (pp. 41–59). Kohlhammer.

Anneken, V. (2009). Behindertensport ist Teilhabe. *B&G Bewegungstherapie und Gesundheitssport, 25*(5), 190–194.

Anneken, V. (Ed.). (2013). *Inklusion durch Sport. Forschung für Menschen mit Behinderung*. Sportverlag Strauß.

Anneken, V., & Bungter, T. (2015). Rehabilitationssport. In M. Wegner, V. Scheid, & M. Knoll (Eds.), *Handbuch Behinderung und Sport* (pp. 216–225). Hofmann.

Baumann, C. (2004). *Menschen mit geistiger Behinderung im organisierten Sport. Eine organisationssoziologische Untersuchung zu Partizipationsbestrebungen im Deutschen Behindertensportverband*. Diss. Univ. Bielefeld.

Biermann, J., Pfahl, L., & Powell, J. J. W. (2020). Mehrebenenanalyse schulischer Inklusion. Zwischen globaler Diffusion der Inklusionsrhetorik, behinderten Bildungskarrieren und institutionellen Pfadabhängigkeiten in Deutschland. In T. Dietze, D. Gloystein, V. Moser, A. Piezunka, L. Röbenack, L. Schäfer, G. Wachtel, & M. Walm (Eds.), *Inklusion – Partizipation – Menschenrechte: Transformation in die Teilhabegesellschaft?* (pp. 195–201). Klinkhardt.

Biermann, J., & Powell, J. J. W. (2021). *Internationale disability studies*. Springer VS.

BMAS (Bundesministerium für Arbeit und Soziales). (2016). *Zweiter Teilhabebericht der Bundesregierung über die Lebenslagen von Menschen mit Beeinträchtigungen. Teilhabe – Beeinträchtigung – Behinderung*. BMAS.

BMAS (Bundesministerium für Arbeit und Soziales). (2021). *Dritter Teilhabebericht der Bundesregierung über die Lebenslagen von Menschen mit Beeinträchtigungen. Teilhabe – Beeinträchtigung – Behinderung. 2021*. BMAS.

Breuer, C., Giel, T., & Hallmann, K. (2017). Germany. Transformation towards a more private sport sector. In A. Laine & H. Vehmas (Eds.), *The private sport sector in Europe. A cross-national comparative perspective* (pp. 141–157). Springer.

Bundesministerium für Arbeit und Soziales. (2011). *Unser Weg in eine inklusive Gesellschaft: Der Nationale Aktionsplan der Bundesregierung zur Umsetzung der UN-Behindertenrechtskonvention*. Berlin: BMAS <www.bmas.de/SharedDocs/Downloads/DE/PDF-Publikationen/a740-nationaler-aktionsplan-barrierefrei.pdf> (1.2.2021).

Bundesregierung der Bundesrepublik Deutschland. (2014). *13. Sportbericht der Bundesregierung (Unterrichtung durch die Bundesregierung vom 5.12.2014, BT-Drs. Drucksache VI/2152)*. Deutscher Bundestag.

Bundesregierung der Bundesrepublik Deutschland. (2019). *14. Sportbericht der Bundesregierung (Unterrichtung durch die Bundesregierung vom 4.4.2019, BT-Drs. Drucksache 19/9150)*. Deutscher Bundestag.

Dahlmanns, J. (2015). Behindertensport: Strukturen und Qualifizierung. In M. Wegner, V. Scheid, & M. Knoll (Eds.), *Handbuch Behinderung und Sport* (pp. 248–257). Hofmann.

Deutscher Olympischer Sportbund, et al. (2013). Inklusion leben – Gemeinsam und gleichberechtigt Sport treiben. In *Positionspapier des Deutschen Olympischen Sportbundes und der Deutschen Sportjugend zur Inklusion von Menschen mit Behinderung*. DOSB.

Doll-Tepper, G. (2008). Entwicklungen des Sports von Menschen mit geistiger Behinderung aus internationaler Perspektive. In M. Wegner & H.-J. Schulke (Eds.), *Behinderung, Bewegung, Befreiung: Gewinn von Lebensqualität und Selbständigkeit durch Wettbewerbe und sportliches Training bei Menschen mit geistiger Behinderung* (pp. 7–14). Institut für Sport und Sportwissenschaft.

Doll-Tepper, G., & Schönherr, D. (2004). Menschen mit Behinderung und Sport. In Technische Universität Berlin (Ed.), *Barrierefreies Planen und Bauen als interdisziplinäres Handlungsfeld*. TU Berlin.

Ecorys. (2018). *Mapping on access to sport for people with disabilities. A report to the European Commission*. European Union.

Emrich, E., Pierdzioch, C., & Rullang, C. (2013). Zwischen Regelgebundenheit und diskretionären Spielräumen: Die Finanzierung des bundesdeutschen Spitzensports. Sport und Gesellschaft. *Sport and Society, 10*(1), 3–26.

European Commission. (2017). *Special Eurobarometer 472. Sport and physical activity*. European Union.

Guett, M., et al. (2011). All for sport for all: Perspectives of sport for people with a disability in Europe. Summary Report to the European Commission, April 2011.

Haring, M. (2010). *Sportförderung in Deutschland. Eine vergleichende Analyse der Bundesländer*. VS Verlag für Sozialwissenschaften.

Hebbel-Seeger, A., Horky, T., & Schulke, H.-J. (Eds.). (2014). *Sport und Inklusion – ziemlich beste Freunde?! 13. Hamburger Symposium für Sport, Ökonomie und Medien 2013*. Meyer & Meyer.

Heyer, K. (2015). *Rights enabled: The disability revolution. From the US, to Germany and Japan, to the United Nations*. The University of Michigan Press.

Inklusionslandkarte. (2021). https://www.inklusionslandkarte.de/ (31.10.2021).

Innenmoser, J., Abel, T., & Kuckuck, R. (Eds.). (2015). *Behindertensport 1951–2011. Historische und aktuelle Aspekte im nationalen und internationalen Dialog*. Meyer & Meyer.

Jaarsma, E. A., Dijkstra, P. U., Geertzen, J. H. B., & Dekker, R. (2014). Barriers to and facilitators of sports participation for people with physical disabilities: A systematic review. *Scandinavian Journal of Medicine & Science in Sports, 24*, 871–881.

Kiuppis, F., & Kurzke-Maasmeier, S. (2012). *Sport im Spiegel der UN-Behindertenrechtskonvention Interdisziplinäre Zugänge und politische Positionen*. Kohlhammer.

Klenk, C., Albrecht, J., & Nagel, S. (2019). Social participation of people with disabilities in organized community sport. A systematic review. *German Journal of Exercise and Sport Research, 49*(4), 365–380.

Knauer-Berg, O., & Bös, K. (2015). Behindertensport in den Medien. In M. Wegner, V. Scheid, & M. Knoll (Eds.), *Handbuch Behinderung und Sport* (pp. 84–92). Hofmann.
Knoll, M., & Fessler, N. (2015). Freizeit- und Breitensport für Menschen mit Behinderungen. In M. Wegner, V. Scheid, & M. Knoll (Eds.), *Handbuch Behinderung und Sport* (pp. 226–237). Hofmann.
Köpfer, A., Powell, J. J. W., & Zahnd, R. (2021). *Handbuch Inklusion international. Globale, nationale und lokale Perspektiven auf inklusive Bildung*. Barbara Budrich.
Kurscheidt, M., & Deitersen-Wieber, A. (2011). Sport governance in Germany. In C. Sobry (Ed.), *Sports governance in the world: A socio-historic approach* (pp. 259–306). Éd. Le Manuscrit.
Maschke, M. (2008). *Behindertenpolitik in der Europäischen Union: Lebenssituation behinderter Menschen und nationale Behindertenpolitik in 15 Mitgliedstaaten*. VS Verlag für Sozialwissenschaften.
Meier, H., Riedel, L., & Kukuk, M. (Eds.). (2016). *Migration, Inklusion und Integration. Soziologische Betrachtungen des Sports*. Schneider Verlag.
Meier, H., Seitz, S., & Adolph-Börs, C. (2017). *Der inklusive Sportverein. Wie inklusive Vereinsarbeit gelingen kann*. Meyer & Meyer.
Mittag, J., Müller-Schoell, T., & Putzmann, N. (2018). Country report: Germany. In A. Geeraert (Ed.), *National Sports Governance Observer. Final report* (pp. 122–140). Play the Game.
Niehoff, U. (2008). Inklusion durch Sport – Inklusion im Sport. In M. Wegner & H.-J. Schulke (Eds.), *Behinderung, Bewegung, Befreiung: Gewinn von Lebensqualität und Selbständigkeit durch Wettbewerbe und sportliches Training bei Menschen mit geistiger Behinderung* (pp. 30–46). Institut für Sport und Sportwissenschaft.
Petry, K., & Hallmann, K. (2013). Germany. In K. Hallmann & K. Petry (Eds.), *Comparative sport development. Systems, participation and public policy* (pp. 75–86). Springer.
Powell, J. J. W., Felkendorff, K., & Hollenweger, J. (2008). Disability in German, Swiss, and Austrian higher education systems. In S. Gabel & S. Danforth (Eds.), *Disability and the politics of education. An international reader* (pp. 517–540). Peter Lang.
Quade, K. (2015). Die Paralympische Bewegung. In M. Wegner, V. Scheid, & M. Knoll (Eds.), *Handbuch Behinderung und Sport* (pp. 258–266). Hofmann.
Radtke, S. (2011). Inklusion von Menschen mit Behinderung im Sport. *Aus Politik und Zeitgeschichte, 16–19*, 13–19.
Radtke, S. (2018). Inklusion im außerschulischen Sport: eine Bestandsaufnahme der Maßnahmen im organisierten Sport sowie des Forschungsstandes neun Jahre nach Ratifizierung der UN-BRK in Deutschland. *Leipziger Sportwissenschaftliche Beiträge, 59*, 160–194.
Radtke, S., & Schäfer, L. (2019). *Inklusion im Nachwuchsleistungssport. Vereinbarkeit von Schule und paralympischem Leistungssport an Eliteschulen des Sports versus Regelschulen*. Sportverlag Strauß.
Scheid, V., Rank, M., & Kuckuck, R. (2003). *Behindertenleistungssport. Strukturen und Anforderungen aus Athletensicht*. Meyer & Meyer.
Schierl, T., & Bertling, C. (2007). Die Darstellung der Paralympics in den Massenmedien unter Berücksichtigung ihrer gesellschaftlichen und historischen Entwicklung. In K. Lennartz, S. Wassong, & T. Zawadzki (Eds.), *New aspects of sport history. The Olympic lectures*. Academia.
Schliermann, R. (2015a). Leistungssport von Athletinnen und Athleten mit Behinderungen. In M. Wegner, V. Scheid, & M. Knoll (Eds.), *Handbuch Behinderung und Sport* (pp. 238–247). Hofmann.
Schliermann, R. (2015b). Die Deaflympische Sportbewegung. In M. Wegner, V. Scheid, & M. Knoll (Eds.), *Handbuch Behinderung und Sport* (pp. 279–290). Hofmann.
Schlund, S. (2017). *"Behinderung" überwinden? Organisierter Behindertensport in der Bundesrepublik Deutschland (1950–1990)*. Campus.
Statista. (2020). *Mitgliederzahlen des Deutschen Behindertensportverbandes von 2002 bis 2020*. https://de.statista.com/statistik/daten/studie/215960/umfrage/mitgliederzahl-des-deutschen-behindertensportverbandes/ (2.6.2021).

Thieme, L., & Wadsack, R. (2013). Sportförderung, öffentliche. In T. Bezold et al. (Eds.), *Handwörterbuch des Sportmanagements* (pp. 311–316). Peter Lang.

Thomas, N. B., & Guett, M. (2014). Fragmented, complex and cumbersome. A study of disability sport policy and provision in Europe. *International Journal of Sport Policy and Politics, 6*, 389–406.

Tiemann, M. (2010). *Öffentliche Gesundheit und Gesundheitssport*. Nomos.

Tiemann, H., & Radtke, S. (2017). Inklusion im schulischen und außerschulischen Sport im Fokus der Heterogenitätsdimension Behinderung. In D. Dumon et al. (Eds.), *Passionately inclusive: Towards participation and friendship in sport. Festschrift für Gudrun Doll-Tepper* (pp. 209–222). Waxmann.

Waldschmidt, A. (2020). *Disability Studies. Zur Einführung*. Junius.

Waldschmidt, A., & Schneider, W. (Eds.). (2007). *Disability Studies, Kultursoziologie und Soziologie der Behinderung: Erkundungen in einem neuen Forschungsfeld*. transcript.

Wedemeyer-Kolwe, B. (2010). Körpergeschichte. In M. Krüger & H. Langenfeld (Eds.), *Handbuch Sportgeschichte* (pp. 104–113). Hofmann.

Wedemeyer-Kolwe, B. (2011). *Vom "Versehrtenturnen" zum Deutschen Behindertensportverband (DBS). Eine Geschichte des deutschen Behindertensports*. Arete.

Wegner, M., Scheid, V., & Knoll, M. (Eds.). (2015). *Handbuch Behinderung und Sport*. Hofmann.

Wicker, P., & Breuer, C. (2014). Exploring the organizational capacity and organizational problems of disability sport clubs in Germany using matched pairs analysis. *Sport and Management Review, 17*(1), 23–34.

Willig, M., Ramm, D., & Groskreutz, H. (2010). Die Wirkung der Behindertenrechtskonventionen auf die Rehabilitation in Deutschland. Impulse und Perspektiven. *Die Rehabilitation, 49*, 259–265.

Chapter 15
The Netherlands: Towards Inclusive Sport for People with a Disability

Caroline van Lindert and Maxine de Jonge

15.1 Introduction

The Dutch government's disability sport policy has intensified since 2000, when the former sport federations for people with an intellectual and physical disability and the Netherlands Olympic Committee* the Dutch Sports Federation (hereafter NOC*NSF) signed a cooperation agreement encouraged by the Ministry of Health, Welfare and Sport (*ministerie van Volksgezondheid, Welzijn en Sport*, hereafter minVWS). The aim of this partnership was to accommodate sport for people with a disability (hereafter pwd) as much as possible within the mainstream settings of organised sport. Since then, sport for pwd has been implemented within the structures of at least 46 mainstream national sport federations and numerous affiliated sports clubs accommodate members with a disability. Over the past 20 years, government policy with regard to sport and physical activity for pwd has been characterised by (financing) time-limited policy programmes, eventually resulting in a broader national policy programme aimed at inclusive sport and physical activity (hereafter PA) for multiple populations, including pwd. The organisational landscape for disability sport has also changed, resulting in a complex constellation of diverse (disability) sport agents. Nonetheless, sport and PA participation levels of pwd remain much lower than the general population. In this chapter, we describe how sport for pwd in the Netherlands is governed and structured and discuss the sport participation of different groups of pwd. The information in this chapter is based on Dutch research reports, literature, policy documents, open data sources and face-to-face interviews held in early 2020 with experts and representatives from governmental, intermediary and non-governmental agents working in the field of

C. van Lindert (✉) · M. de Jonge
Mulier Institute, Utrecht, The Netherlands
e-mail: c.vanlindert@mulierinstituut.nl

disability sport at the national level (Van Lindert & De Jonge, 2022). The interviews and the writing of the chapter were made possible with support from the minVWS.

15.2 Country Profile

In this section we describe various characteristics of the Netherlands, in regard to (disability) sport policy and participation.

Characteristics of the Netherlands

The Netherlands ranks among the most densely populated European countries (CBS, 2020b). Because of its small size, the Netherlands is easily accessible by public transport, car, bicycle and even on foot. Accessibility and close proximity to amenities are important to the Dutch. This also applies to sport facilities, as the Netherlands has a sport facility per 835 inhabitants, and the average distance from a residence to the closest sport facility is less than 800 metres (Van der Poel et al., 2016). The Netherlands is a prosperous nation. Approximately one-third of the Dutch population has a post-secondary education level (CBS, 2020a; Roeters, 2017). Quality of life in the Netherlands is high, and the Netherlands currently ranks at number 5 on the World Happiness Report (Helliwell et al., 2019). The Dutch population is greying and diversifying. People 65 years or older currently make up 19% of the population, and it is expected they will make up 26% of the population by 2040 (CBS, 2018). At present, approximately 24% of the Dutch population is a first- or second-generation immigrant (CBS, 2020d). The secularisation in the Netherlands has continued to increase in recent years. In 2017, less than half of the Dutch people aged 15 and older joined a religious denomination or ideological group (Schmeets, 2018). The Dutch society was historically divided through social views or religious beliefs. Each group had its own institutions, such as sports clubs, schools and political parties, and traces of this compartmentalisation are still found in today's society. Compartmentalisation made consultation and forming coalitions on social and political level desirable (Breedveld & Hoekman, 2017). Today, national and local governments are still based on coalitions of usually two or more parties. The Netherlands is a decentralised unitary state in which the various territorial units also have independent powers. As concluded by Breedveld and Hoekman (2017), politically, culturally and economically, the Netherlands is an exponent of the Rhineland model. The Netherlands has a relatively large public sector. High taxes support many facilities for disadvantaged groups, access to education for all and relatively small income gaps (see Table 15.1).

Table 15.1 Facts and statistics of the Netherlands

Population (number of inhabitants)	17,440,679[a]
Area (sq. km × 1000)	41.54[b]
Density (number of inhabitants per sq. km)	511[c]
Urban population (% of total population)	91[d]
Political organisation	Parliamentary constitutional monarchy
State structure	Unitary
Provinces	12
Municipalities	355[e]
GDP (per capita, USD)	52,304.057[f]
Official languages	1
EU membership	Since 1952
Welfare model	Rhineland

[a]CBS (2020b)
[b]The World Bank Group (2018b)
[c]The World Bank Group (2018a)
[d]The World Bank Group (2018c)
[e]CBS (2020c)
[f]The World Bank Group (2021)

Sport Profile of the Netherlands

Different characteristics of the Netherlands, for example, high gross domestic product (GDP) and high educational levels, can be considered beneficial in regard to the provision of sport and sport participation in the Netherlands (Hoekman & Breedveld, 2013). The sport participation level in the Netherlands (54%) is among the highest in the EU. The same applies to sports club participation (28%) and volunteering in sport (19%; see Table 15.2). Dutch citizens (aged 12 and older) are highly satisfied (86%) with the opportunities to engage in sport and physical activities in their residential area (European Commission, 2014; Hoekman & Breedveld, 2013; RIVM, n.d.-e; Van der Poel et al., 2016). For other sport characteristics, see Table 15.2.

Mainstream sport and disability sport have become increasingly intertwined over the years. The general sport structure in the Netherlands has been extensively described by Breedveld and Hoekman (2017). In this chapter, we will present the current disability sport structure and discuss recent changes in national sport policy that have impacted disability sport. In general, sport is a shared responsibility of many agents in the landscape. Alliances are forged between agents active within and outside the sport sector. This also applies to disability sport. In that sense, the sport sector reflects the Dutch tradition of forming coalitions as described in the first paragraph. The minVWS is in charge of creating national sport policies (physical education falls under the responsibility of the Ministry of Education, Culture and Sciences [*ministerie van Onderwijs, Cultuur en Wetenschappen*, hereafter minOCW]). The minVWS's ambitions are aligned with its strategic partners NOC*NSF, the Association for Sport and Municipalities (*Vereniging Sport en Gemeenten*, hereafter VSG) and the Association of Dutch Municipalities (*Vereniging Nederlandse Gemeenten*, hereafter VNG). From

Table 15.2 Sport profile of the Netherlands

	Ministry of Health, Welfare and Sport
Government authority responsible for sport	
Membership sports club (% of population 6 years and older)*	28%[a]
Membership fitness or health centre (% of population 6 years and older)*	23%[a]
Membership socio-cultural club that includes sport in its activities (e.g. employees' club, youth club and school- and university-related club) (% of population 6 years and older)	13%[a]
Non-organised sport (alone, informal group) (% of population 6 years and older)	63%[a]
Sport participation, at least once a week (% of population 4 years and older)	54%[b]
Number of national sport federations affiliated with NOC*NSF	77[c]
Number of sports clubs affiliated with NOC*NSF sport federations*	23,500[c]
Number of sports club members	4,314,000[c]
National expenditure for sport in 2019 (€ × 1000)	324,146[d]
Government subsidies NOC*NSF in 2018 (€ × 1000)	52,885[e]
Local budget (municipalities) for sport in 2019 (€ × 1000)	1,114,261[f]
Total working hours of volunteers at sports clubs in 2020 (per week, × 1000)	1869[g]
Volunteering in sport (% of population)	19[h]

*Including sports clubs that are not affiliated with NOC*NSF, in 2018 the Netherlands counted 26,510 sports clubs (CBS, 2020e)
[a]RIVM (n.d.-b)
[b]RIVM (n.d.-d)
[c]NOC*NSF (2018)
[d]Rijksoverheid (n.d.-c)
[e]NOC*NSF (2020)
[f]Van den Dool and Van Eldert (2021)
[g]CBS (2020e)
[h]European Commission (2018)

a theoretical perspective, the relationships between the government and the various agents in the sport sector can be characterised as a co-governance relationship, where the agents in the sport sector and the government operate interdependently (Breedveld & Hoekman, 2017). In 2018, the minVWS, NOC*NSF, VSG and VNG signed the National Sport Agreement 'Sport unites the Netherlands' (*Nationaal Sport Akkoord, Sport Verenigt Nederland*, 2019–2022, hereafter NSA) (Ministerie van VWS, 2018b). The partners formulated ambitions with regard to six policy domains, one of which is 'Inclusive sport & physical activity' (*Inclusief sporten en bewegen*), which is relevant to disability sport. This sub-agreement was developed by the minVWS in collaboration with the 'Alliance for Inclusive Sport and Physical Activity (PA)' (*Alliantie inclusief sporten en bewegen voor iedereen*), which comprises various agents representing specific population groups, including pwd.

Disability in the Netherlands

In the early 2000s, the Dutch government passed several pieces of legislation in order to increase the participation of pwd in society, such as the Equal Treatment on the Grounds of Disability and Chronic Illness Act (Wet Gelijke Behandeling Op Grond van Handicap of Chronische Ziekte, 2003). In 2015, the Social Support Act (*Wet Maatschappelijke Ondersteuning*, WMO), the Youth Act (*Jeugdwet*) and the Participation Act (*Participatiewet*) came into effect with the aim of increasing participation in society by people who cannot do so (completely) independently (Jeugdwet, 2014; Wet Maatschappelijke Ondersteuning 2015, 2014; Participatiewet, 2003). The implementation of these laws lies with the municipalities. In 2016, the Netherlands ratified the United Nations Convention on the Rights of Persons with a Disability (UNCRPD). The act on equal treatment of pwd or chronic illness was amended accordingly, and since 2017, schools, employers and companies have to comply with a general standard of accessibility (Besluit algemene toegankelijkheid voor personen met een handicap of chronische ziekte, 2017). In 2018, the national government initiated the programme 'Unhindered participation' (*Onbeperkt Meedoen*), aiming to implement the UNCRPD into Dutch society (Ministerie van VWS, 2018c). Despite all laws and implementation plans adopted, several studies show that the position of pwd in the Netherlands has not improved. Lack of governmental awareness regarding the mandatory nature of the UNCRPD and wide municipal policy discretion coupled with insufficient policy framework, lack of central control and ineffective UNCRPD implementation monitoring may play a role (Eggink et al., 2020; Knapen et al., 2020; Kromhout et al., 2020; Schoonheim & Smits, 2019; Vermeij & Hamelink, 2021).

Dutch parlance regarding disability has changed considerably over the years, along with developments in perception of 'otherness' of people in society and concepts of disability. Nowadays, person-first language is most commonly used, and the preferred term in the Netherlands for disability is *beperking* or *functiebeperking*, which translates as 'limitation' or 'functional limitation' (or impairment and disability). Since the national programme for the implementation of the UNCRPD (*Onbeperkt Meedoen!*) came into effect in 2018, a broad definition of disability was adopted to avoid stigmatisation and exclusion of people with specific health problems (Ministerie van VWS, 2018c). Following that definition, in this chapter we refer to pwd as persons with impairments or chronic conditions in mental and/or physical functions who experience limitations in the execution of activities and barriers to social participation. This definition aligns with the biopsychosocial model of the International Classification of Functioning, Disability and Health (hereafter ICF) from the World Health Organization (hereafter WHO) (World Health Organization, 2002) and is also used in sport participation research (Van den Dool et al., 2022; Von Heijden-Brinkman et al., 2013). Mental disabilities can be seen as impairments or disorders in intellectual (understanding, learning) and psychosocial functions (e.g. hyperactivity/concentration and autism). In regard to physical disabilities, the Dutch distinguish between mobility and sensory impairments and people with chronic conditions or diseases.

The Netherlands uses the national census and data from specific health care services, education and employment services to estimate the number of people with a disability. Due to the diversity in type and degree of disability and impairments, these approaches do not include all pwd. Statistics Netherlands (*Centraal Bureau voor de Statistiek*, CBS) uses the Organisation for Economic Cooperation and Development (OECD) indicator to collect data on the prevalence of long-term mobility, visual and hearing limitations for people 12 years and older (McWhinnie, 1981; see Table 15.3). People are categorised as having a moderate to severe disability if they answer 'cannot perform this skill' or 'can perform this skill with great difficulty' for at least one of the seven distinguished skills in regard to walking, hearing and seeing. The Global Activity Limitation Indicator (GALI) is used in addition to the OECD indicator, but more often for international comparisons. The GALI comprises a single question regarding the extent to which a person, for at least the past six months, felt limited in activities people usually do due to a health problem (see Table 15.3).

According to the OECD indicator, almost 12% of the Dutch population (12 years and older) experiences at least one limitation in hearing, seeing and/or mobility (Table 15.3). Based on population numbers for this age group in 2019 (CBS, 2021a), this amounts to almost 1.8 million people experiencing one or more physical disabilities. Thirty-one per cent of Dutch people suffer from one or more chronic illnesses or conditions (for six months or longer). This equals around 5.4 million people.

People with intellectual disabilities are not included in the national health census. Based on the normal distribution of intelligence among the population and the use of care and facilities for this group, it is estimated that around 440,000 persons in the Netherlands have a minor to severe intellectual disability (Intelligence Quotient (IQ) < 70). This increases to 1,170,000 persons if people with an IQ between 70 and 85 who are not self-reliant and dependent on special care and support are included (around 6.5% of the total population) (Volksgezondheidenzorg.

Table 15.3 Facts and statistics on disability and chronic conditions in the Netherlands

	Total	Male	Women
OECD limitation (at least 1, hearing, seeing and/or mobility, moderate/severe, % of population, 12 years or older, 2019)	11.9	8.4	15.3
OECD mobility limitation (moderate/severe, % of population, 12 years or older, 2019)	8.7	5.3	12.1
OECD visual limitation (moderate/severe, % of population, 12 years or older, 2019)	3.1	2.2	3.9
OECD hearing limitation (moderate/severe, % of population, 12 years or older, 2019)	3.1	3.1	3.1
Chronic disorder (1 or more, 6 months or longer, % of total population, 2019)	31.2	28.9	33.5
Self-perceived long-term limitations in daily activities (GALI, 4 years or older, 2019)	29.2	26.3	32.1

OECD Organisation for Economic Cooperation and Development, *ADL* Activities of Daily Living, *GALI* Global Activity Limitation Indicator
Source: CBS (2021b)

info, 2021). Data on the prevalence of psychosocial problems is scarce in the Netherlands. In 2019, 11.5% of people aged above 12 years perceived their mental health as poor (CBS, 2021b).

Children with a disability are partially accounted for with the above indicators (De Jonge & van Lindert, 2020). In addition, the minOCW registers the number of children in special education. Around 70,000 children are registered in these schools (De Jonge & Van Lindert, 2020a). But this does not represent the total number of children with a disability or chronic condition in the Netherlands, because children with disabilities also attend mainstream education.

Emergence of Disability Sport in the Netherlands

The history of disability sport and the Paralympic movement in the Netherlands can be divided into four periods (see Fig. 15.1): until 1960 (first steps), 1961–1990 (building a structure), 1991–2000 (expansion and bundling) and 2001 and onwards (restructuring and towards inclusion). The first formal step towards the organisation of sport for pwd in the Netherlands was the foundation of the Deaf Sports Federation (*Nederlandse Doven Sport Bond*, NDSB, now called Royal Deaf Sports Federation, KNDSB) in 1926, after local members of the Amsterdam deaf sports club participated in the 1924 first International Silent Games. In 1945 after World War II, the Dutch Military War and Service Victims Association (*Bond van Nederlandse Militaire Oorlog- en Dienstslachtoffers*), the still-existing BNMO, was founded. The Military Rehabilitation Centre *Aardenburg* in Doorn (MRC) organised small-scale sports activities. In 1952, a Dutch archery team accepted Sir Ludwig Guttmann's invitation to participate at the first International Stoke Mandeville Games. After 1950, disability sport increasingly acquired its own identity. The first two sports clubs for wheelchair users in the Netherlands were founded in 1954, as a result of rehabilitation patients' desire to continue practising sport post discharge. The Netherlands sent a team to the 1960 International Stoke Mandeville Games in Rome, which are considered the first Olympic Games for pwd.

In 1961, the Dutch Disabled Sports Federation (*de Nederlandse Invaliden Sportbond*, NIS) was created by the BNMO and MRC as a result of the urge to organise sport for non-veterans with a physical disability. In 1973 a separate organisation was created for sport for people with an intellectual disability (*Nederlandse Sportbond voor Geestelijk Gehandicapten*, NSG). Between the late 1960s and early 1980s, an increasing number of local sports clubs and several national sports federations were established[1] for veterans and for civilians with various disabilities. In

---

[1] Such as the Federation Disabled Horse Riding (Federatie Paardrijden Gehandicapten, FPG, 1967), the Foundation Water Sport for Disabled (Stichting Watersport met Gehandicapten, SWG, 1974), the National Federation Sport Open Days Disabled (Landelijke Federatie Sport Instuiven Gehandicapten, LFSIG, 1974) and the Sport Federation for the Visually Impaired (Sportfederatie Visueel Gehandicapten Nederland, SVGN, 1981).

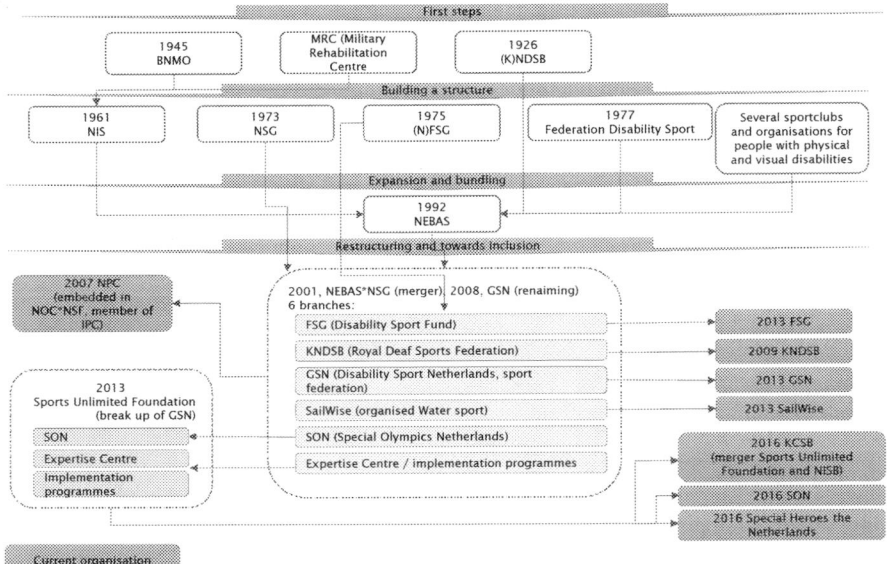

Fig. 15.1 Timeline history of disability sport in the Netherlands*. *BNMO=Dutch Military War and Service Victims Association; (K)NDSB=(Royal) Dutch Deaf Sports Federation; NIS=Dutch Disabled Sports Federation; NSG=Dutch Sports Federation for persons with intellectual disability; (N)FSG=(National) Disability Sport Fund; NEBAS=Dutch Association for Adapted Sports; NPC=National Paralympic Committee; NOC*NSF=Netherlands Olympic Committee*Dutch Sports Federation. Source: authors' own work

addition, in 1975, the National Disability Sports Fund was established (*Stichting Nationaal Fonds Sport Gehandicapten*, NFSG) to raise and distribute funds for the benefit of sport for pwd. The organisation still exists as the Disability Sports Fund (*Fonds Gehandicaptensport*, FSG) and plays a crucial role in the landscape today. A turning point for the position of disability sport in the Netherlands came in 1976 with the participation of Dutch athletes at the Paralympic Summer Games in Toronto and the Paralympic Winter Games in Sweden, which raised the media's and the broader public's attention for disability sport in the Netherlands.

In the 1980s, the Paralympic Games were organised in Arnhem and the World Games for people with disabilities followed ten years later in Assen. In those years, the Dutch began to accept disability sport at the highest level as elite sport. In 1987, motivated by the need to cut back on subsidies, a bundling of the disability sport organisations into one national umbrella organisation was promoted (Tweede Kamer der Staten-Generaal, 1987, 1990). This resulted in the merger of the Dutch Disabled Sports Association (NIS) with several other disability sports associations to form the Dutch Association for Adapted Sports (*Nederlandse Bond voor Aangepast Sporten*, NEBAS) in 1992. The NSG (intellectual disability) stayed independent. In 1993 the KNDSB (deaf sport) joined the new association.

In 2000, during the Sydney Paralympic Games and under the supervision of the minVWS, NEBAS, NSG and NOC*NSF signed an agreement with the aim to intensify their cooperation. The declaration stated that the organisations would share responsibility in integrating sport for pwd into the mainstream sport settings of the national sport federations. The resulting project was entitled 'organisational integration' and ran from 2000 to 2008. Around 40 sport federations agreed to officially integrate sport for pwd into their federations (Notté et al., 2011). NOC*NSF facilitated the participation of Team NL and took over responsibility for the Dutch Paralympic team from the 2004 Games onwards. In 2007, in order to become a member of the International Paralympic Committee (IPC), NOC*NSF established a National Paralympic Committee, embedded within the organisational structures of NOC*NSF. In the same period, NEBAS and NSG intensified their partnership and ratified an agreement to merge in 2001 to create NEBAS*NSG, an umbrella organisation that strove for better sport opportunities for people with physical and intellectual disabilities. In 2008, NEBAS*NSG changed its name to the Disability Sport Netherlands foundation (*Stichting Gehandicaptensport Nederland*). In 2009, the KNDSB (deaf sport) separated itself again. Around 2013, the role and function of Disability Sport Netherlands were re-evaluated. The organisation broke up into several independent organisations, one of which was the expertise centre that came to be known as the Sports Unlimited foundation (*Stichting Onbeperkt Sportief*). The sports federation branch of Disability Sport Netherlands continued as an independent organisation and still exists today under the same name (*Gehandicaptensport Nederland*, GSN). The last major transformation in the landscape of disability sport was made in 2016, with the merger of the expertise centre (*Stichting Onbeperkt Sportief*) with the Dutch Institute for Sport and Physical Activity (*Nederlands Instituut voor Sport en Bewegen*, NISB), resulting in the Knowledge Centre for Sport and Physical Activity (*Kenniscentrum voor Sport en Bewegen*, KCSB). Special Olympics Netherlands (*Special Olympics Nederland*, SON), a former part of the disintegrated Disability Sport Netherlands, still functions as an independent organisation today. Special Heroes the Netherlands (*Stichting Special Heroes Nederland*), an organisation for the implementation of stimulation programmes for pwd, came into existence as a result of the collapse of the Sports Unlimited foundation. Due to the break-up of the former Disability Sport Netherlands foundation, the landscape for disability sport has become increasingly splintered as organisations try to fill the vacuum. There was no longer a national agent that fulfilled the multiple roles of developing knowledge, stimulating, organising and promoting sport for and by pwd. The Dutch disability sport landscape is dynamic in its nature. It remains to be seen how the next stage (inclusion) will unfold (De Heer, 2000; Von Heijden-Brinkman et al., 2013; Meijer, 2014; Notté et al., 2011; Pegels, 1985; Verhaag, 2013).

15.3 The Current Organisation of Disability Sport

Structure of Disability Sport

Many different agents are involved in the provision of sport and PA for pwd in the Netherlands (see Fig. 15.2). However, there is no single organisation in charge that unites all organisations under a shared vision. We provide a brief description of the roles of the different organisations below based on previous research (Van Lindert & De Jonge, 2022).

Governmental Agents

The minVWS is in charge of creating national sport policies, including for pwd. The current policy is the NSA. In addition, the minVWS provides grants to various organisations active in the domain of (elite) sport and/or PA for pwd. The minVWS stresses the importance of collaboration between the various agents in order to reach policy goals and takes it upon itself to facilitate partnerships between other agents.

At the provincial level, the provinces include pwd in their sport policy (Reitsma & Hoekman, 2019). Provinces are indirectly involved in the implementation of sport policy through their respective provincial sport councils (*provinciale*

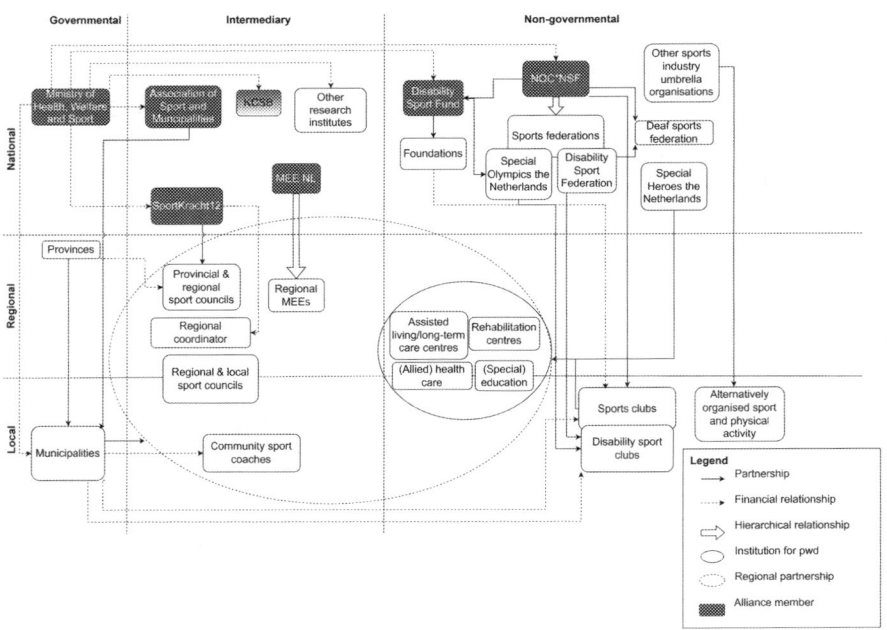

Fig. 15.2 Agents involved in the Dutch disability sport landscape. Source: Van Lindert & De Jonge, 2022: adapted by the authors

sportraden), which act as intermediary support agents. The provincial sport councils are united at the national level through Sportkracht12.

At the local level, almost all municipalities have policy goals relevant to sport and PA for pwd (Gutter & Van Lindert, 2020a). The municipalities are involved in various activities aimed towards enabling pwd to participate in sport and PA, such as minimising financial barriers, employing community sport coaches (*buurtsportcoaches*, hereafter CSC), regional partnerships with neighbouring municipalities, planning and improving sport provision and increasing visibility of sport opportunities. Some municipalities have local sport councils that assist the municipality in the implementation of policy.

Intermediary Agents

Various intermediary agents are active in regard to disability sport and often serve as connecting agents between agents at the governmental and non-governmental levels. MEE the Netherlands is a national association consisting of 20 regional MEE chapters. MEE aims to help people with a non-visible disability in various domains of life. In the past few years, MEE has focused more on guiding people with a non-visible disability towards sport and this is incorporated in some of the regional chapters. The regional MEEs work with national sport federations (NSFs), Disability Sport Fund (*Fonds Gehandicaptensport*, FSG), provincial and regional sport organisations, NOC*NSF, Special Olympics the Netherlands (SON) and Special Heroes the Netherlands. MEE is a member of the Alliance for Inclusive Sport and PA.

Sportkracht12, also member of the Alliance, is a network for the 12 provincial sport councils. The network is well integrated at the regional and local levels. Sportkracht12 has been involved in the development and implementation of national sport policy for pwd since 2015.

Next to the 12 provincial sport councils, the regional sport councils and municipal sport councils are active at the regional or local level, respectively. The regional sport councils can serve a group of municipalities in regard to disability sport; municipal sport councils serve a single municipality. Each individual sport council can also match supply and demand for disability sport at the corresponding level and develop new activities and programmes. Each provincial sport council has a provincial consultant for disability sport. The consultant advises the regional coordinators and helps to translate national policy to the regional and local levels. The regional coordinators are active at the regional level and are responsible for coordinating the 43 'regional partnerships for adapted sports' and facilitate sport and PA for various groups of people, including pwd (Volksgezondheidenzorg.info, n.d.). The purpose of the regional partnerships is to create and optimise the regional network for sport and PA for pwd. The regional partnerships consist of various agents within a region that enable pwd to participate in sport or PA, such as municipalities, special schools, health care institutions and sports clubs. Sometimes, pwd are included in the regional partnerships as 'experts by experience'. The regional coordinator can be employed by a municipality, the regional sport council or a local sport council. Regional coordinators work closely with CSC at the local level. In close cooperation with Disability Sport Fund, the regional partnerships provide an overview of sport programmes and activities for pwd in the area (province, region or municipality), published on the online community platform Unique Sports (*Uniek Sporten*).

The Association for Sport and Municipalities (*Vereniging Sport en Gemeenten*, VSG) is the umbrella organisation for municipal sport policymakers and also a member of the Alliance. The VSG's role is to create and implement policies, promote awareness about inclusive sport among their members and support them with information in regard to grant opportunities, the appointment of CSC or new data through meetings and social media. Since 2008, the national government has provided funds to employ CSC (Ministeries van VWS et al., 2018). The CSC establish connections between local sport agents and organisations from other sectors, such as education and health care, in order to ultimately provide better opportunities for local citizens to participate in sport and PA close to home. CSC are seen as important intermediary professionals in guiding people with a disability towards sport and PA. They connect sports providers with organisations that work with pwd (e.g. schools and health care providers), organise sport activities for pwd and support sports clubs in welcoming pwd (Gutter & Van Lindert, 2020b).

In the Netherlands, various institutions conduct research, educate professionals and/or disseminate information or expertise in order to improve sport for pwd. One of the institutions is the Knowledge Centre for Sport and Physical Activity (*Kenniscentrum Sport en Bewegen*, hereafter KCSB). KCSB is funded by the min-VWS and is responsible for collecting information about sport and PA (for pwd), making the information accessible and sharing it with various organisations such as governments, civil servants, sport federations, sport programmes and activities, and health care institutions. Other research institutions include the Mulier Institute, the National Institute for Public Health and Environment (*Rijks Instituut voor Volksgezondheid en Milieu*, hereafter RIVM), the Dutch Institute for Health Services Research (NIVEL), universities and universities of applied sciences.

Non-governmental Agents

Various non-governmental agents play a direct role in creating policies and sport programmes for pwd. NOC*NSF is the national umbrella organisation for the Dutch Olympic and Paralympic Committee and the national sports federations. Elite para sport is fully integrated, but a National Paralympic Committee (NPC) still exists, embedded within the organisational structures of NOC*NSF. In terms of elite sport, NOC*NSF's goal is to win more medals in more sports. In terms of mainstream sport, the goal is to get more people involved in sport and to experience joy in sport, including pwd. NOC*NSF creates policy (for the sport federations) and also has a role in implementing national policy. NOC*NSF is member of the Alliance for Inclusive Sport and PA.

Seventy-seven national sport federations (NSFs) in the Netherlands are members of NOC*NSF, including Special Olympics Netherlands (SON) and Disability Sport Netherlands (*Gehandicaptensport Nederland*, GSN). Research on the national sport federations, conducted by the Mulier Institute in 2020, shows that 46 NSFs support sport for pwd within their federations (Gutter, De Jonge, et al., 2021). The federations develop, strengthen and expand programmes, events and activities for pwd. This is a direct result of the ongoing integration process. The level of integration of sport for pwd within the federation differs per federation; some federations are more active than others depending on the available capacity (budget and personnel). Sport federations partner with foundations and receive funding from various funds to execute some of the programmes and activities for pwd.

GSN functions as a safety net for sports (clubs) that are not (yet) adopted by national sport federations. Approximately 200 clubs (mostly disability specific) are members of GSN. It is the sport federation for several types of sports specifically for pwd: boccia, bocce, goalball, blind football, motor activity training programme (MATP), sledge hockey, wheelchair rugby and showdown. GSN serves sports clubs specifically for pwd and uses its unique expertise and skills to implement, advise or supervise programmes for (sport for) pwd. GSN works closely with organisations outside of the sport sector that work for pwd, which brings GSN in close contact with pwd, and ultimately gives them a clearer overview of issues pwd face in daily life. In addition, GSN helps municipalities with the content for 'inclusive sport and physical activity' in their local policy and is in charge of a project funded by the minVWS, in partnership with the Royal Deaf Sports Federation (*Koninklijke Doven Sport Bond*, KNDSB) and NOC*NSF, to integrate deaf sport into the NSFs. Furthermore, GSN is leading a collaborative project with the aim of promoting sport participation among people with a visual impairment.

SON uses sport as a means to achieve the inclusion and acceptance of people with an intellectual disability in society. Every two years municipalities organise the Special Olympics National Games under the supervision of SON. SON sends Dutch athletes to the Special Olympics World Games. The aim behind these events is to bring awareness and create support for sport for people with intellectual disabilities. In addition to their events, they also work with other organisations, such as sport federations and sports clubs to provide sustainable and inclusive sport opportunities for people with an intellectual disability.

The KNDSB used to be the sport federation for deaf people in the Netherlands. However, as of January 1, 2022, KNDSB is no longer responsible for organisation of deaf sport. These have been integrated over the past two years into the national sport federations. Now, the KNDSB's role is to provide information and knowledge to GSN regarding (1) the handling of people with a hearing impairment in sport and (2) organising and financing the participation of people with a hearing impairment in international championships and the Deaflympics.

While NOC*NSF is the umbrella organisation for the sport federations, other industries within the sport sector are represented by other branch organisations. The fitness industry is represented at the national level by *NL Actief* and the interests of the swimming pool industry are represented at a national level by the National Swimming Council (*Nationale Raad Zwembaden*, NRZ). In terms of sport for pwd, these organisations share information and offer courses and certifications in regard to providing sport for pwd for local fitness clubs and swimming pools.

Several fundraising agents raise and distribute funds to enable pwd to participate in sport and PA and to support other agents in their activities for pwd at a local, regional or national level. The Disability Sport Fund (*Fonds Gehandicapten Sport*, FSG) plays a unique role in the landscape of sport for pwd, because of its contribution to implementation of national policy goals. FSG is a member of the previously mentioned Alliance for inclusive sport and PA and receives a subsidy from the minVWS to maintain the online community platform Unique Sports where pwd from across the country find their sport.

Several foundations (not funds) in the Netherlands focus on sport for pwd. These are often, but not always, established by a (former) (para-)athlete.[2] The foundations use funding from donations and sponsors to organise sport events for pwd and/or develop and implement projects related to sport and PA for pwd or people with chronic illness. Foundations work together with several national and local agents (e.g. sports providers, (special) schools, primary care and allied health professionals and municipalities).

Special Heroes the Netherlands is a non-profit organisation that aims to use sport and cultural activities to stimulate the physical, mental and social development of pwd. They implement various programmes in (special) education, long-term care centres, rehabilitation centres and hospitals.

Organised sport consists of approximately 23,500 federation-affiliated sports clubs that offer sport at the local level. Sports clubs can receive assistance in recruiting members or tailoring and strengthening their programmes for pwd from local organisations, such as municipalities, local sport councils and CSC; from regional organisations such as the regional and provincial sport councils and the regional coordinator; and from national organisations such as NOC*NSF, foundations, funds and NSFs. In a national sport club survey conducted by the Mulier Institute in 2020, 68% of mainstream sports clubs state they have one or more members with a disability, chronic condition or psychosocial disorder. Nineteen per cent of them have specific teams or groups for pwd. In the majority of sports clubs, members with a disability participate in the mainstream activities (Gutter, Van Lindert, et al., 2021). Besides mainstream sports clubs, sports clubs specifically for pwd also offer sport activities. Alternatively organised sports include sports offered by commercial providers (e.g. fitness centres and swimming pools) and other organisations (e.g. schools, health care institutions and social work). Alternatively organised sports providers can receive support from local agents (such as CSC), regional organisations and national sport industry organisations to help them in recruiting clients or improving their programming for pwd. Some alternatively organised sports providers offer specific hours or groups for pwd. Other providers include pwd in mainstream programming.

---

[2] For example, the Bas van de Goor Foundation, the Ester Vergeer Foundation, the Richard Krajicek Foundation, the Johan Cruyff Foundation, the Edwin van der Sar Foundation, the Dirk Kuyt Foundation, the Mentelity Foundation and the Disabled Child (het Gehandicapte Kind).

Secondary Agents

Several organisations have an indirect role within the sport and PA landscape for pwd. Primary care providers and allied health professionals, such as physical therapists, rehabilitation specialists and lifestyle coaches can refer pwd to sport and PA programmes. Some offer sport programmes for pwd, such as walking groups or medical fitness. Health insurance companies play an indirect role in stimulating sport and PA among pwd. They subsidise physical therapy and rehabilitation treatment, lifestyle interventions and (sport) mobility aids. Assisted living and long-term care centres organise sport and PA programmes for residents and/or clients on their own or in partnership with other parties, such as Special Heroes the Netherlands. Another option is that centres work with other parties, such as the regional MEE organisations and the regional coordinator to help residents/clients find a fitting sport or PA programme, potentially outside of the centre. Commercial (business) partners and sponsors, such as the lottery, provide funding for various programmes and organisations that play a direct role in the landscape. The (special) education sector is directly and indirectly involved in the organisation of sport for children with a disability. Some (special) schools offer after-school sport programming for their students. Special schools also serve as a resource for programmes that are looking for participants with a disability, such as Special Heroes. The educational sector also plays a role in educating students who will ultimately provide sport programming for this group, such as physical education teachers, CSC, personal trainers and fitness instructors, or go on to create sport policy or programmes for pwd, such as civil servants and sport federation employees.

Steering of Disability Sport

Legislative Framework

The Netherlands has no statute or law that specifically addresses sport. From a political-legal perspective, the manner in which the Dutch national government intervenes in sport is an expression of the popular will and is underpinned by the right to sport established in (international) laws, treaties and conventions, such as the Constitution (Ministerie van BZK, 2018), the European Sports Charter (Council of Europe, 2020) and the Treaty of Lisbon (European Union, 2007). Whether or not the Dutch national government should intervene in sport remains a political consideration in which the collective and meritorious goods in and outside the field of sport are weighed against each other (Van der Poel & Pulles, 2013). In 2020, the Dutch Sport Council (*Nederlandse Sportraad*, NSR) issued a recommendation arguing for a legal framework for sport and a greater role for the national government. According to the Dutch Sport Council, the lack of a sport act contributes to the fact that neither the government nor the sport sector has a clear vision or direction, which results in regional differences in the organisation and financing of sport and unsolved issues, for example, the sport sector's inability to find an effective solution to increase sport participation in minority groups (Nederlandse Sportraad, 2020). The lack of a clear direction also applies to the landscape for disability sport, as we saw in the previous section.

Several laws touch upon (sport for) pwd, such as the law regarding the equal treatment of pwd, as mentioned before (Wet Gelijke Behandeling Op Grond van Handicap of Chronische Ziekte, 2003). The Social Support Act (Hoekstra et al., 2019; Wet Maatschappelijke Ondersteuning 2015, 2014) makes municipalities responsible for increasing the societal participation of citizens who are not self-reliant, for example, persons with a disability or chronic illness. The decentralised nature of the Social Support Act allows municipalities to implement the law at their own discretion, resulting in differences across municipalities (Van der Veer et al., 2011). Because of the idea that sport can contribute to social participation, municipalities are increasingly linking sport to the Social Support Act. Therefore, pwd can use this act to apply for personalised guidance or support in practising sport, such as sport mobility aids and caretakers.

Policy Framework

In the Netherlands, the minVWS is responsible for creating (temporary) policies and programmes for sport, including for pwd, at a national level. There are several policies applicable to disability sport (Hoekstra et al., 2019). The overarching aims of these programmes and initiatives are to *'achieve a sporting society in which everyone can enjoy sport and physical activity, suitable and safe opportunities for sport and physical activity are available for everyone, and elite sport inspires and brings people together'* (Rijksoverheid, n.d.-c). Consistent with the principle of subsidiarity, the minVWS assumes the provision of sport to be a municipal responsibility (Ministerie van VWS, 2011). Municipalities are thus one of the main parties funding sport in the Netherlands. In regard to disability sport, 40% of the municipalities have specific policy goals in regard to disability sport and in 42% of the municipalities attention to disability sport falls under the goals for inclusive sport in general (Gutter & van Lindert, 2020). Provinces have no formal task with regard to sport, yet nowadays all 12 provinces mention sport in their coalition agreements for 2019–2023 and sport for pwd is explicitly mentioned in eight of them. The aim of the majority of these policies is to 'attend to and support pwd' (Reitsma & Hoekman, 2019).

The most recent national policy programme in regard to sport is the National Sport Agreement (NSA), which runs from 2018 to 2022 (Ministerie van VWS, 2018b). Relevant to disability sport is the sub-agreement 'Inclusive Sport and Physical Activity'. The overarching aim is to allow every Dutch person to have a life-long enjoyment of sport and PA and remove barriers people may face due to their background. In contrast to previous sport policy programmes in regard to disability sport, this sub-agreement focuses on several minority groups, not solely on pwd. The NSA will be followed up with a new policy in 2023.

The NSA is reflected at the municipal level in local sport agreements, in which different local parties (e.g. municipality, sports clubs, health care organisation, CSC and citizens) collaborate to make and implement plans regarding the aims of the NSA. 'Inclusive Sport and Physical Activity' is incorporated in almost all local agreements of municipalities that have such plans (Pulles et al., 2020). From a theoretical perspective, the development and implementation of policy plans under the NSA and local sport agreements can be seen as a form of network governance or collaborative governance in which policy is co-created (Pulles et al., 2020; Torfing et al., 2019). The underlying assumption is that complex issues cannot be solved by a government alone and cooperation is required with organisations from civil society, the business and wider community (see Emerson et al., 2012).

At national level, the 'Alliance for Inclusive Sport and PA' plays an important role in implementing plans in regard to the sub-agreement 'Inclusive sport and PA'. The Alliance and individual agents receive funding to implement specific programmes for improving the preconditions to inclusive sport and PA, such as financial accessibility, social accessibility, accessible transport and sport mobility aids and accessible facilities. One of the goals is to raise awareness for the importance of inclusive sport with sport organisations and to encourage providing a welcoming atmosphere at local clubs, including for pwd. Local sports providers can apply for mini-grants from NOC*NSF to strengthen or create sport programmes for target groups, including pwd.

Furthermore, the NSA aligns strongly with the aforementioned Community Sport Coaches (CSC) regulation. Despite the changeability of Dutch national sport policy due to elections, the CSC regulation has been an important structural element of national governments' sport policy since 2008 (Ministeries van VWS et al., 2018). As of 2020, 332 of the 355 municipalities use this regulation to employ CSC. The CSC regulation is a form of decentralised policy in which the municipalities have discretionary power, meaning they have the freedom to appoint the CSC according to local demands (Van Lindert et al., 2017). Nevertheless, monitoring shows that in 72% of these municipalities one or more CSC focus on pwd (Van Stam & Heijnen, 2020).

The NSA aligns with a similar agreement from another policy domain, the National Prevention Agreement (*Nationaal Preventie Akkoord*, NPA). The NPA tackles smoking, obesity and alcohol consumption in order to improve the health of Dutch people. The national government co-signed the NPA with over 70 organisations (Ministerie van VWS, 2018a). The NPA contains specific actions to improve motor skills among children with a disability and to promote a healthy lifestyle among people with intellectual disabilities.

In regard to elite para sport, the NSA's sixth sub-agreement entitled 'Elite sport that inspires' (*Topsport die inspireert*) is relevant. It strives to optimise a high performance sport climate and support for talented and high performance athletes, including para-athletes. This includes combining events for Olympic and Paralympic sports and developing a clear vision on the future of Paralympic sport, which was published by the Dutch Sport Council in 2022 (Nederlandse Sportraad, 2022).

Support of Disability Sport

Financial Framework

There are several subsidising mechanisms for organisations involved in disability sport, including the government, private foundations, the lottery and sponsors. The minVWS funds several organisations that organise sport for pwd through grants and government programmes. The framework regulation on subsidies (Kaderregeling subsidies OCW, SZW en VWS, 2016) and the VWS subsidies framework act (Kaderwet VWS-subsidies, 1998) allow the minVWS to subsidise activities in the field of sport (of national significance) and public health and sport institutions that contribute to the realisation of national objectives. The regulations do not explicitly mention pwd (Hoekstra et al., 2019). In 2019, the minVWS's expenditure for sport increased greatly compared to previous years, mainly due to the NSA. In 2019, the expenditure was €324.1 million, compared to €86.2 million in 2018 (Rijksoverheid, n.d.-c). In the years prior to the NSA, disability sport was a specific item in the budget of the minVWS. The subsidies for disability sport programmes fell under the budget for the national sport policy programme 'Sport and PA in the Neighbourhood' (*Sport en Bewegen in de Buurt*, 2012–2018). The yearly budget fluctuated: in 2012 minVWS spent €4.2 million on disability sport, in 2015 €3.1 million, and in 2018 €1.6 million (Rijksoverheid, n.d.-a, n.d.-b). In 2019, €1.752 million of the total budget was spent on subsidies under the sub-agreement 'Inclusive sport and PA' as part of the NSA (Rijksoverheid, n.d.-c). Investments in inclusive sport contribute to improving the possibilities for sport for pwd, but it is no longer possible to determine the exact amount intended for disability sport.

In 2019, €40 million was spent on the development of elite sport such as NOC*NSF's 'high performance sport and talent' programme, which also falls under the umbrella of the NSA. This also includes investments in elite para sport. The yearly budget for elite sport has remained stable. In 2019, the minVWS spent an additional €13.2 million on the support for elite athletes with and without a disability who meet the NOC*NSF regulations for a high performance status. Furthermore, the minVWS financially supports the organisation of elite (Paralympic) sport events (€7.6 million) (Rijksoverheid, n.d.-c).

The minVWS cover 40% of the salary costs for the deployment of CSC. In 2019, a total of €61 million was deposited in the municipal fund for that purpose (Rijksoverheid, n.d.-c). Municipalities finance the remaining 60% of the salary costs. A small proportion of CSC (220 FTE of a total of 3468 in 2020) work for pwd or people with chronic disease (Van Stam & Heijnen, 2020).

In 2019, municipalities spent more than €1.1 billion on sport (Van den Dool & Van Eldert, 2021). Three quarters of the municipal budget for sport is intended for maintenance and management of sport facilities, and the remaining quarter of the budget is spent on stimulating sport participation among residents, including vulnerable groups. Through low rental rates for municipally owned sport facilities, a form of 'hidden' subsidy for local sports clubs, municipalities (try to) ensure that sport remains affordable for their citizens. In addition, Dutch municipalities spent almost €1.4 billion on public PA facilities. It is impossible to untangle what proportion of the total municipal budget on sport is for pwd.

As previously mentioned, the sport domain is the responsibility of the municipality and the national government. However, 10 of the 12 provinces have a sport budget. This budget ranges from half a million to €6.25 million. This money typically comes from the province's economic, health and social portfolio (KPMG, 2019). As with the municipal budgets, it is unclear what proportion of the provincial budgets are spent on sport for pwd.

Other funding mechanisms for organisations for disability sport include foundations, lotteries and sponsors (see also section 'Structure'). For example, in 2018, apart from other income sources, FSG raised €1.7 million from private donations and €1.1 million from company donations through the 1% FairShare programme. Companies participating in the 1% FairShare programme pledge to donate 1% of the amount they would spend on sport sponsorship to FSG. FSG in turn donates this money to sport organisations for pwd such as local clubs and invests the budget in its own programmes such as the online platform Unique Sports (Fonds Gehandicaptensport, 2020). In 2019, the Friends Lottery (*Vriendenloterij*) donated €61.8 million to various charities and organisations to promote health and wellness. A portion of these donation recipients are organisations dedicated to sport for pwd (VriendenLoterij, 2020). Commercial sponsors also contribute financially to organisations for sport for pwd. For example, Coca-Cola Nederland donated €25,000 to SON in 2018 (COCA-COLA Nederland, n.d.). Parties can also apply for money from one of the many foundations for sport for pwd. Each foundation has its own application procedure and criteria.

NOC*NSF uses these various sources to fund sport for pwd. In 2019, NOC*NSF received €52.9 million from minVWS, €44.5 million from lottery organisations and €18.4 million from sponsors. NOC*NSF used this money for various purposes. It is unclear what portion is intended to para sport (NOC*NSF, 2020). Funded through the NSA, NOC*NSF provides sports clubs with microgrants (€850 per grant) to help them to strengthen and renew their activities for people who face barriers in/towards sport or PA participation (including but not limited to pwd). In addition to the microgrants, sports clubs also receive money from their members, sponsors and the municipalities. Organisations that provide sport for pwd—such as Special Heroes the Netherlands, SON and FSG—receive money from the minVWS, sponsors and donations.

Governance and Management Support

In the Netherlands, the agents involved in (disability) sport may operate independently from each other. Each agent has its own resources and own governance structure (Breedveld & Hoekman, 2017). However, goals and interests become intertwined because agents depend on government subsidies to implement special programmes or to keep sport financially accessible to every citizen. Sport agents have to balance their own goals with those of the national government.

In order to support municipalities in developing and implementing sport agreements at the local level, the minVWS provides municipalities with a manual and a local sport advisor. The minVWS also provides support for further integration of disability sport, evidenced by the current project regarding deaf sport.

NOC*NSF and the sport federations support regional partnerships between organised and alternatively organised sports providers, the government and the private sector (see section 'Structure'). The regional coordinator is at the heart of these partnerships (see section 'Intermediary Agents'). NOC*NSF is also in regular contact with regional and provincial sport councils to promote sport for pwd. NOC*NSF and the individual sport federations offer clubs advice and tips for recruiting and maintaining pwd and also provide information for para sport coaches. The provincial and regional sport councils provide information and support to regions and municipalities, CSC, regional coordinators, sports clubs and health care organisations, in order to create and maintain sport opportunities for pwd.

GSN and some other sport federations offer support for clubs for creating sport opportunities for pwd. This support is most often provided through guidebooks and can include information on where/how to recruit members with a disability, information about specific disabilities, accessibility, recruiting volunteers and sexual harassment prevention. NOC*NSF, along with some sport federations, such as GSN, offers additional courses or trainings for coaches and referees on how to work with people with specific disabilities.

Level of Integration

Agents in the field of disability sport in the Netherlands have difficulty in precisely defining the concept of inclusion. Some see 'inclusion' as a policy term and refer to the NSA. Disability sport agents agree that inclusion is the opposite of exclusion. Including pwd in sport should be promoted, exclusion should be avoided at all costs. However, the activities or settings considered to be more or less inclusive for pwd are under debate. The discussion about inclusion in the Netherlands revolves primarily around the context in which pwd can participate in sport and secondarily about the activities that pwd can practise within those settings. According to agents, the context in which pwd can participate in sport moves along the continuum from exclusion (pwd are not welcome to participate), to segregation (pwd participate in their own group/club), to integration (pwd participate in their own group within a mainstream sports setting) and ends at inclusion (pwd participate together with people without disabilities). Some disability sport agents consider sports clubs specifically for pwd (a separate or segregated setting) as less preferable. In the Netherlands, mainstream sports clubs are believed to facilitate social encounters between people with and without disabilities and thus social integration of pwd in the wider society. However, most agents agree that pwd should have ample opportunities and free choice to participate in sport activities and sport settings that suit their own needs, wishes and abilities. If an individual with a disability prefers practising sport in a segregated setting, this should be no issue (Van Lindert & De Jonge, 2022). As mentioned in the paragraph on 'Structure', the majority of sports federations and sports clubs have members with a disability or chronic condition, policy attention or organised activities for pwd (Gutter, De Jonge, et al., 2021; Gutter, Van Lindert, et al., 2021). Furthermore the majority of sports clubs are willing and see possibilities to accept (more) members with a (certain type of) disability or chronic condition. Potential barriers to accepting (more) members are lack of interest or demand from pwd to become member and lack or shortage of (qualified) trainers, coaches and volunteers (Gutter, Van Lindert, et al., 2021).

15.4 Sport Participation by People with Disabilities

Monitoring and Evaluation

Since 2014, the minVWS, in cooperation with RIVM, Mulier Institute and Statistics Netherlands (*Centraal Bureau voor de Statistiek*, CBS), monitors trends and developments in sport participation using 19 key indicators. These key indicators provide the foundation for national sport policy.

The most important data source for sport participation and PA is the annual national health survey/biannual national lifestyle monitor (GE/LSMA, *Gezondheidsenquête/Leefstijlmonitor*), carried out by Statistics Netherlands in cooperation with RIVM. In the annual national health survey, participants are asked to list which types of physical activity (including sports) they participate in (maximum of four sports, physical education and school swimming lessons do not count as sport) and the frequency of participation (days per week, average time spent doing that sport per day, how many weeks per year). They are also asked to report if they are members of a sports club, fitness centre, swimming pool or other sports provider. Questions about sport participation are for people aged 4 and older. Questions about disability are for people aged 12 and older (using the OECD indicator, see section 'Disability in the Netherlands'). The data are representative of the Dutch population. In 2019, the weekly sport participation for people with one or more physical disabilities in the Netherlands aged 12 years and older was much lower than the general population (23.6% vs. 52.8%). The same goes for people with one or more chronic conditions (41.6%) (RIVM, n.d.-c).

Not all types of disability are well-represented in these surveys and barriers and facilitators in regard to sport participation are not measured. Various organisations carry out additional studies. For instance, NIVEL monitors the care and living situation of people with an intellectual disability and their relatives, including sport, using the NIVEL Panel Living Together. The Mulier Institute was granted government subsidies to carry out national monitoring studies on disability sport in 2008 (Van Lindert et al., 2008) and 2013 (Von Heijden-Brinkman et al., 2013) under the supervision of disability sport agents. The Mulier Institute has since then carried out numerous studies, commissioned by the minVWS and agents in the field, including a monitoring study on proxies of people with an intellectual disability commissioned by SON (Van Lindert et al., 2020). Under the current NSA, the Mulier Institute monitors the sub-agreement of inclusive sport and PA by surveying various agents in the field of disability sport. In addition, the Mulier Institute, in collaboration with RIVM, prepared an in-depth report on the participation in sport and PA of adults with a disability and/or chronic condition for the age group 18–79 years, using trend data from the national health survey/lifestyles monitor. The data are published in a research report (Van den Dool et al., 2022) and on the RIVM website for key indicators concerning sport (RIVM, n.d.-a). The results of this study are presented below. The minVWS builds its sport policy programmes to a large extent on monitoring data, in fact, the 2008 and 2013 monitors led to major policy adjustments in regard to disability sport.

Sport Participation

Weekly Participation in Sport

In 2019, 53% of the Dutch population aged 18–79 participated in sport on a weekly basis (see Table 15.4). Sport participation seems to have increased since 2001 (48%). However, weekly sport participation by people with one or more moderate to severe physical disabilities (mobility, hearing and/or visual limitation) aged 18–79 lags far behind that of the general population (26%). Since 2001, sport participation for this group has remained fairly constant. People with mobility limitations show the lowest sport participation rates (23%). People with one or more chronic conditions have a higher weekly sport participation rate (44%). Their participation has increased over time (40% in 2001). For people with both a physical disability and a chronic condition, weekly participation in sport was 25% in 2019 (see Van den Dool et al., 2022).

Table 15.4 Weekly sport participation population aged 18–79, by disability (OECD indicator, moderate and severe) and chronic condition (per year, in percentages)

	2001	2007	2013	2019
	(n = 5279)	(n = 5206)	(n = 5713)	(n = 7216)
Population, n > 5200	48	50	52	53
Physical disability (one or more), n > 660	28	32	31	26
– Mobility limitation, n > 360	22	26	20	23
– Hearing limitation, n > 125	28	31	43	27
– Visual limitation, n > 170	32	32	36	26
Chronic condition, n > 1730	40	42	42	44
Chronic condition and physical disability, n > 460	24	28	28	25

Sources: CBS-Gezondheidsenquête (2001–2013), Gezondheidsenquête/Leefstijlmonitor CBS in cooperation with RIVM (2014–2019), in: Van den Dool et al., 2022: adapted by the authors

Recreational Cycling and Walking

Persons with one or more physical disabilities participate in recreational walking and cycling (not in table). In the general population (aged 18–79), 52% is active in cycling and 72% in walking on a weekly basis (data 2019). For persons with one or more physical disabilities, the numbers were 37% resp. 65% in 2019. Persons with mobility limitations participate less frequently in both activities (33% resp. 61%). The participation in walking and cycling by persons with chronic condition does not differ much from the average population (50% resp. 74% in 2019). When sport participation and recreational walking and cycling are combined, data from the annual health survey show that an increasing share of the general adult Dutch population is active in all three activities on a weekly basis (90% in 2019 compared to 84% in 2001). Data on persons with chronic condition show only minor differences (88% in 2019; 82% in 2001). The weekly participation in sport, cycling and walking is much lower in persons with physical disabilities, but there is an increase over time (76% in 2019; 69% in 2001). Again, persons with mobility limitation show the lowest participation rates (72% in 2019; 64% in 2001) (Van den Dool et al., 2022).

Participation by Socio-demographic and Health Variables

Weekly sport participation by people with one or more physical disabilities differs depending on socio-demographic and health characteristics (see Table 15.5). Especially older people with a physical disability and pwd with a lower socio-economic status participate far less in sport compared to pwd on average. Moreover, persons with both a mobility limitation and a chronic condition (especially diabetes) show lower participation rates. Persons with physical disabilities who use mobility aids participate less frequently in sport (23%), whereas people with physical disabilities who use anatomic aids participate more (34%). The weekly sport participation of pwd who live alone (25%) is somewhat lower than those who live with another parent (29%) or with a partner (29%, not in Table 15.5). Pwd with a non-Western migration background (22%) also participate less in sport than those with a Dutch (29%) or Western migration background (28%, not in Table 15.5) (Van den Dool et al., 2022).

Sport Participation Details

The biannual national lifestyle monitor includes more detailed questions on sport participation than the annual national health survey. Combined results for the years 2017 and 2019 show that adults with a physical disability had less experience with

Table 15.5 Weekly sport participation, by socio-demographic and health variables, persons with physical disabilities (OECD indicator, moderate and severe) and chronic condition, population aged 18–79 (2017–2019, in percentages)

NB: variable count per cell	Population ($n = 21{,}767$)	Physical disability (1 or more)[a] ($n = 2297$)	Mobility limitation ($n = 1689$)	Hearing limitation ($n = 543$)	Visual limitation ($n = 529$)	Chronic condition ($n = 7711$)
General population	54	28	25	28	28	44
Age						
18–49 years	60	35	30	39	39	52
50–64 years	49	26	23	24	24	40
65–79 years	**42**	**25**	**23**	**25**	**22**	**38**
Highest completed education (25–79 years)						
Lower	**34**	**20**	**19**	**21**	**17**	**28**
Middle	50	32	29	33	32	43
Higher	68	42	38	*	*	61
Income						
Lower	**41**	**19**	**18**	*	*	**32**
Middle	51	29	25	30	30	43
Higher	68	46	42	*	*	61
Most important condition (last 12 months)						
Diabetes	34	**18**	**17**	*	*	33
Musculoskeletal condition	43	26	25	24	23	38
Stroke, heart attack, heart disease	37	23	22	*	*	35
Depression	41	22	19	22	*	36
Obesity	40	23	21	*	*	34
Combination of chronic condition and physical disability	27	27	**24**	26	26	27
Use of tools/aids						
Mobility-related tools (e.g. wheelchair, stick)	30	**23**	**23**	*	*	27
Anatomic-related tools (prosthesis, orthosis)	49	34	33	*	*	42

(*continued*)

Table 15.5 (continued)

NB: variable count per cell	Population ($n = 21{,}767$)	Physical disability (1 or more)[a] ($n = 2297$)	Mobility limitation ($n = 1689$)	Hearing limitation ($n = 543$)	Visual limitation ($n = 529$)	Chronic condition ($n = 7711$)
Incontinence aids	37	26	26	*	*	33

*Number of observations less than 150
Sources: Gezondheidsenquête/Leefstijlmonitor CBS in cooperation with RIVM (2017–2019), in: Van den Dool et al., 2022: adapted by the authors
[a]Physical disability (one or more) is a combination of mobility, visual and/or hearing disability

sport earlier in life than the general adult population (see Table 15.6). A large portion of the population with one or more physical disabilities does not participate in sport at all (60%). In 2017–2019, 20% of the general adult population aged 18–79 was member of a sports club, compared to 8% of adults with physical disabilities and 13% of adults with chronic disease. One-third of the general population that participates in sport on a weekly basis is a member of a sports club, compared to almost a quarter of people with a physical disability who participate in sport on a weekly basis. Persons with a disability are more often members of swimming pools or fitness centres than sports clubs. Persons with a physical disability are far less involved in sport lessons, training groups or competitions than the average population and even persons with chronic condition (Van den Dool et al., 2022).

Type of Sport

The biannual national lifestyle monitor (from RIVM and CBS) contains information on participation in different types of sport and exercise (see Fig. 15.3) (Van den Dool et al., 2022). The most popular form of exercise in the Netherlands is walking, followed by cycling and sport. As previously described, pwd are less active in all three activities compared to the general population. The most popular sport discipline among the general population (active and inactive persons with and without disabilities) is fitness/aerobics (25%). Fifteen per cent of persons with physical disabilities practise fitness/aerobics. If we look specifically at persons with a physical disability who participate sport on a weekly basis, we see that 53% participate in fitness/aerobics (not in figure). This is more than other regularly active population groups. Data show that only a small percentage of pwd engage in endurance sports, field sports, indoor sports, swimming sports or other sports.[3]

---

[3] Endurance sports: sports in the public space aimed at continuous movement, such as running, cycling and roller skating. Field sports: sports practised on the fields of official sport accommodations, such as football, hockey, tennis, cricket and baseball. Indoor sports: sports that take place in indoor sport accommodations, such as volleyball, badminton and basketball. Swimming sports: sports that take place in a body of water and involve swimming, such as lap swimming and water polo.

Table 15.6 Details of sport participation by disability and chronic condition, population aged 18–79 (2019, in percentages)

	Population ($n = 6641$)	Physical disability (1 or more)[a] ($n = 787$)	Chronic condition ($n = 1936$)	Neither ($n = 4462$)
History in sport				
Never participated in sport	7	16	10	5
Used to participate in sport	23	37	28	20
Participated in sport but not continuously	26	23	27	25
Always participated in sport a little	29	15	22	32
Always participated in sport a lot	15	8	13	17
Sport frequency (last 12 months)				
Not	33	60	46	27
1–11 times	7	7	6	7
12–39 times	10	7	10	11
40 times or more per year	50	26	38	55
Sport context (population)				
Only member of sports club	14	6	9	16
Only membership of swimming pool/fitness centre	23	14	21	25
Both	6	2	4	7
Neither	57	78	66	53
Sport context (weekly sport participants)				
Only member of sports club	23	17	19	24
Only membership of swimming pool/fitness centre	40	39	45	38
Both	11	6	9	11
Neither	27	37	27	26
Type of sport participation (weekly sport participants)				
Lesson, course, training	37	22	33	38
Competition, tournament or sport event	27	13	20	29
Both	17	6	12	18

(*continued*)

15 The Netherlands: Towards Inclusive Sport for People with a Disability

Table 15.6 (continued)

	Population (n = 6641)	Physical disability (1 or more)[a] (n = 787)	Chronic condition (n = 1936)	Neither (n = 4462)
Neither	53	71	59	51

Sources: Gezondheidsenquête/Leefstijlmonitor CBS in cooperation with RIVM (2019), in: Van den Dool et al. (2022): adapted by the authors

[a]Physical disability (one or more) is a combination of mobility, visual and/or hearing disability

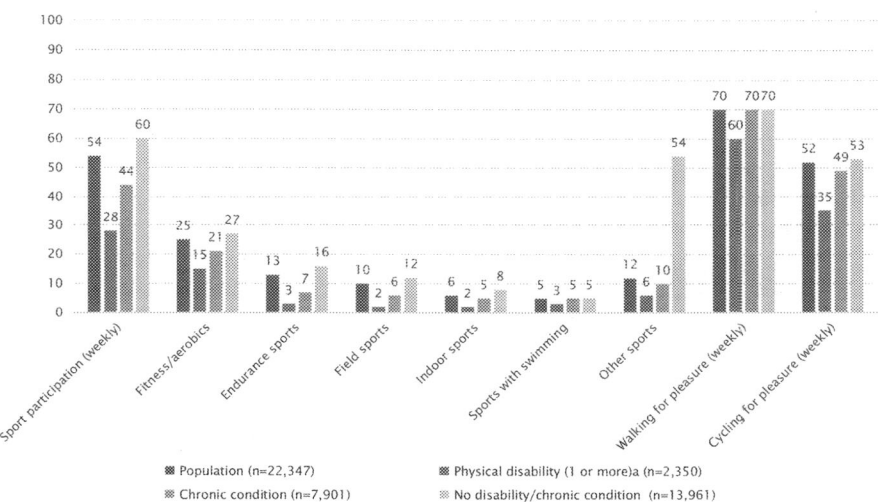

Fig. 15.3 Weekly participation in categories of sport, including walking and cycling for pleasure, by disability and chronic condition, population aged 18–79 (2017–2019, in percentages). [1]Physical disability (one or more) is a combination of mobility, visual and/or hearing disability. Sources: Gezondheidsenquête/Leefstijlmonitor CBS in cooperation with RIVM (2017–2019), in: Van den Dool et al., 2022: adapted by the authors

If we break down the sport participation by persons with a physical disability by visual, hearing and mobility limitation, we see that the latter group participates less often in endurance sport and field sports. However, they participate more often in swimming sports (not in figure). Persons with a visual limitation participate more often in field sports and less often in swimming sports than persons with a hearing limitation. The five most popular sports for each type of disability (in order of decreasing popularity) are (Van den Dool et al., 2022):

- Mobility impairment: fitness, swimming, gymnastics, cycling and yoga
- Visual impairment: fitness, running, cycling, gymnastics and ballet/dance
- Hearing impairment: fitness, running, swimming, cycling and yoga

Persons with Intellectual Disability

People with an intellectual disability are not included in the national surveys. Data on this group is collected through other surveys. In an online panel survey among 1000 proxies of people with mild and moderate intellectual disability, 90% of people with an intellectual disability participated at least once in the last year (2020) in sport and/or PA. Thirty-three per cent participated in sport on a weekly basis, much lower than the general population (54% in 2019; RIVM, n.d.-d). Children and youth (age 4–11, 36%; and 12–25 years, 47%) have a higher level of sport participation than adults (27%) and elderly (12%) with an intellectual disability (Van Lindert et al., 2020). The majority of those who participate in sport or leisure time PA do so in an unorganised manner (36%). Almost a quarter (23%) are members of a sports club. From the members, almost half (47%) of them are members of an association especially for pwd. People with intellectual disabilities also engage in sport in the health care setting or at a fitness centre. Swimming, fitness, football, horse riding and therapeutic sports are the most important types of sport for people with an intellectual disability (Van Lindert et al., 2020).

Children with Disabilities

Data on the sport and PA behaviour of children with disabilities in the Netherlands is scarce. A monitoring system to gather data on this subject is in preparation by the Mulier Institute in cooperation with RIVM. Sport participation of these children is often researched through proxies and small, ad hoc research projects. These studies generally show that children with disabilities participate less in sport and are less often member of a sports club than their peers without disabilities (De Jonge & Van Lindert, 2020a).

Barriers and Facilitators

According to the ICF model (World Health Organization, 2002), various factors (e.g. personal, social and environmental) can positively or negatively influence the functioning and social participation of pwd, including participation in sport. A good understanding of these factors is essential to enable the inclusion of pwd in sport. However, these aspects are not included in the population surveys mentioned earlier and are therefore examined separately. Furthermore, various stakeholders groups, such as CSC, sports clubs, sport federations and municipality officers, have little knowledge of motives, wishes and barriers experienced by pwd in terms of sport participation, and lack the competencies to study these. A lack of insight into the wishes and needs can create a misalignment between policy, organised sport activities and the needs of pwd (Gutter, De Jonge, et al., 2021; Gutter, Van Lindert, et al., 2021; Gutter & Van Lindert, 2020b, 2020a).

Barriers

People with a physical disability experience various barriers towards participation in sport. Personal barriers include the inability to participate in sport during a flare-up or period in which their impairment is worse and inability to participate at the level of other participants. Pain and fatigue or lack of energy hinder participation as well (De Jonge et al., 2020; Hoogendoorn & De Hollander, 2016; Von Heijden-Brinkman et al., 2013). Data from the annual health survey show that people who have experienced pain (in the last four weeks) participate less in sport than the average population. Health-related barriers to participate in sport are experienced more often by persons with a physical disability or chronic condition compared to the general population (Van den Dool et al., 2022). Lack of motivation or interest can be a hindrance for inactive persons.

The most prominent environmental barriers experienced by persons with physical disabilities are considered 'organisational factors', such as finances and transportation (Von Heijden et al., 2013). Other barriers are 'sport opportunities' (e.g. lack of sport opportunities nearby and lack of (experienced) coaching) and 'social environment' (doctor's advice, no one to exercise with or fear of judgement). Environmental factors do play a role, but it remains unclear if these factors prevent pwd from engaging in sport, in a less desirable sport setting for those who are already active or in withdrawal from sport.

Personal barriers, such as lack of interest, seem to be the most prevalent among persons with an intellectual impairment. Physical disabilities and poor (perceived) health are also barriers within this population. Lack of expert guidance in sport is experienced as an obstacle, especially with young children. They often need help to participate in sport, for example changing clothes and with the activity itself. Transportation and lack of sport opportunities nearby can also be an obstacle to participate in sport for this group (Haarmann et al., 2019; Hoogendoorn & De Hollander, 2016; Van Lindert et al., 2020; Von Heijden-Brinkman et al., 2013).

Children with a disability face various barriers towards sport participation, including lack of interest, lack of time, unfamiliarity with the possibilities, negative past experiences, insufficient opportunities in the region, insufficient guidance during the activity and lack of assistive devices (Van Lindert et al., 2008; Von Heijden-Brinkman et al., 2013). Children with certain behavioural disorders, such as attention deficit hyperactivity disorder (ADHD) and obsessive-compulsive disorder (OCD), face barriers related to emotional and behavioural regulation while participating sport. These include a short temper, short attention span, impulsiveness, difficulty listening, difficulty dealing with loss (ADHD) and conflict with authority (coaches and referee). Children with anxiety and/or depression face barriers such as stress and social contact in regard to sport participation. Children with autism have difficulty in communication, empathy and fixations, which limits their sport participation (Breedveld et al., 2010).

Facilitators

The motivation to participate in sport for pwd does not differ much from the general Dutch population. Health benefits, improved fitness, enjoyment, relaxation and social contacts are the main reasons for people with a physical disability to participate in sport. Persons with a physical disability more often mention advice from a caregiver as a reason to participate in sport. Other reasons include gaining self-confidence, the feeling of participating in society and learning to use assistive devices (De Jonge et al., 2020; Hoogendoorn & De Hollander, 2016; Von Heijden-Brinkman et al., 2013). Support from family members, peers and health care professionals also facilitates sport participation in this group.

For persons with intellectual impairment same motivations play a role, but in a different order of importance. According to relatives, enjoyment and relaxation come first, followed by health or improved fitness and fun and social interaction. Other important motives are gaining self-confidence, releasing energy or aggression and being outdoors (Van Lindert et al., 2020). Furthermore, support from family and caregivers is crucial for this group.

For children with a disability, improved fitness, social interaction, enjoyment and gaining self-confidence are important motivators to participate in sport according to parents (De Jonge et al., 2020).

15.5 Conclusion

In the Netherlands, a large number of agents are active in the disability sport landscape, under no clear direction. However, stimulating sport participation is a common objective by these agents. Although the agents represent individual interests, they often work together to achieve their goals. The minVWS deliberately brings parties together under the NSA in order to create more harmony in the landscape. Pwd are receiving more attention in sport policy at the national, regional and local levels, as policymakers are aware of the importance of improving possibilities for pwd to participate in sport. This is probably the result of 20 years of policy on this subject in combination with the improved image of pwd in sport. Dutch citizens' attitudes towards the participation of pwd in sport have become more positive in the last decade (Van Lindert & De Jonge, 2020). Pwd are welcomed in many sports clubs and integration is well underway. It remains to be seen whether this progresses towards inclusion in the sense that pwd will have the same opportunities and possibilities as people without disabilities. There are still countless obstacles that pwd encounter on their way to an active living. A large proportion of pwd still does not participate in sport today. In the last 20 years, we see no progress in the sport participation levels. However, it is difficult to link policy directly with participation numbers. Behavioural change is complex and it takes many years before changes become apparent. However, we don't know if participation rates would have declined without the 20 years of policy measures. At the same time, policy programmes and initiatives were of a fragmented nature (time limited) and not well integrated under a long-term strategy. Thus, it remains uncertain whether effects of these programmes can be found in participation rates or if they should be found in other layers of the system (Hawe et al., 2009). More research is needed based on other indicators to uncover (un)expected results of all those initiatives and to determine which factors are helpful or counter-productive. Take the impact of the COVID-19 pandemic as an example of a counter-productive factor. In the past years, despite the extra attention to the importance of inclusive sport and PA (NSA), the pandemic resulted in pwd experiencing more obstacles to participate in sport and PA and (possibly) lower participation rates (De Boer et al., 2021; De Jonge & Van Lindert, 2020b; RIVM, n.d.-d). The measures to counter the pandemic did not sufficiently take into account the (im)possibilities of pwd to stay active. It remains to be seen whether or not the impact of the pandemic is temporary.

Acknowledgements This chapter was made possible with the financial support of the minVWS and the Mulier Institute. The data collection and desk research for this chapter was part of a monitoring study on inclusive sport and PA by people with disabilities in 2020 and 2021. The chapter would not have been completed without the valuable input of experts and agent representatives we interviewed.

References

Besluit algemene toegankelijkheid voor personen met een handicap of chronische ziekte. (2017). *Besluit algemene toegankelijkheid voor personen met een handicap of chronische ziekte.* https://wetten.overheid.nl/BWBR0039653/2017-06-21

Breedveld, K., Bruining, J. W., van Dorsselaer, S., Mombarg, R., & Nootebos, W. (2010). *Kinderen met gedragsproblemen en sport: bevindingen uit de literatuur en uit recent cijfermateriaal.* Mulier Instituut.

Breedveld, K., & Hoekman, R. (2017). The Netherlands: How the Interplay Between Federations and Government Helps to Build a Sporting Nation. In J. Scheerder, A. Willem, & E. Claes (Eds.), *Sport policy systems and sport federations* (pp. 201–219). Palgrave Macmillan UK. https://doi.org/10.1057/978-1-137-60222-0_10

CBS. (2018). *Prognose bevolking; kerncijfers, 2018–2060.* https://opendata.cbs.nl/statline/#/CBS/nl/dataset/84345NED/table?dl=2453C

CBS. (2020a). *Bevolking; onderwijsniveau; geslacht, leeftijd en migratieachtergrond.* https://opendata.cbs.nl/statline/#/CBS/nl/dataset/82275NED/table?ts=1595339126147

CBS. (2020b). *Bevolkingsteller.* https://www.cbs.nl/nl-nl/visualisaties/bevolkingsteller

CBS. (2020c). *Gemeentelijke indeling op 1 januari 2020.* https://www.cbs.nl/nl-nl/onze-diensten/methoden/classificaties/overig/gemeentelijke-indelingen-per-jaar/indelingperjaar/gemeentelijke-indeling-op-1-januari-2020

CBS. (2020d). *Hoeveel mensen met een migratieachtergrond wonen in Nederland?* https://www.cbs.nl/nl-nl/dossier/dossier-asiel-migratie-en-integratie/hoeveel-mensen-met-een-migratieachtergrond-wonen-in-nederland-

CBS. (2020e). *Sportclubs; personeel, exploitatie, ledental, gebruik accommodaties.* https://opendata.cbs.nl/#/CBS/nl/dataset/70256NED/table?ts=1634296428130

CBS. (2021a). *Bevolking; geslacht, leeftijd en burgerlijke staat, 1 januari.* https://opendata.cbs.nl/#/CBS/nl/dataset/7461bev/table

CBS. (2021b). *Health and health care; personal characteristics.* https://opendata.cbs.nl/statline/#/CBS/en/dataset/83005ENG/table?ts=1626702486322

COCA-COLA Nederland. (n.d.). *Investeringen in gezondheid en welzijn.* https://www.cocacolanederland.nl/duurzaamheid/maatschappij/onze-investeringen-in-gezondheid-en-welzijn-

Council of Europe. (2020). *European Sports Charter.* https://www.coe.int/en/web/sport/european-sports-charter

De Boer, D. R., Hoekstra, F., Huetink, K. I. M., Hoekstra, T., Krops, L. A., & Hettinga, F. J. (2021). Physical activity, sedentary behavior and well-being of adults with physical disabilities and/or chronic diseases during the first wave of the COVID-19 Pandemic: A rapid review. *International Journal of Environmental Research and Public Health, 18*(12), 6342. https://doi.org/10.3390/ijerph18126342

De Heer, W. (2000). *Sportbeleidsontwikkeling 1945–2000.* De Vrieseborch.

De Jonge, M., & Van Lindert, C. (2020a). *Het sport- en beweeggedrag van kinderen met een beperking: een verkenning.* https://www.mulierinstituut.nl/publicaties/25738/het-sport-en-beweeggedrag-van-kinderen-met-een-beperking/

De Jonge, M., & Van Lindert, C. (2020b). *Invloed van de coronamaatregelen op actieve mensen met een beperking, factsheet 2020/36.* Mulier Instituut. https://www.mulierinstituut.nl/publicaties/25613/invloed-van-de-coronamaatregelen-op-actieve-mensen-met-een-beperking/

De Jonge, M., Van Lindert, C., & Van den Dool, R. (2020). *Behoeftenonderzoek mensen met een beperking.* Mulier Instituut. https://www.mulierinstituut.nl/publicaties/25411/behoeftenonderzoek-mensen-met-een-beperking/

Eggink, E., Woittiez, I., & De Klerk, M. (2020). *Maatwerk in meedoen. Een vergelijking van zelfredzaamheid, hulpbronnen en kwaliteit van leven tussen mensen met en zonder een verstandelijke beperking.* Sociaal en Cultureel Planbureau. https://www.scp.nl/publicaties/publicaties/2020/12/03/maatwerk-in-meedoen

Emerson, K., Nabatchi, T., & Balogh, S. (2012). An integrative framework for collaborative governance. *Journal of Public Administration Research and Theory, 22*(1), 1–29. https://doi.org/10.1093/jopart/mur011

European Commission. (2014). *Special Eurobarometer 412/Wave EB80.2. Report - Sport and physical activity.* European Commission. https://doi.org/10.1007/978-1-137-06127-0

European Commission. (2018). *Special Eurobarometer 472 Report - Sport and physical activity (Vol. 8, Issue December 2017, p. 133).* European Commission. https://doi.org/10.2766/483047

European Union. (2007). *Treaty of Lisbon. Amending the treaty on European Union and the treaty establishing the European Community. (2007/C 306/01).* European Union. https://eur-lex.europa.eu/legal-content/EN/TXT/?uri=CELEX%3A12007L%2FTXT

Fonds Gehandicaptensport. (2020). *Jaarverslag Fonds Gehandicaptensport 2019.* Fonds Gehandicaptensport. https://joostbloom.nl/fgs2019/111/#zoom=z

Gutter, K., De Jonge, M., & Van Lindert, C. (2021). *Sporten en bewegen voor mensen met een beperking: aandacht van sportbonden voor inclusief sporten en bewegen.* Mulier Instituut. https://www.mulierinstituut.nl/publicaties/26140/sporten-en-bewegen-voor-mensen-met-een-beperking-aandacht-van-sportbonden-voor-inclusief-sporten-en-bewegen/

Gutter, K., & Van Lindert, C. (2020a). *Sporten en bewegen voor mensen met een beperking: beleid en activiteiten van gemeenten, factsheet 2020/34.* Mulier Instituut. https://www.mulierinstituut.nl/publicaties/25621/sporten-en-bewegen-voor-mensen-met-een-beperking-beleid-en-activiteiten-van-gemeenten/

Gutter, K., & Van Lindert, C. (2020b). *Sporten en bewegen voor mensen met een beperking: de inzet van de buurtsportcoach, factsheet 2020/41.* Mulier Instituut. https://www.mulierinstituut.nl/publicaties/25670/sporten-en-bewegen-voor-mensen-met-een-beperking-de-inzet-van-de-buurtsportcoach/

Gutter, K., Van Lindert, C., & Van Kalmthout, J. (2021). *Sporten en bewegen voor mensen met een beperking: aanbod van verenigingen.* Mulier Instituut. https://www.mulierinstituut.nl/publicaties/25793/sporten-en-bewegen-voor-mensen-met-een-beperking-aanbod-van-verenigingen/

Haarmann, A., Voss, H., & Boeije, H. (2019). *Sporten en bewegen door mensen met een lichte verstandelijke beperking: Belemmeringen en mogelijkheden.* Nivel. https://www.nivel.nl/en/publicatie/sporten-en-bewegen-door-mensen-met-een-lichte-verstandelijke-beperking-belemmeringen-en

Hawe, P., Shiell, A., & Riley, T. (2009). Theorising interventions as events in systems. *Am J Community Psychol Jun, 43*(3–4), 267–276. https://doi.org/10.1007/s10464-009-9229-9

Helliwell, J. F., Layard, R., & Sachs, J. D. (2019). World Happiness Report 2019. New York: Sustainable Development Solutions Network. https://s3.amazonaws.com/happinessreport/2019/WHR19.pdf

Hoekman, R., & Breedveld, K. (2013). The Netherlands. In K. Hallman & K. Petry (Eds.), *Comparative sport development: Systems, participation and public policy* (Vol. 8, pp. 119–134). Springer. https://doi.org/10.1007/978-1-4614-8905-4_10

Hoekstra, F., Roberts, L., Van Lindert, C., Martin Ginis, K. A., Van der Woude, L. H. V., & McColl, M. A. (2019). National approaches to promote sports and physical activity in adults with disabilities: examples from the Netherlands and Canada. *Disability and Rehabilitation, 41*(10), 1217–1226. https://doi.org/10.1080/09638288.2017.1423402

Hoogendoorn, M. P., & De Hollander, E. L. (2016). *Belemmeringen en drijfveren voor sport en bewegen bij ondervertegenwoordigde groepen.* RIVM.

Jeugdwet. (2014). https://wetten.overheid.nl/BWBR0034925/2021-07-01

Kaderregeling subsidies OCW, SZW en VWS (2016). *Kaderregeling subsidies OCW, SZW en VWS.* https://wetten.overheid.nl/BWBR0037603/2021-01-01

Kaderwet VWS-subsidies. (1998). *Kaderwet VWS-subsidies.* https://wetten.overheid.nl/BWBR0009455/2016-08-01

Knapen, J., Zonneveld, E., Menting, J., Hulsbosch, L., & Boeije, H. (2020). *Monitoring Onbeperkt meedoen! Tweede meting overkoepelende indicatoren: 2016–2019.* Nivel. https://www.nivel.nl/sites/default/files/bestanden/1003884.pdf

KPMG. (2019). *Brancherapport Sport.* https://www.kennisbanksportenbewegen.nl/?file=9752&m=1573120314&action=file.download

Kromhout, M., Van Echtelt, P., & Feijten, P. (2020). *Sociaal domein op koers? Verwachtingen en resultaten van vijf jaar decentraal beleid.* https://www.scp.nl/publicaties/publicaties/2020/11/16/sociaal-domein-op-koers

McWhinnie, J. R. (1981). Disability assessment in population surveys: Results of the O.E.C.D. Common Development Effort. *Revue d'Epidemiologie et de Sante Publique, 29*(4), 413–419.

Meijer, G. (2014). *Casus Olympische Spelen voor gehandicapten Arnhem 1980.* Mulier Instituut. https://www.mulierinstituut.nl/publicaties/14441/casus-olympische-spelen-voor-gehandicapten-arnhem-1980/

Ministerie van BZK. (2018). *Grondwet voor het Koninkrijk der Nederlanden 2018* (p. 10). Ministerie van Binnenlandse Zaken en Koninkrijkrelaties. https://www.denederlandsegrondwet.nl/9353000/1/j4nvih713kb91rw_j9vvkl1oucfq6v2/vkwrfdbpvatz/f=/web_119406_grondwet_koninkrijk_nl.pdf

Ministerie van VWS. (2011). *Programma Sport en Bewegen in de Buurt. Vergaderjaar 2011–2012, Kamerstuk 30234 nr. 54.* Ministerie van Volksgezondheid, Welzijn en Sport. https://zoek.officielebekendmakingen.nl/kst-30234-54.html

Ministerie van VWS. (2018a). *Nationaal Preventie Akkoord. Naar een gezonder Nederland.* Ministerie van Volksgezondheid, Welzijn en Sport. https://www.rijksoverheid.nl/onderwerpen/gezondheid-en-preventie/documenten/convenanten/2018/11/23/nationaal-preventieakkoord

Ministerie van VWS. (2018b). *Nationaal Sportakkoord. Sport Verenigt Nederland.* (p. 37). Ministerie van Volksgezondheid, Welzijn en Sport. https://www.mulierinstituut.nl/publicaties/23878/nationaal-sportakkoord/

Ministerie van VWS. (2018c). *Programma VN-Verdrag Onbeperkt Meedoen! Implementatie VN-verdrag inzake de rechten van mensen met een handicap.* https://www.rijksoverheid.nl/onderwerpen/rechten-van-mensen-met-een-handicap/documenten/rapporten/2018/06/01/programma-vn-verdrag-onbeperkt-meedoen

Ministeries van VWS, OCW, SZW, & VNG. (2018). *Bestuurlijke afspraken Brede regeling combinatiefuncties*. https://sportindebuurt.nl/bestanden/Bestuurlijke afspraken Brede regeling combinatiefuncties 2019 tm 2022 ondertekend.pdf

Nederlandse Sportraad. (2020). *De opstelling op het speelveld. Naar een sterke sportbranche voor een vitale samenleving*. https://www.nederlandse-sportraad.nl/documenten/publicaties/2020/11/19/de-opstelling-op-het-speelveld

Nederlandse Sportraad. (2022). *Gelijkwaardig en inclusief - advies over de doorontwikkeling van paralympische topsport*. Nederlandse Sportraad. https://www.nederlandse-sportraad.nl/adviezen/documenten/publicaties/2022/03/31/gelijkwaardig-en-inclusief%2D%2D-advies-over-de-doorontwikkeling-van-paralympische-topsport

NOC*NSF. (2018). *Lidmaatschappen NOC * NSF over 2018*. https://nocnsf.nl/media/1080/ledentalrapportage-nocnsf-2018-sportonderzoek.pdf

NOC*NSF. (2020). *Jaarrekening NOC*NSF 2019* (Vol. 31, Issue 0). Arnhem: NOC*NSF. https://nocnsf.nl/media/2946/04a3-nocnsf-definitieve-jaarrekening-2019-incl-controleverklaring.pdf

Notté, R., Van Kalmthout, J., & Van Lindert, C. (2011). *Monitor Integratie van Gehandicaptensport binnen reguliere sportbonden*. W.J.H. Mulier Instituut. https://www.mulierinstituut.nl/publicaties/8995/monitor-integratie-van-gehandicaptensport-binnen-reguliere-sportbonden/

Participatiewet. (2003). *Participatiewet*. https://wetten.overheid.nl/BWBR0015703/2021-07-01

Pegels, J. (1985). *Met Pijl en Boog naar Engeland. De geschiedenis van de gehandicaptensport in Nederland*. Uitgeverij De Vrieseborch.

Pulles, I., Reitsma, M., Hoogendam, A., Nafzger, P., & Van der Poel, H. (2020). *Monitor Sportakkoord "Sport verenigt Nederland". Van akkoord naar uitvoering. Voortgangsrapportage november 2020*. Mulier Instituut. https://www.mulierinstituut.nl/publicaties/25687/monitor-sportakkoord-sport-verenigt-nederland-van-akkoord-naar-uitvoering/

Reitsma, M., & Hoekman, R. H. A. (2019). *Sport in provinciale coalitieakkoorden 2019–2023*. https://www.mulierinstituut.nl/publicaties/25228/sport-in-provinciale-coalitieakkoorden-2019-2023/

Rijksoverheid. (n.d.-a-a). *Rijksbegroting, 2012, verantwoording, jaarverslag en Slotwet Volksgezondheid, Welzijn en Sport, 2012*. https://www.rijksbegroting.nl/2012/verantwoording/jaarverslag,kst181512_12.html

Rijksoverheid. (n.d.-b-b). *Rijksbegroting, 2018, verantwoording, jaarverslag en Slotwet Volksgezondheid, Welzijn en Sport 2018*. Rijksoverheid. https://www.rijksbegroting.nl/2018/verantwoording/jaarverslag,kst260574_12.html

Rijksoverheid. (n.d.-c-c). *Rijksbegroting, 2019, verantwoording, jaarverslag en Slotwet Volksgezondheid, Welzijn en Sport 2019*. Rijksoverheid. https://www.rijksfinancien.nl/jaarverslag/2019/XVI/onderdeel/423442

RIVM. (n.d.-a-a). *Kernindicatoren. Verdiepend onderzoek. Sporten en bewegen met een langdurige aandoening of een lichamelijke beperkingen*. Retrieved 13 June 2022, from https://www.sportenbewegenincijfers.nl/verdiepend-onderzoek/AandoeningBeperking

RIVM. (n.d.-b-b). *Sport en bewegen in cijfers, kernindicatoren, clublidmaatschap en andere sportverbanden*. Retrieved 10 December 2020, from https://www.sportenbewegenincijfers.nl/kernindicatoren/clublidmaatschap

RIVM. (n.d.-c-c). *Sport en bewegen in cijfers, kernindicatoren, sportakkoord: Inclusief sporten en bewegen*. Retrieved 23 April 2021, from https://www.sportenbewegenincijfers.nl/beleid/sportakkoord/inclusief-sporten

RIVM. (n.d.-d-d). *Sport en bewegen in cijfers, kernindicatoren, sportdeelname wekelijks*. Retrieved 24 September 2021, from https://www.sportenbewegenincijfers.nl/kernindicatoren/sportdeelname-wekelijks

RIVM. (n.d.-e-e). *Sport en bewegen in cijfers, kernindicatoren, tevredenheid sport- en beweegaanbod (2018)*. Retrieved 6 October 2020, from https://www.sportenbewegenincijfers.nl/kernindicatoren/tevredenheid-sport-en-beweegaanbod

Roeters, A. (2017). *Employment*. The Netherlands Institute for Social Research. Time Use in the Netherlands: Edition 1. https://digital.scp.nl/timeuse1/employment/

Schmeets, H. (2018). *Wie is religieus, en wie niet? CBS Statistische Trends oktober 2018.* (p. 20). Den Haag: Centraal Bureau voor de Statistiek. https://www.cbs.nl/nl-nl/achtergrond/2018/43/wie-is-religieus-en-wie-niet-

Schoonheim, J., & Smits, J. (2019). *Schaduwrapportage Verdrag inzake de rechten van personen met een handicap in Nederland.* Alliantie VN-verdrag Handicap. https://iederin.nl/wp-content/uploads/2019/12/Schaduwrapport-VN-verdrag-Handicap.pdf

The World Bank Group. (2018a). *Population density (people per sq. km of land area).* https://data.worldbank.org/indicator/EN.POP.DNST?locations=NL

The World Bank Group. (2018b). *Surface area (sq. km) – Netherlands.* https://data.worldbank.org/indicator/AG.SRF.TOTL.K2?locations=NL&view=chart

The World Bank Group. (2018c). *Urban population (% of total population) (Netherlands).* https://data.worldbank.org/indicator/SP.URB.TOTL.IN.ZS?locations=NL

The World Bank Group. (2021). *GDP per capita (current US$) - Netherlands (2020).* https://data.worldbank.org/indicator/NY.GDP.PCAP.CD?locations=NL

Torfing, J., Sørensen, E., & Røiseland, A. (2019). Transforming the public sector into an Arena for co-creation: Barriers, drivers, benefits, and ways forward. *Administration & Society, 51*(5), 795–825. https://doi.org/10.1177/0095399716680057

Tweede Kamer der Staten-Generaal. (1987). *Sportbeoefening door gehandicapten. Tweede Kamer. Vergaderjaar 1987–1988, Kamerstuk 16 709, nr. 10. Verslag van een mondeling overleg.* Tweede Kamer der Staten Generaal. https://repository.overheid.nl/frbr/sgd/19871988/0000099607/1/pdf/SGD_19871988_0001815.pdf

Tweede Kamer der Staten-Generaal. (1990). *Tweede Kamer, vergaderjaar 1990–1991, 21 800 XVI, nr. 30. Brief van ministerie van Welzijn, Volksgezondheid en Cultuur.* Tweede Kamer der Staten Generaal. https://repository.overheid.nl/frbr/sgd/19901991/0000031603/1/pdf/SGD_19901991_0005093.pdf

Van den Dool, R., & Van Eldert, P. (2021). *Monitor sportuitgaven gemeenten 2019: een overzicht van de uitgaven in 2019 plus samenhangende vraagstukken.* Mulier Instituut. https://www.mulierinstituut.nl/publicaties/25879/monitor-sportuitgaven-gemeenten-2019/

Van den Dool, R., Van Lindert, C., Van den Berg, S., & Wendel-Vos, W. (2022). *Deelname aan sport en bewegen door mensen met een beperking. Stand van zaken eind 2019.* Mulier Instituut. https://www.mulierinstituut.nl/publicaties/26505/deelname-sport-en-bewegen-door-mensen-met-een-beperking/

Van der Poel, H., & Pulles, I. (2013). *De sportinfrastructuur in Nederland: Gezien in vogelvlucht.* https://www.mulierinstituut.nl/publicaties/12751/de-sportinfrastructuur-in-nederland/

Van der Poel, H., Wezenberg-Hoenderkamp, K., Hoekman, R. H. A., Bakker, S., Davids, A., Hoffmans, W., Van Lindert, C., Lucassen, J. M. H., Rewijk, D., Schadenberg, B., & Scholten, V. (2016). *Sportaccommodaties in Nederland: kaarten en kengetallen.* Mulier Instituut/Arko Sports Media. https://www.mulierinstituut.nl/publicaties/21399/sportaccommodaties-in-nederland/

Van der Veer, J. C. V., Schalk, J., & Gilsing, R. (2011). Decentralisatie: maatwerk of uniformiteit? Het Wmo-beleid van Nederlandse gemeenten. *Beleid En Maatschappij, 38*(3), 262–282. http://www.boomlemmatijdschriften.nl/tijdschrift/benm/2011/3/benm_1389-0069_2011_038_003_002

Van Lindert, C., Brandsema, A., Scholten, V., & Van der Poel, H. (2017). *Evaluatie Buurtsportcoaches. 'De Brede impuls combinatiefuncties als werkend proces'.* Mulier Instituut. https://www.mulierinstituut.nl/publicaties/22940/evaluatie-buurtsportcoaches/

Van Lindert, C., & De Jonge, M. (2020). *Houding ten aanzien van sporten door en voor mensen met een beperking, factsheet 2020/38.* Mulier Instituut. https://www.mulierinstituut.nl/publicaties/25619/houding-ten-aanzien-van-sporten-door-en-voor-mensen-met-een-beperking/

Van Lindert, C., & De Jonge, M. (2022). *Inclusief sporten en bewegen voor mensen met een beperking. Landschap en betekenissen.* Mulier Instituut. https://www.mulierinstituut.nl/publicaties/26684/inclusief-sporten-en-bewegen-voor-mensen-met-een-beperking/

Van Lindert, C., De Jonge, M., & Balk, L. (2020). *Ontmoetingen tussen sporters met en zonder verstandelijke beperking: 1-meting #PlayUnified.* Mulier Instituut. https://www.mulierinstituut.nl/publicaties/25669/ontmoetingen-tussen-sporters-met-en-zonder-verstandelijke-beperking/

Van Lindert, C., De Jonge, M., & Van den Dool, R. (2008). *(On)beperkt Sportief. Monitor sportdeelname van mensen met een handicap 2008.* https://www.mulierinstituut.nl/publicaties/5554/onbeperkt-sportief/

Van Stam, W., & Heijnen, E. (2020). *Monitor Brede Regeling Combinatiefuncties 2020.* https://www.mulierinstituut.nl/publicaties/25683/monitor-brede-regeling-combinatiefuncties-2020/

Verhaag, M. (2013). *Paralympische beweging en Nederland. Mijlpalen en archieven.* Mulier Instituut. https://www.mulierinstituut.nl/publicaties/12088/paralympische-beweging-en-nederland/

Vermeij, L., & Hamelink, W. (2021). *Lang niet toegankelijk. Ervaringen van Nederlanders met een lichamelijke beperking als spiegel van de samenleving.* Sociaal en Cultureel Planbureau. https://www.scp.nl/publicaties/publicaties/2021/06/08/lang-niet-toegankelijk

Volksgezondheidenzorg.info. (2021). *Verstandelijke beperking. Cijfers & Context. Huidige situatie.* https://www.volksgezondheidenzorg.info/onderwerp/verstandelijke-beperking/cijfers-context/huidige-situatie#node-prevalentie-van-verstandelijke-beperking

Volksgezondheidenzorg.info. (n.d.). *Sport op de kaart. Regionale samenwerkingsverbanden aangepast sporten in 2021.* Retrieved 13 June 2022, from https://www.sportenbewegenincijfers.nl/kaarten/onbeperktbewegen/beleid

Von Heijden-Brinkman, A., Van den Dool, R., Van Lindert, C., & Breedveld, K. (2013). *(On)beperkt sportief 2013: monitor sport- en beweegdeelname van mensen met een handicap.* https://www.mulierinstituut.nl/publicaties/12543/onbeperkt-sportief-2013/

VriendenLoterij. (2020). *Jaarverslag 2019 VriendenLoterij.* VriendenLoterij N.V. https://publicaties.vriendenloterij.nl/vriendenloterij-jaarverslag-2019/page/1

Wet gelijke behandeling op grond van handicap of chronische ziekte. (2003). https://wetten.overheid.nl/BWBR0014915/2020-01-01

Wet maatschappelijke ondersteuning 2015. (2014). https://wetten.overheid.nl/BWBR0035362/2020-07-01

World Health Organization. (2002). *Towards a common language for functioning, disability and health. International Classification of Functioning, Disability and Health (ICF).* https://www.who.int/publications/m/item/icf-beginner-s-guide-towards-a-common-language-for-functioning-disability-and-health

Chapter 16
Switzerland

Julia Albrecht, Siegfried Nagel, and Christoffer Klenk

16.1 Introduction

In 2014, Switzerland ratified the United Nations Convention on the Rights of Persons with Disabilities that demands the possibility to participate both in mainstream and in disability-specific sports activities. However, only 18% of Swiss mainstream sports clubs provide services for people with disabilities. Thus, disability sport in Switzerland is still mainly separated from non-disabled sport and there are even different disability sports federations for different disability forms. Regarding policies, the Federal Sports Promotion Act (2011) names sport as an important social domain where integration takes place without explicitly mentioning people with disabilities. Furthermore, in the Federal Disability Equality Act (2002), there are no concrete statements on equality in sport. However, the Federal Concept for Sports for All (2015) mentions that there should be enough low-threshold and target-group specific sports offers for people with disabilities, as all people should have the opportunity to exercise regularly throughout their lives. In this chapter, we describe the roles of the organisations in Swiss disability sport and we present quantitative data from the project Social Inclusion and Volunteering in Sports Clubs in Europe ($n = 31$ mainstream sports clubs in Switzerland; $N = 959$ members, thereof 53 with disabilities). Furthermore, we include qualitative data from eight separate training groups only for people with disabilities and eight integrative/inclusive training groups where people with and without disabilities practise together.

J. Albrecht (✉) · S. Nagel · C. Klenk
Institute of Sport Science, University of Bern, Bern, Switzerland
e-mail: julia.albrecht@nct-heidelberg.de

© The Author(s), under exclusive license to Springer Nature Switzerland AG 2023
C. van Lindert et al. (eds.), *The Palgrave Handbook of Disability Sport in Europe*, https://doi.org/10.1007/978-3-031-21759-3_16

16.2 Country Profile

Characteristics of Switzerland

Despite its small size (see Table 16.1), the mountainous country Switzerland has four different language regions: German (the main language of 62.6% of the population), French (22.9%), Italian (8.2%), and Romansh-speaking (0.5%) (Eidgenössisches Department für auswärtige Angelegenheiten [EDA], 2017). About 37.5% (30.2% first generation and 7.3% second generation) of the country's population has a migration background (Bundesamt für Statistik [BFS], 2019). Due to the federalist structure as well as the direct democracy, the 26 cantons and 2250 municipalities have a high degree of autonomy and freedom of action (EDA, 2018). The Swiss welfare system can be classified as liberal because the free market plays an important role or as a soft guarantee as every citizen has the right to participate in all social systems (Esping-Andersen, 1990; Opielka, 2005). Switzerland has a very high living standard as the gross domestic product (GDP) per capita takes third place in the world (OECD, 2018).

Sport in Switzerland

The sports system in Switzerland (see Table 16.2) consists of the public sector with sports policy institutions at the national, regional, and local levels, the voluntary sector, and a market sector that has grown over the past decades (Kempf & Lichtsteiner, 2015). About 75% of the Swiss population practise sports regularly at least once a week (Lamprecht et al., 2020). Swiss Olympic—the umbrella organisation of the voluntary sports sector in Switzerland—represents the interests of 86

Table 16.1 Figures of Switzerland

Population (number of inhabitants)[a]	8,544,527
Area (km^2)[b]	41,285
Density (inhabitants/km^2)	207
Urbanisation rate (%)[c]	74%
Political organisation[d]	Direct democracy
Structure of the state[d]	Federalist
Number of provinces (cantons)[d]	26
Number of municipalities[d]	2250
GDP per capita (US dollars)[e]	70,485
Number of official languages[f]	4
EU membership	No
Welfare model[g]	Liberal welfare system/soft guarantee

Source: [a]BFS (2019a), [b]ARE (2020), [c]The World Bank Group (2020), [d]EDA (2018), [e]OECD (2018), [f]EDA (2017), [g]Esping-Andersen (1990)

Table 16.2 Sport profile of Switzerland

Government authority responsible for sport	Federal Office of Sport (BASPO)
Membership sport club (% of population)[a]	33%
Membership fitness or health centre (% of population)[b]	19%
Sport participation, at least once a week (% of population)[c]	75%
Number of national sport federations	86
Number of sport clubs	19,000
Number of sport club members[a]	2,800,000
National budget for sport (€ × 1,000,000)	228

Sources: [a]Lamprecht et al. (2017), [b]Klostermann et al. (2020), Lamprecht et al. (2020)

national sports federations and their sports clubs. In particular, Swiss Olympic advocates organised sport in Switzerland, supports, and coordinates the activities of member federations, fulfilling tasks and services at a superordinate level. There are currently about 2.8 million (33%) members out of 8.5 million people in Switzerland who actively or passively belong to a sports club that is a member of a federation that belongs to Swiss Olympic (Lamprecht et al., 2017). About 22% of the general adult population are active members in one of the nearly 19,000 sports clubs that are a core element of the Swiss sports landscape. With their sports programmes and other activities, sports clubs can contribute to public welfare, for example, public health and social integration (Nagel et al., 2020). However, so-called fitness activities are mainly practised in private fitness facilities. About 19% of the Swiss population are members of one of the approximately 1000 fitness, health, and sports centres (Klostermann et al., 2020).

The Federal Office of Sport (BASPO, Bundesamt für Sport), as part of the Federal Department of Defence, Civil Protection and Sport, is responsible for the development and shaping of national sports policy. The Federal Act on the Promotion of Sports and Exercise (Sports Promotion Act; SpoFöG, Sportförderungsgesetz, Bundesgesetz über die Förderung von Sport und Bewegung, 2011) provides a legal framework to support private initiatives in sports, particularly those of sports clubs and federations. Despite this Federal Act, the national government has no direct legal obligation to sports clubs and vice versa. This is the result of the traditional principles of subsidiarity and autonomy. This means that sports clubs can plan their programmes without direct public intervention and only get support and funding if necessary. In this context, the Youth and Sports programme (J+S, Jugend und Sport) that supports sports clubs has to be highlighted. The BASPO distributes over 100 million Swiss Francs (CHF) (€95 million) per year to clubs engaged in the promotion of youth sports. Overall, the national budget for sports stimulation and sports facilities amounts to about CHF240 million (€228 million).

The 26 cantons are responsible for the regional development, construction, and maintenance of sports-related infrastructure and implementation of J+S programmes. However, there are big differences in how the cantons use profits from lotteries for sports promotion and the support of special programmes in sports clubs.

There are also large differences between municipalities when it comes to the support and funding of sports clubs. However, in most municipalities, sports clubs can use public sports facilities for free or by paying a moderate fee.

Disability in Switzerland

The Swiss Federal Statistical Office (BFS, 2020) defines disability according to the Federal Law on the Elimination of Discrimination Against People with Disabilities (Disability Equality Act; BehiG, Behindertengleichstellungsgesetz, Bundesgesetz über die Beseitigung von Benachteiligungen von Menschen mit Behinderungen, 2002). It defines people with disabilities from a biopsychosocial perspective as persons who have a permanent health problem, that is, organic impairment or functional restriction, and who are moderately or severely restricted in activities of everyday life. Accordingly, almost one-fifth of the Swiss population has a disability, including movement, seeing, hearing, and other impairments, but only around 4% suffer from severe disability (see Table 16.3; BFS, 2020, data of 2017; for Swiss terms for disability, see Appendix). The BehiG (2002) aims to prevent, reduce, or eliminate disadvantages to which people with disabilities are exposed so that they can fully and effectively participate in social life. The Disability Equality Act uses a similar definition of disability as the United Nations Convention on the Rights of Persons with Disabilities (UN CRPD, 2006) and the demands already point in the direction of the far more detailed UN CRPD which was only ratified in 2014 in Switzerland. However, there are still shortcomings in the legislation and implementation of the UN CRPD (Inclusion Handicap, 2019) and also in the Swiss Disability Equality Act (Egger et al., 2015). Furthermore, Inclusion Handicap (2019)—the umbrella organisation of organisations for people with disabilities in Switzerland— criticises that there are no plans to analyse and adapt current federal legislation in the light of the UN CRPD. The main deficiencies are that there is no protection against workplace discrimination in the private sector, no inclusive labour market and education system, insufficient protection against discrimination of persons with disabilities by private persons, and the system of decision-making by representation (Inclusion Handicap, 2019). Furthermore, according to Inclusion Handicap (2019), there is no community life with equal opportunities for choice for many people with

Table 16.3 Facts and statistics on disability in Switzerland (2017; population aged 15 and over in private households)

Prevalence of one or more disabilities, total (% of the population)	1,264,000 (18%)
… thereof with severe disability, total (% of the population)	285,000 (4.1%)
Prevalence of severe/total movement impairment, total (% of the population)	67,000 (1.0%)
Prevalence of severe/total seeing impairment, total (% of the population)	77,000 (1.1%)
Prevalence of severe/total hearing impairment, total (% of the population)	78,000 (1.1%)

Source: BFS (2020)

disabilities, especially for people with mental and intellectual disabilities, including restrictions on the choice of residence and type of housing, despite some progressive measures in federal legislation.

Emergence and Rise of Disability Sport in Switzerland

Swiss Deaf Sport was founded in 1930 as the oldest disability sports association in Switzerland (PluSport, 2019). Procap was founded in 1930 as the Swiss Invalids Association and today it is the largest member association of and for people with disabilities in Switzerland.

In 1956, Sport Handicap Geneva association (SH Geneva) was founded as the first Swiss sports group to offer and organise sports for people with movement disabilities. In 1959, the Swiss Grouping for Paraplegics (Para Group) of the Swiss Association for Paralytics and rheumatics (ASPr) was founded for athletes in wheelchairs. In 1966, SH Geneva and the Para Group decided to merge (Cornaton et al., 2018). Also in 1966, three members of the Para Group founded Wheelchair Club (RC, Rollstuhlclub) Kriens.

In 1956, the Swiss Working Group for Disability Sport (Schweizerische Arbeitsgruppe für Invalidensport) was founded on the initiative of a priest suffering from polio who approached General Guisan (PluSport, 2020b). Since disability sport should be organised not only for but also by people with disabilities, the Working Group was transformed into the Swiss Sports Federation for Invalids (SVIS, Schweizerischer Verband für Invalidensport) in 1960 and the Swiss Federation for Disability Sport (SVBS, Schweizerischer Verband für Behindertensport) in 1977. When in 1960 the SVIS was established, SH Geneva became an affiliate and the ASPr with its Para Group became a partner of SVIS. The focus of SVIS was medical and medico-social in the sense of rehabilitation and social reintegration through sport but not for recreational purposes or competitive practice as the SVIS had a high involvement of the army and doctors. By contrast, SH Geneva was self-organised by a core of people with disabilities and people who were deeply involved in the world of disability. In 1968, the splitting of the disability movement into two distinct entities took place when RC Kriens separated from the SVIS and became a simple member of the Para Group because the club wanted to train for competitions and not for rehabilitation purposes (Cornaton et al., 2018). Since its foundation, the SVIS and later SVBS have developed from a self-help organisation of people with disabilities to a federation that focuses on sport and not on disability (PluSport, 2020b). In 2000, the Federation received its current name PluSport Disability Sport Switzerland (Behindertensport Schweiz).

Later in the development of Swiss wheelchair athletics, the Swiss Paraplegics Association (SPV, Schweizer Paraplegiker-Vereinigung) was founded as a self-help organisation (PluSport, 2019) in 1980, playing a central role in the development of successful Swiss wheelchair racers (Frenkiel, 2018). RC Kriens and six other clubs were initial members (SPV, 2005). SPV's sport policies were based on considerable

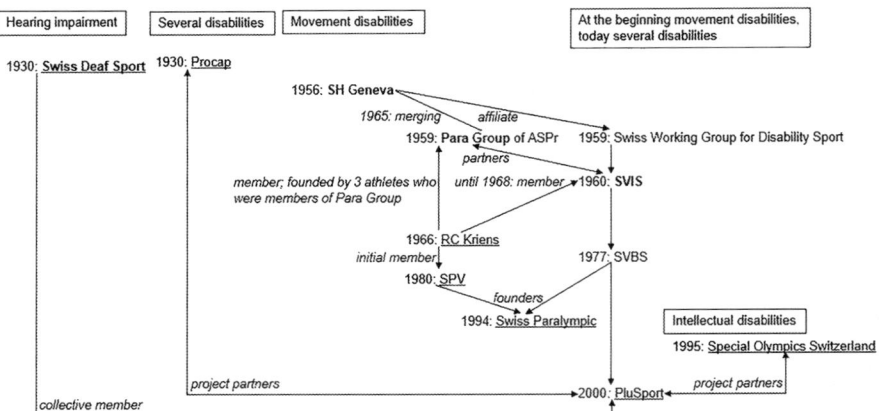

Fig. 16.1 The emergence of disability sport in Switzerland. Organisations in bold are among the founders of Swiss disability sport. Underlined organisations still exist

human and financial means, an advanced medical environment, good sports infrastructure, and the recruitment of former champions (Frenkiel, 2018).

In the 1980s, a group of committed individuals offered sport for people with intellectual disabilities and Special Olympics Switzerland was established as a foundation in 1995 (Special Olympics Switzerland, 2022). To support elite disability sport the SPV and PluSport founded the national Paralympic Committee Swiss Paralympic in 1994 (see Fig. 16.1).

16.3 The Disability Sport System

Structure of Disability Sport

Governmental Agents

There are various governmental agents, whereby at the national level the *Federal Office of Social Insurance* (BSV, Bundesamt für Sozialversicherungen) plays a crucial role as the most important funding agency for disability sport organisations. The BSV is subordinate to the Federal Department of the Interior (EDI, Eidgenössisches Department des Inneren) and supports disability sport with financial grants of the Disability Insurance (IV, Invalidenversicherung).

The *Federal Office for the Equality of Persons with Disabilities* (EBGB, Eidgenössisches Büro für die Gleichstellung von Menschen mit Behinderungen) was established in 2004 and belongs to the EDI. Its task is to promote equality for people with disabilities and to work for the elimination of disadvantages for people with disabilities.

The *BASPO* promotes (high-performance) sport and physical activity for the Swiss population. As a public body, it is responsible for the implementation and administration of the politically decided policies and programmes and the funding (Ibsen et al., 2016). With its Sub-Department of "Integration and Prevention," it is also responsible for the target group of people with disabilities. This Sub-Department is committed to fair, safe, and integrative sports and is involved in the promotion of equal access and participation of all people in sport. It encourages behaviour to anchor the positive values of sport in society (BASPO, 2020).

Governmental school departments at the regional level manage sport and physical activity at mainstream and special needs schools regarding both, finances and contents with exact specifications of the curriculum.

At the local level, sport departments supply sport facilities and partly financially support sports clubs.

Intermediate Agents

The intermediary level does not exist in Switzerland. This means there are no intermediate organisations that function as a link between the governmental and non-governmental agents in Swiss disability sport.

Non-governmental Agents

Various non-governmental agents play a role in disability sport in Switzerland. However, PluSport, Swiss Paralympic, and Special Olympics Switzerland are the central actors in Swiss disability sport because they bring together most memberships of people with disabilities.

PluSport is the umbrella organisation and competence centre of Swiss disability sport. It promotes the sport of people with disabilities from popular to high-performance sport with the goal of integration and inclusion (PluSport, 2020b). Thereby, PluSport is responsible for all target groups in different sports, including different age groups and different forms of disability, however, with a focus on physical disabilities.

Swiss Paralympic, as the national Paralympic committee, supports Swiss elite disability sport to ensure regular participation of athletes from different kinds of sports in national and international competitions (Swiss Paralympic, 2020c). The organisation manages the selection of athletes for competitions as well as the financing and organisation of their participation. Furthermore, they carry out publicity work and sensitisation to guarantee professional conditions for athletes and spectators and successfully network in politics, disability organisations, sports federations, sports clubs, and with sponsors (Nagel & Adler Zwahlen, 2016). Moreover, they offer sports consulting for sport-interested people with disabilities (Swiss Paralympic, 2020b).

Wheelchair Sports Switzerland (RSS, Rollstuhlsport Schweiz) of the SPV offers sports consulting for the entry into wheelchair sport and a sports camp to try eight types of sport (SPV, 2020c).

Swiss Olympic as the non-governmental umbrella organisation of Swiss sport and the National Olympic Committee of Switzerland represents the interests of 86 sports federations with about 19,000 sports clubs (Lamprecht et al., 2017). In this dual function, Swiss Olympic creates the best possible conditions for sporting success on an international level (Swiss Olympic, 2020). PluSport and RSS are members of Swiss Olympic and Swiss Paralympic.

Special Olympics Switzerland, as an independent national foundation to support sports of people with intellectual disabilities, acts as a project partner of PluSport.

Swiss Deaf Sport is a collective member of PluSport.

Procap Sport has 30 sports groups with over 1500 active members (Procap, 2020b). It belongs to the self-help organisation Procap, which has over 21,000 members in around 40 regional sections. In addition to its local sports groups, Procap Sport organises regional and every other year national sports events for people with disabilities.

The *Swiss Equestrian Federation* and *Swiss Cycling* are separately mentioned in Fig. 16.2., as they included and therefore are responsible for para-equestrian and para-cycling, respectively.

The local level is the most important administrative level for sport including disability sport and sports clubs are the main promoters of both elite and mainstream sport in Switzerland.

All the mentioned non-governmental agents have partner-like relationships. Within the individual federations, there are bottom-up decision-making structures between the inter units from the local, regional, and national levels. As in a representative political system, decision-making power lies with members or individual

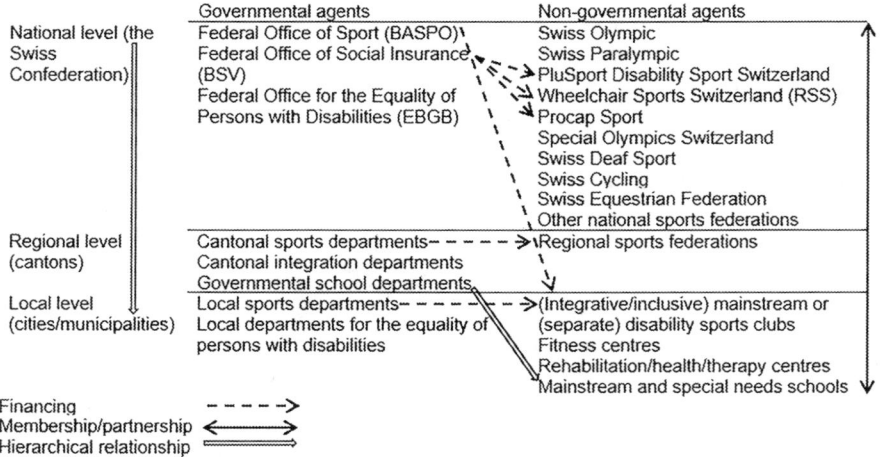

Fig. 16.2 Disability sport framework for Switzerland

member federations that send representatives at the regional and national levels. However, the financing flows from the top down.

Secondary Agents

In addition to (disability) sports organisations, many other interconnected organisations, with relationships in various forms to governmental and non-governmental agents, play an important role in the provision of disability sports activities although they do not have the creation of policies or sports programmes for people with disabilities as a core task. The core tasks of these organisations are in the areas of self-help and health care. Therefore, their field of activity includes or is connected to disability sport.

Inclusion Handicap, the disability umbrella organisation, represents the interests of people with disabilities in various political matters and advocates all relevant related issues in society. Important issues are the UN CRPD (2006), mobility, construction, and above all social insurance regulations. Moreover, the organisation ensures that people with disabilities can participate on an equal basis in cultural life as well as in recreational, leisure, and sports activities. As PluSport is a member of Inclusion Handicap, they share common interests in the field of leisure, culture, and sports with a cooperative relationship (PluSport, 2020e).

The *Swiss Paraplegics Centre* (Schweizer Paraplegiker-Zentrum) is a national and international leader in cross-sectional, back, and respiratory acute and rehabilitation medicine that belongs, like the SPV, to the Swiss Paraplegics Group. As the affiliated Sports Medicine (Sportmedizin) Nottwil motivates, advises, and accompanies athletes with and without disabilities of any age and discipline, it is also relevant to Swiss disability sport. For this, the Sports Medicine Nottwil cooperates amongst others with the SPV, Swiss Olympic, Swiss Paralympic, Swiss Deaf Sport, and PluSport (Sportmedizin Nottwil, 2020).

Cerebral, the Swiss Foundation for the Cerebral Palsy Child (Schweizerische Stiftung für das cerebral gelähmte Kind, 2020), supports persons affected, institutions, and organisers, as well as specialists in various matters, including recreation and leisure. For example, Cerebral supports foundations with special schools, like the Foundation Aarhus in the financing of camps, the acquisition of mobility equipment suitable for people with disabilities, or the equipment with the necessary infrastructure in the residential groups (Stiftung Aarhus, 2020). Foundations like Aarhus, in turn, cooperate with federations like PluSport to offer sports activities, in this case, football, for children and adolescents with disabilities.

INSOS, the branch association of social institutions with services for people with disabilities in Switzerland (Soziale Institutionen für Menschen mit Behinderungen Schweiz, 2020), represents the interests of 800 service providers and 60,000 people with disabilities. The association provides impetus, support, advice, and a network. As the organisation is committed to the implementation of the UN CRPD (2006) and an inclusive society, it supports its member institutions in the provision of sport for people with disabilities and as part of this especially recruits and motivates participants for the Special Olympics World Games.

Pro Infirmis, as a non-profit and politically independent umbrella organisation for regional and local disability organisations, runs counselling centres throughout Switzerland and supports people with physical, intellectual, and psychological impairments. The organisation promotes together with those affected the independent and self-determined life of people with disabilities and is committed to ensuring that people with disabilities can actively participate in social life including sport and are not disadvantaged (Pro Infirmis, 2020).

Insieme is the umbrella organisation of parents' associations for people with intellectual disabilities. It cooperates with the disability organisations like Inclusion Handicap, INSOS, PluSport, and Special Olympics; self-help organisations like Cerebral; the EBGB and the BSV as governmental actors; and international partners like the Austrian and German Counselling (Lebenshilfe). The organisation is committed to legal frameworks and social conditions that allow people with intellectual disabilities to lead a dignified life. The common goal of Insieme is that people with intellectual disabilities belong to our society. They should live among us—independent, self-determined, and as normal as possible. Therefore, its regional clubs, which in turn are partly members of Pro Infirmis, support people with intellectual disabilities and their relatives with offers for holidays, educational and leisure activities including sport, opportunities for relief, and exchange of experience (Insieme, 2020).

Steering of Disability Sport

Legislative Framework

To date, there are no decrees or laws regarding sport specifically aiming for people with disabilities neither at the national nor at the regional level, and Switzerland is a country with non-interventionist sports legislation.

At the national level, the Swiss Federal Constitution, article 68, lays down the promotion and development of sport (Nagel & Adler Zwahlen, 2016). Having regard to that article, the Sports Promotion Act (2011) names sport as an important social domain where integration takes place, however, without explicitly mentioning people with disabilities. The Federal Disability Equality Act (2004) as the legal framework for governmental, non-governmental, and secondary agents obliges the federation, cantons, and communities to set conditions that facilitate participation, integration, and equal opportunities in social life for people with disabilities (Nagel & Adler Zwahlen, 2016). Although there are no concrete statements on equality in access to sports, it is included in the obligations as it belongs to social life. The Federal Concept for Sports for All (Breitensportkonzept Bund; Eidgenössisches Department für Verteidigung, Bevölkerungsschutz und Sport, 2015) explicitly focuses on people with disabilities and mentions that there should be enough low-threshold and target-group specific sports offers for people with disabilities, as all people should have the opportunity to exercise regularly throughout their lives (Eidgenössisches Department für Verteidigung, Bevölkerungsschutz und Sport, 2015). Despite the ratification of the UN CRPD (2006) in 2014, there is, as yet, no legally binding transposition into concrete law. Therefore, there is no legislative guideline for actors, but thus far only value-oriented, normative, and idealistic statements.

At the regional level, about half of the 26 cantons have a cantonal sports concept. In addition, nearly half of the cantons have a law regarding sport and/or the promotion of physical activity, and the majority of cantons have sport-specific laws. According to cantonal sports concepts, cantons are responsible for the development, construction, and maintenance of a cantonal sport-related infrastructure as well as the implementation of the national J+S programme (Ibsen et al., 2016).

Policy Framework

Steering of (disability) sport in Switzerland is not uniformly centralistic, but it takes place both through governmental agents such as the BASPO, the BSV, and the EBGB, and through non-governmental agents such as Swiss Olympic, PluSport, and Special Olympics (see Fig. 16.2.).

Governmental and non-governmental agents in the disability (sport) system are independent entities. However, there is a financial relationship as the governmental agents finance the (disability) sports federations under the principle of subsidiarity.

The principal reason why the Swiss government, the cantons, and municipalities publicly promote and subsidise sport are the assumed or assigned positive social effects, such as social integration of specific target groups like people with disabilities, accumulation of cultural and social capital, and health promotion (Lamprecht et al., 2017). As these external effects are expected to be particularly significant in sports clubs (e.g., Braun & Finke, 2010), sport policy mainly aims at club sport, which can be seen for example in the provision of the sports infrastructure by the municipalities. Therefore, federations at the national and regional levels and sports clubs at the local level share the same aims for the use of sport to achieve social benefits (Nagel & Adler Zwahlen, 2016).

Switzerland's ratification of the UN CRPD (2006) in 2014 made it easier for disability organisations to exert political influence although some of the non-governmental and secondary agents already actively do policy work through lobbying, partnerships, and so on. In this context, PluSport as a non-governmental agent influences issues relevant to disability sports policy through its representation of interests, cooperation, and participation in relevant committees at a national level, as PluSport is closely linked to the BASPO in terms of sport, education, and integration/inclusion. Currently, the focus is on the recognition and role of disability sport. Thus, with the commitment of PluSport's Policy and Sports Commission, it has already been possible to bring several disability sports policy positions to Parliament. At the regional and local levels, PluSport supports its federations and sports clubs by providing advice on organisation and media processing and thus exerts influence on national, regional, and local political bodies. Also, PluSport as an umbrella organisation directly carries the concerns of its members into national politics as far as possible and reasonable (PluSport, 2020e).

In 2011, PluSport, Procap Sport, and the Swiss Paraplegics Association (SPV) founded the Interest-Community Sport and Handicap that cooperates with other sports organisations to promote and implement equality in sport. An important goal of this interest-community is to exploit synergies with other organisations like Swiss Deaf Sport as a collective member of PluSport, foundations like Special Olympics Switzerland as a project partner of PluSport and institutions for people with disabilities.

At the regional level, the main objectives of cantonal disability policy in Bern are, for example, equality, autonomy, personal responsibility, freedom of choice, and participation and involvement in social life (Gesundheits-, Sozial- und Integrationsdirektion Kanton Bern, 2020). Therefore, cantons also support in various ways organisations in the pursuit of integration or inclusion and equal access to sport for people with disabilities.

At the local level, policy programmes and interventions concerning disability sport are less supported and targeted than at the regional level, partly because policy objectives widely vary between municipalities. Moreover, responsibilities between sports departments and departments for the equality of persons with disabilities are often not clearly defined, although cooperation would be appropriate.

The collaborative governance structure and direct interaction within policymaking and the implementation process between governmental and non-governmental agents in Switzerland can be seen as co-governance (Skelcher, 2000) as partnerships bring together public and voluntary sector actors that operate between and around the core institutions of democratic government. For example, the BASPO as a governmental actor has a cooperation agreement with Swiss Olympic as a non-governmental actor.

Indirectly, the Invalidity Insurance (IV, Invalidenversicherung) has an impact on sport participation of people with disabilities as people with an IV card receive discounts for culture, sport, and education, for example, reduced fees for swimming pools (MyHandicap, 2020). However, the IV does not subsidise sports material like specific wheelchairs or prostheses. For this, athletes with disabilities can apply for a fund from PluSport (PluSport, 2020d).

Financial, Governance, and Managerial Support

Financial Framework

Regarding subsidising mechanisms for organisations involved in disability sport, financial support comes mainly from the governmental side and goes primarily to specific disability (sport) organisations such as PluSport, Procap (Sport), and the SPV.

Together with the EBGB and in collaboration with various disability sports federations, the BASPO is committed to the equalisation and participation of people with disabilities in sport. This is done via education and training, higher compensation for J+S offers aimed at young people with and without disabilities, advice, and cooperation in the development of guidelines for obstacle-free building, and support for civil society projects (BASPO, 2019a). In this regard, the J+S programme, which is funded by the BASPO, offers specialised courses regarding the integration of people with disabilities and/or a migration background (Nagel & Adler Zwahlen, 2016). Thereby, J+S promotes the joint sports activities of children and young people with and without disabilities (J+S, 2019). Although there are no financial grants available for sports clubs participating in the adults sports programme Switzerland (ESA, Erwachsenensport Schweiz), which is run in cooperation with cantons, sports federations, and private sports providers, ESA coaches receive free training and may participate in the J+S courses on preventive and integrative action (ESA, 2017).

In the National Sports Facility Concept (NASAK, Nationales Sportanlagenkonzept), accessibility for people with disabilities is not explicitly mentioned, as it is a requirement for new facilities and those that are being renovated. Accessibility can therefore be a problem for older existing sports facilities that have not yet been renovated.

PluSport (about CHF5,000,000 (€4,753,000) per year), Procap (about CHF7,000,000 (€6,655,000) per year, only part for the area of sport), and the SPV (about CHF2,000,000 (€1,901,000) per year) receive financial grants for specific purposes within disability sport from the BSV (BSV, 2015).

Aside from this, disability (sports) organisations rely on donations from private persons and companies that are tax-deductible. These can be increased through public presence as is, for example, done by Swiss Paralympic (Swiss Paralympic, 2020c).

Cantons support the construction and maintenance of sports facilities and also sports clubs in municipalities, using profits from lotteries (Swisslos, 2020). Here as well, people with disabilities are not explicitly mentioned but may also profit from the support of mainstream sport and associated infrastructure.

In Switzerland, the local authorities often pay some form of a lump sum to local sports clubs, including disability sports clubs. And approximately three-quarters of all Swiss sports clubs exclusively or partially rely on public sports facilities (Stamm et al., 2015), for which about half of the clubs only pay a relatively low yearly flat rate or even nothing. The economic value of this support from local authorities for sports clubs is relatively high although there are large differences concerning how much and in what manner sports clubs are supported (Lamprecht et al., 2017).

Support and programmes by non-governmental agents also vary between cantons and municipalities. For example, in St. Gall there is the programme "Sportverein-t" that aims, amongst other measures, to improve the integration of people with disabilities. Participating clubs receive higher funding from the lotteries (Interessengemeinschaft der St.Galler Sportverbände, 2020).

Governance and Management Support

On the one hand, there is independent governance of governmental and non-governmental agents due to the separation of the system. On the other hand, there is also shared governance, and organisations involved in disability sport are supported in their governance and management, for example, through cooperation between governmental and non-governmental agents such as the BASPO and Special Olympics or the EBGB and PluSport.

Sports clubs and sports organisations are supported and governed under general rules and regulations according to the Federal Constitution, which also applies to other voluntary organisations (Ibsen et al., 2016). Also, the BASPO is not only involved in the general training of J+S instructors and coaches but since 2015 also offers courses for the integration of people with disabilities and/or a migration background through sport, as well as in promoting equality (BASPO, 2019b). In the courses on the integration of people with disabilities, a core concern is to show instructors and coaches ways for joint sports activities and training for children and young people with and without disabilities, for example, with the basic and advanced module "Sport and Handicap" (BASPO & J+S, 2016). Furthermore, issues on sport and integration of people with disabilities and a migration background will be embedded in the basic course across all sports.

PluSport concentrates particularly on the promotion of young talent among amateur athletes, athletes, sports club directors, and managers (PluSport, 2020c). Measures for the development of new sports offers, networking of partnerships, and creation of events—with the acquisition of members, talents, managers, and board members—are implemented in the framework concept for sport and athlete development (short FTEM Switzerland: foundation, talent, elite mastery), which was devised by the BASPO and Swiss Olympic (Grandjean et al., 2015). As PluSport is committed to seamlessly combining popular sport, top-class sport, and the promotion of young talents, this framework aims to improve coordination and systematics of sports promotion, to increase the level of competitive sports, and to keep people in sport for life.

Furthermore, PluSport cooperates with various organisations and institutions such as universities, rehabilitation centres, and institutions for people with disabilities and participates at congresses and sports events to increase public awareness (PluSport, 2020c). As coordinator between athletes and specialists in the field of disability sport, PluSport supports the development of new sport offers for people with disabilities and is responsible every year for over 80 training and further education courses of disability sport coaches of PluSport and its partner organisations, amongst them Procap Sport (PluSport, 2020a).

Special Olympics Switzerland offers courses in the field of sports for dealing with people with disabilities and on Special Olympics in general. The foundation also cooperates with sports clubs and sports events through the development of training concepts and inclusive conditions and carries out quality control to ensure quality. For relatives, schools, specialist agencies, institutions, and interest groups, Special Olympics helps with the development of a useful network (Special Olympics Switzerland, 2020).

The SPV, with its department RSS and its partner organisations BASPO and ESA, offers a target group needs-oriented and high-quality training course for coaches in wheelchair sports. The education aims to train coaches for wheelchair sports in the wheelchair clubs and in the association and to maintain the quality of movement and sports lessons or sport-specific training organised by the technical commissions to the highest possible level (SPV, 2020a).

Swiss Paralympic is more responsible for elite sport and therefore creates selection concepts for sports organisations (Swiss Paralympic, 2020a).

The BASPO also supports selected projects by mainstream sport organisations that serve the integration of people with disabilities (BASPO, 2019a).

> The current project of the Swiss Football League "Radio Blind Power—bringing the visually impaired closer to the ball" is an example of corporate social responsibility (CSR) by mainstream sport organisations. Here, live matches of the Super League are broadcast via audio transcription for passive sport consumption (Swiss Football League SFL, 2020).

Level of Integration or Inclusion

Disability sport in Switzerland is often practised in separate settings and there are different disability sports federations for different disability forms. Therefore, people with disabilities often take part in separate sports activities specifically organised for people with disabilities (Klenk et al., 2017). However, according to the BASPO (2019b) and PluSport which both agree with the UN CRPD (2006), disability sport should also take place in integrative/inclusive settings where people with and without disabilities exercise together so that people with disabilities have the right to choose (Valet, 2018). An example of this is the Unified programme by Special Olympics which promotes regular sports activities in sports clubs and at sporting events where people with and without intellectual disabilities practise together (Special Olympics Switzerland, 2020). Consequently, disability sport in Switzerland can be practised in a spectrum ranging from a categorical separate setting with peers of the same disability to a fully inclusive setting where people with and without disabilities exercise and compete together without any modifications or adaptions (Misener & Darcy, 2014).

16.4 Sport Participation by People with Disabilities

Monitoring and Evaluation

Despite the ratification of the UN CRPD in 2014, "Sport Schweiz," the regular sports monitor in Switzerland, has not yet considered the category of disability in its latest reports (Lamprecht et al., 2014, 2020) and, to date, the government does not invest in or stimulate the evaluation of sports programmes or interventions for people with a disability. Consequently, there still remains a lack of data.

Therefore, in this chapter, we mainly refer to the Swiss data from the project Social Inclusion and Volunteering in Sports Clubs in Europe (SIVSCE). In 2016, data were collected by online questionnaires on the meso level of mainstream sports clubs ($n = 31$) (Breuer et al., 2017) and the micro level of sports club members ($N = 959$, response rate: 26%) who voluntarily participated in the survey (van der Roest et al., 2017).

Furthermore, to comprehensively analyse sport participation of members with disabilities in sports clubs and the relevant personal and environmental factors, we conducted a multiple case study in the German-speaking part of Switzerland, which was funded by the BASPO. Data were collected from 2016 to 2017 on the meso level of 16 training groups in 14 sports clubs and training groups that were recruited via snowball sampling. Three integrative/inclusive training groups were theoretically selected for in-depth case studies (Yin, 2014) where data were also captured on the micro level of participants ($N = 14$ participants, 10 of whom have a disability) with a triangulation of methods and data sources (Albrecht et al., 2019).

In both studies, we differentiate between the following disability forms: physical disability (e.g., mobility impairment, problems in the musculoskeletal system), visual impairment, hearing impairment, intellectual disability (e.g., Down syndrome, mental disability), and psychosocial/behavioural problems (e.g., autism, ADHD). In the SIVSCE project, there is an additional category of chronic diseases (e.g., asthma, diabetes, multiple sclerosis, cardiovascular disease).

Sport Participation

Participation in Sport Clubs

According to the BFS (2020), 18% of the Swiss population has a disability. According to data from SIVSCE only 53 (7%) out of 730 valid responses for the respective question of the surveyed Swiss mainstream sports club members indicated to have at least one form of disability. Thus, to date, people with disabilities appear to be underrepresented in Swiss mainstream sports clubs.

Sport Participation Frequency

Of the 53 Swiss sports club members with disabilities in the sample of the SIVSCE project, 26% ($n = 14$) do not actively practise sport in the club, compared to only 15% ($n = 100$) of the members without disabilities. However, when sport-active in the club there are no significant differences in the sport participation frequency between people with (median = 1 time a week) and people without disabilities (median = 1 time a week) (Likert scale from 1 = less than once a month to 5 = 3 times a week or more). When compared to other members with disabilities (median = 4; Likert scale: 0 = not sport-active in the club, 1 = less than once a month, 2 = 1–3 times a month, 3 = 1 time a week, 4 = 2 times a week, 5 = 3 times a week or more), members with a physical disability (median = 0) are less frequently active. Context factors such as age, gender, and level of education show no effect on the frequency level in both groups.

Sport and Club Participation Form

Regarding the sports club system, 18% of the Swiss mainstream sports clubs also provide services for people with disabilities (Lamprecht et al., 2017). Thus, those clubs can be considered as integrative/inclusive. However, all the surveyed members in the SIVSCE project participate in mainstream forms of sport and none of them practises specific forms of sport for people with disabilities or chronic diseases or sport for rehabilitation. Moreover, they all practise sport in a group together with members without disabilities. One participant with a visual impairment additionally practises in a special group consisting of people with disabilities only. In the BASPO project, 3 out of 15 training groups offer adapted forms of sport. These are wheelchair line dance, goalball, and rafroball.[1] From the 16 training groups in the BASPO project, 8 training groups are specific disability training groups, and in 8 training groups, people with and without disabilities practise together.

Sport Type

The members with disabilities surveyed in the SIVSCE project most often play tennis ($n = 13$). Other quite common sports amongst members with disabilities are swimming ($n = 7$) and football ($n = 6$). Further practiced sports are volleyball

---

[1] Rafroball is an inclusive form of handball for people with and without disabilities, for example, the size of the goal is adapted to the movement possibilities of the goalkeeper, which was developed by four Swiss men in the 1990s (Association Rafroball, 2020).

($n = 3$), water polo ($n = 3$), alpine skiing ($n = 3$), snowboarding ($n = 2$), handball ($n = 2$), ice hockey ($n = 2$), triathlon ($n = 2$), athletics ($n = 1$), ball sport ($n = 1$), fitness/aerobic ($n = 1$), and running ($n = 1$). Four participants stated that they practise a different sport.

The training groups in the BASPO project offer swimming ($n = 4$), football ($n = 3$; among them case 1), floorball ($n = 2$), athletics ($n = 1$; case 2), climbing ($n = 1$), dancing ($n = 1$), goalball ($n = 1$; case 3), multisport ($n = 2$), and rafroball ($n = 1$).

Type of Sport Club

Only mainstream sports clubs that do not have special measures, that is, specific programmes and initiatives for people with disabilities, to increase the participation of people with disabilities in the form of targeted sports activities, special teams, cooperation with organisations or municipalities, and reduced membership fees or compensation for disability participated in the Swiss survey of the SIVSCE project. Therefore, the members mentioned primarily participate in mainstream sports clubs. However, in the BASPO project, 9 out of 14 sports clubs are disability sports clubs. Furthermore, PluSport has around 90 disability sports groups, with about 12,000 active members and 2000 coaches (PluSport, 2019, 2020b); the SPV has 27 wheelchair clubs with 517 athletes (SPV, 2020b); Swiss Deaf Sport consists of 14 disability-specific sports clubs (Swiss Deaf Sport, 2020); and Procap Sport has 30 sports groups (Procap, 2020a). Furthermore, Special Olympics also supports the participation of people with disabilities in mainstream sports activities with the programme Unified (Special Olympics Switzerland, 2020).

Participation by Type of Impairment or Disability

Nineteen members with a chronic disease, 14 with a visual impairment, 11 with a physical disability, 8 with a psychosocial/behavioural problem, 6 with a hearing impairment, and no members with an intellectual disability participated in the Swiss member survey of the SIVSCE project (multiple answers possible).

In the BASPO project, there are members with an intellectual disability and with a physical disability in all eight separate training groups; four groups have members with a psychosocial/behavioural problem and only two groups with a visual impairment. From the eight training groups where participants with and without disabilities practise together, there are seven groups with participants with a physical disability, three groups with participants with an intellectual disability, and two groups with participants with a visual impairment. All groups have participants with congenital disabilities. In four separate groups and in five integrative/inclusive groups, there are members with acquired disabilities.

Volunteering

In the SIVSCE project, 37 members with disabilities (70%) are voluntarily active as coach/instructor ($n = 12$), as referee/official ($n = 4$), and in other tasks connected to the sports activity ($n = 6$). Moreover, there are also board members amongst them ($n = 9$) and members of one or more committees ($n = 8$). Members with disabilities are also active in other forms of club leadership/management ($n = 3$) and funding activities ($n = 5$) as well as in administration, office work, or the like ($n = 8$). They volunteer in technical work and services ($n = 3$) and contribute to the organisation of club activities, tournaments, or the like ($n = 15$). Participants with disabilities are responsible for communication ($n = 9$), driving to matches, tournaments, or the like ($n = 9$), as well.

In the BASPO project, in two separate training groups and five integrative/inclusive training groups, members with disabilities (6%) are also voluntarily active as (assistant) coaches ($n = 7$), on the board ($n = 2$), and as weight room manager ($n = 1$).

Barriers and Facilitators

As results from both projects rest upon low numbers of respondents, the barriers and facilitators discussed below are indicative. However, these results from Switzerland are in line with existing international results (see reviews of Jaarsma et al., 2014; Shields et al., 2012).

Barriers

When asked about restrictions (multiple answers possible), Swiss mainstream sports club members with disabilities in the SIVSCE project mainly mention personal restrictions ($n = 18$ out of 53 surveyed members) as they often have physical problems ($n = 9$) or it is hard for them to find sports activities that suit them ($n = 5$). Other personal difficulties are that the disability acts very differently depending on the (time of) day ($n = 4$) or that it is difficult for them to concentrate ($n = 2$). Interestingly, in the SIVSCE project, no persons with intellectual disabilities answered the questionnaire. Possibly because they find it difficult to participate in the questionnaire form. However, this tendency also appears in the BASPO data, where all separate training groups have members with intellectual disabilities, but in only two out of seven training groups, participants with and without disabilities practise together.

Seven surveyed members with a disability see social restrictions as a relevant problem. They mainly mention that it is difficult for them to be around many people at the same time ($n = 3$), that it is difficult for them to be part of a team ($n = 3$), and that it is difficult for them to find people with whom they can do sport on an equal footing ($n = 2$). One surveyed person does not feel welcome and accepted as people have trouble with her disability ($n = 1$) and one member with a visual impairment does not have a buddy ($n = 1$). Only three surveyed members see structural restrictions as a possible barrier: sports activities ($n = 2$) and facilities ($n = 2$) are not adapted for people with a disability, the staff are not trained to attend to people with a disability ($n = 1$), and due to the disability participating in sports activities is expensive ($n = 1$).

However, some disadvantages due to the disability have to be accepted as was pointed out by a visually impaired athlete from the BASPO project when he said: "If you are 100% reliant on public transport, ... you have to accept that it takes you longer to get [to training]" (participant 8). Interestingly, participants seem to accept these hindering factors relatively easily. A coach saw waiting for sprint prostheses and a lack of technical support for almost one year as a significant issue, but for the athlete herself (participant 7) it was not worth mentioning.

Facilitators

Diverse social support is an environmental facilitator for both recreational and competitive athletes in the BASPO project. Their teachers ($n = 2$) or caregivers ($n = 3$) bring most of the children to the training in case study 1. A mother always accompanies only one participant to training. Interestingly for both athletes in case study 2, social support and acceptance even increased over time due to their successful performance. Now, the parents and siblings actively support the sports (competition) and everyday life. One athlete was very enthusiastic about sports from an early age and initially joined the club with a friend when looking for a suitable sport, as soccer did not work well anymore with his visual impairment. This social support was especially valuable as the friend could help him with travel to the training sessions. One athlete joined the club on her own initiative by seeking contact with a disability sports federation, where she met another athlete who was already in the club, which is close to her place of residence. Now, the parents and siblings support the two athletes by accompanying them to competitions as well as by supporting them in their everyday life. Participant 7 illustrates it this way: "I still live at home ... [and] ... it happens from time to time when my mother cooks ..., that something is saved for me and I am very happy when I come home at half-past nine after training."

In case study 3, most of the participants have a supportive social network consisting of family and friends who support them individually. Furthermore, external people are always ready to help as timekeepers or goal judges at tournaments or on other occasions.

Participants in case study 1 experience that their social environment not only accepts but also is proud of their participation in special training. In contrast to the other cases, the athletes in case study 2 state that to be awarded with honours is nice, but in the end, they do the sport for themselves. This shows that they have a very high intrinsic motivation, as they are active in an elite setting and of course want to perform well.

In all cases, the athletes appreciate that all are treated equally as the following quote shows: "I like that we are all coached in the same way and he [coach] doesn't say you can make one more break than the others or something like that. I must train just as hard. I like that, that's very positive" (participant 7).

That the training infrastructure in all cases is accessible for the forms of disability and easily reachable by public transport or car is an important structural facilitator.

> Case study 1 is a good example of practice, where the professional premier league football club cooperates with Special Olympics and special needs schools to stimulate sport participation of children and adolescents with disabilities. Since 2013, the club has offered training where a disability group is integrated into a regular club in the context of CSR. Biweekly special training (predecessor of the Unified programme) for children and adolescents with disabilities from special needs schools and young refugees from refugee hostels takes place in the stadium and is especially open to beginners, as there is no talent reward.

16.5 Conclusion

Various governmental, non-governmental, and secondary agents aiming to support sport participation of people with disabilities play an important role in Swiss disability sport. Governmental agents are mainly responsible for financing and the legislative framework, whereas non-governmental agents are largely responsible for implementation. However, despite the diverse field of institutions and the cooperative relationship between the different agents, there are still shortcomings in the structure of the Swiss disability sport system. People with disabilities are underrepresented in sport—both in general and in sports clubs, as participation rates are lower compared to the population without disabilities. Only 18% of Swiss mainstream sports clubs provide services for people with disabilities (Lamprecht et al., 2017). Moreover, the systemic and historically grown separation of the mainstream and the disability sport systems in Switzerland may encourage sports activity of people with disabilities in a separate rather than an integrative/inclusive mainstream setting, a separation that even applies to people with different forms of disability. Consequently, as proposed by the UN CRPD (2006), people with disabilities should have equal access to sports in both separate and integrative/inclusive settings, general sports participation by people with disabilities should be enhanced, and, more specifically, access to mainstream sport participation should be facilitated. This appears to be crucial because when people with disabilities are sport-active, participation frequency of people with disabilities is equivalent to that of people without disabilities and so they are equally socially integrated. Participants in the BASPO project also articulated this issue. However, results, especially regarding volunteering, have to be interpreted with caution as mainstream sports club members with disabilities in the SIVSCE project possibly face fewer barriers to social integration than people with disabilities who are active outside of mainstream sport settings.

Currently, there are also significant efforts at various levels in Switzerland to encourage sports to be more inclusive for people with disabilities. Regarding this, the dual structure of disability and mainstream sport should be evaluated at the macro level to assess appropriateness or whether disability and mainstream sports federations should merge. Furthermore, in the steering of disability sport, the legislative framework could be enhanced by integrating the UN CRPD (2006) into the existing Disability Equality Act (2002) and the Sports Promotion Act (2011) which may lead to a higher obligatory nature for implementation. Regarding financial, governance, and managerial support, separate disability sports federations and clubs are well supported. However, there is action required especially regarding the financial resources, for mainstream sports federations and clubs to implement integrative/inclusive sport. Moreover, regarding infrastructure, access could be facilitated, for example, by including accessibility as an important aspect in the NASAK especially in the extension of existing buildings. One of the most common structural barriers in the SIVSCE project is that facilities are not adapted for people with a disability, while in the BASPO project, accessible infrastructure is viewed as an important facilitator.

On the meso level of sports organisations, adaptions have to be implemented to increase the possibilities for people with disabilities sport participation. That people with disabilities on their own initiative invented rafroball indicates there is a lack of adapted forms, especially for people who do not want to participate in sports for people with disabilities or chronic diseases or sport for rehabilitation. Also in the SIVSCE project, a frequently mentioned barrier is that sports activities are not adapted for people with a disability. A variety of social support is an important facilitator for people with disabilities sport participation, not only family and friends should support and help sport participation but also caregivers and teachers should be sensitised about their crucial role, for example, within their education. Moreover, contact persons and information from (disability) sports organisations could help to get more people with disabilities into sports and socially integrated into a sport setting.

Implications for future research are to improve national surveys that gather extensive comprehensive longitudinal data and allow robust statements about development. This requires the integration of specific indicators to gain a detailed overview of people with disabilities sport participation as well as preferences and possible difficulties to implement measures to facilitate sport participation. This means that the BFS should obtain further differentiated statistics on people with disabilities, especially concerning different disability forms and key figures on sport, such as sports activity level. Of particular interest here are the data of people with disabilities who are not or are no longer active in sport and their views on access to sport. For the "Sport Schweiz" monitor, this means that the monitoring should be expanded by the integration of central key figures specifically for the sports behaviour of people with disabilities—in general, and in sports clubs in particular. Moreover, data in the context of sports clubs and training groups and how integration/inclusion can work, both from the perspective of the people concerned and from the perspective of organisations, is needed.

References

Albrecht, J., Nagel, S., & Klenk, C. (2019). Social integration in sports clubs of young members with disabilities in Switzerland: A multiple-case study. In European Association for Sociology of Sport (Ed.), *Sports and the environment—Policies, values and sustainability: Book of abstracts. 16th European Association for the Sociology of sport conference* (pp. 73–74). University of South-Eastern Norway.

Association Rafroball. (2020). *Integration—Rafroball*. https://rafroball.org/rafroball/integration/?lang=de

Braun, S., & Finke, S. (2010). *Integrationsmotor Sportverein: Ergebnisse zum Modellprojekt "spin—Sport interkulturell"* [integration engine sports club: Results of the model project "spin—Sport intercultural"]. VS Verlag für Sozialwissenschaften. https://doi.org/10.1007/978-3-531-92480-9

Breuer, C., Feiler, S., Llopis-Goig, R., & Elmose-Østerlund, K. (2017). *Characteristics of European sports clubs: A comparison of the structure, management, voluntary work and social integration among sports clubs across ten European countries* (social inclusion and volunteering in sports clubs in Europe report) Odense.

Bundesamt für Sozialversicherungen. (2015). *Vereinbarte maximale IV/AHV-Beiträge an Organisationen der privaten Behindertenhilfe* [Agreed maximum IV/AHV contributions to private disability assistance organisations]. https://sozialversicherungen.admin.ch/de/d/6370/download

Bundesamt für Sport. (2019a). *Sport und handicap*. https://www.baspo.admin.ch/de/sportfoerderung/fairness%2D%2D-ethik-und-sicherheit/sport-und-integration/sport-mit-handicap.html

Bundesamt für Sport. (2019b). *Sport und integration*. https://www.baspo.admin.ch/de/sportfoerderung/fairness%2D%2D-ethik-und-sicherheit/sport-und-integration.html

Bundesamt für Sport. (2020). *Integration und Prävention* [Integration and prevention]. https://www.ehsm.admin.ch/de/uebersicht/integration-praevention.html

Bundesamt für Sport, & Jugend+Sport. (2016). *Integratives Handeln: Sport und handicap* [integrative action: Sport and handicap]. http://www.jugendundsport.ch/internet/js/de/home/ethik/downloads_querschnittsthemen.parsys.23831.downloadList.32622.DownloadFile.tmp/2016handicapdweb.pdf

Bundesamt für Statistik. (2019). *Bevölkerung nach Migrationsstatus*. https://www.bfs.admin.ch/bfs/de/home/statistiken/bevoelkerung/migration-integration/nach-migrationsstatuts.html

Bundesamt für Statistik. (2020). *Gesundheit: Taschenstatistik 2019* [Health: Pocket statistics 2019]. Neuchâtel. Eidgenössisches Department des Inneren. https://www.bfs.admin.ch/bfs/de/home/statistiken/gesundheit/erhebungen/sgb.html

Bundesgesetz über die Beseitigung von Benachteiligungen von Menschen mit Behinderungen. (2002). (2002 & rev. 01.01.2020). https://www.admin.ch/opc/de/classified-compilation/20002658/index.html

Bundesgesetz über die Förderung von Sport und Bewegung. (2011). SR 415.0 (2011 & rev. 01.01.2013). https://www.admin.ch/opc/de/classified-compilation/20091600/index.html

Cornaton, J., Schweizer, A., Ferez, S., & Bancel, N. (2018). The divisive origins of sports for physically disabled people in Switzerland (1956–1968). *Sport in Society, 21*(4), 591–609. https://doi.org/10.1080/17430437.2016.1273596

Egger, T., Stutz, H., Jäggi, J., Bannwart, L., Oesch, T., Naguib, T., & Pärli, K. (2015). Evaluation des Bundesgesetzes über die Beseitigung von Benachteiligungen von Menschen mit Behinderungen—BehiG: Integraler Schlussbericht. Im *Auftrag des Eidgenössischen Departements des Innern—Generalsekretariat GS-EDI/Eidgenössisches Büro für die Gleichstellung von Menschen mit Behinderungen EBGB*. Bern. Büro für Arbeits- und Sozialpolitische Studien BASS AG. https://www.zhaw.ch/storage/sml/institute-zentren/zsr/projekt-evaluation-behig-integrale-Fassung-2015.pdf

Eidgenössisches Department für auswärtige Angelegenheiten. (2017). *Die Sprachen—Fakten und Zahlen*. https://www.eda.admin.ch/aboutswitzerland/de/home/gesellschaft/sprachen/die-sprachen%2D%2D-fakten-und-zahlen.html

Eidgenössisches Department für auswärtige Angelegenheiten. (2018). *Politisches System der Schweiz—Fakten und Zahlen*. https://www.eda.admin.ch/aboutswitzerland/de/home/politik/uebersicht/politisches-system-der-schweiz%2D%2D-fakten-und-zahlen.html

Eidgenössisches Department für Verteidigung, Bevölkerungsschutz und Sport. (2015). *Breitensportkonzept bund* [Federal Concept for sports for all]. https://www.admin.ch/ch/d/gg/pc/documents/2698/Sport_Breitensportkonzept-Bund_de.pdf

Erwachsenensport Schweiz. (2017). *Über esa [About ESA]*. https://www.erwachsenen-sport.ch/de/ueber-esa.html

Esping-Andersen, G. (1990). *The three worlds of welfare capitalism*. Polity Press.

Frenkiel, S. (2018). The development of Swiss wheelchair athletics. The key role of the Swiss Association of Paraplegics (1982–2015). *Sport in Society, 21*(4), 610–621. https://doi.org/10.1080/17430437.2016.1273600

Gesundheits-, Sozial- und Integrationsdirektion Kanton Bern. (2020). *Behindertenpolitik* [disability policy]. https://www.gef.be.ch/gef/de/index/soziales/soziales/behinderung/Behindertenpolitik_Kanton_Bern.html

Grandjean, N., Gulbin, J., & Bürgi, A. (2015). *Rahmenkonzept zur Sport- und Athletenentwicklung in der Schweiz: FTEM Schweiz*. https://www.swissolympic.ch/dam/jcr:5dab6dca-d7f6-4ae2-b55a-d4618087d591/Rahmenkonzept_zur_Sport-_und_Athletenentwicklung_DE.pdf

Ibsen, B., Nichols, G., & Elmose-Østerlund, K. (2016). *Sports club policies in Europe: A comparison of the public policy context and historical origins of sports clubs across ten European countries* (social inclusion and volunteering in sports clubs in Europe report). University of Southern Denmark, Department of Sports Science and Clinical Biomechanics.

Inclusion Handicap. (2019). *Erstes Staatenberichtsverfahren der Schweiz vor dem UNO-Ausschuss für die Rechte von Menschen mit Behinderungen: Eingabe im Hinblick auf die List of Issues*. Bern. Inclusion Handicap. https://www.inclusion-handicap.ch/admin/data/files/asset/file_de/546/dok_eingabe_loi_bf_26082019.pdf?lm=1566998857

Insieme. (2020). *Angebot [Offer]*. https://insieme.ch/insieme/angebot/

Interessengemeinschaft der St.Galler Sportverbände. (2020). *Sport-verein-t*. https://www.igsgsv.ch/sport-verein-t/

Jaarsma, E. A., Dijkstra, P. U., Geertzen, J. H. B., & Dekker, R. (2014). Barriers to and facilitators of sports participation for people with physical disabilities: A systematic review. *Scandinavian Journal of Medicine & Science in Sports, 24*, 871–881. https://doi.org/10.1111/sms.12218

Jugend+Sport. (2019). *Integration [Integration]*. https://www.jugendundsport.ch/de/themen/integration.html

Kempf, H., & Lichtsteiner, H. (2015). *Das System Sport—in der Schweiz und international* [The sports system—in Switzerland and international]. Bundesamt für Sport (BASPO).

Klenk, C., Albrecht, J., & Nagel, S. (2017). *Bedingungen der Teilhabe von Kindern und Jugendlichen mit Behinderungen am Vereinssport: Abschlussbericht* [Conditions for the participation of children and adolescents with disabilities in sports clubs: Final report] [research report]. University of Bern, Institute of Sport Science.

Klostermann, C., Lamprecht, M., Stamm, H., & Nagel, S. (2020). Current situation of fitness sport in Switzerland. In J. Scheerder, H. Vehmas, & K. Helsen (Eds.), *The rise and size of the fitness industry in Europe: Fit for the future?* (pp. 373–388). Palgrave Macmillan. https://doi.org/10.1007/978-3-030-53348-9_17

Lamprecht, M., Bürgi, R., Gebert, A., & Stamm, H. (2017). *Sportvereine in der Schweiz: Entwicklungen, Herausforderungen und Perspektiven [Sports clubs in Switzerland: Developments, challenges and perspectives].* Bundesamt für Sport.

Lamprecht, M., Bürgi, R., & Stamm, H. (2020). *Sport Schweiz 2020: Sportaktivität und Sportinteresse der Schweizer Bevölkerung [Sports Switzerland 2020: Sports activity and interest of the Swiss population].* Bundesamt für Sport. https://www.sportobs.ch/inhalte/Downloads/Bro_Sport_Schweiz_2020_d_WEB.pdf

Lamprecht, M., Fischer, A., & Stamm, H. (2014). *Sport Schweiz 2014: Sportaktivität und Sportinteresse der Schweizer Bevölkerung [Sports Switzerland 2014: Sports activity and interest of the Swiss population].* Bundesamt für Sport.

Misener, L., & Darcy, S. (2014). Managing disability sport: From athletes with disabilities to inclusive organisational perspectives. *Sport Management Review, 17*, 1–7. https://doi.org/10.1016/j.smr.2013.12.003

MyHandicap. (2020). *Vergünstigungen für Menschen mit Behinderung [Benefits for people with disabilities].* https://www.myhandicap.ch/recht-behinderung/ermaessigungen-rabatte-iv-bezueger/

Nagel, S., & Adler Zwahlen, J. (2016). Switzerland. In *sports club policies in Europe: A comparison of the public policy context and historical origins of sports clubs across ten European countries (Social inclusion and volunteering in sports clubs in Europe report)*, pp. 86–89: University of Southern Denmark, Department of Sports Science and Clinical Biomechanics.

Nagel, S., Stegmann, P., Bürgi, R., & Lamprecht, M. (2020). Switzerland: Autonomous sports clubs as contributors to public welfare. In S. Nagel, K. Elmose-Østerlund, & B. Ibsen (Eds.), *Sports economics, management and policy. Functions of sports clubs in European societies: A cross-national comparative study* (pp. 289–314). Springer.

OECD. (2018). *GDP per capita.* https://data.oecd.org/gdp/gross-domestic-product-gdp.htm

Opielka, M. (2005). Der "weiche Garantismus" der Schweiz: Teilhaberechte in der Sozialpolitik. *Bulletin NFP, 51*(2), 1–6. http://www.snf.ch/SiteCollectionDocuments/nfp/nfp51/NFP51_Bulletin2_d.pdf.

PluSport. (2019). *Informationsbroschüre Ausbildung [Information brochure education].* https://www.procap.ch/fileadmin/user_upload/customers/redesign_procap/Sich_engagieren/Freiwilligenarbeit/PluSport_Infobroschuere_de.pdf

PluSport. (2020a). *Ausbildung und Weiterbildung im Sport [Education and training in sport].* https://www.plusport.ch/de/ausbildung/#c408

PluSport. (2020b). *Behinderung, Handicap, Bewegung, Sport [Disability, handicap, movement, sports].* https://www.plusport.ch/de/plusport/#c3971

PluSport. (2020c). *Förderung des Nachwuchses im Bereich Behindertensport [Promotion of young talent in the field of sports for the disabled].* https://www.plusport.ch/de/sport/nachwuchsfoerderung/

PluSport. (2020d). *Nachwuchsförderung im Leistungssport für junge Talente [Promotion of young talents in competitive sports].* https://www.plusport.ch/de/sport/nachwuchsfoerderung/nachwuchsfoerderung-spitzensport/junge-sporttalente/#c15297

PluSport. (2020e). *Sport & Politik [Sports & politics].* https://www.plusport.ch/de/inklusion/sport-politik/#c15091

Pro Infirmis. (2020). *Organisation [Organization].* https://www.proinfirmis.ch/ueber-uns/organisation.html

Procap. (2020a). *Sportgruppen [Sport groups].* https://www.procap.ch/de/angebote/reisen/sport/sportgruppen.html

Procap. (2020b). *Über uns [About us].* https://www.procap.ch/de/ueber-uns.html

Schweizer Paraplegiker-Vereinigung. (2005). *Unsere Geschichte.* https://www.spv.ch/de/wer_wir_sind/unsere_geschichte/

Schweizer Paraplegiker-Vereinigung. (2020a). *Ausbildung [Education]*. https://www.spv.ch/de/was_wir_tun/rollstuhlsport_schweiz/ausbildung/

Schweizer Paraplegiker-Vereinigung. (2020b). *Rollstuhlsport Schweiz [Wheelchair Sports Switzerland]*. https://www.spv.ch/de/was_wir_tun/rollstuhlsport_schweiz/

Schweizer Paraplegiker-Vereinigung. (2020c). *Sportberatung Buchen [Book a sports consultation]*. https://www.spv.ch/de/was_wir_tun/rollstuhlsport_schweiz/sportberatung_buchen/

Schweizerische Stiftung für das cerebral gelähmte Kind. (2020). *Hilfsangebote [Support services]*. https://www.cerebral.ch/de/hilfsangebote

Shields, N., Synnot, A. J., & Barr, M. (2012). Perceived barriers and facilitators to physical activity for children with disability: A systematic review. *British Journal of Sports Medicine, 46*, 989–997. https://doi.org/10.1136/bjsports-2011-090236

Skelcher, C. (2000). Changing images of the state: Overloaded, hollowed-out, congested. *Public Policy and Administration, 15*(3), 3–19. https://doi.org/10.1177/095207670001500302

Soziale Institutionen für Menschen mit Behinderungen Schweiz. (2020). *INSOS Schweiz [INSOS Switzerland]*. https://insos.ch/

Special Olympics Switzerland. (2020). *Unified*. https://specialolympics.ch/angebote-projekte/unified/

Special Olympics Switzerland. (2022). *Geschichte*. https://specialolympics.ch/ueber-special-olympics/geschichte/

Sportmedizin Nottwil. (2020). *Verbände und partner* [associations and partners]. https://www.paraplegie.ch/sportmedizin/de/ueber-sportmedizin/ueber-uns/verbaende-und-partner

Stamm, H., Fischer, A., Nagel, S., & Lamprecht, M. (2015). Sport clubs in Switzerland. In C. Breuer, H. Hoekman, S. Nagel, & H. van der Werff (Eds.), *Sport clubs in Europe: A cross-national comparative perspective* (pp. 401–417). Springer.

Stiftung Aarhus. (2020). *Leitbild [Mission statement]*. https://www.aarhus.ch/stiftung-aarhus/leitbild/

Swiss Deaf Sport. (2020). *Verband—über uns [Association—About us]*. https://www.sgsv-fsss.ch/de/swissdeafsport/verband-ueber-uns/#1504368353873-a753dc7a-82a2

Swiss Football League SFL. (2020). *Radio blind power*. https://www.sfl.ch/sfl/corporate-social-responsibility/barrierefreiheit/radio-blind-power/

Swiss Olympic. (2020). *Über uns [About us]*. https://www.swissolympic.ch/ueber-swiss-olympic/ueber-uns.html

Swiss Paralympic. (2020a). *Selektionskonzepte [Selection concepts]*. https://www.swissparalympic.ch/selektionskonzepte/

Swiss Paralympic. (2020b). *Wie kann ich einsteigen? [How can I get in?]*. https://www.swissparalympic.ch/sport/wie-kann-ich-einsteigen/

Swiss Paralympic. (2020c). *Über uns [About us]*. https://www.swissparalympic.ch/ueber-uns/

Swisslos. (2020). *Jeder Swisslos-Kunde unterstützt automatisch den Schweizer* sport [Every Swisslos customer automatically supports Swiss sport]. https://www.swisslos.ch/de/informationen/guter-zweck/verwendung-der-lotterieertraege/gewinn-fuer-den-sport/filmmaterial.html

United Nations. (2006). Convention on the rights of persons with disabilities. https://www.un.org/development/desa/disabilities/convention-on-the-rights-of-persons-with-disabilities/article-1-purpose.html

Valet, A. (2018). About inclusive participation in sport: Cultural desirability and technical obstacles. *Sport in Society, 21*, 137–151. https://doi.org/10.1080/17430437.2016.1225920

van der Roest, J.-W., van der Werff, H., & Elmose-Østerlund, K. (2017). *Involvement and commitment of members and volunteers in European sports clubs: A comparison of the affiliation, voluntary work, social integration and characteristics of members and volunteers in sports clubs across ten European countries* (social inclusion and volunteering in sports clubs in Europe report). University of Southern Denmark, Department of Sports Science and Clinical Biomechanics.

Yin, R. K. (2014). *Case study research: Design and methods* (5th ed.). Sage.

Chapter 17
Hungary: Rise of Attention Given to Disability Sports

Szilvia Perényi and Zsuzsanna Szilárd

17.1 Introduction

The development of sports for people with disabilities in Hungary began as early as 1912 with the foundation of the first Deaf-Mute Sports Club (SSC, Siketek Sport Clubja). Increased attention, however, was only given to this area starting from the 1980s when disability-specific sports federations were founded. The aim of this chapter is to introduce the development processes, functions and mechanisms of sports for people with disabilities in Hungary. Beyond the legislative environment, funding resources, infrastructure availability and sports participation are touched upon through the lens of all disability groups and connecting organisational structures, thus, clubs and federations. The foundation of the Hungarian Paralympic Committee (MPB, Magyar Paralimpiai Bizottság) in 1997 and the establishment of a state secretariat office for disability sports in 1999 created special attention for disability issues in the sports sector in Hungary. The law of 1998 on equal treatment and equal opportunities was a very valuable asset also in international comparison (Act XXVI, 1998). The developmental process included the structure of disability sports, legal and financing environment, media attention as well as overall social awareness. As a result, the approach and the consideration of disability sports today are similar to non-disability sports. Its inner structures reflect both disability groups and the national and international sports federation structures. Disability sports have become widespread in Hungary as a result of both health and social rehabilitation considerations. Even though resources, in particular financial, show some differences in comparison to non-disability sports, athletes with disabilities

S. Perényi (✉)
Hungarian University of Sports Science, Budapest, Hungary

Z. Szilárd
Semmelweis University Pető András Faculty, Budapest, Hungary

and their trainers are better recognised and remunerated today, and the budget available is also increasing yearly. Leisure sports for people with disabilities are linked to the National Leisure Sports Federation (MSZSZ, Magyar Szabadidősport Szövetség).

17.2 Country Profile

Characteristics of Hungary

Hungary is located in the Carpathian Basin in Central Europe. Its capital is Budapest, located in the centre of the country. The country has dominantly basin nature. The total length of the Hungarian border is 2238 km, which is shared with Austria, Slovakia, Ukraine, Romania, Slovenia, Croatia and Serbia (I1, MEK, 2020).

Hungary is a relatively small country with a territory of 93,030 km^2 and a population of 9772 million as of 2019. Hungary is divided into 7 regions, 20 municipalities and the capital. In total 30% of the total population is concentrated in Budapest and its agglomeration, and 70% of the population lives in cities and urban communities (Table 17.1). There are 3155 settlements altogether in Hungary, out of which 346 are cities.

Hungary is a republic, and the official language is Hungarian. The vast majority of the country's population is Hungarian; however, under the Nationality Act, 13

Table 17.1 Statistical data of Hungary based on the 2021 census

Population (number of inhabitants)	9,604,000 persons
Area (km^2)	93,030 km^2
Density (inhabitants/km^2)	103 person/km^2
Urbanisation rate (%)	70% of the population lives in cities and urban communities, and 30% of the total population is concentrated in the capital and its agglomeration
Political organisation	Parliamentary republic
Structure of the state	Republic
Number of counties	20
Number of settlement	3155 settlements (198 districts)
GDP per capita (EUR)	24,380
Number of official languages	1
EU membership	May 1, 2004
Welfare model	Central-Eastern European model

Source: Central Statistical Agency of HUN and https://eacea.ec.europa.eu

ethnic groups (Bulgarian, Gypsy, Greek, Croatian, Polish, German, Armenian, Romanian, Ruthenian, Serbian, Slovak, Slovenian and Ukrainian) are recognised as national minorities. A large Hungarian minority population lives in Transylvania, Ukraine, Serbia and Slovakia. The dominant religion is Catholic, but all religious affiliations are free to be practised. A census is carried out every 10 years in Hungary, data from the 2021 census is available (KSH, 2022).

Sport in Hungary

Sport in Hungary is overseen by the State Secretariat of Sports in the Ministry of Human Resources, which is also responsible for allocating state funding. At a local level municipalities also have a critical role. Besides, the civil sector with sports clubs, sports federations and sports umbrella organisations provide sporting opportunities at all levels, including for people with disabilities. Sport today is an important segment of society in Hungary; talents of Hungarian people are highly valued, in which sporting success is articulated. In 2000, the issue of sport was raised to ministerial level in the administration of the current government, and in 2010 it was declared to be a "strategic state sector". In this process, reorganisation procedures and the implementation of new funding systems were put in place, which was combined with refurbishing the legal environment as well. The strategy also reached the education and health sectors. Daily physical education classes were implemented in primary and high schools, and the theme "*sport as a medicine*" was acknowledged, followed by rethinking training and funding of sports professionals (Perényi, 2013). In order to reach goals in the development of sport, facilities were constructed and reconstructed (Géczi & Bardóczy, 2017); also major continental and world events were staged (Stocker & Szabó, 2017). Team sports gained special attention; the private sector was called upon by funding tax-deduction schemes like the "Corporation and dividend tax" (TAO—Társaság adó és osztalékadó) and by providing services at large events (Perényi et al., 2017) (Table 17.2).

Disability in Hungary

At the beginning of the nineteenth century, little attention was given to the needs of people with disabilities in Hungary; therefore, the establishment of institutions which specialised in the education of children with disabilities was considered a great success in Hungary. The first organised activities considering the degree of disability severity were open for people with hearing impairments, followed by the visually and then by the mentally disabled. The first deaf-mute institute established in 1802 by András Cházár (1745–1816) is still functioning today, where children from the age of nine were taught vocations, but there was initially no general education in the programme. Later Antal Simon (1772–1808) created learning through

Table 17.2 Sport country profile of Hungary

Government authority responsible for sports	Ministry of Defence
Membership sports club (% of population)*	4%
Membership fitness or health centre (% of population)*	8%
Membership socio-cultural club that includes sports in its activities (e.g. employees' club, youth club, school- and university-related club) (% of population)*	3%
Sport participation, at least once a week (% of population)*	24%
Number of national sports federations**	53
Number of sports clubs***	12,500 +
Number of sports club members**	Approximately 500,000
National budget for sports (€ × 1,000,000)**	562 euro (2014)
National budget for sports federations (€ × 1000)	n.d.
Local budget for sports (€ × 1,000,000)	n.d.
Share of economic value of volunteers in sport in the GDP (%)*	4%

EMMI, KSH* *n.d* not defined
Sources: *Special Eurobarometer 472, 2017 (European Commission, 2017)

writing-reading procedures and Antal Schwarczer (1780–1834) developed the technique for establishing study groups according to the development levels of children. The training of special professionals (doctors and educators) in the Teacher Training School in Pest started in the 1850s; educational materials were developed, and the teaching of voice-speech began by Károly Fekete (1822–1889). However, despite the efforts, the education lacked a systematic approach and uniformity for those involved (Tóthné Kälble, 2019; EU-COM, 2010; Europa-Hungary, 2020; Nádas, 2018a, 2018b).

The first institution for the visually impaired was founded in 1826, combining vocational and intellectual training. A public educational system was proposed from the 1870s onwards, but differentiated education was not achieved until the beginning of the twentieth century. The Pest Institute of the Blind recommended the training of parents, educators and pastors and provided guidance on the causes, symptoms, prevention, treatment, education and integration of blindness (Fónagy, 2015).

The establishment of educational institutions for children with mental disabilities was delayed until the second half of the nineteenth century; previously these children were kept at home or sent to insanity centres. The first institution was opened in 1875 by Jakab Frim (1852–1919). For those with severe mental disabilities, the "Budapest Institute for Idiots and Intellectually Retarded" was established, which was a healing, educational, training and nursing institution. Music and exercise were the two most important training tools in their programme. In 1887, a need to ensure kindergarten and nursery facilities according to severity levels and to provide primary school training for those with minor disabilities in separate classes emerged. Consequently, by the turn of the century, the foundations of the structure for segregated special education system still operating today in Hungary had been established for children with slight mental disabilities in educational institutions, while for the more serious cases nursing institutions were established (Kálmán & Könczei, 2002; Nádas, 2018a, 2018b).

Today, official definitions and expressions have been developed in connection with disabilities in Hungary (Tóthné Kälble, 2019) and they are clarified by the interpretative provision of the law. According to the LXII Act 2013, amendment of Act XXVI 1998, a person with a disability is a *"person who duratively or permanently lives with sensory, communication, physical, mental, psychosocial impairment, or any accumulation thereof, which creates environmental, social and other significant obstacles and restricts or impedes effective and equal social participation in interactions"* (Act LXII, 2013). In public education, the term "Special Educational Need" (SNI, Sajátos Nevelési Igény) is used instead of the term "disability". The law of CXC for 2011.4. § 25. rules that the special educational need of a child can be certified on the basis of expert opinion, as a result disability or other psychological development disorders (severe learning, attention or behavioural control disorder) can be diagnosed and treatment received (Act III, 1993; Act C, 1999; Act CXXV, 2003; Act XCII, 2007; Act CXXV, 2009; Act CXC, 2011).

Disability is determined on the basis of medical, pedagogical or social criteria. In daily conversation, "people with disabilities" (fogyatékkal élők) is the most commonly used term in health care and research, and it is considered by the levels of limitation in physical condition or in exercised activities, that is, in action, or by physical differences. The vocabulary of mental disability (szellemi fogyatékosok) and visual impairment (látás sérültek vagy vakok, gyengénlátók) varies by the area of expertise such as special education, law, medicine or psychology (Act LXII, 2013; NEFMI, 2011a, b). Tóthné Kälble et al., 2015). The definition of autism has also evolved over the last decade; today it is called spectrum disorder. Hearing loss (hallás sérültek) is an umbrella term with sub-categories. In general, the severity of a disability is determined on the basis of the International Classification of Diseases (IDC), including hearing impairment. In its regulation the Ministry of Human Resources (EMMI) draws attention to the fact that hearing loss may limit the development of conceptual thinking on a linguistic basis, which may affect the development of the entire personality (EMMI32, 2012; Zöld Könyv, 2005; EU-COM, 2010).

Today, the environment to help people with disabilities is instantly developing in Hungary with mostly integrated services available. Statistics based on the 2011 census (conducted every 10 years in Hungary) show that 595,187 people live with some kind of disability (Table 17.3), which was 5.99% of the total population at that time (9,938,000 persons). Within the different classifications of disability groups in relation to the total population, physical disabilities (2.34%) show the highest rate in comparison to other forms—site impairment (0.74%), hearing impairment (0.63%), psychological and inner-organ impairment (0.47%) and mental disorder (0.43%).

It appears that age plays a significant role in the distribution of disability forms. Table 17.3 shows that, with the exception of mental disabilities and autism, cases start growing after the age of 50. In 2011 72% of persons with disabilities were

Table 17.3 Disability forms by age and proportion in relation to total population in 2011

Type of disability	Age									Total (N)	Within total population (%)
	–14	15–19	20–29	30–39	40–49	50–59	60–69	70–79	80–		
Physical disability	4573	2391	5256	9573	16,861	50,416	5643	51,059	35,647	232,206	2.34
Site impairment	2344	1717	3238	4377	5811	12,555	12,695	14,593	161	7343	0.74
Blind	247	186	457	699	780	1358	1635	1724	1968	9054	0.09
Mental disorder	6094	4083	7307	7719	6076	5182	305	1854	1414	42,779	0.43
Autistic	2598	735	1071	364	165	88	46	32	21	512	0.05
Psychological impairment	1648	1059	2804	5216	7392	1277	6897	4517	3962	46,265	0.47
Hearing impairment	1596	865	1864	2827	3831	8005	10,959	14,055	19,012	63,014	0.63
Deaf	378	264	645	1025	119	1544	1366	1141	1018	8571	0.09
Deaf and blind	124	61	141	172	245	592	603	583	741	3262	0.03
Speech impairment	2151	760	1422	1746	1767	2559	2057	132	746	14,528	0.15
Other speech impairment	1962	598	1114	1070	1076	1614	1637	1123	719	10,913	0.11
Inner-organic impairment	216	764	1546	2618	4224	11,887	10,379	8224	4846	46,648	0.47
Other	260	105	146	205	267	519	364	261	150	2277	0.02
Unknown	2329	999	1687	2803	3961	8804	7756	5507	3274	3712	0.37
Total population with disabilities	28,464	14,587	28,698	40,414	53,646	117,893	115,874	105,993	89,618	595,187	5.99

Source: KSH (Central Statistical Agency) Census 2011

above this age; in the case of physical disabilities this proportion grows to 83% in this age group (KSH, 2003).

In the 2011 census, the largest segment of the population classified as disabled ($N = 595,187$) were people with physical disabilities (39.0%) followed by those with mental and psychological (16.0%), visual (14.0%) and hearing (13.0%) impairment.

In regards to perceived barriers, 72.5% of people experienced barriers in daily life due to disabilities. The level of barriers is greatest in relation to daily life (43%) and to transport (40%), less in self-sufficiency (20%), in communication (10%) and in community life (8%), all increasing with age (KSH, 2011). No perceived barrier was reported by 8%. According to people with disabilities, social services for daily life, logistics at home, in the workplace and transportation seem to require development. It must be stated, however, that during the past decade numerous infrastructural developments were made to city public services in Hungary. This includes improved accessibility of buses, trams, metro and bus stations, and accessibility requirements when building new facilities or renovating old sports facilities. Therefore, the results of the next census are expected to show fewer perceived barriers for people with disabilities (Pálhegyi, 1987; Marton, 2008; Juhász, 2004; Könczei, 2006).

According to data from the Central Statistical Agency of Hungary, the proportion of children with Special Educational Needs (SNI—Sajátos Nevelési Igény) is 3.0% among pre-schoolers aged 3–6 in 2016; and out of the nearly 10,000 children affected, 82.2% took part in integrated education. Primary school children with SNI needs ($N = 55.3$ thousand) in 2018 had a share of 7.6% of the total population, and 71.1% of them participated in integrated education. The number of SNI students showed no change in comparison to previous academic years; however, the overall number of primary school pupils declined, and integration records increased. Secondary education shows similar slightly increasing trends both in the number of students affected and in the proportion of integration. With the exception of vocational schools and skills-development schools, where youth is taught exclusively in connection to their specific needs (additionally those who cannot progress with other pupils), almost all SNI pupils in other types of schools receive integrated education (KSH, 2016a, 2016b).

Emergence or Rise of Disability Sport in Hungary

The history of organised disability sport takes us back to the beginning of the twentieth century when the first sports clubs for the deaf were established in special schools in Hungary. As a pioneer initiative for the people with hearing impairment, the Hungarian Deaf Sports Club was founded in Budapest in May 1912. It was the third association of its kind following Berlin in 1900 and Vienna in 1904. Since this historical start several sport clubs were founded to assist people in sporting activities, although organising competitions among these clubs as national sports federations were not established until later. Also, due to the lack of a national federation,

Hungary could not be part of the six nations (Belgium, Czechoslovakia, France, Great Britain, the Netherlands and Poland) establishing the International Silent Games, the deaf version of the Olympic Games initiated by E. Rubens-Alcais, a deaf French man. However, Hungarian clubs did send athletes to participate in the first Silent Games held in Paris in 1924 along with Italy and Romania. Hungary was also part of the seven nations that founded the "International Committee on Quiet Sports" at the café de la Porte Dorée in August 1924. In the second Silent Games held in Amsterdam in 1928, the Hungarian Vilma Kraszner won medals in 50 m backstroke, 200 m freestyle and 100 m pectoral fins with huge success. In 1937, Hungarian sports diplomacy also showed at the Seventh Congress of Deaf Athletes which was held in Budapest with the participation of 114 representatives from 14 nations. The congress gave a tribute to the 30th anniversary of the foundation of the Deaf Institute of Festetics Street of Budapest and the 25th anniversary of the first Deaf Sport Club (1912) in Hungary (Nádas, 2018a, 2018b).

Organised sport for people with *physical disabilities* in Hungary was formulated slightly later, during the late 1920s. The doctors and educators of the National Home for Crippled Children established in 1903 recognised the rehabilitation value and human-shaping power of the sport for their students. As a result, the Sports Association of Cripples (NYSE—Nyomorékok Sport Egyesülete) was established in 1929—the legal successor of this establishment still functions today as "Mozgásjavító" (Mozgásjavító Óvoda, Általános Iskola, Gimnázium, Kollégium, Egységes Gyógypedagógiai Módszertani Intézmény—Kindergarten, Elementary and Specialised Secondary School, Unified Special Education Methodology Centre and Students' Residence). Through regular school physiotherapy, sports activities and home competitions, students developed to a level where they could participate in integrated sports competitions, including table tennis, athletics and football in Budapest. After World War II, as a consequence of the political decisions of the time (1945–1952), the "Crippled Home" with a complex rehabilitation activity with a high European reputation was demolished. Parallel to the restructuring of the institution, the widely acknowledged teaching and healing training methods including complex sporting activity-related therapeutic care suffered as well. Up until the 1970s, being a person with a disability in Hungary created a persona non grata status for those involved. The new beginning was initiated by teachers András Fejes (1946–2020) and Zoltán Tauber (1946–2020) and students of the demolished primary school by founding the Halassy[1] Sports Club (HOSC) in 1970. The first sports were table tennis, archery, chess and sitting volleyball, and later the divisions of swimming, bowling and small-court football joined. The first large-scale international sport competition called "spartakiad" for people with disabilities in Hungary was organised by HOSC in 1971. From the 1980s a large number of sport clubs were formed for this population in Hungary (Tóthné Kälble, 2014; Nádas, 2018a, 2018b).

---

[1] Halassy Olivér, amputee water polo player competing among able bodied athletes; two-time Olympic Champion, 1932,1936; silver medalist in 1928 Games; four-time European Champion swimmer and water polo player.

People with *visual impairments first* began to play sports through chess in Hungary. In the special School of the Blind József Zichó, a blind music teacher, initiated the activity in the late 1940s. As a result of the integrated competitions, a department was founded in 1950 with support from the Blind Association (advocacy). In 1957, the athletics department was founded and in 1959 the importance of chess increased. The formation of the International Chess Federation of the Blind in 1960 and the International Sports Federation of the Blind in 1981 gave great impetus to international and national development. The 1976 Paralympic Games in Toronto were the first to include visually impaired athletes. Goalball sports as team sports started in 1981 in Hungary (Fónagy, 2015; Nádas, 2018a, 2018b).

Sports and competition opportunities for *people with mental disabilities* were available from the 1970s and operated through a special school system. For a quarter of a century, people with mental disabilities could participate in two sports, athletics and football. In 1992, by founding the Hungarian Sport Federation for People with mental Disabilities or MÉS, Magyar Értelmi Fogyatékosok Sportszövetsége (from 2006 Hungarian Parasport Federation, MPSZ, Magyar Értelmi Fogyatékosok Sportszövetsége), three mental disability sport competition categories were created. School sport was managed by FONESZ (Fogyatékosok Nemzeti Sportszövetsége—National Sports Federation for the Disabled), which continued to operate as FODISZ (Fogyatékosok Diák-, és Szabadidősport Szövetség—Disability Student and Leisure Sports Association) from 2010. At that time, injury-specific sports federations were also transformed and in 2012 they were transformed into the Federation for Sport Organisations of People with Disabilities (FMSZ, Fogyatékkal élők Sportszervezeteinek Magyarországi Szövetsége), which ceased to exist without a successor. The Competition Sports Association of the Disabled (FOVESZ, Fogyatékosok Versenysport Szövetsége) carries out the tasks related to sport.

The Hungarian Special Olympics Association (MSOSZ—Magyar Speciális Olimpiai Bizottság) was founded in 1989, providing people with mental disabilities the opportunity to compete in 12 sports (Hungarian Olympic Committee, 2012).

17.3 The Disability Sport System

Structure of Disability Sport

In Hungary, there were delays in relation to functions essential to health and social rehabilitation considerations. Efforts made in the 1970s and 1980s came to fruition in disabled sport only 20 years later (Czeglédy, 2002). Several sport-related associations were founded to assist people with disabilities, in which the democratic change in 1989–1990 played a significant role (Perényi, 2013). The structure, legal, funding and policy environment of the sport for people with disabilities gained larger attention in 2000 when the newly established Ministry of Youth and Sport created the

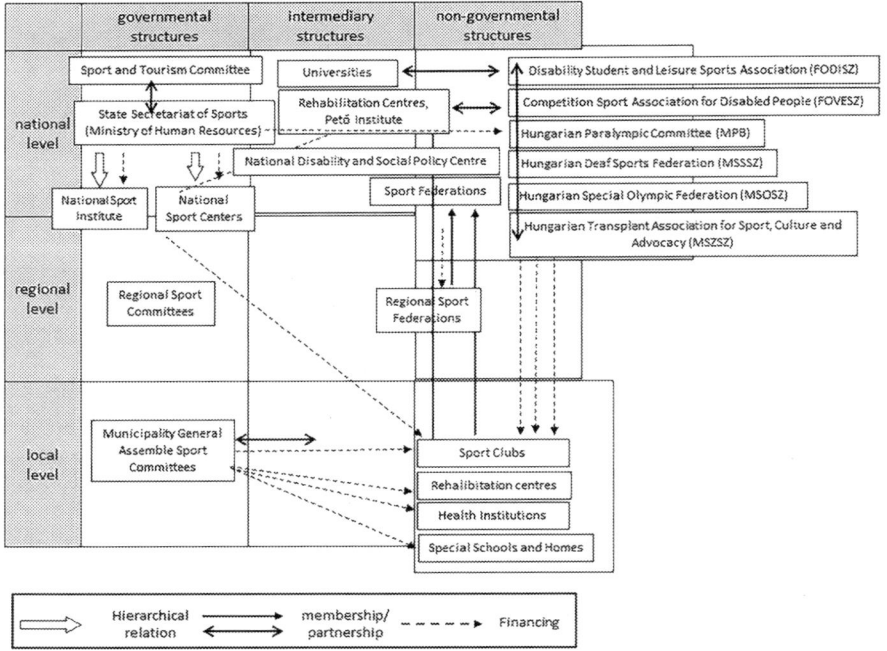

Fig. 17.1 Disability sports framework for Hungary. *As of June 2022 the State Secretariat of Sports from the Ministry of Human Resources was transferred under the Ministry of Defence. Source: Developed by author as an adaptation to disability sport using Perényi (2013)

Deputy State Secretary for Disability Sport. Disability sport structure follows the logic of able bodied sport in Hungary at governmental and non-governmental levels, with intermediary sections (Fig. 17.1).

Governmental Agents

At a governmental level, several platforms are responsible to secure rights for people with disabilities as declared in the Constitution of Hungary. The first level is a ministerial level; the second is the committees of the Parliament of Hungary; and the third is a right protection agency to control the first two. The Ministry of National Resources (EMMI, Emberi Erőforráspok Minisztériuma) is the supreme body where the issues for people with disabilities are represented at the highest level. In particular, the Secretary of State for Social Affairs and Social Inclusion is responsible for promoting the professional concept of legislation on equal opportunities for people with disabilities, the rights of people with disabilities and the provision of equal opportunities. Sport for people with disabilities is overseen by the State Secretariat of Sports. Standing Committees of the Parliament include the Subcommittee on People with Disabilities and the Sports and Tourism Committee. Governmental agencies such as the National Sport Institute and the National Sports

Centres are responsible for issues related to sport for people with disabilities. The same applies to regional sports committees and municipality sports committees at the local level.

At the state level, the issue of disability appears in the standing committees and non-profit organisations, which, together with the stakeholders, are responsible for the implementation of equal opportunities and social acceptance of people with disabilities. There is a disability-specific non-governmental organisation for each branch of disability.

Intermediate Agents

Intermediate organisations function in Hungary as link between governmental and non-governmental agents. For example, the National Disability and Social Policy Centre Nonprofit Ltd (Nemzeti Fogyatékosságügyi- és Szociálpolitikai Központ Közhasznú Nonprofit Kft. formerly known as Nonprofit Ltd for Equal Opportunities for Disabled Persons) aims to promote the widest possible social acceptance and complex rehabilitation of the disabled through its professional programmes. Based on the principle of *"nothing about us, without us"*, it works closely with advocacy and professional organisations, national and international professionals and institutions of people with disabilities (OFP, 2015).

The Klebelsberg Centre (KLIK, Klebelsberg Központ) offers all students with disabilities access to sport activities of their choice through functions of the Competition Database (VESPA) since 2008. There are currently more than 9000 registered students (Act CLXXII, 2011, 2018; Act XXXIX, 2019). The integration of students with disabilities into sports is accomplished in cooperation with the National Association of Students and Leisure Sports for the Disabled (FODISZ, Fogyatékosok Diák-, és Szabadidősport Szövetség).

Within schools and between schools in special education, competition-like sporting events provide regular physical activities, training and competition opportunities. Those interested or talented may join integrated sports clubs, special clubs or student sports clubs. Persons with disabilities have the opportunity to engage in physical activity in health and rehabilitation centres and through subscribed rehabilitation processes as part of the available framework for sports preparation. However, in some cases, a lack or shortage of available integrated options, material conditions (accessibility) or personnel (trained professionals) hinder participation. Similarly to adult sport, student sport is organised on the basis of competitive logic (Nemzeti köznevelésről szóló 2011. évi törvény; Kőpatakiné, 2009; Sáringerné Szilárd, 2015).

In recent years higher education institutions have offered courses for disabled students and created the circumstances for them. In 2019 the University of Physical Education (TE, Testnevelési Egyetem), in cooperation with the NPC (National Paralympic Committee), introduced the inclusive sports trainer training programme among other sport-related training programmes. By doing so it acknowledged that students with disabilities have special needs in PE classes and these can be fulfilled by suitably qualified professionals. Specialised training for sports serving people with disabilities means a focal point to change how sports professionals think about sport and inclusion and creates higher prestige and acceptance for both athletes and professionals (Tóthné Kälble et al., 2015; Csányi, 2001; Csányi et al., 2004; Orbán-Sebestyén et al., 2018).

Non-governmental Agents

Non-governmental organisations in Hungary exist in each of the disability categories not only in general, but also specifically in sport for relevant groups. There are several large umbrella organisations in the country, which are not sports organisations, but they also have tasks and activities in relation to physical activities and leisure sports for people with disabilities. They use sport as an instrument in their activities to promote active and healthy living and serve social inclusion and personal development goals. Sports umbrella organisations in Hungary function to specifically cater sport for people with disabilities. After the political changes in 1989, the Hungarian Sports Federation for the Disabled and the Hungarian Special Olympics Association were formed. International sports and sports diplomacy influenced the Hungarian developments in the area. In 1983, Hungary joined the International Sports Organisation for the Disabled. In 1986, they organised the World Sitting Volleyball Championships and in 1991 the third general meeting of the IPC was held in Budapest.

Today the following umbrella organisations function in Hungarian disability sports, noting that some of them were reorganised over the years or continued operation as new organisations (Fig. 17.1):

1. Disability Student and Leisure Sports Association (FODISZ, Fogyatékosok Diák-, és Szabadidősport Szövetség) incorporating the abolished the National Sports Federation for the Disabled (FONESZ Fogyatékosok Nemzeti Sportszövetsége)
2. Competition Sport Association for Disabled People (FOVESZ, Fogyatékosok Versenysport Szövetsége) incorporating the abolished The Hungarian Sports Federation of Visually Impaired and Disabled Persons (MLMS, Magyar Látássérültek és Mozgáskorlátozottak Sportszövetsége) and the Hungarian Parasport Association (MPSZ, Magyar Parasport Szövetség)
3. Hungarian Paralympic Committee (MPB, Magyar Paralimpiai Bizottság)
4. Hungarian Deaf Sports Federation (MSSSZ, Magyar Siketek Sportszövetsége)
5. Hungarian Special Olympic Association (MSOSZ, Magyar Speciális Olimpiai Szövetség)
6. Hungarian Transplant Association for Sport, Culture and Advocacy (MSZSZ, Magyar Szervátültetettek—Országos Sport, Kulturális és Érdekvédelmi—Szövetsége)

The above sports umbrella organisations have members nationwide. In all disability categories there are altogether 470 sports organisations, mostly sports clubs, out of which 124 are located in the capital (26%). Disability-specific or integrated assistance to affected persons and their families is available throughout the country—see more under "Sport Participation".

The Sports Association of Students with Disabilities (FODISZ) provides school and student sports by organising and conducting local and national championships. Initially, disability-specific sports associations were formed. After this, they merged, and in 2012, the Competition Sport Association for Disabled People (FOVESZ) took over the management (HOC, 2012). FODISZ organises 450 events a year with its county member organisations, most of which are leisure sports events (150–300). However, they are also connected to the ascendant Olympiad. Some 200 sports professionals work in these competitions across the country and involve around 8000 children and young people in 50 locations and 12 sports. FODISZ assists sports organisations to obtain competition licences. Hungarian leisure sports events organise a "chance" race for people with disabilities, so they can participate in able bodied sporting events (Fótiné Hoffmann et al., 2015; Hungarian Olympic Committee, 2012).

The Hungarian Paralympic Committee (MPB, Magyar Paralimpiai Bizottság), established in 1991, operates independently as a sports umbrella organisation overseeing the national teams and Paralympic participation for people with disabilities (Perényi, 2013). Its structure, roles, functions and rights are very similar to the Olympic Committee. However, its funding is downscaled for its needs, but acknowledging that financial support is raising year by year. MPB is a member of the International Paralympic Committee (IPC) and represents and assists goals, symbols and the Paralympic movement. It also cooperates with national sports organisations for the different disability groups, sports federations and sports clubs listed above. The MPB also has the responsibility of ensuring accessibility to sports facilities, particularly ensuring sports training centres have the capacity to receive athletes with disabilities for training and competition, but also facilitating spectator accessibility to facilities and information. The MPB also has the responsibility to provide sports for students with disabilities and leisure sport in general. In this undertaking it cooperates with governmental and other non-governmental organisations. It also helps these organisations with their international competition procedures (Nádas, 2018a, 2018b).

Sport for people with *hearing impairments* is organised by the Hungarian Hearing Impaired Sports Association (MHSSZ) founded in 1997, which took over the role of the Sports Committee of the Hungarian Deaf established in 1968 by 7 sports clubs and 19 county organisations. The MHSSZ is the central national governing body of physical education and sport for deaf and hard-of-hearing people living in Hungary. The organisation is a member of the International Committee of Sports for the Deaf (ICSD) and the European Deaf Sports Organisation (EDSO). It currently has 43 member organisations in 17 sports. The biggest sports club in Hungary is the *Deaf Sports Club in Budapest*. Teams regularly participate in leagues along with hearing players and occasionally organise tournaments (e.g. mixed volleyball) that anyone can enter. The majority of deaf/hard-of-hearing students and athletes participate in national competitions in an integrated way (Tóthné Kälble, 2019).

Sports for the *visually impaired* is organised by the Blind Students' Sports Union since 1999. This organisation provides sporting opportunities for the visually impaired in five special institutions, seven classes in national and international competitions. It also organises exhibition competitions as part of social recognition and integration. From 2008, a joint competition started for pupils in integrated schools. It became a member of the Hungarian Handball Federation (MKSZ, Magyar Kézilabda Szövetség) and the Budapest Sports Federation for People with Disabilities. The Parasport Subcommittee of the MKSZ helps to organise the competitions, but also leisure sport gains increasing popularity (Nádas, 2018a, 2018b).

Secondary Agents

Two higher education institutions—Eötvös Loránt University Bárczi Gusztáv Faculty of Special Needs Education and Semmelweis University Pető András Faculty—started training professionals to support people with disabilities. There are several organisations, such as rehabilitation centres, special schools and care facilities in Hungary that play a role in the recruitment or referral of participants and are involved in training coaches for disability sport but do not have direct policy formulation impact on disability sport. These organisations, however, create sport programmes for people with disabilities and influence these programmes through the education of professionals or by helping people with disabilities. Here mostly universities shall be mentioned, particularly the University of Physical Education with its recent (2019) special training programme for professionals working in the sector as PE teachers or coaches. Another fine example is the Pető Institute based on the conductive pedagogy method, which is an internationally acknowledged educational system. Its habilitation and rehabilitation procedure was developed by András Pető (1893–1967) in the 1940s. Since 1963 in the Mozgássérültek Nevelő- és Képzőintézete (Training and Educational Institute for the Physically Disabled) professionals, so-called conductors, are trained for the treatment of children having suffered brain damage or dysfunction during or immediately after birth, or as a result of an injury or a stroke. By applying Pető's methodology and with the assistance of a specially trained teacher (the conductor) disabled persons of any age will have a chance to solve the tasks of life independently by active learning throughout the educational process.

Currently, the practice-oriented four-year conductor training is offered at the Pető András Faculty of Semmelweis University. In its own training institutes at the kindergarten and school level, it performs public education, rehabilitation and habilitation tasks, providing early development and adult rehabilitation. Due to its originality and uniqueness, the Pető Method was the first to win the Intellectual Hungaricum title in the Hungaricum Klub qualification system. It also received the Hungarian Heritage Award and Prima Primissima Award in 2013. Started in 1958 based on sports journalist votes the "Athlete of the Year" title is awarded in Hungary annually; since the year of 2000 athletes in Paralympic sports are also acknowledged for their achievements. Since 2013 FMSZ organises a day of "Acceptance-Sports-Activities" in which students in higher education may try parasports and meet para-athletes.

Steering of Disability Sport

Legislative Framework

The Ministry of Human Resources is the responsible governmental organisation for overseeing and guaranteeing the rights of people with disabilities. That includes the tasks given to the State Secretariat of Sport to create the adequate legal environment necessary for equal opportunities for people with disabilities in sport. Act I. 2004 on Sport, followed by its amendments (2011, 2018, 2019), regulates sporting opportunities for people with disabilities both in competitions and in leisure sports. As it states, "Disability sports federations are national sports federations set up for offering sports activities, following the basic injury-specific disability branches and are used for competition and leisure for people with disabilities" (Act I, 2004). Accordingly, the injury-specific federations are subject to the provision of the rights and obligations laid down in this law and other legislation for "securing sports participation and sports competition for people with the different categories of disabilities" (Amendments of 2004 Act on Sports), as summarised in Fig. 17.1.

Disability sport–related legislation, however, must consider general legal frameworks and control units in Hungary for disability issues. Therefore, the Equal Opportunities Act of 1998 (Act XXVI, 1998) and the National Disability Council (OFT, Országos Fogyatékosügyi Tanács), which are responsible for reviewing legislation affecting people with disabilities, should be considered during legislative procedures. OFT has delegates from government agencies, national NGOs and smaller organisations functioning in the area of sport, culture, employment and advocacy and has the responsibility to propose decisions and programmes and initiate discussions.

In the case of building new sport facilities, the Government Decree (OTÉK) on national urban planning and construction requirements 253/1997 (XII. 20) prohibits deviation of accessible usability for all. The 2008 Amendment of OTÉK was a very important step towards accessibility because it significantly expanded and detailed the rules for barrier-free design in urban planning including facilities in general, thus, in sports as well. Sport and the training of sports professionals in higher education must apply to the National Public Education Act (Act CXC of 2011, amended in 2014) and the National Higher Education Act (Act CCIV, 2011). This ensures no discrimination, provides advantages in considerations for persons with disabilities and also orders institutional tasks in relation to services offered. The allocation of 1% of personal income tax also applies to sports and leisure organisations including those in disability sport (Act CXXVI of 1996, Act 4/A. Sect (1)).

Policy Framework

From 2000, the Deputy State Secretariat for Disability Sport began addressing the role of sport for people with disability. In general sport was acknowledged to serve health prevention, health and professional development, but also talent management in sport and athletic careers and overall in society. Such policy aspects have been implemented widely also for disability sports. For example, in 2017 the Hungarian Parliament appointed national days to celebrate disability sports. February 22 became the Hungarian Parasport Day, while June 4 the Sports Day of the Deaf. From 1984, the "Do sport with us!" competition was held annually with the participation of 200–300 children with disabilities each year. Since 2009, this competition has gained an international momentum under the new name "Playing Without Borders." Since 2010, a "Movement Improvement Cup" was held to prepare athletes for Paralympic sports and for skill competitions.

The promotion of rehabilitation sports, student sports and leisure and competitive sports became the focus also for people with disabilities. For example, the "MERI Sports Day" (Brave) is organised annually to promote sports for people with reduced mobility showcasing a diversity of sports that are available for people with disabilities. At the event, tryouts are assisted by professional help for all types of disability groups. The annual event started as a joint programme of the National Association of Disabled People's Associations (MEOSZ) and the National Institute of Medical Rehabilitation (OORI) in 2008, and the programme was supported by the Hungarian Paralympic Committee from the beginning. From 2017 onwards, the National Association of Students and Leisure Sports for the Disabled (FODISZ) also participated in the event.

The policy also promotes fair play and integration. For example, it is possible to adapt sport for deaf athletes through football referees waving flags and start whistles being replaced by light signals when running and swimming. To further emphasise equal access and integration, nowadays, there are deaf judges who communicate in sign language in the same way as most athletes; and sign language interpreters also assist in communication among participants. The participation of deaf athletes is regulated in integrated sports. Athletes with hearing loss of at least 55 decibels in both ears are allowed to participate in competitions using only their natural hearing capacities in competitions; thus, athletes are not allowed to wear hearing aids, or cochlear implants.

Financial, Governance and Managerial Support

Financial Framework

In the year 2000, the Ministry of Sports created a State Secretariat for the sports of persons with disabilities and the leadership position was filled by a former Olympic and Paralympic Champion fencer, Pál Szekeres. Besides the attention raised for disability sports, funding channels also opened up at an unprecedented manner. Clubs and federations received funding for equipment, facilities, training and competition costs. The funding was raised year by year, and the circumstances for sport became much better for people with all kinds of disabilities.

The disability sport was addressed in the scheme of the 2010 new sport funding system as well. This process also reached the structures and organisations, but the clearer structure allowed for more transparent mechanisms and a base for receiving funding for delegated tasks for organisations. The "tax-benefit" scheme given to companies, called "TAO" (Bardóczy, 2012) in case of the first five (2011–2017), then the six (since 2018) ball sports (football, basketball, handball, ice hockey and water polo, volleyball), also provides for the disability sports such as wheelchair basketball or sitting volleyball. All sporting facilities—such as artificial football turfs, arenas for basketball and handball, ice rinks and swimming pools—are built and renovated (Géczi & Bardóczy, 2017) to serve people with disabilities. All other funding programmes, such as the programme for 16 successful Olympic sports or the remedial funding programme for 20 other Olympic and non-Olympic sports take inclusive consideration for athletes with different disabilities as well.

Funding for disability sports has also grown over the years. As Table 17.4 shows, the total funding available for disability sports grew by more than 60% between 2018 and 2020. It should be mentioned, however, that the funding available for disability sports is much less than for sport in general; proportionate statistics in reflection to the proportion of the population is not available. Within disability sport also as in Olympic sports, the one-third two-thirds share is applied (Perényi & Bodnár, 2015; Perényi, 2020), sports included in the programme of the Paralympic Games receive higher share from the available funding. It should be emphasised, however, that the allocation of financial support shows more diversity in terms of targeted goals, organisations and causes. The proportion of allocated available funding between Paralympic and non-Paralympic sports shows less of a difference. Starting from 2005 the proportions stabilised around the two-thirds and one-third levels in favour of Paralympic sports (Fig. 17.2).

Funding available for the Paralympic sports through the Hungarian Paralympic Committee also shows a large increase over the past 15 years. As Fig. 17.2 shows over 4.5 times more funding helped Paralympic athletes in 2020 than in 2005.

Hungarian disability sport (SO, MPB, FODISZ) is supported by the state through the State Secretariat of Sports (EMMI) today. FODISZ and SO receive state funding

Table 17.4 Available state funding for disability sports (in million Euro) between 2018 and 2020

State support for disability sports	
years	Total funding
2018	1.68
2019	1.78
2020	2.71

Source: MPB (Hungarian Paralympic Committee)

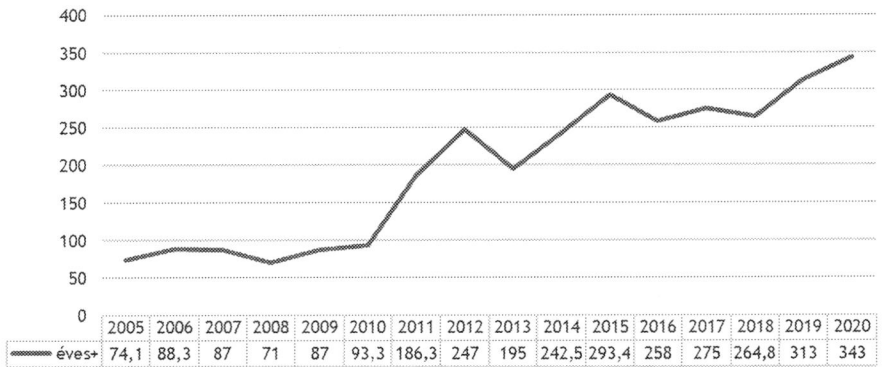

Fig. 17.2 State support for the Hungarian Paralympic Committee (MPB) between 2005 and 2020 in million HUF. Source: MPB (Hungarian Paralympic Committee)

through the Hungarian Paralympic Committee (MPB), but sponsors and tender funds also assist its operation.

Level of Integration of Inclusion

The status and the prestige of being a Paralympic athlete have increased in sport and in society. Performance at the Paralympic Games is compensated by increasing attention in the media and equal remuneration to Olympic athletes. Inclusion and integration is in focus; people with disabilities can participate in sport freely and they are able to become members of a regular sports club. They participate in activities together with able bodied people in an increasing manner (Nádas, 2018a, 2018b).

The website and the YouTube channel of the Hungarian Paralympic Federation also function as a knowledge centre. They distribute training and coaching materials and create films and books on athletes and coaches. They also develop guidelines on how clubs can implement overall policy items. Disability sports are also promoted in schools, the performance of para-athletes is acknowledged and the "National Parasport and the National Deaf Sport Day" was enacted.

The fact that sports federations also connected with the disability sport system facilitates integrative sport opportunities for people with disabilities. This way they provide sporting opportunities in their facilities for people with disabilities and also organise competitive events, especially in fencing, swimming, volleyball, basketball and hand(goal)ball.

Paralympic athletes are integrated into general athlete support schemes as well, and they are included in programmes created for talented athletes such as the "Sports Stars," the Sport XXI. and the Heracles programmes (SportXXI, 2007). In these programmes, talented Olympic and Paralympic athletes can gain financial support for both their sport and educational endeavours. The prize money for medals won in world and continental championships and the Olympic Games also refers to the Paralympic Games. The coaches of para-athletes are included in the "Gerevich" scholarship fund and in the "state coach" programme run by the National Society of Coaches (MET, Magyar Edzők Társasága).

17.4 Sport Participation by People with Disabilities

Monitoring and Evaluation

A systematic monitoring system of Hungarian sport is still lacking. Currently, a national sport information system is still under development, and therefore more in-depth data describing the population is not available. Similar to the able bodied sport system, athletes compete with competition licences. However, in disabled sport the umbrella organisations of respective sports keep track of the number of athletes.

The evaluation system is based on the performance of athletes in international competitions and the Paralympic, Deaf-Mute or Special Olympic Games. Hungarian athletes with disabilities won a total of 144 medals altogether at Paralympics Games (gold: 31; silver: 50; bronze: 63) and 129 medals at Deaf and Mutes Games (Siketlimpia) (gold: 47; silver: 46; bronze: 36). Monitoring programmes on disability sport for inclusion, sport stimulation or sports participation at grass roots level are also lacking. Developments towards setting up monitoring programmes in a systematic and structured way are expected in the near future.

For control and citizen protection, organisations protecting equal opportunities and human rights exist in Hungary for sports. These include the Equal Treatment Authority (EBH, Egyenlő Bánásmód Hatóság), the Hungarian Helsinki Committee (MHB, Magyar Helsinki Bizottság) and the Society for Civil Liberties (TASZ, Társaság a Szabadságjogokért).

Sport Participation

Survey data for disability sports is very limited. Participation numbers are recorded by sports umbrella organisations and sports federations. Based on the administration of the five main umbrella sports organisations for people with disabilities, the total number of athletes with a competition permit in 2016 was 16,665, out of which FODISZ counted the largest population with 13,426 athletes (Table 17.5).

Competitions are mostly held by disability sports federations and their member organisations, sports clubs in most cases. In some sports, athletes with disabilities also participate in the able bodied competition system, as the international trend towards integrative competition was also received with willingness in Hungary as

Table 17.5 Total number of participants affiliated with disability sports umbrella organisations (year of 2018)

Umbrella organisations in disability sports	Persons with disabilities
Paralympic sports (all sports)	908
MSOSZ	1759
MSZSZ	215
FODISZ	13,426
MHSSZ	357
Total	16,665

Source: MPB (Hungarian Paralympic Committee)

stated before. Accordingly, federations also keep track of athletes with disabilities as demonstrated in Table 17.6. Although majority of athletes with disabilities are registered in disability sports federations, it seems that the number of athletes registered in sports federations is balanced between Budapest and the rest of the country. While sports federations provide more opportunities for elite and competitive athletes, less competitive and performance-oriented sport happens in connection to disability sports organisations. Umbrella organisations, such as FODISZ or the Special Olympic organisation, register the majority of their athletes in the countryside (Gősi, 2017) providing sporting opportunities from grass roots level to elite for people with disabilities.

People with disabilities are also increasingly participating in mass sporting events such as street running events and marathons. As part of CSR activities and event sponsors, increasing opportunities and awareness are given for disability sport, for example in the Budapest marathon and half-marathon (Perényi & Bodnár, 2015). Runners also support relevant causes through their participation (Gősi, 2017).

Barriers and Facilitators

The biggest barrier for people with disabilities to take part in sport is the concern for their health condition, followed by the lack of confidence in exploring their abilities in an alternative following their injury. Additionally, a lack of information for parents of children with disabilities can be noticed. All these concerns are tackled by increasing sources of information available for all parties involved. Rehabilitation centres and civil organisations are offered for people with disabilities and their parents, where they are oriented and assisted in the process of how to find the right sport and how to include that sport as part of their rehabilitation later in their life. Also, in informal groups families and individuals helping each other, mentors and role models are emerging across all disability groups. Through this process several persons with disabilities become engaged with sports clubs where sport professionals, including coaches, will support them to enter regular sporting activities and, as soon as it is adequate for them, sports competitions (Nádas, 2018a, 2018b).

Table 17.6 Total number of registered participants with disabilities[a] in national sports federations with capital and countryside breakdown (2018)

Name of national federations	Total number of participants	Capital (Budapest)	Countryside
Sport-specific federations			
Hungarian Tennis Federation	4	4	0
Hungarian Dance Sport Federation	4	4	0
Hungarian Triathlon Federation	7	3	4
Hungarian Taekwondo Federation	8	8	0
Hungarian Cycle Sports Federation	8	5	3
Hungarian Rugby Federation	12	12	
Hungarian Curling Federation	14	14	0
Hungarian Shooting Federation	15	8	7
Hungarian Ski and Snowboard Federation	15	10	4
Hungarian Track and Field Federation	28	3	25
Hungarian Powerlifting Federation	29	29	0
Hungarian Kayak-canoe Federation	30	15	15
Hungarian Basketball Federation	32	10	22
Hungarian Fencing Federation	34	13	21
Hungarian Bowling Teke Federation	42	16	26
Hungarian Rowing Federation	52	27	25
Hungarian Swimming Federation	59	33	26
Hungarian Table tennis Federation	60	36	24
Hungarian Judo Federation	66	21	45
Hungarian Skander Federation	84	61	23
Hungarian Handball Federation (goalball)	91	41	40
Hungarian Volleyball Federation	96	23	63
Hungarian Boccia Federation	120	53	67
Umbrella organisations			
Hungarian Transplant-Sport Federation	215	86	129
Hungarian Deaf and Mute Sport Federation	357	166	191
Hungarian Special Olympic Federation	1759	423	1336
FODISZ	13,426	1691	11,735
Total	16,667	2815	13,831

[a]Competitive/elite and grass roots level participants. Source: Nádas (2018a, 2018b)

17.5 Conclusion

By reviewing sports for people with disabilities in Hungary a heroic historical path can be witnessed. The process starting as early as the nineteenth century supported people and recognised the need for physical activity and sports as a tool for their development, health and quality of life. The foundation of the Hungarian Paralympic Committee in 1997, and the establishment of the State Secretariat Office for Disability Sports in 1999 created special attention for disability issues in the sports sector in Hungary. The law of 1998 on equal treatment and equal opportunities was also a very valuable asset in international comparison.

The development process has positively impacted sports for people with disabilities, including the legal and sports financing environment, raising media attention and overall social awareness. As a result, the approaches and considerations of sports for people with disabilities have become more similar to able bodied sports today. Its inner structure reflects both disability groups and the structure of national and international sports federation. It is in contact with government organisations, antidoping authorities, and health and educational institutions, and through the National Paralympic and Special Olympic Committee, it has connection to the Paralympic and Special Olympic Movement. Sports for people with disabilities have become widespread in Hungary as a result of health and social rehabilitation considerations. Even though resources, particularly financial resources, show some revealing differences in comparison to able bodied sports, para-athletes and their trainers are better recognised and remunerated today, and the budget available is increasing yearly.

In general we can state that the current policy system in Hungary stimulates participation of people with disabilities in sport and provides opportunities for those motivated and talented to build an athletic career. The success of disability sport lies in the systematic and strategic approach and cooperation of the different levels of organisations. However, grass roots sport still needs more support and promotion among those in rehabilitation and in general for disability groups. This implies, especially in the current pandemic period, that people with disabilities may be more vulnerable and therefore need to be treated more carefully and with increased attention. Despite this difficult period, which at times involved restrictions on freedom, disability sport was able to function through sports club, registered athletes and closed-door competitions and matches. Although drop-outs were registered and leisure sports suffered, for example, fitness clubs were restricted, open-air activities were encouraged and initiated during the pandemic.

References

Bardóczy, K. (2012). A sportolás hatása a mozgássérült emberek életminőségére [The impact of sports on the quality of life of people with disabilities]. In Vári, A. (szerk.), *Sport és egészség* (pp. 229-240). Budapest: Semmelweis Kiadó.

Czeglédy, K. (2002). *A sportolók mozgásszervi rehabilitációja*. Országos Sportegészségügyi Intézet.

Csányi, Y. (2001). Az együttnevelés fontosabb tényezői, feltételei. Bevezető a sorozathoz. In: Csányi, Y. (Eds.), *Mozgáskorlátozott gyermekek integrált oktatása-nevelése*. Útmutató szülőknek és szakértői bizottságoknak, Fogyatékos Gyermekek, Tanulók Felzárkóztatásáért Országos Közalapítvány, Budapest.

Csányi, Y., Fótiné, H. É., Kereszty, Z. S., Nagyné, K. I., & Willumsen, J. (2004). *Inklúziós tanterv és útmutató a magyarországi pedagógusképzés számára.* GYISM, OM.
Csányi, Y., & Keresty, Z. S. (2009). *Inklúziós tanterv és útmutató a magyarországi pedagógusképzés számára* Oktatási segédanyag. Aktualizált kiadás. SzCSM, Budapest.
Fejes, A. (1984). Az emberi rehabilitáció hazai úttörője, dr. Halassy Olivér. In Mozgáskorlátozottak Országos Szövetsége (szerk.), *Halassy Olivér* (1909-1983): Emlékkönyv. Budapest: Magyar Paralimpiai Bizottság.
Gál, A., Dóczi, T., & Sáringerné Szilárd, Z. S. (2014). A fizikai aktivitás és a sport magyarországi dimenzióinak feltárása. Társadalmi befogadás a sportban és a sport által (szociális inklúzió). *Összegző tanulmány a TÁMOP 6.1.2/11 sz. c. projekt keretében végzett kutatás eredményeiről.* 156 oldal.
Géczi, G., & Bardóczy, G. (2017). Tendency of Hungarian sport facilities development between 2010 and 2016. *Magyar Sporttudományi Füzetek XVI. A sportirányítás gazdasági kérdései,* 78–90.
Gősi, Z. S. (2017). A sportszövetségek bevételi szerkezetének és vagyonának változása 2011-2015 között. *Magyar Sporttudományi Füzetek XVI. A sportirányítás gazdasági kérdései,* 91–99.
Fótiné, H. É., Berencsi, A., Lénárt, Z., Tóthné Kälble, K., & Vámos, T. (2015). Nemzetközi kitekintés az inkluzív testneveléssel kapcsolatos kutatásokra a sajátos nevelési igényű tanulók szemszögéből. In L. Révész & T. Csányi (Eds.), *Tudományos alapok a testnevelés tanításához. II. kötet: A testnevelés és az iskolai sport neveléstudományi, pszichológiai és kommunikációs szempontú megközelítései.* Magyar Diáksport Szövetség.
Juhász, F. (2004). *Irányelvek a funkcióképesség, a fogyatékosság és a megváltozott munkaképesség véleményezéséhez.* Medicina Könyvkiadó.
Kálmán, Z., & Könczei, G. (2002). *A Taigetosztól az esélyegyenlőségig* (p. 19). Osiris.
Könczei, G. (2006). *A fogyatékosság definíciója Európában—összehasonlító elemzés.* ELTE, Bárczi Gusztáv Gyógypedagógiai Főiskolai Kar.
Kőpatakiné, M. M.. (2009). Az együttműködés magyarországi gyakorlata—A nemzetközi együttműködés első tapasztalatai. *Oktatáskutató és Fejlesztő Intézet.* http://www.ofi.hu/tudastar/reszorszagos/egyuttmukodes
Kőpatakiné, M. M. (2004). Közben felnő egy elfogadó nemzedék. *Új Pedagógiai Szemle, 54*(2), 38–48.
Marton, K. (2008). Rejtőzködő fogyatékos-közösségek és a többségi társadalom. *Világosság, 11–12,* 233–239.
Nádas, P. (2018a). *Árnyékban született csillagok. Paralimpiatörténeti tanlmányok I* (Vol. Meosz, pp. 1–483). Magyar Paralimpiai Bizottság.
Nádas, P. (2018b). *Árnyékban született csillagok. Paralimpiatörténeti tanlmányok II* (Vol. Meosz, pp. 499–931). Magyar Paralimpiai Bizottság.
Nádas, P., & Kőpatakiné, M. M. (2008). Fogyatékossággal kapcsolatos fogalmak- pedagógiai szempontból. In *Ismerkedő könyv. A paralamipai sportágak- társadalmi befogadás- szemléletváltás* (p. 144).
Orbán-Sebestyén, K., Sáringerné Szilárd, Z., & Hunyadi, K. (2018). Inkluzív sportoktatás az integrált szemléletű nevelésben—A Testnevelési Egyetem Inkluzív sportoktatói szakirányú továbbképzésének előzményei. *Testnevelés, Sport, Tudomány, 3*(1–2), 73–78.
Pálhegyi, F. (1987). A fogyatékosság bélyegének pszichodinamikája. In F. Pálhegyi (Ed.), *A gyógypedagógiai pszichológia elméleti problémái* (pp. 79–86). Tankönyvkiadó.
Perényi, S. (2013). Hungary. In K. Hallmann & K. Petry (Eds.), *Comparative sport development—System, participation and public policy* (pp. 87–99). Springer.
Perényi, S. (2020). Hungary: Potentials for civil initiatives in sports, 151–182. In Siegfried Nagel, Karsten Elmose-Østerlund, Bjarne Ibsen, Jeroen Scheerder (eds.) *Functions of sports clubs in European societies a cross-National Comparative Study,* 385. Springer International Publishing, Sports and economics management and policy, Springer Switzerland AG.

Perényi, S., & Bodnár, I. (2015). Sports clubs in Hungary. In C. Breuer, R. Hoekman, S. Nagel, & H. van der Werff (Eds.), *Sport clubs in Europe, a cross-national comparative perspective* (Sports economics, management and policy) (pp. 221–247). Springer.

Perényi, S., Szerovay, M., Bodnár, I. (2017). HUNGARY: Filling the Gaps in the Strategic State Sector. In Antti, Laine; Hanna, Vehmas (Eds.), *The Private Sport Sector in Europe: A Cross-National Comparative Perspective* (pp. 18, 175–192). Cham, Svájc: Springer International Publishing.

Sáringerné Szilárd Zs. (2015). *Mozgásos tevékenységek összetett képességfejlesztő hatása inkluzív óvodáskorú közösségben*. Kiadó: Dr. Molnár Andrea, Ovi-Foci Közhasznú Alapítvány 2015. 50 oldal Dr, Molnár Andrea, Ovi-foci Közhasznú Alapítvány 2015. ISBN 978–963–12-2356-9.

Sipos-Onyestyák, N., Perényi, S., Farkas, J., Gősi, Z., & Kedelényi-Gulyás, E. (2019). Az európai sportágazati szakember-fejlesztés lehetőségei: az ESSA-Sport projekt bemutatása és előzetes, eredményei. *Testnevelés, Sport, Tudomány, 4*(1–2), 47–59.

Stocker, M., & Szabó, T. (2017). A hazai sportirányítás szerepe és tevékenysége a kiemelt hazai sportesemények esetében. *Magyar Sporttudományi Szemle, 18*(73), 21, 56–77.

Tauber, Z. (1991). A mozgássérült sportolók rehabilitációjának történeti áttekintése Magyarországon. In Péter, I. (szerk.), *Mozgáskorlátozottak sportja* (pp. 15–28). Budapest: Országos Mozgássérültek Rehabilitációs Központja.

Tóthné Kälble, K. (2019). *Szakirodalmi áttekintés a sajátos nevelési igényű tanulók fittségi vizsgálatairól. A NETFIT® sajátos nevelési igényű gyermekekre történő adaptációjának megalapozása*. Magyar Diáksport Szövetség, Budapest. Retrieved, August 23, 2020, from https://www.researchgate.net/publication/338449679_

Tóthné Kälble, K., Fótiné, H. É., Lénárt, Z., Kälbli, K., Fótiné, H. É., & Lénárt, Z. (2015). Az adaptált fizikai aktivitás és az adaptált testnevelés fejlődése és jelentéstartalmának sokszínűsége a nemzetközi és hazai színtéren. In L. Révész & T. Csányi (Eds.), *Tudományos alapok a testnevelés tanításához. II. kötet: A testnevelés és az iskolai sport neveléstudományi, pszichológiai és kommunikációs szempontú megközelítései*. Magyar Diáksport Szövetség.

Tóthné Kälble, K., Lénárt, Z., Berencsi, A., Fótiné, H., Vámos, T., Lénárt, Z., Berencsi, A., Fótiné, É., & Vámos, T. (2014). A fogyatékos személyek iránti pozitív attitűd szerepe az inkluzív testnevelés oktatásban. *Magyar Sporttudományi Szemle, 15*(58), 65.

Fónagy, Z. (2015). *A Pesti Vakok Intézete—A szociális gondoskodás változatai a 19. században*. Retrieved August 16, 2020, from https://mindennapoktortenete.blog.hu/2015/03/29/vakok_intezete_pest

Laws and Documents

EU-COM (2010). Európai fogyatékosságügyi stratégia 2010–2020. M*egújított elkötelezettség az akadálymentes Európa megvalósítása iránt. Európai Bizottság.* http://eur-lex.europa.eu/legal-content/HU/TXT/PDF/?uri=CELEX:52010DC0636&from=ens

Europa-Hungary. (2020). *Political-social-and-economic-background-and-trends of Hungary*. Retrieved August 22, 2020, from https://eacea.ec.europa.eu/national-policies/eurydice/content/political-social-and-economic-background-and-trends-35_hu

European Commission. (2002). *Definitions of disability in Europa—A comparative analysis. 10. Emberi méltóság korlátok nélkül. Méltóképpen másképp Fogyatékosügyi projekt. 201/2. Ájor Projektfüzetek. 45.o.*

Hungarian Olympic Committee. (2012). *A Magyar Olimpiai Bizottság sportfejlesztési irányai és területei 2012*. Budapest.

I1 MEK. (2020). *Az ország fekvése, földrajzi helyzete és határai. Magyar Elektronikus Könyvtár*. Retrieved August 22, 2020, from http://mek.niif.hu/02100/02185/html/99.html

KSH (2011). Central Statistical Agency - *Census 2011*. http://www.ksh.hu/nepszamlalas/?lang=en

KSH (2016a). Central Statistical Agency. http://www.ksh.hu/docs/hun/xftp/idoszaki/mo/mo2016.pdf
KSH (2016b). Central Statistical Agency. *SNI students (Riport sajátos neveklési igényű tanulókról). VÍRISOS a doksi.* Retrieved, August 23, 2020, from https://www.ksh.hu/docs/hun/xftp/idoszaki/oktat/oktatas1819.pdf
KSH (2003). Central Statistical Agency. *Népszámlálás, 12. A fogyatékos emberek helyzete.* KSH.
European Commission (2017). Special Eurobarometer 412. (n.d.). *Sport and physical activity (Wave EB80.2). Brussels: European Commission, Directorate-General for Education, Youth, Sport and Culture.* Accessed December 10 2018, from https://ec.europa.eu/commfrontoffice/publicopinion/archives/ebs/ebs_412_en.pdf
Zöld Könyv. (2005). *"A demográfiai változások kihívása, a nemzedékek közötti szolidaritás új formái"*, 2
Act III. (1993). 1993. évi III. törvény a szociális igazgatásról és szociális ellátásokról.
Act XXVI. (1998). 1998. évi XXVI. törvény a fogyatékos személyek jogairól és esélyegyenlőségük biztosításáról.
Act C. (1999). 1999. évi C. törvény az Európai Szociális Karta kihirdetéséről.
Act CXXV. (2003). 2003. évi CXXV. törvény az egyenlő bánásmódról és az esélyegyenlőség előmozdításáról.
Act XCII. (2007). 2007. évi XCII. törvény a Fogyatékossággal élő személyek jogairól szóló egyezmény és az ahhoz kapcsolódó Fakultatív Jegyzőkönyv kihirdetéséről.
Act CXXV (2009). 2009. évi CXXV. törvény a magyar jelnyelvről és a magyar jelnyelv használatáról.
NEFMI (2011a). 38/2011. (VI. 29.) NEFMI rendelet a Jelnyelvi Tolmácsok Országos Névjegyzékéről.
NEFMI (2011b). 62/2011. (XI.10.) NEFMI rendelet a jelnyelvi tolmácsszolgálatok működésének és a jelnyelvi tolmácsszolgáltatás igénybevételének feltételeiről.
Act CXC (2011). *Act CXC. on children with special needs {törvény a sajátos nevelési igényű gyermekekért} (SNI) CXC for 2011. 4. § 25. "Special Education Need" (SNI, Sajátos Nevelési Igény) Law of CXC for 2011. 4. § 25.*
EMMI32 (2012). Document on children with hearing impered. Ministry of Human Resources, Budapest.
Act LXII (2013). Fogyatékos személyek jogairól és esélyegyenlőségük biztosításáról szóló 1998. évi XXVI. törvény 2013. évi LXII. módosítása. (LXII Act 2013 amendment of Act XXVI 1998 on the rights and equal opportunities of persons with disabilities).
OFP (2015). 1653/2015. (IX.14.) Korm. határozat az Országos Fogyatékosságügyi Program végrehajtásának 2015-2018. évekre vonatkozó Intézkedési Tervéről.
Act I (2004). 2004 Act on Sports and its 2011 & 2018 Amendments (2004. évi I. törvény a sportról, és annak módosításai 2011, 2018).
Act CLXXII. (2011). 2011. évi CLXXII. törvény a sportról szóló 2004. évi I. törvény módosításáról.
Act CLXXII (2018). 2018. évi CLXXII. törvény a sportról szóló 2004. évi I. törvény módosításáról.
Act XXXIX (2019). 2019. évi XXXIX. törvény a sportról szóló 2004. évi I. törvény módosításáról.
Act CXC (2011). A nemzeti köznevelésről szóló 2011. évi CXC. Törvény (2014. módosítás).
Act CCIV. (2011). A nemzeti felsőoktatásról szóló 2011. évi CCIV. törvény (Nftv.)
SportXXI. (2007). 5/2007. (VI. 27.) OGY határozat a Sport XXI. Nemzeti Sportstratégiáról. http://njt.hu/cgi_bin/njt_doc.cgi?docid=110484.156866
Act CLXXII (2011). CLXXII. Törvény. (2011). *CLXXII. Törvény a sportról szóló 2004. évi I. Törvény módosításáról [Act CLXXII amending act I of 2004 on sport].* Accessed November 13, 2018, from http://njt.hu/cgi_bin/njt_doc.cgi?docid=139772.203174

Chapter 18
Disability Sport in Lithuania

Jurate Pozeriene and Diana Reklaitiene

18.1 Introduction

This chapter will provide an overview of disability sport in Lithuania, its structure and policies. The policies and programmes concerning disability sport are realized by public authorities, non-governmental sport organizations and municipalities at different levels, from local to national. However, the level of integration is still not clear and the process continues. Non-governmental organizations at different levels attempt to improve policies and programmes to provide inclusive settings for disability sport, but the process depends on the two largest state organizations—the Ministry of Education, Science and Sports as well as the Ministry of Social Affairs and Labour, which funds national disability sports programmes. Furthermore, we will present what is known about sports participation of people with disabilities in Lithuania and challenges of Lithuanian disability sport.

J. Pozeriene (✉)
Department of Health Promotion and Rehabilitation, Lithuanian Sports University, Kaunas, Lithuania
e-mail: jurate.pozeriene@lsu.lt

D. Reklaitiene
Department of Coaching Science, Lithuanian Sports University, Kaunas, Lithuania
e-mail: diana.reklaitiene@lsu.lt

© The Author(s), under exclusive license to Springer Nature Switzerland AG 2023
C. van Lindert et al. (eds.), *The Palgrave Handbook of Disability Sport in Europe*, https://doi.org/10.1007/978-3-031-21759-3_18

18.2 Country Profile

Characteristics of Lithuania

Lithuania (in Lithuanian: *Lietuva*), officially the Republic of Lithuania (in Lithuanian: *Lietuvos Respublika*), is a country in Eastern Europe, the largest of the three Baltic states. The country is situated along the southeastern shore of the Baltic Sea, to the southeast of Sweden and Denmark. It is bordered by Latvia in the north, Belarus in the east and south, Poland in the south and Kaliningrad region (Russian exclave) to the southwest. Lithuania holds a 90-kilometre-long area of the Baltic Sea coast. As the National Geographic Institute of France confirmed in 1989, the geographic centre of Europe lies just 24 kilometres northwest of Vilnius. Total area of the country is 65,300 sq. km. Nearly one third of the territory is covered by forests, 4.5% by inland waters. There are over 2800 lakes larger than 0.5 hectares in size, and 18 rivers longer than 100 kilometres in Lithuania.

Lithuania has an estimated population of 2.8 million people in 2019; its capital and largest city is Vilnius. Other major cities are Kaunas and Klaipėda. Lithuanians are Baltic people. The official language, Lithuanian, is one of only two living languages (together with Latvian) in the Baltic branch of the Indo-European language family. For further facts and statistics we refer to Table 18.1.

For centuries the southeastern shore of the Baltic Sea was inhabited by various Baltic tribes. In the 1230s the Lithuanian lands were united by Mindaugas, who was

Table 18.1 Facts and statistics of Lithuania

Official Country Name	Lithuania
Area (km^2)	65,300
Capital city	Vilnius
Official EU language	Lithuanian
Population (number of inhabitants)[a]	2,794,090
Ethnic groups	86.4% Lithuanians; 5.7% Poles; 4.5% Russians; 1.5% Belarusians; 1.0% Ukrainians; 0.9% other
Density (inhabitants/km^2)[b] m	43
Political organization	Parliamentary Republic
Structure of the state	Unitary
Number of counties	10
Number of municipalities	60
GDP per capita (US dollars)[b]	18.427
EU Membership	2004
Currency	Euro
Welfare model[c]	Eastern European

Sources: [a]Eurostat (2018), [b]World Economic Outlook Database (October 2020), [c]Lauzadyte-Tutliene et al. (2018)

crowned as the King of the Grand Duchy of Lithuania, the first Lithuanian state, on the 6th of July in 1253. During the fourteenth century, the Grand Duchy of Lithuania was the largest country in Europe: present-day Belarus, Ukraine and parts of Poland and Russia were territories of the Grand Duchy of Lithuania. With the Lublin Union of 1569, Lithuania and Poland formed a voluntary two-state union, the Polish–Lithuanian Commonwealth. The Commonwealth lasted more than two centuries, until neighbouring countries started systematically dismantling it from 1772 to 1795, with the Russian Empire annexing most of Lithuania's territory. In the aftermath of the World War I, Lithuania's Act of Independence was signed on 16 February 1918, declaring the re-establishment of the sovereign state. Starting in 1940, Lithuania was occupied first by the Soviet Union and then by Nazi Germany. As the World War II neared its end in 1944 and the Germans retreated, the Soviet Union reoccupied Lithuania. On 11 March 1990, the year before the break-up of the Soviet Union, Lithuania became the first Soviet republic to declare independence. Lithuania is a parliamentary republic with the head of government—the prime minister—and the head of state—the president—who appoints the prime minister. The Parliament is a single-chamber legislative body. The country is divided into 60 municipalities, with directly elected mayors.

The most important sectors of Lithuania's economy in 2018 were wholesale and retail trade, transport, accommodation and food services (32.2%), industry (21.9%) and public administration, defence, education, human health and social work activities (14.3%) (Official website of the European Union, 2020).

As a country with a long history, pagan roots and a very rich folklore, Lithuania has many old customs that are still practised today. Whether they are about the change of seasons, the celebration of nature, or Christmas and Easter superstitions.

Sport in Lithuania

After Lithuania restored its independence in 1990, all spheres of public life, including sport, faced significant changes and challenges. Lithuania dropped the so-called Soviet Sport Governance Model, which had been based on purely state management and professional sport have not officially existed. The Lithuanian National Olympic Committee (LNOP), which was re-established in 1988, and the newly established Department of Physical Education and Sports near the Government of Lithuania played a great role in reforming the Lithuanian sports system, searching for new directions and making international contacts (National Olympic Committee, 2020). Gradually, the Lithuanian system developed towards the leading European countries sports governance model. A club system was developed according to the example of Western countries, the federations of various sports gained total independence and new non-governmental sports organizations were founded (Cingiene, 2017; Cingienė & Gobikas, 2019).

In 1992, the Constitution of Lithuania (Republic of Lithuania, 1992) was adopted by Lithuanian citizens in the referendum. Article 53 of the Constitution stipulated that the State promotes physical culture in the society and supports sport, meaning sport became a constitutional value in Lithuania. In 1995, the Parliament of Lithuania adopted the Law on Sports and Physical Education, which became the foundation for the legal regulation of sports in Lithuania. The Sports Law divided sports governance functions between the state institutions and non-governmental organization self-governance bodies, laid down legal grounds for professional sport and established the main principles for the organization of sports events. Nevertheless, during the past two years, the governing model of Lithuanian sport system has been redesigned. The Ministry of Education, Science and Sport became responsible for the formation, coordination and implementation of sports policy.

The 2011–2020 National Sports Development Strategy (Government of the Republic of Lithuania, 2014) emphasizes the social mission of sport and the importance of creating conditions to include all social groups into physical education and sports activities. This strategy covers the majority of domains (sport clubs, athlete medical care centres, sports facilities, sport management, sport science, media and other areas) and aims to promote a healthy lifestyle to the broader society and particularly young people. The Strategy has many dimensions, including: recommendations for the general population and elite sports; policy changes to upgrade the infrastructure and urban planning in order to improve opportunities for sport activities; implementation of a clearly formulated national campaign for physical education (PE) and public awareness of physical activity. More specifically, this strategy includes initiatives to encourage young people to participate in voluntary sports activities; recommendations for establishment and implementation of minimum standards for local sports and health infrastructure; environmental changes to encourage children, teenagers and elderly people as well as individuals with disability to participate in sports and provide healthy and active lifestyle.

Currently, sport is regulated by the following laws of the Republic of Lithuania:

- Law on Sport (No. XIII-1540, Republic of Lithuania, 2018)
- Law on the Development of Non-Governmental Organizations (No. XII-717, Republic of Lithuania, 2003)
- Law on Associations (No. XI-1653, Republic of Lithuania, 2015a)
- Law on Charity and Support (No. X-461, Republic of Lithuania, 2005)
- Law on Volunteering (No. XI-1500, Republic of Lithuania, 2011a)
- Law on Local Self-Government (No. XII-883, Republic of Lithuania, 2014)
- Law on the Social Integration of the Disabled (No. IX-2228, Republic of Lithuania, 2004)
- Anti-Doping Convention and Additional Protocol to the Anti-Doping Convention
- International Convention for the Suppression of Doping in Sport

Eurobarometer survey regarding physical activity was carried out for the European Commission and the results showed that 37% of Lithuanians exercise or do sport regularly; 22% of Lithuanians exercise or do sport at least once a week, 15% exercise more than five times a week. About 8% are members of a sport club, only 1% are members of a health/fitness clubs and 6% of another type of club (e.g. employees' club, youth club, school—and/or university related club or other).

Researchers conducted that, in 2016, 80.1% of adolescents were insufficiently physically active (Guthold et al., 2020).

There are 41 national Olympic sports federation in Lithuania. The most popular sports in Lithuania are: basketball, track-and-field athletics and swimming. Sport profile of Lithuania is presented at Table 18.2.

Disability in Lithuania

The United Nations (UN) Convention on the Rights of People with Disabilities and its Optional Protocol (hereinafter referred to as the Convention) was ratified by the parliament of Republic of Lithuania and enacted as the Law on the Ratification of the UN Convention on the Rights of People with Disabilities and its Optional Protocol (2010). But major concepts regarding disability are consolidated in Article 2 of the Law of the Republic of Lithuania on Social Integration of People with Disabilities (IX-2228, 2004):

- *A person with disabilities* is an individual with a disability category, or with less than 55% working capacity and/or with special needs requirements, as recognized under the above Law.
- *Disability* is a long-term deterioration of health due to the disorder of bodily structure and functions and adverse environmental factors, resulting in diminished participation in public life and decreased possibilities of functioning.
- *Working capacity* is individual capacity to implement previously acquired professional competence or acquire new professional competence or perform fewer demanding tasks in terms of professional competence.

Table 18.2 Sport profile of Lithuania

Government Authority Responsible for Sport	Ministry of Education, Science and Sports
Membership sport club (%)	7 (in 2017)
Membership fitness or health centre (%)	1 (in 2014)
Membership socio-cultural club that includes sport in its activities (e.g. employees' club, youth club, school- and university-related club) (%)	Data is not available
Sport participation, at least once a week (%)	27 (in 2014)
Number of national Olympic sport federations	41
Number of sport clubs	approx. 1290
Number of sport club members	23,291
National budget for sport (€ × 1,000,000)	13.6
Local budget for sport (€ × 1,000,000)	0.5
Share of economic value of volunteers in sport in the GDP (%)	0.9

Sources: Special Eurobarometer 4,722,018; Lithuanians statistics, 2018; Ministry of Social Security and Labor, 2018

- *Special need* is the need for special assistance arising from the person congenital or acquired long-term health condition (disability or loss of working capacity) and adverse environmental factors.

The definition of the person with disabilities is also provided in the official document 'Technical Requirements STR 2.03.01:2001 Buildings and territories'—Requirements related to the needs of people with disabilities (Valstybės žinios [Official Gazette], 2001): *people with disabilities*—people with impaired functions of parts of body, including movement, visual, auditory, manipulative disorders, that cause partial or complete restriction for people to move around and have access to environmental elements.

The main legal act regulating the disability assessment system is the Law on the Social Integration of the Disabled. Regarding the law, which entered into force in 2005, significant changes were made regarding the terminology of disability (see Table 18.3) as well as data collection. The Law incorporates new concepts and definitions, introduces new definitions of the 'disabled' and 'disability', substituting the old 'invalid' and 'invalidity'. All discriminative provisions highlighting the exclusiveness of an individual with disabilities were removed. The model of social integration of the disabled was set to be more similar to the models of the EU member states, thus legally enforcing equal rights and opportunities of the disabled in the society.

According to the statistical data of the Ministry of Social Security and Labour (2018), there were 230,609 people with a disability in Lithuania—8.2% of the population in 2018. Since 2012, this number has declined slightly due to emigration, low fertility, healthier lifestyles and improved health care services.

Table 18.3 Changes of disability sports terminology from 1991 until today, from Lithuanian to English

1991	Today
Invalidumas [invalidity]	Neįgalumas [Disability]
Invalidas *[invalid/handicapped]*	Asmuo, turintis negalią/neįgalusis *[Person with a disability/Disabled]*
Vaikai invalidai *[Invalid children]*	Neįgalūs vaikai/vaikai, turintys specialiųjų poreikių *[Children with disabilities/children with special needs]* Moksleiviai, turintys specialiųjų mokymosi poreikių [Students with special educational needs]
Invalidų sportas *[Invalid sport]*	Neįgaliųjų sportas *[Disability sport]*
Sportininkas invalidas *[Invalid athlete]*	Neįgalusis sportininkas *[Athlete with a disability]*
Kūno kultūra specialiosioms grupėms/gydomojo kūno kultūra *[Physical education for special groups/therapeutic physical training]*	Taikomasis fizinis ugdymas/taikomoji fizinė veikla *[Adapted Physical Education/Adapted physical activity]*

Sources: Vasiliauskas and Ivaškienė (2001), Lithuanian Law on the Ratification of the UN Convention on the Rights of Persons with Disabilities (2010)

Statistically, people with disabilities are divided into levels, presenting the concepts of severe, moderate and mild disability, percentage of working capacity and level of special needs:

- People under 18 (with certain exceptions) with a defined level of disability (severe, moderate or mild)
- People of working age with a defined level of working capacity (55% or less)
- People (various age) with a defined level of special needs (constant care, help, purchase and maintenance of a car, reimbursement of transport costs)

Statistics in Lithuania in year 2018 show that distribution in the population of people with disabilities is 55% people with moderate disability, 30% with a mild disability and 15% with severe disability (World Bank group, 2020).

There are no official statistics about people with disabilities regarding the type of disability (hearing, visual, mental, or physical). More statistical data on children with special educational needs is available in Lithuania, which is based on the conclusion of the pedagogical/psychological assessment. Those children have a right to pedagogical, psychological, special–pedagogical, social–pedagogical and special help provision, with special educational and technical aids.

Most children with special education needs as well as with disabilities in Lithuania are educated in regular schools together with their peers without disability (Table 18.4).

With a rapid process of integration of children with a disability into the mainstream educational setting in Lithuania, comprehensive schools have more children, who, in addition to general needs, have special educational needs: the majority of children with special educational needs (88.0%) attend classes with their peers and 2.9% attends special classes in regular schools. About 9.1% attend special schools for the disabled with severe disabilities (Ostasevičienė et al., 2015).

Table 18.4 School setting of children with special needs in Lithuania

	Academic year			
	2015/2016	2016/2017	2017/2018	2018/2019
General education classes (inclusion)	34,032	34,143	34,093	35,711
Special classes in general education settings (partial integration)	986	1023	1110	1159
Special schools	3638	3680	3656	3686
Total	38,656	38,5846	37,860	40,556

Source: Ostasevičienė et al. (2015)

Emergence or Rise of Disability Sport in Lithuania

Organized disability sports in Lithuania started around 1984–1985. The first competition for physically impaired people took place on August 18, 1984 in Pasvalys district. 34 most active disabled people from various Lithuanian cities and districts participated in disc and grenade throws, basketball free throws, pneumatic shooting, weight lifting. The first Sport and Health Club for the Disabled 'Draugystė' was established in 1985 (Vasiliauskas & Ivaškienė, 2001).

After the re-establishment of Lithuania's independence in 1991, fundamental changes started in Lithuanian sports, including the sports for the disabled. A long and difficult process has begun—reorganization of legal framework of sports, establishment of disability sports clubs, medical, social, educational and vocational rehabilitation system has been reorganized too (Vasiliauskas & Ivaškienė, 2001). At the national level, in 1992 the Lithuanian Invalid Affairs Council under the Government of the Republic of Lithuania was established for improvement, development and management of integration process for people with disability. This Council also took responsibilities for disability sports under the umbrella of the National Rehabilitation Programme for the Disabled. From 1994, the Department of Physical Education and Sports near the Government of the Republic of Lithuania took responsibilities for the development of elite disability sports.

18.3 The Disability Sport System

Structure of Disability Sport

Figure 18.1 displays the organization of disability sport in Lithuania at national, regional and local levels.

Governmental Agents

At the national level, the Ministry of Education, Science and Sports is solely responsible for general sport policy formation, coordination and implementation as well as guides disability sport policy, legislation and financing, including sports facility construction.

Department for the Affairs of the Disabled near the Ministry of Social Security is responsible for planning, organization and coordination of tools of social integration of people with disabilities in order to create equal rights and opportunities for disabled people to participate in public life. The Department implements different social programmes, projects and policies including disabilities sports.

At the local level all 60 municipalities (12 cities and 48 districts) are responsible for sports. Sport departments in municipalities play an important role in the

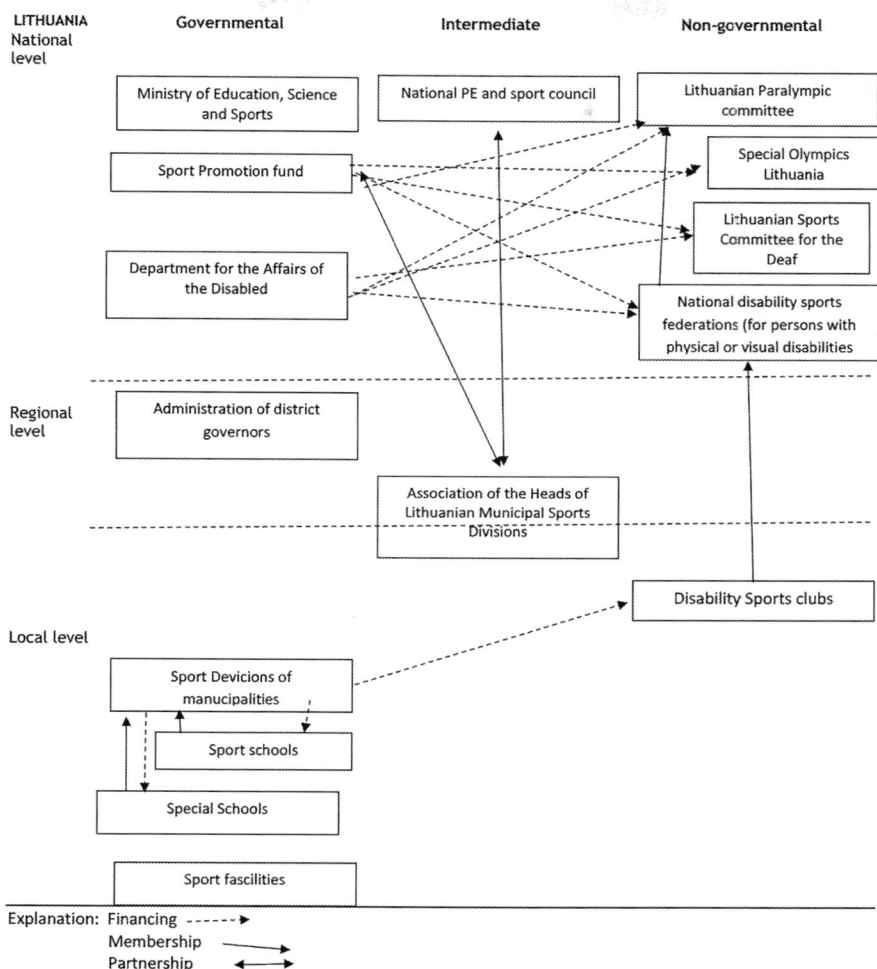

Fig. 18.1 Disability sport structure Lithuania

organization of sport at the local level: they are responsible for the implementation of disability sport policy, for the operation and maintenance of sports facilities, for the funding of sport activities, for awarding some grants and payments to high performance athletes and so on. There are 84 public sports education centres (sport Schools) but only 359 children and youngsters with disabilities are participating in sport activities organized in these centres (Official Statistic Portal, 2020).

Intermediate Agents

The National Physical Education and Sport Council (hereinafter the Council) was established with the aim to encourage the interest of all public administration institutions and non-governmental organizations in physical education and sport as well as their cooperation. The Council consists of representatives of governmental institutions and representatives of non-governmental sport organizations. The Council mainly has an advisory function and is responsible for 'the promotion of physical activity and sport and seek that the development of physical activity and sport would be in compliance with the international regulations on PE and sport' (National Report: Analysis of Labour Market Realities and Challenges in the Sport and Physical Activity Sector, 2019).

The Association of the Heads of Lithuanian Municipal Sports Departments (further—AHLMSD) is the main jurisdiction on the regional level. The association consists of representatives from local councils and from regional/local sport organizations. AHLMSD members can express their opinion and make an impact on the strategic decisions. The president of the Association is also a member of the board of the Sports Financing Fund and the Council (National Report: Analysis of Labour Market Realities and Challenges in the Sport and Physical Activity Sector, 2019).

Non-governmental Agents

The most important non-governmental disability-focused organizations are the Lithuanian Paralympic Committee, the Lithuanians Deaf Sports Association and the Special Olympics Lithuania. The Committee has a traditional way of organizing and governing sports, physical activity and recreation for their members, which are mainly disability-specific clubs.

The Lithuanian Paralympic Committee (LPC) was founded in 1990 and was involved in International Paralympic Committee in 1991 (Lithuanian Paralympic Committee, 2015a). The Committee includes two federations—the Lithuanian Blind Sports Federation (LBSF) and the Lithuanians Sports Federation for the Disabled (LSFD). The federations include around 30 sports clubs with more than 2500 members with disabilities (Lithuanian Paralympic Committee, 2015b). The main objectives of the LPC are to promote, disseminate and to develop the disability sport in Lithuania in partnership with other sport organizations. Also, to coordinate the activities of sport federations, to provide services for disability sport federations, to initiate new programmes, to debate and represent the interests of LPC members (Rėklaitienė et al., 2015).

The Lithuanian Sports Committee for the Deaf (until 2007 the federation) was established in 1990. The Committee is responsible for the sport and physical activity of the deaf and hearing impaired and includes six sport clubs all over Lithuania. The committee involves these sports—badminton, basketball, the Greek Roman wrestling, track and field, table tennis, volleyball and orienteering.

The Special Olympics Lithuanian (SOL) was founded in 1989 and includes seven local clubs, about 38 special schools. The mission of SOL is to provide year-round sports training and athletic competition in a variety of Olympic–type sports for children and adults with an intellectual disability, giving them continuing opportunities to develop physical fitness, demonstrate courage, experience joy and participate in the sharing of gifts, skills and friendship with their families, other Special Olympics athletes and the community. SOL is organizing about 48 competitions per year and other development programmes such as Athlete Leadership, Young Athletes, Unified Sports and so on (Ministry of Social Security and Labour, 2018).

The Lithuanian disability sports organizations covers 23 different sports. Each year, about 100 championships of various sports for disabled are held in the country (in 2017, 97 championships were organized, in 2018, 99), attended by more than 3500 athletes with disabilities; four events were held for schoolchildren and children with disabilities (for example, deaf schoolchildren's games, children's sports competition 'Brave, Strong and Quick', basketball and football tournaments of special education schools), attended by more than 400 children, six to seven health and fitness events (the Lithuanian Disabled Games, Special Olympics of Care Homes, events under the framework of the European Special Olympics Football and Basketball Weeks, summer and winter sports festivals for persons with mobility and visual impairments) attended by nearly 1500 athletes with disabilities. In 2017–2018, 57 different training camps were organized for more than 1000 disabled athletes (Ministry of Social Security and Labour, 2018).

At the local level, there are 105 legal organizations (about 50 sport clubs) across the country, where 2449 people with disabilities do sports (according to the 2018 data). However, the total number of people with disabilities who participate in sports is small and makes up only 2% of all disabled people (Reklaitienė & Poerienė, 2013). In Lithuania, the disabled are not sufficiently encouraged and only few measures are taken to enable them to participate more actively in sports, physical and recreation activities. The sport facilities are also not accessible enough to provide sport activities for disabled on the equal basis with others (Reklaitienė et al., 2016).

Secondary Agents

The Sport for All association founded in 1991 is an independent non-governmental organization uniting 17 voluntary sport associations with around 450 clubs and more than 1800 volunteers (Sport for All association, 2020). The association's main objectives are to enhance people's health and social well-being through physical education and sport, to promote healthy lifestyles and to organize physical education, grassroots sport and recreation activities for people of different age. The association provides clubs with organizational and methodological assistance while organizing competitions, championships, promotion and the organization of joint festivals and workshops.

Steering of Disability Sport

Legislative Framework

One of the most important legislation related to sports, as well as disability sports is the Law on Sports (Lithuanian Republic, 2018). The law defines competencies of Government and municipal institutions regarding the sports sector (Republic of Lithuania, 2018-10-18, XIII-1540). This law

- lays down the principles of sport and regulates the competence of state and municipal institutions in the field;
- regulates the organization of sport and the competences of non-governmental sports organizations;
- controls the training of athletes, development of a system of competitions;
- regulates activities of sports specialists and the basis of the professional sport development; and
- defines principles of the organization of sports competitions and events as well as lays down the requirements for sports facilities.

According to this law, disability sports are based on

(i) equality—the aim is to create conditions for all to participate in sports, without discrimination on the grounds of their disability and social or economic status;
(ii) continuity—state, municipal and non-governmental sports organizations should create appropriate conditions for people with disabilities to be continually involved in sport activities; and
(iii) freedom of choice—it means that individuals with disabilities have the right to choose freely the forms of physical activity and sports, establish associations that unite their members on a sport basis.

In the Lithuanian Law on Education (Xii-2213, 2015b) is written: 'A municipality in which territory the student with special educational needs to reside, shall take care of the accessibility of education environment (for sport and physical education as well) and has an obligation to adapt the school environment, by providing psychological, special–pedagogical, special– and social–pedagogical assistance, by supplying technical aids and special teaching aids for schools.' It is recognized In the Law of Sport that sports of the disabled means organized sports activities for people with temporary or full physical and/or mental disability. The aim of such activities is to strengthen health and/or seek best possible sport results. The law states that physical education and sport should comprise education of children and youth in the field of physical education and sports as well as promotion and enhancing physical activity and sports for adults and people with disabilities. Some concepts regarding disability sport is written in the Law on Social Integration of People with Disabilities (IX-2228, 2004). The Law on Construction (Valstybės žinios (Official Gazette) No. 101–3597, 2001) states that the design, construction, reconstruction or inspection of buildings and civil engineering works must be carried out in such a way that they would accommodate the specific needs of the disabled, that covers the infrastructure for sport and physical activity as well.

Policy Framework

Policy formation at the national level is performed by Parliament, Government and ministries (Ministry of Education, science and sport, Ministry of Health, etc.), also other state institutions (Department of Statistics, Department of Disability Affairs, etc.). The Parliament of the Republic of Lithuania approves disability sports strategy, which sets out the priorities, long-term goals and trends of the content change on the recommendation of the government.

At the national level the Ministry of Education, Science and Sports is solely responsible for the sports policy formation, organization, coordination and controls its implementation at the state level. But there is no separate department or council for development of disability sport. The Ministry has established only the Sport group, in which only one specialist is responsible for disability sports.

Other state institutions or non-governmental organizations perform the functions assigned to them by Lithuania's sports law, other laws and Government resolutions in the field of sport and create conditions for the development of the sport.

For a long time, Lithuania did not have a long-term or short-term disability sports strategy, which caused many problems in this area. Due to a lack of funding, financial savings and irrational use of funds, Lithuanian municipal sports facilities and equipment for disability sport does not meet the requirements, sports infrastructure and outdoor recreation are outdated or non-existent, there is a lack of qualified disability sports specialists (Požėrienė et al., 2014a, 2014b; Reklaitienė et al., 2016).

In recent years, attempts have been made to solve problems mentioned above, to rationalize the use of funds for different disability sports and physical education, to develop public programmes, to reduce social exclusion and to increase integration into society through sport, to improve accessibility to sports, to create and upgrade sports facilities. However, it is still lack of cooperation and control between institutions, not all the projects and programmes are implemented purposefully, municipalities are short of specialized and accessible sports facilities. Lithuania does not have a modern system for the formation and implementation of disability sports policy, which requires responsible diligent work as well as certain review of regulations and monitoring of their implementation (Reklaitienė et al., 2016).

On the other hand, the legal framework for disability sport and inclusion is also an integral part of national decision making. The Sports Law (2018-10-18, No. XIII-1540), Law on Social Services (2006-01-19, X-493) Law on Equal Treatment (2003-11-18, IX-1826), the Convention on the Rights of Persons with Disabilities (ratified by Lithuanian Parliament 2010-05-27, XI-854), Law on the Social Integration of the Disabled (2004-05-22, IX-2228) state that everyone is equally entitled to participate in sports and physical activity at all levels and chosen roles. According to the regulation for constructions approved by the Ministry of

Environment of the Republic of Lithuania all buildings in the public environment must be adapted for the disabled.

However, various politicians, abled-bodied and disability sport organizations have different interpretations of priorities in disability sport area as well as understanding about the implementation and monitoring of these legislations. The sport for disabled among the wider population is still perceived as activities and services which should be organized for separate groups in segregated environment (Požėrienė et al., 2014a, 2014b; Reklaitienė et al., 2016; Stankevičiūtė et al., 2017).

Financial, Governance and Managerial Support

Financial Framework

The Sport Financing Fund (hereinafter the Fund) receives 2.5% of the annual income from alcohol and manufactured tobacco excise and not less than 10% from the lottery and gambling tax. The Fund supports physical activity and sports projects in five areas: (i) promotion of physical activity; (ii) purchase of sports inventory and equipment; maintenance and construction of sports facilities; (iii) organization of sports events; (iv) development of sports science and education as well as professional training; and (v) maintenance and repair of existing sports facilities. The fund had increased from €6.6 million in 2018 to €13.6 million in 2019 (Government of the Republic of Lithuania, 2019). The important rule of the fund financing distribution is that at least 10% of the whole fund should be used to implement projects promoting sports activities for the disabled.

The responsible administrator on the governmental level is the Ministry of Education, Science and Sports. The ministry is in charge of distributing the state's sport subsidies to all national level sport associations through the Sport Financing Fund, including the LPC. The financing of elite (high-skills) sports programme comes from the state budget. The budget of implementation of the high-level sports programme of Disability sports organization is showed in Table 18.5. Total budget for elite disability sport in 2020 is less than €1 M (€840,000).

Table 18.5 Budget for sports organizations in Lithuania

Sport Organization	Budget
Lithuanian Paralympic Committee	€85,662
Lithuanian Sports Federation for the Blind	€166,543
Lithuanian Sports Federation for the Disabled	€135,837
Lithuanian Sports Committee for the Deaf	€410,708
Lithuanian Special Olympics Committee	€41,250
Total	€840,000

Source: Ministry of Education, Science and Sport (2020)

In 2020, the amount of subsidies for non-governmental organization or disability sports clubs was organized through the Ministry of Social Affairs and Labour. 90 sports organizations (there are 105 legal organizations at the local level) received financing (€349,923 from the state budget and €245,195 from municipalities' budget) and developed physical activities programmes for the disabled under the umbrella of the state programme 'Integration of the Disabled People Through Physical Education and Sport'. The activities were performed in 46 municipalities (Department for the Affairs of the Disabled, 2020).

But as it was mentioned above, all the activities for the disabled are usually organized separately for special population and there is no actual inclusion of the disabled into general sport society. All activities are foreseen mainly for the organizations for the disabled, which are really exclusive and do not encourage activities together with able-bodied people (Department for the Affairs of the Disabled, 2017).

Governance and Management Support

The Ministry of Education, Science and Sports

1. takes part in shaping the policy of the Republic of Lithuania in the field of sport;
2. draws a long-term physical activity and sports strategy and development programme, strategic action plans of the institution, control their implementation;
3. approves a list of strategic sports;
4. disposes of state budgetary appropriations;
5. coordinates activities of the organizations acting in the system of physical activity and sport;
6. cooperates with the Lithuanian communities abroad in the field of physical activity and sport;
7. sets the qualification requirements for heads of State physical activity and sports institutions, coaches and specialists, their performance evaluation, granting of categories and so on;
8. promotes the development of the physical activity and sport information system and sports science; and
9. accumulates and analyses statistical information about physical activity and sport.

Other ministries and state institutions within their competence, participates in the formation of a physical education and sports policies, implementing and creating conditions for the development of physical education and sports. For example, the Ministry of Social Security and Labour develops physical activity and sport of the disabled as a mean of their integration into society, support the initiatives and programmes of physical activity of family and community. The Ministry of Health develops the principles of healthy lifestyle, draw up and coordinate programmes for enhancing physical activity, draws up drafts of legal acts related to enhancement of physical activity, participate in solution of the issues regarding the use of doping in sports, lay down the requirements for health check-ups for athletes (Karnickas & Zaleskis, 2010; Gedvilaitė, 2011; Cingienė & Gobikas, 2019).

The municipal departments for PE and sports implement sport policy in the municipality. They set up and close PE and sports institutions, fund the activities of sport schools, sport clubs and other non-governmental sports organizations which acts within the municipal territory, but do not carry out public administration functions. Municipalities implement a strategy of the development of sports facilities in the municipality, ensure their accessibility to the residents, can fund participation of teams in national and international competitions, carry out educational sport activities (Kriščiūnas, 2019).

Non-governmental sports organizations, such as Paralympic, Deaflympics and Special Olympics, Sport for All movements in Lithuania, have the right to connect into associations in accordance with the procedure and for the purposes laid down by the laws. Sport clubs may be established for sport amateurs and for professional athletes. Disability sport clubs are public legal organizations whose purpose is to meet public interests in sport, to unite people with disabilities for physical activity, healthy lifestyle, to aim at qualitative and quantitative results of professional and recreational sports.

The national disability sports committees and federations must be recognized by the Ministry of Education, Science and Sports. These organizations organize official national championships and form national sports teams of Lithuania as well as represent Lithuania in international competitions.

Level of Integration of Inclusion

The Lithuanian Ministry of Social Affairs and Labour (2019) from the year 2016 implemented a sport integration project 'Integration of the Disabled People Through Physical Education and Sport'. The project's goal was to include children, youth and adults with disabilities in physical activities together with people without disabilities. This can be seen as a different approach for integration and inclusion, as the funding was raised for sports clubs for the disabled or other disability organizations to implement the reverse inclusion.

There is no monitoring and evaluation system for disability sport integration processes in Lithuania (Lithuanian Disability Forum, 2015). Only few individual initiatives for the process evaluation was done in Lithuanian Sports University. The university has established the strategic research area in the field of Empowerment of People with disabilities through physical activity and sports. The conducted studies showed that some National Sports Federations had taken responsibility of disability sport, for example track and field, cycling or swimming, but all-inclusive activities are implemented only on elite level.

18.4 Sport Participation by People with Disabilities

Monitoring and Evaluation

The first Report on the implementation of the Convention was done by the Ministry for Social Affair and Labour and published in 2012. Lithuanian Disability Forum prepared the parallel report for UN about the implementation of the Convention, emphasizing how the implementation affected participation of people with disabilities in recreation, leisure and sport. The official report for UN was done in 2017 and 2018.

There are no systematic surveys and studies conducted in Lithuania that relate to sport participation of people with disabilities. Most of the data is possible to receive from financial reports of sport federations or other disability organizations. For example, in 2018 Lithuanians Sports Federation for the Disabled organized 32 competitions at national level and there were 678 participants. 90 disability sports organizations participated in the state programme 'Integration of the Disabled People Through Physical Education and Sport'. According to the reports of the projects, 3328 (of which 2897 adults and 431 children with disabilities) participated in continuous sport activities and 3240 (of which 2958 adults and 282 children with disabilities) participated in one-time sport activities or events. But this data does not show the full picture to analyse the participation of people with disabilities in sports.

On the other hand, sport clubs for people with disabilities are distributed very unevenly in Lithuania. The majority of such clubs are located in the largest cities of Lithuania. People with disabilities are unable to receive sport services anywhere else. The statistical data do not reflect the real distribution of sport activities and involvement of the disabled all over Lithuania, because in some regions people with disabilities are totally inactive.

Sport Participation

Participation level in physical activity among all the population was estimated for the first time at the national level in Lithuania in 2002. According to Lithuanian sports information centre (2014) 20.6% of Lithuanian population participated in organized sport activities, 46.8% in non-organized sport activities and 36.8% haven't participated at all. As compared to the data of Eurobarometer in 2018, 51% of the Lithuanian population was not engaged in sport activities; however, 75% was engaged in other kind of physical activities (European Commission, 2018).

There are no official statistics on people with disabilities participating in sports, what sports they are involved in, or whether sports are adapted for people with disabilities. For example, the report of Ministry of Social Affairs (MSA) in 2019 indicated total number of people with disabilities involved in 'Integration into Society Through PE and Sports' programme. There were 4583 in total, 3289 of them participated in regular activities and 3153 participated in non-permanent activities (Ministry of Social Security and Labor, 2018).

Barriers and Facilitators

Lithuania's Disabilities Department and Ministry of Social Affairs and Labour (2019) evaluated the effectiveness of the implementation of the Convention on the Rights of People with Disabilities in Lithuania. The results showed that 33.9% (573 respondents) of disabled people have access to sports and recreational facilities, 32.2% (545 respondents) have no access and 33.8% (572 respondents) did not have any opinion regarding this question.

Rėklaitienė et al. (2015) made the research and identified barriers for sport participation among young people with disabilities. Most of the barriers for participation in sport activities comes from logistical problems, lack of instructors and volunteers, lack of accessible facilities as well as poor economic situation of respondents. The situation is better among adults with disabilities, because they have more support from social services.

Barriers

The barriers arising in the inclusive sport system, which influence a lower physical activity among people with disabilities, are lack of collaboration, negative attitude towards disability overall, lack of teachers' competence and low funding possibilities. The important aspect is the parents' attitude. They still lack information about possibilities for their children to participate in physical activities. Parents are still ashamed of their children and/or wants to hide them and not show them to society. They don't want their children to participate in special sport club activities if the child is studying in integrated educational setting. On the other hand, there is no clear system to guide disabled into sport. The children who live or study in special institutions have a possibility to participate in various kind of sport (Reklaitienė et al., 2016).

There is no data available on what is happening in the community level concerning sport activities, or any other services for the disabled, for example, information and consulting services, organization and provision of psychological assistance for the disabled and their family members, the activities for increasing independence, regular sports and cultural activities. The only information available is from the financial statements of the organizations.

It should be noted that according to the data of the Education Management Information System, only about 10% of secondary schools are accessible for wheelchair users, and only 0.3% of schools are fully accessible for the blind in Lithuania. It means, that students or young adults with disabilities do not have any possibility to participate in PE or sports activities and it is necessary to emphasize that accessible environment is necessary not only for students with disabilities, but also for teachers and parents, who may also have a disability.

Facilitators

National legislation provides state subsidies for the adaptation of sports facilities for the disabled and construction supervision in order to ensure equal access to sports facilities for all. This means that the whole construction or reconstruction process is controlled from the approval of the project to the handover of the building in order to ensure the accessibility for the disabled. Nevertheless, the data shows that 32 municipalities did not ensure the effective implementation that at least 30% of public buildings that provide social, educational, health and cultural services would be adapted for people with disabilities. No public transport was adapted for disabled people in 34 municipalities (Rėklaitienė et al., 2015, 2015, 2016).

There are 1611 gyms, 50 swimming pools, 599 stadiums, 272 tennis courts, 6 athletics indoor stadiums and other sport facilities In Lithuania (Official Statistic Portal, 2020). But there is no data how many sports facilities are adapted and accessible for people with disability. Till now there is not valuable control mechanism to evaluate the accessibility.

18.5 Conclusion

Although the social model of disability in Lithuania is implemented by the law, the medical model of disability is still rooted in the society, and the capacity and abilities of the disabled are assessed from the medical aspect. Disability sports and physical activity for the disabled in Lithuania have been organized mainly in segregated settings.

Lithuanian laws regulating disability sports define guidelines for physical activity, but there is no developed national strategy for the development of disability sports. Because of that, there is need to provide the analysis of the current situation of sports for the disabled in Lithuania, define strategic goals and outline guidelines for further development of the sport for disabled. This is especially relevant for the training of young athletes with disabilities, as now the existing system is encouraging only highly skilled athletes in Paralympic sports, but does not create the preconditions for preparing a shift.

There is lack of data regarding the sport participation of people with disabilities. We still need to answer the following questions—whether conditions are created for people with disabilities to participate in mainstream sports activities, and whether they are physically active enough or not and find out the reasons for that. The participation data is accessible only from Paralympics, Special Olympics, sports for the blind and Deaf Sports Committees. The monitoring of ongoing disability sport integration processes in Lithuania is not processed at all. There are only separate initiatives to monitor and investigate the process. We need to increase the research and systematic monitoring to evaluate the disability sport process and give the recommendations regarding the improvement, motivation and barriers for participation and so on.

References

Cingiene, V. (2017). Lithuania: The organization and governance of sport. In J. Scheerder, A. Willem, & E. Claes (Eds.), *Sport policy systems and sport federations*. Palgrave Macmillan. https://doi.org/10.1057/978-1-137-60222-0_9

Cingienė, V., & Gobikas, M. (2019). Formation of sports public policy within the context of hierarchy governance. *Public Policy and Administration, 18*(3), 35–45. https://doi.org/10.5755/j01.ppaa.18.3.24719

Department for the Affairs of the Disabled. (2017). *Neįgaliųjų ir kitų visuomenės narių nuomonės apklausa, įvertinant Jungtinių Tautų Neįgaliųjų teisių konvencijos įgyvendinimo efektyvumą Lietuvoje (Survey of the opinion of the disabled and other members of the society, assessing the effectiveness of the implementation of the United Nations Convention on the Rights of Persons with Disabilities in Lithuania)*. http://www.ndt.lt/wp-content/uploads/Lietuvosne%C4%AFgali%C5%B3j%C5%B3-draugijosataskaita-2017.12.07-GALUTINI.pdf.\

Department for the Affairs of the Disabled. (2020). *Skirtas finansavimas (financing)*. https://www.smm.lt/uploads/documents/Sportas/programos/2020/AMSP%201%C4%97%C5%A1%C5%B3%20paskirstymo%20lentel%C4%97.pdf downloaded 31.7.2020.

European Commission. (2018). *Sport and physical activity (Special Eurobarometer 472)*. Brussels: European Commission.

Eurostat. (2018). *Sport statistics* (2018 ed.) European Union. https://ec.europa.eu/eurostat/documents/4031688/8716412/KS-07-17-123-EN-N.pdf/908e0e7f-a416-48a9-8fb7-International Monetary Fund (2020). World Economic Outlook Database. Washington: IMF. https://www.imf.org/en/Publications/WEO/weo-database/2020/October/. Downloaded 07.05.2020.

Gedvilaitė, A. (2011). Kūno kultūros ir sporto strategijos formavimas Lietuvoje (Physical Education and Sports Strategy formation in Lithuania). *Management Theory and Studied for Rural Business and Infrastructure Development, 5*(29), 74–80.

Government of the Republic of Lithuania. (2014). *2011–2020 metų valstybinės sporto plėtros strategijos įgyvendinimo tarpinstitucinis veiklos planas. (The inter-institutional action plan for the implementation of the National Sports Development Strategy 2011–2020)*. Resolution No 112 on 5 February 2015. Available at https://www.e-tar.lt/portal/lt/legalAct/79300c30a88b11e4a82d9548fb36f682 Downloaded 05.03.2020.

Government of the Republic of Lithuania. (2019). *Dėl sporto rėmimo fondo lėšų paskirstymo proporcijų, sporto rėmimo fondo administravimui skirtų lėšų dalies nustatymo ir sporto rėmimo fondo lėšomis finansuojamų sporto projektų finansavimo tvarkos aprašo patvirtinimo (On the approval of the Description of the order of determining the proportions of the allocation of assets from the sports support fund, the allocation of the funds for the administration of the sports fund and funding of the sports projects financed by the sports fund)*. Vilnius: Government Office.

Guthold, R., Stevens, G. A., Riley, L. M., & Bull, F. C. (2020). Global trends in insufficient physical activity among adolescents: A pooled analysis of 298 population-based surveys with 1·6 million participants. *Lancet Child Adolescent Health, 4*, 23–35. https://doi.org/10.1016/S2352-4642(19)30323-2

Karnickas, L., & Zaleskis, J. (2010). Sport Governance in Lithuania. *The International Sports Low Journal, 3*, 116–117.

Kriščiūnas, D. (2019). Implementation of sports policy in municipal administrations and councils: The case of Lithuania. *Humanities studies, 1*(77), 100–109. https://doi.org/10.30839/2072-7941.2019.177718

Lauzadyte-Tutliene, A., Balezentis, T., & Goculenko, E. (2018). Welfare State in Central and Eastern Europe. *Economics and Sociology, 11*(1), 100–123. https://doi:10.14254/2071-789X.2018/11-1/7.

Lithuanian Disability Forum. (2015). *Alternatyvi ataskaita dėl JT neįgaliųjų konvencijos įgyvendiinimo Lietuvoje (Alternative report on the implementation of the UN Convention on the Rights of Persons with Disabilities in Lithuania)*. Asociacija Lietuvos neįgaliųjų forumas.

Lithuanian Paralympic Committee. (2015a). *About us*. http://www.lpok.lt/Default.aspx?Lang=EN Downloaded 17.05.2020.

Lithuanian Paralympic Committee. (2015b). *History of the LNOC*. https://www.ltok.lt/en/history-of-the-lnoc/. Downloaded 17.05.2020.

Lithuanian Sports Information Centre, LSIC. (2014). http://www.sportinfo.lt/. Downloaded 17.05.2020.

Minister of Environment of the Republic of Lithuania. (2001). *The regulation Technical Requirements STR 2.03.01:2001 Buildings and territories – Requirements related to the needs of persons with disabilities*. Valstybės žinios (Official Gazette), No 53–1898.

Ministry of Education, Science and Sport. (2020). *Neįgaliųjų sporto organizacijų 2020 m. aukšto meistriškumo sporto programoms įgyvendinti skiriamos valstybės biudžeto lėšos (State budget funds for disability Sports organizations for implementation sport programs for high-skilled athletes with disabilities in 2020)*. Vilnius.

Ministry of Social Security and Labor. (2018). *Neįgaliųjų socialinės integracijos veiklos rezultatų bei jungtinių tautų neįgaliųjų teisių konvencijos ir jos fakultatyvaus protokolo 2018 m. stebėsenos ataskaita (Monitoring report of 2018 results of social integration activities for people with disabilities regarding implementation of UN convention on the rights of disabled persons and its optional protocol)*. Vilnius: Ministry of Social. http://www.ndt.lt/wp-content/uploads/JT_neigaliuju_teisiu_konvencijos_stebesenos_ataskaita_GALUTINE.pdf Downloaded 05.03.2020.

Ministry of Social Security and Labour. (2018). *Statistics on social integration. Annual Reports*. Available at: https://socmin.lrv.lt/uploads/socmin/documents/files/veikla/veiklos%20ataskaitos/SADM%202018%20metu%20veiklos%20ataskaita.pdf Downloaded 10.09.2020.

National Olympic Committee. (2020). *About LNOC*. https://www.ltok.lt/en/about-lnoc/. Downloaded 17.05.2020.

National Report: Analysis of Labour Market Realities and Challenges in the Sport and Physical Activity Sector. (2019). *ESSA-Sport project, Lithunia*. Mykolas Romeris University.

Official Statistic Portal. *Lietuvos švietimas, kultūra ir sportas (Lithuanian education, culture and sports)* 2020. https://osp.stat.gov.lt/lietuvos-ssvietimas-kultura-ir-sporta-2020/spotrto-organizaciju-veikla

Official website of the European Union. *Lietuva*. https://europa.eu/european-union/about-eu/countries/member-countries/lithuania_lt Downloaded 17.05.2020.

Ostasevičienė, V., Gaižauskienė, A., Požėrienė, J., & Rėklaitienė, D. (2015). *Inkliuzinio fizinio ugdymo poveikis vaikų, turinčių specialiųjų poreikių, emocijų ir elgesio savybių raiškai. (monografija) (The effect of Inclusive Physical Education on the Emotions and Behavior of Children with Special Needs)*. Kaunas: Lietuvos sporto universitetas, 223 p.

Požėrienė, J., Rėklaitienė, D., & Ostasevičienė, V. (2014a). *Lietuvos sporto universiteto studentų požiūris į inkliuzinę fizinę veiklą (Attitudes of Lithuanian Sports University students towards inclusive physical activity)*. Paper presented at Lithuanian scientific conference 'Athlete Training Management and Factors Determining Athlete Working Capacity' held at Lithuanian Sports University, Kaunas, 8 December (pp. 309–317). : LSU.

Požėrienė, J., Rėklaitienė, D., & Ostasevičienė, V. (2014b). *APA Professionals Training in Lithuania*. Paper presented at European Congress of Adapted Physical Activity held at Madrid

Polytechnical University, Madrid, Spain, 29 September—2 October (pp. 98–98). Madrid: Universidad Politécnica de Madrid, Fundación Sanitas.

Reklaitienė, D., & Poerienė, J (2013). Accessibility of physical activity facilities in local surroundings according to elderly with disabilities. *Sport Bilimleri Dergisi=Hacettepe Journal of Sport Sciences: 19th International Symposium of Adapted Physical Activity,* 24 (2, Special Issue), 191–195.

Rėklaitienė, D., Požėrienė, J., & Leveckytė, V. (2015). *Perspectives and problems of Paralympic movement in Lithuania.* Paper presented at the 20th International Symposium on Adapted Physical Activity, held at Wingate Institute, Netanya, Israel 11–15 June (pp. 129–129). Netanya: Wingate Institute.

Reklaitienė, D., Pozeriene, J., & Ostaseviciene, V. (2016). The accessibility for people with disabilities – new challenge and possibilities for fitness and recreation services development. *Transformations in Business & Economics,* 15(2B), 699–708.

Rėklaitienė, D., Selickaitė, D., & Požėrienė, J. (2015). *Moving away from special education towards inclusive education: what is successful practice of organizing physical education for children with intellectual disabilities.* Paper presented at the 20th International Symposium on Adapted Physical Activity, held at Wingate Institute, Netanya, Israel 11–15 June (pp. 89–89). Netanya: Wingate Institute.

Republic of Lithuania. (1992). *Constitution of the Republic of Lithuania.* Valstybės Žinios (Official Gazette), No 33–1014. Available at: https://www3.lrs.lt/home/Konstitucija/Konstitucija.htm Downloaded 05.03.2020.

Republic of Lithuania. (2003). *Law on development of non-governmental organisations.* Available at: https://e-seimas.lrs.lt/portal/legalAct/lt/TAD/d415a500124111e48595a3375cdcc8a3?jfwid=tsp3ux4t8 Downloaded 05.03.2020.

Republic of Lithuania. (2004). *Law on Social Integration of the Disabled.* Valstybės žinios (Official Gazette), No 83–2983. Available at: https://www.e-tar.lt/portal/lt/legalAct/TAR.199156E4E004/cWWgldtkIu Downloaded 05.03.2020.

Republic of Lithuania. (2005). *Law on charity and sponsorship.* Available at: https://e-seimas.lrs.lt/portal/legalAct/lt/TAD/TAIS.281044?jfwid=-pw6828l4q Downloaded 05.03.2020.

Republic of Lithuania. (2006). *Law on social services.* Valstybės Žinios (Official Gazette), No X-493. Available at: https://e-seimas.lrs.lt/portal/legalAct/lt/TAD/TAIS.277880 Downloaded 05.03.2020.

Republic of Lithuania. (2010). *Law on the ratification of the United Nations convention on the rights of persons with disabilities and its optional protocol.* Valstybės žinios (Official Gazette), No 67–3350.

Republic of Lithuania. (2011a). *Law on Volunteering.* Available at: https://www.ilo.org/dyn/natlex/docs/ELECTRONIC/90083/103623/F-476544576/LTU90083.pdf Downloaded 05.03.2020.

Republic of Lithuania. (2011b). *Nutarimas dėl 2011–2020 metų valstybinės sporto plėtros strategijos patvirtinimo (Resolution on the approval of the 2011–2020 National Sports Development Strategy).* Available at https://www.e-tar.lt/portal/lt/legalAct/TAR.5149504F601C Downloaded 05.03.2020.

Republic of Lithuania. (2015a). *Law on associations.* Available at: https://e-seimas.lrs.lt/portal/legalAct/lt/TAD/066670f3168011e5bfc0854048a4e288?jfwid=-n126u3s5u Downloaded 05.03.2020.

Republic of Lithuania. (2015b). *Law on education.* Available at: https://e-seimas.lrs.lt/portal/legalAct/lt/TAD/df672e20b93311e5be9bf78e07ed6470?jfwid=rivwzvpvg Downloaded 05.03.2020.

Republic of Lithuania. (2018). *Law on Sports (I-1151).* Available at: https://e-seimas.lrs.lt/portal/legalAct/lt/TAD/TAIS.23317/GtjmbabxaW?jfwid=-1n2mj5n8o Downloaded 05.03.2020.

Republic of Lithuania. (n.d.). *Law on Self-Government.* Available at: https://e-seimas.lrs.lt/portal/legalAct/lt/TAD/c18a8ae0f55e11e3b62ec716086f051f?jfwid=1bc6m4zi8x Downloaded 05.03.2020.

Sport for All Association. (2020). *Apie mus. (About us).* http://www.sportasvisiems.lt/lt/asociacija/apie_mus Downloaded 17.05.2020.

Stankevičiūtė, I., Požėrienė, J., & Rėklaitienė, D. (2017). *Neįgalaus jaunimo įtraukimas į aktyvias laisvalaikio veiklas Kauno mieste (Involvement of disabled youth in active leisure activities in Kaunas).* Paper presented at Lithuanian Scientific Conference 'Control of athletic training and factors affecting athletic performance', held at Lithuanian Sports University, Kaunas, 21 December (p. 45) Kaunas: LSU.

Vasiliauskas, K., & Ivaškienė, V. (2001). *Fiziškai neįgalių žmonių fizinis ugdymas ir saviugda (Physical education and self-education of physically disabled people).* Kaunas.

World Bank group. (2020). *Negalios politika ir negalios vertinimo sistema Lietuvoje (Disability policy and disability assessment system in Lithuania).* Brussels and Vilnius.

World Economic Outlook Database. (2020). *WEO Data: October 2020 Edition.* https://www.imf.org/en/Publications/WEO/weo-database/2020/October Downloaded 10.10.2020.

Chapter 19
Structure of the Analysis on the Development and Situation of Disability Sports Policy in Slovenia

Mojca Doupona and Simona Kustec

19.1 Introduction

Sport for athletes with disabilities (SAWD) began in Slovenia only after the World War II as a result of the rehabilitation of those affected. The umbrella organisation is Zveza ŠIS-SPK, a federation of disability organisations funded by the Foundation *for* Funding Disability and Humanitarian Organisations (FIHO). Due to the new inclusive legislation in the field of sport, Zveza ŠIS-SPK connects with the national branch associations, creates new opportunities and improves the system in cooperation with Ministry of Education, Science and Sport (MIZŠ, Ministrstvo za izobraževanje, znanost in šport) and National Olympic Committee—Association of Sport Federations (OKS-ZŠ, Olimpijski komite Slovenije—Združenje športnih zvez). There is a need for interdisciplinary and systemic interdepartmental integration, as the field of SAWD is currently opaque and fragmented into individual sectors such as: sport, education, health and social affairs. In Slovenia, the system and structure of disability sport is less researched and discussed. There is not much literature nor accurate data on the number of programmes and active athletes with disabilities. Data on the number of athletes with disabilities can only be found in the field of elite para-sport. We also observe differences between sports for athletes with intellectual disabilities and athletes with physical disabilities. In terms of personnel and funding, SAWD is completely underserved compared to sport in general. At the implementation level, we find some inclusive sports programmes, but they are not systematically funded. An important source of funding is the local community and sponsors, but it is only realised in some, mostly urban or larger municipalities.

M. Doupona (✉)
Faculty of Sport, University of Ljubljana, Ljubljana, Slovenia
e-mail: Mojca.doupona@fsp.uni-lj.si

S. Kustec
Faculty of Management, University of Primorska, Koper, Slovenia

SAWD relies heavily on the existing sports system in Slovenia, which is not comparable to the small population of people with disabilities in terms of criteria, so the criteria need to be adapted.

19.2 Country Profile

Slovenia is a small but topographically diverse country in Central Europe with a population of 2 million (Table 19.1). Slovenian citizens are known of giving a remarkably high value to the top athletes' results on the world sport stages, and being themselves at the same time highly active in the recreational part of sport activity in comparison with other European citizens, and regardless of various socio-demographic determinants (ISSP, 2009).

Characteristics of Slovenia

Slovenia was part of Yugoslavia for most of the twentieth century. As the northernmost state of the former state, it historically participated more than other former republics in the Western Europe modernisation processes and occupied the most economically advanced position, which made it attractive to immigrants from other Yugoslav regions. The majority of the population today are ethnic Slovenes, the two main ethnic minorities are Italians and Hungarians. With the disintegration of Yugoslavia and the emergence of an independent state, Slovenia changed its

Table 19.1 Facts and statistics of Slovenia

Population (Number of Inhabitants)[a]	2,111,461
Area (km^2)[a]	20,271
Density (inhabitants/km^2)[a]	103
Urbanisation rate (%)[b]	19.4–46.0
Political organisation[c]	A democratic republic
Structure of the state[c]	Unitary
Number of provinces[a]	12
Number of municipalities[a]	212
GDP per capita (US Dollars) on 6th of April 2021[d]	25,144
Number of official languages[a,e]	1
EU Membership[a]	2004
Welfare model	Eastern European social model (Koren, 2015)

Sources: (a) SIStat (2020), (b) EUROSTAT (2017a), (c) GOV.SI (2020a, 2020b) and (d) ZŠRS Planica (Grujić, 2020)
[e]Language: Slovenian, and also Italian and Hungarian in ethnically mixed regions

socio-political system from a communist to a democratic multi-party system. In 2004 it became economically and politically integrated with Western Europe and joined NATO and the EU. The economy in the twenty-first century is largely based on services and trade. With the changes of social system (1991), significant changes in commercialisation and the partnership between state and private capital occurred. In the late eighties when political processes, connected with Slovenian independence become very straightforward, the legal and institutional changes of the whole system affected the field of sport as well.

Sport in Slovenia

Organisation of Slovenian sport has always been in accordance with a traditional European pyramid model of sport according to which the major part of sport organisations are being represented in the frameworks of the grass-roots sports clubs at the local level of municipalities, following by the regional and national sport associations and OKS-ZŠZ on the top of the pyramid. Sport in general is supposed to be governed by the principles of high self-autonomy and cooperation between individual sport organisational levels. Even though the key democratic institutions and responsibilities were defined in 1991, the sports field suffered from a lack of contextual changes to the old socialist legislation before 1998 when the Sports Act finally came into force. Pursuant to Articles 1–3 of the Sports Act (1992) sport encompasses the broader aspects of human life and foresees the involvement of both state and civil society players, who should work together co-operatively. The most important legislation supplementing the Sports Act is the National Programme of Sport in Slovenia introduced in 2000, according to which the state co-creates the conditions for the development of sport at the national and local level, and through international and bilateral co-operations (NPS, 2000) (Table 19.2).

Disability in Slovenia

In Slovenia, different terms are in use when dealing with sports activity of people with disabilities, such as: disability sport, sport for persons with special needs, rehabilitation sport, therapeutic rehabilitation, sport for the locomotory impaired, adapted sports activity, Paralympics, Special Olympics, disability sport and so on. By means of the said terms, we try to define the diverse, complex and demanding developments in the field of involvement in sports associated with various types and levels of impairment in individuals. There is no data on the actual number of included athletes with diverse abilities (Filipčič et al., 2016; Sambolec, 2012; Štrumbelj, 2015; Štrumbelj et al., 2012). According to SORS (2014), we do not have accurate data on the number of persons with disabilities in Slovenia, but this number is estimated at 160,000 to 170,000 persons (disabled workers, children and

Table 19.2 Sport profile of Slovenia

Government Authority Responsible for Sport	Ministry of Education, Science and Sport
Membership—sports club (% of population)	–
Membership—fitness or health centre (% of population in 2017)[g]	10.3%
Membership—socio-cultural club that includes sporting activities (e.g. employees' club, youth club, school- and university-related club) (% of population)	–
Sport participation, at least once a week (% of population)[f]	78.3
Number of national sport federations[a]	75
Number of sports clubs (NPŠZ members of OKS-ZŠZ)[a]	2705
Number of sports clubs' members (NPŠZ members of OKS-ZŠZ)[a]	59,538
National budget for sport (€ × 1,000,000)[d]	29.25
National budget for sport federations[h] (€ × 1000)[e]	69,322.40
Local budget for sport (€ × 1,000,000)[d]	107.37
Share of economic value of volunteers in sport in the GDP (%)[c]	0.013

Sources: (a) OKS-ZŠZ (2020/21), (b) EUROSTAT(2017b), (c) PROSTOVOLJSTVO.ORG (2021), (d) ZŠRS Planica (Grujić, 2020) & FIHO (2019), (e) AJPES (2021), (f) Mediana Survey (2019) and (g) FZS (Gerlovič et al., 2019)

[h]The data are calculated from the annual balance sheets of national sports federations. Government revenues as well as own revenues of associations, sponsorships, membership fees and others are considered

Table 19.3 Facts and statistics on disability in Slovenia, age 6 to 26

	Data Captured on 30/9/2020	% of Population
Prevalence of intellectual disabilities	133	0.9
Prevalence of moderate/severe hearing disabilities	169	1.2
Pupils with speech and language disorders	1629	11.5
Prevalence of moderate/severe seeing disabilities	68	0.5
Prevalence of one or more moderate/severe physical disabilities	157	1.1
Prevalence of psycho-social (behavioural) disabilities	509	3.6
Prolonged illness	1356	9.5
Pupils with deficits in individual areas of learning	5872	41.3
Pupils with autistic disorders	227	1.6
Pupils with multiple disorders	4104	28.9
Total:	14,224	100

Source: MIZŠ (2020)

adolescents with special needs, military and war invalids and moderate, severe and severe mental and the most severely physically handicapped). Table 19.3 presents detailed data on children and young people with disabilities who are included in regular and special compulsory schooling programmes. However, we were unable to obtain data on adults with various disabilities.

Table 19.4 Number of athletes included in the Zveza ŠIS-SPK 2020 by age

	2020
12 years and younger	11
12–23 years	93
23 years and older	2329
Total	2433

Source: Zveza ŠIS-SPK (2020)

More detailed data on the number of included athletes with disabilities are therefore kept mainly at the competitive level. Indicative data on the number of people with disabilities involved at the recreational level can be found at the FIHO Foundation (Table 19.5). However, we do not have data on the number of athletes with disabilities included in all sports associations or NPŠZ, with the exception of the Zveza ŠIS-SPK (Table 19.4), which is the umbrella association for athletes with disabilities in Slovenia. The latter information is essential for the entire review and it is believed that this will be the next step in the development of sports for the disabled in Slovenia. Inclusion at the level of the NPŠZ is the direction of the International Paralympic Committee, which we follow.

With Slovenia's accession to the European Union, some key international conventions, charters, strategies and action plans were adopted, which directed us towards an inclusive sports society. The trend of sports development in the world (Zakrajšek, 2014) is based on ensuring equal opportunities for all athletes, regardless of the abilities of the individual, and Slovenia follows this direction. The inclusion of athletes with different abilities in normal sports environments at all levels, recreational and elite, rehabilitation and schooling, professional, at all ages and in all sports, is one of the fundamental national interests. Gradual legislative changes "from the top down" set the appropriate systemic framework for action in practice. We can also say that inclusion in Slovenian sport is carried out "from the bottom up," as we find quite a few inclusive programmes in different environments such as kindergartens, schools, sports associations and sports associations, disability associations and disability associations, rehabilitation programmes in health care and social inclusion programmes in the field of mental health and elsewhere. The *Resolution on the National Programme of Sport of the Republic of Slovenia 2014–2023* (2014) (hereinafter NPŠ) divides programmes into four areas, namely: sports in the educational system, leisure sports education and extracurricular sports activities, competitive sports and sports for people with different abilities.

Emergence or Rise of Disability Sport in Slovenia

In the 1990s, ten national disability organisations decided to establish a new Sports Federation for the Disabled of Slovenia (Zveza ŠIS-SPK, Zveza za šport invalidov Slovenije—Slovenski paralimpijski komite). Thus, from the Federation of Disability Sports Societies it became the Federation of National Sports Societies.

Slovenian athletes with disabilities participated for the first time at the fourth Summer Paralympic Games held in 1972 in Heidelberg. From then on, they participated in the national representation of Yugoslavia, and since 1992, they have been taking part in all international competitions as the national representation of Slovenia. Up to now, Slovenian athletes won 14 gold, 15 silver and 20 bronze medals in the following sports: alpine skiing, athletics, goalball, table tennis, volleyball, swimming and shooting. The first medals were won by Jože Okoren and Pavla Sitar Benček in 1972 in Heidelberg. They both competed in athletics. The only bronze medal was won by Franc Komar at the 1984 Winter Games in Innsbruck. The first gold medal under the flag of Slovenia was won by Franjo Izlakar in Barcelona in 1992. First he won gold in shot put, and then in discus throw. He then set a world record with a ball and a Paralympic record with a discus. At the last Paralympic Games in Rio de Janeiro 2016, both Slovenian representatives stood on the podium in the same discipline, air rifle standing. Veselka Pevec won a gold medal and Franček Gorazd Tiršek a silver.

19.3 The Disability Sport System

Disability sport was addressed in Slovenia and throughout the world after the Second World War. The physical and mental rehabilitation of war invalids finds its way into sports activities in medical centres such as The University Rehabilitation Institute, Republic of Slovenia (URI-Soča, Univerzitetni rehabilitacijski Inštitut Republike Slovenije—Soča) in Ljubljana. These soon grow beyond the health framework and competitive disability sport emerges. In the journal of the Association of Paraplegics of Slovenia (2020) titled *50 Years of Sport of Slovenian Paraplegics* we can find information about the first participation of selected 20 athletes who formed an escort team and participated for the first time in the Paralympic Games, which took place in Heidelberg in 1972.

If the beginnings of disability sport were linked to the field of health, development to date has taken place mainly in the field of social protection in the form of good financial support for various programmes run by disability organisations, which, however, only to a lesser extent also carry out sports and recreational activities. Thus, it prevailed that the disability sport stuck under the label of rehabilitation, socialisation and recreation, that is, unequal treatment compared to sport in general, despite the excellent representation of elite sport throughout the period until today. Many medals at the biggest European and world competitions and Paralympic Games testify to the excellence of Slovenian disability sport. However, only recently has the status of elite athletes with disabilities begun to equal that of non-disabled athletes. The main central organisation for athletes with disabilities in Slovenia today is Zveza ŠIS-SPK.

In Slovenia, the system and structure of sport for athletes with disabilities are less researched and discussed. There is not much literature and also no accurate data on the number of programmes and active athletes with disabilities. Accurate data can only be found in the field of elite, competitive sports. To get a better insight into the current situation, we conducted seven interviews with some current key figures in the field of sport for athletes with disabilities, namely: (1) Polona Sladič, head coach of Zveza ŠIS-SPK and Slovenian Shooting Federation; (2) Jože Okoren, former para-athlete, now official in Zveza ŠIS-SPK; (3) Franc Pinter Anćo, current athlete, pair shooter (4) Damijan Lazar, president of Zveza ŠIS-SPK; (5) Vladimir Kukavica, the director of FIHO; (6) Aleš Remih, the director of Sports Foundation; and (7) Boro Štrumbelj, professor at the Faculty of Sport in Ljubljana, former director of Sport Directorate, active in Slovenian Swimming Association, president of Expert Council of Zveza ŠIS-SPK and author of professional articles and publications on sport for athletes with disabilities in Slovenia.

Structure of Disability Sport

The structure of disability sport in Slovenia is diverse and opaque. It is built on the existing sport system, which is based on a pyramidal structure (Fig. 19.1). The pyramid structure is a fundamental concept of all spheres and levels (legislation; relations between actors, organisations and decision-makers; type of funding etc.), to which we add the specifics of disability sport, as disability sport is the domain of different spheres, such as: Zveza ŠIS-SPK at OKS-ZŠZ level, Ministry of Health (MZ, Ministrstvo za zdravje) and Ministry of Labour, Family, Social Affairs and Equal Opportunities (MDDSZ, Ministrstvo za delo, družino, socialne zadeve in enake možnosti), at the level of the line MIZŠ, *FIHO,* National Council of Disability Organisations of Slovenia (NSIOS, Nacionalni svet invalidskih organizacij Slovenije), social welfare institutions, disability associations and unions, university programmes that train personnel in the field of disability sport and a rehabilitation centre such as URI-Soča.

The types of sports programmes intended for athletes with disabilities that we recognise in Slovenia are: Rehabilitation (URI-Soča), recreation and socialisation (sports clubs, disability organisations, Special Olympics Slovenia, education) and elite sports (Zveza ŠIS-SPK and NPŠZ).

Programmes for athletes with disabilities are often divided into two major subgroups and also implemented in different organisations: sports programmes for athletes with physical disabilities and sports programmes for athletes with intellectual disabilities (Fig. 19.2).

There are specific organisations of disability sport, but they are not officially incorporated into the structure of sport, since they primarily represent the field of the people with disabilities, that is, they take place in the field of social and health care. The need for inter-ministerial cooperation has been recognised but not introduced at system level. The URI-Soča, which is extremely important for athletes with disabilities, as many people meet different sports for the first time there, is programmatically and financially completely unrelated to the line MIZŠ as a health facility. The *FIHO* is also completely unrelated to the sports sector. The cooperation

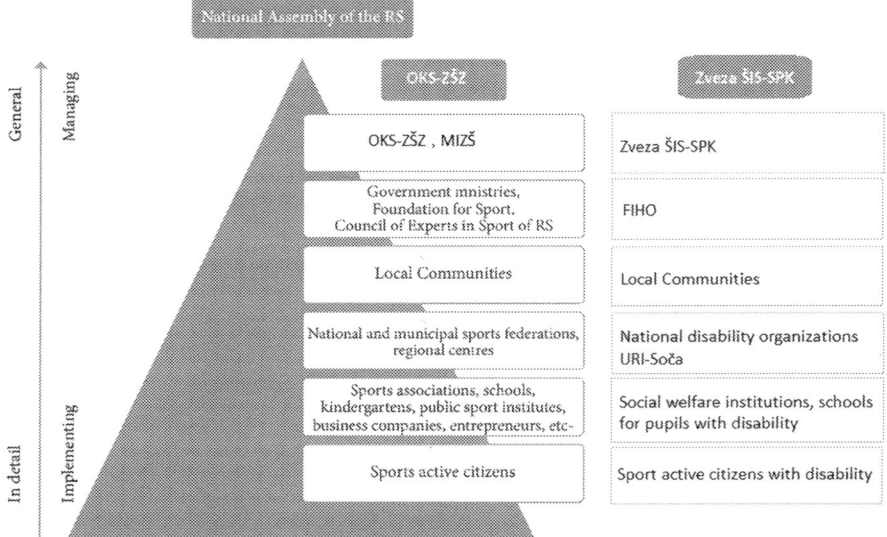

Fig. 19.1 Pyramid structure of sport as defined in the NPŠRS 2014–2023 (Jurak, 2014), with adds for disability sport. Source: Jurak, 2014 (left side), authors' own work (right side)

between OKS-ZŠZ and the Zveza ŠIS-SPK has started in the last three years. Moreover, there is a strong sense of disconnectedness and inconsistency at the level of cooperation between municipalities and the state. Some municipalities already fund disability sports programmes at the local level, but many do not fund them at all. Municipal tenders also differ from each other and do not have the same criteria. Sport in the Slovenian school system is a completely separate field. The lack of transparency of organisations offering sports programmes for potential athletes with disabilities means that only a small number of children and youth with disabilities participate.

Governmental Agents

Major state or national institutions of critical importance to disability sport are: (1) National Assembly of the Republic of Slovenia (DZ-RS, Državni zbor Republike Slovenije), (2) Sports Directorate at the MIZŠ, (3) *OKS*-ZŠZ and (4) Zveza ŠIS-SPK. The state bodies that influence disability sports are the same as those that influence sports in general, along with a few others, but Zveza ŠIS-SPK in particular plays a central role. However, according to the law, Zveza ŠIS-SPK can only affiliate organisations for people with disabilities, not sports organisations. OKS-ZŠZ is therefore automatically superior to it, although they should be equal. State organisations, on the other hand, prepare laws and regulations and take care of supervision. The strength of the influence of individual institutions at this level varies.

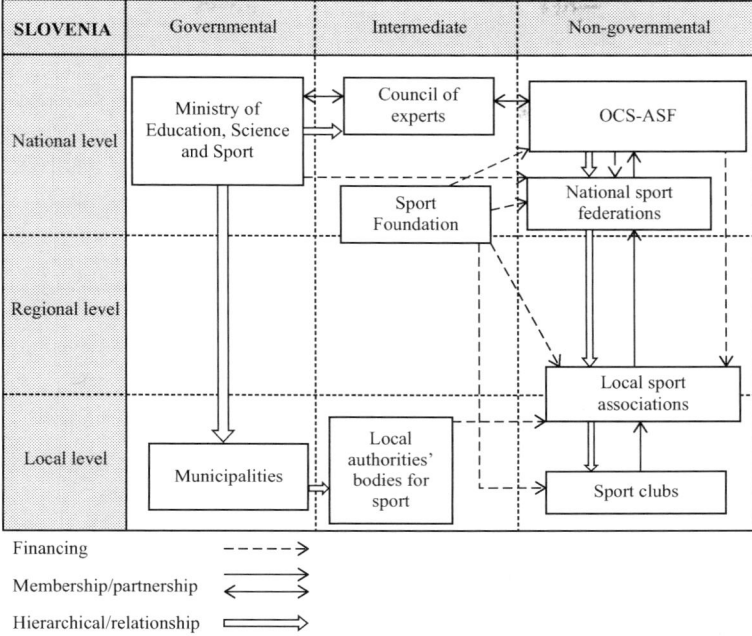

Fig. 19.2 Sport framework of Slovenia. Source: Scheerder et al. (2007)

Intermediate Agents

The main institutions at the intermediate level of disability sport are the following (1) line ministries: MIZŠ, MDDSZ, MZ, (2) Expert Council *for* Sport *of the* Government of the Republic of Slovenia, (3) NSIOS, (4) FIHO and (5) Sports Foundation (FŠO, Fundacija za šport). At this level, inter-ministerial cooperation should take place, but in practice it is not realised. As mentioned earlier, each organisation operates completely independently of the other. There is no institution that collects data on disability sport from all these "intermediary" institutions.

Non-governmental Agents

Non-governmental organisations in the field of disability sport are: (1) national and municipal sports federations, (2) regional centres, (3) public sports institutions, (4) social institutions, (5) sports clubs, (6) associations and federations of people with disabilities and (7) educational institutions. Among the non-governmental organisations listed, we find various sports programmes for athletes with disabilities, but the problem remains that the institutions are not connected.

Secondary Agents

The main actors at the secondary level are (1) local communities and (2) businesses, individual entrepreneurs. Local authorities have a special status in Slovenia, as they have a certain autonomy in relation to the government. With regard to legislation, their activities are dependent on the government, although operationally they act quite independently. They are an extremely important source of funding and support for non-profit organisations in the local area.

The key to the life of an individual athlete with a disability is support from the local community, support from municipal resources and support from vulnerable businesses that are aware of their social responsibility by supporting athletes and other similar individuals and groups (cultural workers, volunteers etc.) in the local area. This was also presented in an interview by Jože Okoren (2020), who emphasised that the local environment is important because not all people with disabilities live in Ljubljana or in larger cities. After rehabilitation, they go to their home environment and want to work, study and live there.

Steering of Disability Sport

Inclusion in sport was outlined on the basis of EU guidelines (Zakrajšek, 2014) with the new Sports Act (2017) and regulations. According to the experts (Štrumbelj, 2020; Kukavica, 2020; Remih, 2020; Lazar, 2020), Slovenia is at a stage where it is necessary to implement inclusion down to the lower levels of the pyramid. At the moment there are no financial resources for this, there is no plan, although at the lowest level of the pyramid, that is, in clubs, institutes, schools and so on, some inclusive sports programmes are running completely independently.

Relationships

From the organisational point of view, we note that there are two types of sports organisations in Slovenia. On the one hand, there are national branch sports federations (NPŠZ, nacionalne panožne športne zveze) which, under the auspices of the OKS-ZŠZ, are completely subordinated to the competitive system and usually have no place for recreational programmes, and on the other hand, there are federations which exclusively promote recreational activities, such as Slovenian Sokol Union and Sports Union of Slovenia. Both recreational and elite sport are systematically regulated differently, which consequently also has an impact on disability sport, which for the time being is still treated separately from sport in general in the legislation. In disability sport, there is no clear demarcation between recreational and competitive sport programmes. More emphasis is placed on para-disciplines within the activities of Zveza ŠIS-SPK, which according to legislation and statutes is a disability association and not a sports association. There is also a distinct difference between programmes for athletes with a physical disability and programmes for athletes with intellectual disability. For decades, the latter operated exclusively within the Special Olympics framework that supports socialisation and recreational inclusion. Within its system it also conducts competitions, but only with the aim of cooperation and not with a selected choice of competition systems, as otherwise a top sport does. The latter has changed in the last three years. Athletes with intellectual disabilities already compete in para-swimming disciplines and inclusive judo. This creates an additional barrier for politicians and decision-makers in equal treatment, as the prevailing mentality is that athletes with intellectual disabilities are not capable of elite sport. Boro Štrumbelj (2020) mentioned in an interview that cooperation with disability organisations is very poor, as athletes with paraplegia are otherwise well organised, as are the deaf, but not everyone else. They are often not recognisable, limited to a narrow circle of members, in contrast to the proactivity of Zveza ŠIS-SPK.

Legislative Framework

Today, the disability sport is legally equal to sport, which, according to experts, was favoured by Slovenia's accession to the European Union (EU). The trend of sport development in the world is inclusion, which means equal opportunities for all athletes regardless of disability. The current Sports Act (2017) has legally equalised the status of the Slovenian Paralympic Committee and the Olympic Committee of Slovenia, which gives the Paralympic Committee the opportunity to independently regulate the field of disability sport.

The rights of athletes with disabilities are written down in documents dealing with persons with disabilities in general, as well as in documents regulating the field of sport and, last but not least, in documents relating exclusively to disability sport. The Slovenian legal bases for the operation of disability sport are the following documents:

- Sports Act (Official Gazette of the Republic of Slovenia, No. 29/17, 21/18 – ZNOrg in 82/20)
- Resolution on the National Programme of Sport of the Republic of Slovenia 2014–2023 (NPŠ) (Official Gazette of the Republic of Slovenia, No. 26/14)
- Strategy of the Sports Federation for the Disabled of Slovenia – Slovenian Paralympic Committee (Zveza ŠIS-SPK) for the period 2019–2029
- Action plan of the Strategy ŠIS-SPK

Slovenian practice in the field of disability sport is at the beginning of the transformation process according to the modern EU directives. Regulations are still being harmonised with laws. Gradual changes from above set the systemic framework for action in practice, which currently lags far behind and relies mainly on voluntary work. The latter is a practice from the past, rooted in both the National Programme of Sport and the Societies Act (Official Gazette of the Republic of Slovenia, No. 64/11—official consolidated text and 21/18—ZNOrg).

The challenges of the process of transformation and equalisation of the disability sport with the sport of the non-disabled and the related fusion into a single Slovenian sport according to the principles of inclusion are first reflected in the small number of young athletes with disabilities. The quantity is the basis and criterion for co-financing of various programmes in sport, which are defined in bylaws:

- Rules on co-financing the annual sports programme at state level (Official Gazette of the Republic of Slovenia, No. 68/19 in 91/20), hereinafter referred to as LPŠ
- Rules on the criteria for co-financing the annual sports programme at state level (Official Gazette of the Republic of Slovenia, No. 22/15, 1/16, 1/17, 29/17 – ZŠpo-1 in 11/18)

Disability sports programmes are financially supported by the *FIHO*. The funds are directly received by the Zveza ŠIS-SPK as an association of disability organisations in the field of sports and some other disability organisations. The legal basis is wide and published on the FIHO website, but let us mention here only the basic laws:

- Gaming Act (Official Gazette of the Republic of Slovenia, No. 14/2011; ZIS-UPB3)
- Ownership Transformation of the Lottery of Slovenia Act (Official Gazette of the Republic of Slovenia, No. 44/96, 47/97, 102/07, 26/11, 109/11, 58/12 in 29/17 – ZŠpo-1)

As Vlado Kukavica (2020), its director, said, FIHO is a public corporation and the only systemic financer of the activities of disability and humanitarian organisations in Slovenia, through which the state fulfils its welfare state obligation. Managed by civil society, it has the legal basis for funding recreational and sports programmes for people with disabilities and others.

It is important that the rights of top athletes are becoming equal in practise, as reflected in the following legal acts:

- Bloudek Awards Act (Official Gazette of the Republic of Slovenia, No. 112/05)
- Act Regulating the Supplement to Pensions for Work and Outstanding Achievements in Sports (Official Gazette of the Republic of Slovenia, No. 34/17)
- Rules on the reimbursement of the education and training costs of elite athletes (Official Gazette of the Republic of Slovenia, No. 46/18)
- Conditions, rules and criteria for the *registration* and *category* ranking of *athletes* in the Republic of Slovenia (Expert Council *of the* Republic of Slovenia *for* Sport, 19. 4. 2017)
- Rules on granting scholarships for athletes in the Republic of Slovenia (based on the Agreement on co-financing scholarships for talented athletes in the Republic of Slovenia, concluded on 22 December 2011 by OKS-ZŠZ, MIZŠ and the FŠO)

According to Polona Sladič (2020), the adoption of the Act Regulating the Supplement to Pensions for Work and Outstanding Achievements in Sports was beneficial for people with disabilities, as the Paralympic medal was also recognised as a sufficient basis for a pension supplement.

Other acts interfering with the field of disability sport are:

- Disability action plan API 2014–2021
- Equalisation of Opportunities for Persons with Disabilities Act (Official Gazette of the Republic of Slovenia, No. 94/10, 50/14 in 32/17)
- Pension and Disability Insurance Act (Official Gazette of the Republic of Slovenia, No. 96/12, 39/13, 99/13 – ZSVarPre-C, 101/13 – ZIPRS1415, 44/14 – ORZPIZ206, 85/14 – ZUJF-B, 95/14 – ZUJF-C, 90/15 – ZIUPTD, 102/15, 23/17, 40/17, 65/17, 28/19 in 75/19)
- Personal Assistance Act (Official Gazette of the Republic of Slovenia, No. 31/18)
- Non-Governmental Organisations Act (Official Gazette of the Republic of Slovenia, No. 21/18)
- Rules on the operation and financing of the sports ombudsman (Official Gazette of the Republic of Slovenia, No. 69/17)

Policy Framework

Slovenian disability sport policy is oriented towards local needs (Mihorko et al., 2014). Stakeholders in the field of disability sport, such as athletes with disabilities, coaches in the field of disability sport, presidents and directors of key institutions, point to the under-provision of the field in terms of co-funding of programmes and staff, mass, the establishment of transparent criteria, equal opportunities compared with non-disabled people and transparent integrated regulation of the sector.

Financial, Governance and Managerial Support

Financial Framework

Disability sports programmes are financially mostly supported by the *FIHO*. The funds are directly received by the Zveza ŠIS-SPK. The financing of disability sport in Slovenia is non-transparent due to the unclear structure of disability sport, which originated in the field of health and is still based on the concept of disability. At the level of funding for recreational and elite sports programmes for people with disabilities, there are no regulations. Therefore, it is not entirely clear who can apply for funding, where, when, how and for which programmes. Traditional funding channels exist mainly through the Zveza ŠIS-SPK, which should, modelled on OKS-ZŠZ, cover mainly elite sport, but which due to the disorganised nature of the field also looks after individual members at the level of associations. The biggest gap is in the inclusive programmes for athletes with disabilities that take place in individual divisional federations according to the EU model and guidelines (Zakrajšek, 2014).

The following is a compilation of some financial data from various sources, indicating the incoherence of systems at national and local level. In disability sport programmes, the largest financial contribution at the state level comes from the FIHO, which otherwise funds only disability organisations. All sports clubs and associations that implement inclusion in the NPŠZ are completely exempt from this.

Table 19.5 shows data from FIHO for the period 2015–2019, which indicates that the organisation allocates approximately 11 million euros per year to programmes run by disability organisations. Of this amount, between 7–9% of the funds are earmarked for disability sport in these organisations. The sports umbrella association with the status of a disability organisation the Zveza ŠIS-SPK receives from this fund annually between 20–40% of all FIHO funds earmarked for disability sport, which amounts to an average of almost 400,000 EUR.

The Zveza ŠIS-SPK also receives funding from the MIZŠ and, to a lesser extent, from the FŠO. Aleš Remih (2020), director of FŠO, said that the organisation is in the process of changing the rules that will further define this area of sport, as well as allow the dedication of more resources and attention to this area.

Table 19.6 shows the amount of co-financing in the period 2017 to 2019 (Grujić, 2020) according to the Institute of Sport of the Republic Slovenia Planica (ZŠRS Planica, Zavod za šport Republike Slovenije Planica). MIZŠ co-finances the top sports programmes of the Zveza ŠIS-SPK and FŠO co-finances programmes such as magazine, several sport divisions, leadership of members and sports results.

As mentioned above, NPŠZ, which through their members (federations, clubs etc.) include athletes with disabilities on an equal and inclusive basis, currently do not receive systemic funds. Sports clubs can only apply for funding for disability sport in local tenders. However, the positions in the public tenders do not reflect the actual circumstances. The Guidelines for Sport and Recreation for People with Disabilities (Mihorko et al., 2014) state that on average only 8% of the planned funds for disability sport were spent at the local level. This means that there are many opportunities for funding sports activities for people with disabilities that are underused by both sports clubs and clubs for people with disabilities.

Table 19.7 shows data from three co-funded programmes by Slovenian municipalities in 2016–2018, namely: disability sport, year-round sports programmes for teaching sports to children and youth with special needs, and sports events for children and youth with special needs at regional and national levels.

The great discrepancy between sport in general and sport for athletes with disabilities is also reflected in the unpaid work of coaches of top athletes with disabilities. MIZŠ co-finances the salaries of professionally trained coaches within the framework of the so-called national branch sports schools (NPŠŠ, nacionalne panožne športne šole). Under this program, no one is employed in the field of disability sports. A partial explanation can be found in the organisation of disability sports within Zveza ŠIS-SPK, which, according to the Sports Act is an association of disability organisations and not an association of sports organisations or sports branch associations.

Table 19.5 FIHO tenders for disability organisations by year (2015–2020) and the number of participants in funded sports programmes

	All FIHO programmes in EUR	Sports and Recreation FIHO funds in EUR	Share of FIHO Funds for Sports in %	FIHO Funds for the Zveza ŠIS-SPK in EUR	Share of All FIHO Funds for the Zveza ŠIS-SPK in %	Share of FIHO Funds for Sports of the Zveza ŠIS-SPK in %	No. Participants in FIHO-Funded Sports Programmes	Of all No. Participants Maximum for the Programme of the Zveza ŠIS-SPK: Communication and Informing
2015	11,538,150.00	785,088.71	6.80	142,730.12	1.24	18.18	53,673	35,000
2016	11,916,450.00	968,777.11	8.13	340,557.39	2.86	35.15	21,815	no data
2017	11,349,000.00	974,254.52	8.58	374,020.27	3.30	38.39	57,332	35,000
2018	11,370,450.00	990,643.36	8.71	373,032.30	3.28	37.66	63,656	39,800
2019	11,011,682.00	1,053,401.44	9.57	391,147.87	3.55	37.13	64,343	41,000
2020	11,163,750.00	no data	–	–	–	–	–	–

Source: FIHO, 2020

Table 19.6 Financing of the Zveza ŠIS-SPK according to the source of financing in the period 2017–2019

	2017	2018	2019
MIZŠ	97,432.00	115,737.00	153,337.00
FŠO	40,397.00	10,262.88	22,167.22
Total	137,829.00	125,999.88	175,504.22

Source: ZŠRS Planica (Grujić, 2020)

Table 19.7 Co-financed disability sports programmes at the local level in the period 2016–2018 in EUR

All Municipalities Together	2016	2017	2018
1. Disability sport	129,395.39	140,341.38	183,429.85
2. Year-round sports programmes for physical education of children and youth with special needs	26,134.92	29,475.78	58,669.09
3. Sports events for children and youth with special needs at regional and national level	3131.00	700.00	1534.86
Total	158,661.31	170,517.16	243,633.80

Source: ZŠRS Planica (Grujić, 2020)

Governance and Management Support

The main support body for the sports system in Slovenia is ZŠRS Planica. The Institute provides support in the implementation of tasks of national and local importance defined in the National Programme of Sport, mainly in the areas of physical education, sports recreation, quality sports, elite sports, disability sport, professional and development tasks, and sports facilities. ZŠRS Planica publishes an annual report entitled Sport in Figures, which presents statistical data on sport in the Republic of Slovenia in the form of tables and charts (Grujić, 2020). But the publication does not have data on the number of all sports programmes and programme participants in Slovenia, such as sports and recreation programmes for disability organisations, which are crucial for the development of disability sports. It also does not have an overview of the number of athletes with disabilities in the NPŠZ, nor does it have an overview of which clubs, other than Zveza ŠIS-SPK, involve athletes with disabilities at all or have developed appropriate programmes and staff.

Another important pillar of support for disability sport, where mainly information about registered and categorised athletes is collected, is the *OKS-ZŠZ*. In cooperation with the Zveza ŠIS-SPK, it mainly collects information about competitive athletes and decides on the guidelines of Slovenian sport at various levels and in various bodies at the highest level. OKS-ZŠZ also conducts trainings for coaches, organises congresses and other. The systems of the two organisations (ZŠRS Planica & OKS-ZŠZ) are not interconnected.

Level of Inclusion

The legislation in the field of disability sport in Slovenia is quite inclusive, which is an excellent basis for further steps. In JR LPŠ we find co-funding of disability sports programmes at the state level—national championships for people with disabilities along with non-disabled people. This is an inclusive solution. Also the programmes and professional work at the Zveza ŠIS-SPK (programme "Become an Athlete"), at NPŠZ (inclusive programmes at the level of recreation and competitions), at disability organisations (support of FIHO), in the school system (Festival Play with me etc.) and at the MIZŠ (compliance with EU directives), OKS-ZŠZ (in cooperation with the MIZŠ and others—Human Resources Development in Sports) are inclusive or at least in favour of inclusion. Inclusion is a process or better a situation in which all actors in society work towards equal opportunities for every member of society. Inclusion in sport means sport for athletes with diverse abilities and is based on creating equal opportunities for all and establishing environments where all stakeholders work towards equal inclusion. In the practice of sports environments, the togetherness and the will are palpable, so we can say that the sports society is on the way to inclusion. Of course, it is necessary to continue with the regulation of the field, because without sufficient financial support it will be impossible to continue building.

On the level of inclusion in sport and in the context of shooting, Polona Sladič (2020) highlighted the Slovenian Shooting Federation, which enabled certain shooters with disabilities to participate in Shooting Federation. Although this seems normal today, it was not always so: *"When this happened for the first time, there were complaints that a shooter with a spinal injury was sitting while shooting and therefore had an advantage."* In 2013 Slovenia integrated the rule that shooters with disabilities in the SH1 category (backless category) can shoot in the National League.

The example described is the highest degree of inclusion we can and will expect. Considering the fact that it is already implemented in some sectors, we can say that disability sport in Slovenia has already reached the highest level of inclusion in some sectors. And this success must be systematically supported and the models of good practice must be transferred to all sports. In some sports, such as judo, athletes can already participate at all levels, from training in clubs to competing at the highest level. In most other sports, this is systematically promoted within Zveza ŠIS-SPK, but according to some experts (Lazar, 2020; Štrumbelj, 2020; Sladič, 2020; Okoren, 2020) this does not work for young people.

19.4 Sport Participation by People with Disabilities

The National Programme of Sport of the Republic of Slovenia (NPŠRS) 2014–2023 states that there are approximately 170,000 people in Slovenia with the status of a person with a disability, which is approximately 8.5% of the population (NPŠRS

2014–2023). The same document uses two terms in disability sport, which usually refer to two age groups, namely: children and youth with special needs and people with disabilities (adult or senior sports programmes). The Disability Action Plan 2014–2021 (API) states: »*People with disabilities are not a uniform group, but are defined by various functional limitations, such as: people with intellectual disabilities; people with visual, hearing and mobility impairments; people who face various everyday obstacles in all aspects of human life; older people who require care.*« In the area of recreational sports activities, there are currently very few programmes for this population, from both a competitive and a recreational standpoint (Jurak, 2014; Mihorko, 2014). Sports programmes in which athletes with disabilities participate take place at different levels and in different organisations, such as: Zveza ŠIS-SPK, in clubs and associations with the status of a disability organisation, in inclusive sports clubs, in primary schools with adapted programmes, in social care institutions, within the Special Olympics of Slovenia and in the URI-Soča. In all areas (school, club, association and rehabilitation) we can find programmes at the recreational level, while in the educational area, sports clubs and at association, competitions also take place.

Jože Okoren (2020) recalls the establishment of disability organisations in the 1960s, along with recreational and elite sports: "Each group of people with disabilities was organised independently: Deaf, blind, paraplegics, people with cerebral paralysis, multiple sclerosis, dystrophies, Special Olympics, in total about 15–16 disability organisations."

More detailed data on the number of included athletes with disabilities is mainly kept at the competitive level. Evidence on the number of participants at the recreational level can be found at the FIHO. However, in Slovenia data on the number of included athletes with disabilities in sports federations or in NPŠZ are not available. Judo athletes with disabilities, for example, are already registered within the OKS-ZŠZ like other athletes, but the data does not show that they are athletes with disabilities. The latter is evidence of full inclusion, but we learn that sometimes so-called positive discrimination[1] is needed, especially when we want to exercise certain rights or benefits, since formal equality generally perpetuates or even reinforces actual inequality (Cerar, 2006).

---

[1] Positive discrimination measures are generally characterised in theory and practised by various terms, such as positive action, positive measures, special measures, temporal measures and so on. The terms positive discrimination and preferential treatment have become widely used, especially in the field of legal theory. In Anglo-American law, positive discrimination is usually referred to as affirmative action, but in constitutional law theory, the term reverse discrimination is often used. The term positive differentiation is also used in the social sciences (e.g. sociology). The EU acquis and the Slovenian acquis have so far used "softer" terms, such as "positive action" or "special (positive) action" (Cerar, 2006).

Monitoring and Evaluation

Data on programmes and the number of athletes with disabilities were obtained from: Zveza ŠIS-SPK, OKS-ZŠZ, ZŠRS Planica and FIHO. An important description of activities and developments in the field of disability sports can also be found in the annual API report of MDDSZ, based on Disability Action Plan 2014–2021. Below we present data on the number of included athletes with disabilities, obtained from the previously mentioned sources.

Sport Participation

Tracking participation rates in sports programmes for children, youth and adults with disabilities is extremely challenging. Most importantly, it again demonstrates the importance of understanding and distinguishing between recreational programmes and competitive programmes. For the latter, the statistics are simpler because the basic criterion for an athlete to be registered within the OKS-ZŠZ is to participate in an official competition. According to the data presented in Table 19.5, the sports and recreational programmes promoted by FIHO, which are exclusively for people with disabilities and not for sports organisations, reached 64,343 members in 2019, of which 41,000 members are involved in the programme of Zveza ŠIS-SPK titled "Communication and Informing" alone. 23,343 members are included in other sports and recreation programmes. According to the data of the MIZŠ, 10,397 children and youth with special needs are included in educational programmes at the primary and secondary school level in the school year 2020/21. According to ZŠRS Planica, 60 students were enrolled in OŠPP sports programmes in the 2018/19 school year. In 2020, 104 athletes up to the age of 23 and 2329 adults are enrolled in the programmes of the Zveza ŠIS-SPK. As of 8 January 2021, there are a total of 246 registered and 70 categorised athletes in the disability sport disciplines who compete in the official systems of the Zveza ŠIS-SPK.

Barriers and Facilitators

Barriers

The field of disability sports in Slovenia is at an important stage of development and is focused on inclusion. The overarching Sports Act, adopted in 2017, enables inclusion, as do bylaws and regulations. Some sports programmes implemented in sports federations, disability organisations and schools are already inclusive. However, for inclusion in sport to fully come to life, a number of barriers still need to be addressed, such as:

- the missing link between sport, health, social affairs and education;
- the harmonisation of certain criteria that otherwise apply to the general population, such as the division of sports into classes based on the rules on co-financing the annual sports programme at state level (Official Gazette of the Republic of Slovenia, No. 68/19 and 91/20);
- only two coaches associated with Human Resources Development and Sport are employed for a fixed period of time;
- NPŠZ have not yet applied for MIZŠ tenders intended for people with disabilities, such as the pilot programme for linking sports and disability and charity associations and clubs, and the reasons for this can be found in the lack of knowledge of the field, lack of practice and no precise criteria;
- according to Sports Act (2017, Article 46), professional work in sport can only be carried out by a professional who has the appropriate sports education, but in disability sport, coaches are also professionals from other fields such as social work, physiotherapy, special education and the like, and as such cannot be funded;
- inclusion is only partially implemented at local level because, unfortunately, there are currently only a few municipalities that fund it;
- annual sports events should be combined into one common event at national level for all athletes regardless of disability; and
- according to OKS-ZŠZ (2020), on 3 December 2020, only three out of a total of 115 athletes were employed in public administration.

Facilitators

Quite a few projects in sport for athletes with disabilities promote inclusion in sport, such as:

- Slovenian legislation in the field of disability sports is inclusive and it is important that it continues to be implemented;
- the project "Human Resources Development in Sport 2016–2022" has recruited the first two coaches in the field of disability sport;
- the programme "Become an Athlete" was launched by Zveza ŠIS-SPK together with Lidl Slovenia. The aim of the programme is to change the view of sport from the perspective of young people with disabilities, to raise public awareness and thus to break down prejudices about the inclusion of young people with disabilities in sports programmes;
- currently, three athletes with disabilities are employed in public administration (OKS-ZŠZ, 2020);
- many sports federations are open to the inclusion of athletes with disabilities under their auspices, such as Slovenian Judo Federation, which is the first and currently the only branch federation in Slovenia to also operate the Paralympic judo discipline for the blind under its auspices; and
- an important recognition of athletes with disabilities has been demonstrated by their inclusion in the rights under the Act Regulating the Supplement to Pensions

for Work and Outstanding Achievements in Sports (Official Gazette of the Republic of Slovenia, No. 34/17) and thus many top athletes who have won medals in the highest competitions of world and Paralympic rank have received adequate pensions with the enactment of this Act.

19.5 Conclusion

Today we can say that we are witnessing a process of inclusion from the top down and vice versa. Both legislation and the various programmes in sports and disability associations make it possible to begin the process of inclusion. However, we lack the links between legislation and practice, systemic regulations, bylaws and some additional political will to regulate the field especially in a transparent way. The worst part is funding, as many disability sports programmes are run by coaches on a volunteer basis. In practice, disability sport is run professionally, but without earmarked funding for elite sport and without clear demarcation and support for the mass.

It would be useful to organise centres where experts can link all levels and help players in the field of disability sport to apply properly for tenders, inform them about opportunities, programmes, staff and the like.

The fact that MIZŠ's support unit, ZŠRS Planica, does not have all the key data in the field of disability sports in Slovenia leads us to the conclusion that we do not yet have an overview of important information on the basis of which we could build an effective inclusive system in all areas: programmes, personnel, funding, interdisciplinary and interdepartmental cooperation and the like.

We notice that there is a lack of young talent, that the structure of athletes with disabilities is older.

The concept of elite disability sport has also not yet been accepted and internalised. This means that despite legislation, the sport sector has not yet changed the mentality that athletes with disabilities are first and foremost athletes and only secondarily people who need adjustments in certain circumstances. So we are still at a stage where we see, for example, an athlete with a disability as a person with a disability and not as an athlete. But the situation is slowly changing for the better, mainly thanks to effective media support and the introduction of inclusive legislation. We believe that soon we will only talk about sport and not about disability sport.

In terms of the Covid-19 pandemic, we are seeing major problems and a decline in fitness among formerly active athletes. Athletes living in social care facilities who were unable to attend training regularly were particularly affected, although the situation has changed and some athletes are now able to undertake training. We also have a recent study on the consequences of a pandemic in school children. Through regular measurements, a sharp decline in the physical performance of school children was detected at the Faculty of Sport in Ljubljana (Jurak et al., 2021), where it was found that the first two months of self-isolation reversed more than ten years of health gains achieved through public health policies and physical activity interventions. After our collective efforts, manifested outwardly by maintaining a physical distance, we must now re-engage socially and physically, with particular attention to those who are otherwise most powerless and marginalised.

References

Ajpes. (2021). *Agencija Republike Slovenije za javnopravne evidence in storitve*. https://www.ajpes.si

Cerar, M. (2006). *IUS-INFO*. Available from https://www.iusinfo.si/medijsko-sredisce/kolumne/10150

Conditions, rules and criteria for the registration and category ranking of athletes in the Republic of Slovenia. (2017). *Expert Council of the Republic of Slovenia for Sport (19. 4. 2017)*. Available from https://www.gov.si/zbirke/delovna-telesa/strokovni-svet-republike-slovenije-za-sport/

Eurostat. (2017a). *Selected indicators by degree of urbanisation*. https://ec.europa.eu/eurostat/web/degree-of-urbanisation/statistics-illustrated

Eurostat. (2017b). *Public opinion – Sport and physical activity*. https://ec.europa.eu/commfrontoffice/publicopinion/index.cfm/survey/getsurveydetail/instruments/special/surveyky/2164

Filipčič, T., Štrumbelj, B., Lamovec, I., Burja, C., Petrović, N., Janežič, S., … Tanšek, G. (2016). Priročnik za izvajanje interesnih programov športa otrok, mladine in odraslih s posebnimi potrebami. In T. Filipčič in B. Štrumbelj (ed.). Ljubljana: Zveza za šport invalidov Slovenije – Paraolimpijski komite.

Fundacija za financiranje invalidskih in humanitarnih organizacij v Republiki Sloveniji /FIHO/. (2019). Available from https://fiho.si/

Gerlovič, D., Kucler, T., Sila, B., & Hosta, M. (2019). *Športna dejavnost Slovencev s poudarkom na fitnes aktivnostih: raziskava Fitnes zveze Slovenije*. Fitnes zveza Slovenije (FZS).

GOV.SI. (2020a). *About Slovenia*. https://www.gov.si/en/policies/state-and-society/about-slovenia/

GOV.SI. (2020b). *Slovenia država*. https://www.gov.si/zbirke/projekti-in-programi/30-let-samostojnosti-slovenije/slovenija-drzava/

Grujić, S. (2020). *Review of sport in the Republic of Slovenia from 2015 to 2020*. Ljubljana. Zavod za šport Republike Slovenije Planica (ZŠRS Planica). Available from https://www.zsrs-planica.si/2011/11/29/publikacija-sport-v-stevilkah-012011/

ISSP Research Group, International Social Survey Programme (ISSP). GESIS Cologne Germany ZA4850, Data Version 2.0.0 (2009–10–29). Available from https://www.gesis.org/en/issp/modules/issp-modules-by-topic/leisure-time-sports

Jurak, G (ed.). (2014). *National programme of sport in Republic of Slovenia 2014–2023*.

Jurak, G., Morrison, S. A., Kovač, M., Leskošek, B., Sember, V., Strel, J., & Starc, G. (2021). A COVID-19 crisis in child physical fitness: Creating a barometric tool of public health engagement for the Republic of Slovenia. *Frontiers in Public Health, 9*. https://doi-org.nukweb.nuk.uni-lj.si/10.3389/fpubh.2021.644235

Koren, M. (2015). *Evropski socialni model: Slovenija in primerjava z Bolgarijo*.

Kukavica, V. (2020). *Šport invalidov v Sloveniji [interview]*. MIZŠ.

Lazar, D. (2020). *Šport invalidov v Sloveniji [interview]*. MIZŠ.

Mediana Survey. (2019). *Mediana Sporto brands Adria*. https://www.mediana.si/kontinuirani-projekti/

Mihorko, B., Štrumbelj, B., Čander, J., & Cimerman Sitar, M. (2014). *Smernice za šport in rekreacijo invalidov*. Društvo vojnih invalidov.

National Programme of sport in the Republic of Slovenia. (2000). Offcial Gazette of the Republic of Slovenia, No. 24/2000, 31/2000 corr. Available from https://www.uradni-list.si/glasilo-uradni-list-rs/vsebina?urlid=200024&stevilka=1065

Olimpijski komite Slovenije – Zveza športnih zvez. (2020). Available from https://www.olympic.si/sportniki/dvojna-kariera/poklicna-integracija/zaposlovanje-vrhunskih-sportnikov

Okoren, J. (2020). *Šport invalidov v Sloveniji [interview]*. MIZŠ.

Prostovoljstvo.org. (2021). *Prostovoljstvo danes*. https://www.prostovoljstvo.org/o-prostovoljstvu/prostovoljstvo-danes

Remih, A. (2020). *Šport invalidov v Sloveniji [interview]*. MIZŠ.

Resolution on the National Programme of Sport of the Republic of Slovenia 2014–2023. (2014). Official Gazette of the Republic of Slovenia, No. 26/14. Available from http://www.pisrs.si/Pis.web/pregledPredpisa?id=RESO99

Rules on co-financing the annual sports programme at state level. (2019). Official Gazette of the Republic of Slovenia, No. 68/19 and 91/20. Available from http://www.pisrs.si/Pis.web/pregledPredpisa?id=PRAV13863

Sambolec, L. (2012). *Vključevanje otrok s posebnimi potrebami v dodatne športne dejavnosti (Diplomsko delo)*. Fakulteta za šport.

Scheerder, J., Van Tuyckom, C., & Vermeersch, A. (2007). *Europa in beweging: sport vanuit Europees perspectief*. Academia Press.

SiStat. (2020). *Republic of Slovenia Statistical Office*. https://pxweb.stat.si/SiStat/en

Sladič, P. (2020). *Šport invalidov v Sloveniji [interview]*. MIZŠ.

Sports Act. (2017). Official Gazette of the Republic of Slovenia, No. 29/17, 21/18 – ZNOrg and 82/20. Available from http://www.pisrs.si/Pis.web/pregledPredpisa?id=ZAKO6853

Štrumbelj, B. (2015). Šport otrok in mladostnikov s posebnimi potrebami v vzgojno- izobraževalnem sistemu. V M. Kovač in M. Plavčak (ur.). *Zbornik 28. posveta športnih pedagogov Slovenije*. : Zveza društev športnih pedagogov Slovenije.

Štrumbelj, B., Filipčič, T., Mihorko, B., Šolar, A., Gačner, D., Čander, J., & Ledinek, M. (2012). *E- časopis ŠME št.1: Modeli vključevanja otrok in mladine invalidov v športne dejavnosti*, pridobljeno s. http://www.zsis.si/2012/09/21/e-asopis-me-t1-modeli-vkljuevanja-otrok-in-mladine-invalidov-v-portne-dejavnosti/

Štrumbelj, B. (2020). *Šport invalidov v Sloveniji [interview]*. MIZŠ.

Zakrajšek, A. (2014). *Modeli integracije paraolimpijskih športov v panožne zvez in športna društva vsvetu in možnosti integracije v Sloveniji*.

Chapter 20
Portugal: Pathways of Sport for People with Disabilities

Leonardo José Mataruna-Dos-Santos, Anabela Vitorino, and Nuno M. Pimenta

20.1 Introduction

Portugal is a country in the extreme southwest of Europe, between the Atlantic Ocean and Spain, with a territory area of 92,212 km^2 and a population of just above 10 million people, of which 6.1% are people with disabilities (INE, 2001). The participation in sport of people with disabilities first formally began in Portugal in the 1940s. However, it was not until the 1972 Paralympic Games in Heidelberg that a Portuguese team first participated at this level (CPP, 2021). Since then, disability sport in Portugal has been given progressive steps and has been used as an instrument for promoting social integration, health and other positive outcomes, for people with disabilities.

L. J. Mataruna-Dos-Santos (✉)
Canadian University Dubai, Dubai, UAE

Portugal Olympic Academy, Lisbon, Portugal
e-mail: leonardo.mataruna@cud.ac.ae

A. Vitorino
Sport Sciences School of Rio Maior—Polytechnic University of Santarém, Santarém, Portugal

Research Center in Sports Sciences, Health Sciences and Human Development (CIDESD), Vila Real, Portugal

Life Quality Research Centre (CIEQV), Leiria, Portugal
e-mail: anabelav@esdrm.ipsantarem.pt

N. M. Pimenta (✉)
Sport Sciences School of Rio Maior—Polytechnic Institute of Santarém, Santarém, Portugal

Interdisciplinary Centre for the Study of Human Performance (CIPER), Lisbon, Portugal

Centro de Investigação Interdisciplinar em Saúde (CIIS), Lisbon, Portugal
e-mail: npimenta@esdrm.ipsantarem.pt

Organised sport for people with disabilities in Portugal is arranged at educational, recreational, therapeutic and competitive levels with some crossover between them. However, in stark contrast to sports for able-bodied participants, a national plan for disability sports has never been implemented nor developed. Accordingly, it has been considered that "there is no disability sport in Portugal, but rather circumstantial sporting practice, more or less framed, aiming at sporadic competitive participation" (Santos & Rodrigues, 2012). Nevertheless, there have been some promising steps, such as those given by the Portuguese Swimming Federation or the equivalent financial support given to Olympic and Paralympic athletes, which are nevertheless insufficient to aim for a broader participation and inclusion of people with disabilities in sport. This chapter provides a timely exploration of the historical context, social and cultural aspects related to disability sport in Portugal.

20.2 Country Profile

This section of the present chapter presents general characteristics of Portugal and some details of the Portuguese sport system and also furthers details of the overall framework of disability sport in Portugal. This is intended to give the reader a good background and insight about the context of Sport in Portugal.

Characteristics of Portugal

Located in the oldest border on the European continent with Spain, Portugal has influences from Mediterranean weather and Iberian Peninsula characteristics (see main characteristics in Table 20.1). Portuguese territory also includes two autonomous regions comprised of the archipelagos of Madeira and the Azores. Madeira is also best known as the birthplace of the famous Portuguese football player Cristiano Ronaldo and Ronaldo has personally supported social foundations and charities for people with disabilities, including initiatives involving disability sports and events there. Madeira is made up by four islands, while the archipelago of Azores encompasses nine islands. Portugal, including the archipelagos, has a semi-presidential political system and a gross domestic product (GDP) of 179 billion euros. This places it among the 50 largest economies in the world, with a positive outlook and growth predicted in the medium term (Statista, 2021).

The Portuguese climate is in favour of outdoor sport activities, and it is characterized by mild winters and nice summers. However, in the North precipitation is higher and temperatures are lower, but the temperature range is widest in the interior region. The projects and programmes for outdoor sports such as surfing, cycling, and hiking have increased in the last decade. The country has a population of 10.31 million people, representing about 2% of the European Union's total population,

Table 20.1 Demographic data and country characteristics

	n	Position	Score
Total population	10,168 M	–	–
People with disabilities (2001 Census)	636,059	–	–
Hearing	84,172		
Physical disability (motor—one or more)	156,246		
Visual	163,569		
Cerebral palsy	15,009		
Intellectual	70,994		
Other disabilities	146,069		
Special students (2010–2011)	46,950	–	–
Special students (2010–2011)	88,023	–	–
People attending rehabilitation programmes in the country	13,950	–	–
Inequality	16%	–	–
Human Development Index	–	38th	0.864
Global Peace Index (GPI) 2020	–	3rd	1.247
Social Progress Index 2020	–	21st	87.79
Well-being	–	87th	5.0
Happy Planet Index 2016	–	79th	24.8
Life expectation (year)	80.3	–	–
PIB—gross domestic product (GDP)—US$	257.39B	–	–
Average household net-adjusted disposable income per capita 2021 in US$ per year	21,203	–	–

Source: Adapted from: (OECD, 2021; Statista, 2021; UN, 2020; Worldometer, 2021)

with 115,4 inhabitants/km^2 in the population density, with higher concentrations along the coastal strip.

Historically, Portugal officially became a kingdom in 1139, and remained a kingdom for the next 800 years. The establishment of the first Portuguese republic began in 1910 and the start of disability sport with institutions or groups in the country started a few decades later on with sporting activities for those with hearing impairments. These events are not well or systematically documented though.

Globally wise Portugal is a very safe and peaceful country and the Global Peace Index ranks Portugal third globally, only behind Iceland and New Zealand. In the Human Development Index (HDI), Portugal occupies the 38th position of the 189 countries involved (Table 20.1). This index is divided in three different dimensions: human development, long life, decent living standards. The Quality of Life Index also reports a general perception of the country with regard to the opportunities but is not specific of people with disabilities (Table 20.2). The data reported here is commonly used by United Nations agencies, and other international institutions, as a barometer of societal well-being.

Finally, Portugal's position in the Better Life Index, from the Organisation for Economic Co-operation and Development (OECD), is above average in a few key performance indicators such as personal security, work-life balance and housing but below average in indicators such as health status, civic engagement, income and

Table 20.2 Quality of life index in Portugal—2021

	Place
General classification	3rd
Leisure options	4th
Personal happiness	3rd
Health and well-being	21st
Safety and security	10th
Digital life	24th
Travel and transportation	22nd
Quality of the environment	11th

Source: Adapted from: (OECD, 2021)

wealth. 68% of people falling in the age bracket of 15–64 are paid employees while 48% of adults between 25 and 64 years of age have completed upper secondary education; the former KPI is in line with the OECD average while the latter is significantly lower than the OECD average (78%) (OECD, 2021).

Sport in Portugal

Coinciding with the end of monarchy in Portugal there was the introduction of a wide variety of sports to the country in the early twentieth century, such as football and basketball (Crespo, 1977). Foreigners had a significant influence in the spread of physical activities while the educated classes played a pivotal role in both the adoption of new cultural habits and the popularisation of sports among the citizens. The Portuguese government took a lead in promoting the importance of physical education and employed the method developed by Pehr Henrik Ling (Andrea, 2015). The Oporto Lisbon cycling race was one of the earliest official sporting events held in the country after the establishment of the Republic (Barroso, 2001) and professional sport began to follow later with cycling and boxing being early adopters. The Portugal contingent first participated in the 1912 Summer Olympic Games and 1972 Paralympic Games (IOC, 2021; IPC, 2020).

The development of sport in Portugal was heavily influenced by the interests of three distinct sectors of Portuguese society at the turn of the twentieth century (Fernandes et al., 2011). These were the military, the medical profession and scholars, with the military, in particular, emphasising the fencing, swimming and gymnastics exercises. This class-based attitude towards sports and the type of sports in which members of different tiers of society engage in is still felt in Portugal today so, whilst sport presents itself as an attractive vehicle for inclusion and well-being, an adequate support framework is required to ensure that this can take place across all of society, including the most disadvantaged.

Portugal presents one of the lowest sport participations levels in Europe (Eurobarometer, 2017). This is a result of individual characteristics and choices of the population but is also the result of numb policies regarding sport and physical activity participation, for many decades. Historical issues may also play a role. Portugal does not have the virtuous trio of: a healthy population, high-level competition and a world-class professional sports industry.

Portugal supports sports participation financially, particularly those included in the Olympics, with funds which come "from the national budget and from several lottery pools, but funding is fairly inferior to that of its European comparators. Even when the most recent lottery to benefit sport, the Euromillions, is taken into account, the overall conclusion remains unchanged" (Fernandes et al., 2011). The government body responsible for implementing the Portuguese sport policy and governing sport in Portugal is the Portuguese Institute of Sport and youth (IPDJ—Instituto Português do Desporto e Juventude), which works under the State's Secretary for Sport and Youth wish is the special body of the Ministry of Education, dedicated to Sport (Fig. 20.1). The Sport system if mainly funded by the state-owned lottery pools which are managed by the Santa Casa da Misericórdia de Lisboa. Municipalities are also a big support to local clubs mainly focusing on grassroots sports. Several local private companies and businesses also often support sport, both grassroots and higher competitive levels. Here the Portuguese system is not seen as supporting

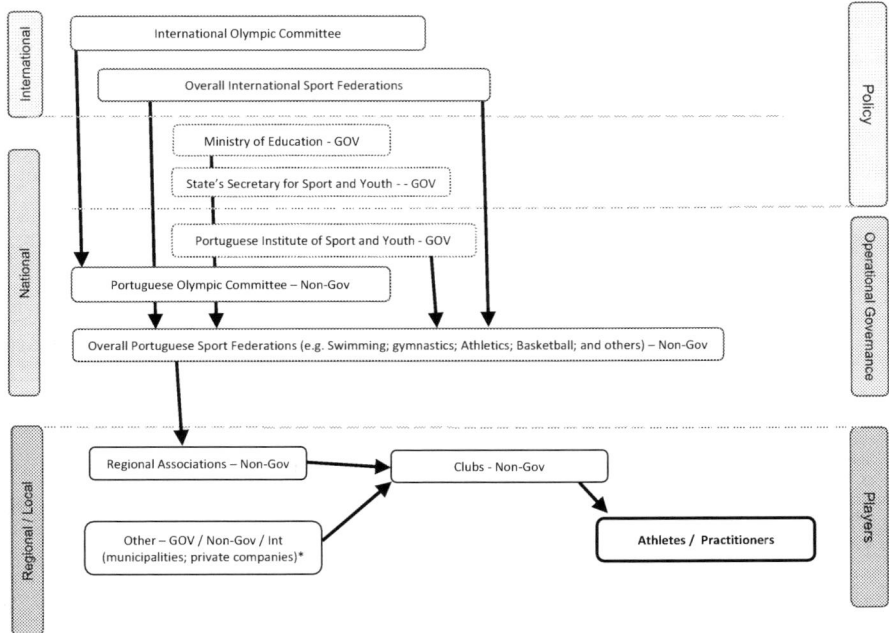

Fig. 20.1 Organogram of able-bodied sport governance in Portugal (GOV—Governmental, Int—intermediary, Non-Gov—Non-governmental agents; arrows represent hierarchical and/or financial relationships). Source: authors' own artwork; data publicly available online on institutional websites of the Portuguese Institute of Sport and Youth (https://ipdj.gov.pt) and the Portuguese Olympic Committee (https://comiteolimpicoportugal.pt)

sport financially in the same way as has been seen, successfully, in the UK. It was argued that Portugal's relative failures in the Olympic Games stem from insufficient funding and that the lottery funding model has been poorly adopted in the country (Fernandes et al., 2011).

Disability in Portugal

The Portuguese Census found that 6.1% of the overall population had some form of disability, summing 639,059 people with disabilities, and that there was a greater prevalence of disabilities on the mainland (6.2%) than the islands (4.8% in Madeira). Figure 20.2 uses this data to detail disabilities in Portugal, as assessed by the 2001 census (INE, 2001). The 2001 census was the last to report data of disabilities following a medical model. The data itself, also, is slightly flawed in that many disabilities are counted but not classifiable. For instance, people reporting more than one disability were classified as "Other." The criterion for defining a disability in the Census changed between 2001 and 2011 with this change leading to an increase in the number of people reported as having a disability in Portugal (INE, 2001, 2011). The 2011 Census numbers show 1,088,412 women and 704,307 men with any limitation, totalling 1,792,718, representing 30% of the entire Portuguese population (INE, 2011). The gigantic increase in the prevalence of persons with disabilities from the 2001 Census to the 2011 Census, relies on different methodologies used: 2001 Census quantified the number of persons with disabilities based on the medical model (hearing disabilities; intellectual disabilities; motor disabilities and so on…), while the 2011 Census used the social model, which takes into account contextual factors (WHO, 2002). This shift in how disabilities were viewed and classified following the 2001 Census came with the unanimous endorsement of the

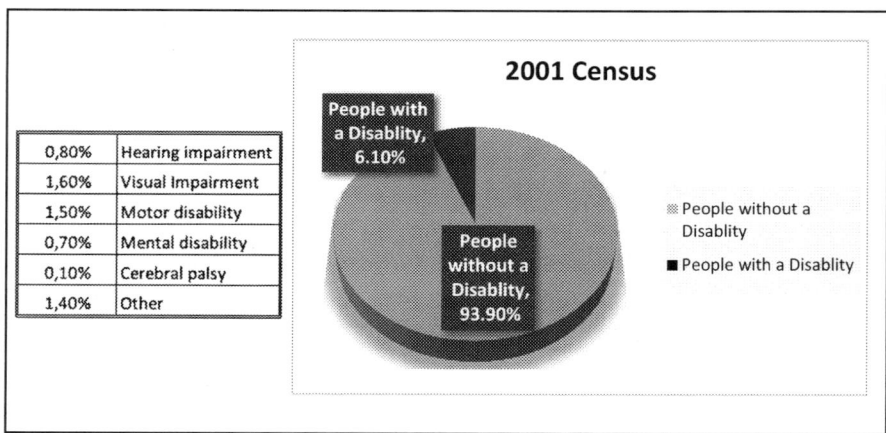

Fig. 20.2 Percentage of the population without and with disabilities by disability type in Portugal. Source: data of Census 2001 (INE, 2001)

ICF whilst, in parallel, all members of the World Health Organization advocated for progressive changes on how physical activity and sports for persons with disabilities were viewed and organised (WHO, 2002). According to the INE (2012), there was a change in this context, with the data being presented based on the concept of disability, that is, the assessment based on diagnoses of disabilities was replaced by a self-assessment that privileges functionality. In other way, disability is redefined as a result of a dynamic interaction between the person and the context, according to the International Classification of Functioning, Disability and Health of the World Health Organization (ICF) (WHO, 2004). This fact can make comparative analyses between these two census records difficult.

Portugal was one of the first countries to proactively implement this new framework and by 2003 the ICF classifications were enshrined in national law (Deliberation no. 10/2003, published in "Republic Diary," II Series, no. 5, 7 January). In 2011, no data was collected on the medical aetiology of disabilities but rather on the functional capacities or limitations of the individual. This was based on the Washington Group short set of questions (Madans et al., 2011) and is in line with the perspective of the second level of the International Classification of Functional, Disability and Health model which classifies the activity, functions and the individual perspective of the person (WHO, 2002). As a consequence, a huge number of persons not diagnosed with any specific disability (from a medical model standpoint), may be considered persons with disabilities, because they cannot perform certain tasks. This is the case of many older adults which, despite not having any particular disability, may have lost some functional capacities associated with ageing. Therefore, the exact number of persons with specific disabilities in Portugal is currently unknown. Current data shows that 17.8% of people between the ages of 15 and 65 years old were found to have difficulties in performing at least one of the basic activities included in the Washington Group short set of questions and that 10% were not able to accomplish two or more (INE, 2011).

One of the few attempts in Portugal to catalogue and begin to address systemic issues related to disability was the work carried out by the National Rehabilitation Secretariat (SNR—Secretariado Nacional de Reabilitação), currently the National Institute for Rehabilitation (INR—Instituto Nacional de Reabilitação) (Anacleto, 2018). In 1995 the SNR conducted the "National Survey on Incapacities, Disabilities and Disadvantages" (INIDD—Inquérito Nacional de Incapacidades, Deficiências e Desvantagens). The data here showed that the 11 main origins of disability in Portugal were common illness (40%), occupational disease (2%), work accident (4%), domestic accident (3%), traffic accident (3%), other accidents (2%), war (1%), senility (5%), childbirth (5%), pregnancy (4%), heredity (12%) and other origins (16%) (SNR, 1995).

Emergence or Rise of Disability Sport in Portugal

The emergence of organised sport for people with disabilities in Portugal occurred at around the same time of World War II and was based on initiatives proposed by a man widely regarded as the father of disability sports, Sir Ludwig Guttmann

(Scruton, 1979). Prior to this, in 1934, the first Recreational Group for the Deaf was established in Oporto, a major city in the northern region of Portugal and the second city of the whole country. Twenty years later (1954), a similar group was established in Lisbon, the country's capital. These groups started promoting physical activity and sports practice for the deaf and are widely regarded as being the vanguard of organised sport for people with disabilities in Portugal. Sousa et al. (2013) produced a full seminal retrospective analysis of the developments during these periods and, through these, it is possible to observe the progression of disability sports in Portugal. Of particular interest is that prior to the 1970s Paralympic sports in Portugal received very limited attention but has since experienced considerable growth and focus. Following the seminal work of Sousa et al. (2013), the timeline of this progression is split into four distinct phases (Fig. 20.3), including the creation of the Portuguese Federation of Sport for Persons with Disabilities (FPDD—Federação Portuguesa de Desporto para Pessoas com Deficiência) and the Portuguese Paralympic Committee (CPP—Comité Paralímpico Português):

Phase I—before 25 April 1974 (the Carnation Revolution):

The Portuguese Association for the Deaf was established in 1958 soon after the creation of the Recreational Group for the Deaf in Lisbon in 1954 and, together with the counterpart Oporto, were already promoting and organising sporting competitions for deaf people. Typical of the emergence of sports for people with disabilities elsewhere, and prompted by the initiatives of Sir Ludwig Guttmann, there was a major emphasis on rehabilitation and treatment of people with disabilities in Portugal during this phase. The Colonial War of 1961 to 1974, in the Portuguese African colonies, was the cause of many injuries and subsequent disabilities, and so the number of people with disabilities in Portugal steadily increased and, with this, created a need for an adequate and coordinated response. Several rehabilitation centres were advocating for such a response from the Portuguese state and, in 1955, a group of Portuguese based medical doctors specialising in rehabilitation, visited Stoke Mandeville Hospital in England. This marked a turning point in the approach

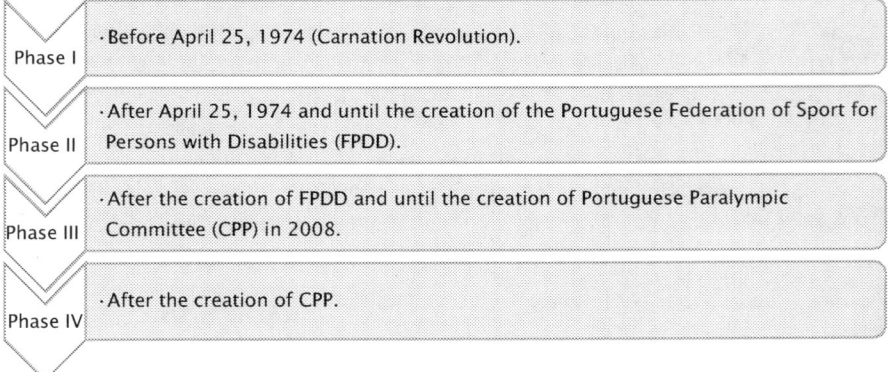

Fig. 20.3 Historical timeline of disability sport emergence and rise. Source: authors' own artwork, adapted from (Sousa et al., 2013)

to disability sports in the country. Still, during this phase, Portugal had no organised system or structures for promoting or governing disability sport. However, prompted by the Stoke Mandeville visit, Portugal's first participation in the Paralympic games occurred in 1972 in Heidelberg, Germany, and in the next year, Portuguese athletes with disabilities also participated in the international games of Stoke Mandeville.

Phase II—after 25 April 1974 (the Carnation Revolution) and until the creation of FPDD in 1998:

The Carnation revolution (25 April 1974) was when the Portuguese military took down the dictatorship in power in Portugal, and implemented the democracy that still endures today. After the Carnation Revolution, Portugal underwent a period a major social and economic transformation. During this period, there was a significant growth in the number and reach of sports associations and the spread of sport across all of society with the concept of 'sport for all' (Council of Europe, 2021). In 1977, Portugal founded two key institutions: The National Rehabilitation Secretariat (currently called National Institute of Rehabilitation—INR) and the Sport General Directorate (currently called Portuguese Institute of Sport and Youth—IPDJ). These two institutions shaped the transformation of sport for people with disabilities in Portugal. However, during this period of national transformation, Portugal did not take part in two consecutive Paralympic games (1976 and 1980) and only chose to resume its official participation at the 1984 New York Games. This was not, at least by contemporary standards, a full participation though, as the sole representatives of the team here, and in 1988, were drawn from the Portuguese Association of Cerebral Palsy (APPC—Associação Portuguesa de Paralisia Cerebral). This was because there was not yet any formal structure devoted to organising and regulating Portuguese Paralympic participation and the APPC was very proactive and took the responsibility for organising and financing a team themselves. It was also during this period, in 1987, that the Special Olympics movement began in Portugal.

Phase III—after the creation of FPDD and until the creation of CPP in 2008:

This third phase lasted two decades and was marked by the foundation of the FPDD in 1988 and characterised by significant development and proliferation of sports for people with disabilities. This included significant focus on, and progress in, organisation, policy, funding and, importantly, the overall promotion and visibility of disability sports. The FPDD led disability sport participation in national and international events, including Portugal Paralympic participations in 1992 Barcelona, 1996 Atlanta, 2000 Sydney, 2004 Athens and 2008 Beijing. During this period, specific associations by area of disability were created (visual, hearing, motor, intellectual, and cerebral palsy) and the Portuguese teams competed widely across these. Paralympic participation was no longer limited in Portugal to specific disabilities or groups.

The Special Olympics, an international non-governmental organization aiming to provide year-round sports training and athletic competition in a variety of Olympic–type sports for children and adults with an intellectual disability, was established in Portugal. The first Portuguese participation in International Games happened in 2007 Shanghai with 21 athletes.

Phase IV—after the creation of the CPP:

In this final phase of development, the CPP was established on 26 September 2008. The CPP leads the Olympic movement in Portugal for people with disabilities and has assumed the responsibility for all Portuguese Paralympic participation. This, for the first time in Portugal, saw a genuine attempt made at the development of a sporting project specifically focused on athletes with disabilities performing at elite levels. Additionally, under this remit, the CPP aimed at promoting inclusion and to fight for the rights and equality of athletes under the Paralympic axiom of "Equality, Inclusion and Sport Excellence.

20.3 The Disability Sport System

This section of the present chapter presents specific details of the organization and framework of disability sports in Portugal. Specifically, this section presents the framework of how disability sport is structured how it is governed in Portugal, from a governmental level down to the stakeholders and the players on the field. Different aspects such as Policy endeavours and legislative framework, as well as financial charter of disability sport is tackled. This is intended to give the reader a greater insight about the organization and framework of Sport in Portugal.

Structure of Disability Sport

Portugal is still in the process of moving from a paradigm based on the medical and rehabilitative model, to the more modern bio-psycho-social paradigm, aligned with the ICF, which is established in the national law since 2003. The country's system of organisation for disability sport governance reflects this long transitory stage and currently there are two main powers in place in Portugal: the Ministry of Education and the Ministry of Solidarity, Employment and Social Security. Each of these two main governmental decision centres have their own chain of structures, subsidiaries and dependencies that constitute the structure in place to rule disability sport. Correspondingly, the organisations that are responsible for the direct governance of disability sport, under the national governmental agents (Fig. 20.4), are the CPP and the FPDD. After the establishment of the FPDD, in 1988, sport for people with disabilities in Portugal became its full responsibility but, following the creation of the CPP, in 2008, different sports began to move from under the FPDD and became nested instead under their mainstream sport federations, particularly those which compete in the Paralympic Games (e.g. all swimming, adapted or not, is now under the Portuguese Swimming Federation). There are though some disability sports for which a regular national sport federation does not exist, such as both Boccia and Goalball and, in these cases, the sports and athletes have remained within the FPDD structure leaving them responsible for governance, including the organising of competitions. The same situation applies to non-Paralympic sports.

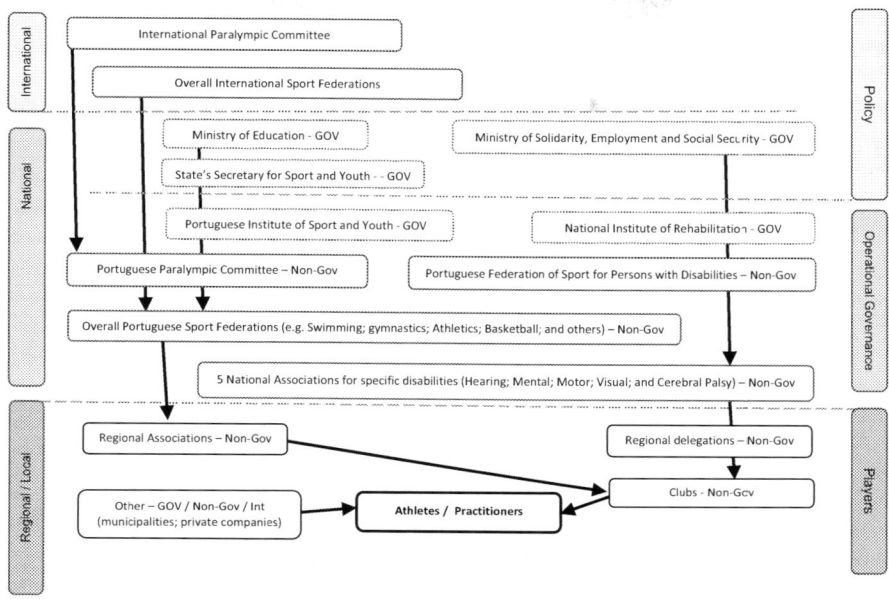

Fig. 20.4 Organogram of disability sport governance in Portugal (GOV—Governmental, Int—intermediary, Non-Gov—Non-governmental agents; arrows represent a hierarchical and/or financial relationship). Source: authors' own artwork; data publicly available online on institutional websites of the Portuguese Institute of Sport and Youth (https://ipdj.gov.pt), the Portuguese Paralympic Committee (https://paralimpicos.pt), the National Institute of Rehabilitation (https://www.inr.pt/inicio) and the Portuguese Federation of Sport for Persons with Disabilities (https://fpdd.pt/novo/)

Governmental Agents

At the governmental level in Portugal, all sports sit under the responsibility of the Ministry of Education (Ministério da Educação). In the case of disability sports, there is also an important intervention by the Ministry of Solidarity, Employment and Social Security (Ministério da Solidariedade, Emprego e Segurança Social), particularly for aspects regarding social support to people with disability, and also regarding the regulation of sports and competitions that are not under regular sport federations. Each Ministry cover many fields of the public organization, beyond sports, therefore they are organized into many departments, called State's Secretaries. In the Ministry of Education there is a specific department responsible for sport, which is the State's Secretary of Sport and Youth (Secretaria de Estado do Desporto e Juventude). The domestic policy agenda for Portuguese sporting practice and competition is set at this level. In the Ministry of Solidarity, Employment and Social Security there is a specific department which is the State's Secretary for the inclusion for people with disabilities (Secretaria de Estado para a Inclusão das Pessoas com Deficiência). This focus on applying Portuguese inclusion policy and regulates sports that are not under de mainstream sport federations (e.g. Boccia, Goalball and other).

The Ministry of Education is also responsible for the entire Portuguese Education System and this includes the Division of School Sports which regulates competitions and practice rules for all sports participation within the schools (not including Physical Education which is part of the formal curricula). Many children with disabilities start their sport participation in schools and many will only ever have the opportunities to compete at this level, particularly in regions with less population and less sport opportunities and clubs, because of funding and organisational issues outside of the statutory education sector. This makes the Ministry for Education a significant player in Portuguese disability sports, albeit not at the elite level.

Intermediate Agents

To operationalise and regulate the implementation of the Portuguese sport policy on the ground, and to make sure everything and all stakeholders, follow the laws and regulations, the Portuguese government have long created the National Institute of Sport and Youth. This is a public institute and its leadership is appointed by the government but it acts more at an executive level and serves as the operational link between the government and the stakeholders and players on the ground. In the case of disability sport, there is another national institute that plays an important role. Operating under the Ministry of Solidarity, Employment and Social Security, specifically under the State's Secretary for the inclusion for people with disabilities, the National Institute of Rehabilitation is also an operational and regulatory governmental branch, in this case, responsible for making sure that inclusion laws are adequately applied and that proper support is provided to persons with disabilities to make sure that barriers are removed and/or can be overcome by persons with disabilities to participate in sports, and also regulates sport participation in disability sports that are not under de mainstream sport federations (e.g. Boccia, Goalball and other).

Non-governmental Agents

At the non-governmental level there are many stakeholders involved. At the top, organizing sport participation, are the CPP, specifically for Paralympic participation, and the overall mainstream sport federations. Mainstream sport federations work together with a network of regional associations/delegations to regulate sport and competitions, and the participation of clubs and athletes. In Portugal, the government delegates many roles and responsibilities to the mainstream sport federations including regulating clubs, coaches, athletes, competitions and other aspects of the regulations of each specific sport. For this reason, the Government, in the form of its operational arm IPDJ, assigns the special status of public utility to sport federations to delegate responsibility of helping make sport available for all. From this standpoint, sport federations have a great responsibility in the promotion of sport and sport opportunities, particularly of disability sports. Some sport clubs may also be given the special status of public utility, but in this case it will have to be attributed by the Ministry, after the club have applied for it. To be given the special status of public utility a sport club have to be non-profit and have to show great value for the community and the country, and show great work done in the promotion of important values and sports for all. This will give the club special tax framework and other privileges to allow the club to better pursue its service to the public.

For non-Paralympic sports, mainstream sport federations respond directly to the National Institute of Sport and Youth, as well as to their international organizations that regulate the specific sport. In Paralympic sports, mainstream sport federations also work together with the CPP to contribute to the Portuguese Paralympic participation which is organized by the CPP. For those specific sports not included under mainstream sport federations (e.g. Boccia, Goalball, and other), competitions clubs, coaches and athletes are under the responsibility of the FPDD, which responds to the National Institute of Rehabilitation and, from this standpoint, falls outside the mainstream sport system, however are still under public regulation and domain.

The Special Olympics Portugal is also a non-governmental that works together with the mother-organization to provide meaningful sport participation experiences to persons with intellectual disabilities. This organization lands outside of the national sport system.

There are also other agents working directly with athletes, including people with disabilities, namely municipalities and private companies, promoting physical activity and sports for people with disabilities. An example of this are swimming schools which operate within municipal swimming pools. Swimming schools offer swimming tuition and recreation, including for persons with disabilities, without being directly involved in competition. Sometimes these clubs act as talent spotters for sport clubs and so form a pathway into competitive sports, but this is not their sole, or even main, remit. On the Portuguese coast privately run surf schools have followed this model too and in recent years have seen significant growth.

Secondary Agents

There is legislation in place in Portugal which stipulates that athletes in organised sports events have mandatory insurance before their participation and that athletes complete a medical exam organised by their sport federations or their association. From this standpoint, insurance companies, medical and health professionals, and institutions in Portugal act as stakeholders in the sport sector and contribute to a safe, healthy, and sound sport practice and competition even though they are not necessarily involved in promoting sport and sport opportunities.

Steering of Disability Sport

In previous decades, disability sport in Portugal was organised under the governance of the FPDD, which remit grew following Portugal's participation in the Paralympic games of Barcelona (1992), Atlanta (1996), Sydney (2000), Athens (2004) and Beijing (2008) as these boosted the profile of Paralympic sports in the county. The country used Paralympic sport to promote sport participation and educational perspectives for all people, but with a particular focus on those with disabilities. A challenge here was that legislation in and around sport was predominantly designed with mainstream or regular sport in mind and so there were gaps in provision and oversight. Nonetheless, the sport for all philosophy was adopted to try to include all people from Portuguese society. London (2012), Rio (2016) and Tokyo (2020) Paralympic Games, following the creation of the CPP, in 2008, saw a consolidation of the Portuguese Paralympic participation and the disability sports programme in Portugal.

This mainstreaming of disability sport in Portugal should not breed complacency though. Most obviously the visibility of people with disabilities in sport needs to be improved and television exposure, the creation of advertises and broadcast of competitions should share more than just sporting results and outcomes to help to develop role models with disabilities in the country. The media promotion can create an accountable campaign of sensibilisation developed exclusively to this population and their relatives and families using the diversity of media communication. This has the dual benefit of promoting the acceptance of disability and in encouraging young people with disabilities to participate in sports. Less obvious to the general public is that the Portuguese sporting bodies and federations are behind in adopting sport management styles which are specifically tailored to Paralympic athletes. Too often the measures, metrics and approaches used are copied from able-bodied sports, and they are not always suitable or optimal.

In 2018 the Ministry of Education conducted legislative initiatives to level the amounts given as support and prizes to both athletes with and without disabilities. As a result, the prizes and financial support given to top athletes with disabilities were highly increased to reach the same amounts as given to top able-bodied athletes. This was a major step in Portuguese policy to warrant equality of opportunities and conditions for top athletes. Still, Portugal currently lacks a national strategy in place for promoting disability sports at the grassroots level and talent identification.

Legislative Framework

Portuguese constitutional law enshrines the right of access to sport to all citizens (no. 1 of Article 79 of the Portuguese constitutional law) and assumes that it is the state's duty to cooperate with schools, sports associations and clubs promoting, stimulating, guiding and supporting sports practice and culture. Accordingly, the

Portuguese Basic Law of Physical Activity and Sport (Law no. 5/2007, published in *Diário da República* no. 111/2007, Series I, of 16 January) states in Article 12: "Everyone is entitled to physical activity and sport, regardless of their ancestry, sex, race, ethnicity, language, origin, religion, political and ideological convictions, education, economic and social and sexual orientation." This legal document further determines how organised physical activity and participation in sport is organised in Portugal. In Article 13 of this cornerstone legal document, the competencies and responsibilities of the CPP are outlined with explicit regard to persons with disabilities and their related competitions. In the same document, Article 29 makes clear that it is the state and national and regional institutions responsibility to promote physical activity and participation in sport by persons with disabilities, including proper technical help, adjusted to any specific requirements or needs of the individual. This envisages both a full integration and social participation of people with disabilities on equal terms and opportunities to those experienced by, and available to, able-bodied people. This regulation assumes that sport is a vital factor in the formation of both the individual and a well-functioning and inclusive society. By making provision for the practice of sports by citizens with disabilities, as can be seen in the determinations contained in Articles 5, 26, 32, 70 and 82, the legislature in Portugal places sport in an elevated role in society.

Likewise, Law no. 38/2004, of 18 August—the Basic Law for the Prevention and Rehabilitation and Integration of People with Disabilities—makes reference to the value of inclusion in sporting provision for citizens with disabilities. Most specifically this concerns sport and recreation as measures for recreation and rehabilitation (Article 25). In addition, it establishes that "it is up to the State to adopt specific measures necessary to ensure the access of people with disabilities to the practice of sport and to enjoy their free time" (Article 38), including access to the practice of high competition sport (Article 39). In covering recreation, rehabilitation and the practice of elite sports, Portuguese law covers the full spectrum of need for citizens with disabilities wishing to be involved, at any level, in playing or practising sport.

Here Portugal was one of the first countries in the world to adopt into law (Deliberation no. 10/2003, published in "*Diário da República*," II Series, no. 5, of 7 January) the rationale of the ICF and, therefore also, the endorsement of the WHO (2002).

In 2018 the Ministry of Education issued a new law (portaria no. 332-A/2018 de 27 de dezembro de 2018), putting on the same level the individual support and prizes given to top athletes, regardless of having disabilities or not. The prize money for medals in the major international events for each sport was levelled for able-bodied athletes and those with disabilities. The prize money for a Paralympic gold medal, which was previously of 20,000 euros, increased to 50,000 euros, which was the same as for an Olympic gold medal. Also, the financial support given to athletes who are eligible and are preparing for Paralympic or Olympic participations became the same for all athletes, regardless of having a disability or not. This was a major step in Portuguese policy to warrant equality of opportunities and conditions for top athletes. Still, Portugal currently lacks a national strategy in place for promoting disability sports at the grassroots level and talent identification.

The National Sport for All Program (IPDJ, 2021) was drawn up in accordance with the international guidelines of the "Sport for All" movement and adopted the definition established in the "European Charter for Sport" (Council of Europe, 2021), in which sport is understood and accepted to be "all forms of physical activities that, through organized or unorganized participation, aim at the expression or improvement of physical and mental condition, the development of social relationships or the achievement of results in competition at all levels." The numbers of sport participation in Portugal are still very modest and are among the lowest observed in Europe (Eurobarometer, 2017).

Policy Framework

The paradigm shift in Portuguese legislation with regard to the inclusion of people with disabilities in sport took place ahead of that of other countries in Europe, and indeed the wider world, and ensured that Portugal moved from using a medical model of disability to a bio-psycho-social model. Following the ICF rationale (as endorsed by the WHO) the sport system for persons with disabilities was kept organised by the FPDD, and not by the specific federation for the related regular sport. This replaced the older model which had emerged during the growth of disability and Paralympic sports in the country in the 1990s and aimed at ensuring a more consistent provision for all athletes in all sports, including those which have no able-bodied equivalent.

The discussion of transfer of governance of selected sports and their competitions to their respective regular sporting federation only started in 2006 on the initiative of the FPDD. These discussions were inspired by initiatives that took place in that same year, particularly related to the transfer of governance of adapted equestrian sports from the International Paralympic Committee to the International Equestrian Federation. Currently most disability sports are ruled under their mainstream sport federation and only a few sports (e.g. Boccia, Goalball and other) are kept under the FPDD.

Financial, Governance and Managerial Support

Financial Framework

Whilst Portuguese law makes equal provision for all citizens and there is, on paper, an equity and equality in the Olympic and Paralympic perspective for sport in the country. However, there are some differences in both the coverage and support for both fields. Particularly at the sport clubs. Some good practices are available, happily, like Oporto Football Club (FCP—Futebol Clube do Porto), where the same level of resources (coaching, physical preparation, physiotherapy, medical staff and other support services) are available for both athletes with and without disabilities. But this seems not yet the norm and should inspire others (Pimenta et al., 2022).

There is little established literature and no consensus around the financing of disability sports and sports for people with disabilities in Portugal and, generally, greater governance and transparency is required here. Despite the low availability of data and published sources regarding funding, several funding sources can be identified, such as:

1. Public funds made available to support clubs attributed to them by the state and allocated according to the number of athletes (this is often made through municipalities)
2. Direct financial support to athletes who compete at elite levels and are classified in the top three in international competitions for their discipline
3. Private sponsorship of disability sports of all levels (clubs and athletes)
4. Athletes, or their families and friends, self-funding participation

Governance and Management Support

The Basic Law on the Sports System introduced in Portugal by Law 1/90 is the first to specifically enhance physical activity and sports for persons with disabilities within the existing sport systems and structures. Prior to this, between 2009 and 2011, support provided for sports performed by persons with disabilities was limited, and relied only on those covered by the CPP, the FPDD and Special Olympics—Portugal. Since 2009 and 2010, scholarships to support athletes and trainers and allowances for the preparation of activities were made available as part of the Paralympic Preparation Program (London 2012) and since 2018 the financial support to top athletes were balanced to those of athletes without disability, which represented a substantial increase. Still the support given to athletes exercising training and competing at lower levels, including grassroots and recreational sports, is still not at the same level. The INR is the main public stakeholder responsible for assuring that barriers are eliminated (e.g. architectural barriers, or other) and to warrant support to people with disabilities to allow them the opportunity to participate in sports. Being a country with fairly limited resources within the context of Europe, Portugal is often faced with challenges in extending the reach of such support to all persons with disabilities and to all barriers or needs experienced by people with disabilities. Despite the commitment and effort of the INR, and all other entities involved in the management of the support to people with disabilities, Portugal is still far from an easy inclusion of persons with disabilities in society and in sports. A lot of work is still to be done in this matter and deeper resources seem needed for this challenge.

Level of Integration or Inclusion

Both inclusion and integration are hard concepts do define and scattered definitions are available. In this chapter we assume that integration is "to be in" and inclusion is "to be part of," including "having a choice," "having a sense of belonging" and "being heard." Dedicated sporting provision for people with disabilities in Portugal has grown over time, however it is still often a segregated system. For example, most children with disabilities are integrated in regular schools in Portugal and there are a lot of children with disabilities participating in disability sports, such as Boccia together with able-bodied colleagues, however these sports are hardly included in the regular curricula of Physical Education classes to pupils of all abilities. This blunts the awareness and understanding needed for fostering inclusive sport and inclusive societies, and interest about disability sport in the future. Schools are often the only place where children with disabilities have the opportunity to experience any sports. This underscores the social role of schools to foster inclusion. Aligned with this view, the Special Olympics movement has been giving several steps in Portugal by implementing important initiatives such as "Unified Schools" aiming to empower youth and educators to be leaders of change to create a more inclusive world. Special Olympics Portugal is currently promoting 11 sports (athletics, basketball, football, equestrian, gymnastics and table tennis are the most popular), the Special Olympics Portugal has other development programmes, such as Family Support Network (FSN), Young Athletes, Law Enforcement Torch Run (LETR), Unified Sports, Unified Schools, Unified Champions Schools, Motor Activities Training Program (MATP) (Special Olympics, 2021).

Regarding the sport system, the supply of disability sports is scarce and mainly focused on main urban areas. Most mainstream sport clubs do not offer opportunities for children with disabilities to participate in sports. Also, the inclusion of disability sports under the responsibility of mainstream sport federations has begun not many years ago and is still in process. A good example of inclusion is the Portuguese Swimming Federation whose tries to include adapted swimming competitions in the same agenda as regular swimming. The Portuguese Swimming Federation argues that they like to "bring all of the swimming family together" and that "there are only athletes," meaning that doesn't matter one's condition, one should be treated and respected as an athlete. The Portuguese Swimming Federation stands as a good example and an example of good practice in the inclusion of disability sport under its responsibility. This can be also observed in the number of athletes (Table 20.3).

Fontes (2009) critiques that the system of policies, as opposed to laws, related to disability sports produced in Portugal is characterised by a lack of organisation and planning which, in turn, leads to a lack of impact in execution. The author argues that emphasising this link between disability and economic deprivation and social exclusion does not mean, however, that the former is the cause and these the result. Poverty does not result from disability, but from the way it is socially constructed, as well as physical, social and psychological barriers erected in relation to disability and people with disabilities. This idea of disability as a social construction and synonymous with oppression by a flawed society is a recent concept but one which rings true to the experience of marginalised athletes with disabilities in Portugal and over the world. Inclusion and opportunity must be developed in the society, structurally, in policy, in schools since young ages, and also through campaigns and effective initiatives that ensure that people with disabilities are able to participate and be included in society.

Table 20.3 Disability sport participation in numbers only of people with disabilities in mainstream (regular) sport federations, in 2019

Federation	Sport	Male			Total Male	Female			Total Female	Total Overall
		≤18	19–35	>35		≤18	19–35	>35		
Federação Portuguesa de Ténis	Tennis	–	4	9	13	–	–	–	–	13
Federação Portuguesa de Tiro	Shooting	–	–	3	3	–	–	–	–	3
Federação Portuguesa de Atletismo	Athletics	8	41	25	74	7	23	7	37	111
Federação Portuguesa de Campismo e Montanhismo	Camping and Mountaineering	–	–	2	2	–	–	–	–	2
Federação Portuguesa de Remo	Rowing	–	13	10	23	–	2	5	7	30
Federação Portuguesa de Desporto Universitário	University Sports	–	3	–	3	–	–	–	–	3
Federação Portuguesa de Desportos de Inverno	Winter Sports	–	–	1	1	–	–	–	–	1
Federação Portuguesa de Vela	Sailing	–	12	19	31	–	3	2	5	36
Federação Portuguesa de Tiro com Arco	Archery	–	2	–	2	–	1	–	1	3
Federação Portuguesa de Ginástica	Gymnastics	7	29	13	49	28	31	9	68	117
Federação Portuguesa de Triatlo	Triathlon	–	2	5	7	–	–	–	–	7
Federação Portuguesa de Canoagem	Canoeing	4	5	5	14	–	–	–	–	14
Federação Portuguesa de Voleibol	Volleyball	–	–	–	–	–	–	–	–	0
Federação Portuguesa de Ciclismo	Cycling	–	10	21	31	–	–	1	1	32

(*continued*)

Table 20.3 (continued)

Federation	Sport	Male			Total Male	Female			Total Female	Total Overall
		≤18	19–35	>35		≤18	19–35	>35		
Federação Portuguesa de Basquetebol	Basketball	4	40	69	113	–	–	4	4	117
Federação Portuguesa de Golfe	Golf	–	9	11	20	–	2	3	5	25
Federação Portuguesa de Badminton	Badminton	2	1	–	3	2	–	–	2	5
Federação Portuguesa de Ténis de Mesa	Table tennis	3	51	–	54	–	3	–	3	57
Federação Portuguesa de Natação	Swimming	*	*	*	141	*	*	*	61	202
Federação Portuguesa de Desportos para pessoas com Deficiência	Multisport*	3	539	396	938	7	154	132	293	1231
Total		31	761	589	1522	37	65	31	487	2009

Source: Authors' own work (based on primary data provided by FPDD)

20.4 Sport Participation by People with Disabilities

This section of the present chapter presents data and details regarding participation in disability sport in Portugal. Specifically, this section presents known number about disability sport participation and identifies the difficulties in monitoring this participation in Portugal. Additionally, barriers and facilitator to disability sport are identified. This is intended to give the reader a greater insight about disability sport participation in Portugal, and to help find opportunities to strive towards a higher and more inclusive disability sport participation.

The growth and mainstreaming of sports played by people with disabilities in Portugal, and of Paralympians themselves, was well demonstrated by the following statement from Portuguese Prime Minister António Costa on saying goodbye to the Paralympic athletes leaving for the Games in Tokyo 2021:

"We assume, in the preparation of this Olympic and Paralympic cycle, the commitment of equality between those who are preparing for both games, whether in prizes or scholarships. In each Olympic cycle, we have a duty to try to take another step, to do as you do, to go a little further," he said. For this reason "the debate and the work that we have to do for the next cycle is post-Olympism, that of after ceasing to practice sports, the continuation of life and the use of knowledge and unique abilities that only high-performance sport, which only by overcoming those who participate in these games, allow them to acquire" (República Portuguesa, 2021).

Here António Costa made clear that the gap in perception and public appreciation for Olympians and Paralympians in the country is closing and must continue to be closed, but also that the Paralympics are, in Portugal, now rightly recognised as being an elite sporting event. The Prime Minister was clear in stating that Paralympians have brought 92 medals to Portugal over the years that there is an expectation that the cohort embarking to Tokyo would move this total past 100. This competitive, medal and target driven nature is a far cry from the recreation and rehabilitative attitudes which dominated the state view of disability sports in past decades.

Monitoring and Evaluation

In spite of an increase in awareness and perception about disability sport is not yet resulting nor relying in a well-organized and structured system that allow a systematic throughout monitoring and both accurate and up-to-date data about disability sport participation, characteristics, heterogeneity and other that would permit a good planning, supported allocation of resources, precise needs assessment and so on, in order to catalyse and promote the sustainability of disability sport.

Sport Participation

In the absence of national systematized data about disability sports, several sources were consulted in order to collect bit and pieces of data that may elicit an overview of disability sport participation in Portugal. These results are not suggestive of very cheering results regarding disability sports participation. Lack of time or a lack of interest are the main reasons cited for individuals not undertaking or engaging in physical exercise programmes or sporting activities in Portugal. Women tend to be less engaged with 78% saying they never practice physical exercise or sport compared to 68% of men.

The last data reported by the Special Olympics, Portugal accounts for a total of 3708 Athletes and Unified Partners people, 221 coaches and 68 competitions held in 2019 (before COVID-19) (Special Olympics, 2021). In the 2019 Abu Dhabi Special Olympics Games the number of Portuguese athletes participating and representing the country was 34 athletes, which was lower than the previous year (49) in Los Angeles, USA (Special Olympics, 2021). The winter sports in the organisation do not have the same relevance than summer sports for Portugal and Portuguese athletes. This organisation is considered to implement excellent cooperation programmes in partnership with other sport institutions, demonstrating efficiency in youth unified actions (Dowling et al., 2010).

As mentioned, data regarding sport participation in Portugal is not abundant, particularly for disability and adapted physical activity. The data reported in Table 20.3 is primary data that was requested directly from FPDD to all mainstream sport federations, and also data from FPDD itself. From a total of 28 sport federations, only 20 responded regarding the number of registered athletes with disabilities participating in disability sports events (Table 20.3). The total number of athletes registered without disabilities was not disclosed by the federations.

Available data and research demonstrates that participation in competitive disability sports has decreased over the years in Portugal (Santos et al., 2013). The highest participation was observed in 2005/2006 with 2911 athletes and has been decreasing ever since, reaching 2304 people in 2012/2013 with 207 sport clubs involved in disability sports competitions (Santos et al., 2013). The number of athletes with disabilities are carefully monitored by the federations as, before the registration to compete in organised competition, national policy dictates that all people must have approval by a physician to compete. This policy, well-intended as it may be, is an obvious barrier to participation for many athletes with disabilities but could also allow good data regarding the characteristics of athletes with disabilities. However, due to the confidentiality of medical data, those characteristics are never known in detail.

Santos et al. (2013) also reported on the participation of pupils with disabilities in sports at school. The most popular disability sport in schools is Boccia with 858 young athletes in the school year of 2010/2011. Participation in Boccia has steadily increased over the years from 63 young athletes in 2001/2002 to 856 in 2010/2011 whilst Goalball is also available as an option to play in some schools and had 119 children participating in 2010/2011. Additionally, 567 children were participating in "other disability sports" run by 61 teams in the same year. Sadly, very little year on year or comparative data is available publicly. According to data from the FPDD, competitive sports was practised by a total of 2304 athletes (1670 were male) in the season of 2012/2013 (Santos et al., 2013). In this season, the most popular sport was athletics (track and field) with 447 athletes, followed by swimming with 288 athletes and football (soccer) with 283 athletes. Data from 2019/2020 season shows a different scenario (Table 20.2). In competitive sports, Boccia and Goalball have the lowest participation. An increase in the participation of athletes with disabilities from 187 in 2012 to 272 in 2014 was also reported in adapted surf events (Matos, 2015).

Regarding informal participation in disability sport, to our knowledge, there is no consistent data available with national or even regional coverage. Such a survey to people with disabilities would be important to assess the level of participation in sports of such target group. This data could help define strategic plans and policy but haven't been done so far. Nevertheless, if we consider national data for population, regarding sport participations, it seems very likely that the participation of people with disabilities in informal disability sport or overall adapted physical activity is very low. Such data would be a good addition to Eurobarometer.

Barriers and Facilitators

Discussion in this chapter to date has made clear that there are a number of social, economic and structural barriers which are liable to preventing participation of athletes with disabilities in Portugal. These can play a critical role in either preventing persons with disabilities from participating in physical activity and sport or, when properly addressed and mitigated, promoting such participation. The former are commonly referred to as barriers to physical activity and sport, and the latter are referred to as facilitators. Literature regarding disability sport and physical activity is richer regarding the barriers than facilitators with the barriers to participation in physical activity and sport receiving more attention from policy makers and policies. There has been, and is, a lot of concern and legislation aimed at eliminating barriers and creating inclusive environments, including removing physical barriers in sport facilities, in transport, and overall commuting infrastructures (Shields et al., 2012; Shields & Synnot, 2016). Whilst these barriers certainly still exist a more recent systematic review suggested that the barriers to physical activity in persons with disabilities would be related more to health issues, motivation, preferences, financial issues, physical fitness and transportation (Bossink et al., 2017). It is likely too that the Covid-19 pandemic will have created another barrier for athletes with disabilities.

Taliaferro and Hammond (2016) acknowledge the diversity of barriers to participation and inclusion and suggest that all barriers to disability sport and physical activity fit into three major themes: (a) organisational barriers, (b) individual constraints and (c) external influences. Still, other barriers referred to as social barriers, including the attitudes of family members, of the staff from social care and similar institutions, of colleagues and the overall society, have been suggested to play roles that are equal or greater than those listed by Taliaferro and Hammond (Shields & Synnot, 2016).

In Portugal, barriers to disability sport and physical activity may be perceived differently according to the specific needs of the person with disability. A global systematic review highlighted that, for persons with intellectual disabilities, the financial issues, lack of transportation and lack of knowledge of disability sport opportunities may play a greater role (Bodde & Seo, 2009) in preventing participation than is the case for athletes with physical disabilities. Accordingly, barriers to disability sport and physical activity may also be perceived differently in different countries, depending on their laws, culture, the individual level of disability, sport development and other more general factors. Country-specific barriers, especially those which are pertinent or systemic to Portugal, will be addressed ahead in this section.

There have been far fewer studies of facilitators to participation than those looking at the barriers. Often, when these studies do take place, we see discussions addressing facilitators as the opposite of barriers and a common example of this to consider that physical barriers of sport facilities are a barrier to disability sport and that as such a building without physical barriers is a facilitator. This may be true but it does not account for the compounding of barriers and the fact that they rarely occur in isolation. Tellingly, the facilitator that seems to trump all others in encouraging sporting participation is the role played by the primary caregiver (Taliaferro & Hammond, 2016). This is a key element that may act as both a key facilitator and a barrier, depending on their attitudes and how they act towards sport yet very little policy focus is aimed at promoting positive attitudes, or practically assisting, the primary caregivers of people with disabilities.

Barriers

There is a paucity of studies exploring the barriers to disability sport in Portugal. Several barriers have been suggested for disability sport (Ferreira, 1993) including the geographical dispersion of athletes and participants which hinders the organisation of a competitive framework and limits competition in disability sport, therefore further reducing participation opportunities; a lack of proper resources and facilities for regular practice of disability sports; a lack of institutional support, particularly those provided by governmental authorities; financial constraints that affect institutions working with people with disabilities which means that sport and participation is not viewed as a priority. This list of barriers has recently been updated and extended, stressing particularly the inadequacy of many sport facilities for people with disabilities, a lack of public support and interest, lack of human support and willing caregivers and lack of sporting opportunities (Marmeleira et al., 2018). In line with the summary of barriers suggested by Taliaferro and Hammond (2016) and Couto and colleagues (2018) suggest that the most common barriers to disability sport in Portugal are linked to personal, social, environmental and organisational factors.

Facilitators

At the time of writing many different private entities and the government are pushing forward initiatives to promote sport for people with disabilities. This is a new trend and, despite slow progress in the field over the last decade, is promising. The growth in legislation and laws dedicated to enabling people with disabilities to be included in sport is believed to be a factor behind this growth in private financial support.

In the Olympic cycle the government usually uses the high-performance results from the Paralympic Games to highlight the investment in the public polices of the people with disabilities and prior to Tokyo 2021 authorities announced that the preparation of this Olympic and Paralympic cycle is regarded on equal terms. This commitment to equality between those who are preparing for both games, whether win prizes or scholarships, tends to show a balance among the public policies and the disability sports. In each Olympic cycle, the debates of conventional athletes and Paralympic athletes is repeated regarding the balance of opportunities and access to funding available to both. In the post-Olympism perspective, is important that the clubs, federation, and other non-governmental organizations (NGOs) promoting disability and disability sports do not become entangled in these debates and do not waver in supporting and promoting sport for all. The continuation of elite sport is essential but also is the sporting participation and involvement of people with disabilities. Portuguese Prime Minister Costa in highlighting the medal tallies of Paralympians over the years ahead of the Tokyo Games served the disability sport agenda well by avoiding the idea that Paralympians are not elite athletes in the same way that able-bodied Olympians are and by treating them, and their achievements as equals.

In general, social projects, specialist schools, and NGO's bear the responsibility for recruiting and encouraging people to undertake sporting and physical activities. In a Portuguese context it is necessary too to think about provision across the whole country, and not just what is available in the main four big cities that already have structure and critical mass to promote improvements in the quality of life of people with disabilities through sporting initiatives. People with disabilities in small urban centres and villages cannot realistically have access to the same provision as those in larger cities but this does not mean that opportunities should not be made available to them. There is a real danger that sport for people with disabilities in some areas of Portugal is still seen through the rehabilitative lens which was prevalent nationally in the mid twentieth century.

Portuguese constitutional law recognises that the state is responsible for designing and promoting policies for the rehabilitation and inclusion of people with disabilities and support for their families, with initiatives that raise awareness and involve the whole of society in these objectives (República Portuguesa, 2021). The INR has made available, in some cities, the Inclusion Counter Centre (Balcão da Inclusão), that is responsible for informing and orientating people with disabilities and their families, or even organization interested or involved directly or indirectly with disability, about local provision and opportunities, help eliminating barriers and making way for facilitators. This is excellent frontline support for those able to access it but (it very accessible) but information regarding Sport in not yet a priority. The good work of these centres and progressive national policy also does not address the lack of institutional support in promoting disability sport, and so this barrier goes unaddressed. Increasing the number of sport specialists and coaches, with knowledge and competencies regarding disability sports could also help mainstreaming disability sport and fostering inclusion making it seamless and natural.

20.5 Conclusion

Portugal has come a long way regarding disability sports. From the initial perspective, fully focused on rehabilitation, to a contemporary biopsicosocial perspective, there is still a lot to be done. Portuguese legal framework is rather progressive and supportive of inclusion but with low financial support and strategic plans in place, the path still looks rather long to envisage higher disability sport participation and natural inclusion of persons with disabilities into sport. Albeit having gone a long way and, seemingly, on a good direction, Portugal seems to show rather modest numbers of disability sport participation, which seems in line with overall sport participation in the country. The modest supply of disability sport opportunities, particularly by mainstream sport clubs, may play a role, and the low financial resources available to grassroots disability sport and low promotion of overall adapted physical activity may be also to blame. Still there are examples of good practices, including the progressive inclusion of disability sports into mainstream sport federations, such as what the Portuguese Swimming Federation did; or the support given to disability sports in line with all other sports by mainstream sport clubs, as FCP. But a lot needs to be done to promote broader participation in disability sport. Some Barriers and facilitator were identified and may support further strives for an unnoticed and natural inclusion of disability sports. Schools and education seem a privileged environment to put efforts into place to foster the needed long term and sustainable changes in society.

References

Anacleto, L. P. Q. (2018). *O Impacto do Dia Paralímpico nos Participantes dos eventos de Caldas da Rainha e Évora*. [RELATÓRIO FINAL DE ESTÁGIO CURRICULAR NO COMITÉ PARALÍMPICO DE PORTUGAL, Universidade Lusófona de Humanidades e Tecnologia – Faculdade de Educação Física e Desproto]. https://recil.ensinolusofona.pt/bitstream/10437/9004/1/Relatório%20de%20Estágio%20Curricular_CPP_Lu%C3%ADsa%20 Anacleto.pdf

Andrea, M. (2015). A propósito de Ling, da ginástica sueca e da circulação de impressos em língua portuguesa. *Revista Brasileira de Ciências do Esporte, 37*(2), 128–135.

Barroso, M. (2001). *História do Ciclismo em Portugal*. CTT.

Bodde, A. E., & Seo, D. (2009). A review of social and environmental barriers to physical activity for adults with intellectual disabilities. *Disability and Health Journal, 2*(2), 57–66. https://doi.org/10.1016/j.dhjo.2008.11.004

Bossink, L. W. M., van der Putten, A. A., & Vlaskamp, C. (2017). Understanding low levels of physical activity in people with intellectual disabilities: A systematic review to identify barriers and facilitators. *Research in Developmental Disabilities, 68*, 95–110. https://doi.org/10.1016/j.ridd.2017.06.008

Council of Europe. (2021). *Recommendation CM/Rec(2021)5 of the Committee of Ministers to member States on the Revised European Sports Charter*. Council of Europe. https://rm.coe.int/recommendation-cm-rec-2021-5-on-the-revision-of-the-european-sport-cha/1680a43914https://rm.coe.int/recommendation-cm-rec-2021-5-on-the-revision-of-the-european-sport-cha/1680a43914

Couto, L., Freitas, L., Corredeira, R., Cunha, M., & Sousa, A. (2018). Barreiras à Prática de Atividade Física Adaptada: A Perspetiva dos Familiares. *Revista Científica da FPDD – Desporto e Atividade Física para Todos, 4*, 22.

CPP. (2021). *Portuguese results at the games*. Comité Paralímpico de Portugal. https://paralimpicos.pt/en/portugueses-nos-jogos-paralimpicos

Crespo, J. (1977). História da educação física em Portugal: os antecedentes da criação do INEF. *Ludens, 2*(1), 45–52.

Dowling, S., McConkey, R., Hassan, D., & Menke, S. (2010). *'Unified gives us a chance' An evaluation of Special Olympics Youth Unified Sports® Programme in Europe/Eurasia* (p. 96). University of Ulster & Special Olympics. http://media.specialolympics.org/resources/sports-essentials/unified-sports/Final-Report-Unified-Sports.pdf

Eurobarometer. (2017). *Sport and physical activity: Report* (p. 85). European Commission. Directorate General for Education, Youth, Sport and Culture. https://data.europa.eu/doi/10.2766/483047

Fernandes, A. J. S., Tenreiro, F. J. S., Quaresma, L. F. S., & Maçãs, V. M. O. (2011). Sport policy in Portugal. *International Journal of Sport Policy and Politics, 3*(1), 133–141. https://doi.org/10.1080/19406940.2011.548136

Ferreira, L. (1993). Desporto para Todos/Desporto Adaptado. *Revista Integrar, 1*, 42–45.

Fontes, F. (2009). Social policies and the Disabled in Portugal: From charity to social citizenship. *Revista Crítica de Ciências Sociais, 86*, 73–93. https://doi.org/10.4000/rccs.233

INE. (2001). *CENSO2001 (Resultados Definitivos)* (p. 648) [Census 2001]. Instituto Nacional de Estatística.

INE. (2011). *Censos2011 (Resultados Provisorios)* (Census 2011; Número Census 2011, p. 143). Instituto Nacional de Estatística.

INE. (2012). *Censos 2011 Resultados Definitivos – Portugal*. Instituto Nacional de Estatística, I.P.

IOC. (2021). *Portugal*. International Olympic Committee. https://olympics.com/ioc/portugal

IPC. (2020). *Tokyo 2020 Paralympic Games set to engage global audiences on digital*. International Olympic Committee. https://www.paralympic.org/news/tokyo-2020-paralympic-games-set-engage-global-audiences-digital

IPDJ. (2021). *Programa Nacional de Desporto para Todos*. Intituto Nacional do Desporto e Juventude. https://ipdj.gov.pt/programa-nacional-de-desporto-para-todos

Madans, J. H., Loeb, M. E., & Altman, B. M. (2011). Measuring disability and monitoring the UN Convention on the Rights of Persons with Disabilities: The work of the Washington Group on Disability Statistics. *BMC Public Health, 11*(Suppl 4), S4. https://doi.org/10.1186/1471-2458-11-S4-S4

Marmeleira, J. F. F., Fernandes, J. M. G. A., Ribeiro, N. C., Teixeira, J. A., & Gutierres Filho, P. J. B. (2018). Barreiras para a prática de atividade física em pessoas com deficiência visual. *Revista Brasileira de Ciências do Esporte, 40*(2), 197–204. https://doi.org/10.1016/j.rbce.2017.12.001

Matos, D. S. F. S. (2015). *Perfil do praticante do subsetor desportivo do Surf adaptado: Estudo de caso da SURFaddict* [Master Thesis, University of Lisbon – Faculty of Human Kinetics]. https://www.repository.utl.pt/bitstream/10400.5/10369/1/Dissertação%20Duarte%20F.%20S.%20Matos.pdf

OECD. (2021). *OECD's Better Life Index. Organisation for Economic Co-operation and Development – Economic Surveys Portugal*. https://www.oecdbetterlifeindex.org/countries/portugal/

Pimenta, N. M., Dekkers, V., & SEDY team. (2022). *Collection of Inclusion Best Practices 2021—SEDY2 project*. Sport Empowers Disabled Youth Project – ERASMUS+. https://www.inholland.nl/onderzoek/publicaties/collection-of-inclusion-best-practices-2021

República Portuguesa. (2021). *Primeiro-Ministro afirma que os portugueses estarão com os atletas paralímpicos*. República Portuguesa – XXII Governo. https://www.portugal.gov.pt/pt/gc22/comunicacao/noticia?i=primeiro-ministro-afirma-que-os-portugueses-estarao-com-os-atletas-paralimpicos

Santos, J. P., Almeida, M., Oliveira, C., Fernandes, R., & Cruz-Santos, A. (2013). Desporto Adaptado em Portugal: Do conceito à prática. *Revista Brasileira de Atividade Física & Saúde, 18*(5), 623.

Santos, J. A., & Rodrigues, N. M. (2012). Adapted sport. Which values should guide it? *Revista Portuguesa de Ciências Do Desporto, 12*(3), 128–113.

Scruton, J. (1979). Sir Ludwig Guttmann: Creator of a world sports movement for the paralyzed and other disabled. *Spinal Cord, 17*, 52–55. https://doi.org/10.1038/sc.1979.13

Shields, N., & Synnot, A. (2016). Perceived barriers and facilitators to participation in physical activity for children with disability: A qualitative study. *BMC Pediatrics, 16*(1), 1–10. https://doi.org/10.1186/s12887-016-0544-7

Shields, N., Synnot, A. J., & Barr, M. (2012). Perceived barriers and facilitators to physical activity for children with disability: A systematic review. *British Journal of Sports Medicine, 46*(14), 989–997. https://doi.org/10.1136/bjsports-2011-090236

SNR. (1995). Inquérito Nacional de Incapacidades, *Deficiências e Desvantagens*. Secretariado Nacional de Reabilitação. https://www.inr.pt/documents/11309/217178/inquerito_nacional_as_incapacidades_deficiências_e_desvantagens.pdf/2c379e4b-6edd-43ba-93de-5188b47c5bb0

Sousa, A., Corredeira, R., & Pereira, A. L. (2013). Desporto Paralímpico em Portugal: Da sua génese à atualidade. *Revista Portuguesa de Ciências do Desporto, 13*(1), 93–112.

Special Olympics. (2021). *Special Olympics—Portugal Factsheet* (p. 1). Special Olympics – Portugal.

Statista. (2021). *Gross domestic product (GDP) per capita in Portugal 2026*. Statista. https://www.statista.com/statistics/372340/gross-domestic-product-gdp-per-capita-in-portugal/

Taliaferro, A. R., & Hammond, L. (2016). I don't have time: Barriers and facilitators to physical activity for adults with intellectual disabilities. *Adapted Physical Activity Quarterly, 33*(2), 113–133. https://doi.org/10.1123/APAQ.2015-0050

UN. (2020). *Human Development Index (HDI)*. United Nations Development Programme. http://hdr.undp.org/en/content/human-development-index-hdi

WHO. (2002). *Towards a Common Language for Functioning, Disability and Health—ICF* (WHO/EIP/GPE/CAS/01.3; p. 22). World Health Organization. https://cdn.who.int/media/docs/default-source/classification/icf/icfbeginnersguide.pdf

WHO. (2004). *CIF – Classificação Internacional da Funcionalidade, Incapacidade e Saúde*. Lisboa: Direcção-Geral de Saúde.

Worldometer. (2021). *Portugal Population*. Worldometer. https://www.worldometers.info/world-population/portugal-population/

Chapter 21
Disability Sport in Spain

Javier Pérez Tejero and Cati Lecumberri Gómez

21.1 Country Profile

Spain's Characteristics

Spain is a country of southern Europe, sharing the Iberian peninsula with Portugal and having a northern border with France and Andorra, and has 46,934,632 inhabitants (Spanish Statistical Office—INE, 2019). Spain's population is equivalent to 0.61% of the total world population. Spain ranks number 30 in the list of countries by population, with a population density of 93 per square kilometre. The total land area is 498,000 km^2, and just over 82% of the population is urban. The median age in Spain is 43.6 years. Spain is a unitary parliamentary constitutional monarchy, with a head of government (the President) and a head of state (the King). A council of ministers is the executive branch and is presided over by the president. Spain is a unitary state, composed of 17 autonomous communities and two autonomous cities, with varying degrees of autonomy. The Spanish economy is the fifth largest in Europe, behind Germany, the United Kingdom, Italy and France, and the fourth largest in the Eurozone, based on nominal gross domestic product (GDP) statistics. In 2012, Spain was the 12th largest exporter in the world and the 16th largest importer, and it is listed 25th in the UN Human Development Index (HDI) and 28th in GDP per capita by the World Bank; thus, it is classified as a high-income

---

J. Pérez Tejero (✉)
Faculty of Physical Activity and Sport Sciences - INEF, Department of Health and Human Performance, Universidad Politécnica de Madrid, Madrid, Spain
e-mail: j.perez@upm.es

C. Lecumberri Gómez
Instituto Nacional de Educación Física Cataluña—INEFC, Universidad de Barcelona, Barcelona, Spain
e-mail: clecumberri@gencat.cat

© The Author(s), under exclusive license to Springer Nature Switzerland AG 2023
C. van Lindert et al. (eds.), *The Palgrave Handbook of Disability Sport in Europe*, https://doi.org/10.1007/978-3-031-21759-3_21

Table 21.1 Facts and statistics of Spain

Population (number of inhabitants)[a]	46,934,632
Area (km²)	498,000
Density (inhabitants/km²)[b]	513
Urbanisation rate (%)[c]	93
Political organisation	Parliamentary constitutional monarchy
Structure of the state	Centralised, with competences delegation to the autonomous communities
Number of provinces (autonomous communities)	17
Number of municipalities	8131
GDP per capita (in USD, 2017)[d]	28,156.82
Number of official languages	1 official and 6 co-official (including Spanish sign language)
EU membership	Since 1986
Welfare model	Mediterranean model

Sources: (a), (b), (c) INE (2019); (d) The World Bank (2017)

economy and among the countries of very high human development. The most important sectors of Spain's economy in 2016 were the wholesale and retail trades, transport, accommodation and food services (23.4%); public administration, defence, education, human health and social work activities (18.9%); and industry (17.8%). Spain is the country with the third largest number of UNESCO World Heritage Sites, after Italy and China (Table 21.1).

Sport in Spain

Sport is growing in cultural importance in Spain, in both quantitative and qualitative measures. In the Spanish Constitution of 1978, regulation of the sporting phenomenon achieved definitive recognition. Until then it had not been subject to global regulation. In the Spanish Constitution, the Supreme Rule of the Spanish state, the importance of sport and physical activity is recognised through Articles 43.3 and 148.1.19. In Spain the public sport sector exists at three levels of administrative regional government: the central government, the autonomous communities and the local government. In addition, the subjective realm in the sporting arena is completed with the involvement of many private players, among them—not only for their importance but also through their peculiar legal status—Spanish sports federations. The organisation of sport in Spain is based on a system of mutual collaboration between the public and private sectors: both sectors share responsibility for the promotion and development of physical activities and sports (Leardy et al., 2018; Deloitte, 2018) (Table 21.2).

Table 21.2 Sport profile of Spain

Government authority responsible for sport	Ministry of Education, Culture and Sport
Membership sport club (%)[a]	8.4
Membership fitness or health centre (%)[b]	10
Membership socio-cultural club that includes sport in its activities (e.g. employees' club, youth club, school- and university-related club) (%)	–
Sport participation, at least once a week (%)[a]	46.2
Number of national sport federations[a]	66
Number of sport clubs[a]	67,512
Number of sport club members[a]	3,867,000
National budget for sport (2021—%GDP)[c]: national (€ × 1,000,000)	251—0.02%
National budget for sport (2018—%GDP)[a]: regional (€ × 1,000,000)	358—0.03%
National budget for sport federations (€ × 1000)[b]	66,000
Local budget for sport (2018—%GDP)[a]: local (€ × 1,000,000)	2340—0.19%

Sources: (a) CSD (2020a); (b) Lifefitness (2019); (c) CSD (2020c)

Disability in Spain

In Spain the term most used today to refer to disability is 'persons with disabilities' (PwD),—recognised by Spanish legislation and by the United Nations Convention on the Rights of PwD (Ratification instrument of November 23rd, 2007). According to the last disability, personal autonomy and dependency situations (EDAD, Encuesta de Discapacidad, Autonomía personal y situaciones de Dependencia) survey by the Spanish Statistical Office (INE, Instituto Nacional de Estadística), the overall population in Spain numbers 47 million. Of these, 3,847,900 are PwD with a further 269,400 residents in centres, which means the total number of people living with a disability is just over four million, accounting for 9% of the total population (EDAD, INE, 2008). Over half (59.8%) of the total amount of PwD are women. If we look at their distribution by households, there are 3.3 million Spanish households that have at least one person living with a disability (20% of the total). The definition for disability used in the survey is as follows:

'Disability' is any important limitation to carry out the activities of daily life that has lasted or is expected to last more than one year and has its origin in an impairment. It is considered that a person has a disability even if they have overcome it with the use of external technical aids or with the help or supervision of another person (except in the case of wearing glasses or contact lenses) (INE, 2008).

Forty-four types of impairment classified into eight groups were considered in the survey: vision; hearing; communication; learning and application of knowledge and task development; mobility; self-care; domestic life; and interactions and personal relationships (Torralba et al., 2017). EDAD (INE, 2008), also presents differences in the rate of disability based on region, sex and age, the latter being higher in women and as the population increases. Up to approximately 45 years old, the proportion of PwD is higher in men than in women, but from that point on, disability

Table 21.3 Facts and statistics on disability in Spain

Prevalence of physical disabilities (movement) (% of population)	3.3
Prevalence of severe mental disorders (% of population)[a]	2.4
Prevalence of hearing disabilities (% of population)	2.0
Prevalence of seeing disabilities (% of population)	1.7
Prevalence of mental disabilities (% of population)	1.6
Prevalence of visceral disabilities (% of population)	1.3
Prevalence of nervous system disabilities (% of population)	1.1
Prevalence of other disabilities (% of population)	0.8
Not available	0.6
Prevalence of speech disabilities (% of population)	0.2

Source: EDAD (INE, 2008); (a) Confederación Salud Mental España (2019)

rates increase, especially in women. Approximately half of PwD in Spain are over 65 years old, most of them women. Almost 80% of women 90 years and older have a disability. Of the total number of people aged six years and older with disabilities, 74.0% (2.8 million) have difficulties performing basic activities of daily living, of which 65.1% are women. Half of them would be considered as having a 'total disability', that is, they cannot perform activities without aid. When dealing with types of impairment, the most frequent are those affecting bones and joints (in 39.3% of PwD), hearing (23.8%), vision (21.0%) and mental-related impairments (19.0%) (Table 21.3).

Emergence of Disability Sport in Spain

In Spain, the first steps towards sport for PwD took place some years later than in the international arena. The beginnings of sport for PwD in Spain are located in 1958 in Barcelona, under the inspiration of Dr. Guttmann's philosophy. There, in that year, the Provincial Council inaugurated the 'Hogares Mundet' care complex to accommodate homeless children and young people, among whom there were a good number of residents affected by polio sequelae. The head of the centre, Joan Palau, encouraged sports activity among these young PwD. Also, in the early 1960s, Dr. Ramón Sales, at the 'Vall d'Hebró' Hospital (also in Barcelona) and Dr. Miquel Sarrias at the National Association of Civil Invalids (ANIC, Asociación Nacional de Inválidos Civiles; today the 'Guttmann Institute' Neurorehabilitation Hospital) introduced sport as a rehabilitation tool in the clinical setting (Palau & García, 2011). In 1968 the Spanish Sports Federation for Disabled (FEDM, Federación Española de Deportes de Minusválidos; a multi-disability and multisport federation) was founded, led by Guillermo Cabezas. This federation existed until the development of the Royal Decree of Sports Federations of December 20, 1991, which designed a new structure for disability sport in Spain. This decree recognised five new disability-specific sports federations: in 1993 the Spanish Federation of Sports for the Blind (FEDC, Federación Española de Deportes para Ciegos) and the

Spanish Federation of Sports for People with Cerebral Palsy (FEDPC, Federación Española de Deportes para Personas con Parálisis Cerebral y Lesión Cerebral) were created; the old FEDM became the current Spanish Sports Federation for People with Physical Disabilities (FEDDF, Federación Española de Deportes para Personas con Discapacidad Física) and two others were created: Sports for People with Intellectual Disabilities (FEDDI, Federación Española de Deportes para Personas con Discapacidad Intelectual) and Sports for the Deaf (FEDS, Federación Española de Deportes para Sordos). On September 6, 1995, the Spanish Paralympic Committee (CPE, Comité Paralímpico Español) was created, as a coordination entity for all sports practised in Spain by PwD with international representation, in collaboration with the Higher Sport Council (CSD, Consejo Superior de Deportes) and the Spanish sports federations, mainly with the five Spanish sports federations of PwD.

As for the sports results, the great leap in quality that the Barcelona 92 Games brought to the international Paralympic movement also took place in the Spanish teams' sports level, which managed to get into the select group of world powers, with their 107 medals and fifth place in the global medal table. In the last 2016 Games in Rio de Janeiro, the Spanish Paralympic team reached 11th position with 31 medals. Paralympic sport has a tremendous positive recognition in Spanish society. A crucial milestone was the creation of the 'Plan for Supporting Paralympic Sport' (ADOP) in 2005, where public institutions and more than 20 private entities sponsor the training and technical preparation of the Spanish Paralympic athletes.

21.2 The Organisation of Disability Sport in Spain

Structure

Governmental Agents

In Spain, the Ministry of Culture and Education is responsible for sport at the national level, mainly through CSD, an autonomous body that directly exercises the power of the general state administration in the field of sport. It exercises the functions granted to it by the 1990 Act on Sports, its statute and the rest of the legal sport system (Lecumberri, 2020a). The National Council on Disability and the Royal Board on Disability (both belonging to the Ministry of Social Rights and the 2030 Agenda) are also bodies at the national level with responsibilities in the sport area. At a regional level, the different autonomous communities (regions) also have competences in sport: most of them have their own sport legislation; the institution in charge of executing sport programmes, including those dealing with disability sport, is the General Directorate of Sport, normally through strategic plans per region. At a local level, municipalities, town halls and deputations are in charge of providing sport services to the citizens through municipal facilities, sports centres and services of a private nature or under concession, and those activities carried out in educational centres. They also work in collaboration with sport clubs, sport associations and the associative movement of disability at a local level (Fig. 21.1).

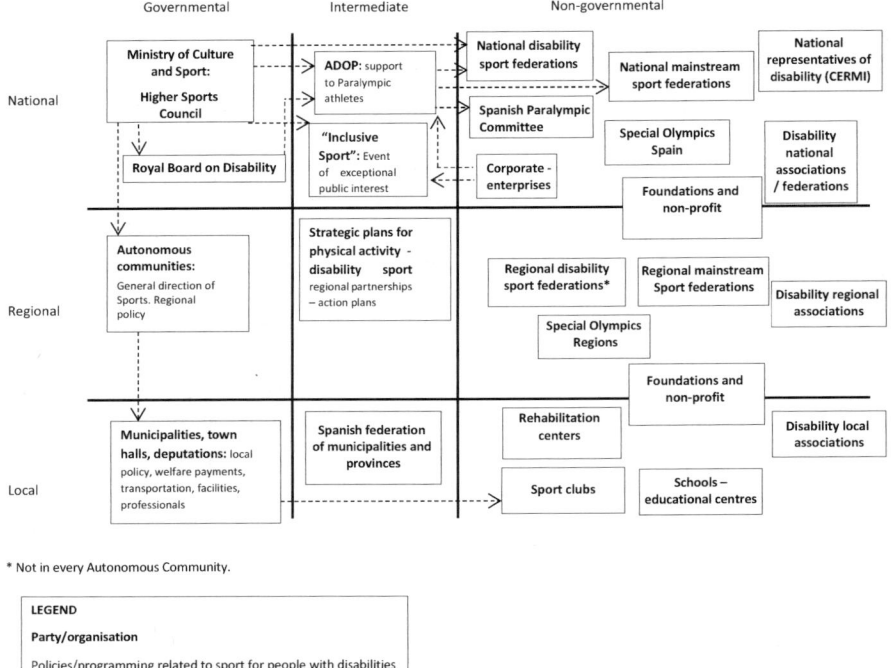

Fig. 21.1 The structure of disability sport in Spain

Intermediate Agents

The Support Programme for Paralympic Sport (ADOP, Ayuda al Deporte Objetivo Paralímpico) is a programme designed to assist elite sports for PwD in Spain to prepare for the Paralympic Games. It was created in 2005, and has supported sportspeople competing in all the Paralympic Games since then. Funding for the ADOP comes from companies and businesses who sponsor athletes, events, federations and teams. For the next Paralympic Games in Tokyo, almost 30 brands are sponsors of the ADOP, apart from the Ministry of Culture and Sport (MCD, Ministerio de Cultura y Deporte) and the Royal Board on Disability: the sponsors have exceeded just over 16 million euros with their contributions so far. At a regional level, the General Directorate of Sports in every community usually run strategic programmes to develop sport activities for PwD at a regional level: for instance, in the Basque Country, the 'Euskadi Plan for Adapted Sport 2015–2020' (Reina, 2018) or the actual 'Plan to Promote Physical Activity and Inclusive Sports' in the Community of Madrid (2018). Also at a regional level, the different actions for mainstream sport promotion include PwD, giving them the same consideration and support and even, in many cases, applying positive discrimination measures.

Non-governmental Agents

The CPE has the same nature and similar exercise functions to those of the Spanish Olympic Committee (COE), but with respect to athletes with physical, sensory and intellectual disabilities, declaring itself a public utility entity regarding its object, nature and functions in the sports field (Mendoza et al., 2018). CPE, apart from its main mission (to prepare the Spanish Paralympic team to compete at the Games) is very active in sport promotion activities, programmes for youth with disabilities sport development (i.e. for swimming, track and field, and cycling) and book editions (Ríos et al., 2014; Spanish Paralympic Committee, 2018) and media coverage of disability sport. Sports federations have a crucial role in disability sport in Spain, and we find two types of these: specific disability sports federations and mainstream sports federations (Olympic sport federations with the modality practised by PwD within). The result is the coexistence of two organisational realities, which are described below:

(a) Sports under the umbrella of disability sports federations:

- FEDC: Paralympic sports: athletics; alpine skiing; Nordic skiing; five-a-side football; goalball; judo; and swimming. Other sports: chess; and shooting.
- FEDDF: Paralympic sports: athletics; wheelchair basketball; boccia; fencing; alpine skiing; Nordic skiing; powerlifting; swimming; wheelchair rugby; snowboarding; Olympic shooting; and seated volleyball. Other sports: motor racing; amputee football; power wheelchair hockey; wheelchair paddle; and wheelchair slalom.
- FEDDI: Paralympic sports: athletics; and swimming. Other sports: basketball; alpine skiing; Nordic skiing; indoor football; rhythmic gymnastics; golf; horse riding; paddle tennis; petanque; and sports skills tests for those with more severe disabilities.
- FEDPC: Paralympic sports: athletics, boccia, alpine skiing, Nordic skiing and swimming. Other sports: wheelchair slalom, seven-a-side football.
- FEDS: athletics; chess; basketball; pool; bowling; cycling; cross-country; darts; winter sports; football; indoor football; mountaineering; mountain biking; swimming; paddle tennis; petanque; fishing; tennis; and table tennis.

(b) Sports integrated into Olympic sports federations:
– Paralympic sports:

- Badminton: Spanish Badminton Federation.
- Cycling: Royal Spanish Cycling Federation (RFEC, Real Federación Española de Ciclismo).
- Horseback riding: Royal Spanish Horseback Riding Federation.
- Canoeing: Royal Spanish Canoeing Federation.
- Rowing: Spanish Rowing Federation.
- Taekwondo: Royal Spanish Taekwondo Federation.
- Table Tennis: Royal Spanish Table Tennis Federation.
- Wheelchair Tennis: Royal Spanish Tennis Federation.

- Archery: Royal Spanish Federation of Archery.
- Triathlon: Spanish Triathlon Federation.

– Other sports or sports discarded from the Paralympic Games' programme:

- Golf: Royal Spanish Golf Federation.
- Karate: Royal Spanish Karate Federation.
- Sailing: Royal Spanish Sailing Federation.
- Surfing: Spanish Surfing Federation.

Sport clubs in Spain are the main support for the practice of sports for PwD, in the different modalities and for all disabilities, from the first stages of promotion and grassroots sports to the stage of high performance. They offer not only their services, facilities, technicians and so on, but also their support through communication channels to give visibility and the greatest possible echo to sport for PwD in their communities (Sanz et al., 2018). They mainly work at a local level, providing access and continuous sport practice. From a total of 67,512 sport clubs in Spain (MCD, 2020) there are 1108 registered in a sport federation recognised by the CPE, which accounts for 1.6% of the total. In many of the cases in Spain, disability sport clubs are developed or under the umbrella of a given disability service provider at a local level, and in recent years many mainstream clubs have started to offer the adapted modality among their services, giving another example of the integration process. Clubs with a greater number of PwD are those of the FEDDI.

Another crucial institution in Spain is Special Olympics, established in Spain in 1991. In 2006 the Special Olympics Spain Foundation was established and obtained the recognition of the CSD, being a member of the CPE from 2011. Currently, Special Olympics Spain, whose headquarters is in Barcelona, has a presence in 13 autonomous communities, in addition to Ceuta and Melilla, through an autonomous branch of the Special Olympics itself or through collaboration agreements with other entities. Its reach nationwide extends to 16,000 athletes and 4500 people, including volunteers and coaches, with participation in 16 sports modalities (Special Olympics, 2020). In light of this, foundations have become forerunners of sport for PwD in Spain. Thus, there has been a significant increase in civil society in the promotion and implementation of actions in relation to physical and sporting activities for PwD, either through foundations or through socially responsible policies of companies that want to link their image either to the sporting values or through sponsorship actions (Reina, 2018).

The non-governmental disability service providers and representatives are well-developed in Spain. The Spanish Committee of Representatives of People with Disabilities (CERMI) is the main representative platform of PwD in Spain, as an umbrella organisation. It is not a specific association for the promoting of sports for people with disabilities, but it has developed different initiatives dealing with sport, such as the support of the book 'White Paper on Sport for Persons with Disabilities' (Leardy et al., 2018). Also, in May 2019, CERMI established its Committee on Sports for PwD, in order to incorporate sport into the agenda of the associative movement.

Steering

Legislative Framework

The main legislation in Spain relevant to disability sport is Act 10/1990, of October 15, on Sport, having already been operating for more than three decades, it is the main legislative frame for sport and also for disability sport. Article 40 of this law states that 'it is the responsibility of the Government to establish the conditions for the creation of state-level sports federations, in which athletes with physical, mental, sensory and mixed disabilities may be integrated'. Five disability groups were recognised: physical; cerebral palsy; visual disability; intellectual disability; and hearing disability, corresponding to the FEDDF, FEDPC, FEDC, FEDDI and FEDS, respectively. In addition, it is important to highlight Article 70 of Act 10/1990, which states: 'sport facilities […] must be accessible, without barriers or obstacles that hinder the free movement of people with a physical disability or advanced age'. In February 2019, a blueprint of a new sport law was presented by the Ministry of Presidency, Relations with Courts and Equality (MPCE, 2019a), focusing on the promotion of real and effective equality and inclusion in sports, and it reinforces governance and transparency in sports entities. One of the main objectives of this law is to guarantee the equality of PwD and the promotion of their sporting activity. The legal consideration of the general interest in inclusive sport is highlighted, as well as the programmes to promote it, its support and visibility. The structure of the disability sport federations for PwD from previous acts will be maintained, but the integration into mainstream sport federations will be mandatory when this becomes the case at the international level. In addition, all federations, regardless of whether they have athletes with disability or not, will have to create a specific inclusive sport commission. From a broader legislative view, already in the 1978 Spanish Constitution the right of PwD are recognised in general terms of equality, freedom, dignity and non-discrimination (Articles 9.2, 10.1 and 14, respectively) and from the perspective of health-care protection, physical education and sport (Article 43). Particular attention is paid to PwD in Article 49, which states that

> the public authorities shall draft policies in the fields of social welfare, treatment, rehabilitation and integration for people with physical, sensory and mental handicaps, providing them with the specialist care they require and affording them special protection for the enjoyment of the rights granted in this section to all citizens.

Crucial legislations to the rights of PwD in Spain were the following:

- Act 13/1982, of April 7th, on the social integration of the handicapped (first Act about PwD in Spain after 1978 Constitution).
- Act 51/2003 of December 2nd on Equal Opportunities, Non-Discrimination and Universal Access by Disabled Individuals. Spanish Official Gazette (BOE) n° 289 of December 3rd.
- Act 27/2007 of October 23rd by virtue of which Spanish sign languages are recognised and means of support are regulated for oral communication by the deaf, hard of hearing, and blind and deaf. BOE n°. 255 of October 24th.

- Ratification instrument of November 23rd, 2007, BOE n° 96 of April 21st, 2008, of the International Convention on the Rights of Persons with Disabilities (ICRPD) drafted in New York on December 13th, 2006 by the UN General Assembly.
- Royal Decree 1276/2011 on Legal Adaptations for Compliance with the ICRPD and Royal Decree 422/2011, by virtue of which the Regulation on Basic Conditions for Disabled Persons' Participation in Political Life and Electoral Processes is approved.
- Royal Legislative Decree 1/2013 of November 29th, by virtue of which the amended text of the General Act on the Rights of Persons with Disabilities and their Social Inclusion is approved. BOE n° 289 of December.
- Act 8/2013 of December 9th on Improvements to the Quality of Education (BOE n° 295 of December 10th) is the actual educational law, which insisted on the goals of promoting people's full personal and professional development.

Apart from the above-mentioned national laws in Spain, Autonomous Communities have competences in health services, social affairs, education and sport promotion, so attention to PwD is taken into consideration from regional laws and programmes within regions. Also at a municipal level, direct services to the citizens are implemented and they are based on the perspective of normalisation and accessibility, including physical activity and sport provision, as this is the main administration dealing with sport budgets (Pérez-Tejero & Casas, 2019), and also the one closest to the citizens. In the case of sport, most Autonomous Communities have their specific sport law, where PwD and their rights are present.

Policy Framework

There have been several coordinated and cooperative actions between the state administration and those intermediate and non-governmental organisations to ensure the right of PwD to access to sport in conditions of equality and non-discrimination, accessible goods and services. The main one in recent years was the Integral Plan for Physical Activity and Sports 'A+D' (CSD, 2009) outlining a series of measures at three levels (health and scholar age, specific collective—also PwD—and transversal), taking into account the different groups of the Spanish population and their access to the practice of physical activity and sport. In this plan, disability sport had the following aims: (a) to generalise the practice of physical activity and sport for citizens with disabilities, preferably in an inclusive environment and close to their social and family context; (b) to guarantee access and use and enjoyment in the design of sports facilities as a fundamental element in equal opportunities; and (c) to improve the training and specialisation of sports managers and public awareness. However, the A+D plan was not implemented, but it provided a real update of the needs of disability sport and also a framework from which many regions (with competences in sport) could be inspired in order to design and to apply policies dealing with PwD and sport. At regional and municipal levels, we can highlight some common policies applied in the recent years, which provide the actual context for disability sport at this level. For instance, most of the regions have their own sport legislation, but also strategic plans to promote disability sport in coordination with federations and clubs. Other important actions are the following (adapted from Reina, 2018):

- Policies providing positive discrimination: the application of public prices for the use of sports services, specific subsidies for non-profit entities whose corporate purpose is the protection and support of PwD in sport, aid to sport clubs for transfers, accompaniment, support for sport competitions and athlete scholarships for academic and sports activities or total subsidies for travel costs and transport of materials to official competitions.
- To provide the same consideration and recognition (even at the financial level) to athletes with or without disability, reaching a given standard. Also, to provide specific programmes for labour inclusion of high-level athletes when they finish their sporting career.
- To promote and to coordinate, sometimes in collaboration with the sports federations of the autonomous community, grassroots or school sports for PwD: example of good practices are the 'Special Sport Games' in Extremadura or 'Parainclusive Games' in the region of Madrid.
- To support athlete development and competition at regional and local levels, for a given sport modality from its cultural tradition ('*pelota valenciana*' in the Community of Valencia), geographic characteristics (adapted winter sports in Aragón), to highlighting the presence of a famous Paralympian in the region (like the Paralympic swimmer Xavi Torres in Balearic Islands).
- To promote sport for PwD for health purposes and improvement of the quality of life. Some outstanding examples can be found with the Hospi-Esport Programme (Martínez, 2008), for health and incorporation in health-oriented physical activity in the rehabilitation phase, mainly in Catalonia and Valencia.
- Thanks to the cultural and social value of their sports achievements, athletes with disabilities are being included in the recognition sport galas at regional and municipal levels.
- To promote collaboration between different councils of the same autonomous government to promote sport for PwD: for instance, culture and sports, together with education (continuous training for physical education teachers/sport coaches regarding inclusion, or development of educational programmes like 'Inclusive Sport at School' in different regions (Pérez-Tejero et al., 2013), social affairs ('Mental Health' sport leagues, or physical activity-oriented health in day-care centres in different regions), or health (the already mentioned 'Hospi-Esport' programme).

Thus, inclusive sport is that sport in which people both with and without disabilities can practise together, adjusted to the possibilities of the practitioners and maintaining the objective of the sport speciality in question; it is also an attitude towards sports practice at all levels, fostering awareness, knowledge and respect for difference: surely inclusive sport is one of the best ways to carry out disability sports promotion programmes (Pérez-Tejero, 2013). Nowadays, this idea is impregnating the general sport context in Spain; one recent signal of this is the non-legislative proposal that urges the government to protect and promote inclusive sport between people with and without disabilities (Servimedia, 2020).

Support

Financial Framework

Sport in Spain has developed thanks to public investment and spending. While the state and regional administration were in charge of coordinating the investment for federated and competitive sports, the local administration focused on the creation and exploitation of sports facilities and on allowing access to sport for all (Leardy, 2018). According to the *Yearbook* of *Sports Statistics* (MCD, 2020), in 2018 the state spent almost 175 million euros and the autonomous communities 358.2 million euros, while local entities spent 2.340 million euros (MCD, 2020). So local authorities (municipalities) are key in sport provision, aiming to increase as much as possible the rate of sports practice and give access to practice to all sectors of the population. From 2010, sport has been considered a 'preferential good' at the local level, along with education or health, with independent spending programmes. Likewise, the municipal responsibility includes the 'promotion of sports and sports facilities and leisure time occupation', maintaining the obligation to provide service for sports facilities in populations greater than 20,000 inhabitants. In this context, disability sport has been greatly recognised in the last 10 years; however, there still remains a lot to do in order to provide equal access and physical activity and sport possibilities to PwD. The other major source of municipalities' funding for sport is the organisation of sports activities and therefore it is essential that these activities must be designed for all people, of course including PwD.

At this level, closer to the citizens, sport clubs, associations and foundations are in charge of disability sport. These entities have enormous financing problems in carrying out their activities. In sports for PwD, often clubs are disability-specific and related with a disability service provider, so functions are performed in most cases by associations and foundations that are not sport based in their origin, but rather include physical activity and sport as one more among the options that they offer to their associates (Leardy, 2018). However, there are specific clubs for Paralympic sports, sports for people with intellectual disabilities or for deaf people and, more importantly, more and more sections of disability sport are being created in mainstream clubs of all modalities, in an inclusive way (Pérez-Tejero, 2013). The main sources of financing for the activities promoted by these entities correspond to the fees of the users themselves, the subsidies they receive from public institutions (mainly municipalities) and the sponsorship from private entities (Leardy, 2018).

The limitations that disability sports clubs experience are frequently compensated by the regional sport federation for disability sport, which is not present in all regions and its format differs from one to another (a multi-disability sport federation like in Baleares or Valencia versus a disability-type sport federation, like the national format, as in Madrid or Catalonia). While in mainstream sport, regional federations play an intermediate function between grassroots sport and highly competitive sports and, therefore, they organise federated competitions in their modality and implement sports athlete development programmes. In the case of sports for PwD, these federations have to also perform sports promotion through the creation of schools and recruitment activities, among others. And all this without neglecting the competitive aspect, with regard to both regional championships and participation in national competitions (Leardy, 2018).

In the case of these regional federations, their main source of financing is the subsidies they receive from the corresponding regional administrations, although by directly imparting activities in schools or similar networks they also receive income from user fees. It is important to highlight that, due to the economic difficulties of the regional federations for disability sport (when they exist) and the low number of athletes, the long-term development programmes in disability sport are very sparse in Spain, and mainly supported directly by the CSD, very often in coordination with the mainstream sport federations with adapted modality and/or the disability sport federation—for instance, for the organisation of national championships at school age. In line with this, another important policy in recent years to promote sport participation at school age has been the inclusion of athletes with disabilities at the official mainstream national championships in athletics, swimming, cross-country, badminton, table tennis, rugby and triathlon, and also reverse integration in wheelchair basketball. It has been possible, with the support of the CSD, for those sport federations interested to afford policies and sport rules to welcome inclusion in official competitions (CSD, 2020b). Related to this, and only for individual sport modalities, since 2010 the CPE, in coordination with the respective sport federation, has promoted the 'Paralympic Promises' funded by corporate entities by a given sport, in order to detect, to prepare and to train future elite athletes with disability.

With regard to the national disability sport federations, their income distribution is as follows: 65% comes mainly from own resources and 35% from outside resources, 33.5% as subsidies from CSD and also the remaining 1.5% from the CPE (Deloitte, 2018); however, no data are available for budgets dealing with adapted modalities in mainstream sport federations.

As mentioned before, the ADOP programme was a milestone in the support for Paralympic sport in Spain from 2005: through the CSD and the area of Social Services (now part of the Ministry of Health, Consumption and Social Welfare), and in coordination with the CPE, they managed to get a series of large companies in our country to support economically these athletes and their preparation, which has been a very fruitful formula. The total budget for the Tokyo Paralympic Games would be similar to that for the Rio de Janeiro 2016 Games, which was 21 million euros (Leardy, 2018). ADOP was recognised by the government as being of exceptional public interest, allowing enterprises to financially support the preparation and training of Paralympic athletes, with tax benefits for those businesses. Finally, one of the more recent steps in inclusive sport promotion, and one that has created exceptional public interest, is the incorporation of 'Inclusive Sport' in the 2018

State General Budget Law (MPCE, 2019b), which allows the financing of different inclusive sport actions and programmes from enterprises' investment in the event.

Another important source of economic support for disability sport in Spain has been the Spanish Association for the Blind (ONCE, Organización Nacional de Ciegos Españoles): since 1988 to the present day, ONCE has invested 75.4 million euros in sports programmes and policies, including the celebration of the 1992 Paralympic Games in Barcelona, an event that marked a turning point in terms of the visibility of the image of disability in Spain, contributing 40% of the total cost (about 24 million euros; Reina, 2018). ONCE is the largest non-governmental institution in contributing to sport for PwD: during the last decade an average annual expenditure of 1.1 million euros per year has been dedicated to this purpose. In the 2017 financial year, the ONCE Foundation allocated 1.43 million euros to sport activities of the FEDDF (including the national Wheelchair Basketball League), FEDDI, FEDPC, FEDS, CPE and, Special Olympics Spain.

Governance and Management

In the Spanish sport institutions Act 19/2013 on transparency, access to public information and good governance is applicable. It has been the CSD who over the years have been supporting sport actors, and mainly sports federations, as non-profit and private organisations with public delegation on sports. Reporting on annual activities has to be completed yearly to the CSD, transparency being a key requisite (Act 10/1990 on Sport). Transparency comprises two main areas: institutional information and statistical, budget and economic information (CSD, 2015). Also, and from 2015, sports federations need to follow the Code of Good Governance of the Spanish Sports Federations (MCD, 2015), a requisite to fully operating with the supervision of CSD. In 2020, the transparency of Spanish National Sport federations was assessed for the third time by Transparency International Spain (2020) and the 65 sports federations were assessed on 32 different indicators; 30 sports federations obtained a score of 100 (out of 100). In the case of disability sport federations in Spain, the FEDDF, FEDPC achieved 100 points, the FEDDI 93.75, the FEDC 90.63 and the FEDS 81.25.

To support the integration processes in sport federations, between 2009 and 2011 there was a consultancy service for them at CSD, with the support of the CPE. Also in 2011 the 'First National Congress in Adapted Sport (CONDA): Moving Towards Integration Together' organised by the CSD, CPE and the Regional Government of Castilla la Mancha was celebrated in Toledo with great success (Pérez-Tejero & Sanz, 2011); however, these events stopped, coinciding with the economic crisis. The last action in this regard from the governmental agents was the 'Round Table for Inclusive Sport' promoted by the CSD between 2018 and 2020. The table was a space for dialogue between sports federations, the CPE, the Directorate General for Disability Policies (Ministry of Health), the Spanish Federation of Municipalities and Provinces (FEMP), academic experts and athletes with disabilities, aiming to elaborate a roadmap for some strategic lines of inclusive sport in the Spanish sports system that was presented in May 2020 (CSD, 2020a).

Level of Integration

At the international level, in 2004 the International Paralympic Committee decided in its General Assembly in Cairo to place its trust in the integration process. Some Paralympic sports modalities such as cycling, horse riding, rowing, tennis and table tennis were transferring the government and management of each sport to their respective international Olympic Federation. This integration process is gradually moving to each country by mandate of the international federations, and in Spain it began in 2009. The most significant process—due to its volume, complexity and importance—was in cycling, whereby the licences from the five Spanish disability sport federations of this sport were transferred to the RFEC. Similar processes took place between 2009 and 2012 in the federations of horse riding, archery, sailing, table tennis and tennis, all of which were previously included among the disciplines of sports federations of PwD. In recent years, the process was much simpler in those federations whose disciplines did not previously exist in entities of PwD, such as taekwondo, canoeing, triathlon, badminton, surfing and rowing. However, at the time of publishing this work, important Paralympic sports such as wheelchair basketball, swimming or athletics have not even initiated an approach on how to begin the integration process, either internationally or in Spain (Leardy & Sanz, 2018). As we see, in Spain integration processes have been initiated, but there is still much more to do. In order to promote the process and to guarantee the access of PwD to sport in Spain, several actions must be transversal and involve all areas of the community: sports; education; social; and even business (Lecumberri et al., 2009). With the publication of the *White Book of Sport for PwD in Spain* (Reina, 2018), an ad hoc survey was performed to discover the perception of the integration process of PwD in the mainstream sport structures, with the questions put to sportsmen and women (from the grassroots to elite level), managers, clubs, federations, medical staff and families. From 373 answer received, more than 75% were in favour of the integration processes, 12% against and 13% unsure.

21.3 Sport Participation by People with Disabilities in Spain

Monitoring and Evaluation

In Spain, 53.5% of the population aged 15 and older practised sport in the last year; most of them (86.3%) with vigorous intensity, at least once a week. Age, sex and educational level are crucial variables, as notable differences by sex show that sport participation continues to be higher in men than in women, even if considered in annual terms (59.8% in men, compared to 47.5% in women), or observed in weekly terms (50.4% versus 42.1% in women). These are results from the Sports Habits Survey in Spain 2015 (MCD, 2020) a part of the National Statistical Plan developed by the MCD. The project had the support of the INE in certain aspects of the sample design. This is a sample survey conducted on a sample of 12,000 people aged 15 and older living in the country and provides information on the habits and practices of Spanish sport. However, no information is provided regarding PwD, so no data are available regarding this group. Nowadays we have to rely on different indicators to infer their participation in sport.

Sport Participation

Even knowing of this lack of information, we can affirm that the involvement of PwD in sport, as in other social and cultural aspects, is far from the ratios recommended for health and far from the rates of the general population. Nowadays, there is a lack of measures and initiatives to alleviate the situation. In contrast, as mentioned, there is plenty of legislation to promote physical activity and sport as a right for this population. Regarding leisure time, data from EDAD (INE, 2008) indicates that only 28.3% of the population with disabilities dedicated their free time to performing some type of physical exercise. However, although the majority do not practise it, physical exercise appears as the first option (with 23%) in the list of activities to which PwD would like to dedicate their free time, but cannot do so because of their disability (Fig. 21.2). Nowadays, the situation for PwD in Spain is very well known by the general population and recognised at the general level, because of all the work performed over many decades by the disability associations and disability services providers, and also because of the achievements of our Paralympic athletes.

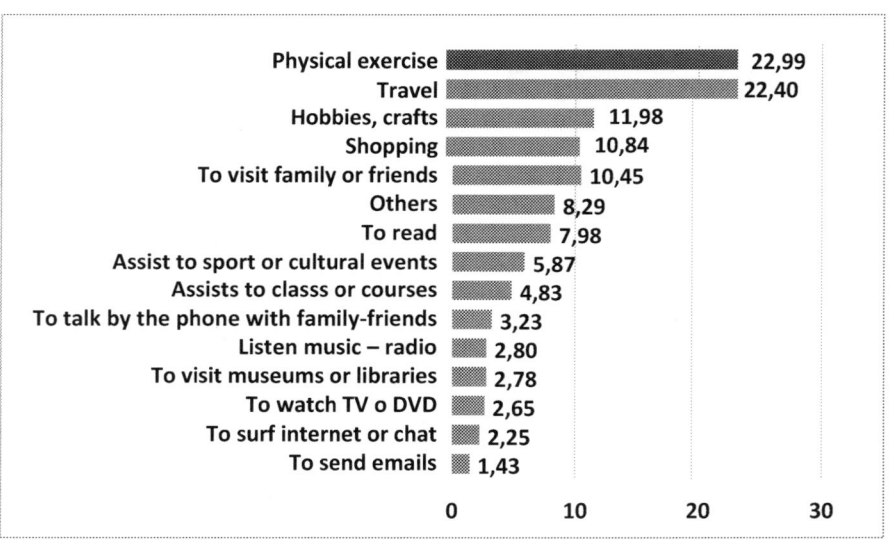

Fig. 21.2 Percentage of people with disabilities that would like to spend their leisure time in a given activity but cannot because of disability. Source: EDAD, INE, 2008

Table 21.4 Number of athletes with disability with a licence at a given Spanish disability sport federation by gender, year 2019

Disability Sport Federation	Total	Men	%	Women	%	Clubs
FEDDF	1687	1407	83.4	280	16.6	156
FEDDI	6377	4639	72.7	1738	27.3	268
FEDC	1841	1417	77.0	424	23.0	**
FEDPC	1514	960	63.4	554	36.6	118
FEDS	772	631	81.7	141	18.3	47
Mainstream sport federations*	725	569	85.8	94	14.2	***
	12,916	9623	74.9	3231	25.1	

*Data from Pérez-Tejero and Ocete (2018); **no data available; ***see Table 21.5
Source: MCS, 2020

One possible indicator of sport practice is a sport licence in a sport federation. In the field of sport licences we gathered data recently published by the MCD (2020), for which we see that the FEDDI is the federation with the highest number of licences presented (6377 in total) among the five sport federations specific to a given disability group (as defined in Sect. 21.2.1). Table 21.4 shows the number of licences in the latest official statistics available on these five federations, along with the number of licences for athletes with disabilities in conventional (mainstream) sports federations. In total, nearly 13,000 PwD had a sport licence in any of these sport federations. It should be noted that there is a significant gender inequality in sport licences: for every three men practising sport with disability, there is only one woman with a licence. Thus, from this data we can analyse this gender distribution, also including the number of PwD licences in mainstream sports federations (Pérez-Tejero & Ocete, 2018). In this context, the result of the process of integration over the past years has developed the sport opportunities for PwD.

The average percentage of licences for athletes with disabilities in the mainstream sports federations accounts for 0.26%. In total numbers, licences for persons with disabilities in these 14 federations together account for 725 athletes in total, a number similar to the 772 licences that FEDS has (the lowest number from those five sport federations for a given group of disability). Therefore, adding the latest available figures, we find from the data available that 12,916 PwD in Spain had a sport licence in 2018. A comparison with the mainstream population could be the following: firstly, in the general population 8.3% of people have a sport licence: 3,945,510 sportspeople in 2019 (MCD, 2020), from a total population of 47,329,981 (INE, 2019). For the PwD sector, this percentage stands at 0.31%, as there are only 12,916 sports licences out of a total of 4,117,300 persons with disabilities in Spain, and only a quarter of them are held by women. This fact shows very clearly the lack of access for the Spanish population with disabilities to sport both as a service in leisure activities and as access to sports competition (sports licences).

In addition, addressing disability in a population statistically is very complex, as the criteria for defining a disability situation can be different, and surveys use different methodologies. For example, for some statistics, the disability certificate is used (statistics of the Community of Madrid, for instance) while other criteria are based

Table 21.5 Number of licences for athletes with disabilities in mainstream Spanish sports federations by gender

	Men	Women	Total	Women with Disability	Men with Disability	Total with Disability	% Disability on Total	Clubs
Badminton	4429	3136	7565	7	27	34	0.45	258
Dance sport	1404	3606	5010	1	3	4	0.08	154
Cycling	72,059	3812	75,871	17	182	199	0.26	3796
Golf	192,414	79,451	271,865	2	48	50	0.02	594
Horse riding	15,793	34,912	50,705	28	30	58	0.57	824
Karate	46,539	18,413	64,952	–	–	–	–	1458
Mountaineering	149,671	72,885	222,556	–	–	–	–	2631
Canoeing	7476	2362	9838	–	–	56	0.57	316
Rowing	8003	3559	11,562	–	–	–	–	133
Taekwondo	28,340	14,024	42,364	–	–	6	0.01	747
Tennis	57,394	22,833	80,227	6	74	80	0.10	1230
Table tennis	7566	1063	8629	2	85	87	1.01	455
Archery	13,717	3869	17,586	4	31	35	0.20	435
Triathlon	22,840	4920	27,760	10	61	71	0.26	1038
Sailing	30,058	11,929	41,987	17	28	45	0.11	451

Source: Pérez-Tejero & Ocete, 2018

on the degree of functioning in activities of daily living (INE, 2008). It would therefore be advisable to include the population with disability in sociological and statistical studies dealing with general population sport habits, such as the survey of sport habits in Spain, performed in 2015 (MCD, 2020).

Barriers and Facilitators

As was noted above, just over 28% of the population with some kind of disability uses leisure time to practise physical exercise or sport. Analysing the reasons why the percentage of participation of PwD is not higher, there are issues regarding barriers and facilitators for practice. For Abellan and Januário (2017), the main barriers influencing access to sport in the group of people with intellectual disabilities were lack of access to public spaces, high financial costs to travel and to participate in activities, lack of peers, lack of professional training and lack of consistent practical opportunities. These barriers to sport participation are also conditioned by the gender factor, where once again women experience additional barriers (Lecumberri, 2020b). A very recent study, focusing on Spanish university students with disabilities and their access and enjoyment of sport (Reina et al., 2019), contacted 417 of them, indicating that the main barriers, in order of importance, were: the lack of sport programmes on offer; the small number of students with disabilities; lack of initiative from university sports services; poor dissemination and visibility; stereotypes and negative attitudes; poor communication between the different services; lack of action protocols; deficiencies in the training of professionals; poor accessibility to sports facilities; lack of resources; lack of support; lack of agreements; lack of constancy from students with disabilities; and lack of time. In contrast, as facilitators of practice (also by importance) they indicated the following: good sport opportunities; staff predisposition; good information dissemination; awareness and attitudes; positive communication between services; initial interview related to sport; training and professional qualification; accessible facilities; availability of specific material; volunteerism; collaboration with external entities; incentives/athletic scholarships/fee exemption (Reina et al., 2019).

However, Spain has worked very hard in recent decades to enhance the enabling factors of sport for PwD. The acquisition of motor skills, greater financial capacity, motivation and determination of the person, educational background and family support (both as companions of practice and as practitioners themselves) are essential to facilitating sports activities for PwD. Access for men and women with disabilities in sport should be managed and promoted by public policies removing barriers and promoting universal accessibility. Although clearly typified in the national laws, there remains a way to go to fully provide adequate access to sport for PwD in Spain.

21.4 Conclusions and Recommendations

Sport for people with disabilities in Spain is a recognizable and transforming reality; below we highlight the most remarkable conclusions and practical recommendations from the present chapter.

- In Spain there is a clear determination to use sport as a tool for social integration of PwD. Although the beginning of sport of PwD was late in Spain when compared with the rest of Europe, because of the Franco dictatorship (1939–1975), nowadays it has a strong organisational structure and great social recognition, especially Paralympic sport.
- MCD is responsible for sport at the national level in Spain, mainly through CSD at the governmental level, while regions have competences in sport and disability, so programmes and initiatives are coordinated at this level. At a local level, municipalities, town halls and deputations are in charge of providing sport services to the citizens through municipal facilities, sports centres and services; they also work in collaboration with sport clubs, sport associations and the associative movement of disability at a local level, with technical and economic difficulties many times. Social awareness and sensibility makes administrations to support this groups.

- Federated sport for PwD is well structured, with five national disability sport-specific sport federations and 16 mainstream national sport federations with inclusion of the adapted/Paralympic modality. CPE coordinates the preparation of elite athletes for Paralypic Games, with governmental and corporate support from specific programmes (i.e. ADOP). Deaf sport and Special Olympics are also well recognised at the national level. Disability service providers and associations play a crucial role in services for PwD (with CERMI as umbrella organisation), also in the access to physical activity and sport promotion.
- The strong legislative support for sport and disability in Spain contrasts with the lack of access to physical activity and sport practices by this population. For instance, 8.4% of the general population had a sport licence (federated sport; MCD, 2020) while for PwD this figure was only 0.31%, with only a quarter being women. Participation in physical activity and sport by PwD is a booming practice but it needs more organisational, training and awareness actions to promote their participation at all levels, and also the visibilisation of disability sport role models in the media.
- Especially in the last years the concept of inclusion in sport is impregnating the general sport context in Spain, with several initiatives that promote the generation of new sport contexts for PwD, the sport participation between people with and without disabilities. Also, a large number of mainstream sport federations already provide participation for PwD through integration processes in the last years.
- Exercise, physical activity and sport are the preferred activity of PwD, when asked what they would do in their spare time if they could. That is why sports services of any kind should be available and accessible, in direct coordination with users and/or the disability representatives. Active participation of PwD in this process is key to successful first contact and adherence to exercise, the view and support of the families and the role of the disability associations, which are very well structured and have so much history in Spain.
- However, there are still many barriers that hinder the practice of sports for PwD who want to exercise: lack of activities offered; lack of training of pre-service sport bachelors, sport professional and sport coaches; lack of accessibility to facilities; precarious sport schedules; and cost of the (adapted) sport equipment, are some of the main barriers.
- The intervention regarding athletes with disabilities must be multidisciplinary, where the staff of each team act in one of the multiple dimensions of the athlete. At the same time, these professionals must be trained in sports and health maintenance techniques and tactics specific to adapted sport or modality. The training of professionals takes on a crucial dimension and it is the responsibility of sports administrations and federations to invest in this training, both officially and continuously.
- It is necessary to plan a coordinated grassroots sport network aimed at promoting access to sport, to identify and to recruit new athletes with disabilities, in coordination with the structures of conventional sport and the disability associations as

two main pillars. Likewise, it is necessary to invest in an efficient management of sport for PwD, contributing to their visibility and empowerment.
- No data on sport habits of Spanish PwD are available, so a future survey must include this dimension. The percentage of 0.31% of the total population of PwD (estimation) having a sport licence, when the figure for the general population stands at 8.3%, reveals their actual lack of access to sport.
- Inclusion in sport in recent years has moved from a philosophy to a reality in Spain, as a way to promote the sport opportunities for PwD and to promote adapted sports to the main public: this is influencing how sport is provided and organised and also how sport policy is evolving.
- The success of sport as a tool for social inclusion for PwD is not only conditioned by public policies or by the economic resources allocated to that end, but will be determined also by the coherence and joint coordination of all agents, resources and the social spheres around the environment of the PwD, and their own actions in achieving the same objective: real inclusion through an active and self-oriented physical activity and sport participation.

The disability sport sector in Spain has been suffering from the Covid-19 situation, as has the rest of the sport industry in Spain, as a non-essential sector. After the nine-week lockdown between March and April 2020, disability sport leagues were cancelled and access to regular physical activity for the whole population was limited, especially for PwD when compared with general population (Moscoso-Sánchez, 2020). Many initiatives for training and physical activity at home were developed (like those provided by CPE during lockdown to Paralympic athletes, for instance, providing sport equipment at home or training screening), especially online. Gradually, the back to normal situation is facilitating access to sport (mainly in open air activities), always with the development of anti-Covid-19 protocols by sport providers. Without doubt, for most PwD in Spain, Covid-19 had a negative impact on their daily life and their access to physical activity and sport.

Acknowledgements The authors thank the support of the 'Fundación Sanitas' Chair in Inclusive Sport Studies at the Universidad Politécnica de Madrid for the development of this chapter.

References

Abellán, J., & Januário, N. (2017). Barreras, facilitadores y motivos de la práctica deportiva de deportistas con discapacidad intelectual. *Psychology, Society and Education, 9*, 419–431.
Act 10/1990, of October 15, on Sport. https://www.boe.es/buscar/act.php?id=BOE-A-1990-25037 (10.08.2019).
Act 13/1982, of April 7th, on the social integration of the handicapped (BOE n° 103 of April 30th). https://boe.es/buscar/pdf/1982/BOE-A-1982-9983-consolidado.pdf (15.01.2021).
Act 19/2013, of December 9, on Transparency, Access to Public Information and Good Governance. https://boe.es/buscar/doc.php?id=BOE-A-2013-12887 (19-12-2020).

Act 27/2007 of October 23rd by Virtue of which Spanish Sign Languages are recognised and Means of Support are Regulated for Oral Communication by the Deaf, Hard of Hearing, and Blind and Deaf. BOE n° 255 of October 24th. https://www.boe.es/buscar/act.php?id=BOE-A-2007-18476 (19.12.2020).

Act 8/2013 of December 9th on Improvements to the Quality of Education (BOE n° 295 of December 10th). https://www.boe.es/buscar/pdf/2013/BOE-A-2013-12886-consolidado.pdf (15.01.2021).

Community of Madrid. (2018). *Plan to promote physical activity and inclusive sport.* https://www.comunidad.madrid/servicios/deportes/plan-fomentar-actividad-fisica-deporte-inclusivo (15.01.2021).

Confederación Salud Mental España. (2019). *Una estrategia en defensa de la salud mental.* https://www.efesalud.com/estrategia-defensa-salud-mental/ (27.11.2019).

CSD. (2009). *Integral plan for physical activity and sports.* http://www.planamasd.es/ (04.01.2020).

CSD. (2015). *Transparency Act Obligations.* http://estaticos.csd.gob.es/prensa/ley_transparencia.pdf (12.12.2020).

CSD. (2020a). *Master plan for inclusive sport.* https://www.csd.gob.es/sites/default/files/media/files/2020-12/Plan%20Director%20Deporte%20Inclusivo%202020%20def.pdf (12.12.2020).

CSD. (2020b). *Spanish championships in school age by regional teams (CESA 2020).* https://www.csd.gob.es/sites/default/files/media/files/2019-10/NORMAS%20GENERALES%20CESA%202020.pdf (05.01.2021).

CSD. (2020c). *El CSD contará en 2021 con 251 millones de presupuesto, la mayor cantidad del siglo para el deporte español – CSD will have a budget of 251 million in 2021, the highest amount of the century for Spanish sport.* https://www.csd.gob.es/es/el-csd-contara-en-2021-con-251-millones-de-presupuesto-la-mayor-cantidad-del-siglo-para-el-deporte-espanol (16.11.2020).

Deloitte. (2018). *International comparative study on high level sport models.* https://fep.es/prensa/07062018_ADESP_Estudio_comparativo_internacional_modelos_deporte_alto_nivel.pdf (05.01.2021).

INE. (2008). *Survey on disabilities, personal autonomy and dependency situations (EDAD, in Spanish).* https://www.mscbs.gob.es/ssi/discapacidad/informacion/encuestaEdad2008.htm (15.01.2021).

INE. (2019). *Spain: Population figures at 1 January 2019.* https://www.ine.es/en/prensa/cp_e2019_p_en.pdf (10.08.2019).

Leardy, L. (2018). Inversión en materia de deporte de personas con discapacidad. In Leardy, L., Mendoza, N., Reina, R., Sanz, D., & Pérez-Tejero (Coords), *El libro blanco del deporte para personas con discapacidad en España* [The white paper on sport for PwD in Spain] (pp. 261–270). : SPCCPE, Fundación ONCE & CERMI.

Leardy, L., Mendoza, N., Reina, R., Sanz, D., & Pérez-Tejero, J. (Coords.) (2018). *El libro blanco del deporte para personas con discapacidad en España* [The white paper on sport for PwD in Spain], Madrid: SPC, Fundación ONCE & CERMI. https://www.cermi.es/es/colecciones/libro-blanco-de-deporte-de-personas-con-discapacidad-en-espa%C3%B1a (19.12.2020).

Leardy, L., & Sanz, D. (2018). Historia sumaria del deporte de personas con discapacidad en España. In L. Leardy, N. Mendoza, R. Reina, D. Sanz, & J. Pérez-Tejero (Coords), *El libro blanco del deporte para personas con discapacidad en España* [The white paper on sport for PwD in Spain] (pp. 27–36). Madrid: SPC, Fundación ONCE & CERMI.

Lecumberri, C. (2020a). Recomanacions legislatives per a l'aplicació de les polítiques de génere en els clubs esportius. *Quadern Dones i esport, 13,* 22–32.

Lecumberri, C. (2020b). Els esports I el génere. *Viure en familia, 85,* 38–41.

Lecumberri, C., Puig, N., & Maza, G. (2009). *Deporte e integración social. Guía de intervención educativa a través del deporte.* Fundación Barcelona Olímpica.

Lifetness. (2019) *Fitness market in Spain.* https://lifefitness.es/sites/g/files/dtv376/f/Zoom%20Mercado%202019_LifeFitness.pdf (10.08.2019).

Martínez, J. O. (2008). Hospi-Sport Cataluña: Filosofía, estructura y aplicaciones. En J. Pérez-Tejero (Coord.), *Discapacidad, calidad de vida y actividad físico deportiva: La situación actual mirando hacia el futuro* (pp. 239-250). Plan de Formación. Comunidad de Madrid.

MCD. (2015). *Code of Good Governance of the Spanish Sports Federations (2015)*. https://www.feb.es/Documentos/Uploads/CBG%202015.pdf (14-12-2020).

MCD. (2020). *Yearbook of sports statistics*. https://www.culturaydeporte.gob.es/dam/jcr:47414879-4f95-4cae-80c4-e289b3fbced9/anuario-de-estadisticas-deportivas-2020.pdf (05.01.2021).

Mendoza, N., Sanz, D., & Reina, R. (2018). Las personas con discapacidad y el deporte en España. Introducción general. In Leardy, L., Mendoza, N., Reina, R., Sanz, D. & Pérez-Tejero, J. (Coords), *El libro blanco del deporte para personas con discapacidad en España* [The white paper on sport for PwD in Spain] (pp. 27–36). Madrid: SPC, Fundación ONCE & CERMI.

Moscoso-Sánchez, D. (2020). El contexto del deporte en España durante la crisis sanitaria de la COVID-19. *Sociología del deporte, 1*(1), 15–19.

MPCE. (2019a). *Government approval of the blueprint of the new sport law*. https://www.lamoncloa.gob.es/consejodeministros/Paginas/enlaces/010219-enlaceleydeporte.aspx (05-01-2021).

MPCE. (2019b). *Event of exceptional public interest 'Inclusive Sports' program*. https://www.boe.es/diario_boe/txt.php?id=BOE-A-2019-3189 (05.01.2021).

Palau, J., & García, M. A. (2011). Historia del deporte adaptado a las personas con discapacidad física. Deportistas sin adjetivos. In M. Ríos, (Coord.) *Deportistas sin adjetivos: El deporte adaptado a las personas con discapacidad física*. Madrid: HSCCSD, Royal Board of PwD, SPC.

Pérez-Tejero, J. (Ed.). (2013). El Centro de Estudios sobre Deporte Inclusivo: Cuatro años de fomento del deporte inclusivo a nivel práctico, académico y científico. *Serie de Cuadernos del CEDI 1*. Madrid: Universidad Politécnica de Madrid, Fundación Sanitas y Psysport.

Pérez-Tejero, J., Barba, M., García, L., Ocete, C., & Coterón, J. (2013). *Deporte inclusivo en la escuela* [Inclusive sport at the school]. Serie 'Publicaciones del CEDI – 3'. Madrid: Universidad Politécnica de Madrid, Fundación Sanitas, Psysport. http://deporteinclusivoescuela.com/ (05.01.2021).

Pérez-Tejero, J., & Casas (2019). Analysis of labour market realities and challenges in the sport and physical activity sector: Spain national report. In *European sector skills alliance for sport and physical activity (ESSA-Sport)*. Lyon: European Observatory of Sport Employment (EOSE). https://www.essa-sport.eu/wp-content/uploads/2020/01/ESSA_Sport_National_Report_Spain.pdf (12.12.2020).

Pérez-Tejero, J., & Ocete, C. (2018). Personas con discapacidad y práctica deportiva en España. In Leardy, L., Mendoza, N., Reina, R., Sanz, D., & Pérez-Tejero, J. (Coords). *El libro blanco del deporte para personas con discapacidad en España* [The white paper on sport for PwD in Spain] (pp. 55-77). Madrid: SPC, Fundación ONCE & CERMI.

Pérez-Tejero, J., & Sanz, D. (Eds.). (2011). Avanzando juntos hacia la integración: CONDA I. Serie 'Publicaciones del CEDI – 2'. Madrid: Universidad Politécnica de Madrid, Fundación Sanitas, Psysport.

Ratification instrument of November 23rd. (2007). BOE n°. 96 of April 21st 2008, of the Convention on the Rights of Persons with Disabilities, drafted in New York on December 13th 2006 by the UN General Assembly. https://www.boe.es/buscar/doc.php?id=BOE-A-2008-6963 (19.12.2020).

Reina, R. (2018). El ecosistema del deporte de personas con discapacidad en España. In Leardy, L., Mendoza, N., Reina, R., Sanz, D., & Pérez-Tejero, J. (Coords.) *El libro blanco del deporte para personas con discapacidad en España* [The white paper on sport for PwD in Spain] (pp. 87-170). Madrid: SPC, Fundación ONCE & CERMI.

Reina, R., Roldán, A., Candela, A., & Castillo de Albornoz, A. (2019). *Práctica deportiva de universitarios con discapacidad: Barreras, facilitadores y empleabilidad* (resumen ejecutivo). Fundación ONCE and Universidad Miguel Hernández. https://comunicacion.umh.es/files/2019/05/07-05-19-estudio-deporte-y-discapacidad.pdf (28.03.2020).

Ríos, M., Ruiz, P., Carol, N. (Coords). (2014). La inclusión en la actividad física y deportiva: La práctica de la educación física y deportiva en entornos inclusivos. Editorial Paidotribo.

Royal Decree 1276/2011 on Legislative Adaptations for Compliance with the ICRPD. BOE n° 224 of September 17th. https://www.boe.es/eli/es/rd/2011/09/16/1276 (19.12.2020).

Royal Decree 1835/1991, of December 20, on Spanish Sports Federations and Register of Sports Associations. https://www.boe.es/buscar/act.php?id=BOE-A-1991-30862 (12.12.2020).

Royal Legislative Decree 1/2013, of November 29, which approves the Consolidated Text of the General Law on the Rights of Persons with Disabilities and their Social Inclusion. https://www.boe.es/buscar/doc.php?id=BOE-A-2013-12632 (27.11.2019).

Sanz, D., Palencia, I., Reina, R., & Leardy, L. (2018). Deporte base y deporte de competición en personas con discapacidad en España. In Leardy, L., Mendoza, N., Reina, R., Sanz, D., & Pérez-Tejero, J. (Coords), *El libro blanco del deporte para personas con Discapacidad en España* [The white paper on sport for PwD in Spain] (pp. 211-241). Madrid: SPC, Fundación ONCE & CERMI.

Servimedia. (2020). *El PSOE pide al Gobierno que impulse el deporte inclusivo entre personas con y sin discapacidad*. https://www.servimedia.es/noticias/1332090 (16.11.2020).

Spanish Constitution. (1978). BOE n° 311 of December 29th. https://www.boe.es/diario_boe/txt.php?id=BOE-A-1978-31229 (17-12-2020).

Special Olympics. (2020). *Special Olympics España*. http://specialolympics.es/ (14.12.2020).

Torralba, M. A., Braz, M., & Rubio, M. J. (2017). Motivos de la práctica deportiva de atletas paralímpicos españoles. *Revista de Psicología del Deporte, 26*, 49–60.

Transparency International Spain. (2020). *INFED sports federations transparency index 2019*. http://www.rfhe.com/wp-content/uploads/2020/05/Informe-de-Transparencia-Internacional-Sobre-Federaciones-Deportivas-Espanolas-Tercera-Edicion.pdf (15.12.2020).

Chapter 22
Turkey (Republic of Turkey): Disability Sports, Policies and Implementations

Yeşim Albayrak Kuruoğlu

22.1 Introduction

Disability sports policies in Turkey are based upon adaptation, accessibility, participation, rehabilitation and success. The outcomes of these issues are currently insufficient. Additionally, there is no systematic policy for training Paralympic athletes. Participation and sustaining the training of athletes with disabilities in Paralympic sports is primarily provided through the initiative of families. In Turkey, investment in and supporting disabled sports are important issues in terms of reaching more people with disabilities (PwDs). This chapter briefly explains disability sport, its structure and policies, and some of the ways it is implemented in Turkey.

22.2 Country Profile

Characteristics of Turkey

Turkey, known officially as the Republic of Turkey, is a transcontinental Eurasian country. Its location at the crossroads of Europe and Asia makes it a country of significant geostrategic importance. Turkey is a democratic, secular, unitary, constitutional republic. It was founded by Mustafa Kemal Atatürk in 1923, which marked the end of the long reign of the Ottoman Empire (Meral & Turnbull, 2016; PwC, 2020). Before the establishment of the Republic of Turkey, Turkish civil law was linked to religion. With the reforms of 1926, a number of new legal codes were established based in part on the Swiss Civil and Italian penal codes. Following these

Y. A. Kuruoğlu (✉)
School of Physical Education and Sports, Haliç University, Istanbul, Turkey
e-mail: yesimkuruoglu@halic.edu.tr

© The Author(s), under exclusive license to Springer Nature Switzerland AG 2023
C. van Lindert et al. (eds.), *The Palgrave Handbook of Disability Sport in Europe*, https://doi.org/10.1007/978-3-031-21759-3_22

changes, the independence of the judiciary-including the constitutional court and the courts responsible for criminal, civil and administrative matters-has been ensured by the Constitution (Brittannica, 2020). Article 3, implicitly, and Article 10, explicitly, ban (defining the term "Turkish" based on citizenship rather than on ethnicity) the division of the Turkish nation into sub-entities; they also prohibit references in law to the other ethnic groups as being separate from the rest of Turkey, under the theory of the indivisibility of the nation (Constitution of the Republic of Turkey, 1982a, 1982b). Turkey's 81 provinces are administered by governors, who are appointed by the Council of Ministers, subject to the approval of the president. Provinces are divided into districts and sub-districts (Meral & Turnbull, 2016; Britannica, 2020).

Turkey has been integrating with Europe and western culture through membership in organisations such as the Council of Europe, North Atlantic Treaty Organisation (NATO), Organisation for Economic Co-operation and Development (OECD), Organisation for Security and Co-operation in Europe (OSCE) and the G-20 major economies. Turkey began full membership negotiations with the European Union (EU) in 2005, having been an associate member of the European Economic Community (EEC) since 1963. A customs accord between Turkey and the EU was signed in 1995 (PwC, 2020). Table 22.1 shows some facts and statistics about Turkey.

Turkey is a secular country with no official religion since the constitutional amendment in 1928 and later strengthened by its founder and the first president Mustafa Kemal Atatürk's Reforms and the appliance of laicism on 5 February 1937 (Brittannica, 2020).

Table 22.1 Facts and statistics of Turkey

Population, million (2019)	82.6
Area	783,356 km^2
Urbanisation rate (%)	75,63
Political organisation	Presidential constitutional republic
Structure of the state	Unitary
Capital city	Ankara
Number of provinces	81
Number of municipalities	1397
Currency	Turkish Lira (TRY)
Official Language	Turkish
Religious beliefs (%)[b]	Islam (98), Christianity (<1), Judaism (<1),other (<1)
GDP, current USD billion[a]	754.8
GDP per capita, current USD[a]	9140
Life expectancy at birth, years (2018)	77.2
Employment rate (Q2, 2020) (%)	45.5
Literacy (age 6 and over) (%)	96.2

Sources: OECD (2020), [a]World Bank (2020), [b]Global Religious Project (2016)

Sport in Turkey

Turkey is one of the few countries which has an article related to sports in its Constitution. Article 59 of the Constitution emphasises: "The State takes measures to develop the physical and mental health of Turkish citizens of all ages and encourages the spread of sports among the masses. The State protects successful athletes" (Constitution of the Republic of Turkey, 1982a).

Physical activities and sports in Turkey extend back to the Ottomans and further into the antiquity of Central Asia where Turks originate from. Archery, horseback riding and wrestling have always been considered as traditional sports in Turkish sport culture. Football (soccer) was established as an organised sport prior to the founding of the republic and helped cultivate the post-Ottoman Turkish national identity. Fenerbahçe, Galatasaray and Beşiktaş Sports Clubs were established at the beginning of the twentieth Century and they still remain the most prominent of the national football and other amateur sports clubs (Mansour, 2017).

The Ministry of Youth and Sports, Directorate General for Sport Services, Directorate General for Youth, Directorate General for *Spor-Toto* (Organisation for betting in sport games; its income is used for sponsoring sports at the national level), the Ministry of National Education, local authorities, the Turkish National Olympic Committee, the Turkish National Paralympic Committee, the Turkish Football Federation and independent sports federations, universities, sports clubs and higher units of sports clubs in Turkey have active roles in managing and conducting sports services (The Turkish Ministry of Youth and Sports, 2020).

Sport in Turkey is being encouraged and supported mostly by the state and sports clubs are given financial or equipment aid. The main targets of the sports policy of the state are to increase the number of athletes, to attain success at international sports competitions, to prepare a suitable sports environment for encouraging and providing for every individual at every age to engage in sports activities (Turkish Cultural Foundation, 2020). Sports facilities with large capacities and investments have been encouraged since 1993 when Turkey first declared its candidature for 2000 Summer Olympic Games. Although it has never been successful, Turkey was a candidate for hosting the Summer Olympic and Paralympic Games five times (2000, 2004, 2008, 2012 and 2020) with its candidate city Istanbul. A remarkable increase in the number of sports facilities, sports clubs, private organisations and athletes has helped the development of the perception of sponsorship and sports marketing in the last two decades (Albayrak Kuruoğlu & Ünlü, 2014).The managerial structure and organisation of sport in Turkey is relevant to the effort to become a full member of the European Union. For example, the establishment of a Sport Council was proposed in 2001. Another proposal was to establish the Turkish Sports Institution to replace the Directorate General for Youth and Sports in 2007. Neither of them has ever been brought to real life. The structure of the sport in Turkey has still not achieved the desired result, yet. The state manages the sport in the form of a higher board that supports and supervises it. (İmamoğlu, 2011).

The type of sports federations are listed under four categories in Turkey. They are the sports federations of Summer Olympic Games, sports federations of Winter Olympic Games, sports federations of Paralympic Sports and other sports federations. According to the National Olympic Committee of Turkey (*TMOK, Türkiye Milli Olimpiyat Komitesi*), there are totally 61 registered sports federations running under these four categories (Turkish National Olympic Committee, 2020). In Turkey, sport is still treated as a public service and based on state obligations arising from the Constitution. Sports services, which are treated as public services, are provided through federations (Çolakoğlu & Solmaz, 2017). Turkish Football Federation became autonomous in 1994, where other sports federations in 2004. However, except football, most of them still rely and are funded by the state because of the explanation given above (İmamoğlu, 2011).

Table 22.2 shows the sport profile of Turkey according to the 2017 Activity Report and Corporate Financial Status and Estimations Report of Directorate General for Sport Services operating under the Ministry of Youth and Sports.

Disability in Turkey

Positive approaches have usually been exhibited for PwDs in the Turkish States throughout the history. For example, we see the first written classification about intellectual disabilities and a chapter about hydrocephalus in the book "Zahire-i Muradiyye" by Turkish physician Mü'min ibn-i Mukbil in 1437, during the Ottoman period (Mukbil, 1437). Organisations for charity and social services including services for PwDs became institutional bodies in the Nineteenth Century. Among these, the Red Crescent Society (*Kızılay*), founded in 1868, and *Darülaceze* (a name for "nursing home" in Ottoman), established in 1895, are the institutions that have survived until today in the Republic of Turkey since the Ottoman period. Darülaceze has been providing services to the PwDS, elderly and orphans regardless of religion, language and gender since its foundation (Ünlü, 2018; Ersoy & Dikici, 2018).

The historical process of disability rights is divided into two periods before and after the Republic, too. Actions regarding PwDs were taken from the *medical model* point of view until the 1950's. However, social actions such as founding schools for PwDs were seen during the Ottoman period. The first two schools for individuals with hearing and vision impairments were established in Istanbul in 1889, served until 1919 and in Thessaloniki (now part of Greece) between 1909 and 1913. Chronological development of educational institutes between the late Ottoman Empire and the early Republic of Turkey for students with disabilities is shown in Table 22.3 (Albayrak Kuruoğlu et al., 2018; Doğan, 2019; Canpolat, 2020a).

PwDs in Turkey could not be part of the political agenda, and they remained as a quiet group of society until 1967. Development of social security policies were given a priority from the thirty first government (1969–1970), until the forty third government (1979–1980), while direct policies about PwDs were not taken into consideration. Fortunately, the government's (1989–1991) programme highlighted

Table 22.2 Sport profile of Turkey

Government authority responsible for sport	Ministry of Youth and Sports Directorate General for Sports Services
Membership sport club (% of population)	No data
Membership fitness or health centre (% of population)	No data
Membership socio-cultural club that includes sport in its activities (e.g. employees' club, youth club, school- and university-related club) (% of population)	No data
Sport participation at least once a week (% of population)	No data
Number of national sport federations	61
Number of sport clubs[a]	15,828
Number of sport club members	No data
National budget for sport (USD million)[a]	261,954
National budget for sport federations (USD million)[a]	20,637
Local budget for sport	No data
Share of economic value of volunteers in sport in the GDP (%)	No data
Federations of Summer Olympic Games (n)	29
Paralympic sports federations (n)	4
Federations of Winter Olympic Games (n)	5
Other sports federations (n)	23
Number of registered athletes in sport clubs[a]	4,907,955
Number of registered female athletes in sport clubs[a]	1,646,102
Number of registered male athletes in sport clubs[a]	3,261,853
Football stadiums (n)	1327
Multi-purpose sports saloons (n)	842
Other (n)	524
Local stadiums (provinces & districts) (n)	333
Youth centres (n)	313
Swimming pools (n)	131
Track and field tracks (n)	55

Sources: Directorate General for Sport Services Activity Report (2017a), [a]Directorate General for Sport Services Corporate Financial Status and Estimations Report (2017b)

Table 22.3 Chronological establishment of schools for students with various disabilities between the late Ottoman and early Republic of Turkey

Date	Name of the School and Province
1921	School for Deaf and Blind in Izmir
1944	School for Deaf and Mute in Istanbul
1949	Rehabilitation Centre in Ankara
1952	School for Blind in Ankara
1950–1980	Schools for Deaf, Mute, Blind, Physical, Intellectual impairments
1980–present	Schools until now

Sources: Albayrak Kuruoğlu et al. (2018), Doğan (2019)

the issue of disability. In this programme, it was stated that PwDs would be supported in terms of their employment (Mumcu, 2018).

It is seen that the development of social rights and policies for PwDs in Turkey is more late when compared to other European countries. The reasons for the delayed emergence of social rights and policies can be considered as the characteristics of Turkey's welfare system, the protective and conservative family structure and the country's social solidarity traditions. All actions such as promoting and ensuring the rights and fundamental freedoms of PwDs have been set at the level of national policy in Turkey.

Turkey's present constitution was founded in 1982. It has been amended 16 times since 1982. Two sources of law have an influence on persons with disabilities. One of them is the Constitution of Turkey. The other is its comprehensive Turkish Disability Act (TDA), which was established in 2005. The TDA can be defined as a framework law on disability. Moreover, Turkey has taken a keen interest in social policy applications and legal regulation(s) for PwDs since the mid-1990s such as forming the Administration of Disabled People (1997), holding the first National Disabled People's Council (1999) and introducing the Turkish Disability Act (2005) (Özgökçeler & Alper, 2010). Turkey signed the United Nations Convention on the Rights of Persons with Disabilities (UNCRPD) on 30 March 2007. The TDA was restructured in 2014, in line with the obligations stipulated by the UNCRPD (UN, 2005; OHCHR, 2015).

Disability rates in Turkey are estimated at 15% of the population. The reason for "estimating" is because, inspecting PwDs has been an issue since the early times of the Republic. The traditional Turkish family and society structure has a solidarity and protectionist feature in terms of its own cultural, moral and human values (Metin, 2017).

The incidence of disability in Turkey increases by age, and the incidence of physical, vision, hearing and intellectual disabilities is higher in rural than urban areas, while the incidence of chronic illnesses is higher in urban than rural areas (Meral & Turnbull, 2016). Table 22.4 indicates the type of impairments and their prevalence in the population.

Table 22.4 Type of impairments, population and prevalence

Type of Impairment	Population #	Prevalence (%)
Visual	280,872	11.09
Hearing	231,323	9.13
Mute	41,372	1.63
Physical	388,081	15.32
Intellectual	494,357	19.52
Emotional/Mental	217,519	8.59
Chronic disease	1130.311	44.62
Other	67,224	2.65

Source: Directorate General for Disabled and Elderly (2019)

The terms of impairment, disability and handicapped were adopted in Turkish language when the World Health Organisation (WHO) developed a classification system called the International Classification of Impairments, Disabilities and Handicaps (ICIDH) in 1980. Impairment, disability and handicap refer to *yetersizlik*, *özürlülük* and *engellilik* consecutively in Turkish. The WHO's *medical model* point of view at that time caused confusion and led to interchanging misuse when these words were translated, although each of them has different explanations. Due to the theoretical differentiation of approaches to the issue of disability since the 1980s and in order to change the social perception of disability and stigma created by the ICIDH disability classification, the WHO developed the International Classification of Functioning, Disability and Health (ICF) system in 2001 (Bilsin & Başbakkal, 2014). In Turkish, the expressions such as "sick, handicapped, blind, deaf" when expressing disability show that disability is accepted as an individual medical problem and often cause a negative impression. According to the ICF classification and the United Nations Convention on the Rights of Persons with Disabilities (UNCRPD), preventing humiliation of PwDs is primarily done through correcting the existing words in the language. Some words expressing disability in Turkish are not fully compatible with the ICF classification system. Therefore, the term "*özürlü*" which carries a meaning of "defects" is still being used in some legislation and official terms. Fortunately, after signing the UNCRPD on 30 March 2007 and restructuring the TDA in 2014, most terms from the *medical model were* converted into terms from the *social model*. For example; the term "özürlü (with defects)" was converted into "*engelli* (person experiencing obstacles/barriers). For example, *işitme engelli* refers to "person with hearing impairment." Although the official Turkish name *Türkiye İşitme Engelliler Spor Federasyonu* has an exact meaning of "*Turkish Sports Federation for People with Hearing Impairment*" the official English name of this federation is accepted as "Turkish Deaf Sports Federation." The Paralympic sports federations in Turkey have been named according to their specific needs and rules (Albayrak Kuruoğlu et al., 2018; TMOK, 2020). Table 22.5, shows the terms of disability and common words of disability sports in Turkish and in English as well as their converted forms.

Rise of Disability Sport in Turkey

The Republic of Turkey, which was formerly the Ottoman Empire, was among the defeated states of the First World War (WWI). The independence war of this latest Turkish state of the era ended with the establishment of the Republic of Turkey in 1923, where almost everything started from scratch in all aspects of life such as adopting the Latin alphabet, establishing a new civil law, appliance of laicism and so on. Fortunately, Turkey did not take part in the Second World War (WWII), as the state had been already trying to recover in many fields after WWI. It is well known that disability sports began to emerge in Europe due to its use in the rehabilitation of disabled soldiers and civilians after the WWII. Turkey's absence from the WWII

Table 22.5 Changes of the terms disability and disability sports from Turkish to English

Terms of Disability in Turkish		Converted Terms
Özürlü (*person with defects/person who feels sorry*)	→	Engelli (*person experiencing obstacles or barriers/person with obstacles in life*)
Engelli birey (*person with obstacles/handicapped/disabled*)	→	Özel gereksinimli birey (*person with special needs*); Yetersizliği olan birey (*person with impairments*)
Engellilerde fiziksel aktivite ve spor (*disabled physical activity and sports*)	→	Özel gereksinimli bireylerde fiziksel aktivite ve spor (*physical activity and sports for the people with special needs*)
Engelli sporları (*disabled sports*)	→	Paralimpik sporlar (*Paralympic dports*)
Engelli spor branşlarıları (*disabled sports branches*)	→	Uyarlanmış spor branşları (*adapted sports branches*)
Engellilerde fiziksel aktivite (*physical activity for disabled people*)	→	Uyarlanmış fiziksel aktiviteler (*adapted physical activities*)
Türkiye Özürlüler Spor Federasyonu (1990) (*Turkish Sport Federation for People with Defects/Suffering*)	→	In 2000 this federation was divided into four separate federations for people with physical, visual, hearing and intellectual impairments (see the information in the section Rise of Disability Sport in Turkey).
Türkiye Zihinsel Engelliler Spor Federasyonu (2000) (*Turkish Sport Federation for the Mentally Disabled*)	→	Türkiye Özel Sporcular Spor Federasyonu (2009) (*Turkish Special Athletes Sports Federation*)
Engelsiz aktiviteler (*activities without obstacles*)	→	The term "engelsiz" (*without obstacles*) is commonly preferred, especially for the names of the projects regarding disabled people.

Source: Translations by the author

can be considered as the major reason for the late development of disability sport. Disability sport was mostly implemented at the schools for PwDs on irregular basis during the early times of the Republic. In 1969, the Turkish Federation of Deaf-Mute Sport Clubs was founded under the accreditation of the International Committee for the Silent Sports (CISS). This federation gathered the schools, sports clubs and individuals with hearing/speaking impairments that had been operating desultory, although it was not recognised by the governmental bodies or the National Olympic Committee of Turkey (State Planning Organization, 1983).

We see the phrase "persons with special status" in Turkey's "Fifth Five-Year Development Plan of 1983," which stated the need for sports for PwDs for the first time. According to the 1983 development plan, PwDs were considered as lonely individuals; thus, sport was an opportunity for them to escape from isolation. It was also claiming that sport should be treated as a valuable rehabilitation tool (State Planning Organisation, 1983).

Turkey did not take part in the international disability sports competitions until 1992 although participated in the earlier Olympic Games. However, there is a record about a young Turkish swimmer who was living in the United Kingdom at that time and participated individually in Stoke Mandeville Games in 1957 (State Planning Organisation, 1983). The rise of disability sport in Turkey is mainly based on "the Sports Council," which was convened in Ankara on 8–11 May 1990. In accordance with the decisions taken there, the Turkish Sports Federation for People with Defects (*Türkiye Özürlüler Spor Federasyonu*) was established on 21 November 1990 under the governance of the General Directorate of Youth and Sports. The aim of the federation was explained as: "to develop sports activities for disabled athletes, to spread these activities throughout the country, to make sports a part of rehabilitation and to plan and implement the necessary effort for providing modern environments for disabled athletes to take part in international events." In 1997, the word "defect" in the name of the federation was replaced by the word "obstacle or handicap" and the official name of the federation was changed to the "Turkish Sports Federation for People with Obstacles/Handicapped (*Türkiye Engelliler Spor Federasyonu*)" (see Table 22.5). Individuals with physical, intellectual, hearing and visual impairments were participating in sport activities and competitions under this federation until 2000. It was decided to divide the federation and four separate federations were founded in 2000, whose official English names are as follows:

1. Turkish Sports Federation for the Physically Disabled (*Türkiye Bedensel Engelliler Spor Federasyonu*)
2. Turkish Deaf Sports Federation (*Türkiye İşitme Englliler Spor Federasyonu*)
3. Turkish Blind Sports Federation (*Türkiye Görme Engelliler Spor Federasyonu*)
4. Turkish Sports Federation for the Mentally Disabled. (This name was changed to "Turkish Special Athletes Sports Federation" [*Türkiye Özel Sporcular Spor Federasyonu]* in 2009.)

When the explanations above are examined chronologically, it can be seen that the rise of disability sports in Turkey is progressing in direct proportion to Istanbul's candidature process for the Olympic Games in the period from 2000 to 2023, which has previously mentioned in the section "Sport in Turkey" of this chapter. Candidate cities bidding to host the Olympic Games are also required to organise the Paralympic Games and commit to any facilities and organisations for 5000 disabled athletes within 15 days of the end of the Olympics. Turkey has successfully bid and hosted the 23rd Summer Deaflympics in 2017. The 23rd Summer Deaflympics was organised with the participation of 1000 volunteers in Samsun on 18–23 July 2017. Around 3104 athletes from 96 countries competed in 21 sports, using 28 venues (Directorate General for Sports Services, 2017). Starting from the mid-80s to the present, whether for physical activity and/or rehabilitation purposes or for performance purposes, the importance given to disability sports continues to increase in Turkey.

22.3 The Disability Sport System

Structure of Disability Sport

The structure of disability sports in Turkey can be examined in two sections as governmental and non-governmental agents. As mentioned in the previous section, disability sport in Turkey was formerly based on the formation of the first sport federation which was related to all disability groups in 1990. Although it was decided to divide into four separate federations, governance and management of them have not been changed dramatically since 2000's. In Turkey, sport is still considered as public service supported and financed by the government through federations. Sports federations are characterised as "independent" under the government supervision, while sports clubs operate as non-governmental organisations. Except football, all sport federations are identified as "independent" instead of "autonomous," because of their government-depended formation (İmamoğlu, 2011).

Figure 22.1,demonstrates the structural breakdown of the administrative agents of disability sports in Turkey. The arrows indicate both financial and hierarchical relationships between the agents.

Governmental Agents

Disability sport is mainly managed by the Ministry of Youth and Sports in Turkey. Other national ministries such as the Ministry of Family, Labour and Social Service, Ministry of National Education and Ministry of Environment and Urbanisation support sport services for PwDs as well. The Ministry of Youth and Sports carries out duties by means of the following service units:

- Directorate General for Youth Services
- Directorate General for Projects and Coordination
- Directorate General for Education, Culture and Research
- Directorate General for Sport Services

The Directorate General for Sport Services and the disability sports federations operating under this service are presented in Fig. 22.1.

The Ministry of National Education provides the curriculum of Physical Education, Physical Education and Sports, Games and Exercises specific to students in Special Education Schools and inclusion classes in schools where the national education programmes are carried out (Canpolat, 2020a).

Local governments are the supporters of national ministries in Turkey. For example; The Directorate General of Youth and Sports has representative offices in 81 provinces as the Provincial Directorate of Youth and Sports. There are also district directorates working under provincial directorates. The obligations concerning local governments have improved the services received by PwDs after the 2000s. Thus, local governments started to play an active role, especially in integrating PwDs into social life such as organising physical and recreational activities.

There are a total of 1397 municipalities in Turkey. This number consists of 30 metropolitan, 51 provincial, 519 metropolitan district, 400 district and 397 town municipalities. Metropolitan municipalities and other municipalities are obliged to provide services for PwDs within their duties and responsibilities. The services provided by municipalities for the PwDs have become widespread after 1990s and legal regulations have been made since 2005 (Uludağ Güler & Çakı, 2021). In Turkey, municipalities provide sport or recreational activities according to their

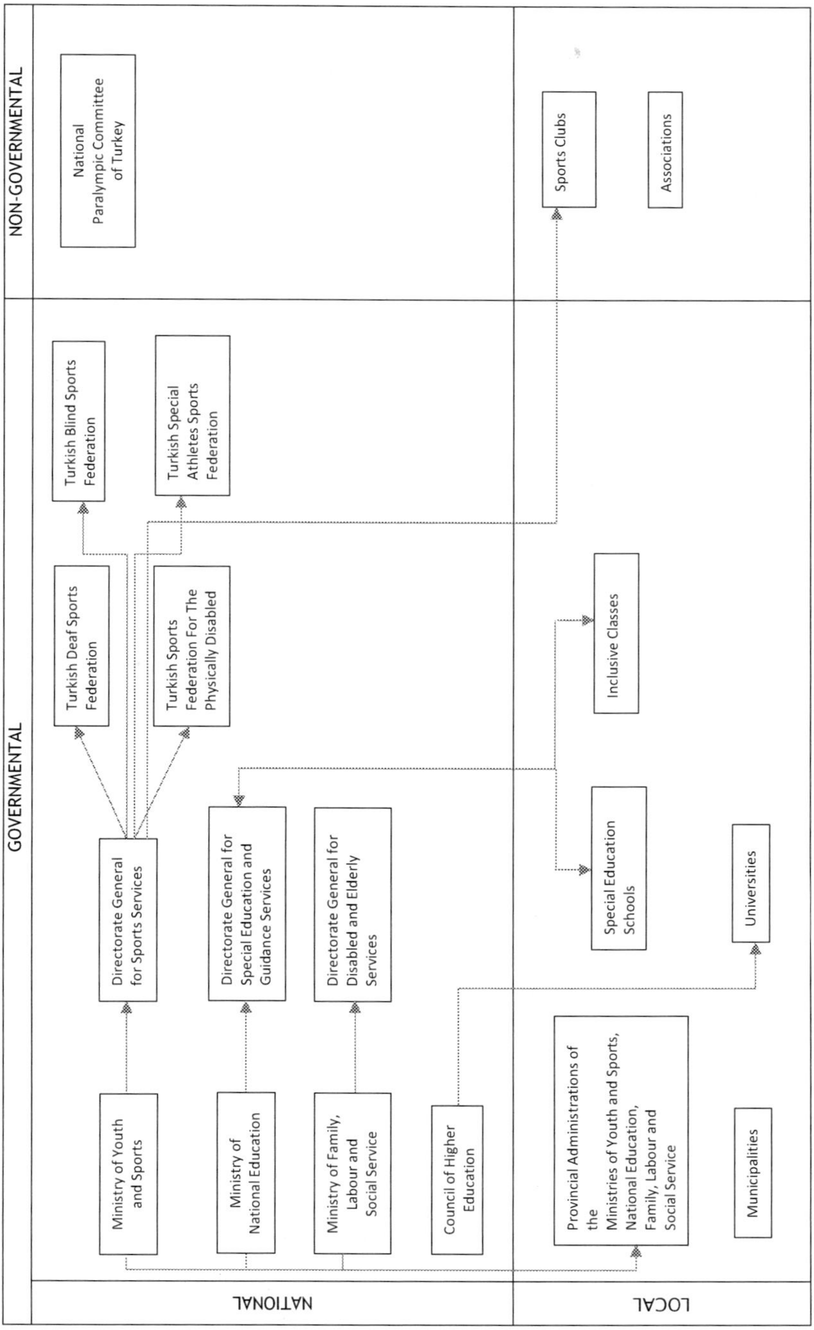

Fig. 22.1 Agents of disability sports in Turkey. Sources: Canpolat (2020a), Ministry of Foreign Affairs (www.mfa.gov.tr)

geographical situation, number of sport experts who can serve PwDs and sport facilities which are suitable for adapted activities. Turkey has established "Province Sport Centres for PwDs (*Engelliler İl Spor Merkezi*)" in all of its 81 provinces. According to 2017 data, there are 20 sports clubs for PwDs operating under the governance and managerial support of municipalities in Turkey. These clubs mostly undertake the task of training athletes with disabilities for the competitions (Canpolat, 2020a; TESYEV, 2020; Kalaycı & Akin, 2019).

The Regulation of Counselling and Coordination of PwDs in Higher Education Institutions includes the rights of students with disabilities and the services they should receive. Participating in intramural sports or benefiting from the university's sport or recreational facilities are among those services. "Adapted Physical Education and Sports" courses are taught either selectively or compulsorily in the higher education programmes of the Faculties of Sports Sciences and the Schools of Physical Education and Sports. A Department of Exercise and Sports Education for the Disabled is located in two of the state and two of the private universities in Turkey (Yüksek Öğretim Kurumu, 2020).

These governmental agents mentioned above provide sport services for PwDs both directly and in cooperation with non-governmental entities.

Non-governmental Agents

Non-governmental agents are the bodies that take an active role in eliminating the barriers that exist for PwDs to participate in physical activity and sports in Turkey. They operate in cooperation with official government bodies such as ministries in order to enhance the inclusion of PwDs in physical activity and sports (Aydın et al., 2018). For example, The Turkish Spastic Children Association is one of the associations among non-governmental agents which used to play an important role in developing the Special Olympics in Turkey. The Special Olympics was organised under this association's name as a result of an agreement signed with the Kennedy Foundation in 1982. The Special Olympics is supported by the Ministry of National Education and it has been in the Turkish Special Athletes Sports Federation activity programme (Canpolat, 2020a). The Turkey Disabled Sports, Education, Assistance and Education Foundation (TESYEV) is also one of the important non-governmental association established in 1999 in order to provide an accessible environment and elevate the quality of life of PwDs. The Association of Sports and Educational Sciences in Disabled Individuals (EBSED) is a new association founded by the trainers of Paralympic athletes and academicians. Its mission is to provide more adapted sports opportunities to especially young PwDs, contribute the education of trainers who wish to work in the field of disability sports. These two associations are two of the examples of strong non-governmental bodies in terms of unions/associations which provides scholarships to athletes with disabilities during their education, recruit their trainers or facilitate the related adapted sport equipment's (TESYEV, 2020; EBSED, 2020).

In Turkey, non-governmental organisations established for the purpose of carrying out sports activities are registered as "sports clubs," those aimed for leisure are registered as "youth clubs" and those aimed for both activities are registered "youth and sports clubs." Sports clubs can be founded only for implementing disability sports or they can also include both disability and normal sports branches. According to its responsibility and function, sports clubs can operate with the characteristics of a school or a public education centre for PwDs (Devecioğlu et al., 2015).

Steering of Disability Sport

Legislative Framework

In the Constitution of Republic of Turkey (1982a, 1982b), section of "The Rights and Missions about Education and Teaching," Article 42 it is stated that "One of the duties of the government is to provide education for the individuals with special needs." In the section "The Rights About Working Conditions," Article 50, it is emphasised: "It is the government's duty to protect individuals with physical and mental impairments in working life." The "Social Security" section, Article 61, mentions the precautions which the government should take in order to adapt PwDs into social life as well as protecting them against any harm (Constitution of the Republic of Turkey, 1982a, 1982b).

In the first periods of development plans between 1960 and 1990, measures for PwDs mostly recognised them as people who need care and protection in Turkey. Such measures were replaced by the ones which aimed to ensure equal participation of PwDs in social life. Some legislative arrangements about PwDs that were put into place after 2008. One of the arrangements concerning sports indicates: "Persons with disabilities can benefit free of charge or with reduced fees from the sports facilities and activities of Directorate General of Youth and Sports and sport federations throughout the 81 provinces of Turkey" (OHCHR-Turkey, 2015).

In Article 58, regarding "Protection of Youth" in the Constitution, legal commitments and duties of the state for protecting the youth are defined and thus the broadest legal framework in relation to youth is defined. The Directorate General for Sport Services, which operates under the Ministry of Youth and Sport, not only is responsible for the youth activities, but also its duties cover every population from various demographic characteristics.

The National Youth and Sports Policy Document (*Ulusal Gençlik ve Spor Politikası Belgesi*) is drawn up in accordance with the following provision of Article 18 of the Legislative Decree Number 638 on the Organisation and Duties of the Ministry of Youth and Sports dated 3 June 2011: "National Youth and Sports Policy Document is drawn up by the Ministry and submitted to the approval of the Council of Ministers with the purpose of providing coordination and cooperation between public institutions and organisations which carry out policies and activities directly or indirectly affecting young people and sports. The National Youth and Sports

Policy Document is reviewed and updated every four years as a minimum. In the updating process of the National Youth and Sports Policy Document, recommendations of the relevant public institutions and organisations, sports federations and non-governmental organisations are taken into consideration." In this document, the definition of young people is described more specifically and the term "disadvantaged young people" is legally included. Young people with disabilities are considered as one of the target groups. Preventing young people with disabilities from being subjected to social exclusion is indicated as important policy in the document. Sport is mentioned as the strongest tool to bring all youth together for providing mutual understanding (Gündoğdu & Asal, 2017).

Policy Framework

According to the National Youth and Sports Policy Document, PwDs are emphasised in terms of "disadvantaged people." The document outlines the necessity to continue sports and rehabilitation for disadvantaged people via cooperation amongst the institutions within the scope of studies conducted to help people having physical, emotional, mental or behavioural disorders or deficiencies form birth or as a result of disease or accidents (European Commission, 2017).

The policies regarding sports for PwDs in terms of "disadvantaged people" are listed in Table 22.6.

Financial, Governance and Managerial Support

All sports federations are headquartered in the capital city Ankara. The regulations about the managerial and financial support of independent sport federations were issued in the National Official Gazette on July 19th, 2012 with the number 28358 (National Official Gazette, 2012). Managerial structuring of four disability sports federations is in the following form: General Assembly, Board of Directors, Supervisory Board, Disciplinary Board and General Secretariat. Revenues of disability sports federations in Turkey include: A certain amount transferred from The Directorate General for Sports Services' budget; grants from individuals and institutions; registration and transfer fees; appeal and penalty fees; the fees of broadcasting rights from national competitions; advertising and sponsorship fees, donations and other. Revenues of disability sports federations are exempt from taxes and fees (National Official Gazette, 2012).

The Directorate General for Sports Services (2014) emphasises "financial aid" as one of its four strategic goals for promoting disability sports in the Strategic Plan of 2015–2019. Table 22.7 shows the amount of financial aid which the disability sports federations received according to the 2017 Activity Report of Directorate General for Sport Services.

Table 22.6 Policies and stakeholders regarding sport for disadvantaged people emphasised in the National Youth and Sports Policy Document of Turkey

Policies	Stakeholders
Accommodating sport facilities for the access of disadvantaged people	The Ministry of Youth and Sports, the Ministry of Family and Social Policies, the Ministry of Environment and Urban Planning, the Ministry of National Education, Local Authorities, the Council of Higher Education, sports federations and non-governmental organisations
Carrying out activities for disadvantaged people in educational institutions	The Ministry of Youth and Sports, the Ministry of Family and Social Policies, the Ministry of National Education, the Council of Higher Education, universities, media institutions, sports federations, non-governmental organisations
Rehabilitation of disadvantaged people through sports	The Ministry of Youth and Sports, the Ministry of Family and Social Policies, the Ministry of National Education, the Ministry of Health, the Council of Higher Education, universities, sports federations, non-governmental organisations
Conducting studies in order to increase the athletic performance of disadvantaged people	The Ministry of Youth and Sports, the Ministry of Family and Social Policies, the Ministry of Health, the Ministry of National Education, local authorities, the Council of Higher Education, sports federations and non-governmental organisations

Source: Turkish Ministry of Youth and Sports (www.gsb.gov.tr)

Table 22.7 Financial aid received by the disability sports federations according to the 2017 Activity Report of Directorate General for Sports Services

Disability Sport Federations	Financial Aid Received in 2017
Turkish Sports Federation for the Physically Disabled	27,397.26 USD
Turkish Deaf Sports Federation	30,735.61 USD
Turkish Blind Sports Federation	27,397.26 USD
Turkish Special Athletes Sports Federation	82,191.78 USD
Total: 167,721.91 USD	
*1.00 USD = 3.65 TRY in 2017	

Source: Directorate General for Sport Services (2020)

In 2017 the financial aid given to all sports federations in Turkey was 20,637,243 USD. The total financial aid given to disability sports federations accounts for only 0.8% of this total amount.

Level of Integration and Inclusion

Efforts to prepare the "Joint Inclusion Memorandum," which is considered the National Action Programme of member and candidate countries for fighting against social exclusion, are one of Turkey's obligations in its EU candidacy process that have been ongoing since 2004. According to the 2019 statistical report of the Directorate General for Disabled and Elderly, 72.9% of students with disabilities were in primary education, 13% were in special education classes and 14.1% were in special education schools, during the 2017–2018 school year (Directorate General for Disabled and Elderly, 2019). In Turkey, pupils with disabilities who are having inclusive education can find chance to participate in physical education and sport courses with their counterparts. However, most physical education and sports teachers still have a lack of knowledge adapting most of the physical skills. It is because teachers receive "adapted physical education course" for one semester during their higher education (Canpolat, 2020b).

Local governments are offering physical, recreational and sport activities in their own geographical region, too. Municipalities are organising structured physical activities for PwDs if only they have enough staff and related physical environment. According to Uludağ Güler and Çakı (2021), the sports activities organised by 30 metropolitan municipalities in Turkey for the PwDs were included under the heading of arts, culture and social activities. Unfortunately art, culture and social activities constitute 13.2% of the total services. Uludağ Güler and Çakı (2021) argue that, it is because the services such as education, vocational training, health aids are prioritised over arts, culture and sports services. Hopefully, it is known that PwDs can benefit from local sports facilities with other people during open hours, if the facilities are equipped accessible (Albayrak Kuruoğlu & Uzunçayır, 2020). For example, the only scout group consisting of PwDs in Turkey was established at the Centre for Disabled in Izmir Metropolitan Municipality. It is reported that 120 PwDs and 40 normally developed counterparts and 15 young volunteers have been involving in the practices of this group since 2018 (Kavili Arap et al., 2021).

22.4 Sport Participation by People with Disabilities

Monitoring and Evaluation

In Turkey, it is hard to report the total number of sport participating PwDs as no data can be found especially regarding local information. It can be said that the participation of PwDs in sports and art usually depends on the economic status of these individuals in Turkey. For this reason, PwDs who participate in sports and art activities by their own means hardly included in the statistical data. The available information is limited to the licensed athlete monitoring provided by disability sports federations (Canpolat, 2020b).

Table 22.8 Number of participants in four major disability sports federations of Turkey, in 2019

Sports Federation	Number of Athletes		Total Number of Athletes	Number of Sport Branches
	Men	Women		
Turkish Special Athletes Sports Federation	10,149	3283	13,432	14
Turkish Sports Federation for the Physically Disabled	3155	486	3641	16
Turkish Deaf Sports Federation	8532	1727	10,259	24
Turkish Blind Sports Federation	2488	688	3176	8
Total	24,324	6184	30,508	

Source: Directorate General for Sport Services (www.shgm.gsb.gov.tr)

Sport Participation

According to Directorate General for Sports Services operating under the Ministry of Youth and Sports, the number of recorded participants who joined the organisations of the four disability sports federations in 2019 is shown in Table 22.8. The number of participants who join the local activities (organised by municipalities of the provinces or districts) is hard to estimate since there is no statistics about this subject.

The Turkish Deaf Sports Federation reported 117 sports clubs and the Turkish Blind Sports Federation reported 252 sports clubs operating under the related branches of these sports federations. The information regarding the number of sports clubs for the Turkish Sports Federation For The Physically Disabled and Turkish Special Athletes Sports Federation was not available. However, according to the 2017 Activity Report of the Directorate General for Sports Services, the total number of active licensed athletes with disabilities was reported as 13,257. Total number of participants was increased to 30,508 in 2019 as mentioned in Table 22.8. The number of licensed athletes with disabilities is about 1.2% when compared to the disability population (Directorate General for Sports Services, 2017). Although the 2015–2019 strategic plan of the Directorate General for Sports Services stated that the monitoring will be carried out every six months (Directorate General for Sports Services, 2013), the obtained information is still limited to related sports federations' websites.

Table 22.9 shows the related sport branches of the disability sport federations.

In Turkey, the Ministry of Youth and Sport publishes a report concerning its activities every year. Activities related to PwDs are as follows:

(i) "Engelsiz Kamp (Camp without obstacles)": 1253 young people with various disabilities have been joining the summer camps (contains sports and recreational activities) which were organised in different provinces.
(ii) "29 Ekim Farkındalık Koşusu (29th September Awareness Run)": 29th September 1923 is the founding day of Republic of Turkey. In 2019, this activity was organised with the route from Istanbul to Ankara. Para-athletes and special athletes were included for this festive running activity.

Table 22.9 Sport branches of the disabled sport federations in Turkey

Sports Federation	Name of the Sport Branches	Number of Sport Branches
Turkish Special Athletes Sports Federation	Track and field, basketball, equestrian, cycling, bowling, boccia, gymnastics, football, futsal, skiing, table tennis, tennis, volleyball, swimming	14
Turkish Sports Federation for the Physically Disabled	Amputee football, wheelchair basketball, shooting, arm wrestling, archery, swimming, sailing, wheelchair tennis, badminton, track and field, sitting volleyball, table tennis, weightlifting, boccia, skiing, wheelchair dancing	16
Turkish Deaf Sports Federation	Basketball, volleyball, handball, taekwondo, badminton, track and field, cycling, bowling, futsal, wrestling, tennis, swimming, skiing, judo, karate, table tennis, beach volleyball, golf, orienteering, shooting, sailing, chess, curling	23
Turkish Blind Sports Federation	Track and field, football, futsal B2-B3, goalball, weightlifting, judo, chess, swimming	8

Source: Directorate General for Sport Services (2020)

(iii) "Sportif Yetenek Tarama Projesi (Sports Talent Screening Project)": The aim of this project is to screen and monitor children from 81 provinces of Turkey. In the 2017–2018 period, 869 children with disabilities were included and tested. Children who had the potential to be future Paralympic athletes were selected to participate in "Fundamental Movement and Athletic Skills Education." The number of talented participants with disabilities were recorded as 3551 in the 2018–2019 period.

(iv) "Antrenörler Engelleri Aşıyor Projesi (Trainers Are Overcoming Obstacles Project)": With the aim of training adapted sport trainers, this project has already been completed. Trainers who certificated from this project were provided with work in these sport centres. It was reported that 4652 trainers were certified and 3931 PwDs had benefited from these centres between May 2018 and May 2019 and 4652 between May 2019 and January 2020 (Ministry of Youth and Sport, 2020).

Barriers and Facilitators

Barriers

In Turkey, incentives that increase the mobility of PwDs and facilitate their social lives were raised at the same time with the EU countries. There isn't any incompetence in the adoption of laws. However, it is not easy to track due to the lack of mechanisms and civil initiatives for inspection. It is believed that there was a gap between legal regulations and practices (Meral & Turnbull, 2016; Mumcu, 2018). Although the importance of physical activity and sports for PwDs is considered from the point of social policies; statistics and scientific studies examining the effectiveness of implementations are rare. Disability sports clubs are usually government-dependent in terms of serving unless they have their own sports facilities. The budget for disability sports federations in Turkey increased tenfold between 2008 and 2014. Despite this, disability sports federations operate in dozens of sport branches on low budgets. The reason is not because of low priority, but the opportunities such as facilities, equipment, number of experts are limited and the demand from this population have not yet reached the desired degree. In recent years, Turkey's international achievements in Paralympic sports have increased the demands of PwDs who want to involve in sports which gives hope in terms of future investments (Çınarlı & Ersöz, 2010; Mumcu, 2018). In Turkey there are shortcomings in the planning and implementation of projects in disability sports. The reason for these shortcomings may be due to the fact that stakeholder institutions do not work with a project-based system (Canbolat, 2020b).

Individual barriers are also one of the parameters regarding participating in disability sports. According to Albayrak Kuruoğlu and Uzunçayır (2020), transportation and accessibility are important factors in terms of motivation for PwDs, because it is hard to reach facilities by public transport. Another study conducted by Kızar et al. (2018) revealed that one of the major barriers considering the needs and opportunities of the PwDS to participate in sports was the inadequate physical conditions of sports facilities. Participants of the study mentioned that sports facilities were not meeting their special needs such as accessing locker rooms, entrances and exits (Kızar et al., 2018).

Facilitators

In Turkey, most of the articles required by member states relating to EU compliance laws and the UNCRPD are under the responsibility of local governments. Centres for PwDs have been established to provide services in many local government units in order to enable PwDs to participate in society, to ensure social harmony and to eliminate discrimination. These centres are providing counselling, prevention, care, rehabilitation, orientation, personal development and support services for PwDs. Recreation and sports activities are organised and implemented mostly by municipalities in this particular centres (Mumcu, 2018). According to Tekkurşun-Demir and İlhan (2020), there is a need for obtaining individual information about the challenges and facilitators about sports participation of PwDs. Their study was based on implementing a questionnaire with individual items and it was found that the mean score of the motivational level of the athletes with physical impairments was higher than the athletes with visual and hearing impairments. Motivation of PwDs for sports participation is an important parameter in terms of participating and sustaining involvement in sports (Tekkurşun-Demir & İlhan, 2020).

The joint mission of the four disability sports federations in Turkey is to establish the archive of athletes with disabilities, to increase the recognition of athletes with disabilities in cooperation with schools, clubs, media, as well as to ensure their integration in the society and to represent them at the highest level in international activities. Each federation creates its own archive. Information about past athletes can be obtained from the relevant department of the Federation. It is provided as a report to the ministry upon request. The procedures and principles about awarding (cash or by other means) the athletes, sports clubs, coaches and trainers who have achieved outstanding success in national and international sports activities are based on the Law No. 3289 dated on May 05, 1986 (National Official Gazette, 2010). One of the other facilitating practices of physical activity and sports for PwDs is tax incentives in Turkey. The state has made legal arrangements about regulating tax deduction for sponsorship in sports. In Turkey taxes are partially waiving for encouraging investments and development of sports (Çınarlı & Ersöz, 2010).

22.5 Conclusion

The systematic struggling process of PwDs living in European countries against social barriers has led to a change in the political view of PwDs over the last fifty years. In Turkey, the effects of this change have been observed since 2000 because PwDs were formerly considered individuals who needed protection or should be kept hidden at home. This is still a traditional point of view accepted in various regions of the country. The process of Turkey's integration into the European Union has provided opportunities for PwDs to participate in society and work force. The number of PwDs participating in sports in Turkey is increasing day by day due to development and success in Paralympic sports. It is necessary to know the number of the athletes and branch distributions for future structuring. Facility planning should be done according to the numbers and the needs of athletes with disabilities. However, regarding data is still insufficient and unknown as well as the budget allocated for the participation of PwDs in sports is not enough when compared to other countries in Europe. Turkey has to put more effort in terms of providing, monitoring and evaluating disability sports services throughout the country.

In Turkey, the Covid-19 pandemic has caused disruptions in physical activity and sports implementations in every means. Due to the fact that staying indoors for a long time can have a negative impact on mental and physical health, PwDs under the age of 20 were allowed to go to parks and gardens during curfews in Turkey.

The Ministry of Youth and Sports decided to postpone activities in all sports federations during the first year of the pandemic. Down Syndrome Association of Turkey is continuing to provide online exercise programmes (yoga, Zumba) by the help of volunteered experts on certain days of the week (Down Syndrome Association of Turkey, 2021). Metropolitan Municipalities are also providing online exercise courses from their social media accounts which are visible to public. Since the Covid-19 restrictions in Turkey ended in July 2021, the postponed recreational and sports activities for PwDs have been continuing with precautions.

References

Albayrak Kuruoğlu, Y.& Ünlü, H. (2014). *The analysis of Turkey's olympic education implementations according to olympic legacy and candidature process*. 13th International Sports Science Congress, 07–09 November, Konya, Turkey.

Albayrak Kuruoğlu, Y., & Uzunçayır, D. (2020). Statements of parents about the impact of adapted swimming education on children with special needs. *Ulusal Spor Bilimleri Dergisi, 4*(2), 174–186. https://doi.org/10.30769/usbd.826474

Albayrak Kuruoğlu, Y., Uzunçayır, D., &Camekan, E. (2018). *The impact of aquatic exercises on physical fitness levels of intellectually disabled children*. Disability Sport Conference, Research Centre Business in Society, 03-05 September 2018, Coventry University, United Kingdom.

Aydın, H., Gül, Ö., & Aydın, M. (2018). Kurumsal bakım ve rehabilitasyon sürecinde sporun önemi, kamu ve sivil toplum kuruluşu işbirliği: Aile, Çalışma Ve Sosyal Hizmet Bakanlığı ile Aile ve Sosyal Politikalar Gençlik Spor Kulübü. *Akademik Sosyal Araştırmalar Dergisi, 6*(80), 627–644.

Bilsin, E., & Başbakkal, Z. (2014). Dünyada ve Türkiye'de engelli çocuklar. *Ege Üniversitesi Hemşirelik Fakültesi Dergisi, 30*(2), 65–78.

Britannica. (2020). https://www.britannica.com/place/Turkey/Constitution (Accessed on 31.07.2020).

Canpolat, B. (2020a). Disability Sports Management in Turkey (Book chapter in Turkish). *Sporda Yeni Akademik Çalışmalar-5* (Editors: Mehmet Ilkim, Enes Beltekin) ISBN 978–605–258-937-3, p.41–63, Akademisyen Yayınevi, Ankara.

Canpolat, B. (2020b). The need of physical education and sports teachers for disabled students. *Sivas Cumhuriyet Üniversitesi Spor Bilimleri Dergisi, 1*(1), 17–28.

Çınarlı, S., & Ersöz, G. (2010). Engellilere yönelik spor hizmetlerinin gelişimi açısından sponsorluk ve vergisel düzenlemelere ilişkin öneriler. *Süleyman Demirel Üniversitesi Sosyal Bilimler Enstitüsü Dergisi, 12*(2), 141–156.

Çolakoğlu, T., & Solmaz, S. (2017). Spor federasyonlarında uygulanan bağımsızlık paradoksu. *Atatürk Üniversitesi Beden Eğitimi ve Spor Bilimleri Dergisi, 19*(3), 24–25.

Constitution of the Republic of Turkey. (1982a). *Law No: 4709.* Date of Approval: March 10, 2001. (Amended 2001. Retrieved on March 14, 2013 from www.byegm.gov.tr/content.aspx?s=tcotrot).

Constitution of the Republic of Turkey. (1982b). *Law No: 2709.* Date of Approval: October 18, 1982. Official Gazette: Date: 09/11/1982, Issue: 17 863 (repeated); Published in the Law: Series: 5, Volume: 22, Page: 3, amended09/23/2010.

Devecioğlu, S., Çoban, B., & Karakaya, Y. E. (2015). Spor kulüplerinin yönetim modellerinin değerlendirilmesi (Assessment of the management models of sports clubs). *Dumlupınar Üniversitesi Sosyal Bilimler Dergisi, 31*, 51–68.

Directorate General for Disabled and Elderly. (2019). *Engelli ve Yaşlı İstatistik Bülteni (Bulletin of Disabled and Elderly).* https://www.ailevecalisma.gov.tr/media/51832/mayis-istatistik-bulteni.pdf (Accessed on 06.07.2020).

Directorate General for Sport Services. (2017a). *Spor Hizmetleri Genel Müdürlüğü Faaliyet Raporu (Activity Report of Sport Services).* https://shgm.gsb.gov.tr/Public/Edit/images/SGM/faaliyet%20Raporları/FAALİYET%20RAPORU_2017.pdf (Accessed, 29.07.2020).

Directorate General for Sport Services. (2017b). *Kurumsal Mali Durum ve Beklentiler Raporu (Report of Corporate Financial Status and Estimations).* https://shgm.gsb.gov.tr/Public/Edit/images/SGM/StratejiBütçe/2017%20Yılı%20Kurumsal%20Mali%20Durum%20Ve%20Beklentiler%20Raporu.pdf (Accessed on 05.12.2020).

Directorate General for Sport Services. (2020). *Sport Federations.* https://shgm.gsb.gov.tr/federasyonlar/?p=0 (Accessed, 11.07.2020).

Doğan, A. (2019). Special Education in Turkey (Book chapter in Turkish). *Türk Eğitim Tarihi* (Editors: Mustafa Kılınç, Songül Keçeci Kurt) ISBN 978–605–80114-3-4, p. 439–463, Pegem Akademi, Ankara.

Down Syndrome Association of Turkey. (2021). https://www.downturkiye.org/down-sendromlular-icin-online-egitimler (Accessed on 29.10.2021).

EBSED (Engelli Bireylerde Spor ve Eğitim Bilimleri Derneği). (2020). http://www.ebsed.org/?SyfNmb=2&pt=HAKKIMIZDA (Accessed on 05.10.2020).

Ersoy, A. F., & Dikici, E. (2018). Institutions related to social work activities In the Ottoman period. *Third Sector Social Economic Review, 53*(2), 576–594. https://doi.org/10.15659/3.sektor-sosyal-ekonomi.18.07.946

European Commission. (2017). *Youth policies in Turkey.* https://eacea.ec.europa.eu/national-policies/sites/youthwiki/files/gdlturkey.pdf (Accessed on 03.07.2020).

Global Religious Futures Project. (2016). *Pew Research Center.* http://www.globalreligiousfutures.org/countries/turkey#/?affiliations_religion_id=0&affiliations_year=2020&region_name=All%20Countries&restrictions_year=2016 (Accessed on 05.12.2020).

Gündoğdu, Ş. M., & Asal, Ö. (2017). A decision support system for the determination of disadvantaged youths by National Youth and Sports Policy. *Türkiye Sosyal Araştırmalar Dergisi, 21*(2), 293–310.

İmamoğlu, A. F. (2011). Türkiye'de sporun yönetsel yapısı içinde spor federasyonları. *Gazi Beden Eğitimi ve Spor Bilimleri Dergisi, 16*(2), 3–10.

Kalaycı, S., & Akin, A. (2019). Engellilere yönelik yerel sosyal hizmetlerde belediyelerin yeri: Malatya Büyükşehir Belediyesi (The role of municipalities in local social work for the disabled: The Metropolitan Municipality of Malatya). *Selçuk Üniversitesi Sosyal Bilimler MYO Dergisi, 22*(2), 663–676.

Kavili Arap, S., Yücebaş, E., & Arap, İ. (2021). Local governments' goal of life without barriers: The case of the Izmir Metropolitan Municipality. *Anemon Journal of Social Science of Mus Alpaslan University, 9*(1), 139–156.

Kızar, O., Savucu, Y., Yücel, A. S., & Kargün, M. (2018). Türkiye'deki spor tesislerinin engelliler için yeterlilik düzeyinin incelenmesi. *Turkish Studies, 13*(26), 829–848.

Mansour, M. (2017).Chapter II Sports in Turkey. *Windows into Turkish Culture* (Editors; Danielle V. Schoon and Melinda McClimans), Pressbooks The Ohio State University.

Meral, B. F., & Turnbull, H. R. (2016). Comparison of Turkish disability policy, the United Nations Convention on the rights of persons with disabilities, and the core concepts of U.S. disability policy. *Alter, 10*(3), 221–235. https://doi.org/10.1016/j.alter.2016.02.001

Metin, B. (2017). The role of local governments in the social policy for the disabled: The Case of Keçiören Municipality. *Gazi Universitesi Iktisadi ve Idari Bilimler Fakultesi Dergisi, 19*(1), 320–344.

Mü'min ibn-i Mukbil. (1437). *Zahire-i Muradiyye.* İstanbul: Süleymaniye Yazma Eser Koleksiyonu (Süleymaniye Handwritten Collection), No: 3585.

Mumcu, H. E. (2018). *Engelli Politikaları: Avrupa Birliği Ülkeleri ile Türkiye Karşılaştırması.* ISBN 978 605 258 2017, Akademisyen Kitabevi, Ankara.

National Official Gazette. (2010). *Spor Hizmet ve Faaliyetlerinde Üstün Başarı Gösterenlerin Ödüllendirilmesi Hakkında Yönetmelik (Regulation on the reward of those who have shown outstanding success in sports services and activities).* https://www.resmigazete.gov.tr/eskiler/2010/11/20101103-6.htm (Accessed on 24.04.2021).

National Official Gazette. (2012). *Bağımsız Spor Federasyonları Çalışma Usul ve Esasları Hakkında Yönetmelik (Regulations on the operation principles of independent sports federations).* https://www.resmigazete.gov.tr/eskiler/2012/07/20120719-7.htm (Accessed on 24.04.2021).

OECD. (2020). *Population (indicator).* https://doi.org/10.1787/d434f82b-en (Accessed on 31.07.2020).

OHCHR-Turkey. (2015). (Office of the United Nations High Commissioner for Human Rights) General Directorate of Services for Persons with Disabilities and the Elderly. *Contribution to the Questionnaire from OHCHR Special Rapporteur on the Rights of Persons with Disabilities.* https://www.ohchr.org/EN/Countries/ENACARegion/Pages/TRIndex.aspx (Accessed, 11.09.2020).

Özgökçeler, S., & Alper, Y. (2010). An Assessment of the Turkish Disability Act in view of social model. *Uludag University, Faculty of Economics and Administrative Sciences, Business and Economics Research Journal, 1*(1), 1–33.

PwC. (2020). *Worlwide Tax Summaries: Turkey Overview* (Reviewed, 22 Jan 2020) https://taxsummaries.pwc.com/turkey (Accessed on 31.07.2020).

State Planning Organisation. (1983). Spor komisyonu raporu. *V. Beş Yıllık Kalkınma Planı Özel İhtisas Komisyonu Raporu.* Yayın No:302, Ankara https://www.sbb.gov.tr/wp-content/uploads/2018/11/5-Spor_OIK302.pdf (Accessed on 14.02.2021).

Tekkurşun-Demir, G., & İlhan, E. L. (2020). Motivation of athletes with disabilities for sports participation. *Ankara University Faculty of Educational Sciences Journal of Special Education, 21*(1), 49–69. https://doi.org/10.21565/ozelegitimdergisi.490063

TESYEV (Türkiye Engelliler Spor, Yardım ve Eğitim Vakfı). (2020). http://tesyev.org/tr/anasayfa (Accessed on 05.10.2020).

The Directorate General for Sports Services. (2014). *Stratejik Plan 2015–2019.* https://shgm.gsb.gov.tr/Public/Edit/images/SGM/StratejiBütçe/SGM_Stratejik%20Plan%20_%202015-2019_(04,01).pdf (Accessed on 14.02.2021).

Turkish Cultural Foundation. (2020). *Lifestyle: Sports.* http://www.turkishculture.org/lifestyles/sports-228.htm (Accessed on 31.07.2020).

Turkish Ministry of Youth and Sports. (2020). *The National Youth and Sports Policy Document.* https://gsb.gov.tr/public/edit/files/Mevzuat/TheNationalYouthandSportsPolicyDocument(1).pdf (Accessed on 03.09.2020).

Turkish National Olympic Committee. (2020). *National Sport Federations.* https://www.olimpiyatkomitesi.org.tr/Detail/About-Us/National-Sports-Federations/26/1/1 (Accessed on 06.09.2020).

Uludağ Güler, Ç., & Çakı, N. (2021). The evaluation of metropolitan municipalities' services for disabled people by content analysis method. *Turkish Journal of Geographical Sciences, 19*(1), 92–127. https://doi.org/10.33688/aucbd.847546

United Nations. (2005). *Law on disabled people and on making amendments in some laws and decree laws.* https://www.un.org/development/desa/disabilities/wpcontent/uploads/sites/15/2019/11/Turkey_Turkish-Disability-Act-TDA-No.-5378-of-2005.pdf (Accessed 01.09.2020).

Ünlü, E. (2018). Individuals with intellectual disabilities in the Ottoman Period. *Electronic Turkish Studies, 13*(27), 1563–1574. https://doi.org/10.7827/TurkishStudies.14597

World Bank. (2020). https://www.worldbank.org/en/country/turkey/overview (Accessed on 31.07.2020).

Yüksek Öğretim Kurumu. (2020). *Yüksek Öğretim Bilgi Yönetim Sistemi.* https://istatistik.yok.gov.tr/ (Accessed on 04.10.2020).

Chapter 23
The Landscape of Sport for Persons with a Disability: A System Within a System

Caroline van Lindert, Jeroen Scheerder, and Ian Brittain

23.1 Introduction

Disability is part of the human condition and many people will experience some form of disability at some point in life (World Health Organization & The World Bank, 2011). This is the reality for a quarter of the population in EU member states (European Commission, 2021; Grammenos & Priestley, 2020). Unfortunately, persons with a disability (pwds) face numerous barriers to participate in various domains of life, including sport and physical activity (hereafter PA) (European Commission, 2021; United Nations, 2019). Disability is often a reason for not participating in sport and PA, resulting in lower participation levels among pwds. Participation in sport and PA by pwds, however, is considered a human right and is promoted by the United Nations Convention on the Rights of Persons with Disabilities (hereafter UNCRPD) (United Nations, 2006) and the European disability strategy *the Union of Equality* (European Commission, 2021). Cross-national comparative data on the various ways disability sport is delivered throughout Europe and of sport participation by pwds is mostly lacking. But, it is considered necessary to draw attention to (the reasons for) this group's underrepresentation in sport.

C. van Lindert (✉)
Mulier Institute, Utrecht, The Netherlands
e-mail: c.vanlindert@mulierinstituut.nl

J. Scheerder
Department of Movement Sciences, KU Leuven, Belgium

Policy Research Centre on Sports on behalf of the Flemish Government, Brussels, Belgium

I. Brittain
Centre for Business in Society, Coventry University, Coventry, UK

© The Author(s), under exclusive license to Springer Nature Switzerland AG 2023
C. van Lindert et al. (eds.), *The Palgrave Handbook of Disability Sport in Europe*, https://doi.org/10.1007/978-3-031-21759-3_23

This handbook is an attempt to fill this gap and aims to explore the various ways sport for pwds is governed and organised across Europe, as well as the extent to which and how pwds participate in sport. The following questions have led the editors and contributors in their work (see Chap. 1):

- At the national, regional and local levels, which governmental, intermediate and non-governmental agents are involved in delivering sport for pwds, what are their roles and what is the nature of the relationships between the relevant agents in the disability sport system?
- At the national, regional and local levels, what kind of policies and legislation apply to sport for pwds and to what extent do they promote inclusion in sport among pwds?
- How, and to what extent, do pwds participate in sport and what are the facilitators and barriers towards their participation in sport?
- What are the methods and challenges in collecting sport participation data with regard to pwds?

Making Comparisons

This handbook is written from a cross-national perspective based upon a collection of 19 country-specific chapters (see Chaps. 4–22) from different regions in Europe (see Fig. 2.2 in Chap. 1). The selection of countries is based on the willingness to cooperate by the contributors and the availability of useful data in the respective countries. As a result of our convenience sample, we cannot provide a complete overview of disability sport in Europe as a whole. However, we believe that the data in this handbook provides a reasonable indication of the various ways sport is delivered in Europe. The country-specific chapters in this handbook present both up-to-date data and in-depth descriptions and analyses, based upon a rigorous theoretical and conceptual framework as described in Chap. 1. Similar to Hallmann and Petry (2013) and Scheerder et al. (2017), we consider it useful to mainly 'describe differences' (and similarities) in this handbook. All authors followed a relatively strict set of guidelines to draw a clear picture of the policy and structure of disability sport and sport participation by pwds in their country. The critical reader might argue that this approach is rather superficial. However, without gathering and describing up to date material on these topics in the first place, a cross-national comparison would not be possible at all, since this data cannot be found in existing databases. The value of this handbook lies partly in presenting the available data in a well-organised manner and revealing potential data gaps.

As for the comparison, in this chapter we consider a number of possible explanations for variations between countries (see Scheerder et al., 2017). Firstly, we observe differences in the country profile, for example, the social, welfare, economic, cultural or political climate (see Esping-Andersen's distinction into different welfare states, 1990). For instance, the importance attached to grassroots sports varies from country to country. Scheerder et al. (2017) argue that in the Scandinavian countries, but also in Belgium and the Netherlands, grassroots sports and club-organised sports are very important policy issues, whereas in Anglo-Saxon countries more importance is attached to elite sports. Cultural values that shape the political system and society in general will influence the way disability sport is defined and delivered. This is also true for the importance attached to the inclusion of minority groups in society and sport, for example, pwds and the way disability is viewed in a country (see Chap. 2). Also, geographical differences may cause differences between countries. For example, a small country size and high population density may lead to shorter travel distances between home and sport facilities (see e.g. the Netherlands), while a large country with low population density in rural areas may negatively impact the opportunities to participate in sport (see e.g. the Scandinavian countries and Iceland).

Another explanation for cross-national variations can be found in the steering and organisation of (disability) sport, as well as the division of responsibilities within each country. This chapter will provide various examples of this.

Path dependency can offer another explanation for the international variations in the disability sport systems and participation. As Scheerder et al. (2017) argue, once a certain path has been embarked upon, it is difficult to change course completely (see Green & Collins, 2008). For instance, if a country decides to focus on certain sport disciplines (in elite sport development), or, in the case of disability sport, on developing elite sport instead of grassroots opportunities, it will be difficult to implement a broader policy and focus on other sport disciplines or on grassroots sports as well, because they have been supported less in the meantime and institutional settings are not prepared. This is partly why we asked contributors to pay attention to the history of disability sport in their country.

In this chapter, by taking a helicopter view, we provide an overview of the similarities and differences in the delivery of disability sport and participation by pwds between the countries in this handbook. First, we discuss how the contributing authors understand disability in their country, as we believe this may influence the position of pwds in sport. Second, we give an overview of how disability sport in European countries emerged according to the contributors. The main parts of this chapter concern answering the main questions of this book with regard to the structure, the policy and participation in sport by pwds. We conclude this chapter with a critical analysis of some limitations of the current handbook and the data described in the chapters, and with a summary of recommendations for future policy and research in the field of disability sport.

23.2 Disability Is Part of the Human Condition

To understand the position of pwds in sport in the various countries in Europe, we need to understand pwds' position in those societies in general. Sport is a social phenomenon and reflects norms and values that are prevalent in the broader society

(Coakley, 2015). Based on the descriptions in the country-specific chapters, we mainly observe that developments in society and in certain policies, on national and international levels, have an influence on how sport is delivered for pwds. Almost all contributors make reference to the UNCRPD and its ratification by the countries involved. The UNCRPD not only challenges countries to take serious steps in recognising equal rights for pwds to participate in society, but also offers a framework to define what is meant by disability in the countries involved. For instance, in Denmark "the acknowledgement, that 'disability results from the interaction between persons with impairments and attitudinal and environmental barriers that hinders their full and effective participation in society on an equal basis with others' (United Nations, 2006) is therefore—at least on paper—a guiding principle in both governmental and grass-root work" (see Chap. 4, page XX). With alignment to this definition, contributors from more or less all counties involved describe a move away from the medical model of disability in favour of the social model of disability, human rights practices and/or the so-called biopsychosocial model of the World Health Organisation's (WHO) International Classification of Functioning Disability and Health (ICF model) (World Health Organization, 2002; see also Chap. 2). The proposed interconnection between biology, psychology and socio-environmental factors influences standpoints and value systems in the societies involved and presumably also in sport.

Defining disability is considered difficult by most contributors and we see that they mainly rely on existing international standards. It remains to be seen whether the definitions chosen are also put into practice. We do see that contributors attempt to describe the development of socially accepted terminology, reflecting that disability in society is becoming more normalised.

In most chapters, the contributing authors mention the existence of national acts, laws and/or regulations that focus on equality of treatment for pwds and/or elimination of discrimination against pwds. These acts are meant to improve accessibility to, and integration or inclusion of, pwds in various domains of society (e.g. education, work, social services, etc.).

All contributing authors present data on the prevalence of disability. However, this data is hard to compare because different methods and definitions were used to determine which proportion of the population has a disability. In some cases the definition is broad, resulting in one figure representing all pwds in the country. In other cases the definition distinguishes between type and severity of the disability, resulting in disaggregated prevalence figures for, people with a visual, hearing or mobility impairment for example. The ICF model and its previous versions, has also had an influence on the methods of measuring disability in several countries. For instance, in the Netherlands and in Portugal, questions in census or survey questionnaires, are based on the second level of the ICF model, which highlight the functional capacities or limitations and individual experiences. In Chap. 2 we presented comparable data on the prevalence of disability using EU-survey data (Eurostat, 2022a, 2022b). We discussed the efforts that are being made worldwide to promote the use of standardised questions. To be able to compare disability-related issues within populations, including sport, it is of utmost importance that governments and governing bodies in sport include both indicators related to sport and to disability in (sport participation and PA) population surveys (see Recommendations).

23.3 Long History of Organising Sport for Persons with a Disability

In each country, sport for pwds developed at its own pace and direction. However, a number of similarities stand out in the emergence of disability sport in the countries involved in our handbook. We have identified four phases in the history of disability sport.

In Europe, the first phase in the emergence of disability sport before and shortly after the Second World War is characterised as a pioneering phase. In about half of the countries involved, disability sport started to emerge at the beginning of the twentieth century (sometimes even late nineteenth century), according to the descriptions of the contributing authors. The starting point seems to coincide to a large extent with the establishment of the first deaf sport clubs or federations in the respective countries and the participation by deaf athletes in the *International Silent Games* from 1924 onwards. As deduced from the country-specific descriptions, in the other half of the countries (see Belgium, Iceland, Ireland, Lithuania, Northern Ireland, Slovenia, Spain, Sweden and Turkey) disability sport did not develop until after the Second World War. Many of the contributing authors refer to the emergence of disability sport due to its use in the rehabilitation of war victims after the Second World War and reference the influence of sir Ludwig Guttmann, Director of the Spinal Unit at Stoke Mandeville Hospital in the United Kingdom. In Turkey, however disability sport developed late, mainly due to its absence from the Second World War. In Portugal, in addition to the emphasis on rehabilitation and treatment of pwds after the Second World War, the Colonial War of 1961 to 1974 caused many more injuries and disabilities, requiring a response.

The second phase in the development of disability sport in the European countries is more or less characterised by an expansion of opportunities to participate in sport (or in some countries 'adapted physical activity', hereafter APA) for citizens who acquired a physical disability not during war but due to other causes, for women and children with a disability (in educational settings), for persons with non-motor disabilities, such as a visual impairment, an intellectual disability and so on. Contributing authors make note of the establishment of numerous types of sport clubs and national federations for specific types of disabilities during this phase of expansion. In this phase, some contributors mention increased attention from their governments for improving opportunities for disability sport and some authors mention a shift from competitive sport towards more attention to leisure and grassroots sports or APA.

In many countries, contributing authors note that names of federations are being adapted to more appropriate use of language, according to changes in how societies view pwds in general, and to address the needs and wishes of persons with various types of disabilities instead of solely war victims. Addressing a larger group of pwds and striving for more efficiency has been an incentive for mergers of federations in several countries. The establishment of National Disability Sport Federations (hereafter NDSF) and/or National Paralympic Committees (hereafter NPC) as a result of those mergers can best be seen as the third phase in the development of disability sport in Europe.

As mentioned at the start, not all countries have gone through these changes at the same time or at the same pace. This also applies to what we might call the last phase in the development of disability sport, namely that of 'mainstreaming' disability sport, or the integration and/or inclusion of disability sport. A number of authors explicitly take the effort to write about a process of integrating or including sport for pwds into the mainstream sport structure in their country. The Netherlands, Norway and Sweden seem to tackle this issue the most extensively. In the Netherlands and Norway disability sport is (almost) fully integrated in the mainstream sport settings of the National Sport (Con)federations (hereafter NSCF, NSF) and National Olympic Committees (hereafter NOC). Sweden is working towards dismantling the Swedish Parasport Federation and the inclusion of athletes with disabilities in special sports federations. In other countries, Disability Sport Federations (hereafter DSFs) push forward on inclusion by addressing this issue more often, or by merging the various Disability Sport Federations into one umbrella NDSF of NPC (see Finland).

23.4 The Structure and Steering of Sport for Persons with a Disability

Organisational Landscape of Sport for Persons with a Disability: Unique, But Complex

According to the descriptions of the contributing authors, the landscape or structure of disability sport is more or less built on the existing structures for sport in the respective countries. The sport structure can be built, for instance, on the pyramid model of sport, like in Slovenia, or a 'Sport for All' model like in Iceland and other Nordic countries.

If we have a closer look at the landscape of disability sport, however, we can conclude that disability sport adds specific elements to the sport system giving it its own dynamics. This does not mean that the disability sport system stands alone. It is, in all countries, closely interconnected with the sport system in general. In some cases, elements of the general sport structures and disability sport structures become more intertwined, due to the inclusion of disability sport in mainstream sport provision or due to inclusive sport policy. In Chap. 2 we defined 'mainstreaming' as the policy of integrating the responsibility for sport provision for pwds into non-disabled sport organisations (Kitchin et al., 2019; Kitchin & Howe, 2014). This sometimes makes it hard to distinguish between mainstream sport and disability sport, as is mentioned, for instance, in the chapters of the United Kingdom and the Netherlands, and is clearly the case for Norway.

Contributing authors paint similar pictures of the disability sport system in their country as being complex, fragmented, opaque and confusing. Thomas and Guett (2014) came to a similar conclusion in their study of disability sport policy and provision in Europe. The complexity of construing the disability sport landscape is due to the fact that disability sport is the domain of different social spheres, as is mentioned by several contributors, and not just that of sports alone. It combines knowledge and expertise in sports-related matters with that of knowledge and expertise in disability-related matters. A wide range of actors play a role at all levels.

Contributing authors were asked to give an overview of the main agents in the disability sport system at the national, regional and local levels and to make a distinction between governmental agents, intermediate agents and non-governmental agents, using the framework from Hallmann and Petry (2013) (see Scheerder et al., 2017). In Fig. 23.1 we have combined the information provided by the contributors and construed a composite framework for disability sport. For readability purposes we alternatively use the words 'disability sport' and 'sport for pwds'. The use of the term 'disability sport' however does not imply that sport for pwds is a separate system, set apart from the general sport system.

Governmental Agents at the National Level

In all countries, contributing authors mention that a ministry or several ministries are the main governmental agents at the national level. In general, the state bodies that are responsible for disability sport are the same as those that influence sport in general. Sport, and thus disability sport, is usually the responsibility of the ministry of Education and/or Culture. Other policy domains that are reflected in the names of ministries responsible for (disability) sport are health, welfare, youth, science, social affairs, tourism, media and the interior. Sports is part of the name of a (sub) national ministry or office responsible for disability sport in several countries (Austria, Belgium, Lithuania, Ireland, the Netherlands, Slovenia, Switzerland and Turkey). Within the ministries usually a special unit, secretariat or directorate on sport governs disability sport. Key roles for ministries, directorates or councils in charge of (disability) sport are amongst others the distribution of funds, the formation of overarching national legislation and policies with regard to (disability) sport. Other types of national governmental agents that were mentioned often have an indirect influence on disability sport, for instance, by promoting equal rights and opportunities for social participation for pwds in society at large, by supporting access to health care and rehabilitation services or supporting access to physical education (PE). Some contributing authors stress the importance of PE and APA in (special) schools because it is there that children with a disability often are introduced to sports for the first time.

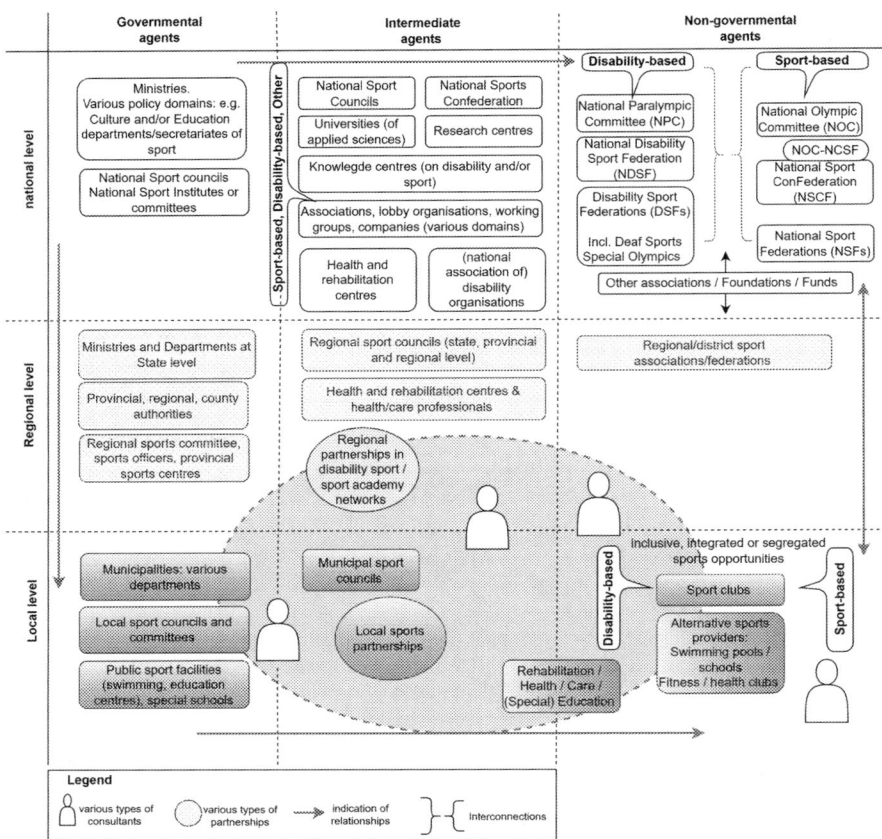

Fig. 23.1 Composite framework for disability sport in Europe. Source: Authors' own interpretation based on data from Chaps. 4–22

Besides ministries, some countries have sport councils residing under government responsibility, see, for instance, the National Sports Council in Finland, Sport Vlaanderen in Flanders, Belgium, the National Sport Institute in Hungary, the National Institute of Sport & Youth in Portugal, or the Higher Sport Council in Spain. Sport councils often have a more administrative and coordinative function in regard to disability sport.

Governmental Agents at the Regional Level

Contributors from around half of the countries mention governmental agents at the regional level. In countries with a federal state structure, such as Austria, Belgium, Germany, the United Kingdom and Switzerland, regional governments or departments have a role in disability sport. In other countries, such as Finland, the Netherlands, Norway, Sweden, Spain and Turkey, regional authorities, like counties, provinces or autonomous communities, are mentioned as having a role in disability sport. Obviously, the regional level plays a more significant role in the countries with a federal state structure. Roles are, amongst others, forming state level sport policies and legislation, the distribution of subsidies and acting as a link between national- and local-level sport policy agents.

Governmental Agents at the Local Level

In almost all cases, the most important governmental agents in the disability sport landscape can be found at the local level. Local governmental authorities, like (sport departments at) municipal councils and sport committees are responsible for the actual implementation of disability sport policy and often formulate their own local policies as a form of devolution of government duties. Local authorities play a central role in (supporting) the provision of community sport and leisure activities. They facilitate and support local partnerships between agents from various sectors, they work on the removal of barriers to participation, invest in the maintenance of sport facilities, fund sport activities and facilitate in transport for pwds or in getting access to sport aids and so on. Local departments from other policy domains, like education, welfare and equal rights, family services, are mentioned occasionally as important indirect influential agents, because they facilitate social participation in general by pwds.

Intermediate Agents as Linking Pin

Contributors listed various types of intermediate agents with a role in disability sport in their countries. However, contributing authors of four countries did not mention the existence of these kinds of agents (Iceland, Portugal, Switzerland and Turkey). Intermediate agents in all cases function as a link between the governmental and non-governmental agents. Intermediate agents can have various formal structures, from semi-governmental (see the arm's length principle in the United Kingdom for the sport councils), to public-private, to non-profit. Intermediate agents can be 'sport-based' (e.g. a sport council) or 'disability-based' (e.g. a national disability centre of expertise) or can be other types of agents (e.g. health insurance). In most cases, the agents can act autonomously from government. The agents have important roles in the disability sport landscape. They are independent bodies with an advisory or executive role, are supportive to the creation of sport programmes for pwds, produce and distribute knowledge with regard to disability-related matters, distribute funds, maintain networks between various agents active in promoting sport participation among pwds, or act as consultants for sport organisations and pwds, and so on. Contributors also mention universities (of applied sciences), knowledge institutes and research centres as important agents to produce and distribute knowledge about disability (sport) or to educate professionals, or facilitate participation in sport for students with disabilities.

Non-governmental Agents at the National Level

Different types of non-governmental agents play a key role in the disability sport landscape. We can roughly distinguish between 'disability-based' sport agents and 'sport-based' sport agents. An example of a 'disability-based' sport agent at the national level is a National Paralympic Committee (NPC), for example, the Austrian Paralympic Committee. Other forms of 'disability-based' sport agents at the national level are a National Disability Sport Federation (NDSF) and various Disability Sport Federations (DSFs). The first acts as a national umbrella or governing body for all sports activities, federations and/or clubs for various types of impairment groups in a given country, see, for example, the *Zveza ŠIS-SPK*, a federation of disability organisations in Slovenia or the National Sports Federation for Disabled Athletes in Iceland, who have a multi-sports role. The second form consists of federations for sports activities and/or clubs for a specific impairment group or specific type of (adapted) sport, see, for instance, the Lithuanian Deaf Sports Association, the Hungarian Special Olympics Association, or the German Wheelchair Sports Association. A majority of contributing countries have a Deaf sports federation and/or a Special Olympics association. Usually they fall under the umbrella of an NPC or NDSF as a member organisation. An NPC usually is in charge of elite sport (development) and the delegation of para-athletes to the Paralympic Games. An NDSF and the DSFs usually are in charge of developing and promoting (participation in) disability sport at a grassroots level, developing their specific sports (for specific age or impairment groups), supporting regional and local sport agents and in several cases promotion of inclusion of pwds in sport.

'Sport-based' sport agents are what we could call 'mainstream' sport agents or sport agents that have been established for athletes without a disability. At the national level, we find, for example, a National Olympic Committee (NOC), a National Sports Confederation (national umbrella or governing body, NSCF) or a combination of the two (NOC/NSCF) and various National Sports Federations (NSFs) for specific types of sport (e.g. athletics, football, swimming, etc.).

Non-governmental Agents at the Regional Level

Regional non-governmental agents are not mentioned very often by the contributing authors. If they are not mentioned this could mean a regional level is non-existent in the overall disability sport system, as seems to be the case in Iceland and Turkey, or it could mean that besides the regional governmental agents, non-governmental sport agents are not active at the regional level, possibly due to a small country size (see Denmark and the Netherlands). Regional sport agents obviously play an important role in countries with a federal state structure. See the United Kingdom, with, at the regional level, agents like Disability Sport Wales, Activity Alliance and Scottish Disability Sport, or Austria, with, in all nine Austrian states, regional affiliates of the Austrian Disability Sports Organisation. In Belgium, for each language area, there is a regional disability sport organisation. In other countries, district or regional sport associations or councils are active.

Non-governmental Agents at the Local Level

At the local level, the most important non-governmental sport agents mentioned by all contributing authors are the local sports clubs, because they deliver sports activities to pwds. As compared to the national level, authors mention the existence of 'disability-based' and/or 'sport-based' sport clubs where pwds can participate in special groups or together with members without a disability. These sport clubs are often run by devoted volunteers. Other types of sport agents that are mentioned are fitness and health clubs, swimming pools and youth clubs. At the local level, several authors give examples of various types of non-sport agents being part of the disability sport framework, such as rehabilitation centres, health institutions, disability associations, special schools or care facilities, while other contributing authors tend to mention these kind of agents as playing a more secondary role outside of the framework (see Sect. Secondary Agents).

Partnerships and Consultants at the Regional and Local Levels

In some countries there is a system of local or regional partnerships and networks in place for disability sport, at a grassroots or an elite level, at different stakeholder levels. In addition, a number of countries work with various types of consultants, that, for instance, support regional and local agents in establishing activities for individuals with disabilities and recruitment for these activities. Partnerships and/or consultants can be found in Denmark, Finland, Flanders, Belgium, Ireland, the Netherlands and Norway.

Secondary Agents

The contributing authors mentioned various agents that have a more secondary or indirect role in the disability sport framework of their country (see Fig. 23.2). These organisations do not have the installation of policies or sport programmes for pwds

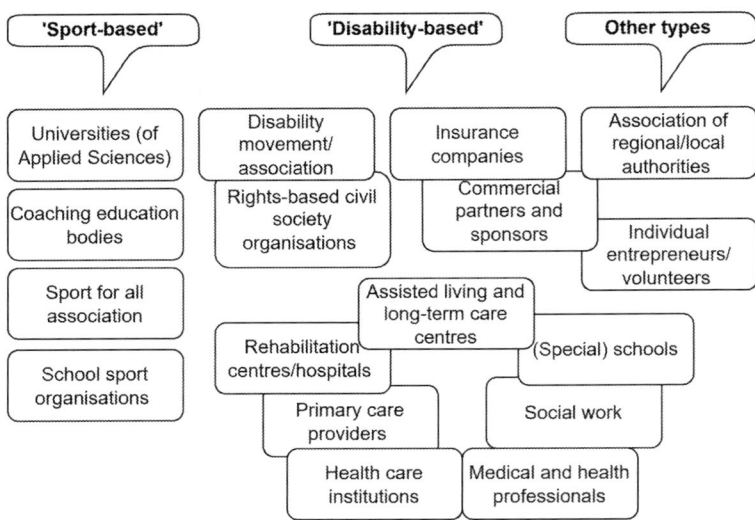

Fig. 23.2 Examples of secondary agents involved in disability sport in Europe. Source: Authors' own interpretation based on data from Chaps. 4–22

as a core task, but are indispensable for pwds or for agents with a direct role in the landscape for various reasons. Important agents and individual professionals are those working in the sectors health care, education and social work. These agents and professionals are in direct contact with pwds for various reasons and can play a role in the recruitment of pwds for sport programmes and activities with agents in the disability sport landscape. Often these agents offer sport and physical activity themselves in their own settings. However, connections between sports professionals and healthcare professionals are not always self-evident due to, for example, cultural differences between the sports and healthcare sectors and the lack of sufficient trust in each other's qualities (see e.g. Leenaars et al., 2016). Other functions of secondary agents are financial and management support for sport programmes, activities and research, the education of (future) coaches, practitioners and policy-makers, representing the interest of pwds and putting inclusion on the agenda.

Typologies of Governing Disability Sport

On closer inspection we find various models or typologies by which the responsibility for policy-making and providing sport for pwds in the organised sport setting is divided among non-governmental sport agents at the national level. See Fig. 23.3.

A first model that could be observed is that 'sport-based' non-governmental sport agents are responsible for disability sport at the national level and stimulate affiliated sport agents to provide sport activities and training for pwds. This model

23 The Landscape of Sport for Persons with a Disability: A System Within a System 573

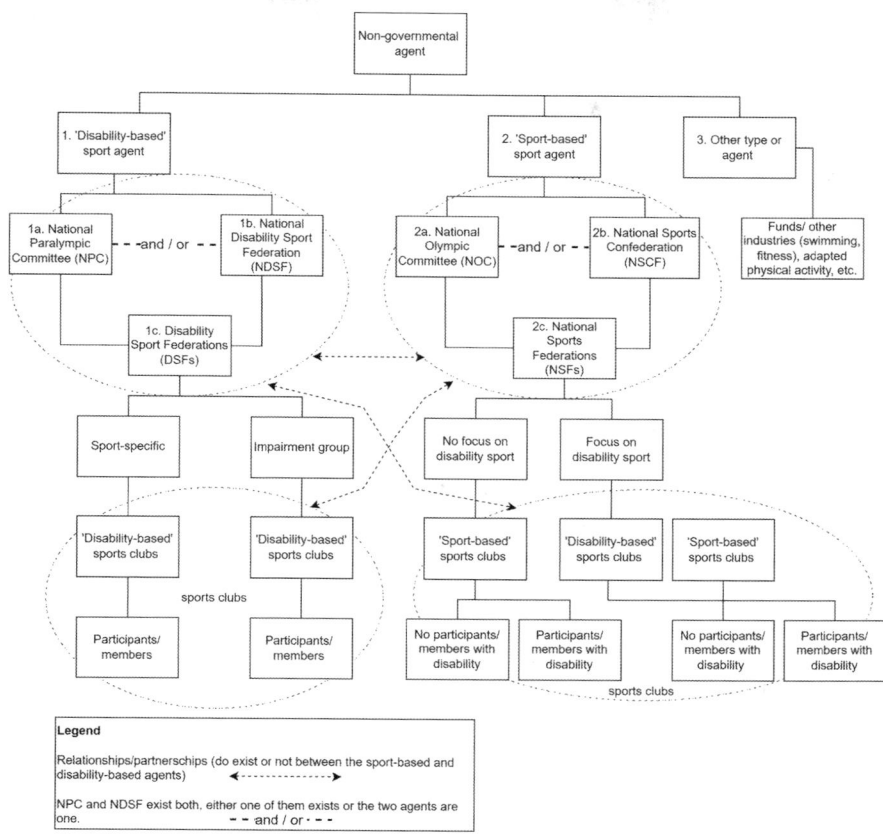

Fig. 23.3 Typologies of governing sport for pwds by non-governmental agents. Source: Authors' own interpretation based on data from Chaps. 4–22

is applicable to Norway and partly to the Netherlands. In both countries a combined 'sport-based' National Olympic (and Paralympic) Committee-National Sports Confederation is responsible for disability sport at the national level. Contributing authors mention this is the result of an ongoing process of many years of integrating disability sport in the 'mainstream' sport setting, making affiliated National Sport Federations (NSFs) responsible for the delivery of sport for pwds within their organised sport settings. In both countries the NOC-NSCF act as National Paralympic Committee to be able to send athletes with a disability to the Paralympic Games. In Norway, separate (National) Disability Sport Federations do not exist anymore. In the Netherlands several 'disability-based' sport agents exist with various roles; for instance, Disability Sport Netherlands still exists for special sports (clubs) that have not been integrated yet, like boccia, and is a member of the NOC-NSCF.

In another model, the National Paralympic Committee (NPC) is in charge of disability sport and simultaneously acts as a National Disability Sport Federation (NDSF). This is, for instance, the case in Finland with the Paralympic Committee. This agent is the result of a recent merger (2020) with the former Finnish Sports Federation of pwds (VAU), which in itself became the umbrella federation of former Disability Sport Federations (DSFs).

Another model we observed is that the NDSF is in charge of disability sport and acts at the same time as an NPC. This is, for instance, the case in Denmark, where Parasport Denmark is considered the primary organiser of sports clubs with programmes for pwds with both mainstream sports clubs with special programmes and disability sports clubs exclusively focusing on disability sport. The NPC is organised under Parasport Denmark.

A fourth model is that the NPC and the NDSF are both responsible for disability sport and have their own goals. This is, for example, the case in Austria. The Austrian Disability Sports Association is responsible for elite sports as well as for sports for all. Its goal is promotion of sport for pwds, supporting the work of regional affiliates and local clubs and representing Austrian disability sport nationally and internationally. The organisation is a member of both the Austrian Paralympic Committee and the Austrian Sports Organisation (umbrella organisation for sports in Austria). The NPC's goal is sending athletes to the Paralympic Games. Mainstream Austrian federal sports federations can become members of the NPC, which supports, promotes and integrates sports for people with a disability.

Within the presented models, we observed that some countries only have an NDSF with a multi-sports and/or multi-impairment group role (e.g. Denmark, Finland, Iceland) and have no affiliated DSFs. Other countries have, next to the NDSF also several DSFs that each represent one sport or one impairment group (e.g. Germany, Ireland, Lithuania). In various countries 'disability-based' sport agents and the 'sport-based' sport agents cooperate. All or some NSFs stimulate disability sport and can take 'disability-based' sport clubs as members. 'Sport-based' sport clubs with members with a disability can on the other hand affiliate with Disability Sport Federations. The conclusion is that there are numerous variations and possibilities to govern disability sport.

The Steering of Sport for Persons with a Disability: Negotiating Interests

Steering is about the relationships between the government and non-governmental (sport) agents and the conditions under which these relationships are built and exist (see Chap. 1). Contributors described the relationships between the relevant agents in the landscape for disability sport and indicated what kind of legislation and policies are relevant or apply to disability sport in their respective countries. These topics were described to a greater or lesser extent according to the available data sources.

Laws and Regulations

With regard to legislation, contributors describe various pieces of legislation that have direct or indirect impact on the way disability sport is delivered or to what extent pwds have access and/or opportunities to participate in sport. Contributors from around half of the countries involved in the handbook make note of a specific sport law, act or decree that regulates various aspects of steering and organising sport and/or ensuring access of citizens to sport or the promotion of sport among citizens of the country (Austria, Belgium, Finland, Hungary, Iceland, Ireland, Portugal, Slovenia, Spain, Switzerland). The sport act, law or decree is an important piece of legislation, often with specified articles on different matters, in which responsibilities or duties are assigned to specific agents. In most cases, the national government and sometimes the local authorities are addressed as an important gatekeeper/advocate responsible for delivering sport according to the framework provided by the law. Laying down matters in a law also has financial implications, resulting in funding of programmes and/or agents that implement what is regulated by the law. To a greater or lesser extent, governing bodies of sport (which can be governmental, intermediate or non-governmental agents) are addressed directly by these laws or acts, 'telling' them what kind of responsibilities, rules or regulations they have to comply with. In other cases, ministries or departments responsible for sport hand over the implementation of the sports law or act to sport governing bodies. It is important to note is that direct reference is not always made to (sport for) pwds in the sport act or law. Sport in general or more specifically the right of access to or equal participation in sport of all citizens in a given country is regulated by these laws and thus indirectly pwds are referenced because they are part of all citizens or are seen as (one of the) disadvantaged groups that need special attention with regards to sport promotion.

In a number of countries, however, pwds or disability sport is referenced directly in the sport law, act or decree, for instance, in Lithuania, where the law states that disability sports are based on equality, continuity and freedom of choice. See the *Bundes-Sportförderungsgesetz* in Austria which defines the promotion of disability sports and the inclusion of pwds into sport as one of its promotional subjects. The Austrian Disability Sport Association and the federal sport federations are required to work together with regard to disability sport. In Belgium, the Decree on Sports Federations regulates the funding mechanisms for the entire sports sector, including the funding procedure for disability sport. In Slovenia, disability sport is legally equal to sport, which was favoured by the country's accession to the EU as mentioned by the contributors. In Portugal and Spain, especially sport law seems to have an important role in promoting sport participation by pwds and tasking the state to establish the right conditions.

Contributors mention several non-sport-related pieces of legislation that have direct or indirect impact on the provision of disability sport or opportunities for pwds to participate in sport. These acts refer to different domains: human rights issues, education, health, work, social services and welfare, disability services, spatial planning and design. Acts in regard to human rights, more specifically in regard to equality and equal treatment of citizens and/or non-discrimination of pwds seem to be important and overarching all other domains. These acts ensure, for instance, that everyone is equally entitled to participate in society, including pwds, and/or that barriers to participation in various life domains should be removed. Contributors regularly mention that these acts or sub-articles, directly refer to participation in sport and PA, but also to participation in education, work and so on. In this sense, the human rights acts provide guiding principles for all these other life domains to undertake actions to prevent pwds from being excluded. In this regard too, the ratification of the UNCRPD is referred to as an important driver for inclusive practices in the country, including sport. In all cases, even if a country does not have specific sport law or legislation, the sport sector can be influenced by these acts in the sense that sport agents have to comply with the responsibility to ensure equal access to sport for pwds and other disadvantaged groups. In other non-sport-related acts, (financial) provisions are regulated to ensure removal of various barriers to participate in sport: for example, the provision of mobility aids (e.g. wheelchair), provision of transportation, accessible sport facilities and so on. Some acts refer to the autonomy of associations, which impacts sport federations' freedom to associate.

Whether these kinds of acts can compensate for the absence of a sport act, or that a sport act and these other acts have reinforcing powers cannot be concluded on the basis of our indicative analyses. Only that having these kinds of acts, in which reference is made to the provision of sport in general, to sport participation by pwds in particular or to ensuring equal access and/or promoting inclusion in sport of pwds, are important for raising awareness and requiring governments and other agents to act correspondingly.

Policies in Regard to Persons with a Disability

With regard to policies, we may conclude that disability sport or promoting sport amongst pwds is not the issue of one single policy plan or programme at the national level, but is addressed through various policy plans and programmes, mostly indirectly. The formulation of policy goals at the national level with regard to sport for pwds is mentioned more or less by over half of the contributing authors. It is not always clear though, whether these goals are solely focused on sport for pwds, or pwds are mentioned as one of the target groups that are addressed by these goals. To our best interpretation, in three countries, contributing authors mention the existence of a specific policy plan or programme for disability sport. See Denmark, for example, where disability sport is added to the three-year framework agreements between the government and non-governmental sport agents. Also, Norway has a separate inclusion plan for pwds. And in Ireland, the Policy on Participation in Sport by pwds was launched by Sport Ireland. Most often however, goals or ambitions with regard to disability sport are implicitly mentioned or 'hidden' as part of general sport policy goals and programmes or within policies of non-sport-related domains.

If goals are mentioned explicitly, they are about promoting participation in sport by pwds, promoting inclusion in sport for pwds, providing equal access to sport for pwds, enhancing health and wellbeing by means of sport or improving accessibility to sport.

If it is not at the governmental level, more often the actual implementation of (implicit) policies in regard to pwds, is performed by non-governmental agents at the national, regional or local level, through programmes, projects and activities. Non-governmental agents may also implement plans or undertake actions regardless of national policy. These actions do not always seem to be coordinated or regulated, but often are a result of negotiations and lobbying. Contributors also mention state (in the case of countries with a federal state structure), regional or local governmental agents are involved in (implementing) policies with regard to sport for pwds.

Whether the existence or absence of specific policy goals or ambitions or specific policy documents (plans, strategies, programmes) with regard to pwds and sport, can be conceived as beneficial or not is an interesting subject for future research. If it is the result of a process of striving for (more) inclusion, that pwds in sport policy automatically become part of the policy in such a way that they no longer need to be specifically referred to, then that could be interpreted positively. However, if at the same time the specific needs of pwds are neglected and this results in an unequal starting position with regards to sport participation compared to persons without disabilities, the effect will probably be negative. This is about the difference between 'equality' and 'equity' as explained in Chap. 2 (see Miller & Katz, 2002). We cannot be certain whether the agents in the landscape of disability sport are aware of the impact of ignoring this difference. Equality, according to Block & Fines (2022:81), means "that all people, regardless of their gender, race, age, class, language, religion, or abilities, are entitled to benefit from public goods, resources, and services". Equity is about taking specific measures to address the specific needs of a certain group which enables this groups equal participation in sport (Block & Fines, 2022; see also Miller & Katz, 2002). For instance, the contributors for the Netherlands stress that in the current inclusive sports policy, pwds are referred to as one of the population groups that perceive barriers towards sport participation because of their background. Focus is on removing barriers to participation, of which some of them specifically apply to pwds, for example, support in applying for special sport equipment. If the absence of a specific focus on pwds within sport policy is the result of ignoring the interests of pwds in the first place, that is not beneficial either, because then sport policy will not be aligned with their needs at all.

Relationships Between the Various Agents

If we now look at the relationships between the various agents in the disability sport landscape, we see various types of relationships: financial, membership/partnership and/or hierarchical relationships. These are shaped in different ways, more or less influenced by the legislative and policy frameworks. In the conceptual framework for this handbook we explained two theories with regard to relationships between governmental and non-governmental agents or between governing bodies and their affiliates: the so-called principal-agent approach (Goodwin & Grix, 2011; Ross, 1973) and the co-governance approach (Groeneveld, 2009; Skelcher, 2000) (see Chap. 1). In order to determine the basis of which model or power relations the relationships are built between and within governmental and non-government agents in the field of disability sport in Europe, more in-depth research is needed. However, based on the descriptions of the contributors, a few things can be observed.

Contributors show few hierarchical relationships between the various agents in the landscape of sport for pwds. The following are examples of those relationships:

- at the governmental level, from ministries to regional departments and/or to municipalities;
- at the national level, from a ministry (governmental level) to sports councils (intermediate level) and from a ministry to sport councils at the (regional) intermediate level; and
- at the non-governmental level, from a national sports governing body to member organisations at national, regional and local levels, both disability-based and sport-based.

Membership/partnership relationships are indicated more often. We see these kinds of relationships most often:

- at the non-governmental level, between a national sports governing body and member organisations at national, regional and local levels, both disability-based and sport-based;
- at the local level, between municipalities and local non-governmental agents, such as sports clubs and schools; and
- at regional and local levels, between various governmental, intermediate and non-governmental levels.

Financial relationships are mentioned quite often. These relationships are, for example,

- from sponsors and funds to various sport agents;
- at the national level, from ministries to intermediate and non-governmental agents;
- at a regional level, from regional governmental agents to regional/district sport councils and federations;
- at the local level, from municipalities to sports clubs; and
- from national governing bodies to local member clubs.

Figure 23.4 shows a simplified representation of the types of relationships between the various agents in the landscape of sport for pwds.

In general, we see that governmental agents are responsible for policy-making at the national or local level with regard to sport for pwds, whereas non-governmental

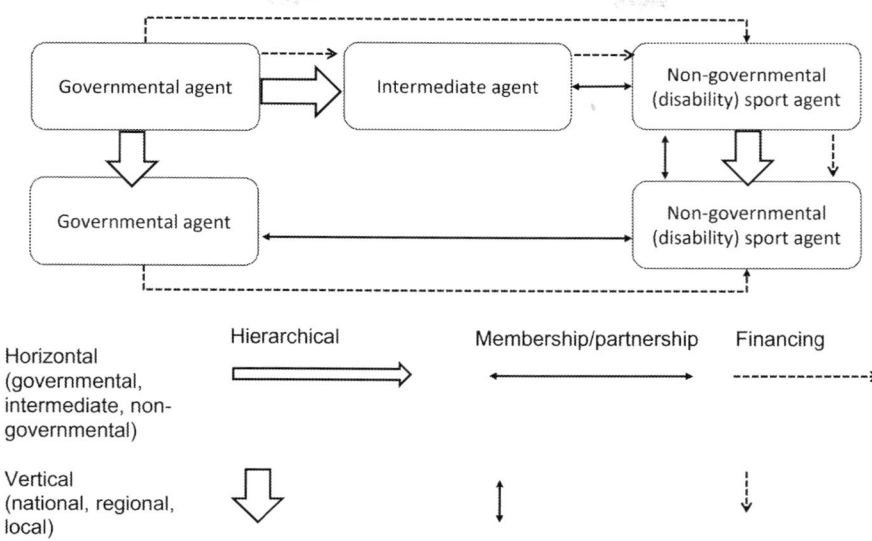

Fig. 23.4 Relationships between agents with regard to disability sport. Source: Authors' own interpretation based on data from Chaps. 4–22

'sport-based' or 'disability-based' sport agents have the 'traditional' role of governing, organising or providing sport (for pwds). As a rough outline, governments have directing, stimulating and/or financing roles and non-governmental agents have organising and implementing roles. In turn, non-governmental agents provide policies for their own member organisations. By supporting agents financially, governmental agents have the power to enforce, to a certain extent, the implementation of policies by non-governmental agents. By doing so the non-governmental agents can be seen as the activity-partners of the government. Whether and to what extent the relationships between the government and non-governmental agents are characterised by hierarchical principles or by principles of co-operation, mutual partnership or co-creation, or whether the government and non-governmental agents operate independently from each other (co-existence) differs by country. To be able to draw firm conclusions in this respect, we need more in-depth research and analyses. As far as we can conclude on the basis of the country-specific descriptions so far, we see in majority that relationships are built on partnerships between the various agents. The governmental agents and non-governmental agents mostly act interdependently. Important to note is that sport agents are not dependent upon government support alone. Often, they have additional financial resources, from public-private sponsorships or foundations. These non-governmental financial resources obviously are very important for sport agents that lack structural partnerships with the government or cannot survive without these resources.

It appears that in most countries, non-governmental sport agents can act, to a greater or lesser extent, autonomously, having their own (democratic) governing principles and making their own decisions. Autonomy, however, does not always imply complete independence from the government. As we already mentioned, sport agents often depend on financial support from the government for their operations and projects. Contributors mention that governments and non-governmental agents work under agreements (e.g. Denmark) or on the basis of approved policy or actions plans with clear goals (e.g. Belgium), which gives the government or sport council at the intermediate level some control over the implementation of plans by the non-governmental agents. In the case of Denmark, it is argued that the non-governmental agents still have large autonomy to act and achieve goals within the framework agreements and act at an arm's length of the government. In the United Kingdom, non-governmental agents also act at an arm's length from the government. The contributors argue this is the result of a shift from a strong hierarchical government towards governance through networks and partnerships (see Skelcher, 2000). The government has less power to deliver policy, however still funds the non-governmental agents. More contributors make note of these kind of co-governance relationships.

Nevertheless, there are exceptions. In Turkey, for instance, the state has an important role in (disability) sport and manages sport as a public service. In countries with a sport law, for instance, in Lithuania or Spain, the organisation of sport, the competences of the non-governmental agents or the inclusion of pwds in sport, is regulated or promoted by law. In those cases, governments might have a stronger position in sport. For Austria, contributors explicitly mention that there are principal-agent relationships defined by laws and regulations.

Whether the government plays an active role in disability sport, clearly differs by country. An active role from the government however, does not necessarily mean that the relationships in the landscape are very hierarchical. For instance, for the Netherlands, contributors mention the government playing an active role in shaping sport policy that focusses on the inclusion of pwds in sport while at the same time stimulating active participation from stakeholders at all levels. In the various countries, partnerships in policy-making and provision of sport for pwds seem very important. In most countries, contributors observe the co-existence of a wide variety of actors at various levels, who cooperate with each other when needed, but simultaneously pursue their own goals in parallel. This might be the result of the broad definition of disability sport we used for this handbook (see Chap. 2). Agents outside the traditional pyramid system of sport (confederation, federations, clubs) are considered important for providing sport for pwds at a grassroots level. This results in a much broader picture of the agents involved (see Fig. 23.1).

Overall, we may conclude that the steering of disability sport in Europe is characterised more by fragmentation and negotiation than by central coordination and alignment of goals and interests of all parties involved.

Integration and Inclusion: Important Elements in Policy and Provision of Disability Sport

The integration and/or inclusion of pwds in sport appear to be important subjects in this handbook. As we described previously in this chapter, contributors referred to inclusive sport and non-sport-related policies and legislations in their countries, which mostly focus on ensuring equal access and promotion of the rights of pwds to participate in society and/or in sport. With regard to the structure and steering of disability sport, almost all contributors talk about varying degrees of cooperation between 'disability-based' and 'sport-based' sport agents (see previous paragraphs). At one end of the spectrum 'disability-based' and 'sport-based' sport agents work more or less separately from one another. In these cases, 'disability-based' sport agents are largely responsible for disability sport and pwds participate to a large extent in separate sport clubs and sport activities for pwds. Our best interpretation is that Iceland would be at this end of the continuum. On the other end of the continuum 'sport-based' agents have taken over responsibility of sport for pwds from the (former) (National) Disability Sport Federation(s) and disability sport is fully integrated in the 'mainstream' sport setting. Our best interpretation is that Norway and the Netherlands could be placed at this end of the continuum. In between, all other countries find their place at varying levels of mainstreaming.

It is difficult to perfectly assess the level of integration or mainstreaming for each country on the basis of the descriptions provided by the contributors. Interpretation errors can easily be made. Beforehand, we did not provide the countries with a list of indicators by which to determine the level of integration or stage in the mainstreaming process. This would be an interesting subject for further research. As for now, with caution, we group countries in three categories, according to the descriptions offered by the contributors (see Fig. 23.5).

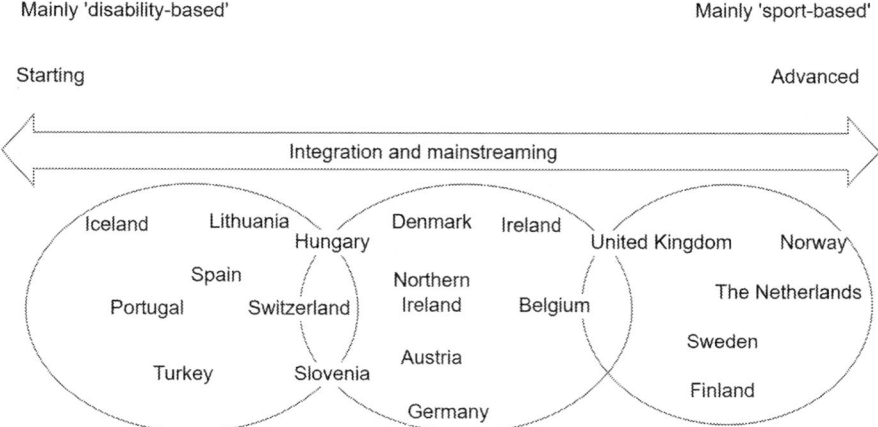

Fig. 23.5 Countries on a continuum of mainstreaming, from mainly 'disability-based' to mainly 'sport-based' (indicative). Source: Authors' own interpretation based on data from Chaps. 4–22

One group of countries is in the beginning of the process of integrating pwds in mainstream sport or is gradually moving towards more cooperation with 'sport-based' sport agents in order to provide opportunities for pwds to participate in sport in settings other than the disability specific sport club or activity. In one or two cases mainstream sport agents may have gained responsibility for a specific type of sport. Another group of countries is somewhere in the middle of the process, with governing bodies encouraging more cooperation between 'sport-based' and 'disability-based' sport agents, transferring responsibilities to a vast number of mainstream sport agents, encouraging sport clubs to open their doors for pwds and so on. In the third group we see countries where mainstreaming is key policy and cooperation between 'disability-based' and 'sport-based' sport agents is more rule than exception, and in some cases has resulted in the abolishment of disability sport federations.

It is important to note that by placing countries on a continuum we do not have the intention to value one system over another, as if mainstreaming all sports for pwds would be the best possible way to organise sport for pwds. It may well be that the described system best fits the country at that specific moment. As the authors for Iceland say: "most people agree that the current system fits Iceland better than moving the sport for individuals with disabilities into the other sports federations" (see Chap. 6, page xx).

As argued in Chap. 2, inclusion of pwds in sport means having the possibility to choose what activity, where, how and with whom a pwd wants to be involved and about taking responsibility in providing that range of choices (Kiuppis, 2018; Misener & Darcy, 2014). It might well be that a pwd rather wants to be active in a separate sport activity with peers with a disability rather than in a mainstream sport club in activities together with peers without disabilities, which could be called full inclusion (see Christiaens & Brittain, 2021). According to the UNCRPD, integrative or separate sport activities can be part of an inclusive sport landscape and all of these different sporting opportunities should be promoted (see Article 30, United Nations, 2006). This implies that inclusion as a concept encompasses both segregation and integration (if self-chosen), as well as being the opposite from those concepts when placed on a continuum (see Committee on the Rights of Persons with Disabilities, 2016). The latter implies there is a certain order in the striving for more inclusion, needing integration as an intermediary step to evolve from segregation to inclusion (Committee on the Rights of Persons with Disabilities, 2016). According to the UN, segregation would then be a situation in which services for pwds are provided in separate environments designed or used to respond to the needs of pwds, in isolation from persons without disabilities. Integration would mean a process of placing pwds in existing mainstream organisations with the expectation that they are able to adjust to the requirements in those organisations. And inclusion would mean a process of systemic reform. In order to break down barriers, changes are necessary in the approaches, structures and strategies of existing organisations and in society at large, and everyone, regardless of disability or other characteristic, are considered part of society (see Committee on the Rights of Persons with Disabilities, 2016). Inclusion thus seems to be a confusing concept with different meanings. Perhaps that is why most contributors refrained from defining the concept in their chapters more precisely. The contributors for Finland however seem to have tackled the difference between integration and inclusion by saying that: "integration refers to the disability sport integration process and transfer of disability sports, athletes with disabilities and programs into mainstream sport federations" and "inclusion is the ultimate goal of these actions and processes and it refers to equal participation opportunities, sense of belonging and being welcomed" (see Chap. 5, page xx). Integration, and thus mainstreaming, however does not guarantee the transition from segregation to inclusion (Committee on the Rights of Persons with Disabilities, 2016). As explained previously in this chapter, special attention and specific measurements targeted at pwds might by necessary to ensure their equal participation and thus inclusion in sport.

To conclude, the main policy approaches in the countries observed resemble more that of a strategy of mainstreaming and integration than that of inclusion, although inclusion as a word or concept is widely used in legislation and policy documents. It seems that countries still have to make further steps in the process of striving for (more) inclusion. This means having a choice, having opportunities to undertake different sports at various levels (from a grassroots to an elite level), being represented in various roles in sport organisations, having a sense of belonging and so on.

23.5 Sport Participation by Persons with Disabilities

Contributors were asked to describe on the basis of available data how, and to what extent, pwds participate in sport and what the facilitators and barriers towards their participation in sport are. Contributors were also encouraged to give information (if available) on the methods and challenges in sport participation data collection for this group and whether some kind of monitoring and/or evaluation system was in place in the respective country. In contrast to the availability of data with regard to the structure and steering of disability sport, far less contributors were able to answer (all) questions on sport participation (monitoring and evaluation), mainly because of the lack of (specific) data. We analysed the descriptions provided by the contributing authors in their chapters to draw some preliminary conclusions with regard to the type of data source that is available, the targeted populations in these data sources and some general trends in sport participation amongst pwds. This overview is probably far from complete, as we expect contributors were challenged to select the most suitable data for this section in their chapters. Population surveys in which data could be distinguished by disability and compared to populations without disability were, for example, preferred over membership figures from (disability) sport federations, as these kinds of data do not reveal participation levels of pwds in organised and non-organised sport compared to general populations or persons without disabilities. Furthermore, the limited word count may have 'forced' authors, which was also applicable to the previous sections, to choose to present the most preferable data or to leave out further details.

Monitoring and Evaluation Is Not Structurally Embedded in the Policy-Making Process

Although most countries ratified the UNCRPD and often have national legislation and/or policies that promote inclusion in sport for pwds, systematic monitoring or evaluation of (the effect of the implementation of) sport policy programmes focussed on pwds or systematic collection of data on sport participation levels in this population is still hard to find in the respective countries within this handbook. Article 31 of the UNCRPD specifically formulates that States Parties should collect appropriate information, including statistical and research data, to enable them to formulate and implement policies to give effect to the UNCRPD. Because inclusion in sports is also part of the UNCRPD (see Article 30), data collection also applies to the area of sports (United Nations, 2006). Contributing authors make note of this deficiency with regret. Only a few countries have taken structural measures to monitor and/or evaluate developments in the structure, steering and/or organisation of disability sport, and/or participation levels of pwds in sport and/or barriers or facilitators experienced by them to participate in sport. The contributors for Finland, for example, make explicit reference to the responsibility of the *National Sports Council* to supervise and monitor the success of sport policy and the impact of government actions in the field of sport and PA and sum up several reports on these matters. In the Netherlands monitoring of trends in sport participation, including amongst pwds, and organisational developments is structural embedded as part of the policy-making process. In Ireland and in the United Kingdom, sport participation in the population, including pwds, is monitored in line with both governments' sport policies. In Northern Ireland sport participation is monitored structurally.

Many authors, however, point out that in their country not much data is available on levels of sport participation amongst pwds. On closer inspection, contributing authors described four different types of data sources with information on sport participation of pwds (see Table 23.1).

Different Types of Population Surveys or Studies

In seven countries results were presented from national population surveys with fairly large samples in which both questions related to sport participation and disability were included and comparisons could be made between pwds and peers without disabilities or the general population. Take, for instance, the Survey of Health, Impairment and Living Conditions in Denmark, the Continuous Household Survey in Northern Ireland, the annual National Health Survey in the Netherlands, the Irish Sport Monitor or the Sport England's Active Lives Adult survey. In one country, Belgium (Flanders), the survey only included pwds (convenience sample). We observe a number of methodological differences between the surveys: in sample size, whether it is a repeated or single measurement (e.g. annual, bi-annual, only

Table 23.1 Available types of data sources for sport participation among persons with a disability in the countries involved in the handbook[a]

Type of Data (Source)	Country
Population surveys or studies on levels of sport participation and/or physical activity, including pwds	Austria, Belgium (Flanders)[b], Denmark, Germany, Ireland[c], the Netherlands[c], Northern Ireland[c], United Kingdom[c]
Surveys or studies specifically targeting children and young people with (and without) disabilities, mostly school based surveys (special and/or mainstream schools in primary and/or secondary education)	Finland, Iceland, Ireland, Northern Ireland, Portugal, United Kingdom
Surveys or studies among mainstream sport clubs (and/or their sport club members)[d]	Belgium/Flanders, Denmark, England/UK, Finland, Germany, Hungary, Iceland, the Netherlands, Norway, Spain, Switzerland
Data from sport federations and sport clubs with programmes, activities, competitions for pwds. (Data from financial, administration, monitoring reports or registration data, on number of clubs, projects, programmes, activities for pwds, or number of sport licences, participants.[e])	Austria, Germany, Hungary, Iceland, Lithuania, Norway, Slovenia, Sweden, Portugal, Spain, Switzerland,

[a]If contributing authors did not mention a specific data source in the respective country this does not necessarily mean the data source is absent in that country. The authors may well have decided not to mention all available sources due to the limited word count or other reasons. Data sources include surveys or studies in the past and more recent studies that have been conducted a single time, and longitudinal studies that provide trend data
[b]No comparison with general population, sample only included pwds
[c]Surveys in these countries are ongoing, enabling analysis of trends
[d]Including countries that participated in the SIVSCE research project as mentioned in Chap. 3
[e]Authors note that these figures are indicative, often estimates, that participants with a disability can be counted twice when participating in several activities, the use or the registration of data based on information of pwds may be restricted due to privacy regulations
Source: Authors' own interpretation of data based on Chaps. 3–22

one or two times), the definition of sport participation (e.g. at least once a year, twice per month, at least weekly), the number of details on sport participation (membership of clubs, type of sport, etc.), whether or not distinction to socio-demographic variables is possible and in the definition of disability (one single question or distinction to type and severity of disability or illness). In two countries specific sets of questionnaires were used to measure disability. The authors for Finland mentioned the use of the *Washington Group on Disability Statistics questionnaire* (see Chaps. 2 and 5) and in the Netherlands the *OECD-indicator* (Organisation for Economic Cooperation and Development) was used to measure disability (see Chap. 15). In four countries the surveys have a longitudinal character which enables analysis of trends in sport participation amongst pwds. This is the case in Ireland, the Netherlands, Northern Ireland and the United Kingdom as far as our interpretation of the country-specific chapters is concerned. In this chapter we will not repeat the results of the surveys mentioned. Comparison of figures would not make sense because of the differences in methods. For a cross-national comparison of sport participation levels amongst pwds we refer the reader to Chap. 3, where data from the Eurobarometer on sport is presented. In this chapter we will sum up some noteworthy trends in sport participation in general based on the contributions.

Surveys Targeting Children with a Disability

A second type of data source contributors of six countries make note of was data collected among children and young people with disabilities (see Table 23.1). These studies are often school-based surveys, where children and young people are included from special and/or mainstream schools in primary and/or secondary education. Figures for children and youth with a disability was compared to children without disabilities. In at least two countries the surveys are ongoing, enabling analysing trends. In general, the presented studies show lower participation rates in physical activity and/or sport for children and youth with a disability in comparison to peers without a disability. School-based surveys can be a valuable addition to the previously mentioned population surveys. Children and youth with a disability are not always included in these surveys or are underrepresented by low numbers. The school-based studies give insight into the specific needs of children with a disability in the school system. In the previous parts of the country-specific chapters, contributors often stressed the importance of physical education in the school system for gaining familiarity with sports, offering in school sports activities or recruitment of participants for out of school sports offerings.

Surveys Among Sports Clubs

A third type of data source mentioned by contributors of six countries is sports club surveys (see Table 23.1). In the sports club surveys mainstream sports clubs are often questioned about having one or more members with a disability. As such these studies shed some light on the level of integration of pwds in mainstream sport settings in these countries. Contributors from three countries make reference to participation at the cross-European research project called SIVSCE (Social Integration and Volunteering in Sports Clubs in Europe). Ten European countries participated in this survey as was mentioned in Chap. 3. Based on this limited number of sports club surveys alone, we see huge differences in the percentage of mainstream sports clubs with one of more members with a disability. Sports club surveys in themselves can be of great value for making sport policy with regard to pwds. With these studies, if used structurally, trends in integrating pwds in clubs can be monitored. For instance, the contributors for Norway and Finland observed an increase of clubs with one or more members with a disability. The studies can also be helpful in identifying barriers and needs for support felt by sports clubs, who are expected or encouraged by their (local) governments and sports federations to be inclusive.

Registration Data from Sport Federations and Clubs

A fourth type of data described by contributors is data from sport federations and sport clubs that have programmes, activities or competitions for pwds (see Table 23.1). Data can come from financial reports, registrations or monitoring reports and may reveal information on the number of affiliated (disability-based) sports clubs and their registered members with a disability, the number of projects, programmes and activities for pwds and their counted participants, or the number of sport licences owned by athletes with a disability or number of para-athletes that are part of the countries' elite programmes. The data sources and figures presented by the authors differ greatly in size or subject and making comparisons would therefore not make sense. Often contributors included these sources to compensate for the lack of data on sport participation levels of pwds from population surveys. This does not imply registration data like this is not valuable. On the contrary, monitoring numbers of clubs, projects and its participants, can shed light on certain developments in providing sport for pwds. When a decline in membership numbers for 'disability-based' sports clubs is observed, as was, for instance, mentioned by the contributors for Austria, this could be explained as diminishing interest from pwds in sport. It may, however, also imply an increasing interest in mainstream sports offers, and thus be a result of inclusion policies. Registration, monitoring or 'counting' numbers often is required as part of framework agreements between sport agents and governments and thus part of the deal to obtain funds. An observed limitation is that figures obtained by registration data may represent an overestimation of unique persons active in disability sport, because the same individual may be counted twice when participating in more than one activity. Furthermore, the collection of personal information on pwds and the use of this data may be restricted due to privacy regulations. Presented figures therefore must be viewed with caution. A last limitation is that registration data from sport agents only gives information on organised participation in sport and/or participation in competitive or elite sport settings amongst pwds, and not on other forms of sport participation.

Indicative Remarks on Sport Participation (Details) Amongst Persons with a Disability

Separate from the cross-national data we have presented on sport participation in Chap. 3, here we sum up a number of indicative trends on sport participation that could be observed in the data provided by the contributors. It should be emphasised that these indicative conclusions should best be confirmed or evidenced with new research data or more extensive analysis of existing data:

- In general, regardless of the data source, the targeted group of pwds or the precise definition of a sports participant, participation levels of pwds in sport and/or PA are much lower than those for peers without disabilities or the population in general. This applies to adults as well as to children and youth with a disability.
- Some socio-demographic characteristics intersect with the negative impact of having a disability on sports participation: being elderly, having lower educational levels and/or lower income levels, living in regions with low household wealth (United Kingdom), being unemployed, being a woman/girl (not the case in Denmark) and being aged 12 years and over (compared to children aged under 12). This means pwds with these characteristics have lower participation levels compared to other pwds.
- When a distinction by type and severity of disability could be made, contributors observed lower participation levels amongst persons with more severe disabilities or illnesses compared to persons with milder forms of disability. Persons with mobility, walking or physical disabilities tend to be less active than those with other types of disabilities. Persons with more than one type of disability or who combine disability with chronic illness also have lower levels of sport participation.
- With regard to the types of sports practiced by pwds, fitness, swimming, cycling and walking seem to be the most popular activities for pwds, excluding differences between countries or between persons with different types of disability.
- Participation in team or competitive sports seem to be less common for pwds than participation in individual or recreational physical activities such as walking, cycling, yoga or swimming. Differences between countries probably have to do with differences in country profile, related to cultural, geographical aspects and so on. In mountainous countries pwds, for example, participate in skiing and in coastal countries adapted surfing.
- With regard to the organisational setting of sport, the surveys that were available indicate, following the contributors, lower sports club membership figures for pwds compared to the general population or persons without disabilities. Furthermore, pwds participate less in sports club settings compared to other organisational forms. Pwds participate more in unorganised or self-organised sport settings or in fitness clubs than in the sports club setting.

Challenges in Data Collection

On the basis of the descriptions provided by the contributors we can conclude that data collection on different aspects of sport participation among pwds is not without its challenges. Collection and interpretation is hampered by various shortcomings or barriers.

First of all, a lack of objective measures to define disability and sport participation causes differences in outcomes and makes comparisons between surveys (and countries) difficult. It makes it hard to uniformly distinguish by type and/or severity of disability and other health-related problems and to distinguish between various details of sport participation. Existing indicators for sport participation, for instance, with regard to the question of when to define someone as a non-sport participant, an irregular or regular sport participant, may not be applicable for or not match with the lived experiences of respondents with a disability. For instance, if we only focus on weekly participants, we might overlook respondents with a disability who are active in sports but don't feel able to participate every week due to their disability. And if we only focus on 'traditional' types of sport (competitive forms, team sports, etc.) we might overlook other activities with a sporting character in which pwds are engaged and so may underestimate their activity levels.

Secondly, specific groups of pwds may be underrepresented or excluded from surveys for various reasons. Surveys often don't present the overall picture for all disability groups. Different surveys are needed for specific groups of pwds. Pwds cannot be easily reached. Registration according to disability goes against privacy regulations, which means pwds cannot be identified from existing population files. If persons with, for instance, visual and/or hearing impairments are included in surveys, this is often with low numbers (corresponding to the lower prevalence figures in the population). This complicates making statistically significant statements for these groups. The experienced inaccessibility of (online) questionnaires for pwds, may also hinder their participation in research. Questions may not be adapted for persons with intellectual impairment and the questionnaire format may not be adapted for persons with visual impairment. In school-based surveys, special schools may be excluded, while children with disabilities may be underrepresented in mainstream schools. In convenience samples, the risk of mainly targeting sports active pwds or persons with less severe disabilities may also lead to bias.

To be able to compare activity levels of pwds with those of the general population or peers without disabilities it is necessary to use large representative population samples. Large samples are also necessary to increase the chance of including pwds in the research. Often these kinds of surveys are expensive and are dependent upon government support and support from a countries statistics office. In the surveys, both indicators on disability and on sport and physical activity have to be included. This requires giving data collection on sport participation among pwds policy priority and reserving the necessary budget by national governments or sports councils. Mostly however this is lacking.

Barriers and Facilitators Towards Sport Participation for pwds

Contributors were asked to give information on the barriers and facilitators towards sport participation experienced by pwds. Most of them were able to give an overview. Descriptions were based on various sources, such as quantitative or qualitative research amongst pwds, insights gathered from experts or practitioners working with pwds, or own observations from the contributors. Although not required in the conceptual framework, some contributors also tuned in on factors that positively or negatively influence policy-making and/or provision of sport for pwds seen from an organisation's, expert's or practitioner's point of view. The contributors' descriptions should in no way be interpreted as evidence for any causal relationship between participation levels in sport amongst pwds and the barriers or motives perceived by them. Scholars have pointed out that in recent years an increasing amount of research has become available on this subject (see also Chap. 1), but that evidence for causal relationships between constraints and participation in sport, recreation and PA is often limited. They suggest that more longitudinal studies with larger samples are needed to improve study quality, generalisation of findings and distinction by type of disability (see amongst others Darcy et al., 2017; Yu et al., 2022).

Not discouraged by this fact, we believe it is helpful to make a short list of factors that were mentioned by the contributors. This list could provide a basis for further research to make meaningful comparisons between groups of pwds and countries. The observed factors can be categorised in different dimensions. The simplest way of categorising is making a distinction between personal and environmental factors, according to the ICF model as explained in Chap. 2 (World Health Organization, 2002). However, we could also categorise in a more refined way. In the literature personal factors are also called intrapersonal factors. Environmental factors are further distinguished into interpersonal factors and environmental or structural factors (see a.o. Darcy et al., 2017; Yu et al., 2022). Darcy et al. (2017) refer to a social model approach to disability, in which it is emphasised that barriers pwds encounter in their lives impact upon social participation, in addition to the possible impacts of an individual's impairment. Yu et al. (2022) refer to the socio-ecological model (see Bronfenbrenner, 1979; Sallis et al., 2008) as a framework to categorise factors (see Fig. 23.6).

We used this framework to categorise factors mentioned across the various country-specific chapters (see Tables 23.2, 23.3, 23.4, 23.5, 23.6). The core concept of the socio-ecological model is that it helps to understand how people, in our case pwds, interact with their environment and how their individual behaviour is influenced (Sallis et al., 2008). To improve participation levels in sport, it is not enough to focus solely on motivation and skills, but to create environments and policies that enable pwds to become active (see Yu et al., 2022). An individual's behaviour is understood by looking at multiple levels of influences: at intrapersonal, interpersonal, organisational, community and policy levels (Sallis et al., 2008; Yu et al., 2022; see Fig. 23.6). An important element of the model is that factors across the levels interact with each other and can have reinforcing impact on an individual's behaviour. For instance, take the reinforcing influence of a low socio-economic status (lack of money) of a pwd on the one hand and high costs of special equipment that is necessary for the person to be able to participate in sport and lack of policy to support pwds with low income on the other hand. Policy factors (see Table 23.6) are mentioned several times by contributors, both as negative and as positive factors influencing the provision of sport for pwds. It is here that

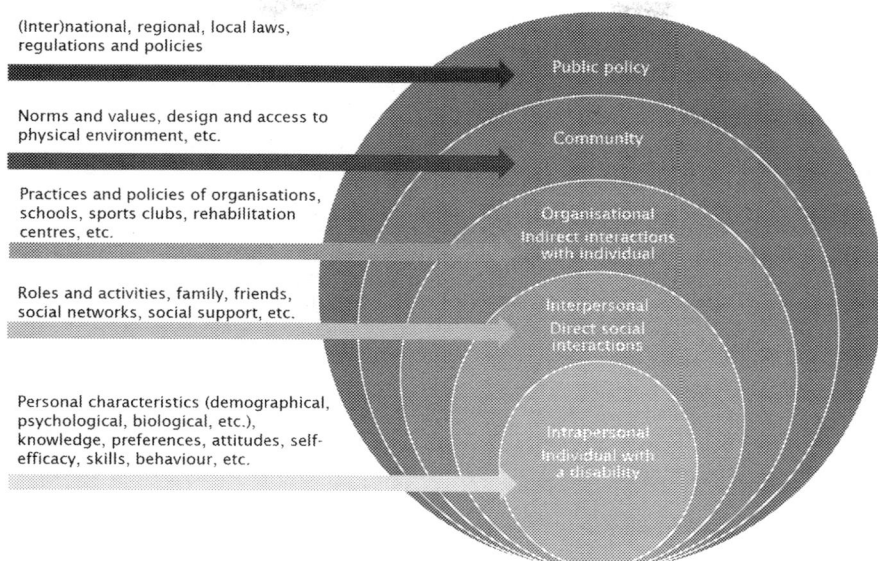

Fig. 23.6 Socio-ecological model applied to sport participation amongst persons with a disability. Source: Adapted by the authors from a.o. McLeroy et al. (1988), Mehtälä et al. (2014), Sallis et al. (2008)

Table 23.2 Individual factors that may influence sport participation by pwds

Dimension	Examples of Barriers Mentioned
Demographic	Age; place of residence
Socio-economic	Income; lack of money; economic struggles
Psychological	Feelings of loneliness; fear of being bullied; fear of judgement; lack of self-confidence; difficult to concentrate; internalised oppression; dealing with loss; negative past experiences with sport; negative school experiences; not feeling welcome
Cognitive	Lack of information, knowledge, awareness of (suitable) sporting opportunities; hard to find a sport
Biological	Concern for health conditions, physical problems, injury/illness/hindrance from the impairment itself; inability to participate in bad period/on specific days; fatigue/lack of energy/pain; short attention span; impulsiveness; difficultly listening
Other	Lack of time; lack of motivation/interest

Source: Authors' own interpretation based on data provided in Chaps. 4–22

specific elements of the structure and steering of disability sport in a specific country, as described in the first parts of the country-specific chapters and in this chapter, can interact with experienced barriers to participate in sport by pwds on personal and environmental levels.

Table 23.3 Interpersonal factors that may influence sport participation by pwds

Dimension	Examples of Barriers Mentioned
Social group	Hard to find people with whom to do sports on an equal footing; no one to exercise with/lack of peers; difficult to be part of a team/to be around many people at the same time; inability to participate at the level of other participants
Social support	Need of special assistance/to be dependent on others for transport; lack of assistance to help with sports practices; lack of information with parents about possibilities for their children
Social norms and attitudes	Attitudes/willingness of primary caregivers; low expectations from teachers, families and peers; parents' attitude/shame

Source: Authors' own interpretation based on data provided in Chaps. 4–22

Table 23.4 Organisational factors that may influence sport participation by pwds

Dimension	Examples of Barriers Mentioned
Economic	High costs of sport/equipment; inadequate sponsorship; high costs to organise activities for pwds with high support needs
Activities	Shortage/lack of (mainstream/adapted) sports offer that is accessible/nearby (for different types and severity of disability); limited choice of different sports; insufficient participants to start a sport; lack of professional training
Expertise/ coaches	Shortage/lack of educated/skilled coaches/instructors/leaders/assistants/ volunteers; lack of experience, knowledge and competence about disability sport; lack of knowledge of motives, wishes and needs of pwds
Sports equipment	Shortage/lack of specialised equipment in sports clubs
Orientation/ attitudes	The goal and performance strategy of local sports club; ableist notion of competitiveness and body ideal; being forgotten to be invited to events
Diversity	Representation and visibility for pwds within sports organisation
Schools	Poor physical education provision in schools

Source: Authors' own interpretation based on data provided in Chaps. 4–22

Motives and Facilitating Factors

Contributors mentioned social reasons/contacts, having fun and enjoyment and improving fitness and health benefits as the most important reasons to participate in sport for pwds. Other motivations contributors mentioned were relaxation, gaining self-confidence, a feeling of being part of society, releasing energy or aggression and learning to use assistive devices. Facilitators that help improving participation levels amongst pwds are amongst others, supportive social networks, a diversity of choice from a range of sports offer, facility proximity, cheaper prices, people to go with, communications from trusted sources, inclusive sport sessions and impairment specific sessions, informal groups helping each other, role models, improved and inclusive community facilities and improved expertise with regard to inclusive sport, physical activity and physical education with trainers, coaches and teachers. Facilitators are often the opposite of the barriers that were mentioned. Important to

Table 23.5 Community factors that may influence sport participation by pwds

Dimension	Examples of Barriers Mentioned
Access and accessibility of facilities	Transportation problems; hard to reach facilities by public transport; high financial costs to travel; lack of accessible and safe spaces/sport facilities to do sport; lack of secondary schools that are accessible; lack of access to public spaces
Access to aids	Specialised or high-tech equipment (e.g. wheelchair) is not readily available/at high cost
Communication	Inaccessible or inefficient communication channels; lack of coverage of a wide range of sports in the media
Organisational networks and cooperation	Lack of coordination and cooperation between sports and disability organisations; ad hoc structures and approaches; fragmented disability sport landscape; shortcomings in the planning and implementation of projects in disability sport
Norms and values	Lack of acceptance form society; negative attitudes towards (athletes with a) disability; ableism; negative and prejudiced characterisations of pwds; lack of a culture of general participation in physical exercise and sport
Geographical aspects	Less sport opportunities in smaller communities/rural areas/low population areas; uneven distribution of sports clubs over country; geographical dispersion of athletes and participants

Source: Authors' own interpretation based on data provided in Chaps. 4–22

Table 23.6 Policy factors that may influence sport participation by pwds

Dimension	Examples of Barriers Mentioned
Support policies	Unclear who pays for equipment; low funding possibilities; lack of institutional support and interest by governmental authorities; financial constraints that affect institutions working with pwds; competition with other organisations to acquire funding and to find sponsors
National policies and regulations	National policy dictates e.g. that all people must have approval by a physician to compete; austerity measures; gap between legal regulations and practices

Source: Authors' own interpretation based on data provided in Chaps. 4–22

note is that among the facilitating factors to improve sport opportunities for pwds, the contributors made reference to various structure- and policy-related aspects. Laws, regulations and policies that promote inclusion or ensure that facilities are accessible for pwds were seen as important facilitators. Other facilitating factors were a stronger leadership, encouragement from national sports federations of local sports clubs to welcome (more) pwds, consultants that support agents, clear plans and strategies, the inclusion process with mainstream sport federations, a high proportion of volunteers, increased budget for disability sport federations and so on. Although we cannot draw causal relationships between structure and policy aspects of disability sport and sport participation of pwds, contributors made it very clear these relationships do exist and are worthwhile examining.

23.6 Limitations

The unique selling point of this handbook, in our humble opinion, is that it provides up to date information on a wide range of topics with regard to sport for pwds across Europe. As such it is a valuable source of data for academics, policy-makers and practitioners in the field of disability sport. However, we are aware of the fact that the selection of countries is based on a convenience sample. We selected contributors that were willing and able to make a contribution. We made an effort to include countries from all regions, but still certain regions are under-represented, for example, Eastern and Southern Europe, with the risk that the perspectives of underrepresented regions are not well included. We do believe, however, that with the coverage of 19 countries, the data in this handbook provides a good, but indicative, understanding of the various ways disability sport is delivered across the European region.

A second limitation of this handbook might be that the data provided by the contributors is not always easy to compare. The contributors were given a conceptual framework with clear instructions as to how to structure the available data. Within that framework there was freedom to highlight country specifics or to leave open topics for which data was lacking. The depth with which the requested topics were described differed. This variability in the data made comparison across countries more difficult. Important to note is the overall descriptions in the country-specific chapters are based on numerous underlying data sources. A systematic comparison of uniform indicators therefore requires more in-depth research (see section 'Recommendations').

A limitation of the handbook may also be that data provided in this handbook may become outdated. Obviously, this is always the case when situations are described in a certain time frame. Contributors have looked back and described the current situation of the structure and steering of disability sport in their country as far as data was available. Changes may occur due to political changes or changes in policies and practices of the agents involved. We don't see this as a disadvantage. To be able to monitor developments in disability sport, having some kind of baseline measurement is very useful. And that is what this handbook provides.

Another limitation of this handbook is that we might have overlooked the voices of pwds themselves. One of the key principles of the UNCRPD is "[c]onsidering that persons with disabilities should have the opportunity to be actively involved in decision-making processes about policies and programmes, including those directly concerning them" (United Nations, 2006:2). Although pwds, as respondents, are included in many of the studies contributors referred to in their chapters, answering questionnaires or being an interviewee is not the same as co-authoring a chapter on the structure and steering of disability sport. We should therefore be aware of the potential bias in the descriptions made by the contributors and editors, especially referring to discussions on the integration or inclusion of pwds in sport. These two concepts might be understood very differently by pwds in comparison to the contributors and the representatives of the various agents in the landscape of disability sport, whom we presume are predominantly non-disabled. This entails a great responsibility and we must therefore ask ourselves whether the terms used in the book with regard to disability and disability sport or sport for pwds, are used in accordance with the meaning attached to them by pwds themselves. As explained in Chap. 1, we have tried to seek common ground with regard to the terms used in this handbook.

23.7 Recommendations

Based on the overview provided in this chapter, we can make a number of recommendations for researchers, policy-makers and practitioners in the field of disability sport.

First of all, to be able to make meaningful cross-national comparisons it is important to develop a uniform set of indicators to measure developments in various aspects of sport for/by pwds. These sets of indicators may focus amongst others on the following aspects of disability sport:

- the structure of disability sport (e.g. who are involved and how?);
- the steering of disability sport (e.g. what legislations and policies are in place and how do they impact disability sport provision, what is the nature of the relationships between the agents involved and how does this impact the provision of disability sport?);
- the organisation of sport for/by pwds (what is the (segregated, integrated, inclusive) sport offer for pwds?);
- the participation in sport amongst pwds (to what extent and how do pwds participate in sport?);
- the facilitators and barriers impacting sport participation (what are reasons for pwds to participate in sport, what motivates them, what hinders them to participate (more) in sport?);
- mediating and moderating factors that impact the provision of sport for pwds;
- the involvement of experts by experience/pwds in the steering and provision of sport for pwds; and
- inclusion processes.

For each of the subjects, project teams, preferably including experts by experience, could be formed that are dedicated towards developing theory and practice based indicators that are applicable across countries. Based on these sets of indicators, research projects could then provide a basis for a more profound analysis of differences and similarities between countries, and moreover, for developing theories on the relationships between various factors influencing the steering and provision of sport for pwds and participation levels amongst pwds. Data collection and monitoring would then support making evidence-based policies with regard to sport for pwds.

In developing indicators and data collection the EU could play a stimulating role. In Article 9.2 of the Union of Equality, the European strategy for the rights of pwds, the European Commission stresses the ambition of the EU to strengthen its data collection on pwds and states that it will work with EU member states in that regard (European Commission, 2021). To be able to distinguish by disability the Commission, for example, wants to promote the use of the Washington Short Set of Questions by which disability could be measured (see The Washington Group on Disability Statistics, 2022, see also Chap. 2). To be able to distinguish sport participation levels by disability, European- and national-level surveys should include an indicator for disability. As is shown in Chap. 3, Eurostat's Eurobarometer on sport still lacks an indicator that determines whether a respondent has a certain disability. Vice versa, surveys that focus on the living conditions of pwds, should include indicators to measure participation in sport and/or PA. A greater awareness (also part of Article 9 of the Union of Equality) of the importance of including indicators on disability and/or sport participation by researchers and representatives from governmental and non-governmental agents with influencing powers is needed to improve opportunities for monitoring and cross-national comparisons.

An opportunity to include disability as a variable in sport-related data collection would be to align with the works of a special Task Force appointed by the European Commission to develop harmonised sport statistics in the EU, including statistics and data on health-enhancing physical activity, social dimensions of sport and Sport Satellite Accounts in the EU (European Commission, 2022). The Task Force's objective is to support evidence-based policy-making at both national and EU levels by harmonising existing methodologies and definitions on sport statistics.

Monitoring integration and inclusion processes in sport should be a focus point too. It appears that inclusion is an important element of national and local policies with regard to sport for pwds in the various countries, stimulated by international and national laws and regulations. The countries are at different developmental stages and can learn from each other by means of exchanging knowledge about what is meant by whom by inclusion and what is the impact of more or less inclusion. Is more inclusion always for the better for pwds or the sport for pwds, or are there disadvantages too? For instance, if inclusion means that pwds can only take part in sport settings together with persons without disability and they would lose other, segregated (own clubs) or integrated (special teams in mainstream clubs), options, would that be beneficial for the promotion of sport participation by pwds or not? Or, if disability sport is governed fully by mainstream sport agents, as is the case in Norway, do athletes with a disability still feel represented by the system and are they still part of the decision-making process of organisations? These are aspects that need to be monitored so that countries can learn from mistakes and successes.

References

Block, M. E., & Fines, A. (2022). Examining physical activity for individuals with disabilities through a social justice lens. *Kinesiology Review, 11*(1), 80–87. https://doi.org/10.1123/kr.2021-0052

Bronfenbrenner, U. (1979). *The ecology of human developments: Experiments by nature and design.* Harvard University Press.

Christiaens, M., & Brittain, I. (2021). The complexities of implementing inclusion policies for disabled people in UK non-disabled voluntary community sports clubs. *European Sport Management Quarterly, 1–21*. https://doi.org/10.1080/16184742.2021.1955942

Coakley, J. (2015). *Sports in society: Issues and controversies* (11th ed.). McGraw-Hill Education.

Committee on the Rights of Persons with Disabilities. (2016). *United Nations Convention on the Rights of Persons with Disabilities. General comment No. 4 (2016) Article 24: Right to inclusive education*. United Nations. https://www.right-to-education.org/resource/general-comment-4-article-24-right-inclusive-education

Darcy, S., Lock, D., & Taylor, T. (2017). Enabling inclusive sport participation: Effects of disability and support needs on constraints to sport participation. *Leisure Sciences, 39*(1), 20–41. https://doi.org/10.1080/01490400.2016.1151842

Esping-Andersen, G. (1990). *The three worlds of welfare capitalism*. Princeton University Press.

European Commission. (2021). *Union of equality: Strategy for the rights of persons with disabilities 2021–2030*. European Commission. https://eur-lex.europa.eu/legal-content/EN/TXT/?uri=CELEX:32022R0720

European Commission. (2022). *Call for experts for a Task Force on harmonised sport statistics in the EU (TF SPORT)*. https://sport.ec.europa.eu/news/call-for-experts-for-a-task-force-on-harmonised-sport-statistics-in-the-eu-tf-sport

Eurostat. (2022a). *Functional and activity limitations statistics. Eurostat statistics explained*. https://ec.europa.eu/eurostat/statistics-explained/index.php?title=Functional_and_activity_limitations_statistics

Eurostat. (2022b). *Self-perceived long-standing limitations in usual activities due to health problem by sex, age and income quintile. HLTH_SILC_12*. https://ec.europa.eu/eurostat/databrowser/view/hlth_silc_12/default/table?lang=en

Goodwin, M., & Grix, J. (2011). Bringing structures back in. The 'governance narrative', the 'decentred approach' and 'asymmetrical network governance' in the education and sport policy communities. *Public Administration, 89*(2), 537–556. https://doi.org/10.1111/j.1467-9299.2011.01921.x

Grammenos, S., & Priestley, M. (2020). *Master tables concerning EU 2020: year 2018. Statistics on Persons with Disabilities (2018)*. European Disability Expertise. https://www.disability-europe.net/downloads/1046-ede-task-2-1-statistical-indicators-tables-eu-silc-2018

Green, M., & Collins, S. (2008). Policy, politics and path dependency: Sport development in Australia and Finland. *Sport Management Review, 11*(3), 225–251. https://doi.org/10.1016/S1441-3523(08)70111-6

Groeneveld, M. (2009). European Sport Governance, Citizens, and the State. *Public Management Review, 11*(4), 421–440. https://doi.org/10.1080/14719030902989516

Hallmann, K., & Petry, K. (Eds.). (2013). *Comparative sport development. Systems, participation and public policy. (Sport Economics, Management and Policy 8)*. Springer Science. https://link.springer.com/book/10.1007/978-1-4614-8905-4

Kitchin, P., & Howe, P. (2014). The mainstreaming of disability cricket in England and Wales: Integration 'One Game' at a time. *Sport Management Review, 17*(February), 65–77. https://doi.org/10.1016/J.SMR.2013.05.003

Kitchin, P., Peile, C., & Lowther, J. (2019). Mobilizing capacity to achieve the mainstreaming of disability sport. *Managing Sport and Leisure, 24*(6), 424–444. https://doi.org/10.1080/23750472.2019.1684839

Kiuppis, F. (2018). Inclusion in sport: Disability and participation. In Sport in society (21, 1, 4–21). Routledge. doi:https://doi.org/10.1080/17430437.2016.1225882.

Leenaars, K. E. F., Florisson, A. M. E., Smit, E., Wagemakers, A., Molleman, G. R. M., & Koelen, M. A. (2016). The connection between the primary care and the physical activity sector: Professionals' perceptions. *BMC Public Health, 16*(1), 1001. https://doi.org/10.1186/s12889-016-3665-x

McLeroy, K. R., Bibeau, D., Steckler, A., & Glanz, K. (1988). An ecological perspective on health promotion programs. *Health Education Quarterly, 15*(4), 351–377. https://doi.org/10.1177/109019818801500401

Mehtälä, M. A., Sääkslahti, A., Inkinen, M., & Poskiparta, M. E. (2014). A socio-ecological approach to physical activity interventions in childcare: A systematic review. *International Journal of Behavioral Nutrition and Physical Activity, 11*(1), 22. https://doi.org/10.1186/1479-5868-11-22

Miller, F. A., & Katz, J. H. (2002). *Inclusion breakthrough: Unleashing the real power of diversity*. Berrett-Koehler Publishers.

Misener, L., & Darcy, S. (2014). Managing disability sport: From athletes with disabilities to inclusive organisational perspectives. *Sport Management Review, 17*(1), 1–7. https://doi.org/10.1016/j.smr.2013.12.003

Ross, S. (1973). The economic theory of agency: The principal's problem. *American Economic Review, 63*(2), 134–139.

Sallis, J. F., Owen, N., & Fisher, E. B. (2008). Ecological models of health behavior. In K. Glanz, B. K. Rimer, & K. Viswanath (Eds.), *Health behavior and health education: Theory, research, and practice* (4th ed., pp. 465–485). Jossey-Bass.

Scheerder, J., Willem, A., & Claes, E. (Eds.). (2017). *Sport policy systems and sport federations. A cross-national perspective*. Palgrave Macmillan.

Skelcher, C. (2000). Changing images of the state: Overloaded, hollowed-out, congested. *Public Policy and Administration, 15*(3), 3–19. https://doi.org/10.1177/095207670001500302

The Washington Group on Disability Statistics. (2022). *WG Short Set on Functioning (WG-SS)*. https://www.washingtongroup-disability.com/question-sets/wg-short-set-on-functioning-wg-ss/

Thomas, N., & Guett, M. (2014). Fragmented, complex and cumbersome: A study of disability sport policy and provision in Europe. *International Journal of Sport Policy and Politics, 6*(3), 389–406. https://doi.org/10.1080/19406940.2013.832698

United Nations. (2006). *Convention on the Rights of Persons with Disabilities (CRPD)*. https://www.un.org/development/desa/disabilities/convention-on-the-rights-of-persons-with-disabilities.html

United Nations. (2019). *Disability and development report. Realizing the Sustainable Development Goals by, for and with persons with disabilities. 2018*. United Nations.

World Health Organization. (2002). *Towards a common language for functioning, disability and health. International Classification of Functioning, Disability and Health (ICF)*. https://www.who.int/publications/m/item/icf-beginner-s-guide-towards-a-common-language-for-functioning-disability-and-health

World Health Organization, & The World Bank. (2011). *World report on disability*. World Health Organization. https://www.who.int/teams/noncommunicable-diseases/sensory-functions-disability-and-rehabilitation/world-report-on-disability

Yu, S., Wang, T., Zhong, T., Qian, Y., & Qi, J. (2022). Barriers and facilitators of physical activity participation among children and adolescents with intellectual disabilities: A scoping review. *Healthcare, 10*(2), 233. https://doi.org/10.3390/healthcare10020233

Index

A
Ableism, 28, 31–32, 259, 261
Active Lives survey, 255, 258
Active Living: No Limits (2016-2021), 217, 223, 225, 233
Activity Alliance, 223, 244, 245, 248, 252, 254, 259, 260, 571
The Act on Equality between Women and Men, Finland, 110
Act on Social Services, Denmark, 82, 89, 91
Adapted physical activity (APA), Finland, v, 114, 118
Affirmative Model, 30–32
Article 18 of the Constitution, Turkey, 549
Article 42 of the Constitution, Turkey, 549
Article 50 of the Constitution, Turkey, 549
Article 58 of the Constitution, Turkey, 549
Article 59 of the Constitution, Turkey, 539
Article 61 of the Constitution, Turkey, 549
Association of Cerebral Palsy (APPC), Portugal, 493
Austerity, UK, 33, 259, 261
Austrian Deaf Sports Confederation (ÖGSV), 272, 275, 276, 282–284, 288
Austrian Disability Sports Confederation (ÖBSV), 267
Austrian Paralympic Committee (ÖPC), 267, 273, 276–278, 280, 282, 285

B
Barriers
 Belgium, 318–320
 Denmark, 86, 96–97, 564
 Finland, 113–115
 Germany, 344
 Hungary, 430
 Iceland, 138–140
 Ireland, 210–211
 Lithuania, 454–455
 The Netherlands, 376–377
 Northern Ireland, 232–233, 376–378
 Norway, 163–165
 Portugal, 507–508
 Slovenia, 479–481
 Spain, 530–531
 Sweden, 187
 Switzerland, 403
 Turkey, 554–556
 United Kingdom, 259–260
Basic Law, Germany, 326, 338
Belgian Paralympic Committee (BPC), 302, 307, 310
Biopsychosocial model, 31, 35, 174, 197, 353, 564
Boin, Victor, 302
Brexit, 62, 238, 261
British Paralympic Association (BPA), 247
Brussels Capital Region, 296, 297, 313
Budapest Institute for Idiots and Intellectually Retarded, 414
Bundes-Sportförderungsgesetz (BSFG), 269, 273, 275, 277–280, 575
Bundes-Sport GmbH (BSG), 270, 274, 275, 277, 278, 280, 288

© The Author(s), under exclusive license to Springer Nature Switzerland AG 2023
C. van Lindert et al. (eds.), *The Palgrave Handbook of Disability Sport in Europe*, https://doi.org/10.1007/978-3-031-21759-3

C

Cara-Sport Inclusion Ireland, 193, 199, 202, 203, 212
Cerebral, the Swiss Foundation for the Cerebral Palsy Child (Schweizerische Stiftung für das cerebral gelähmte Kind), 393
Comité Estatal de Representantes de Personas con Discapacidad (CERMI, Spanish Committee of Representatives of People with Disabilities), 520, 532
Challenges in data collection, ix, 7, 588–589
Characteristics of
  Austria, 268
  Belgium, 296–297
  Denmark, 80
  Finland, 102
  Germany, 326–327
  Hungary, 412
  Iceland, 126
  Lithuania, 438–439
  The Netherlands, 350, 351
  Northern Ireland, 218–221
  Norway, 146–147
  Portugal, 486–494
  Republic of Ireland, 193–196, 218, 223
  Slovenia, 462–463
  Spain, 513–517
  Sweden, 170
  Switzerland, 386–390
  Turkey, 537–538, 542
  United Kingdom (UK), 238–240
Charter of Fundamental Rights of the European Union, 4
Children with a disability, 27, 88, 138, 355, 363, 365, 377, 378, 443, 565, 567, 586
Chronic health disorders, Belgium, 303, 304, 306, 318
Club (-organised setting), Belgium, 299
Club-organised sport, 56, 59, 62–70, 73–75, 295, 300, 303, 304, 307, 309, 311, 563
Coach education, Belgium, 153, 162, 248, 312
Co-governance approach, 578
Comité Olímpico Español (COE, Spanish Olympic Committee), 75, 519
Comité Paralímpico de Portugal (CPP, National Paralympic Committee of Portugal), 485, 492–494, 496–499, 501
Comité Paralímpico Español (CPE, Spanish Paralympic Committee), 517, 519, 520, 525, 526, 532, 533
Community factors, 593
Community sport coaches, the Netherlands, 359, 365
Comparability, 56
Comparative framework, 8, 10, 14
Comparisons, 5, 7, 10, 19, 36, 39, 40, 44, 55–57, 59, 68, 70, 117, 126, 138, 208, 212, 232, 239, 270, 301, 302, 354, 411, 415, 417, 432, 462, 529, 562–563, 584–587, 589, 590, 594–596
Conference of Sports Ministers of the Länder, Germany, 334
Congreso Nacional de Deporte Adaptado (CONDA, National Congress in Adapted Sport), Spain, 526
Consejo Superior de Deportes (CSD, Higher Sports Council), Spain, 517, 520, 522, 525, 526, 531
Country profile
  Austria, 268–274
  Belgium, 296–304
  Denmark, 80–84
  Europe, 462–466
  Finland, 102
  Germany, 326–331
  Hungary, 412–419
  Iceland, 126
  Ireland, 194–200
  Lithuania, 438–444
  The Netherlands, 350
  Northern Ireland, 218–221
  Norway, 146–151
  Portugal, 486–494
  Slovenia, 462–463
  Spain, 513–517
  Sweden, 170–176
  Switzerland, 386
  Turkey, 537–545
  United Kingdom (UK), 238–244
Covid-19 pandemic, 2, 17, 98, 203, 379, 481, 507, 556
Cross-national, ix, x, 5, 7–10, 36, 37, 39, 40, 44, 55, 56, 59, 61, 66, 70, 74, 561–563, 586, 587, 595, 596
Cross-temporal, x, 55, 74, 75

D

The Danish Gymnastics and Sports Association (DGI), 81, 84, 85, 87, 88, 90, 98
Deaf Institute of Festetics Street of Budapest, 418
Department of Communities (DoC), 217–220, 222–225, 227–231

Index 601

Department of Digital, Culture, Media and Sport (DCMS), 245, 250
Department of Tourism, Culture, Arts, Gaeltacht, Sport and Media, 193, 194, 196, 200
Deputy State Secretary for Disability Sport in Ministry of Youth and Sport (2000), Hungary, 420
Deutscher Behindertensportverband (DBS), 334
Development of disability sports, Austria, 17, 272, 274
Devolution, UK, 218, 238, 260
Directorate General for Sport Services, Turkey, 540
Directorate General for Youth Services, Turkey, 546
Disability, v–vii, ix, x, 1–18, 25–49, 55–75, 79–98, 101–119, 125–141, 150–157, 174–185, 197–211, 217–234, 237, 239–255, 267, 270–287, 295–320, 325–345, 349–379, 388–405, 411–432, 437–456, 461–482, 485–510, 513–533, 537–556, 561–596
Disability Act 2005, Ireland, 199
Disability Action Plan 2014-2021, Slovenia, 478, 479
Disability-based, 9, 49, 570, 571, 573, 574, 578, 579, 581, 582, 587
Disability Discrimination, 225
Disability in
    Austria, 267, 270–272
    Belgium, 301–302
    Denmark, 82–83
    Europe, vii, 40–42
    Finland, 103–105
    Germany, 328–332
    Hungary, 413–418
    Iceland, 129–131
    Ireland, 194, 197–198, 202, 203
    Lithuania, 441–443, 455
    The Netherlands, 353–354, 369
    Northern Ireland, 217, 220–221
    Norway, 148–150
    Portugal, 490–491
    Slovenia, 463–465
    Spain, 515–516, 526, 532
    Sweden, 174–175
    Switzerland, 388
    Turkey, 540–543
    United Kingdom (UK), 260
Disability Mainstreaming Policy (DMP), 228
Disability models, 9
Disability sport, 5, 25–49, 55, 79–98, 101, 125–141, 145, 175, 194, 217–234, 237, 267, 295–320, 325–345, 349, 385, 411–432, 437–456, 461–482, 485, 513–533, 537–556, 561
    policy, ix, 5, 6, 9, 10, 18, 119, 217, 240, 349, 350, 444, 445, 473, 567, 569
    system, vii, 7, 10–12, 14, 17, 19, 48, 84–91, 108–115, 119, 131–137, 176–185, 200–207, 222–229, 244–255, 260, 304–313, 332–343, 390–400, 405, 419–429, 444–452, 466–477, 494–502, 545–552, 562, 563, 566, 567, 570
Disability Sport Federations (DSFs), 111, 151, 245, 248, 250, 446, 521, 525–527, 529, 553, 566, 570, 574, 582, 583, 593
Disability Sport Hubs, 223, 224, 227, 228, 232, 233
    Progressive Building Society, 227
Disability Sport Northern Ireland (Disability Sport NI), 221
Disableism, 32
Diversity, vii, ix, 4, 16, 30–32, 82, 160, 163, 201, 207, 229, 233, 234, 254, 260, 271, 309, 332, 340, 354, 426, 427, 498, 507, 592
Donnelly, 2011, 219, 221, 226, 229–233
    SAPAS Survey, 230

E
Educational level, 62, 73, 75, 316, 351, 588
Emberi Erőforráspok Minisztériuma (Ministry of National Resources, EMMI) 2010-, Hungary, 420, 427
Emergence of disability sport
    Austria, 272–273
    Belgium, 302–304
    Denmark, 83–84
    Finland, 105–107, 109
    Germany, 331
    Hungary, 417–419
    Iceland, 130–131
    Ireland, 198–200
    Lithuania, 444
    The Netherlands, 355–357
    Northern Ireland, 221
    Norway, 150–151
    Portugal, 491–494
    Slovenia, 465–466

Spain, 516–517
Sweden, 175–176
Switzerland, 389–390
Turkey, 543–545
United Kingdom (UK), 242–244, 565
Encuesta de Discapacidad, Autonomía personal y situaciones de Dependencia (EDAD, Survey on disabilities, personal autonomy and dependency situations), Spain, 515, 528
Environmental factors, 17, 35, 37, 39, 96, 176, 210, 377, 400, 441, 442, 590
Equality, 4, 30, 33, 46, 89, 102, 112–114, 116, 126, 149, 154, 160, 225, 229, 247, 273, 390, 394, 396, 398, 448, 478, 494, 498–500, 504, 508, 521, 522, 564, 575–577
Equality Act 2010 (EqA 2010), UK, 240, 242, 249, 260
Equality and Anti-discrimination Act, Norway, 149
Equal society, 74
Equal Status Act 2000, Ireland, 197, 204
Equity, 46, 170, 500, 577
EU27, 5, 41, 42, 62, 63, 71–73
EU28, 62, 63, 65–68, 71, 72
EU member state, 4, 5, 15, 17, 18, 57, 59–68, 71–73, 75, 328, 442, 555, 561, 596
Eurobarometer survey (EB), 9, 16, 56–60, 62, 70, 74, 75, 82, 440
European Charter on Sport for All: Disabled Persons, 75
European Commission (EC), vii, 1, 2, 4, 5, 9, 15, 40, 56, 58, 60, 61, 74, 271, 328, 351, 440, 453, 550, 561, 595, 596
European Disability Strategy 2010–2020, 4, 415
European Pillar of Social Rights, 4
European Sport for All Charter, 4, 75
European Union (EU), vii, 1, 2, 4, 5, 7, 15, 18, 40, 41, 57, 59–62, 64, 71–74, 112, 129, 145, 170, 194, 226, 238, 239, 270, 288, 301, 326, 328, 351, 363, 463, 465, 470, 471, 473, 477, 478, 486, 538, 539, 551, 554–556, 575, 595, 596
Exclusion, 2, 27, 43, 183, 194, 312, 353, 368, 449, 502, 550, 551

F
Facilitating factors, 592–593
Facilitators
    Belgium, 318–320
    Denmark, 96–97
    Finland, 113–115, 118, 119
    Germany, 344
    Hungary, 430
    Iceland, 138, 140
    Ireland, 202, 210–212
    Lithuania, 454–455
    The Netherlands, 369, 376–378
    Northern Ireland, 217, 232–233
    Portugal, 504, 507–510
    Slovenia, 479–481
    Spain, 530–531
    Sweden, 187
    Switzerland, 403–406
    Turkey, 554–556
    United Kingdom, 259–260
Federación Española de Deportes para Ciegos (FEDC, Spanish Federation of Sports for the Blind), 516, 519, 521, 526
Federación Española de Deportes para Personas con Discapacidad Física (FEDDF, Spanish Sports Federation for People with Physical Disabilities), 517, 519, 521, 526
Federación Española de Deportes para Personas con Discapacidad Intelectual (FEDDI, Spanish Sports Federation for People with Intellectual Disabilities), 517, 519–521, 526, 529
Federación Española de Deportes para Personas con Parálisis Cerebral (FEDPC, Spanish Federation of Sports for People with Cerebral Palsy), 517, 519, 521, 526
Federación Española de Deportes para Sordos (FEDS, Spanish Sports Federation Sports for the Deaf), 517, 519, 521, 526, 529
Federación Española de Municipios y Provincias (FEMP, Spanish Federation of Municipalities and Provinces), 526
Federal Ministry of Labour and Social Affairs, Germany, 333, 339
Federal Ministry of the Interior, Germany, 333, 340–342
Financial framework
    Austria, 280
    Belgium, 310
    Denmark, 90
    Finland, 111–112
    Germany, 340–341
    Hungary, 426–428

Index 603

Iceland, 135–136
Ireland, 205–206
Lithuania, 450–451
The Netherlands, 366–368
Northern Ireland, 226
Norway, 156–157
Portugal, 500–501
Slovenia, 473–474
Spain, 524–526
Sweden, 182–183, 186
Switzerland, 397–398
Turkey, 550–551
United Kingdom, 252–253
Financial relationships, 88, 108, 224, 395, 489, 495, 578
The Finnish Constitution, Finland, 110
Finnish Paralympic Committee, 106, 107, 112
Fitness, 3, 13, 25, 36, 43, 47, 48, 57, 59, 60, 62–70, 74, 75, 82, 93, 94, 131, 133, 134, 148, 172, 178, 185, 195, 210, 219, 220, 257, 285, 290, 300, 314, 316, 317, 361–363, 369, 373, 375, 376, 378, 387, 402, 432, 440, 447, 481, 507, 571, 588, 592
Flanders, 61, 66, 295–320, 568, 571, 584
Flemish Decree on Sports Federations, 304–307, 309–312, 320
Fogyatékkal élők Sportszervezeteinek Magyarországi Szövetsége (FMSZ, Federation for Sportorganisations of People with Disabilities), Hungary, 419, 425
Fogyatékosok Diák-, és Szabadidősport Szövetség (FODISZ, National Association of Students and Leisure Sports for the Disabled), Hungary, 419, 421–423, 426, 427, 429, 430
Fogyatékosok Nemzeti Sportszövetsége (FONESZ, National Sports Federation for the Disabled), Hungary, 419, 422
Fogyatékosok Versenysport Szövetsége (FOVESZ, Competition Sports Association of the Disabled), Hungary, 419, 422, 423
Foundation for Funding Disability and Humanitarian Organisations, Slovenia, 461
Framework agreement, Denmark, 87, 88, 90, 91, 97, 576, 580
Framework for disability sport, 278, 339, 449, 567, 568
Functioning, 1, 9, 33–39, 376, 413, 425, 441, 530

G
Galtung's Triangle of Violence, 26
Gehandicaptensport Nederland (GSN), 357, 360, 361, 368
German Association of the Blind and Disabled, 335
German Deaf Sport Association (DSG), 335
German Disabled Sports Youth (DBSJ), 335, 342
German Sports Association for the Hard of Hearing (DSSV), 335
Gezondheidsenquête/Leefstijlmonitor (national lifestyle monitor), the Netherlands, 369
Global Action Plan on Physical Activity (GAPPA), 3, 251
Governance and management support
  Austria, 280–282
  Belgium, 310–311
  Denmark, 91
  Finland, 111–112
  Germany, 340–342
  Hungary, 426–427
  Iceland, 135–137
  Ireland, 205–207
  Lithuania, 450–452
  The Netherlands, 367–368
  Northern Ireland, 226–228
  Norway, 156–157
  Portugal, 500–502
  Slovenia, 473–476
  Spain, 526
  Sweden, 178
  Switzerland, 397–399
  Turkey, 550–551
  United Kingdom, 252–254
Governmental agents
  Austria, 273, 567, 568
  Belgium, 305, 567, 568
  Denmark, 84–86
  Finland, 107–108, 569
  Germany, 333–334, 568
  Hungary, 420–421, 568
  Iceland, 131–132
  Ireland, 200–201, 567
  Lithuania, 444–445, 567
  The Netherlands, 358–359, 567, 569
  Northern Ireland, 222
  Norway, 151–152, 569
  Portugal, 495–496, 568
  Slovenia, 468, 567
  Spain, 517, 568, 569
  Sweden, 177–178, 569
  Switzerland, 390–391, 567, 568

Turkey, 546–548, 567, 569
United Kingdom, 246, 568
Grassroots sports, ix, 1, 5, 6, 141, 227, 331, 447, 489, 520, 525, 532
G-sport, Belgium, 303–307, 310
Guttman, Ludwig, 25–49, 127, 130, 242, 244, 355, 491, 492, 516, 565

H

Halassy Sports Club (HOSC), Hungary, 418
Harmonisation, 56
Harmonised data, 55–57
Hierarchical relationships, 13, 88, 308, 546, 577, 578
History, 19, 102, 105, 113, 115, 118, 125, 127, 130, 147, 197, 218, 221, 267, 296, 298, 302, 320, 325, 356, 417, 439, 532, 540, 563, 565–566
History of disability sport in the Netherlands, 355–363
Human rights model, 30, 197

I

ÍF (The Icelandic Paralympic Sport Federation), 128, 130, 131, 133–141
ÍFR (Oldest sport club in Iceland that focuses on athletes with disability), 130
Impairments, 2, 4, 9, 16, 28–30, 32–34, 36–39, 44, 45, 82, 95, 104, 109, 117, 119, 131, 137, 138, 150, 153, 164, 174, 175, 181, 186, 197, 220, 234, 240, 242, 246, 248, 255–258, 260, 272, 301–304, 306, 313, 314, 316–320, 329, 335, 353, 354, 361, 375, 377, 378, 388, 394, 400–402, 404, 413, 415, 417, 419, 423, 447, 463, 478, 487, 515, 516, 540, 542–545, 549, 555, 564, 565, 570, 574, 589, 590, 592
Inclusion, v, vii, ix, 3, 25–49, 86, 101–119, 125, 147, 169–174, 193, 217, 239, 267–288, 295, 329, 355, 391, 422, 449, 465, 486, 521, 546, 562
Inclusion Handicap, Switzerland, 388, 393, 394
Inclusive sports trainer training (UPE), Hungary, 421
Inclusive organisation, Norway, 161
Income inequality, 73, 74
Insieme, Switzerland, 394

INSOS (Soziale Institutionen für Menschen mit Behinderungen Schweiz), 393, 394
Institute of Technology, Tralee, 3, 193–213
Instituto Nacional para a Reabilitação (INR, National Institute for Rehabilitation), Portugal, 491, 493, 501, 509
Instituto Português do Desporto e Juventude (IPDJ, Portuguese Institute of Sport and Youth), 489, 493, 497, 500
Integration process, Norway, 160–165
Intellectual (disability), 6, 75, 83, 91, 106, 130, 136, 159, 163, 175, 177, 178, 198, 212, 277, 303, 318, 319, 331, 335, 354–357, 361, 365, 369, 370, 376, 389, 390, 392, 394, 399, 400, 402, 403, 447, 461, 467, 471, 478, 490, 493, 497, 507, 519, 521, 524, 530, 540, 542, 565
Intellectual impairment, Belgium, 313, 318
Intermediate agents
  Austria, 274–275
  Belgium, 306
  Denmark, 86–87
  Finland, 108–109
  Germany, 334
  Hungary, 421–422
  Ireland, 201–202
  Lithuania, 446
  Netherlands, 359–363
  Northern Ireland, 223
  Norway, 152–153
  Portugal, 496, 569
  Slovenia, 469
  Spain, 518
  Sweden, 178
  Switzerland, 391, 569
  United Kingdom, 246
Internalised ableism, 32
International Charter of Physical Education, Physical Activity and Sport, 3
International Classification of Functioning Disability and Health (ICF-model), 2, 9, 16, 31, 34–37, 39, 40, 104, 197, 198, 301, 353, 376, 491, 494, 499, 500, 543, 564, 590
Interpersonal factors, 592
Intersectional, 4, 31, 212
Intrapersonal factors, 590
ÍSÍ (*The National Olympic and Sport Association of Iceland*), 127, 128, 130, 131, 133–136, 140, 141

Index

J

Jugend trainiert für Paralympics (JTFP), Germany, 342

K

Kazan Action Plan (KAP), 3, 234
Kindergarten, Elementary and Specialised Secondary School, Unified Special Education Methodology Centre and Students' Residence ("Mozgásjavító") (Mozgásjavító Óvoda, Általános Iskola, Gimnázium, Kollégium, Egységes Gyógypedagógiai Módszertani Intézmény), Hungary, 418
Knowledge Centre on Disability (KCB), 85, 86, 96
Kristín Rós Hákonardóttir, 125

L

Lamprecht, M., 386, 387, 392, 395, 398, 400, 401, 405
Language and disability, 33–34
Law on Sport, Lithuania, 440
Law on the Social Integration of the Disabled, Lithuania, 440, 442, 449
Laws and regulations, 149, 155, 250, 468, 479, 496, 575–576, 580, 596
Legislation, ix, 4, 7, 11, 13, 14, 89, 90, 107, 110, 114, 130, 134, 175, 199, 225, 249, 301, 320, 326, 338, 353, 388, 389, 394, 420, 425, 444, 448, 450, 455, 461, 463, 467, 470, 477, 480, 481, 497, 498, 500, 507, 508, 515, 517, 521, 523, 528, 543, 562, 567, 569, 574–576, 581, 583, 584, 595
Legislative framework
  Austria, 278–279
  Belgium, 309
  Denmark, 89
  Finland, 110
  Germany, 338–339
  Hungary, 425
  Iceland, 134
  Ireland, 203–204
  Lithuania, 448–449
  The Netherlands, 363–364
  Northern Ireland, 225
  Norway, 155–156
  Portugal, 498–500
  Slovenia, 471–473

  Spain, 521–522
  Sweden, 181
  Switzerland, 394–395
  Turkey, 549–550
  United Kingdom, 249–250
Leisure and Recreation Act, Denmark, 82, 85, 89, 91
Level of integration and inclusion
  Austria, 282–283
  Belgium, 311–312
  Denmark, 91
  Finland, 112–113
  Germany, 342–343
  Hungary, 428–429
  Iceland, 136–137
  Ireland, 207
  Lithuania, 452
  Netherlands, 368–369
  Northern Ireland, 228–229
  Norway, 160
  Portugal, 501–502
  Slovenia, 477
  Spain, 527
  Sweden, 184–185
  Switzerland, 399–400
  Turkey, 551–552
  United Kingdom, 255
Limitations, 2, 35–42, 57, 75, 83, 92, 104, 105, 117, 150, 220, 234, 242, 285, 301, 313, 341, 345, 353, 354, 370, 371, 375, 415, 478, 490, 491, 515, 524, 563, 564, 587, 594–595
Limitation, the Netherlands, 353, 354, 370, 371, 375
Lithuanian Paralympic Committee (LPC), 446, 450
Local authorities, UK, 246, 252, 253
Local Sports Partnerships (LSP), Ireland, 193, 195, 196, 199–202, 205–207, 210, 212

M

Magyar Paralimpiai Bizottság (MPB, Hungarian Paralympic Committee), 411, 422, 423, 426–428, 432
Magyar Siketek Sportszövetsége (MSSSZ, Hungarian Deaf Sports Federation), 422
Magyar Speciális Olimpiai Szövetség (MSOSZ, Special Olympics Hungary), 419, 422

Magyar Szervátültetettek-Országos Sport, Kulturális és Érdekvédelmi – Szövetsége (MSZSZ, Hungarian Transplant Association for Sport, Culture and Advocacy), 412, 422
Mainstreaming, 39, 47, 199, 212, 228, 498, 504, 509, 566, 581–583
Management training activities, Austria, 282
Measuring disability, 38, 39, 564
Medical model, 29, 103, 455, 490, 491, 500, 540, 543, 564
Medical perspective, Austria, 288
Membership, Austria, 16, 81, 84, 87, 88, 95, 147, 157, 158, 172, 183, 202, 208, 210, 229–231, 255, 258, 283, 284, 288, 332, 335, 336, 343, 345, 391, 402, 538, 583, 585, 587, 588
Membership/partnership relationships, 12, 13, 224, 304, 577, 578
Mental (disability), ix, 1–4, 9, 28, 34, 36, 37, 39, 43, 75, 83, 91–93, 95, 129, 138, 150, 151, 195–197, 204, 205, 219, 220, 240, 250, 251, 258, 259, 272, 301, 303, 304, 306, 308, 313, 318, 320, 329, 345, 353, 355, 362, 389, 400, 413–415, 417, 419, 443, 448, 464–466, 500, 516, 521, 539, 549, 550, 556
Ministerio de Cultura y Deporte (MCD, Ministry of Culture and Sport), Spain, 518, 520, 524, 526, 527, 529–532
Ministry of Culture, Norway, 82, 84–86, 88–91, 96, 97, 149, 151–156, 172, 305, 517
Ministry of Education and Culture, Finland, 101, 103, 107, 111
Ministry of Education, Science and Sport, Slovenia, 461
Ministry of Education, Science and Sports, Lithuania, 440, 449, 452
Ministry of Education, Science and Culture, Iceland, 131, 132, 134, 135
Ministry of Health, Welfare and Sport, the Netherlands, 349
Ministry of Social Affairs, Iceland, 82, 89, 91, 131, 134, 135, 453, 454
Ministry of the Presidency, Relations with the Courts and Equality (MPCE, Ministerio de Presidencia, Relaciones con las Cortes e Igualdad), Spain, 521, 526

Ministry of Youth and Sports, Turkey, 419, 539, 540, 546, 549, 553, 554, 556
Monitoring and evaluation
  Austria, 283
  Belgium, 15
  Denmark, 172
  Finland, 584
  Hungary, 429
  Iceland, 137
  Ireland, 207, 584
  Lithuania, 449, 452
  Netherlands, 353, 376
  Northern Ireland, 208, 229, 584
  Norway, 586
  Portugal, 504
  Slovenia, 479
  Spain, 527
  Sweden, 172, 185
  Switzerland, 400
  Turkey, 552, 556
  United Kingdom, 584
Motives, 248, 318, 319, 376, 378, 590, 592–593

N
National Action Plan on Disability, Austria, 271, 279, 283
National Action Plan on Integration, Germany, 333
National Disability and Social Policy Centre Nonprofit Ltd. (Nemzeti Fogyatékosságügyi- és Szociálpolitikai Központ Közhasznú Nonprofit Kft.), Hungary, 421
National Disability Authority, Ireland, 197, 199, 202, 205, 210, 212
National Disability Inclusion Strategy, Ireland, 197, 198
National Disability Sport Federation (NDSF), 525, 566, 570, 573, 574, 581
National Disability Sport Organisations (NDSOs), UK, 244, 246, 248, 253
National Governing Bodies of Sport (NGBs), Ireland, 193, 195, 201–203, 205–207, 210, 212, 221, 224
National Governing Bodies of Sport (NGBs), UK, 239, 241, 244, 245, 247–249, 253, 255, 260, 261
National health survey, Austria, 285, 369–371, 584

Index   607

National Home for Crippled Children,
    Hungary, 418
National Institute of Rehabilitation, Portugal,
    496, 497
National Olympic Committee (NOC), 174,
    269, 270, 277, 298, 392, 461, 539,
    540, 544, 566, 570
National Paralympic Committee (NPC), 47,
    87, 109, 335, 356, 357, 360, 391,
    421, 566, 570, 573, 574
National Physical Activity Plan, Ireland, 193,
    196, 200, 204, 205
National Programme of Sport of the Republic
    of Slovenia (NPŠRS), 465, 468,
    471, 477
National sport federation, Finland, 109, 115,
    241, 349, 355, 357, 359–361, 494,
    526, 532
National Sport Monitor, Ireland, 195
National Sports Agreement, the Netherlands,
    352, 358, 364–368, 370, 378, 379
National Sports Confederation (NSCF),
    566, 570
National Sports Federations (NSFs), 87, 90,
    91, 101, 107, 109, 111–114, 169,
    173, 184, 269, 360–362, 387, 417,
    425, 431, 452, 566, 570, 573,
    574, 593
National Sports Policy, Ireland, 147, 193, 194,
    196, 200, 203, 204, 207, 387
National Youth and Sports Policy Document,
    Turkey, 549–551
NI Assembly and (Stormont) Executive, 218
NOC*NSF, 349, 351, 352, 356, 357,
    359–362, 365–368
Non-discrimination Act, Finland, 114, 522
Non-governmental agents
    Austria, 276, 571, 575, 580
    Belgium, 303, 306, 571, 575, 580
    Denmark, 87, 571, 580
    Finland, 575
    Germany, 335
    Hungary, 422, 575
    Iceland, 133, 569, 570, 575
    Ireland, 202, 575
    Lithuania, 446, 580
    The Netherlands, 349, 571
    Northern Ireland, 223
    Norway, 573
    Portugal, 493, 497, 569, 575
    Slovenia, 570, 575
    Spain, 575, 580
    Sweden, 178

Switzerland, 391, 569, 575
Turkey, 548, 569, 580
United Kingdom, 569, 580
Nordic Model, Iceland, 102, 126, 173
The Norwegian olympic and Paralympic
    Committee and Confederation of
    Sports (NIF), 145, 147, 148,
    151–158, 160–165
NPŠZ, Slovenia, 465, 467, 470, 474,
    476–478, 480
Nyomorékok Sport Egyesülete (NYSE, Sports
    Association of Cripples),
    Hungary, 418

O
OECD-indicator, 354, 369, 585
Olimpijski komite Slovenije–Združenje
    športnih zvez (OKS-ZŠZ), Slovenia,
    461, 463, 467, 468, 470, 472,
    473, 476–480
Operationalisation, 46, 56, 59, 75, 116
Order (DDO) 2006, Ireland, 220, 225
Organisational factors, 377, 508, 592
Organisational integration, the
    Netherlands, 357
Organisational landscape, 10, 44, 47,
    349, 566–567
Organización Nacional de Ciegos Españoles
    (ONCE, Spanish Association for the
    Blind), 526
ÖSP (Sport club focusing on athletes with
    intellectual disabilities), 130

P
Pan-European, 37, 55–75
Paralympic movement, 6, 25, 47, 48, 277, 355,
    423, 517
Paralympic sport, 6, 107, 109, 111, 113,
    161, 252, 365, 366, 425–427,
    455, 492, 497, 498, 500, 517,
    519, 524, 525, 527, 531, 537,
    540, 543, 555, 556
Parantee-Psylos, 295, 303, 304, 306–308, 310,
    312, 317, 320
Parasport Denmark, 84, 87, 88, 90, 91,
    96, 97, 574
Para sports, 6, 47, 145, 153, 156–159,
    161–163, 165, 223, 306, 308, 360,
    365–367, 461
Pető András Faculty of Semmelweis
    University, Hungary, 424

Physical (disability), 36, 39, 48, 83, 86, 91–93, 95, 97, 106, 130, 159, 308, 329, 349, 353–355, 369–373, 375, 377, 378, 391, 400–402, 415, 417, 418, 461, 467, 471, 507, 521, 565, 588
Physical activity (PA), v–ix, 2–7, 9, 10, 32, 36, 43, 44, 49, 55–75, 86, 92, 93, 98, 103, 104, 106, 107, 109–111, 113, 115–119, 128, 129, 132, 133, 138, 140, 149, 152, 153, 155, 156, 172, 176, 194–196, 199, 200, 202, 204, 205, 207, 208, 210–212, 219, 222, 223, 228–232, 239, 251–253, 255–257, 259–261, 273, 283, 285, 308, 309, 313, 314, 318, 328, 349, 351, 352, 358–367, 369, 370, 376, 379, 391, 395, 421, 422, 431, 440, 446, 448–455, 482, 488, 491, 492, 497, 499–501, 506, 507, 509, 510, 514, 522–524, 528, 532, 533, 539, 545, 548, 552, 554, 556, 561, 565, 572, 576, 584, 586, 588–590, 592, 596
Physical impairment, Belgium, 303, 317
PluSport, Switzerland, 389–399, 402
Policies, v–vii, ix, x, 3–15, 18, 19, 25, 29, 31, 33, 34, 37, 38, 44–47, 75, 79–98, 101, 103, 106, 107, 110, 111, 113–116, 118, 119, 125, 126, 128, 134–137, 141, 147, 149, 151, 154–156, 162, 169, 170, 172, 175, 178, 181, 186–188, 193, 195, 196, 199–205, 208, 212, 213, 217, 218, 220, 223, 225, 228, 232, 237, 239, 240, 244, 246, 248–250, 252, 253, 255, 260, 267, 270, 271, 274, 276, 280, 282, 284, 288, 295, 296, 298, 300, 301, 305, 306, 308–310, 320, 329, 333, 334, 340, 349–353, 358–366, 368–370, 376, 378, 385–387, 389, 391, 393, 395, 396, 419, 424, 426, 428, 432, 437, 440, 444, 445, 449, 451, 452, 461–482, 489, 493–496, 498, 499, 502, 506–509, 520–523, 525, 526, 531, 533, 537–556, 562–564, 566, 567, 569, 571, 574, 576–584, 586, 587, 589, 590, 593–596
Policy factors, 590, 593
Policy framework
    Austria, 282
    Belgium, 61, 311
    Denmark, 61

Finland, 110
Germany, 61, 339
Hungary, 61, 425
Iceland, 134
Ireland, 204
Lithuania, 449
Netherlands, 61, 353, 364
Northern Ireland, 225
Norway, 61
Portugal, 500
Slovenia, 473
Spain, 61, 522
Sweden, 182
Switzerland, 61, 395
Turkey, 549
United Kingdom, 250
Policymaker, 8, 45, 97, 360, 378, 594
Population surveys, 38, 40, 104, 376, 565, 583–587
Portuguese Federation for sport of people with disabilities (FPDD), 492–495, 497, 498, 500, 501, 506
Prevalence of disability, 11, 38, 40, 56, 83, 104, 117, 130, 174, 242, 301, 490, 564
Principal-agent approach, 13, 578
Procap Sport, Switzerland, 392, 396, 399, 402
Profit, 13, 75, 80, 151, 172, 247, 387, 397
Pro Infirmis, Switzerland, 394
Province Sport Centres for PwDs, Turkey, 548

Q

Questionnaire, 6, 56, 58, 60, 62, 117, 160, 162, 208, 285, 313, 318, 340, 400, 403, 555, 564, 585, 589, 594

R

Real Federación Española de Ciclismo (RFEC, Royal Spanish Cycling Federation), 519, 527
Recommendations, 9, 45, 108, 117, 199, 200, 277, 329, 363, 440, 449, 456, 531–533, 550, 563, 594–596
Recreational and psychological value of sport, 26
Regional associations, Germany, 335
Regional network, the Netherlands, 359
Regional sport organisations with Sport Councils, Norway, 165
Regional sports policy and support for sports for PWD, Sweden, 182

Index 609

Registration data, 37, 587
Regjeringen (The Government), 2019,
    Norway, 147, 152, 153, 155, 156
Rehabilitation (URI-Soča), Slovenia, 466,
    467, 478
Rehabilitation Centers, Belgium, 153,
    302, 308
Relationships
    Austria, 267, 270, 275–278, 285–287, 580
    Belgium, 296, 304, 308
    Denmark, 84, 88
    Germany, 325, 332, 338
    Ireland, 195, 203
    Northern Ireland, 219, 224, 233
    Norway, 154–155
    Slovenia, 470–471
    Sweden, 178, 180
Reliability, 56
Rise or emergence of disability sport in
    Austria, 272–273
    Belgium, 302–304
    Denmark, 83–84
    Finland, 105–107, 109
    Germany, 331
    Hungary, 417–419
    Iceland, 130–131
    Ireland, 198–200
    Lithuania, 444
    The Netherlands, 355–357
    Northern Ireland, 221
    Norway, 150–151
    Portugal, 491–494
    Slovenia, 465–466
    Spain, 516–517
    Sweden, 175–176
    Switzerland, 389–390
    Turkey, 543–545
    United Kingdom, 242–244
Royal Board on Disability, Ministry of Social
    Rights and 2030 agenda (Real
    Patronato sobre Discapacidad),
    Spain, 517

S
Sajátos Nevelési Igény (SNI, Special
    Educational Needs) Hungary, 224,
    225, 256, 415, 417, 443, 448
Scatterplot, 74
School-based surveys, 117, 586, 589
Secondary agents
    Austria, 277, 574
    Belgium, 308

Denmark, 574
Finland, 574
Germany, 336, 574
Hungary, 424, 425
Lithuania, 574
The Netherlands, 363, 573
Northern Ireland, 224
Norway, 573
Portugal, 497
Slovenia, 470
Sweden, 179
Switzerland, 393, 394
Sector Responsibility Principle,
    Denmark, 86, 89
Sensory (disability), ix, 1, 4, 34, 39, 41, 42,
    159, 197, 225, 285, 301, 329, 353,
    415, 519, 521
Siketek Sport Clubja (SSC, Deaf-Mute Sports
    Club), Hungary, 411
Sjálfsbjörg (National Association of the
    Disabled in Iceland), 130
Social Code IX, Germany, 329
Social integration and Volunteering in Sports
    Clubs in Europe (SIVSCE), 61, 62,
    65, 67, 74, 94, 400–403, 406,
    585, 586
Social model, 29–33, 35, 82, 103, 220, 455,
    490, 543, 564, 590
Social status pyramid, Belgium, 316, 317
Socio-ecological model, 590, 591
Special Olympics Austria (SOÖ), 267, 273,
    275–278, 280, 284, 285
Special Olympics Belgium (SOB), 303, 307
Special Olympics Finland, 110
Special Olympics Germany, 335, 341
Special Olympics Iceland, 106, 110, 113, 115,
    118, 125, 131
Special Olympics Ireland, 201, 221
Special Olympics Lithuania (SOL), 181,
    446, 447
Special Olympics Netherlands (SON),
    359–361, 367, 370
Special Olympics Northern Ireland, 227, 234
    Special Olympics Ulster, 227, 228, 232
Special Olympics Norway, 154
Special Olympics Portugal, 493, 497, 501,
    502, 505
Special Olympics Slovenia, 478
Special Olympics Spain, 520, 526
Special Olympics Sweden, 179
Special Olympics Switzerland, 390–392, 396,
    399, 402
Special Olympics Turkey, 548

Sport, v, 1–18, 25–49, 55–75, 79–98,
    101–119, 125–141, 145, 169–174,
    193, 217, 237–261, 267, 295,
    325–345, 349–379, 385, 411–432,
    437, 461–482, 485–510, 513–533,
    537–556, 561–596
Sport as a curative factor, 25–26
Sport as a means of Social Re-integration, 26
Sport-based, 6, 9, 49, 70, 524, 569–574, 578,
    579, 581, 582
Sport Councils, UK, 241, 244–246, 569
Sport England, 222, 246, 247, 251–258
Sport Federations, Norway, 150, 151,
    153–158, 160–162, 165
Sport Financing Fund, Lithuania, 450
Sport for all, UK, 245
Sport for persons with a disability,
    44–46, 561–596
Sport in
    Austria, 269–270
    Belgium, 297–299, 302–304, 320, 575
    Denmark, 79–84, 97
    Finland, 102–103, 105–107, 109
    Germany, 325–345
    Hungary, 413, 417–425
    Iceland, 125–141
    Ireland, 193–196
    Lithuania, 439
    The Netherlands, 351–352
    Northern Ireland, 218–219
    Norway, 147–148
    Portugal, 486, 488–489
    Slovenia, 463–464
    Spain, 514–515
    Sweden, 169–174, 177
    Switzerland, 386–387, 392
    Turkey, 539–541
    United Kingdom, 239–240
Sport Inclusion Disability Officers, Ireland
    (SIDOs), 193, 199, 200, 202, 205,
    207, 210, 212
Sporting Future: A New Strategy for an Active
    Nation, UK, 250
Sport Ireland, 193–196, 199–210, 212, 223,
    224, 576
Sport law, 521, 522, 575, 576, 580
Sport Matters: The Northern Ireland Strategy
    for Sport and Physical Recreation,
    2009-2019, 217, 218
Sport Northern Ireland (Sport NI), 217,
    218, 228
Sport participation, vi, ix, 1–18, 37, 40, 43, 47,
    49, 84, 85, 89, 92–97, 115–118,
    135, 137–140, 157, 158, 186, 187,
    207–211, 217, 225, 226, 229–233,
    239, 241, 242, 247, 250, 251,
    254–261, 270, 279, 283–288, 309,
    343–344, 349, 351, 353, 361, 364,
    366, 369–378, 396, 400–406,
    429–430, 453–455, 477–481, 488,
    493, 496–498, 500, 503–510, 525,
    527–533, 552–556, 561, 562, 565,
    569, 575–577, 583, 585, 591–593,
    595, 596
Sport participation by people with disabilities/
    by persons with a disability
    Austria, 64
        membership, 284, 288
    Belgium
        club membership, 316
        by demographic background, 316–317
        French Community and the German-
            speaking Community of Belgium,
            305, 317–318
        frequency, 314–318
        inclusion in mainstream sport, 314
        type of sport, 314–316
    Denmark, 61, 64, 74, 79–98, 571
        sports clubs, 94–96
    Finland, 64, 74, 101–119, 566, 569, 571
    Germany, 61, 66, 325–345
    Hungary, 61, 66, 411–432
    Iceland, 125–141, 565
    Ireland, 194, 197–200, 211, 565, 571
    Lithuania, 64, 65, 437–456, 565, 569
    Northern Ireland
        club membership, 231
        comparison with general
            population, 232
        frequency, 231
        other sport contexts, 232
        type of sport, 231
    Norway
        general disability sport
            participation, 157–160
        paralympic top level sport, 157
    Portugal, 485–510
    Slovenia, 461, 463–465, 473, 477, 479,
        481, 565, 575
    Spain, 61, 66, 513–533, 565, 569
    Sweden, 64, 172, 175–178, 182, 565, 569
    Switzerland
        frequency, 401
        sport and club participation form, 401
        sport clubs, 400
        sport type, 401–402

Index

  by type of impairment or disability, 402
  type of sport club, 402
  volunteering, 403
 The Netherlands
  children with disabilities, 376
  cycling and walking during leisure
   time, 371
  people with intellectual disabilities, 376
  by socio-demographic and health
   variables, 371–373
  sport participation details, 371–375
  type of sport, 373–375
  weekly participation in sport, 370
 Turkey, 540–547, 565
 United Kingdom
  adults (aged 16+), 256
  children and young people (aged 5-16),
   156, 257
  by club membership, 258
  by impairment, 258
  by region, 257
Sport policy of the government: "Sport and
  Physical Activity for all",
  Norway, 156
The Sports Act, Finland, 103, 108, 110, 111,
  114, 463, 474
Sports Act, Slovenia, 463
Sports clubs, the Netherlands, 350–352,
  355, 359
Sports club surveys, 61, 586
Sports Committee for Deaf, Lithuania,
  446, 455
The Sports Confederation of Denmark (DIF),
  81, 84, 85, 87, 88, 90, 98
Sports Development Strategy, Lithuania, 440
Sports federations, Lithuania, 453
Sports for All Policy, Belgium, 309
Sport Vlaanderen, 295, 299–300, 304–307,
  309, 313, 320, 568
S-Sport Recreas, Belgium, 303, 307
Stamm, H., 397
Standing Committees of the Parliament
  include the Subcommittee on
  People with Disabilities and the
  Sports and Tourism Committee,
  Hungary, 420
Start to para-sport project, Belgium, 308
Statistics Norway (SSB), 145, 150, 153, 157
Steering (of disability sport)
 Austria, 575
 Belgium, 308, 575
 Denmark, 89, 574
 Europe, 98
 Finland, 574, 575

 Germany, 337
 Hungary, 575
 Iceland, 574, 575
 Ireland, 575
 Lithuania, 448
 The Netherlands, 584
 Northern Ireland, 224
 Norway, 567
 Portugal, 575
 Slovenia, 575
 Spain, 575
 Sweden, 175
 Switzerland, 575
 Turkey, 549
 United Kingdom, 224
Stoke Mandeville (Games, Hospital), 25, 26,
  242, 244, 302, 355, 492, 493,
  544, 565
Strategy 2025, Sweden, 183–185
Structure (of disability sport)
 Austria, 275
 Belgium, 305
 Denmark, 84
 Europe, 562
 Finland, 107
 Germany, 332
 Hungary, 411
 Iceland, 132
 Ireland, 200
 Lithuania, 444
 The Netherlands, 567
 Northern Ireland, 222
 Norway, 151
 Portugal, 494
 Slovenia, 461
 Spain, 518
 Sweden, 176
 Switzerland, 392
 Turkey, 545
 United Kingdom, 245, 567
Support for disability sport, 11, 311,
  476, 526
Survey, 5, 9, 15, 16, 37–41, 55–62, 74, 75, 79,
  82, 83, 92–94, 96, 104, 111, 113,
  115–118, 127, 128, 138, 139, 176,
  207, 229, 230, 234, 237, 255–257,
  271, 279, 285, 288, 304, 313, 316,
  318, 328, 336, 343, 344, 362,
  369–371, 376, 377, 400, 402, 406,
  429, 453, 506, 515, 527–530, 533,
  564, 565, 583–589, 596
Survey of Health, Impairment and Living
  Conditions in Denmark
  (SHILD), 92

Sustainable Development Goals (SDGs), 3, 4, 212
Swedish Deaf Sports Federation, 175, 185
Swedish Parasport Federation, 169, 174–176, 179, 180, 184, 185, 187, 188, 566
Swedish parliament, 181
Swedish Sports Confederation, 169
Swiss Deaf Sport, 389, 393, 396, 402
Swiss Federal Act on the Promotion of Sports and Exercise (Sports Promotion Act; SpoFöG, Sportförderungsgesetz, Bundesgesetz über die Förderung von Sport und Bewegung, 2011), 387
Swiss Federal Concept for Sports for All (Breitensportkonzept Bund, 2015), 395
Swiss Federal Office for the Equality of Persons with Disabilities (EBGB, Eidgenössisches Büro für die Gleichstellung von Menschen mit Behinderungen), 390, 394, 395, 397, 398
Swiss Federal Office of Social Insurance (BSV, Bundesamt für Sozialversicherungen), 390, 394, 395, 397
Swiss Federal Office of Sport (BASPO, Bundesamt für Sport), 387, 391, 395–406
Swiss Paralympic, 391–393, 397, 399
Swiss Paraplegics Association (SPV, Schweizer Paraplegiker Vereinigung), 389, 390, 392, 393, 396, 397, 399, 402

T
Teacher Training School in Pest (1850s), 414
Theories and models of disability, 28–32
Time-trend, 57, 59, 70
Treaty on the Functioning of the European Union (TFEU), 4
Turkish Blind Sports Federation (Türkiye Görme Engelliler Spor Federasyonu), 545, 553
Turkish Deaf Sports Federation (*Türkiye İşitme Engelliler Spor Federasyonu*), 543, 545, 553
Turkish Disability Act (TDA), 542, 543
Turkish Special Athletes Sports Federation (Türkiye Özel Sporcular Spor Federasyonu), 545, 548, 553
Turkish Sports Federation of the Physically Disabled (Türkiye Bedensel Engelliler Spor Federasyonu), 545, 553
Typologies of governing disability sport, 572–574

U
UN Convention on the Rights of Persons with Disabilities, Austria, 271, 280
UN Convention on the Rights of Persons with Disabilities, Belgium, 301
UN Convention on the Rights of Persons with Disabilities, Denmark, 82
UN Convention on the Rights of Persons with Disabilities, Finland, 110
UN Convention on the Rights of Persons with Disabilities, Germany, 329, 342
UN Convention on the Rights of Persons with Disabilities, Iceland, 130
UN Convention on the Rights of Persons with Disabilities, Ireland, 199, 204
UN Convention on the Rights of Persons with Disabilities, Lithuania, 450
UN Convention on the Rights of Persons with Disabilities, Norway, 149
UN Convention on the Rights of Persons with Disabilities, Spain, 516
UN Convention on the Rights of Persons with Disabilities, Sweden, 169
UN Convention on the Rights of Persons with Disabilities, Switzerland, 385, 388
UN Convention on the Rights of Persons with Disabilities, the Netherlands, 353
UN Convention on the Rights of Persons with Disabilities, Turkey, 542
Union of Equality, 1, 4, 561, 596
United Nations (UN), 2–4, 30, 34, 38–40, 82, 115, 183, 197, 199, 288, 331, 453, 487, 542, 561, 564, 582, 584, 594
United Nations Convention on the Rights of Persons with Disabilities (UNCRPD), 3–5, 7, 9, 16, 18, 30, 34, 38, 39, 110, 331, 333, 338, 339, 343, 353, 385, 388, 393, 395, 399, 400, 405, 406, 542, 543, 555, 561, 564, 576, 582, 584, 594

Index

United Nations Educational, Scientific and Cultural Organisation (UNESCO), 3, 234, 514
The University of Physical Education (UPE, Testnevelési Egyetem), Hungary, 421, 424

V
Validity, 56

W
Washington Group on Disability Statistics questionnaire, 585
Welfare state, 17, 61, 80, 83, 102, 103, 106, 114, 126, 146, 326, 338, 472, 562
Wheelchair Sports Switzerland (RSS, Rollstuhlsport Schweiz), 392
White paper on sport for people with disabilities in Spain (Libro blanco del deporte de personas con discapacidad en España), 520
World Health Organization (WHO), 1–3, 6, 9, 26, 31, 34, 38–40, 47, 59, 174, 197, 208, 212, 271, 314, 353, 376, 490, 491, 499, 500, 543, 561, 564, 590

Y
Youth and Sports (J+S, Jugend und Sport), Switzerland, 147, 150, 387, 397, 398, 419, 539, 540, 545, 546, 549, 553, 554, 556
Youth Sport Trust (YST), 246, 247

Z
ZŠRS Planica, Slovenia, 476, 479, 481
Zveza ŠIS-SPK, Slovenia, 461, 465–468, 470–474, 476–480, 570

Printed in the United States
by Baker & Taylor Publisher Services